American Casino Guide

2015 Edition

Written and Edited By
Steve Bourie

Assistant Editors
Matt Bourie
Christine Bourie

Contributing Writers
Linda Boyd
John Grochowski
Dewey Hill
H. Scot Krause
Jean Scott
Henry Tamburin

This book is dedicated to the memory of my mother,
Terry Bourie, who always enjoyed a good game of chance.

American Casino Guide - 2015 edition

Published By:
Casino Vacations Press, Inc.
P.O. Box 703
Dania, Florida 33004
(954) 989-2766

e-mail: info@americancasinoguide.com
website: americancasinoguide.com

ISBN-13: 978-1-883768-24-9
ISSN: 1086-9018

Table of Contents

About Your Guide

This guide has been written to help you plan your visit to casino gambling areas and also to help you save money once you are there. The first edition of this guide began 23 years ago as an eight-page newsletter and it has continued to grow each year as casino gambling has spread throughout the country. We have listed information on all of the states that offer any type of traditional casino table games or slot machines (including video lottery terminals). We have also included stories to help you understand how casinos operate; how video poker and slot machines work; how to make the best plays in blackjack, craps, roulette and baccarat; and how to take advantage of casino promotional programs. Additionally, we have included a casino coupon section that should save you many times the cost of this book.

Virtually every casino has a "comp" program whereby you can get free rooms, food, shows or gifts based upon your level of play at their table games. If you plan on gambling during your trip to the casino, you may want to call ahead and ask their marketing department for details on their programs. There are also stories in this book to help you understand how "comp" programs work and how to best take advantage of them.

One more suggestion to save you money when visiting a casino is to join their players club. It doesn't cost anything and you would be surprised at how quickly those points can add up to earn you gifts, cash, food or other complimentaries. Also, as a club member you will usually receive periodic mailings from the casino with money-saving offers that are generally not available to the public.

When using this guide please remember that all of the listed room rates reflect the lowest and highest prices charged during the year. During holidays and peak periods, however, higher rates may apply. Also, since the gambling games offered at casinos vary from state to state, a listing of available games is found at the start of each state heading. We hope you enjoy your guide and we wish you good luck on your casino vacation!

Your Best Casino Bets - Part I

by Henry Tamburin

The majority of casino players leave too much to chance when playing in a casino. To put it bluntly, they don't have a clue as to how to play. They are literally throwing their money away with little chance of winning. Luck most certainly has a lot to do with your success in a casino but what really separates the winners from the losers is the skill of the players. Granted, there is no guarantee that you will win, but on the other hand, there is no guarantee that you must lose. My objective in this article is to educate you on the casino games so that at the very least, you'll be able to enjoy yourself in the casino with maximum play time and minimum risk to your bankroll.

Let's begin our understanding of casino gambling by learning how casinos win as much as they do. They don't charge admission, and they certainly don't depend on the luck of their dealers to generate the income they need to pay their overhead. In fact, they guarantee themselves a steady income by having a built in advantage, or house edge, on every bet. Think of it as a very efficient hidden tax that generates them a guaranteed daily profit.

Here's an example of how this works. Suppose we take a coin and play heads or tails. Every time you lose a flip of the coin you pay me $1. Every time you win a flip, I pay you 90¢. Would you play? I hope you said no. Here's why. In this simple game I would have an advantage over you and I created that advantage by not paying you at the true odds of one-to-one (or $1).

Casinos do this very same thing to create their advantage. They simply pay off winning bets at less than the true odds. For example, the true odds of winning a bet on number 7 on roulette are 37-to-1 (the latter means you have 37 chances to lose vs. one chance to win). If you get lucky and the roulette ball lands in the number seven slot, you'd expect the casino to pay you 37 chips as winnings for the one chip you bet on number 7 (37- to-1 payoff). If they did that, the casino's advantage would be zero. However, as I mentioned above, the casinos create their advantage by paying off winning bets at less than true odds. In the case of our bet on number 7, the winning payoff is 35 chips (instead of 37 chips). The two chips the casino quietly kept is what pays their bills. Mathematically, the casino advantage is 5.26% on this bet which simply means day in and day out, the casino expects to win (or keep) 5.26% of all money wagered in roulette.

The casino games with the lowest casino advantage (less than 1.25%), and your best bets, are blackjack, craps, baccarat, and video poker. Now don't sell the ranch and run over to your nearest casino just yet. These games, plus table poker, are your best bets but you must learn how to play these games properly to enhance your chances of winning. Here are some tips to get you started:

BLACKJACK - This is your best casino game, but you must learn how to play your hands (when to hit, stand, double-down, split, etc.). This is known as the basic strategy. Learn it and you can reduce the casino's advantage to virtually zero. And if you learn how to keep track of the cards as they are played (i.e. card counting) you can actually turn the tables on the casino and have the edge over them! Do not try to play blackjack if you haven't learned the correct basic strategy. If you do, your chances of winning are slim. Also, it's wise not to make any side bets that may be offered on your table and please stay away from any game which only pays 6-to-5 for an untied blackjack. Blackjack tournaments are also popular and here players compete against other players with the player with the most chips at the end of the round advancing. Tournament prizes can be substantial. Playing and betting strategy for blackjack tournaments, however, is different than playing blackjack in a casino so bone up on your tournament skills before considering playing in a tournament.

CRAPS - The game of craps intimidates most casino players because of the complicated playing layout and the multitude of bets. In fact craps is an easy game to play. And it also has some of the best bets in the casino (and also some of the worst). Your best bet is the pass line with odds and come with odds. Next best is a place bet on six or eight. Stay away from all other bets on the layout because the casino's advantage is too high. If you really enjoy the game of craps you might consider learning dice control – it's not an easy skill to learn and it requires a lot of practice but if you get good at it, you can have the edge over the casino.

ROULETTE - Every bet on the American roulette layout (with 0 and 00 on the wheel) has a high casino advantage. That goes for bets straight up on numbers that pay 35-to-1, as well as even money wagers on red or black. Atlantic City players get a break. If you bet on an even money payoff bet and 0 or 00 hits, you lose only half your wager. This cuts the casino's advantage in half. Also, some casinos offer a European layout with only one zero. This is a better bet than wheels with 0 and 00.

BACCARAT - Many casinos offer a low stakes version called mini-baccarat. Not a bad game to play. If you bet on the bank hand, the casino's edge is only 1.17%. And when you play baccarat, there are no playing decisions to make which makes the game very easy to play. However, this game is fast with many decisions per hour. It's best to play slowly. One way is to only bet on the bank hand after it wins (meaning you won't be betting on every hand which will slow down your play).

BIG SIX WHEEL - Stay away from spending a lot of time (and money) at this game. The casino's advantage is astronomical (11% to 26%). Its drawing card for the novice player is the low minimum bet ($1). Save your money for the better games.

CARIBBEAN STUD POKER - This popular cruise ship game has found its way to land-based and dockside casinos. Unlike regular table poker where players compete against each other, in this game the players play against the house. But the rules favor the casino and their advantage is about 5%. The part of this game that appeals to players is the progressive jackpot side bet. You should not make this side bet, however, unless the jackpot exceeds $280,000 for the $1 ante and the $1 jackpot bet.

PAI GOW POKER - Strange name for a casino game. The game is a cross between Pai Gow, a Chinese game of dominoes, and the American game of seven-card poker. Players are dealt seven cards and they must arrange (or set) their cards into a five-card poker hand and a two-card poker hand. Skill is involved in setting the two hands which can help reduce the casino's advantage.

SLOT MACHINES - Casinos earn more money from slot machines than all the table games combined. The casino's advantage varies from one machine to another. Typically the higher denomination machines ($1 and up) pay back more than the nickel, quarter and fifty-cent machines. Slots are not your best bet in the casino, but here are a few tips: It's wise to play one coin only in machines where all the payouts increase proportionally to the number of coins played (i.e. there is no jackpot for playing maximum coins). However, if the machine has a substantial jackpot when you play maximum coins, then you should always play the maximum number of coins the machine will accept or you won't be eligible for a bonus payoff for the jackpot. Don't waste hours looking for a machine that's "ready to hit." Join the slot clubs, always use your slot club card when you play, and try to schedule your play time when the casino offers multiple points. Joining is free and you'll be rewarded with discounts and other freebies. Machines that have lower jackpots pay smaller amounts more frequently which means you normally get more playing time for your money. Playing machines that have bonus rounds and fancy graphics may be fun, but the house edge on these machines is usually higher than traditional reel spinning machines. Likewise, the house edge is higher for linked machines that have those life-changing mega jackpots. Some casinos now certify their machines to return 98% or more and these machines are your best bets. Also, consider playing in slot tournaments where you are competing against other players, rather than the house, and the prizes can be substantial.

VIDEO POKER - Your best bet if you enjoy playing slot machines. Skill is involved as well as learning to spot the better payoff machines. For example, on the classic jacks-or-better game, always check the full house and flush payoff schedule. The machines on jacks or better pay nine coins for a full house and six coins for a flush for each coin played. These machines are known as 9/6 machines. They are readily available; seek them out. The same analogy holds for bonus poker, double bonus, deuces wild, jokers wild, etc. video poker games. There are good pay schedules and bad ones, and it's up to you to know the difference and play only the higher paying schedules with the correct playing strategy (readily available on the Internet, in books, and on strategy cards).

KENO - This casino game has a very high casino advantage (usually 20% and up). Stay away if you are serious about winning.

RED DOG - This is the casino version of the old acey-deucey. The stakes are low, but the casino edge is a wee-bit steep (3.5%). If you play, only make the raise wager when the spread between the two cards is seven or more.

SIC BO - This is an asian game in which players bet on the outcome of the roll of three dice. There are lots of bets on the layout, some that pay odds of 150-to-1. However, most have a very high casino advantage. Your best bet is a bet on the big or small wager.

LET IT RIDE - This casino table game is based on the all-American game of poker. Like Caribbean Stud Poker, players compete against the house rather than against each other. What makes this game so unique is that the players can remove up to two of their initial mandatory three bets if they don't think they can win. The objective is to end up with a five-card poker hand of at least 10's or higher. The higher the rank, the greater the payoff; up to 1,000-to-1 for the royal flush. The casino edge is about 3% and about 70% of the hands will be losing hands. If you are lucky enough to catch a high payoff hand, be smart, push your chair back, and take the money and run!

THREE CARD POKER - One of the more successful table games in recent years, you can wager on either the Ante/Play or Pair Plus. You win your Ante/Play bet if your three card poker hand beats the dealer's hand. If you wager Pair Plus, you win money if your three card hand contains at least a pair or higher (the higher the ranking hand, the greater the payout). There are different paytables – the best pays 4-1 for a flush rather than 3-1. The optimum playing strategy is to raise on Q-6-4 or higher and avoid playing the Pair Plus if the flush pays only 3-1.

Henry Tamburin has more than 30 years of experience as a casino player, author, columnist and instructor. More than 7,500 of his articles on casino gambling have been published in numerous national gaming publications including Casino Player magazine. He is also the author of numerous books and instructional videos, edits the popular Blackjack Insider newsletter (www.bjinsider.com), and is the Lead Instructor for the Golden Touch Blackjack course (www.goldentouchblackjack.com). You can visit his web site at http://www.smartgaming.com

Your Best Casino Bets - Part II

by Steve Bourie

In the previous story Henry gave you his choices for your best casino bets based on which ones offer you the best mathematical odds. Now, Henry is a great mathematician who is truly an expert at crunching numbers to figure out what the theoretical odds are, but what about real life? By this I mean - at the end of the week, or the month, or the year, how much does a casino really make from blackjack, or craps, or roulette? Sure, you can do the math to calculate the casino advantage on a bank hand in mini-baccarat as 1.17%, but at the end of the day what percent of those bets on mini-baccarat actually wind up in the hands of the casino? Is it precisely 1.17%? or is it less? or is it more? And, if you knew how much the casino truly averaged on all of the games it offered, which one would turn out to be your best bet based on that information?

To find the answer to this question I began my search by looking at the annual gaming revenue report issued by Nevada's State Gaming Control Board. It lists the win percentages, based on the drop (an explanation of this term later), for all of the games offered by the casinos and you might be surprised at which game had the lowest win percentage. Go ahead and take a guess...nice try, but you're wrong! The answer is bingo, where casinos only won 1.94% of the money they handled!

The first column below lists the actual win percentages based on the "drop" (an explanation of "drop" follows shortly) for Nevada's various games for the fiscal year from July 1, 2013 through June 30, 2014:

GAME	WIN %	ADJUSTED WIN %
Keno	25.93	25.93
Race Book	15.17	15.17
Slot Machines	6.41	6.41
3-Card Poker	31.18	6.24
Sports Pool	6.08	6.08
Let It Ride	24.22	4.84
Pai Gow Poker	21.74	4.35
Pai Gow	18.90	3.78
Roulette	17.53	3.51
Baccarat	13.71	2.74
Craps	13.64	2.73
Mini-Baccarat	11.90	2.38
Twenty-One	11.83	2.37
Bingo	1.94	1.94

Usually bingo would rank as one of the games with the worst odds, but not in Nevada where it's sometimes used as a "loss leader." Just like your local Kmart runs especially low prices on a couple of items to bring you into the store where they believe you'll buy some other items, Nevada casinos use bingo to bring people into their casinos, believing that while they're there they'll play other games and also develop a loyalty to that casino. So, if you're a bingo player Nevada casinos are the best places you'll ever find to play your game.

Before we go on to the other games though you'll need a brief explanation of how the win percentages are calculated and we'll start off with a basic lesson in how casinos do their accounting.

Casinos measure their take in table games by the drop and the win. The drop is the count of all of the receipts (cash and credit markers) that go into the drop box located at the table. Later, an accounting is made to see how much more (or less) they have than they started with. This amount is known as the win (or loss).

What the first column in the table shows you is how much the casinos won as a percentage of the drop. For example, on the roulette table for every $100 that went into the drop box the casino won $17.53 or 17.53%. What it doesn't tell you, however, is how much the casinos won as a percentage of all the bets that were made. In other words, the drop tells you how many chips were bought at that table, but it doesn't tell you how many bets were made with those chips. For example, if you buy $100 worth of chips at a blackjack table and play $10 a hand you don't bet for exactly 10 hands and then leave the table, do you? Of course not. You win some hands and you lose some hands and if you counted all of the times you made a $10 bet before you left the table you would see that your original $100 in chips generated many times that amount in bets. In other words, there is a multiplier effect for the money that goes into the drop box. We know that for every dollar that goes into the drop box there is a corresponding number of bets made. To find out exactly what that number is I asked Henry for some help. He replied that there is no exact answer, but during a 1982 study of the roulette tables in Atlantic City it was discovered that the total amount bet was approximately five times the amount of the buy-in. This means that for every $100 worth of chips bought at the table it resulted in $500 worth of bets being made.

The multiplier effect for the money that goes into the drop box is also dependent on the skill of the player. A blackjack player that loses his money quickly because he doesn't know good playing strategy will have a much lower multiplier than a player who uses a correct playing strategy. For purposes of this story, however, we'll assume that they balance each other out and we'll also assume that all games have the same multiplier of five. We can now return to our win percentage tables and divide by five the percentages for those games that have a multiplier effect. These new adjusted numbers lets us know approximately how much the casinos actually won as a percentage of the amount bet on each of those games. Keep in mind, however, that besides bingo there are three other game categories that do not need to be adjusted: keno, race book and sports pool. They need no adjustment because there is no multiplier factor involved. On these particular games the casinos know the exact total of the bets they take in and the exact total of the bets they pay out.

After calculating our adjusted win numbers we can now go back and take another look at which games are your best casino bets. The worst game, by far, is keno with its 25.93% edge. Next comes the race book with 15.17%, followed by slot machines at 6.41% and then three-card poker at 6.24%

Sports betting has a casino win rate of 6.08% but that number actually deserves a closer look because there are really five different types of bets that make up that figure: football - 6.36%; basketball - 4.86%; baseball - 4.25%; sports parlay cards - 35.14%; and other sports (golf, car racing, etc.) - 7.95%. As you can see, all sports bets carry a relatively low house edge, except for sports parlay cards which you may want to avoid.

Next on our list is let it ride at 4.84%. That's followed by pai gow poker at 4.35%; pai gow at 3.78%; and roulette at 3.51%.

Finally, we come to the four best casino bets that all have roughly the same edge of less than three percent: baccarat at 2.74%; craps at 2.73%; mini-baccarat at 2.38%; and twenty-one (blackjack) at 2.37%.

So there you have it. After discounting bingo, blackjack is your best casino bet! Henry said it was a good game to play and he was right.

An important thing to keep in mind, however, is something else that Henry said about the game of blackjack: "you must learn how to play your hands." You should remember that of all the table games offered in a casino (other than poker), blackjack is the only one that is a game of skill. This means that the better you are at playing your cards, the better you will be able to beat the house average. The 2.37% figure shown is just an average and if you learn the proper basic strategies you should be able to cut it down even more. Good luck!

Casino Comps

by Steve Bourie

In the world of casino gambling a "comp" is short for complimentary and it refers to anything that the casino will give you for free in return for your play in their casino.

Naturally, the more you bet, the more the casino will be willing to give you back. For the truly "high roller" (those willing to bet thousands, tens of thousands or even hundreds of thousands on the turn of a card) there is no expense spared to cater to their every whim, including: private jet transportation, chauffeur-driven limousines, gourmet chef-prepared foods, the finest wines and champagnes, plus pampered butler and maid service in a $10 million penthouse suite. But what about the lower-limit bettor?

Well, it turns out that pretty much any gambler can qualify for comps no matter what their level of play and if you know you're going to be gambling anyway, you might as well ask to get rated to see what you can get on a comp basis.

When you sit down to play be sure to tell the dealer that you want to be rated and they'll call over the appropriate floorperson who will take down your name and put it on a card along with information on how long you play and how much you bet. The floorperson won't stand there and constantly watch you, instead they'll just glance over every once in awhile to see how much you're betting and note it on the card. If you change tables be sure to tell the floorperson so that they can continue to track your play at the new table.

Usually a casino will want you to play for at least three hours and virtually all casinos use the same formula to calculate your comp value. They simply take the size of your average bet and multiply it by: the casino's advantage on the game you're playing; the decisions per hour in your game; and the length of your play in hours. The end result is what the casino expects to win from you during your play and most casinos will return anywhere from 10% to 40% of that amount to you in the form of comps.

So, let's say you're a roulette player that averages $20 a spin and you play for four hours. What's that worth in comps? Well, just multiply your average bet ($20), by the casino's advantage in roulette (5.3%) to get $1.06, which is the average amount the casino expects to make on you on each spin of the wheel. You then multiply that by the number of decisions (or spins) per hour (40) to get $42.40, which is the average amount the casino expects to make on you after one hour. Then, multiply that by the total hours of play (4) to get $169.60, which is the average amount the casino expects to make on you during your four hours of play. Since the casinos will return 10% to 40% of that amount in comps, you should qualify for a minimum of $16.96 to a maximum of $67.84 in casino comps.

One thing to keep in mind about comps is that you don't have to lose in order to qualify. The casino only asks that you put in the time to play. So, in our example if, after four hours of gambling, our roulette player ended up winning $100, they would still be eligible for the same amount of comps.

The last thing to mention about comps is that some casino games require skill (blackjack and pai gow poker), or offer various bets that have different casino advantages (craps) so those factors are sometimes adjusted in the equation when determining the casino advantage in those games. Just take a look at the chart below to see how the average casino will adjust for skill in blackjack and pai gow poker as well as for the types of bets that are made in craps.

Game	Game Advantage	Decisions Per Hour
Blackjack	.0025 (Card Counter) .01 (Good Basic Strategy) .015 (Soft Player)	70
Roulette	.053	40
Craps	.005 (Pass Line/Full Odds) .01 (Knowledgeable) .04 (Soft)	144
Baccarat	.012	70
Mini-Baccarat	.012	110
Pai Gow Poker	.01 (Knowledgeable) .02 (Average)	25

Players Clubs And Comps

by Steve Bourie

Before you start playing any kind of electronic gaming machine in a casino, you should first join the casino's players club to reap the rewards that your play will entitle you to. What is a players club you ask? Well, it's similar to a frequent flyer club, except that in these clubs you will earn cash or comps (free food, rooms, shows, etc.) based on how much money you put through the machines.

Virtually all casinos in the U.S. have a players club and joining is simple. Just go to the club's registration desk, present an ID, and you'll be issued a plastic card, similar to a credit card. When you walk up to a machine you'll see a small slot (usually at the top, or side) where you should insert your card before you start to play. The card will then record how much money you've played in that particular machine. Then, based on the amount you put through, you will be eligible to receive cash (sometimes) and comps (always) back from the casino. Naturally, the more you gamble, the more they will give back to you.

Some casinos will give you a free gift, or some other kind of bonus (extra slot club points, free buffet, etc.) just for joining and since there's no cost involved, it certainly makes sense to join even if you don't plan on playing that much. As a club member you'll also be on the casino's mailing list and you'll probably be receiving some good money-saving offers in the mail. Additionally, some casinos offer discounts to their club members on hotel rooms, meals and gift shop purchases.

While almost no casino will give you cashback for playing their table games, virtually all casinos will give you cashback for playing their machines. The amount returned is calculated as a percentage of the money you put through the machines and it basically varies from as low as .05% to as high as 1%. This means that for every $100 you put into a machine you will earn a cash rebate of anywhere from five cents to $1. This may not seem like a great deal of money but it can add up very quickly. Additionally, some casinos (usually the casinos with the lower rates) will periodically offer double, triple or quadruple point days when your points will accumulate much more rapidly.

One other point to make about cashback is that the vast majority of casinos (about 90%) offer a lower cash rebate on their video poker machines than they do on their slot machines. Generally, the rate is about one-half of what the casino normally pays on its slot machines. The reason for the reduced rate is that video poker is a game of skill and knowledgeable players can achieve a greater return on video poker games than they could on slots. Since the casino will make less money on video poker games they simply reduce their cash rebates accordingly. This is very important to keep in mind, especially if you're a bad video poker player, because you'll probably only be earning half the cash rebate you could be getting by just playing the slots.

Of course, the best situation is to be a smart video poker player in a casino that offers the same cash rebate to all of its player regardless of what kind of machine they play. This way you could be playing a good VP game, combined with a good rebate, and this will allow you to be playing at a near 100% level!

One final point to make about cash rebates is that not all clubs will allow you to get your cashback immediately. In Atlantic City, for example, all of the casinos will send a voucher to your home address which you must bring back to the casino (usually within 90 days) to receive your cash. You should always make it a point to ask if your cashback from the slot club is available immediately. If not, you may find yourself being mailed a voucher that is worthless to you.

While not every casino's club will give you back cash it is standard for every club to allow you to earn "comps" for your machine play. "Comps" is short for complimentaries and it means various things that you can get for free from the casino: rooms, meals, shows, gifts, etc.

Once again, the comp you will earn is based on the amount of money you put through the machines but it is usually at a higher level than you would earn for cashback. After all, the real cost to a casino for a $15 meal is much less than giving you back $15 in cash so the casinos can afford to be more generous.

When it comes to players club comp policies they basically fall into one of three categories. Some casinos have clubs that allow you to redeem your points for either cash at one rate, or comps at a reduced rate that will cost you fewer points. In these clubs, for example, you might have a choice of redeeming your 1,000 points for either $10 in cash or $20 in comps.

Another option (one that is commonly used by many "locals" casinos in Las Vegas) is for the casino to set a redemption schedule for each particular restaurant, or meal. For example: breakfast is 800 points, lunch is 1,200 points and dinner is 1,600 points. These are popular programs because players know exactly what is required to earn their comp.

At the other extreme, many casinos base their comps on your total machine play but won't tell you exactly what's required to achieve it. At the MGM Resorts properties in Las Vegas, for example, you will earn cashback at a set schedule but you'll never quite know what you need to earn a food comp. You just have to go to the players club booth, present your card, and ask if you can get a buffet or restaurant comp. The staff will then either give it to you or say you need some more play on your card before they can issue you a food comp.

And which casinos have the best players clubs? Well, that would really be dependant on what's most important to you. If you're visiting from out of town you would probably want a club that's more generous with room comps so you could save money on your accomodations. However, if you're going to be playing at a casino near your home you would be more interested in which casino offers the best cashback rate and food comps. Whatever the situation, be sure to give most of your play to the casino that offers the best benefits for you and you'll soon be reaping the rewards of players club membership!

Taking Advantage of Players Clubs

by H. Scot Krause

Players clubs originated in Atlantic City nearly 30 years ago as a way to begin recognizing and rewarding the casino's good players. Today, players clubs are the casino's most powerful marketing tool and the player's best benefit the casino has to offer. It's the best of both worlds for both the player and the casino.

To begin, perhaps the word "club" is a little misleading, since there are no dues to pay, meetings to attend or any of the usual aspects associated with joining a club. You do get a players club membership card (also called a player's card) which is your key to unlocking the benefits and rewards of the casino you're playing in.

Typically, your players club membership card is a plastic card, with your identifying number on it, that you will use while playing at any of the casino's slot or video poker machines or while playing table games. It resembles a credit card, but only in its appearance, and is in no way an actual credit card. I mention that because there are some people who actually, mistakenly believe they will be inserting a credit card into their slot machine and play on credit, and therefore they refuse to get their player's card and are basically denied any and all benefits they are entitled to!

So let's start at the beginning and walk through the player's card program, when and why to do it and discuss some benefits, rewards and perks.

When you enter any casino for the first time, ask someone immediately where you can find the players club or players club booth before you put any money into a machine. At the booth, you should find a rather friendly group of employees who will get you started, signed up and get your card for you pronto.

You'll probably need to fill out a short application form or at least give your identification card to the clerk. It's simply a way to register the card in your name. You usually don't need to give your social security number if you don't want to, but always give your birthday and anniversary dates when asked. They help identify you with the casino in case others have your same name and many times the birthday benefits are nothing short of fantastic. Adding your e-mail address and signing up for text messages will also get you additional offers sent to you.

Always ask the players club personnel about how to use the card and any other current promotions or benefits in addition to using your card. There will usually be a brochure or literature available that you can take explaining all the club benefits. There may also be a sign-up bonus such as a free gift, free slot play or free points when you register. Be sure to ask. Sometimes an easily obtainable coupon may be required, and the clerks can tell you where or how to get one. Finally, I like to request two cards when I join, and you might like to do the same. You'll find that you may lose one, or want to play two machines at one time. That's it! You're on your way.

When you're out on the casino floor, you'll notice a slot on the machines that your card fits into. When you decide which machine you want to play, put your card in the slot and leave it in the entire time you play that machine. (Note: Take a moment to look for the card reader slot and not the bill acceptor. If you accidentally put your card in the bill acceptor you'll probably strip the magnetic reader off your card and it won't work).

Most machines will have some type of reader that will display your name, points earned or at least let you know your card has been accepted. It's not a swipe card, and you must leave it in the machine while you play. It's simply counting the coins, or credits, that go through the machine while you're playing and giving you credit in the form of points for the amount of money that cycles through the machine. (Some casinos consider time on the machine as well as money being cycled, but that is a little more rare than in years past). Now, while you're playing, you'll be earning valuable points that become redeemable for anything from cashback to restaurant complimentaries (referred to as "comps") show tickets, gifts, reduced room rates or free rooms, to almost any amenity you may want or require.

Check your card while you're playing to make sure it's working properly. If you sit idle for a period of time while you're ordering a cocktail or what have you, the card reader may stop working and you'll need to reinsert it. Be sure to keep your card in the machine until you have completed your play and cashed all coins or tickets out of the machine. Some clubs base their points on a coin-out system, rather than coin-in and some slot machines actually may pay a bonus when you cash out on certain games!

Your players club rewards are based on total play and your rewards may vary according to point formulas created exclusively for the casino at which you're playing. I do caution you not to continue to play beyond your comfortable gambling range and budget just to earn a point level or comp. Let the comps fall in place as you play or when you return again in the future. Which brings me to another interesting thought. I've heard players refuse to get a card because they believe they won't return to the casino again. First of all, you never know what your future plans may hold. Second, you may earn enough points while you're on this trip to at least earn a small comp or some cash back before you leave.You'll at least get on the casino's mailing list for future specials and events. You may win a jackpot that will allow you to return sooner than you originally thought was possible. And finally, with as many consolidations and buy-outs as there are in the casino business today, the casino you're playing at today may be owned by someone else tomorrow, who may in turn, be closer to your home, and you'll be able to use your points with them. There's just no good excuse not to get a player's card at any casino you visit.

Here are a couple other tips when you plan to visit a casino and need to get a players club card. Sometimes you can apply or sign-up in advance by mail registration or visiting the casino's website on the Internet. They will often mail you the card in advance or have it already prepared for you when you get to the casino. Call and ask ahead of time for this service and you'll save time and won't have to stand in long lines when you hit the casino floor. Sometimes, when you receive your card by mail or Internet sign-up, you'll get additional offers, coupons, gifts and funbook offers along with it. On the other hand you may find a coupon or a rebate offer that offers a bonus if you sign up in person with the coupon in hand. Try to investigate a little before signing up as to which way may be the best way for you to enroll in the club.

Many casinos now also employ players club ambassadors, cash hosts, or enrollment representatives who will sign you up on the casino floor, making it even easier for you to enroll in the club. They often have additional incentives or perks they can give you when you sign up with them. You might also check to see if a card you have from another casino might work where you're playing now. Many casino corporations are beginning to combine their clubs to offer you benefits at any of their respective properties. We're sure to see more of this as consolidations and mergers continue to take place.

Now, let's take a little closer look at the benefits and reasons why you want to belong to these players clubs. Obviously, the casinos want your business and will go to great lengths to have you return. In addition to the points you're earning while playing, which will entitle you to various comps as mentioned previously, your most valuable asset from joining the players club will be your mailing list advantage. Offers to players club members are mailed often and repeatedly for room specials, many times even free room offers, meal discounts (two for ones), and often other free offers. We've been mailed match play offers, double and triple point coupons (and higher), show and movie theater tickets, spa specials, gifts and gift certificates, drawing tickets, and a myriad of other offers.

The casino offers are based on levels of play, and better offers including lavish parties, Superbowl and New Year's Eve invitations, free participation to invited guest slot tournaments, limousine services, and even free round-trip airfare, are offerd to the casino's best players. Don't rule yourself out just because you don't think you'll reach those levels of play to be awarded those opportunities. Everyone is rewarded in some way for even the most nominal play. Just wait until your birthday rolls around and I can almost guarantee you'll get some fabulous offers from the casinos to spend your celebration with them!

Finally, we'll now take a look at some of the myths regarding players clubs and player's cards and dispose of them accordingly. Here are some of the arguments I've heard against players club cards, or excuses as to why players don't use them...

"I never win when I play with my card." The truth is your results would be the same regardless if you had a card in or not. There is no relation between the card counting coins through the machine and what comes up on the screen when you push the button. The card just records how much money is wagered. It has no memory of whether you have won or lost and it doesn't care.

"I don't want to be tracked," or "I don't want the casino to know how much I'm playing," or "I don't want the IRS to have my records." In fact, you do want the casino to track you so you can be rewarded for your play. They have no way of knowing you, or how they can help and reward you unless they know who you are, what you're playing and how much you're spending. The IRS does not have access to your gambling activities, but you, in fact, do. The players club can provide you with a year end win-loss record of your play that may help you offset wins with losses for tax purposes.

"I don't need a card, I'm a local," or "I'm a tourist." Basically, you're one or the other, but either way you still should have a card. The casino's computers usually separate locals from tourists and tailor their offers accordingly. If you're going to play anyway, get a card!

"I always lose those cards." You can always have another card made. Get extras made. Why play without it? It's like losing your wallet. The card has so much value for you, yet you leave it in the machine. You don't forget your airline frequent flier card at the airport, or your grocery savings card when you go shopping, do you?

"I don't need a card, I'm leaving in an hour." It doesn't matter how long you will be staying or how soon you will be leaving. Remember that all-important mailing list, and that you just might return some time in the future or play at a sister property somewhere else. (Don't worry. Most casinos do not sell their mailing list names. They want you for themselves and are very selfish!)

All-in-all, I've never heard of one good reason not to join a players club. In fact, I hope I've given you enough good reasons to always join every players club at every casino you ever visit. Good luck and happy Players clubbing!

H. Scot Krause is a freelance writer, gaming industry analyst and researcher. Scot reports, researches, and specializes in writing about casino games, events, attractions and promotions. His work is regularly featured in several gaming publications and he writes the popular "Vegas Values" weekly column for the American Casino Guide website.

Las Vegas Resort Fees

by Dewey Hill

Resort fees are a growing trend in Vegas. It is more difficult than ever to find a casino hotel that does not charge these fees. Left off advertisements, not included in discounter search prices, hidden in fine print, these fees make booking a room more complicated and potentially much more expensive.

What are resort fees?

Resort fees are per night mandatory charges added to your hotel bill and collected by the hotel/casino, ostensibly for certain amenities, most of which traditionally have come free with any booked room, like free parking, or pool use. Sometimes there are some new amenities like free WiFi, access to the fitness center, free water bottles in the room, a free daily newspaper, or a VIP line pass to avoid crowds at the buffet. Fees are often missing in advertised prices or hidden in the fine print.

Unlike sales taxes, resort fees work like a flat tax; they might add a mere 10-20% to the nightly charges of expensive hotels, but add as much as 50% to inexpensive hotels.

Are there other similar fees?

Yes. Golden Nugget's new $5 "Fremont Experience fee" is an attempt at linguistic distance from the term "resort fee," but it is essentially indistinguishable.

Some casinos are charging a fee for early check-in. If you will be arriving tired, or if you are checking out of one hotel and into another during one trip, avoiding early check in fees may increase the value of your booking and the flexibility of your first day in a casino. These are especially prevalent at Strip and upscale properties. When moving from one hotel to another, call and ask about a free late check out. Often you can leave an hour after the standard checkout and then check your bags at the next hotel with the bellman. Leaving luggage at the Aria is not recommended because there have been many complaints, but most other places it is a common and easy practice to check luggage at the bell desk until the room is ready.

What about comped rooms?

Policies vary. Some casinos automatically waive resort fees for comped rooms, some require that we ask them to be waived, and for others it depends upon how the room is booked. Many will use resort fees as another incentive for higher levels of play. Others charge everyone the same fee even if the room is comped. Sometimes the fee will be waived, but amenities connected with the fee will be denied.

• Caesars Entertainment charges comped rooms for those with the lowest tiered Player's Club status (Gold) but no resort fee is charged those holding a card higher than Gold status.

• Station Casinos and Boyd Casinos and the D and Golden Gate charge no resort fee on any comped room and do not limit amenities.

• Folks getting comped M Life rooms by playing the MyVegas games report that the rules on resort fees change all the time. Sometimes they can book the earned freebies with no fees; other times they have to pay them. Check the fine print on comp offers.

• Some places allow us to pay the resort fee with Player's Card points.

Why would a casino use a resort fee rather than put all charges up front?

• Casinos charging resort fees appear less expensive until the fine print is examined, so that helps in advertising. It also might trick inexperienced Vegas travelers, or those who don't attend to the details of their bills, into believing that what they will be charged is significantly less than it actually will be at check out. Since reporting of hotel room charges often ignores resort fees, media tends to be complicit in this tactic. While in theory the resort fee could easily be mentally added to the posted hotel charge, in practice it is often mentally ignored, even by veteran visitors.

• Discount brokers typically have search engines that arrange the hotels according to price, so that the customer can enter trip dates and make easy comparison based on cost. Because resort fees are not included in the programed rankings of those searches, the casino hotel will see their rooms disingenuously ranked as cheaper than the actual cost.

• Resort fees also help casinos when discount brokers discount any rooms they have been unable to sell in order to liquidate an overstock. In a real sense, a discount broker, when selling any room in a casino hotel that charges a resort fee, can only sell or discount a percentage of that room. The casino still collects the entire resort fee.

• Discounters take a cut of the cost of the room. So a casino that wants to raise prices gets more value from a price raise if it is in the form of a resort fee.

• Resort fees may attract customers who have been paying higher a la carte fees for fitness centers or in-room wifi. A resort fee charges every customer for these amenities. Few use them, but those who do are then subsidized by those who do not. If the resort fee itself is used as a comp for well bankrolled players, the cost of providing amenities is paid for by lower bankrolled guests. Comped rooms may not incur mandatory resort fees, but amenities will be more expensive if paid for individually.

• The fee system allows the casinos to divide their guests into two categories, dividing those who just want a room in Vegas from those who will gamble where they stay.

• In short, the resort fee structure adds an element of flexibility to room charges that the casino hotel can use to their advantage in renting rooms to a variety of customers. Customers lose the transparency and dependability of an agreed upon cost that is determined upfront at the time of booking; casino hotels are able to more fluidly flex the price of the hotel room to match the variegated profile of their customer.

How much are these fees?

• Fees change often and unfortunately the change is usually an increase. Ask what they are before you book and ask again when you confirm your booking. Often new or higher fees apply even for bookings made before the fee was in effect. Further confusing any cost comparisons is that some charge a tax on the fee.

• Fee amounts noted here include taxes on the fee: $28 fees are the highest in Vegas: Red Rock, Green Valley Ranch, Aria, Bellagio, Encore, Mandalay Bay, MGM , Mirage, Caesars, Cosmopolitan, Vdara, Mandalay Bay, Red Rock, THE Hotel, Treasure Island, Palazzo, Venetian, Wynn

• Station Casinos all have resort fees from about $13 to the high rates of $28.

• On the Boulder Strip, Sam's Town and Boulder Station have fees, while Eastside Cannery and Arizona Charlie's do not.

• Silver Sevens has the lowest fee, $3.

• Treasure Island will waive fee for some advertised specials.

• Super 8 next to Ellis Island gets the prize for the most free amenities with NO resort fee: wifi in the room, parking, 24 hour heated pool, free airport pickup/delivery, a guest laundromat and television with twice the number of channels, including TCM and three HBO channels.

• These downtown casinos have resort fees: the newly remodeled Downtown Grand ($20.16), the Plaza ($11.40), the Golden Gate and the D ($22.40), El Cortez ($10.02) and that $5 Fremont Experience fee at the Golden Nugget. The D fees are huge given the reasonable rates for rooms. Comped rooms, even 2-for-1 deals are free of fees.

These casinos DO NOT have resort fees at the time of writing:

• Cannery Casino in North Vegas and Eastside Cannery on Boulder Highway
• Arizona Charlie's Casinos on Boulder and Decatur.
• Best Western associated with Casino Royale
• Super 8 located next to Ellis Island on Koval near Flamingo
• M Resort
• Marriott Grand Chateau
• Skylofts at MGM Grand
• Wynn (suites only, standard rooms have fees)
• Boyd casinos downtown: Main Street Station, Fremont, California

Resort fees can change any day and in all probability have changed since this article went to print. To be certain of accurate, up-to-date information, call the casino hotel and ask before booking any location. Ask the amount of the resort fee and also ask if taxes are charged on the fee or just on the room charge. Ask how it can be waived.

Resort fees often at times will not appear on a printout from a discount broker and are missing in email advertisements or hidden in fine print.

As often as you can, book directly with hotels rather than using a discount broker.

When a room is booked directly, any cancellation or alteration of a reservation will usually not incur other fees that are being charged more often by discounters (i4Vegas for example, generally charges $25 for changes or cancellations). With direct bookings, paperwork will not get lost or misinterpreted. Many discount hotel representatives are talking to you from far away in an English new to them, and that adds to the confusion of a booking and may incur errors.

Only when booking directly with the hotel, rather than with a broker, can you reduce the length of a booking without losing the original sale rate. To modify a discount broker deal, you must cancel the entire first booking and rebook at generally higher current rates.

Also, your play may reduce the cost of your stay if you book directly. Hosts can rarely comp discount broker bookings; they can always comp direct bookings or remove resort fees based on good play.

Some casinos will book directly and match the low price of a discounter. Find a good price, note the source of the site, and call the casino to ask.

However you make your reservation, be sure to make a confirmation phone call directly to the hotel a few days before you arrive. Carefully recheck dates and charges and resort fees. Reconfirm any changes or cancellations. Bring along a printout detailing your purchase. This will save you any surprise at check-in when you are overtired from air travel, anxious to enjoy Vegas, and forced to stand in repeated lines between phone calls to a discounter or while waiting for misinformation to be corrected.

Also pay attention to what you sign when you check in. Hotels with resort fees generally have you agree to the fees when you arrive, but sometimes that is in the fine print.

If you take advantage of Internet name-your-own-price offers or air-hotel package deals, resort fees will not be included in quoted charges, but added on by the hotel afterwards. This is especially frustrating when a discounter searches for a hotel using your set price, but will not tell you the name until you make the reservation, so you can't check on resort fees before booking. When naming your own price, it may be wise to just assume you will pay an additional $20 on average in resort fees.

Are there ways to avoid or modify resort fees?

Developing a playing history with a casino will often generate offers that are free of the resort fees. Boyd never charges for comped mights. The D does not charge even for 2-for-1 offers.

• To avoid the new Caesars entertainment resort fees, at least for one year, apply for the new Total Rewards no fee credit card. Within about 30 days of making application, this will upgrade your player's card to Platinum status for a year. Folks with Platinum status and above do not pay resort fees whether the booking is comped or paid. Gold members pay resort fees even on comped rooms. An added advantage to having the card is that if you use it for minimum purchases to keep it active, your Player's Club points will never expire. Otherwise, CET points are only good for 6 months. It also may make a difference in free drink offers in Atlantic City. Gold card player's are limited in drink choices.

• While Caesars Entertainment charges a $10 fee to make an initial booking on the phone, once you are booked online, you can call and negotiate any changes in hotel bookings for roughly the same time period, but pay no $10 phone fee. Just remind them that your initial booking blocked your ability to see optional offers online. Resort fees are sometimes negotiable in this conversation or the available rates they quote might offset the fees.

• Some convention bookings negotiate a waiver of resort fee. SEMA and AAPEX, which attracts 120,000 participants annually in November, negotiates waived fees for members booking through their site.

• Condos at Signature MGM that are rented out directly by the condo owners, or through third party companies they hire, can be booked without the usual resort fee.

• Some casinos periodically drop resort fees as a come-on in advertised room rate specials. Watch for these deals in advertised specials.

• Sometimes an upgrade can be negotiated with a waived resort fee. This can make the cost of an upgrade to room luxury less expensive.

• After booking, ask for an emailed, detailed description of your charges, and bring a printout to the hotel. If resort fees are implemented or raised after your booking, but before your check-in, a printout of the original booking will often save you added costs.

What methods are there of protest?

• If you have been caught with an unexpected new fee, or a raised fee, argue that your original contract should be honored. Complain at the front desk in a calm, reasoned manner. Ask for a manager. Be prepared to wait.

• If you have done some gambling, have a host review your play before you check out and ask in that review if the resort fee can be dropped. Again, be prepared to wait.

• Complain in writing to the casino, even if you lost the argument at the front desk. Casinos pay attention to letters. You may find you get an offer for a free upgrade or a future stay without resort fee.

• Whenever you cancel a reservation, include the resort fee as one of the reasons for the cancellation.

• Use a comped visit at a resort fee casino hotel, but don't play there that visit. Seed your play for future offers with a casino that does not charge a resort fee on comped rooms, and explain your decision in writing to both casinos.

• Write to any casino that does not charge a resort fee or keeps the fee low. Thank them, and tell them you have decided to move your business to their casino.

• Each time you write to a casino for any reason, remind them that this issue is important to you.

Will it do any good?

The large number of new resort fee charging hotels, suggests that resort fees are with us to stay. Caesars Entertainment tried to market a "no fees" approach. It failed.

However, customer complaints always are noted, even if they are not answered. Regular customers may expect an answer and perhaps, if the letter touches the right nerve, the answer may include a waived fee or a free room upgrade on your next visit.

M casino responded to customer complaints by dropping the practice altogether.

At the very least when booking, be aware that these fees are likely to be charged and how much they add to your booking cost.

Dewey Hill retired from teaching English to travel in the most frugal ways, play poker at the lowest limits, and fish bluegills. His love of Vegas, as well as his disdain for resort fees, keeps him on discussion boards and blogging daily. He collects Vegas experiences at vegasbirthdaybash.blogspot.com.

Slot Machines

by Steve Bourie

Virtually anyone who visits a casino, even for the first time, is familiar with a slot machine and how it operates: just put in your money, pull the handle and wait a few seconds to see if you win. It isn't intimidating like table games where you really need some knowledge of the rules before you play and it's this basic simplicity that accounts for much of the success of slot machines in the modern American casino.

As a matter of fact, the biggest money-maker for casinos is the slot machine with approximately 65 percent of the average casino's profits being generated by slot machine play. As an example, in Nevada's fiscal year ending June 30, 2014 the total win by all of the state's casinos was a little more than $11.2 billion. Of that amount, $6.73 billion, or slightly more than 60 percent, was from electronic machine winnings.

With this in mind, you must ask yourself, "can I really win money by playing slot machines?" The answer is a resounding yes...and no. First the "no" part: in simplest terms a slot machine makes money for the casino by paying out less money than it takes in. In some states, such as Nevada and New Jersey, the minimum amount to be returned is regulated. In Nevada the minimum is 75 percent and in New Jersey it's 83 percent. However, if you look at the slot payback percentages for those particular states in this book you will see that the actual average payback percentages are much higher. In New Jersey it's close to 91 percent and in Nevada it's slightly less than 93 percent. Even though the actual paybacks are higher than the law requires, you can still see that on average for every $1 you play in an Atlantic City slot machine you will lose 8¢ and in a Las Vegas slot machine you will lose 6¢. Therefore, it doesn't take a rocket scientist to see that if you stand in front of a slot machine and continue to pump in your money, eventually, you will lose it all. On average, it will take you longer to lose it in Las Vegas rather than Atlantic City, but the result is still the same: you will go broke.

Gee, sounds kind of depressing, doesn't it? Well, cheer up because now we go on to the "yes" part. But, before we talk about that, let's first try to understand how slot machines work. All modern slot machines contain a random number generator (RNG) which is used to control the payback percentage for each machine. When a casino orders a slot machine the manufacturer will have a list of percentage paybacks for each machine and the casino must choose one from that list. For example, a manufacturer may have 10 chips available for one machine that range from a high of 98% to as low as 85%. All of these chips have been inspected and approved by a gaming commission and the casino is free to choose whichever chip it wants for that particular brand of machine.

In almost all instances, the casino will place a higher denomination chip in a higher denomination machine. In other words, the penny machines will get the chips programmed to pay back around 87% and the $25 machines will get the chips programmed to pay back around 98%. A casino can always change the payback percentage, but in order to do that it usually must go back to the manufacturer to get a new RNG that is programmed with the new percentage. For this reason, most casinos rarely change their payback percentages unless there is a major revision in their marketing philosophy.

And what exactly is a random number generator? Well, it's a little computer chip that is constantly working (as its name implies) to generate number combinations on a random basis. It does this extremely fast and is capable of producing hundreds of combinations each second. When you pull the handle, or push the spin button, the RNG stops and the combination it stops at is used to determine where the reels will stop in the pay window. Unlike video poker machines, you have no way of knowing what a slot machine is programmed to pay back just by looking at it. The only way to tell is by knowing what is programmed into the RNG.

As an example of the differences in RNG payout percentages I have listed below some statistics concerning various slot manufacturers' payback percentages in their slot machines. Normally, this information isn't available to the public, but it is sometimes printed in various gaming industry publications and that is where I found it. The list shows the entire range of percentages that can be programmed into each machine:

Aruze Gaming
Paradise Fishing	88.00% - 90.00%
Ultra Stack Lion	87.20% - 96.00%

Aristocrat
African Storm	87.86% - 94.84%
Batman	88.43% - 88.44%
Jaws	88.70% - 92.00%
The Walking Dead	88.50% - 93.50%
The Rolling Stones	86.00% - 96.00%
Wild Panda	88.00% - 95.00%

Bally Gaming
Betty Boop's Love Meter	87.68% - 87.99%
Black & White 5 Times Pay	84.49% - 96.72%
Black & White Sevens	87.00% - 95.00%
Blazing 7's Double (reel)	88.00% - 95.98%
Cash Spin	85.72% - 88.38%
Hot Shot Progressive	85.41% - 96.01%
Hot Spin	87.59% - 89.99%
Money Talks	88.00% - 96.06%

Money Wheel	85.38% - 96.08%
Poppit!	87.95% - 95.89%
Spin & Win (3-Reel)	83.24% - 94.00%
Titanic	85.19% - 88.46%

GTECH
Bejeweled	86.55% - 89.18%
Deal or No Deal - In it to Win it	86.00% - 96.00%
IC Money	85.20% - 97.02%
Lion Queen	85.01% - 92.01%
Sphinx 3D	86.00% - 92.00%
Tropical Paradise	86.00% - 96.00%

IGT
Avatar - Treasure of Pandora	85.00% -96.00%
Back to the Future	85.90% - 93.50%
Dangerous Beauty 2	87.50% - 98.00%
Diamond Jackpots	87.90% - 96.50%
Elephant King	85.03% - 98.04%
Enchanted Unicorn	85.00% - 98.00%
Fortune Cookie	85.03% - 98.01%
Neon Nights	87.53% - 98.03%
Red White and Blue	85.03% - 97.45%
Sex and The City Multi-Play	89.90% - 94.90%
Texas Tea	87.00% - 97.00%
Wheel of Fortune Secret Spins	89.00% - 93.50%
Wolf Run 2: Into The Wild	85.00% - 98.00%

Konami Gaming
African Diamond	82.13% - 96.03%
Big Africa	85.50% - 98.10%
Dungeons & Dragons	87.20% - 96.10%

WMS Gaming
Alice	87.00% - 96.00%
Reel 'em in/Compete to Win	86.92% - 96.15%
Cash Crop	86.36% - 94.92%
Great and Powerful Oz Stand Alone	86.00% - 96.00%
Great and Powerful Oz Progressive	86.00%
Monopoly Luxury Diamonds	87.90% - 90.02%
Monopoly Real Estate Tycoon	86.00% - 94.00%
Price is Right - Plinko Jackpots	87.00% - 96.00%
Star Trek	84.49% - 93.95%
Wizard of Oz Progressive	86.05% - 86.15%
Wizard of Oz Stand Alone	86.05% - 93.99%

Once again, keep in mind that casinos generally set their slot paybacks based on each machine's denomination. Therefore, penny machines will probably be set towards the lower number and $5-$25 machines will be set towards the higher number.

Okay, now let's get back to the "yes" part. Yes, you can win money on slot machines by using a little knowledge, practicing some money management and, mostly, having lots of luck. First, the knowledge part. You need to know what kind of player you are and how much risk you are willing to take. Do you want to go for the giant progressive jackpot that could make you a millionaire in an instant or would you be content walking away just a few dollars ahead?

An example of a wide-area progressive machine is Nevada's Megabucks where the jackpot starts at $10 million. These $1 machines are located at more than 125 Nevada casinos around the state and are linked together by a computer. It's fine if that's the kind of machine you want to play, but keep in mind that the odds are fairly astronomical of you hitting that big jackpot. Also, the payback percentage is lower on these machines than the average $1 machine. During Nevada's fiscal year ending June 30, 2014 Megabucks averaged a little less than 88% payback while the typical $1 machine averaged a little less than 95%. So, be aware that if you play these machines you'll win fewer small payouts and it will be very difficult to leave as a winner. Unless, of course, you hit that big one! If you really like to play the wide-area progressive machines your best bet is probably to set aside a small percentage of your bankroll (maybe 10 to 15 percent) for chasing that big jackpot and saving the rest for the regular machines.

One other thing you should know about playing these wide-area progressives is that on most of them, including Megabucks, you will receive your jackpot in equal payments over a period of years (usually 25). You can avoid this, however, by playing at one of the casinos that link slot machines at their own properties and will pay you in one lump sum. Be sure to look on the machine before playing to see how it says you will be paid for the jackpot.

Knowledge also comes into play when deciding how many coins to bet. You should always look at the payback schedule posted on the machine to see if a bonus is payed for playing the maximum number of coins that the machine will accept. For example, if it's a two-coin machine and the jackpot payout is 500 coins when you bet one coin, but it pays you 1,200 coins when you bet two coins, then that machine is paying you a 200-coin bonus for playing the maximum number of coins and you may want to bet the maximum two coins to take advantage of that bonus. However, if it's a two-coin machine that will pay you 500 coins for a one-coin bet and 1,000 coins for a two-coin bet, then there is no advantage to making the maximum bet on that machine and you should only bet the minimum amount. To see more on this subject, watch my video titled "The Slot Machine - When to bet Maximum Coins" on our YouTube channel at www.youtube.com/americancasinoguide.

Knowledge of which casinos offer the best payback percentages is also helpful. When available, we print that information in this book to help you decide where to go for the best return on your slot machine dollar. You may want to go to the Las Vegas Strip to see some of the sites, but take a look at the slot machine payback percentages for the Strip-area casinos in the Las Vegas section and you'll see that you can get better returns for your slot machine dollar by playing at the off-Strip area casinos.

The final bit of knowledge you need concerns players clubs. Every major casino has a players club and you should make it a point to join it before you insert your first coin. It doesn't cost anything to join and as a member you will be able to earn complimentaries from the casinos in the form of cash, food, shows, drinks, rooms or other "freebies." Just make sure you don't get carried away and bet more than you're comfortable with just to earn some extra "comps." Ideally, you want to get "comps" for gambling that you were going to do anyway and not be pressured into betting more than you had planned.

Now let's talk about money management. The first thing you have to remember when playing slot machines is that there is no skill involved. Unlike blackjack or video poker, there are no decisions you can make that will affect whether you win or lose. It is strictly luck, or the lack of it, that will determine whether or not you win. However, when you are lucky enough to get ahead (even if it's just a little) that's where the money management factor comes in. As stated earlier, the longer you stand in front of a machine and put in your money, the more likely you are to go broke. Therefore, there is only one way you can walk away a winner and that's to make sure that when you do win, you don't put it all back in. You really need to set a "win goal" for yourself and to stop when you reach it. A realistic example would be a "win goal" of roughly 25 percent of your bankroll. If you started with $400, then you should stop if you win about $100. The "win goal" you decide on is up to you, but keep in mind that the higher your goal, the harder it will be to reach it, so be practical.

And what if you should happen to reach your goal? Take a break! Go have a meal, see a show, visit the lounge for a drink or even just take a walk around the casino. You may have the urge to keep playing, but if you can just take a break from the machines, even it's just for a short time, you'll have the satisfaction of leaving as a winner. If, later on, you get really bored and find that you just have to go back to the machines you can avoid a total loss by not risking more than half of your winnings and by playing on smaller denomination machines. If you made your winnings on $1 machines, move down to quarters. If you won on quarters, move down to nickels. The idea now is basically to kill some time and have a little fun knowing that no matter what happens you'll still leave as a winner.

And now, let's move on to luck. As stated previously, the ultimate decider in whether or not you win is how lucky you are. But, is there anything you can do to help you choose a "winning" machine? Not really, because there is no such thing. Remember, in the long run, no machine will pay out more than it takes in. There are, however, some things you could try to help you find the more generous machines and avoid the stingy ones. Keep in mind that all slot machine payback percentages shown in this book are averages.

Like everything else in life, slot machines have good cycles where they pay out more than average and bad cycles where they pay out less than average. Ultimately, what you want to find is a machine in a good cycle. Of course if I knew how to find that machine I wouldn't be writing this story, instead I'd be standing in front of it with a $100 bill in my hand getting ready to play it. So, I guess you'll have to settle for my two recommendations as to how you might be able to make your slot bankroll last longer.

First, is the "accounting" method. With this method you start with a pre-determined number of credits and after playing them though one time, you take an accounting of your results. If you have more than you started with you stay at that machine and start another cycle. Just keep doing this until the machine returns less than you started with. As an example, let's say you start with a $10 credit voucher. After making 10 $1 bets you see how many credits you have left on the machine. If it's more than $10 you start over again with another 10 $1 bets and then do another accounting. If, after any accounting, you get back less than the $10 bankroll you started with, stop playing and move on to a different machine. This is an especially good method because you have to slow down your play to take periodic accountings and you will always have an accurate idea of how well you are doing.

The other method is even simpler and requires no math. It's called the "baseball" method and is based on the principle of three strikes and you're out. Just play a machine until it loses three times in a row, then move on to another machine. Both of these methods will prevent you from losing a lot in a machine that is going through a bad cycle. To see more on this subject, watch my video titled "10 Tips To Stretch Your Slot Machine Bankroll" on our YouTube channel at www.youtube.com/americancasinoguide

Slot Machine Trends - 2015

by John Grochowski

For generations, it's been said that Charles Fey's Liberty Bell slot was instantly recognizable as the ancestor of modern games. With symbols on three reels and a handle on the side, it had a look and feel that told slot players the games they played weren't all that different from great grandad's day.

But oh, how things have changed in the days of video. With five video reels – and sometimes six – slot machines tempt players with stacked symbols, double symbols, expanding wilds and other treats. And that doesn't even take into account bonusing, 3-D technology and other tools gamemakers use to keep the games fresh, enticing and exciting. Those tools are constantly evolving as technology allows gamemakers to follow their imaginations.

Let's look at where some of the latest trends are taking manufacturers in slot creativity:

BONUSING: Bonus events are expected game features nowdays, but we have to look back only to the mid-1990s to find a time they didn't even exist. That changed with the advent of Wheel of Gold by Anchor Gaming, the first megahit bonus event that affixed a tower with a wheel atop Bally slant-top three-reel slot machines. When a player got the bonus symbol on the reels, a tone would sound and surrounding players would stop and watch the wheel spin for a bonus prize.

International Game Technology licensed Wheel of Gold, turned it into Wheel of Fortune, and the rest is slot machine history.

Around the same time, we started seeing the first video slot machines with bonus events. The fishing round on WMS Gaming's Reel 'Em In made a major impact. Nowadays, the bonuses are getting ever more creative:

**Bally Technologies, where the U-Spin technology for touch-screen wheel spins has been a huge success, opportunities to extend the technology's reach are high priority. With U-Spin, you touch the screen to give a wheel a spin, and the effect is striking.

That includes Titanic, based on the Leonardo DiCaprio box-office smash. Bonus events are selected through a representation of the engine order telegraph --- the wheel-shaped ship's control marked off in segments including stop, slow, half and full, For game purposes the segments correspond to awards and events. In a demo, a quick flick on the touchscreen landed the device on a segment marked "Safe."

That launched the Safe Bonus, which started with another U-Spin, this time of the combination dial on the ship's safe. It landed on a number for a credit award, than opened into a finely appointed ship's room for a pick'em bonus. Touching a vase, a table, and other furnishings brought credit awards.

When you win big, the celebration includes the famous moment in the movie when DiCaprio as Jack Dawson stands on the prow and shouts for the planet to hear, "I'm king of the world!" Slot playing kings and queens also see coins flying across the screen during the classic scene.

From there, Bally has gone to related mechanics such as U-Race, where you touch the screen to guide your driver in NASCAR, U-Play, where you play notes on a virtual piano in All That Jazz , U-Aim to position your cannon in Pirate's Quest and U-Shoot, where you touch the iDeck virtual button panel to position yourself to fire at alien ships in Total Blast. In Cash Wizard Tiki Magic, a follow-up to the popular Cash Wizard, Bally uses a U-Drag format during the Spell Bonus so players can touch and drag different ingredients for their spell potion to win prizes.

** At Multimedia Games, bonusing means first and foremost its popular TournEvent tournament system. TournEvent allows casinos to convert linked machines from regular play to tournament mode in just 10 seconds. Casinos can run tournaments at any time, even in high-traffic areas of the casino instead of shunting them to the dark corners where the setup won't get in the way of regular play. Multimedia also brings interactivity to players through its MoneyBall bonus feature that it layers on top of a variety of base games. In the MoneyBall event, players take aim to direct their ball launch from the top of the screen. There are several themes, including Pinball, Hotel, Tree and UFO.

The variation in themes helps keep the games fresh and full of surprises. Once a player has played one theme, the game selects a different theme the next time they enter into the MoneyBall bonus. It plays plays much like pachinko and pinball, as the player watches the ball hit pins, multi-ball triggers, fireballs for a three-times multiplier. An added feature is a ball lock, which takes players to a bonus-within-a-bonus such as a a wheel spin or special three-reel slot game.

**WMS Gaming, always creative, has licensed Beetlejuice, and developed a game as quirky as the film, with both free spin and pick'em-style bonuses. The playing field is six symbols across and 10 deep. Film character symbols are oversized, taking up two spaces acress, with most also being four symbols deep. Beetlejuice himself is six symbols deep with a 2-by-6 Beetlejuice taking up 60 percent of an oversized two-reel set, the look is striking.

The bonus package is where the film elements really come to the fore. One event that starts with a spin of a wheel on the screen has a giant fly leading the way to the graveyard. There, you pick from funeral cards marked "Deceased" to collect bonuses. Watch out for Beetlejuice, though. He's hiding under some of the cards, and if you pick him three times --- Beetlejuice, Beetlejuice, Beetlejuice --- the bonus round is over.

WMS also is rolling out games for its new Blade slot cabinet, which shortens the distance between its two high-resolution video screens, involves the player with direct and indirect emotive lighting, offers smoother reel animation and even brings video streaming capabilities to the slot floor.

One ice-hot game for the Blade is Cool Jewels, a cascading reels game where wilds next to each other lock and move down the screen together. In an exploding jewels bonus event, the value of the explosions increases as the round continues. In a trial run at the max bet level each jewel was worth 20 credits early in the round, but 500 at the end. That can make for some huge-paying spins.

Megajackpots games always are a highlight at IGT, and one new Megajackpots thriller is Avatar, based on the film favorite. One version is on the Center Stage platform with a huge dual screen overhead. It has multiple bonus features, including free spins, credit awards and scatter pays. Players can customize the games, change the sound and reel backgrounds, and earn experience points to unlock bonus events. You can create a log-on identity so you can pick up where you left off next time you play.

A second game, Avatar Treasures of Pandora, is on IGT's Crystal Core cabinet with a 42-inch LCD display. The button panel also is a touch screen --- a dynamic button panel --- with one physical button called the Super Button. It's a versatile device. You can push it like a button, move it like a joystick, even spin it around. In one bonus event, Willow Glade, you can touch areas on the panel to move to different areas of the glade to make pick'em bonus selections. There are options aplenty.

The Walking Dead from Aristocrat Technologies is loaded with unquiet features, including a Reel Growth format that adds extra spaces to create more potential winners. During normal play, there are six video reels that are each four symbols deep. The middle four reels can grow to five, six or seven symbols deep.

When the reels grow and the zombies start walking, you can anticipate a little gore that's good for the players. In The Horde Bonus, the horde invades the screen and leaves wild symbols behind. During a demo, one zombie took a shot in the head, splattering blood --- and wild symbols --- across the reels. When the blood starts flowing, so do the wins.

With plenty of video clips and imagery from the TV show, Aristocrat anticipates this to be the start of a series of slots.

Among the newest developments are systems-based bonusing that can bring special rewards and events to players on different types of games. At International Game Technology, that includes a suite of bonuses delivered through the Service Window, which casino operators can configure to pop up on games linked through an internal work.

Applications through the suite include Random Riches, which gives you a bonus when you reach a certain betting threshold, and Team Challenge, which can split players into teams even if they're on different banks of machines. In Team Challenge, players then play a game on the player-tracking interfaces to collect their rewards.

Aristocrat Technologies also is delivering targeted bonusing through its Speed Solutions brand. The nRich application gives the players bonusing targets based on their play. What the player sees is a thermometer, and as wagers drive the thermometer to the top, they trigger a bonus game that can be played in the Aristocrat Media Window or on the player tracking system's LCD panel. A variety of interfaces are available for the bonus event, such as a scratch-and-win experience or a claw game.

Incredible Technologies' second The King of Bling game, Iced Out, is a blast, with a couple of new features, One is Iced Out, triggered by diamond symbols on the first two reels. The diamonds are held, and everything else goes into respin mode. The diamonds dance, bounce, sway and spin in time to the music, and the tempo picks up as the wins mount. The respins continue as long as they bring more diamonds, which lock into place. The goal is to ice out the screen, covering it in diamonds.

The Bounce 2 Nite feature involves bouncing a flashy car. Touch the front left bumper, and it raises and bounces down with a crash, revealing bonus credits. Touch other areas of the car, and they bounce too. The awards are random, not determined by where you touch the car. Focus groups just liked making it bounce.

The nRich application uses a player's past performance and gives realistic targets to achieve. While you play your regular game, the application launches that alert you that you're about to hit a goal.

The goal, of course, is to keep you in your seat. The graphics inform you that if you play a little longer, you can reach a goal and collect a bonus or launch a bonus feature. After you reach that goal, a new goal is displayed, then another, all in attainable increments so that there's always a new goal within reach.

GTECH's Galaxis casino systems management portfolio offers a module of bonusing tailored to each individual casino's needs. The Galaxis Bonusing suite gives casinos options including Points Bonusing and Jackpot Bonusing, and the options can be flexibly combined with each other. Galaxis Bonusing modules can be implemented independently of slot machine types, brands, and denomination. They can be applied to any number of machines, and even be connected with the table games pits.

TimeBomb FEVER and OnTarget FEVER were introduced last year. TimeBomb FEVER allows the casino operator to guarantee that a jackpot hits within a specified time, and a random number generator determines exactly when at what games the bonus burst occurs. The casino operator configures the time period and the number of times the jackpot will hit, so one use is to boost play during usually slow times of day.

OnTarget FEVER reserves a reward for a specific player segment. Depending on casino marketing goals, a reward could be targeted at women for ladies night, men on a guys' night out, players club members of more than a year's standing; or new club members.

To the player who's not part of a targeted group, the slot machines play as normal. There are no reduced payback percentages for players not part of the group, nor are there increased percentages for the targeted players. These bonusing systems are separate from that, an extra way to reward loyal players.

3-D TECHNOLOGY: Sphinx has long been a player favorite, with several versions of the game released over the years by Atronic, which was merged into Spielo International, and which today is under the GTECH umbrella. GTECH has turned to Sphinx once more for a real show-stopper of a game, Sphinx 3D. It features some of the best 3D effects you'll find outside big-budget movies. In fact, a few players find it a little too real, a little too intense, and GTECH has included an option to let players damp down the effect a bit.

The main event is spectacular, a journey into the heart of the Sphinx in an aerial trip on the 3D screen. There are eight different flight paths, and two different iterations of each path. It's a high-paying trek that doesn't come up all that often, so you'll rarely take the same path twice.

Coins from a big win seem to jump right off the screen. Players feel like they can reach out and grab them. Stacked wilds? They're truly stacked. Coin-shaped discs depicting a scarab stack up on the same reel position. As the stack grows, it increases the number of times a winner is collected.

Say you have a stack of five scarabs, and the wild symbol is part of a 250-credit win. You collect once, and a scarab is taken away. Then you collect again, and again, and again, and again, until all five scarabs have been removed. It's a new way of stacking wilds that would work effectively only with great 3D. And great 3D is a welcome addition to the Sphinx family.

SYMBOL MAGIC: Modern symbols don't necessarily fit into neat little boxes, one symbol per space, anymore. Regular players know of expanding wilds, where a wild symbol can expand to fill whole columns to create extra winning combinations. Now Mega Symbols that fill whole blocks of spaces are part of the designers' toolkits, as are split symbols where two of the same icon can fit in the same space.

WMS Gaming has launched a concept it calls called Mega Symbols. In Baby Dolls, the game's three characters are a rock band, with a blonde lead singer and two guitarists, one with red hair and one with blue. There are six reels, with the first and last being three symbols deep, and the other four each four symbols deep. When a Mega Symbol hits, it fills all four middle reels. In one test, the blonde singer Mega Symbol came up, and a single image of her face filled 16 spots. Mega Symbols games pay both left to right and right to left, so if you have the Mega Symbol, a matching symbol either on the first or last reel will bring a big winner.

Another intriguing concept is split symbols, pioneered by High 5 Games. High 5 is an independent game developer that has designed games for major slotmakers including Bally, IGT and Aristocrat. Shadow of the Panther is an IGT game that was designed by High 5 Games. It uses split symbols, something that's become a popular part of the High 5 designers' toolkit. On some symbols, there are two panthers in the frame instead of one. The same deal goes for leopards, tigers and other reel symbols.

If a symbol with one panther on the first reel lines up with a symbol with two panthers on the second reel, then you have three in a row and will get a small payback. If both symbols have two panthers, then you have four in a row and get a bigger return. However, if both symbols have only one panther in the frame, then you have only two in a row, and that does not bring a payback at all. By using split symbols, it makes possible big paybacks with 10 symbols on the same payline. I once called up an online version of the game at High 5 Casino on Facebook where the pay table showed a six-credit return per credit wagered on a winning payline if you have three black panthers, rising to eight for four panthers, 10 for five and so on, up to 250 for 10 panthers.

Shadow of the Panther also uses stacked symbols, which in the last few years have been adopted by nearly every slot maker. A stack of the same symbol can fill an entire column. That's great if you get matching stacks next to each other, but a stack on one of the first couple of reels means no winners that don't include that symbol. If you have matching double symbols stacked all the way across, filling the entire screen with 10-symbol pays on a 30-line game, wins can get very, very large. It also leaves a volatile game, where if the double symbols and the matching stacks aren't coming, it can make for fast losses. It's a game for gambling, rather than a game for extended time on device.

MULTIPLE PLAYING FIELDS: In recent years, IGT, Bally and WMS all have released slots with four playing fields --- that is, four sets of video slot reels on the same screen. If you're not a winner on one, perhaps you'll land a big one on another. Maybe you'll even win on all four for a big bonanza.

On IGT's Winner's Choice machines, you can play the same game four times, or mix it up, even playing four different games. Available in the first release were Cleopatra, Treasure of Troy, Siberian Storm, Dazzling Diamond Queen, Super Lotus Flower and Wolf Run.

There's a two-level mystery progressive jackpot, and some cool extra features. The player can choose the music. Tired of listening to Cleopatra's sound package? Then change to Wolf Run. In one bonus event, a wheel shows the silver and gold progressives, as well as icons for each of the six games. You could win one of the jackpots, or you could win free spins on any game --- even one you don't have active. IGT hopes that will introduce players to unfamiliar games, and maybe even make some new fans.

It's a fun player customization feature, part of the ever-evolving range of possibilities that keep the games we play fresh.

John Grochowski writes a weekly syndicated newspaper column on gambling, and is author of the "Casino Answer Book" series from Bonus Books.

Slot Tournaments

by Steve Bourie

Slot tournaments are special contests arranged by casinos where participants who get the highest scores on slot machines within an allotted amount of time, or credits, are awarded cash or prizes. Some slot tournaments are offered free of charge but most require an entry fee.

Virtually every casino today offers slot tournaments and they're used by each casino's marketing department as a promotional tool to generate more business for the casino. An interesting thing about slot tournaments is that they aren't necessarily designed as money-making events for the casino.

Some casinos will give back all of the entry fees in the form of prizes and some won't. Those casinos that give back all of the money are happy to have the tournament's contestants in their hotel rooms and playing in their casino. The thinking at these casinos is that the tournament is generating extra business and they don't have to make money off the tournament itself. These are the best kinds of tournaments to play in but they aren't always easy to find. In other instances the casinos look at tournaments strictly as a money-making venture and they'll keep part of the entry fees for themselves. In either case, tournaments can sometimes provide extra value to you and they are occasionally worth looking into.

Each month Las Vegas Advisor gives information on upcoming tournaments in that city and many gaming magazines do the same for all of the major casinos throughout the country. These publications don't list much more than the required entry fee so you'll have to call each casino for more information on the specifics. You can probably get that information over the phone but it's best to ask for a brochure to be mailed to you. This way, you'll have an official written record of the tournament rules and regulations.

When looking at the prize structure of the tournament be sure to add up the total cash value of all the prizes and compare it to the total amount of money the casino will be getting in entry fees. For instance, if the entry fee is $200 and they're limiting the tournament to 200 entrants then the casino is generating $40,000 in entry fees. Are they offering that much in cash prizes? If so, then it's a good tournament. If they're only offering $25,000 in cash, then the casino is keeping $15,000 and you may want to shop around for a different tournament that offers you more "equity." By equity we mean the value you'll be receiving in relation to the cost to enter. Positive equity means the casino is giving back more in cash and benefits than it's charging to enter the tournament. Negative equity means just the opposite: the casino is charging more than it's giving back in cash and benefits. You should always try to find a positive equity tournament.

Another thing you'll need to add into the equation when considering your equity are the extra "freebies," or discounts, that the casino will add to the package. Most casinos will host a welcoming party for the contestants, plus a free lunch or dinner and an awards banquet at the end when the winners are announced. Generally, all casinos will also offer a discounted room rate to tournament participants and some will even throw in a surprise gift for everyone. If you don't need a room then that benefit won't add anything to the value you'll be receiving but for some players a discounted room rate could mean the difference between a positive and negative equity situation. Each tournament is different and you should be sure to add up the total of all the benefits you'll receive when deciding which tournament you want to enter.

One more thing to keep in mind when looking at a tournament's structure is how the prizes are distributed. If too much is given to the top finishers that leaves less to be distributed among the other contestants. The chances are pretty good that you're not going to win one of the top prizes so it will help if the lower-tier prizes are worthwhile.

One last thing to remember about tournaments is that in many of them it pays to enter early. Most tournaments offer an "early-bird" discount if you enter by a certain date and the entry fee rises after that date. The discount can be as high as 25 percent and, once again, the reduced rate could make the difference between a positive and a negative equity situation.

Once you've found the tournament that offers you the most equity you'll need a strategy for winning. What's the best strategy? Get lucky! Slot tournaments are pure luck and there really isn't anything you can do to help you win. So, just keep pushing that spin button and hope for a good score!

Personally, I only like to play games of skill (like blackjack and video poker) so I usually don't play in slot tournaments. There was, however, one instance where I played in a tournament because of the value it offered.

Keep in mind that the following story took place many years ago, but the information is still valid for comparing the value offered by a slot tournament. My friend and I were planning a trip to Las Vegas to attend the Gaming show at the city's main convention center. This event is held each year and it's the world's largest trade show for the casino industry. The event took place during the middle of the week but we also wanted to stay over for the weekend. Unfortunately, the room rates are much higher on weekends and the hotels usually don't discount their rates very much on those days. After calling around to check rates we decided to look in the Las Vegas Advisor to find out about slot tournaments.

Boulder Station was having its All Treats, No Tricks slot tournament that same weekend. The entry fee was $199 but by entering before a certain date, the fee was reduced to $149 and there was a total of $40,000 in prize money up for grabs. The rules required 268 entrants, or else the total prize money could be reduced, but based on that required number the casino would be receiving $39,932 in prize money (assuming all early entrants) and awarding $40,000 in prize money which made this a slightly positive equity situation. Additionally, everyone received a t-shirt, a welcoming cocktail party, lunch at the Pasta Palace, an awards celebration and a reduced room rate of $25 for Friday and Saturday evening.

We had stayed at Boulder Station before and we both liked the property very much. We called the hotel's reservation department and they told us it would be $99 per night on Friday and Saturday. That was $198 for the two nights, plus 9% tax, for a total of $215.82 By entering the slot tournament our cost would be $149, plus $50 for the room for two nights, plus 9% tax (only on the room), for a total of $203.50 Hey, you want to talk about positive equity? This thing was great! Not only were they giving back all of the prize money, but in this case it was actually cheaper to enter the slot tournament than to get the room by itself!

The rules allowed us to enter as a team for the $149 fee and that also got us into the activities together. At the welcoming party we had an unlimited choice of alcoholic beverages or sodas, plus a large selection of finger sandwiches and other snacks. The Pasta Palace is a good restaurant and we had a great lunch there.

We weren't very lucky in the tournament and didn't finish high in the standings. Actually, we received the lowest cash prize which was $40. That brought our actual cost for the room and the tournament down to $163.50 which was still $52 cheaper than just getting the room by itself. Plus, we got the t-shirt, welcoming party and lunch as an added bonus.

As you can see, we saved some money by entering the slot tournament and we also had a lot of fun. You can do the same thing by checking out some of the tournaments that are available the next time you're planning a trip to a casino. Just use the toll-free numbers in this book to call the casino marketing departments, or visit their websites, for information on current tournaments.

Video Poker

by Steve Bourie

Okay, who knows the main difference between video poker and slot machines? C'mon now, raise your hands if you think you know it. If you said "a slot machine is a game of luck and video poker is a game of skill" then you are correct! When you play a slot machine there is no decision you can make which will affect the outcome of the game. You put in your money; pull the handle; and hope for the best. In video poker, however, it is your skill in playing the cards which definitely affects the outcome of the game.

Okay, who knows the other major difference between video poker and slot machines? Well, you're right again if you said "you never know what percentage a slot machine is set to pay back, but you can tell a video poker machine's payback percentage just by looking at it." Of course if you knew that answer then you also knew that video poker machines almost always offer you better returns than slot machines (provided you make the right playing decisions).

Now for those of you who didn't know the answers to those two questions, please read on. You others can skip the rest of this story as I am sure you're eager to get back to your favorite video poker machine.

First, let's cover the basics. Video poker has virtually the same rules as a game of five card draw poker. The only difference is that you have no opponent to beat and you can't lose more than your initial bet. First, you deposit from one to five coins in the machine to make your bet. You are then shown five cards on the video screen and your goal is to try to make the best poker hand possible from those cards. Since it is a draw game, you are given one opportunity to improve your hand. This is done by allowing you to discard from one, up to all five cards from your original hand. Of course, you don't have to discard any if you don't want to. After choosing which cards you want to keep (by pushing the button below each card), you then push the deal button and the machine will replace all of the other cards with new cards. Based on the resulting final hand the machine will then pay you according to the pay schedule posted on the machine. Naturally, the better your hand, the higher the amount the machine will pay you back.

That's pretty much how a video poker machine works from the outside, but what about the inside? Well, I had a few questions about that so I visited International Game Technology, which is the world's largest manufacturer of video poker machines (as well as slot machines), in January 2001 and spoke to their chief software engineer, James Vasquez. Here's what Jim had to say in answer to some questions about how his company's machines work:

Let's talk about the difference between video poker and slot machines. It's my understanding that with video poker you can't control the number of winning and losing combinations programmed into the computer chip, instead its based on a 52-card deck with a fixed number of combinations. Is that correct?

Vasquez: Yes, assuming there are no wild cards.

When the cards are dealt is it done on a serial basis where it's similar to cards coming off the top of a deck? Or, parallel where there are five cards dealt face up and one card is unseen underneath each of the initial five cards?

Vasquez: It's serial and the five later cards aren't determined until there is more player interaction at the time of the draw.

They aren't determined at the time of the deal?

Vasquez: No. They're determined at the time of the draw. That varies with the jurisdictional regulation actually. Some lottery jurisdictions tell you that you have to draw all 10 at once. Different jurisdictions write into their rules how they want it done, specifically on poker, because it's a simpler game and they understand it. They say they either want all 10 done at once, or however they want.

How is it done in Nevada? All ten at once, or five and five?

IGT: In Nevada it's five and five.

The talk with Jim Vasquez confirmed that in most regulated jurisdictions video poker machines use a Random Number Generator to shuffle a 52-card deck and then choose five cards to display to the player. (By the way, when played without wild cards, there are exactly 2,598,960 unique five-card poker hands that can be dealt to a player.) Then, when the deal button is pushed, the next group of cards is chosen and dealt to the player.

One point must be made here regarding random outcomes in video poker machines. Please note that gaming regulations always require video poker machines to have random outcomes. You should be aware that there are casinos operating in places that do not have gaming regulations. Examples are cruise ships which operate in international waters, some Indian reservations that are not subject to state regulations, and virtually all Internet casinos. You should also be aware that the technology exists for machines to be set so they do not act randomly. These machines can be actually programmed to avoid giving the players better hands and they wind up giving the house a much bigger advantage. These machines are illegal in Nevada, New Jersey, Colorado and all other states that pattern their gaming regulations after those states. You may, however, come across them in unregulated casinos.

One final point you should keep in mind - IGT is not the only manufacturer of video poker machines. There are quite a few others and they may engineer their machines to work in a different manner. Their RNG may not stop in the same way and their draw cards may be dealt differently. IGT, however, is by far the largest and it is the type of machine you will most often encounter in a casino.

Now that you understand how a video poker machine works let's learn how to pick out the best paying ones. In the beginning of this story it was mentioned that "you can tell a video poker machine's payback percentage just by looking at it." That's true, but it takes a little bit of knowledge to know the difference among all the different types of machines. An example of some of the different machines available are: Jacks or Better, Bonus, Double Bonus, Double Double Bonus, Joker Poker and Deuces Wild. To make it even more confusing, not only are there different machines, but each of those machines can have a different pay schedule for the same hand.

Fortunately, every video poker machine's payback percentage can be mathematically calculated. Not only does this let you know which machines offer you the best return, but it also tells you the best playing decisions to make on that particular machine based on the odds of that combination occurring. The bad news, however, is that it's fairly impossible to do on your own so you'll have to either buy a book that lists all of the percentages and strategies or buy a computer program that does the work for you. Take a look at the tables on the next few pages and you'll see some different types of video poker games and their payback percentages (when played with maximum coin and perfect strategy). For those of you with a computer there are several software programs on the market that can determine the exact payback percentage for any video poker machine. They retail for prices from $29.95 to $59.95, but can be purchased at discounted prices at www.americancasinoguide.com/video-poker-software. Besides calculating percentages, they also allow you to play different types of machines and analyze hands to show you the expected return for each play. You can set these games to automatically show you the best decision, or to just warn you if you make a wrong decision.

If you have no desire to get quite that serious about learning video poker then I'll try to provide some general tips to help you out. First, you'll need to find the machines that offer you the highest returns. One of the best is the 9/6 Jacks or Better machine. Of course, you're probably wondering "what is a 9/6 Jacks or Better machine?" Well, the Jacks or Better part refers to the fact that you won't win anything from the machine unless you have at least a pair of Jacks. The 9/6 part refers to the payback schedule on this kind of machine.

As stated earlier, each machine can have a different payback schedule and there are at least 20 different kinds of payback schedules available on Jacks or Better machines. In Las Vegas the two most common Jacks or Better machines you will find are 8/5 and 9/6. Here's a comparison of their pay schedules (per coin, for five-coin play):

Hand	9/6	8/5
Royal Flush	800	800
Straight Flush	50	50
4-of-a-Kind	25	25
Full House	**9**	**8**
Flush	**6**	**5**
Straight	4	4
3-of-a-Kind	3	3
Two Pairs	2	2
One Pair J's	1	1

As you can see, the schedules are identical except for the better payoffs on the 9/6 machines for Flushes and Full Houses. The payback on a 9/6 machine is 99.5% with perfect play, while the 8/5 machines return 97.3% with perfect play. Of course, it doesn't make any sense to play an 8/5 machine if a 9/6 machine is available. Yet, you'll often see lots of people playing an 8/5 when a 9/6 can often be found in the same casino. The reason they do that is because they don't know any better; you do. Always look for the 9/6 machines. They can be usually found in most downtown Las Vegas casinos at the quarter level and in many Strip casinos at denominations of $1 and higher. In other states they won't be found as easily, and sometimes, not at all.

One other common machine you will come across is an 8/5 Jacks or Better progressive. These feature the same 8/5 pay table as above except for the royal flush which pays a jackpot amount that is displayed on a meter above the machine. The jackpot will continue to build until someone hits a royal flush; then it will reset and start to build again. When the progressive jackpot (for five coins) on a 25¢ machine first starts out at $1,000 the payback is only 97.30%, but when it reaches $2,166.50, the payback is 100%.

Another good tip is to restrict your play to the same kind of machine all the time. Each video poker machine has its own particular strategy and what works best on a Jacks or Better machine is definitely much different from what works best on a Deuces Wild machine. I usually only play 9/6 Jacks or Better machines because that is what I practice on and I automatically know the best decision to make all the time. Keep in mind that when you calculate the payback percentage for a video poker machine the number you arrive at is based on perfect play. As an example, a 9/6 Jacks or Better video poker machine has a 99.5% payback with perfect play. This means that, theoretically, it will return $99.50 for every $100 played in the machine, but only if the player makes the correct decision every time. If you make mistakes, and most players do, the return to the casino will be higher. If you play several different kinds of machines it becomes increasingly harder to remember the correct play and you will make mistakes. Therefore, it only makes sense to memorize the correct decisions for one kind of machine and to always play on that same kind of machine (of course, in order to learn those proper strategies, you may want to buy that book or software).

Jacks or Better Pay Table Variations
(Per coin with maximum coin played and perfect strategy)

9/6			9/5	
Royal Flush	800		Royal Flush	800
Straight Flush	50		Straight Flush	50
4-of-a-kind	25		4-of-a-kind	25
Full House	*9*		*Full House*	*9*
Flush	*6*		*Flush*	*5*
Straight	4		Straight	4
3-of-a-kind	3		3-of-a-kind	3
2 Pair	2		2 Pair	2
Jacks or Better	1		Jacks or Better	1
Payback	**99.54%**		**Payback**	**98.45%**

8/6			8/5	
Royal Flush	800		Royal Flush	800
Straight Flush	50		Straight Flush	50
4-of-a-kind	25		4-of-a-kind	25
Full House	*8*		*Full House*	*8*
Flush	*6*		*Flush*	*5*
Straight	4		Straight	4
3-of-a-kind	3		3-of-a-kind	3
2 Pair	2		2 Pair	2
Jacks or Better	1		Jacks or Better	1
Payback	**98.39%**		**Payback**	**97.28%**

7/5			6/5	
Royal Flush	800		Royal Flush	800
Straight Flush	50		Straight Flush	50
4-of-a-kind	25		4-of-a-kind	25
Full House	*7*		*Full House*	*6*
Flush	*5*		*Flush*	*5*
Straight	4		Straight	4
3-of-a-kind	3		3-of-a-kind	3
2 Pair	2		2 Pair	2
Jacks or Better	1		Jacks or Better	1
Payback	**96.15%**		**Payback**	**95.00%**

__Bonus Poker Pay Table Variations__
(Per coin with maximum coin played and perfect strategy)

__7/5 Bonus__

Royal Flush	800
Straight Flush	50
Four Aces	80
Four 2s 3s 4s	40
Four 5s-Ks	25
Full House	*7*
Flush	*5*
Straight	4
3-of-a-kind	3
2 Pair	2
Jacks or Better	1
Payback	**98.02%**

__8/5 Bonus__

Royal Flush	800
Straight Flush	50
Four Aces	80
Four 2s 3s 4s	40
Four 5s-Ks	25
Full House	*8*
Flush	*5*
Straight	4
3-of-a-kind	3
2 Pair	2
Jacks or Better	1
Payback	**99.17%**

__10/7 Double Bonus__

Royal Flush	800
Straight Flush	50
Four Aces	160
Four 2s 3s 4s	80
Four 5s-Ks	50
Full House	*10*
Flush	*7*
Straight	5
3-of-a-kind	3
2 Pair	1
Jacks or Better	1
Payback	**100.17%**

__9/7 Double Bonus__

Royal Flush	800
Straight Flush	50
Four Aces	160
Four 2s 3s 4s	80
Four 5s-Ks	50
Full House	*9*
Flush	*7*
Straight	5
3-of-a-kind	3
2 Pair	1
Jacks or Better	1
Payback	**99.11%**

__10/6 Double Double Bonus__

Royal Flush	800
Straight Flush	50
Four Aces w/ 2, 3 or 4	400
Four 2, 3 or 4 w/A-4	160
Four Aces	160
Four 2,3 or 4	80
Four 5-K	50
Full House	*10*
Flush	*6*
Straight	4
3-of-a-kind	3
2 Pair	1
Jacks or Better	1
Payback	**100.07%**

__9/6 Double Double Bonus__

Royal Flush	800
Straight Flush	50
Four Aces w/ 2, 3 or 4	400
Four 2, 3 or 4 w/A-4	160
Four Aces	160
Four 2,3 or 4	80
Four 5-K	50
Full House	*9*
Flush	*6*
Straight	4
3-of-a-kind	3
2 Pair	1
Jacks or Better	1
Payback	**98.98%**

Deuces Wild Pay Table Variations
(Per coin with maximum coin played and perfect strategy)

Short Pay

Natural Royal Flush	800
Four Deuces	200
Wild Royal Flush	25
5-of-a-kind	15
Straight Flush	9
4-of-a-kind	*4*
Full House	3
Flush	2
Straight	2
3-of-a-kind	1
Payback	**94.34%**

Full Pay

Natural Royal Flush	800
Four Deuces	200
Wild Royal Flush	25
5-of-a-kind	15
Straight Flush	9
4-of-a-kind	*5*
Full House	3
Flush	2
Straight	2
3-of-a-kind	1
Payback	**100.76%**

Not So Ugly (NSU) Deuces

Natural Royal Flush	800
Four Deuces	200
Wild Royal Flush	25
5-of-a-kind	*16*
Straight Flush	*10*
4-of-a-kind	*4*
Full House	*4*
Flush	*3*
Straight	2
3-of-a-kind	1
Payback	**99.73%**

Deuces Deluxe

Natural Royal Flush	800
Four Deuces	200
Natural Straight Flush	50
Wild Royal Flush	25
5-of-a-kind	15
Natural 4-of-a-kind	10
Wild Straight Flush	9
Wild 4-of-a-kind	4
Full House	4
Flush	3
Straight	2
3-of-a-kind	1
Payback	**100.34%**

Now that you've decided which machines to play, you'll need some help with strategy. On the next page is a chart that will give you an excellent simple strategy to use for both 9/6 and 8/5 video poker machines. For each dealt hand, start at the top of the chart, and hold the cards for the first available hand type.

The chart was derived from calculations using the video poker software program called Optimum Video Poker by Dan Paymar. The chart does not take into account any penalty card situations (where the holding of some cards can lessen your chance of getting a straight or a flush), but it will still give you an expected return of 99.5429%, which is within 0.001% off of perfect play. Most players would lose more through inadvertent deviations from a chart with several penalty considerations. Although the chart was created specifically for 9/6 paytables, it can also be used for 8/5 games for a return of 99.29% (within 0.002% of perfect play).

Optimum Strategy Chart For 9/6 Jacks or Better

1. Royal Flush
2. Straight Flush
3. 4 of a kind
4. 4 card Royal Flush
5. Full House
6. Flush
7. 3 of a kind
8. Straight
9. 4 card Straight Flush
10. Two Pairs
11. 4 card Inside Straight Flush
12. High Pair (Jacks or higher)
13. 3 card Royal Flush
14. 4 card Flush
15. 4 card Straight with 3 high cards
16. Low Pair (2's through 10's)
17. 4 card Straight with 1 or 2 high cards
18. 3 card Inside Straight Flush with 2 high cards
19. 3 card Straight Flush with 1 high card
20. 4 card Straight with no high cards
21. 3 card Double Inside Straight Flush with 2 high cards
22. 3 card Inside Straight Flush with 1 high card
23. 3 card Straight Flush with no high cards
24. 2 card Royal Flush (Q-J)
25. 4 high cards (A-K-Q-J)
26. 2 card Royal Flush with no 10
27. 4 card Inside Straight with 3 high cards
28. 3 card Double Inside Straight Flush with 1 high card
29. 3 card Inside Straight Flush with no high card
30. 3 high cards with no Ace (K-Q-J)
31. 2 high cards (Q-J)
32. 2 card Royal Flush (J-10)
33. 2 high cards (K-Q or K-J)
34. 2 card Royal Flush (Q-10)
35. 2 high cards (A-K, A-Q or A-J)
36. 1 high card (J or Q)
37. 2 card Royal Flush (K-10)
38. 1 high card (A or K)
39. 3 card Double Inside Straight Flush with no high card
40. Redraw (All New Cards)

To use the chart just look up your hand and play it in the manner that is closest to the top of the chart. For example: you are dealt (6♣,6♦,7♥,8♠,9♣). You keep (6♣,6♦) rather than (6♦,7♥,8♠,9♣) because a low pair (#16) is higher on the chart than a four-card straight with no high cards (#20). Remember to always look for the highest possible choice on the chart when there are multiple ways to play your hand. As another example: you are dealt (8♣,8♦, J♥,Q♥,K♥). You keep (J♥,Q♥,K♥) rather than (8♣,8♦) because a three-card royal flush (#13) is higher on the chart than a low pair (#16). As a final, but radical, example of how to play your hand by the chart what would you do if you're dealt (6♥,10♥,J♥,Q♥,K♥)? Yes, you have to break up your flush by discarding the 6♥ and go for the royal flush because the four-card royal flush (#4) is higher on the chart than the pat flush (#6). When looking at the 9/6 chart there are a few things that should seem rather obvious:

1) A low pair is relatively good. Of the 40 possible hands, a low pair is #16 which means there are 24 hands worse than a low pair. If you look at the 15 hands that are better than a low pair nine of them are pat hands that require no draw. Of the other six hands, five of them are four card hands and the remaining hand is a three-card royal flush.

2) Don't hold three cards trying to get a straight or flush. Nowhere on the chart do you see that you should hold three cards to try for a straight or flush. In some instances you should hold three cards to try for a straight flush, but never a straight or flush.

3) Rarely draw to an inside straight. Inside straights (6,7,_,9,10) appear only twice on the chart and only in rather bad positions: #27 (with three high cards) and #25 (with four high cards). It is much easier to draw to an outside straight (_7,8,9,10_) where you can complete your straight by getting the card you need on either end. Open end straights appear three times on the chart and in much higher positions than inside straights: #20 (with no high cards), #17 (with one or two high cards) and #15 (with three high cards).

4) Don't hold a kicker. A kicker is an unpaired card held with a pair. For example (8,8,K) or (K,K,9) are examples of hands where an extra card (the kicker) is held. Never hold a kicker because they add no value to your hand!

If you want to make your own video poker strategy charts there are some special video poker programs that can do this for you. For information on buying these programs, go to http://www.americancasinoguide.com/video-poker-software.html With these specialized video poker software programs you can then print out the strategy charts and bring them with you into the casino.

For your information there are exactly 2,598,960 unique poker hands that can be dealt on a video poker machine (when played without a joker). Depending on the strategy that is used, on a 9/6 Jacks or Better machine a royal flush will occur about once every 40,000 hands; a straight flush about every 9,000 hands; four-of-a-kind about every 425 hands; a full house about every 87 hands; a

Other Video Poker Game Pay Tables
(Per coin with maximum coin played and perfect strategy)

Pick'Em Poker (five coin payout)

Royal Flush	6,000
Straight Flush	1,199
4-of-a-kind	600
Full House	90
Flush	75
Straight	55
3-of-a-kind	25
Two Pair	15
Pair 9's or Better	10
Payback	**99.95%**

All American Poker

Royal Flush	800
Straight Flush	200
4-of-a-kind	40
Full House	8
Flush	8
Straight	8
3-of-a-kind	3
Two Pair	1
Pair Jacks or Better	1
Payback	**100.72%**

Double Joker Full-Pay

Natural Royal Flush	800
Wild Royal Flush	100
5-of-a-kind	50
Straight Flush	25
4-of-a-kind	*9*
Full House	5
Flush	4
Straight	3
3-of-a-kind	2
2 Pair	1
Payback	**99.97%**

Double Joker Short-Pay

Natural Royal Flush	800
Wild Royal Flush	100
5-of-a-kind	50
Straight Flush	25
4-of-a-kind	*8*
Full House	5
Flush	4
Straight	3
3-of-a-kind	2
2 Pair	1
Payback	**98.10%**

flush about every 91 hands; a straight about every 89 hands; three-of-a-kind about every 14 hands; two pairs about every 8 hands; and a pair of Jacks or better about every 5 hands. The interesting thing to note here is that both a flush and a straight are harder to get than a full house, yet a full house always has a higher payback. The majority of the time, about 55% to be exact, you will wind up with a losing hand on a 9/6 machine.

The next bit of advice concerns how many coins you should bet. You should always bet the maximum amount (on machines returning 100% or more) because it will allow you to earn bonus coins when you hit the royal flush. Example: for a royal flush on a 9/6 machine with one coin played you receive 250 coins; for two coins you get 500; for three coins you get 750; for four coins you get 1,000 and for five (maximum) coins you get 4,000 coins. This translates into a bonus of 2,750 coins! A royal flush can be expected once every 40,400 hands on a 9/6 Jacks or Better machine and once every 40,200 hands on an 8/5 Bonus Poker machine. The odds are high, but the added bonus makes it worthwhile. If you can't afford to play the maximum coins on a positive machine then move down to a lower denomination machine. And, if you absolutely insist on playing less than the maximum, be sure to play only one at a time. It doesn't make any sense to play two, three or four coins, because you still won't be eligible for the bonus.

One important thing to keep in mind when you look at the total payback on these video poker machines is that those numbers always include a royal flush and the royal flush plays a very big factor in the total return. As a matter of fact, the royal flush is such a big factor on video poker machines that you are actually expected to lose until you get that royal flush. Yes, even by restricting your play to video poker machines with a more than 100% payback you are still expected to lose money until you hit a royal flush. Once you hit that royal flush it will bring your cash back up to that 100% level but until it happens you should be fully aware that you are statistically expected to lose money.

According to video poker expert Bob Dancer, "on a 25¢ Jacks or Better 9/6 machine you will lose at a rate of 2.5% while you are waiting for the royal to happen. Another way to look at this is quarter players who play 600 hands per hour can expect to lose about $18.75 per hour, on average, on any hour they do not hit a royal." You really have to keep in mind that there are no guarantees when you play video poker. Yes, you are expected to get a royal flush about once every 40,000 hands but there are no guarantees that it will happen and if you don't get that royal flush it could cost you dearly.

A final tip about playing video poker concerns players clubs. Every major casino has a club and you should make it a point to join the players club before you insert your first coin. It doesn't cost anything to join and as a member you will have the opportunity to earn complimentaries from the casinos in the form of cash, food, shows, drinks, rooms or other "freebies." When you join the club you'll be issued a card (similar to a credit card) that you insert in the machine before you start to play and it will track how much you bet, as well as how long you play. Naturally, the more money you gamble, the more freebies you'll earn. Just make sure you don't get carried away and bet more than you're comfortable with just to earn some extra comps. Ideally, you want to get comps for gambling that you were going to do anyway and not pressured into betting more than you had planned. Many clubs will also give you cash back for your play and that amount should be added into the payback percentage on the kind of machine you'll be playing. For example, let's say a slot club rebates .25% in cash for your video poker play. By only playing 9/6 Jacks or Better machines with a return of 99.54% you can add the .25% rebate to get an adjusted figure of 99.79%. This means that you are, theoretically, playing an almost even game, plus you're still eligible for other room and food discounts on top of your cash rebate.

"Not So Ugly Deuces" Optimum Strategy

by Steve Bourie

The following strategy chart was created with a software program called Optimum Video Poker by Dan Paymar. The program can be used to practice video poker just like a regular game. However, it can also show you how to use the best strategies, analyze any video poker game, plus it can create customized strategy charts for any video poker game.

To buy this program at a discounted price, or to learn more about it, plus other similar programs, go to: www.americancasinoguide.com/video-poker-software.html

There are numerous pay tables for Deuces Wild games, but keep in mind that this chart only applies to the "NSUD" pay table found in the previous story.

If followed accurately, the expected return (when playing maximum coin) is 99.71%, which is less than 0.012% off of perfect play.

To use the chart, count the number of deuces in the hand that you are originally dealt. Then, hold the first hand-type available in that group.

Four Deuces
1. Just the Deuces

Three Deuces
1. Wild Royal
2. 5 of a Kind
3. Just the Deuces

Two Deuces
1. Wild Royal
2. 5 of a Kind
3. Straight Flush (SF)
4. 4 of a Kind
5. 4 card Royal Flush
6. 4 card SF
7. 4 card Inside SF
8. 4 card SF (2-2-5-6)
9. 4 card SF (2-2-4-5)
10. Just the Deuces

One Deuce
1. Wild Royal
2. 5 of a Kind
3. Straight Flush (SF)
4. 4 of a Kind
5. Full House
6. 4 card Royal Flush
7. Flush
8. 4 card SF
9. 4 card Inside SF
10. Straight
11. 4 card Double-Inside SF
12. 3 of a Kind
13. 4 card SF (Ace low)
14. 3 card Royal Flush
15. 3 card SF
16. 3 card Inside SF
17. Just the Deuce

No Deuces

1. Royal Flush
2. 4 card Royal Flush
3. Straight Flush (SF)
4. 4 of a Kind
5. Full House
6. Flush
7. Straight
8. 4 card SF
9. 3 of a Kind
10. 4 card Inside SF
11. 3 card Royal Flush
12. 3 card Inside SF (Ace low)
13. 4 card Flush
14. 2 Pairs
15. 3 card SF
16. 1 Pair
17. 4 card Straight
18. 3 card Inside SF
19. 3 card Double-Inside SF
20. 2 card Royal Flush (no Ace)
21. 3 card Inside SF (Ace low)
22. 4 card Inside Straight
23. Redraw

Dan Paymar, the creator of Optimum Video Poker, also offers the following advice for using this strategy chart.

Note that any deuces in the dealt hand are included in the hand type description. For example, "4 card Straight Flush" in the "1 Deuce" group could be 2-5♥-6♥-7♥ or 2-9♥-10♥-J♥ (where the non-deuces are all the same suit), but not 2-10♥-J♥-Q♥ since that would be a 4 card Royal Flush which is higher in the chart. A hand such as 2-6♥-8♥-9♥ would not qualify since that would be a 4 card Inside Straight Flush which is lower in the chart.

This strategy is optimized. That is, there are no penalty considerations, and it's simplified in situations that occur infrequently and have very small EV difference. The total net "cost" of this optimization is less than 0.012% off of perfect play and less than 0.005% off of the best published professional strategy for this game. Most players will actually achieve better payback with this strategy than they would with a professional strategy due to many fewer inadvertent deviations from the chart.

Why is this game called "Not So Ugly Deuces"? The original full pay Deuces Wild has the per-coin payoff schedule 1-2-2-3-5-9-15-25-200-800. A game analysis shows that the 5-for-1 payoff for four of a kind contributes over 32% of the game's payback. Many casinos offer this game, but with the quads payoff reduced to 4-for-1. With no strategy change, this reduces the payback by 1/5 of that 32% or more than 6%. This game has the 4-for-1 quads payoff, but increases the payoffs for four other hands. The result, assuming perfect strategy, is 99.726% payback, so many players clubs benefits put it to just about 100%. Multiple points days and/or off-point comps can also make it attractive to advantage players.

The Government's Interest in Your Gambling

by Jean Scott

It's no surprise to anyone, I imagine, that the federal government is interested in what happens in a casino—or anywhere else where gambling occurs. And where there's government, there's paperwork.

The W-2G - Gamblers, if they know anything about gambling paperwork, are probably most familiar with the IRS form W-2G (the G stands for gambling) that applies to "Certain Gambling Winnings." This is the tax form that any for-profit organization issues you—and sends a copy to the IRS—when you win a specified amount while gambling. (Churches and other non-profit organizations are exempt from issuing W-2Gs.)

Most people don't know that there are different rules for when a W-2G must be issued, depending on the form of gambling. For horse and dog racing, jai alai, state lotteries, and some other kinds of wagering, this form must be given for any winnings that are at least 300 times the amount of the bet. However, there's a special rule for bingo and slot machines: You get a W-2G for a gross win that's $1,200 or more, no matter how much your original bet was. And to make it more complicated, keno has its own special rule: a W-2G for any net win of $1,500 or more.

A player will receive a W-2G for a single winning table-game bet if both of the following apply:
1.   The payout is $600 or more and
2.   The winnings are paid at 300-to-1 (or higher).
Some examples would be progressives on Caribbean Stud and Fortune Pai Gow and some bonus bets on Let It Ride.

An important note on W-2G rules for machine play: You don't get a W-2G when you cash out more than $1,200 on a slot machine after a period of play. It's required only for the win of $1,200 or more on one hand or spin. I've heard of players who've had to explain this to green casino employees, especially in Indian casinos.

Also, on multi-line machines, all line winners on one "play" are totaled together and are usually considered one hand. For example, on the usual non-progressive quarter Triple Play machine, a dealt royal gives you a $1,000 win on each of the three lines. When multi-line first came out, there was confusion on this issue. Sometimes it was treated as three separate hands and no W-2G was issued. Occasionally, you might find a casino that still does it this way. However, the common practice is to consider all lines together as one hand, and in this example, you'd be issued a W-2G for $3,000.

Both players and casinos harbor some widespread misconceptions about W-2Gs. First, most players believe (or want to believe) that if you don't get a W-2G, you don't have to report that particular gambling win. And this viewpoint is supported by information in print, even from otherwise accurate gambling writers, seeming to encourage players to look for a machine with a top jackpot under $1,200.

Surprisingly, even the casinos seem to encourage this kind of thinking. I've seen many slot machines with a $1,199 top jackpot that seems to give the appearance of circumventing tax law. Some casinos have reduced the payoffs slightly on some winning video poker hands, so the jackpot is just under the W-2G-issuing amount of $1,200, such as a $5 machine that drops the regular payoff of 250 credits ($1,250) for the straight flush to 239 ($1,195). Or they create a high-limit slot machine that replaces W-2G-generating jackpots on a primary game with lots of bonus wins on a secondary one, keeping each one under that paperwork $1,200 figure.

No matter how shrewdly gambling writers and casinos may seem to be steering you down a different and dangerous path, you're responsible for reporting all gambling wins, and whether you get a W-2G or not has no bearing on that. The fact that many people don't report gambling wins when there's no W-2G evidence won't help you in an IRS audit.

INCOME TAX WITHHOLDING - Federal tax withholding is not required for any amount of winnings from slot machines, bingo, and keno for U.S. citizens who have proper ID and give a Social Security number. However, you may request withholding by the casino for any amount, a handy technique at times to save you the extra paperwork of filing estimated taxes. Casinos will usually do this for you with no problems, but occasionally I've had this request refused, because the particular employee wasn't familiar with the procedure or didn't want to bother with it.

SOCIAL SECURITY NUMBERS - "A couple of years ago, a friend hit a $2,000 royal flush at an Indian casino in Wisconsin. He did not carry his Social Security card with him and, as a result, they wouldn't pay him anything. They did allow him to return later with the card and get his money, but it proved to be a huge hassle."

"One casino in Florida will withhold federal income tax if you cannot present a valid Social Security card—no exceptions—they wouldn't even take my valid military ID card with SSN and photo on it."

The horror stories pour in when the subject of Social Security numbers and casinos is brought up on Internet gambling forums. We all know that identity theft is a big problem and we've been warned not to carry anything that has our Social Security number on it. But the message hasn't seemed to get to some casinos.

The fact is that there's no federal or state law that requires a U.S. citizen to give printed proof of his Social Security number in order to be issued a W-2G and paid a jackpot. He can provide it verbally or write it down. But you may ask how the casino can be sure that a customer gives the correct number. The IRS has provided a form they can give to the player, a W-9 form, Request for Taxpayer Identification Number and Certification (see Appendix A-6). By signing this form, you are certifying, under penalties of perjury, that this is your Social Security number.

I hear your next question already. No, you don't have to give your Social Security number, but in that case, the IRS requires that the casino withhold 28% of the winnings for federal income tax.

As shown by the stories at the beginning of this section, some casinos seem to mix up Social Security cards and ID cards. You do have to show a valid ID or the casino can refuse to pay off a W-2G jackpot until you do. You do not have to show your original Social Security card. In fact, it is written right on your Social Security card that it is not be used as identification.

What can you do if a casino doesn't seem to be following the IRS rules and requires an original Social Security card? I'd ask to speak to a supervisor or even a senior casino executive. One player suggested carrying W-9 forms with you (they can be printed out from the IRS website) and giving one to the casino employee making this mistaken request.

Jean Scott is one of the country's most renowned and successful gamblers. Her first book, The Frugal Gambler, has been a best-seller for many years. She also wrote a sequel, More Frugal Gambling, and a tax guide for gamblers. She provides a complete resource package for video poker players, from beginners to the experienced. For more information on this subject watch Jean Scott's video "Gambling and Taxes" on the American Casino Guide's YouTube channel at youtube.com/americancasinoguide

 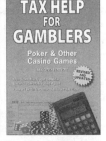

Boyd's Eye View of Video Poker - Blurred Lines

by Linda Boyd

Is there anybody who hasn't seen at least one of the two video versions of Robin Thicke's hit tune "Blurred Lines", with T.I. and Pharrell? I personally liked both the YouTube and Vevo videos of this tongue-in-cheek song.It reminded me more of Robert Palmer's "Addicted to Love" than Marvin Gaye's "Got To Give It Up", but "hey, hey, hey" that's just me. (Marvin Gaye's estate unsuccessfully sued Thicke and friends for plagiarism over the recording.)

I immediately thought of video poker (VP) games when I saw the title and concluded that there are different strokes for different folks. That's because some players want a high risk game and are willing to pay the potential price of a quick bankroll loss that comes with the possibility of big thrill wins. The lines become even more obscured when you factor in the all important theoretical expected return (ER) for various versions of the same game. In other words, what's an acceptable return for one player may not be for another. Throw in a multitude of other variables, like cash for points, comps and other perks and you have quite a blurry distinction between casinos in terms of player benefits.

To Play or Not To Play: Once upon a time there was an abundance of outstanding VP games in the state of Nevada, especially Las Vegas. You might think that with the enormous expansion in the number of casinos nationwide the competition would bring about even better choices. If so, your thinking, logical as it may be, is wrong. That's because along came a myriad of entities with their hands planted firmly in the pockets of casino owners. The more pie slices removed by bureaucracies the fewer pieces left for the patrons. That's exactly what happened in the gaming industry. VP was hit especially hard by management's over-reaction to having the theoretical expected return data (ER) sent to them by gaming manufacturers. Nevermind that you only receive the stated ER with computer-perfect play and that's something few players are skilled enough to do; the ER for less accurate play, of course, is lower. This brings us to the need to make an educated decision of whether or not we still wish to play the game. In fact, another VP writer submitted a scathing article about one of my YouTube videos because I didn't scorn people who chose to play a version of Jacks or Better (JOB) other than 9/6JOB. In fact, I clearly highlighted 9/6JOB explaining the name, showing the pay schedule and the relevant mathematical data associated with the game. I do not, however, see it as my place to ridicule people who choose to play a game in spite of the house's increased edge. My purpose is to present the facts and let players make their own informed decisions about whether or not they still want to play.

Low Variance Games: If you're interested in staying in the game for several hours and not busting your bankroll then look for 9/6 Jacks or Better (9/6JOB). If you can't find it then consider 8/5Bonus Poker (8/5BP) or Not-So-Ugly Deuces (NSUD). The variance for both 8/5BP (20.90) and NSUD (25.62) is higher than 9/6JOB (19.52) but 9/6JOB isn't available anymore in many casinos. NSUD in fact has a higher ER (99.73%) than 9/6JOB (99.54%) but it too is difficult to find. You will need to make sure you locate the right game (free removable pay schedules, games strategies and ER data can be found in my book, "The Video Poker Edge") and know the basic game strategy. As I've said in the past, low variance games increase your promotional equity in the long run since most casinos award entries based on coin in. So in addition to more cash back (it's based on your coin-in as well) by increasing your slot club points, you'll have better odds of winning drawings. I understand that some players find JOB games boring and lament every time they're only paid 125 coins for quads (assuming a 5-coin wager), but statistics don't lie. You should avoid complaining when your high variance DDB (Double Double Bonus) game results in empty pockets and you become a spectator.

Table 1.1: Comparing Jacks or Better Games

Hand/ 5-Coin Bet	9/6 JOB	9/5 JOB	*8/5 JOB
Royal Flush	4000	4000	4000
Straight Flush	250	250	250
4 of a Kind	125	125	125
Full House	45	45	40
Flush	30	25	25
Straight	20	20	20
3 of a Kind	15	15	15
Two Pairs	10	10	10
Jacks or Better	5	5	5
Expected Return	99.5439%	98.4498%	97.2984%
Variance	19.51468	19.49564	19.32326

*Note that 8/5JOB is often found on progressive games and usually the progressive involves only the royal flush. If that's the case, both the ER and variance will be higher in the progressive version than the non-progressive. It's good to have a higher ER but a higher variance increases the risk of running out of bankroll. Also, for computer-perfect play you'll have to make some strategy adjustments as the payout for a royal flush increases. However, make no mistake, given a choice between 8/5JOB progressive and 8/5JOB, always selecting the progressive version is a no-brainer.

Interpreting Table 1.1: Notice that the variances for the three versions of JOB in Table 1.1 are similar to each other, but there's a huge divide when it comes to the ER. All three in fact have a relatively low variance or risk of losing your bankroll but in the absence of other perks I would only play 9/6JOB due to the higher return. I frequently hear players argue that there's "just one coin" difference on "just one hand" between 9/6JOB and 9/5JOB but the data in Table 1.1 tells a different story. You can see that the ER is over 1% higher for 9/6JOB as compared with 9/5JOB; in VP speak that's huge.

For those who know all this and still want to play 9/5JOB because it has the highest ER available within the casino, you've probably made a better decision than playing slots. That's because with video poker you can determine the ER and you can't with slots. Mostly, the ER for slot choices is considerably lower than 98.45%, which you'll get for accurate play on 9/5JOB.

A quick way of spotting low-variance non-deuces games is to check the payouts for frequent hands, like two pair (occurs approximately once every eight hands) and make sure you get a return of double your wager. There are so many deuces wild choices, several are coyote ugly, that you should bring pay tables and ER's with you. I always caution players to avoid unfamiliar games where you don't know either the ER or game strategy.

Only you can assign a value to perks, like comped rooms, food and show tickets. Refer to the "Blurred Lines" section to help you make comparisons.

High Variance Games: If you came to "go big or go home" like some riverboat gamblers, then you'll want a high variance game like 9/6Double Double Bonus (9/6DDB) or Loose Deuces (check the casino's version against your ER tables to make sure it's got a decent theoretical return) and, once more, make sure you know basic game strategy. Be prepared to sit on the sidelines if you run out of money in a hurry because even with computer-perfect play high variance games are risky.

One of the most popular high variance choices is DDB, often found in progressive versions. You used to find an abundance of 10/6DDB (ER 100.0670%, variance 42.17654) but now you have to look harder and most are in Vegas. The bottom line is that if DDB is your passion you'll have to expect lower ER games and a big risk to your bankroll.

Table 1.2: Comparing Double Double Bonus Games

Hand/ 5-Coin Bet	9/6 DDB	9/5DDB	8/5 DDB
Royal Flush	4000	4000	4000
Straight Flush	250	250	250
4 Aces with 2, 3 or 4	2000	2000	2000
Four 2's, 3's or 4's with A-4	800	800	800
4 Aces	800	800	800
Four 2's, 3's, or 4's	400	400	400
4 Fives-Kings	250	250	250
Full House	45	45	40
Flush	30	25	25
Straight	20	20	20
3 of a Kind	20	20	20
2 Pair	5	5	5
Jacks or Better	5	5	5
Expected Return	98.9808%	97.8729%	96.7861%
Variance	41.98498	42.16708	41.99487

Interpreting Table 1.2: Just looking at the variance you can see in real numbers the increased risk of running out of money if you choose DDB over JOB, assuming similar ERs. In the case of many games outside of Nevada most of the DDB versions on the casino floor have low ERs in addition to high variances. Once more notice that the ER decreases by approximately 1.1% every time you're shorted a coin for either a flush or full house. Table 1.3 below will give you realistic hand expectations in terms of the odds.

Table 1.3: 9/6DDB Hand Frequency

Hand: 9/6DDB	Occurs Once In:
Royal	40,799
Straight Flush	9,123
4 Aces with 2, 3 or 4	16,236
Four 2's, 3's or 4's with A-4	6,983
4 Aces	5,761
Four 2's, 3's, or 4's	2,601
4 Fives-Kings	613
Full House	92
Flush	88
Straight	78
3 of a Kind	13
2 Pair	8
Jacks or Better	5

You can see that in spite of the success stories told about big wins in DDB the odds are stacked against you receiving aces with a kicker much less multiple high paying quads in a given session. In fact, if you fail to get your statistical "fair share" of quads you may quickly run out of money due to only an even money return for two pair. That translates to being shorted approximately 500 coins every 800 hands played, assuming a 5-coin wager (two pair occurs once every 8 hands so in 800 hands you'll get two pair 100 times; 5 coins lost times 100 hands equals 500 coins).

As a way of spotting volatile games look for short coin payouts for frequent hands like two pair at the bottom of the pay schedule accompanied by tantalizing big payouts for rare hand combos at the top of the pay table. Make sure you factor in that failure to play accurately will make your ER lower than the mathematical expectation. In fact that's one reason that seemingly "exciting" VP games created by non-playing game-makers rarely survive. Players lose their money quickly due to a combination of incorrect holds and low ERs. Next thing you know the latest "best thing" in video poker has no takers and the machines are gathering dust.

You'll run less money through the casino's devices on average by choosing a risky game because you've increased the odds of quickly running out of bankroll. Some people aren't playing for comps, but you should at least consider the slot cash you're sacrificing before selecting a going for broke VP game. Also, you should expect fewer promo entries whenever the house awards tickets based on coin-in, as most do.

Blurred Lines: Just like Robin Thicke's mega-hit song, there will be blurred lines as to what's good or bad and only your personal preferences can clarify the boundaries. Some video poker pundits are slaves to the ER or theoretical expected return, but they fail to factor in the game's entertainment value. You're in a casino to unwind and have fun, not to earn a living. What's reasonable for one player may not be for somebody else. Here are some specific considerations to help you unravel the tangled comparison issues.

Slot Card Points: There is an easy to use formula that will show you how to determine the value of your slot club points in my book, "The Video poker Edge". You will want to compare the cash awarded for play and can even add that amount to a game's ER. For example, if you're playing 9/5JOB (ER of 98.45%, per Table 1.1) and the slot club points are worth .25%, then the game's actual ER is 98.70% (that's 98.45% +.25%). How about if the house is offering triple points? Then 9/5 JOB would have an ER of 99.20% (99.45% +.75%). True, it's still less than the 99.54% ER of 9/6JOB but it may well be the best game in the house. My point is that you need the skills to properly evaluate a play before making a decision on whether or not to invest your money. Those expecting to earn an income off of the neighborhood casino will probably be out of luck on that goal.

Bounceback Cash: This is money mailed to you by a casino with the stipulation that you must come in person to collect. They know most gamblers will stay and play. Bounceback cash is one of many reasons to give your business to just a few casinos. That's because the amount you receive is based on the level of your play. Many casinos today award bounceback in the form of free play and require that you run the money through a device before you can cash in.

Food Comps: You will be offered either earned or discretionary food comps by most casinos. Earned comps are easy to assess since usually the amount appears on your slot club card. Discretionary comps, however, are up to the host and, like bounceback cash, based on the level of your play. Once more this is a good reason to concentrate play to a few establishments rather than spreading the wealth. You should consider the restaurant choices in terms of your personal preferences in the decision-making process. Also, if casinos are on the brink of closing their doors use your comps ASAP.

Room Comps: Most casinos with rooms will offer free accommodations to their best players. You should make sure "free" means no charge in advance. Resort fees are out of control in some locales (the Vegas Strip, for example) and you may be surprised with a hefty bill upon departure. Just like with other perks tastes vary as to the "best" room and if you won't be using a comped room then it's a worthless perk.

Entertainment Comps: You may not be privy to future entertainment options at any given casino, but you can gauge the value by looking at past bookings. If the casino has been scheduling B List acts, then don't expect Elton John. Keep in mind that even if your favorites appear you'll only be comped when you're a high level player.

Promotions: Some players prefer more chances to win mid-level prizes while others want to go for the gusto with a slim chance for a mega prize; most casinos offer a combination of the two. Nowadays almost all casinos base the number of entries you receive for a drawing on your coin in. That means the more money you run through their devices or spend at the tables the higher your promo equity. Keep in mind that most casinos require that you be present to win and give you a time limit on stepping forward.

Decision Time: Even though the big bite from the profit pie devoured by greedy bureaucracies ultimately wounds players, some establishments will ease the pain with worthwhile perks. Of course the definition of "good" varies between players. It's easy to compare money from the game's ER, slot points, bounceback cash and multiple point promotions but the lines get hazy when you're forced to compare apples to oranges. Creative perks will vary and smart management teams make it a point to find excellent perks that cost them little or nothing.

Linda Boyd, a long-time table game player before turning to video poker, writes for "Midwest Gaming and Travel," "Arizona Player" and other gaming magazines. Her book, "The Video Poker Edge," includes free removable pay schedules and her free strategy cards for the eight most popular games. The second edition is available at amazon.com, Square One Publishers and major bookstores. www.squareonepublishers.com, or see page 28 in this book.

Blackjack

by Steve Bourie

Blackjack is the most popular casino game in America and one of the biggest reasons for that is its relatively simple rules that are familiar to most casino visitors. Blackjack also has a reputation as being "beatable" and although that is true in some cases, the vast majority of players will always be playing the game with the house having a slight edge over them.

At most blackjack tables there are seven boxes, or betting areas, on the table. This means that up to seven people can play at that table and each player has their own box in front of them in which they'll place their bet. Now, before you take a seat at any blackjack table the first thing you should do is to take a look at the sign that's sitting on each table because it will tell you the minimum amount that you must bet on each hand. If you're a $5 player you certainly wouldn't want to sit at a table that has a $25 minimum so, once again, be sure to look before you sit down.

Once you're at the table you'll need chips to play with and you get them by giving your cash to the dealer who will exchange it for an equal amount of chips. Be careful, however, that you don't put your cash down into one of the betting boxes because the dealer might think you're playing it all on the next hand!

After everyone has placed their bets in their respective boxes the dealer will deal out two cards to each player. He will also deal two cards to himself; one of those cards will be face up and the other face down. Now, if you've ever read any brochures in a casino they'll tell you that the object of the game of blackjack is to get a total of cards as close to 21 as possible, without going over 21. However, that really isn't the object of the game. The true object is to beat the dealer and you do that by getting a total closer to 21 than the dealer, or by having the dealer bust by drawing cards that total more than 21.

The one thing that's strange about blackjack is that the rules can be slightly different at each casino and this is the only game where this happens. If you play baccarat, roulette or craps you'll find that the rules are virtually the same at every casino in the U.S. but that isn't the case with blackjack. For example, in most jurisdictions all of the casinos use six or eight decks that are always dealt from a rectangular box called a *shoe* and the cards are always dealt face up. In Las Vegas, some casinos will offer that same kind of game while others will offer games that use only one or two decks that are dealt directly from the dealer's hand and all of the cards will be dealt face down. To make it even stranger, some casinos in Las Vegas will offer both kinds of games in their casinos and the rules will probably change when you move from one table to

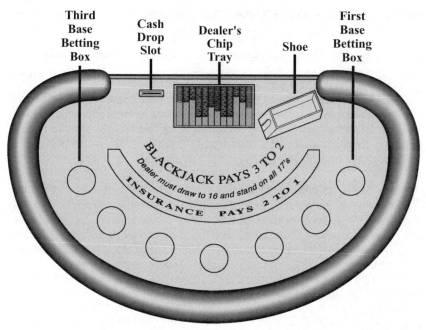

Third Base Betting Box   **Cash Drop Slot**   **Dealer's Chip Tray**   **Shoe**   **First Base Betting Box**

BLACKJACK PAYS 3 TO 2
Dealer must draw to 16 and stand on all 17's
INSURANCE PAYS 2 TO 1

Typical Blackjack Table Layout

another. There can also be other rule variations concerning doubling down and splitting of pairs but we'll talk about those later. For now, just be aware that different casinos can have different blackjack rules and some of those rules will be good for you while others will be bad for you. Hopefully, after reading this story you'll know the good rules from the bad ones and which tables are the best ones to play at.

For our purposes, we'll assume we're playing in a casino that uses six decks of cards that are dealt out of a shoe and all of the player's cards are dealt face up. By the way, whenever you play blackjack in a casino where the cards are dealt face up don't touch the cards. In that kind of game the dealer is the only who is allowed to touch the cards and if you do happen to touch them they'll give you a warning not to do it again - so, don't touch the cards!

After the cards are dealt the players must determine the total of their hand by adding the value of their two cards together. All of the cards are counted at their face value except for the picture cards - jack, queen and king which all have a value of 10 - and the aces which can be counted as either 1 or 11. If you have an ace and any 10-value card you have a blackjack which is also called a natural and your hand is an automatic winner, unless the dealer also has a blackjack in which case the hands are tied. A tie is also called a *push* and when that happens it's a standoff and you neither win nor lose. All winning blackjacks should be paid at 3-to-2, so if you bet $5, you would be paid $7.50. You should avoid playing at any game that pays 6-to-5 (or even money) for blackjacks.

If the dealer has an ace as his up card the first thing he'll do is ask if anyone wants to buy *insurance*. When you buy insurance you're betting that the dealer has a blackjack by having a 10 as his face down card. To make an insurance bet you would place your bet in the area just above your betting box that says "insurance pays 2-to-1" and you're only allowed to make an insurance bet of up to one-half the amount of your original bet. So, if you originally bet $10 you could only bet a maximum of $5 as your insurance bet. After all the insurance bets are made the dealer will check his face down card and if it's a 10 he'll turn it over and all of the insurance bets will be paid off at 2-to-1. If he doesn't have a 10 underneath, the dealer will then take away all of the losing insurance bets and the game will continue. By the way, according to basic strategy, insurance is a bad bet and you should never make an insurance bet.

If the dealer has a 10 as his up card the first thing he'll do is check to see if he has an ace underneath which would give him a blackjack. If he does have an ace he'll turn it face up and start collecting the losing bets that are out on the table. If he doesn't have an ace underneath the game will continue. In some casinos, however, the dealer won't check his hole card until after all of the hands are played out.

If the dealer doesn't have an ace or a 10 as his up card the game continues and the dealer will start with the player to his immediate left to see if they want another card. If a player wants another card they indicate that with a hand signal by tapping or scratching the table with their finger to show they want another card. Taking a card is also known as *hitting* or taking a hit. If a player doesn't want another card they would just wave their hand palm down over their cards. Not taking another card is known as *standing*. The reason hand signals are used is because it eliminates any confusion on the part of the dealer as to exactly what the player wants and it also allows the security people to follow the game on the closed-circuit cameras that are hung from the ceiling throughout the casino.

Keep in mind that the hand signals will be slightly different if you're playing in a casino where the cards are dealt face down and you're allowed to pick them up. In that situation a player would signal that they wanted another card by scratching the table with the edges of the two cards they're holding. If they didn't want another card, they would simply place their two cards under the bet in their box.

In either case, if a player draws another card the value of that card is added to the total of the other cards and the player can continue to draw cards unless he gets a total of more than 21 in which case he busts and loses his bet.

When a player doesn't want any more cards, or stands, the dealer then moves on to the next player and after all of the players are finished then it's the dealer's turn to play. While each player can decide whether or not they want another card the dealer doesn't have that option and he must play by a fixed set of rules that require him to draw a card whenever his total is 16 or less and to stop when his total is 17 or more. If the dealer goes over 21 then he has busted and all of the players remaining in the game will be paid 1-to-1, or even money, on their bet.

If the dealer doesn't bust then each player's hand is compared to the dealer's. If the player's total is higher than the dealer's then they win and are paid even money. If the player's hand has a total that is lower than the dealer's hand then the player loses his bet. If the player and the dealer have the same total then it's a tie, or a push and neither hand wins. After all of the bets have been paid off, or taken by the dealer, a new round begins and new hands are dealt to all of the players.

When deciding how to play your hand there are also three other options available to you besides standing or hitting. The first is called ***doubling down*** and most casinos will allow a player to double their bet on their first two cards and draw only one more card. To do this you would place an amount equal to your original bet right next to it and then the dealer would give you one more card, sideways, to indicate that your bet was a double down. To double down in a game where the cards are dealt face down you would turn up your original two cards and tell the dealer you wanted to double down. Then, after you double your bet, the dealer would give you one more card face down. Some casinos may have restrictions on this bet and may only allow you to double down if the total of your two cards is 10 or 11, but it's always to your advantage if they allow you to double down on any two cards.

Another thing you can do is ***split*** your cards if you have a pair and then play each card as a separate hand. For example, if you had a pair of 8's you would place a bet equal to your original bet right next to it and tell the dealer you wanted to split your pair. The dealer would then separate your two 8's and give you one card on your first 8. Unlike doubling down, however, you are not limited to only getting one card and you can play your hand out normally. When you were finished with your first hand the dealer would then give you a card on your other 8 and you would play that hand out. Although you aren't usually limited to just one card on your splits, there is one instance where that will happen and that happens when you split aces. Almost all casinos will give you just one card on each ace when you split them. Also, if you get a 10-value card with your ace it will only count as 21 and not as a blackjack so you'll only get even money on that bet if you win. Besides splitting pairs you can also split all 10-value cards such as jack-king or 10-queen but it would be a very bad idea to do that because you would be breaking up a 20 which is a very strong hand and you should never split 10's. By the way, if you wanted to split a pair in a casino where the cards are dealt face down you would simply turn your original two cards face-up and tell the dealer that you wanted to split them.

The last option you have is not available in most casinos but you may come across it in some casinos and it's called *surrender*. With the surrender option you're allowed to lose half of your bet if you decide you don't want to play out your hand after looking at your first two cards. Let's say you're dealt a 10-6 for a total of 16 and the dealer has a 10 as his face-up card. A 16 is not a very strong hand, especially against a dealer's 10, so in this case it would be a good idea to surrender your hand and when the dealer came to your cards you would say "surrender." The dealer would then take half of your bet and remove your cards. Surrender is good for the player because in the long run you will lose less on the bad hands you're dealt and you should always try to play in a casino that offers the surrender option.

All right, we've covered the basics of how to play the game of blackjack and all of the possible options a player has, so the next question is how do you win? Well, the best way to win is to become a card counter, but for the average person that isn't always possible so let's start off by taking a look at basic blackjack strategy.

Computer studies have been done on the game of blackjack and millions of hands have been analyzed to come up with a basic formula for how to play your hand in any given situation. The main principle that these decisions are based on is the dealer's up card because, remember that the dealer has no say in whether or not he takes a card - he must play by the rules that require him to draw a card until he has a total of 17 or more. Now, according to these computer calculations the dealer will bust more often when his up card is a 2,3,4,5 or 6 and he will complete more hands when his up card is a 7,8,9,10-value card or an ace. Take a look at the following chart that shows how each up-card affects the dealer's chance of busting:

Chance The Dealer's Up Card Will Bust

2	35%
3	38%
4	40%
5	43%
6	42%
7	26%
8	24%
9	23%
10	21%
Ace	11%

As you can see, the dealer will bust most often when he has a 5 or 6 as his upcard and he will bust the least amount, approximately 11% of the time, when his upcard is an ace. This means it's to your advantage to stand more often when the dealer's upcard is a 2 through 6 and hope that the dealer will draw cards that make him bust. It also means that when the dealer's upcard is a 7 through ace he will complete more of his hands and in that situation you should draw cards until you have a total of 17 or more.

Now let's show you how to play your hands by using the basic strategy and we'll start off with the *hard hand* strategy and hard hand means a two-card total without an ace. A hand with an ace is known as a **soft hand** because the ace can be counted as either a 1 or an 11. So, if you had an ace-6 you would have a soft 17 hand and if you had a 10-6 you would have a hard 16 hand. Later on we'll take a look at how to play soft hands, but for now we'll concentrate on the hard hand totals. Oh yes, one more thing, the following basic strategy applies to casinos where they deal more than one deck at a time and the dealer stands on soft 17, which is the situation you'll find in the majority of casinos today. So, keep in mind that the strategy would be slightly different if you were playing against a single deck and it would also be slightly different if the dealer hit a soft 17.

Whenever your first two cards total 17 through 21, you should stand, no matter what the dealer's up card is.

If your cards total 16, you should stand if the dealer has a 2 through 6 as his upcard otherwise, draw a card. By the way, 16 is the worst hand you can have because you will bust more often with 16 than with any other hand. So, if that's the case then why would you want to ever hit a 16? Well, once again, those computer studies have shown that you should hit a 16 when the dealer has 7 through ace as his upcard because in the long run you will lose less often. This means that yes, 16 is a terrible hand, but you should hit it because if you don't you will lose even more often than when you do take a card.

If your cards total 15, you should also stand if the dealer has a 2 through 6 as his upcard otherwise, draw cards until your total is 17 or more.

The same rules from 15 and 16 also apply if your cards total 14. Stand if the dealer has a 2 through 6, otherwise draw cards until your total is 17 or more. The same rules also apply if your cards total 13. Stand if the dealer has a 2 through 6, otherwise draw cards until your total is 17 or more.

When your cards total 12 you should only stand when the dealer has a 4,5 or 6 as his upcard, remember - those are his three weakest cards and he will bust more often with those cards, so you don't want to take a chance on busting yourself. If the dealer's upcard is a 2 or a 3, then you should take just one card and stop on your total of 13 or more. Finally, if the dealer has a 7 through ace as his upcard then you should draw cards until your total is 17 or more.

Basic Strategy - Single Deck

Dealer stands on soft 17 • Double on any 2 cards • Double allowed after split

Your Hand	Dealer's Upcard									
	2	3	4	5	6	7	8	9	10	A
17	ALWAYS STAND ON HARD 17 (OR MORE)									
16	-	-	-	-	-	H	H	H	H*	H
15	-	-	-	-	-	H	H	H	H*	H
14	-	-	-	-	-	H	H	H	H	H
13	-	-	-	-	-	H	H	H	H	H
12	H	H	-	-	-	H	H	H	H	H
11	ALWAYS DOUBLE									
10	D	D	D	D	D	D	D	D	H	H
9	D	D	D	D	D	H	H	H	H	H
8	H	H	H	D	D	H	H	H	H	H
A,8	-	-	-	-	D	-	-	-	-	-
A,7	-	D	D	D	D	-	-	H	H	-
A,6	D	D	D	D	D	H	H	H	H	H
A,5	H	H	D	D	D	H	H	H	H	H
A,4	H	H	D	D	D	H	H	H	H	H
A,3	H	H	D	D	D	H	H	H	H	H
A,2	H	H	D	D	D	H	H	H	H	H
A,A	ALWAYS SPLIT									
10,10	ALWAYS STAND (NEVER SPLIT)									
9,9	Sp	Sp	Sp	Sp	Sp	-	Sp	Sp	-	-
8,8	ALWAYS SPLIT									
7,7	Sp	Sp	Sp	Sp	Sp	Sp	Sp	H	-*	H
6,6	Sp	Sp	Sp	Sp	Sp	Sp	H	H	H	H
5,5	NEVER SPLIT (PLAY AS 10 HAND)									
4,4	H	H	Sp	Sp	Sp	H	H	H	H	H
3,3	Sp	Sp	Sp	Sp	Sp	Sp	Sp	H	H	H
2,2	Sp	H	Sp	Sp	Sp	Sp	H	H	H	H

- =Stand   H=Hit   D=Double   Sp=Split   *= Surrender if allowed
shaded boxes show strategy changes from chart on next page

Basic Strategy - Single Deck

Dealer stands on soft 17 • Double on any 2 cards • Double <u>NOT</u> allowed after split

Your Hand	Dealer's Upcard									
	2	3	4	5	6	7	8	9	10	A
17	ALWAYS STAND ON HARD 17 (OR MORE)									
16	-	-	-	-	-	H	H	H	H*	H*
15	-	-	-	-	-	H	H	H	H*	H
14	-	-	-	-	-	H	H	H	H	H
13	-	-	-	-	-	H	H	H	H	H
12	H	H	-	-	-	H	H	H	H	H
11	ALWAYS DOUBLE									
10	D	D	D	D	D	D	D	D	H	H
9	D	D	D	D	D	H	H	H	H	H
8	H	H	H	D	D	H	H	H	H	H
A,8	-	-	-	-	D	-	-	-	-	-
A,7	-	D	D	D	D	-	-	H	H	-
A,6	D	D	D	D	D	H	H	H	H	H
A,5	H	H	D	D	D	H	H	H	H	H
A,4	H	H	D	D	D	H	H	H	H	H
A,3	H	H	D	D	D	H	H	H	H	H
A,2	H	H	D	D	D	H	H	H	H	H
A,A	ALWAYS SPLIT									
10,10	NEVER SPLIT (ALWAYS STAND)									
9,9	Sp	Sp	Sp	Sp	Sp	-	Sp	Sp	-	-
8,8	ALWAYS SPLIT									
7,7	Sp	Sp	Sp	Sp	Sp	Sp	H	H	-*	H
6,6	Sp	Sp	Sp	Sp	Sp	H	H	H	H	H
5,5	NEVER SPLIT (PLAY AS 10 HAND)									
4,4	NEVER SPLIT (PLAY AS 8 HAND)									
3,3	H	H	Sp	Sp	Sp	Sp	H	H	H	H
2,2	H	Sp	Sp	Sp	Sp	Sp	H	H	H	H

- =Stand　　H=Hit　　D=Double　　Sp=Split　　*= Surrender if allowed

Basic Strategy - Multiple Decks

Dealer stands on soft 17 • Double on any 2 cards • Double allowed after split

Your Hand	Dealer's Upcard									
	2	3	4	5	6	7	8	9	10	A
17	ALWAYS STAND ON 17 (OR MORE)									
16	-	-	-	-	-	H	H	H*	H*	H*
15	-	-	-	-	-	H	H	H	H*	H
14	-	-	-	-	-	H	H	H	H	H
13	-	-	-	-	-	H	H	H	H	H
12	H	H	-	-	-	H	H	H	H	H
11	D	D	D	D	D	D	D	D	D	H
10	D	D	D	D	D	D	D	D	H	H
9	H	D	D	D	D	H	H	H	H	H
8	ALWAYS HIT 8 (OR LESS)									
A,8	ALWAYS STAND ON SOFT 19 (OR MORE)									
A,7	-	D	D	D	D	-	-	H	H	H
A,6	H	D	D	D	D	H	H	H	H	H
A,5	H	H	D	D	D	H	H	H	H	H
A,4	H	H	D	D	D	H	H	H	H	H
A,3	H	H	H	D	D	H	H	H	H	H
A,2	H	H	H	D	D	H	H	H	H	H
A,A	ALWAYS SPLIT									
10,10	ALWAYS STAND (NEVER SPLIT)									
9,9	Sp	Sp	Sp	Sp	Sp	-	Sp	Sp	-	-
8,8	ALWAYS SPLIT									
7,7	Sp	Sp	Sp	Sp	Sp	Sp	H	H	H	H
6,6	Sp	Sp	Sp	Sp	Sp	H	H	H	H	H
5,5	D	D	D	D	D	D	D	D	H	H
4,4	H	H	H	Sp	Sp	H	H	H	H	H
3,3	Sp	Sp	Sp	Sp	Sp	Sp	H	H	H	H
2,2	Sp	Sp	Sp	Sp	Sp	Sp	H	H	H	H

- =Stand   H=Hit   D=Double   Sp=Split   *= Surrender if allowed

Basic Strategy - Multiple Decks

Dealer stands on soft 17 • Double on any 2 cards • Double <u>NOT</u> allowed after split

Your Hand	Dealer's Upcard									
	2	3	4	5	6	7	8	9	10	A
17	ALWAYS STAND ON HARD 17 (OR MORE)									
16	-	-	-	-	-	H	H	H*	H*	H*
15	-	-	-	-	-	H	H	H	H*	H
14	-	-	-	-	-	H	H	H	H	H
13	-	-	-	-	-	H	H	H	H	H
12	H	H	-	-	-	H	H	H	H	H
11	D	D	D	D	D	D	D	D	D	H
10	D	D	D	D	D	D	D	D	H	H
9	H	D	D	D	D	H	H	H	H	H
8	ALWAYS HIT 8 (OR LESS)									
A,8	ALWAYS STAND ON SOFT 19 (OR MORE)									
A,7	-	D	D	D	D	-	-	H	H	H
A,6	H	D	D	D	D	H	H	H	H	H
A,5	H	H	D	D	D	H	H	H	H	H
A,4	H	H	D	D	D	H	H	H	H	H
A,3	H	H	H	D	D	H	H	H	H	H
A,2	H	H	H	D	D	H	H	H	H	H
A,A	ALWAYS SPLIT									
10,10	ALWAYS STAND (NEVER SPLIT)									
9,9	Sp	Sp	Sp	Sp	Sp	-	Sp	Sp	-	-
8,8	ALWAYS SPLIT									
7,7	Sp	Sp	Sp	Sp	Sp	Sp	H	H	H	H
6,6	H	Sp	Sp	Sp	Sp	H	H	H	H	H
5,5	NEVER SPLIT (PLAY AS 10 HAND)									
4,4	H	H	H	H	H	H	H	H	H	H
3,3	H	H	Sp	Sp	Sp	Sp	H	H	H	H
2,2	H	H	Sp	Sp	Sp	Sp	H	H	H	H

- =Stand　　H=Hit　　D=Double　　Sp=Split　　*= Surrender if allowed
shaded boxes show strategy changes from chart on previous page

Basic Strategy - Multiple Decks

Dealer hits soft 17 • Double on any 2 cards • Double allowed after split

Your Hand	Dealer's Upcard									
	2	3	4	5	6	7	8	9	10	A
17	STAND ON ALL - EXCEPT SURRENDER* AGAINST DEALER'S ACE									
16	-	-	-	-	-	H	H	H*	H*	H*
15	-	-	-	-	-	H	H	H	H*	H*
14	-	-	-	-	-	H	H	H	H	H
13	-	-	-	-	-	H	H	H	H	H
12	H	H	-	-	-	H	H	H	H	H
11	D	D	D	D	D	D	D	D	D	D
10	D	D	D	D	D	D	D	D	H	H
9	H	D	D	D	D	H	H	H	H	H
8	ALWAYS HIT 8 (OR LESS)									
A,8	STAND ON ALL - EXCEPT DOUBLE AGAINST DEALER'S 6									
A,7	D	D	D	D	D	-	-	H	H	H
A,6	H	D	D	D	D	H	H	H	H	H
A,5	H	H	D	D	D	H	H	H	H	H
A,4	H	H	D	D	D	H	H	H	H	H
A,3	H	H	H	D	D	H	H	H	H	H
A,2	H	H	H	D	D	H	H	H	H	H
A,A	ALWAYS SPLIT									
10,10	ALWAYS STAND (NEVER SPLIT)									
9,9	Sp	Sp	Sp	Sp	Sp	-	Sp	Sp	-	-
8,8	ALWAYS SPLIT - EXCEPT SURRENDER* AGAINST ACE IF ALLOWED									
7,7	Sp	Sp	Sp	Sp	Sp	Sp	H	H	H	H
6,6	Sp	Sp	Sp	Sp	Sp	H	H	H	H	H
5,5	D	D	D	D	D	D	D	D	H	H
4,4	H	H	H	Sp	Sp	H	H	H	H	H
3,3	Sp	Sp	Sp	Sp	Sp	Sp	H	H	H	H
2,2	Sp	Sp	Sp	Sp	Sp	Sp	H	H	H	H

- =Stand   H=Hit   D=Double   Sp=Split   *= Surrender if allowed

Basic Strategy - Multiple Decks

Dealer hits soft 17 • Double on any 2 cards • Double **NOT** allowed after split

Your Hand	2	3	4	5	6	7	8	9	10	A
	\<-- Dealer's Upcard -->									
17	STAND ON ALL - EXCEPT SURRENDER* AGAINST DEALER'S ACE									
16	-	-	-	-	-	H	H	H*	H*	H*
15	-	-	-	-	-	H	H	H	H*	H*
14	-	-	-	-	-	H	H	H	H	H
13	-	-	-	-	-	H	H	H	H	H
12	H	H	-	-	-	H	H	H	H	H
11	D/H	D/H	D/H	D/H	D/H	D/H	D/H	D/H	D/H	D/H
10	D/H	D/H	D/H	D/H	D/H	D/H	D/H	D/H	H	H
9	H	D/H	D/H	D/H	D/H	H	H	H	H	H
8	ALWAYS HIT 8 (OR LESS)									
A,8	ALWAYS STAND - EXCEPT D/S AGAINST A DEALER 6									
A,7	D/S	D/S	D/S	D/S	D/S	-	-	H	H	H
A,6	H	D/H	D/H	D/H	D/H	H	H	H	H	H
A,5	H	H	D/H	D/H	D/H	H	H	H	H	H
A,4	H	H	D/H	D/H	D/H	H	H	H	H	H
A,3	H	H	H	D/H	D/H	H	H	H	H	H
A,2	H	H	H	D/H	D/H	H	H	H	H	H
A,A	ALWAYS SPLIT									
10,10	ALWAYS STAND (NEVER SPLIT)									
9,9	Sp	Sp	Sp	Sp	Sp	-	Sp	Sp	-	-
8,8	ALWAYS SPLIT - EXCEPT SURRENDER* AGAINST ACE IF ALLOWED									
7,7	Sp	Sp	Sp	Sp	Sp	Sp	H	H	H	H
6,6	H	Sp	Sp	Sp	Sp	H	H	H	H	H
5,5	D/H	D/H	D/H	D/H	D/H	D/H	D/H	D/H	H	H
4,4	H	H	H	H	H	H	H	H	H	H
3,3	H	H	Sp	Sp	Sp	Sp	H	H	H	H
2,2	H	H	Sp	Sp	Sp	Sp	H	H	H	H

- =Stand   H=Hit   D=Double   Sp=Split   *= Surrender if allowed

D/H=Double if allowed, otherwise hit   **D/S**=Double if allowed, otherwise stand

When your cards total 11 you would always want to hit it because you can't bust, but before you ask for a card you should consider making a double down bet. If the casino allows you to double down then you should do that if the dealer has anything but an ace as his upcard. After you double down the dealer would give you just one additional card on that hand. If the dealer's upcard is an ace then you shouldn't double down. Instead, you should hit the hand and continue to draw until your total is 17 or more. If the casino doesn't allow you to double down then you should just hit your hand and then, depending on your total, play it by the rules you were given for the hands that totaled 12 through 21. Meaning, if you had an 11 and the dealer had a 5 as his upcard, you should take a card. Then let's say you draw an ace which gives you a total of 12. Well, as noted before, if you have a 12 against a dealer's 5 you should stand and that's how you should play that hand.

If your total is 10 you would, once again, want to double down unless the dealer showed an ace or a 10. If the dealer had an ace or a 10 as his upcard you should hit your hand and then use the standard rules for a hand valued at 12 through 21. Therefore, if you had a 10 and the dealer had an 8 as his up card you would want to double down and take one more card. If you weren't allowed to double, then you would take a hit and let's say you got a 4 for a total of 14. You should then continue to hit your hand until your total is 17 or more.

If your total is 9 you would want to double down whenever the dealer was showing a 3,4,5 or 6 as his upcard. If the dealer had a 2 as his upcard, or if he had a 7 through ace as his upcard, you should hit your hand and then use the standard playing rules as discussed before. So, let's say you had a 9 and the dealer had a 4 as his upcard you would want to double down and take one more card. If you weren't allowed to double then you should take a hit and let's say you got a 2 for a total of 11, you would then take another hit and let's say you got an ace. That would give you a total of 12 and, as mentioned previously, you should stand on 12 against a dealer's 4.

Finally, if your total is 8 or less you should always take a card and then use the standard playing rules that were already discussed.

Now, let's take a look at splitting pairs, but keep in mind that the rules for splitting will change slightly depending on whether or not the casino will allow you to double down after you split your cards. Most multiple-deck games allow you to double down after splitting so that's the situation we'll cover first and then we'll talk about the changes you need to make if you're not allowed to double down after splitting.

As noted earlier, when your first two cards are the same most casinos will allow you to split them and play them as two separate hands so let's go over the basic strategy rules on when you should do this.

The first thing you should remember is that you always split aces and 8's. The reason you split aces is obvious because if you get a 10 on either hand you'll have a perfect 21, but remember that you won't get paid for a blackjack at 3-to-2, instead it'll be counted as a regular 21 and you'll be paid at even money. If you have a pair of 8's you have 16 which is a terrible hand and you can always improve it by splitting your 8's and playing them as separate hands.

The next thing to remember about splitting pairs is that you never split 5's or 10's. Once again, the reasons should be rather obvious, you don't want to split 10's because 20 is a great hand and you don't want to split 5's because 10 is a great hand to draw to. Instead, you would want to double down on that 10, unless the dealer was showing a 10 or an ace as his upcard.

2's, 3's and 7's should only be split when the dealer is showing a 2 through 7 as his upcard. Split 4's only when the dealer has a 5 or 6 as his upcard (remember 5 and 6 are his weakest cards!), 6's should be split whenever the dealer is showing a 2 through 6 and finally, you should always split 9's unless the dealer is showing a 7, 10 or ace. The reason you don't want to split 9's against a 10 or an ace should be rather obvious, but the reason you don't want to split them against a 7 is in case the dealer has a 10 as his hole card because in that case your 18 would beat out his 17.

If the casino will not allow you to double down after splitting then you should make the following three changes: For 2's and 3's only split them against a 4,5,6 or 7; never split 4's; and for a pair of 6's only split them against a 3,4,5 or 6. Everything else should be played the same.

Now, let's take a look at how to play *soft hands* and, remember, a soft hand is any hand that contains an ace that can be counted as 1 or 11. For a soft hand of 19 or more you should always stand.

For soft 18 against a 2,7 or 8 you should always stand. If the dealer shows a 9, 10 or an ace you should always take a hit and for a soft 18 against a 3,4,5 or 6 you should double down, but if the casino won't allow you to double then you should just hit.

For soft 17 you should always take a hit, but if the casino allows you to double down, then you should double against a dealer's 3,4,5 or 6.

For soft 16 or a soft 15 you should always take a hit, but if the casino allows you to double down then you should double against a dealer's 4, 5 or 6.

For soft 14 you should always take a hit, but if the casino allows you to double down then you should double against a dealer's 5 or 6.

Finally, for a soft 13 you should always take a hit, but if the casino allows you to double down then you should double against a dealer's 5 or 6.

The last thing we need to cover is surrender which, as noted before, isn't offered in many casinos but it is an option that does work in your favor and if available, you should play in a casino that offers it. The surrender rules are very simple to remember and only apply to hard totals of 15 or 16. If you have a hard 16 you should surrender it whenever the dealer has a 9, 10 or ace as his upcard and if you have a hard 15 you should surrender it whenever the dealer has a 10 as his upcard. That's all there is to surrender.

Now that you know how to play the game and you have an understanding of the basic strategy let's take a quick look at how the rule variations can affect the game of blackjack. As noted before, various computer studies have been made on blackjack and these studies have shown that each rule change can either hurt or help the player by a certain amount. For example, a single-deck game where you can double on any first 2 cards (but not after splitting pairs), the dealer stands on soft 17 and no surrender is allowed has no advantage for the casino when using the basic strategy. That's right, in a game with those rules in effect the game is dead even and neither the casino nor the player has an edge!

Take a look at the following chart and you'll see how some rules changes can hurt you or help you as a player. Minus signs in front mean that the casino gains the edge by that particular amount while plus signs mean that you gain the edge by that amount.

RULES THAT HURT YOU		RULES THAT HELP YOU	
Two decks	-0.32%	Double after split	+0.13%
Four decks	-0.49%	Late surrender	+0.06%
Six decks	-0.54%	Resplit Aces	+0.14%
Eight decks	-0.57%	Double anytime	+0.20%
Dealer hits soft 17	-0.20%		
No soft doubling	-0.14%		
BJ pays 6-to-5	-1.40%		
BJ pays 1-to-1	-2.30%		

As you can see, it's always to your advantage to play against as few decks as possible. The house edge goes up substantially as you go from 1 deck to 2, but the change is less dramatic when you go from 2 to 4, or from 4 to 6, and it's barely noticeable when you go from 6 to 8. You can also see that you would prefer not to play in a casino where the dealer hits a soft 17 because that gives the dealer a slight edge. You would also want to play in a casino where you're allowed to double down on your soft hands or else you would be giving another added edge to the casino.

You can also see from these charts that you would want to play in a casino where you were allowed to double down after splitting cards and you would also want to play in a casino that offered surrender. The other two rules variations that help the player are somewhat rare but they were put in to show you how these rules changes can affect your odds in the game. Some casinos will allow you to resplit aces again if you draw an ace to one of your original aces and this works to your advantage. Also, some casinos will allow you to double down on any number of cards rather than just the first two. In other words, if you got 2-4-3-2 as your first four cards you would then be allowed to double down on your total of 11 before receiving your 5th card. If they allow you to do this then, once again, you have a rule that works in your favor.

The point of showing you these charts is to help you understand that when you have a choice of places to play you should always choose the casino that offers the best rules. So, if you find a single-deck game with good rules you could be playing an even game by using the basic strategy, or at worst be giving the casino an edge of less than one-half of 1%.

Now, there is one way that you can actually have the edge working in your favor when you play blackjack and that's by becoming a card counter. As mentioned before, card counting is not for the average person but it really is important that you understand the concept of card counting and if you think you'd like to learn more about counting cards then it's something you can follow up on later.

Many people think that to be a card counter you have to have a photographic memory and remember every single card that's been played. Fortunately, it's not quite that difficult. Actually, the main concept behind card counting is the assumption that the dealer will bust more often when there are a lot of 10's in the deck and that he will complete more hands when there are a lot of smaller cards in the deck. Now, if you stop to think about it, it makes sense doesn't it? After all, the dealer has to play by set rules that make him take a card until he has a total of 17 or more. If there are a lot of 2's, 3's and 4's in the deck the dealer won't bust very often when he draws cards, but if there are a lot of 10's in the deck then chances are he will bust more often when he is forced to draw cards.

The card counter tries to take advantage of this fact by keeping a running total of the cards that have been played to give him an idea of what kind of cards remain in the deck. If there are a lot of 10 cards remaining in the deck then the counter will bet more money because the odds are slightly in his favor. Of course, if there are a lot of small cards remaining then the counter would only make a small bet because the odds would be slightly in favor of the dealer. Another thing that the card counter can do is to change his basic strategy to take advantage of the differences in the deck.

There are at least a dozen different card counting systems but let's take a quick look at a relatively simple one (it's also the most popular) and it's called the **high-low** count. With this system you assign a value of +1 to all 2's, 3's, 4's, 5's and 6's, while all 10's, Jacks, Queens, Kings and Aces are assigned a value of -1. The remaining cards: 7, 8 and 9 have no value and are not counted.

$$+1 = 2, 3, 4, 5, 6$$
$$-1 = 10, J, Q, K, A$$

When you look at these numbers you'll see that there are an equal number of cards in each group: there are five cards valued at +1 and five cards valued at -1. This means that they balance each other out and if you go through the deck and add them all together the end result will always be a total of exactly zero.

What a card counter does is to keep a running total of all the cards as they're played out and whenever the total has a plus value he knows that a lot of small cards have appeared and the remaining deck is rich in 10's which is good for the player. But, if the total is a minus value then the counter knows that a lot of 10-value cards have appeared and the remaining deck must be rich in low cards which is bad for the player. To give you an example of how to count let's say the following cards have been dealt on the first hand from a single deck:

$$2, 3, 3, 4, 5, 5, 5, 6, = +8$$
$$J, K, Q, A, = -4$$
$$\text{Total} = +4$$

As you can see, there were eight plus-value cards and four minus-value cards which resulted in a total count of +4. This means that there are now four more 10-value cards than low cards remaining in the deck and the advantage is with the player. Naturally, the higher the plus count, the more advantageous it is for the player and counters would be proportionally increasing their bets as the count got higher. The card counter would also be using the same basic strategy we spoke about previously, except for certain instances where a slight change would be called for.

On the other hand, if the count is negative, a card counter will always bet the minimum amount. Of course, they would prefer not to bet at all, but the casinos don't like you to sit at their tables and not bet so the counter has to bet something and the minimum is the least they can get by with.

There is one more important thing to explain about card counting and it's called the **true count**. The true count is a measure of the count per deck rather than a **running count** of all the cards that have been played and to get the true count you simply divide the running count by the number of decks remaining to be played. As an illustration, let's say you're playing in a six-deck game and the count is +9. You look at the shoe and estimate three decks remain to be played. You then divide the count of +9 by three to get +3 which is the true count. As another example, let's say you're in an eight-deck game with a count of +12 and there are six decks left to be played. You divide +12 by six to get +2 which is the true count. To put it another way, a +2 count in a double-deck game with one deck left to be played is the same as a +4 count in a four-deck game with two decks left to be played, which is the same as a +6 count is a six-deck game with three decks left to be played, which is the same as a +12 count in an eight-deck game with six decks left to be played.

For the card counter, it is crucial to always take the running count and then divide it by the number of decks remaining in order to get the true count because all betting and playing decisions are based on the true count rather than the running count.

Of course, if you're playing in a single-deck game the running count and the true count are initially the same. The more you get into the deck, however, the more weight is given to the running count because there is less than one deck remaining. So, if the running count was +3 and only a 1/2-deck remained you would calculate the true count by dividing +3 by 1/2 (which is the same as multiplying by 2/1, or 2) to get a true count of +6. As another example, if the running count was +2 and about 2/3 of the deck remained you would divide +2 by 2/3 (the same as multi-plying by 3/2 or, 1 and 1/2) to get +3.

As you can see, the count becomes much more meaningful as you get closer to the last cards in the deck and that's why casinos never deal down to the end. Instead, the dealer will insert a plastic card about 2/3 or 3/4 of the way in the deck and when that card is reached the dealer will finish that particular round and then shuffle the cards. How far into the deck(s) that plastic card is inserted is known as the ***penetration point*** and card counters always look for a dealer that offers good penetration. The card counter knows that the further into the deck(s) the plastic card is placed the more meaningful the true count will be and the more advantageous it will be for the card counter.

So, now that you know how those card counters keep track of the cards, what kind of advantage do you think they have over the casino? Well, not too much. Depending on the number of decks used, the rules in force, and the skill of the counter, it could be as much as 2% but that would be at the high end. Probably 1% would be closer to the actual truth. This means that for every $1,000 in bets that are made the card counter will win $10. Not exactly a huge amount but there are people out there who do make a living playing the game.

Say No! To 6-to-5 Blackjack Games

by Henry Tamburin

Historically, a blackjack hand has always paid 3:2. So if you bet $10, you will be paid $15 (a 3:2 payoff). This assumes, of course, that the dealer doesn't have a blackjack on the same hand.

Single-deck games have traditionally attracted more blackjack players because they believe they have a better shot at winning playing against one deck. In fact, knowledgeable players who use the basic playing strategy in a single-deck game can reduce the house edge to virtually zero.

Casinos have tried Super Fun 21, a single-deck game with a mix of rules that gives them a higher house edge. However, casino bosses have to pay a royalty for this game, which they dislike. Then, a Las Vegas casino discovered that by simply changing the blackjack payoff from 3:2 to 6:5, they could enjoy a healthy edge on a single-deck game, and not have to pay royalties to anyone. And so was born the 6:5 single-deck game.

The 6:5 payoff alone increases the house edge to almost 1.4 percent (no, that's not a typo). Therefore, the overall casino advantage for a typical 6:5 single-deck game where the dealer hits soft 17 and players can double down after a pair split (DAS) is about 1.45 percent. The latter is nearly nine times greater (gulp) than a traditional 3:2 single deck game being offered nowadays in some casinos, and about three times greater (ouch) than a decent six-deck game.

But instead of talking percentages, let's talk dollars and cents so you can really see how much a 6:5 game costs you. Suppose you play two hours of blackjack at $10 a pop and you are dealt an average of 80 hands per hour. A blackjack occurs about once in every 21 hands, so on average you should expect to get four blackjacks per hour, or a total of eight in two hours. Each of those blackjacks should earn you $15 (with a 3:2 payout on a $10 wager), but instead you are paid only $12 in the 6:5 game. You are shortchanged $3 on every blackjack, so in the course of two hours of play, you have been shortchanged $24. That is an atrocity.

Casinos also love the 6:5 game because it virtually eliminates those pesky card counters, since many find the house edge too tough to beat with card counting. And get this: some brazen Las Vegas casino bosses are trying to implement the 6:5 payoff in double-, six-, and even eight-deck games (no, I'm not joking). This would increase the house edge, on some games, up to an appalling 2%!

6:5 games also have these additional pitfalls, which most players are not aware of:

1. If you wager an amount that is not divisible by 5, your payoff for a blackjack actually gets worse. For example, if you bet $8 and get a blackjack, you'll be paid only $9, which is equivalent to the payoff odds of 5.625:5 rather than 6:5 (casinos will pay 6:5 on the first $5 of your wager, and even money for the remaining $3). When the game was first offered, I bet a red ($5) and pink ($2.50) chip on a hand and was dealt a blackjack. At 6:5 payoff odds, a $7.50 wager should pay an even $9, but the dealer paid me only $8.50. I tried to politely explain to the dealer and then to the shift boss that 6:5 on $5 is $6, and 6:5 on $2.50 is $3 therefore I should be paid a total of $9. My plea fell on deaf years.

2. In a 3:2 game, a player can take even money if he is dealt a blackjack and the dealer shows an ace. However, the math doesn't work in the casino's favor on a 6:5 game, so they won't allow players to take even money.

3. The game is mostly offered on low-limit tables in tourist locations where blackjack players tend to be less sophisticated about the game ("milk the tourists" mentality). Knowledgeable players with limited bankrolls are also faced with this dilemma: either play the 6:5 game with lower betting limits, or play the better 3:2 multiple-deck games, but with higher betting limits. If they opt for the latter, they often get less playtime because they tap out sooner because of overbetting in relation to their modest bankroll. Either way, they get screwed.

4. Casinos often tout their single-deck games on marquees without mentioning the 6:5 payoff. Signage on blackjack tables alerting players to the 6:5 payoff is often minuscule and not read by players. Many players, in fact, don't realize the change in blackjack payoff when they first sit down and play until after it occurs.

The bottom line is that unless players do something about it, the 6:5 game will ultimately ruin blackjack. So what can you do to help?

1. Don't play any 6:5 blackjack games. Instead, play only games that pay 3:2 on a blackjack.
2. Voice your displeasure about the game to a casino supervisor, your casino host, and even the casino manager. Be sure to also tell them you are taking your business to casinos that don't offer this wretched game.
3. Warn your friends and family, who are planning to visit a casino, about this outrageous game.

It's clear that in their attempt to make more money, casinos are actually ruining one of the best games for players. Don't let this happen. Just say NO! to 6:5 blackjack games.

Henry Tamburin is the editor of the Blackjack Insider newsletter (www.bjinsider.com), lead instructor for the Golden Touch Blackjack Course (www.goldentouchblackjack.com) and host of www.smartgaming.com. For a free three-month subscription to his blackjack newsletter, go to www.bjinsider.com/freetrial

Roulette

by Steve Bourie

Virtually all American casinos use a double-zero roulette wheel which has pockets numbered from 1 to 36, plus 0 and 00 for a total of 38 pockets. This is in contrast to Europe where a single-zero wheel is used and the game has always been the most popular in the casino.

There are usually six seats at the roulette table and to help the dealer differentiate what each player is betting every player is assigned a different color chip which they purchase right at the table. Each table has its own minimum chip values and that information is usually posted on a sign at the table. As an example let's say a table has a $1 minimum chip value. This means that when you give the dealer your money the colored chips he gives you in return must have a minimum value of $1 each. So, if you gave the dealer $50 he would ask what value you wanted on the chips and if you said $1 he would give you 50 colored chips.

If you prefer, you could say you wanted the chips valued at $2 each and he would just give you 25 chips rather than 50. You can make the value of your colored chips anything you want and you'll notice that when the dealer gives you your chips he'll put one of your chips on the railing near the wheel with a marker on top to let him know the value of your chips. Later on when you're done playing at that table you must exchange your colored chips for regular chips before leaving. The colored chips have no value anywhere else in the casino so don't leave the table with them.

Besides the minimum chip value, there is also a minimum amount that must be bet on each spin of the wheel. Once again, the minimums are probably posted on a sign at the table. If it says $2 minimum inside/$5 minimum outside this means that when betting on any of the 38 numbers that pay 35-to-1 the total of all your bets must be $2. You could make two different $1 bets or one $2 bet, it doesn't matter except that the total of all your bets on the numbers must be at least $2. The $5 minimum outside means that any of the outside bets that pay 2-to-1, or even money, require that you bet $5 each time. On the outside bets you can't make a $3 bet and a $2 bet to meet the minimums - you have to bet at least $5 every time. After you've exchanged your cash for colored chips you're ready to place your first bet so, let's see what your options are:

You can make a *straight* bet where you only bet on one number and if it comes in you'll be paid 35-to-1. The casino advantage on this bet is 5.26% and by the time you're done with this roulette section I'm sure you'll be very familiar with that number.

Another choice you have is to do a *split*. This is where you put a chip on the line that separates two numbers. If either number comes up you'll be paid at 17-to-1. The casino advantage on this bet is 5.26%.

If you put a chip in an area that splits 4 numbers this is called a *corner* bet and if any one of those 4 numbers comes in you will be paid off at 8-to-1. The casino advantage on this bet is 5.26%.

If you put a chip at the beginning of a row of 3 numbers, this is called a *street* bet and if any one of those 3 numbers shows up you will be paid off at 11-to-1. The casino advantage on this bet is 5.26%.

You can also put a chip on the line between two streets so that you have a *double street* covered and if any one of those 6 numbers come in you'll be paid off at 5-to-1. The casino advantage on this bet is?... you guessed it...5.26%.

The only other bet you can make on the inside numbers is the *5- number* bet where you place one chip in the upper left corner of the number 1 box. If any one of those 5 numbers comes in you'll be paid off at 6-to-1 and what do you think the casino advantage is on this bet? 5.26%? Nope, I gotcha... it's 7.89%. Actually, this is the worst possible bet on the roulette table and the only bet you'll come across that doesn't have a 5.26% house edge on the double-zero roulette wheel. You should never make this bet.

One quick word here about "to" and "for" when discussing odds. Whenever the odds are stated as "to" this means that in addition to the stated payoff you also receive your original bet back. In other words, if you won your single number bet in roulette you would receive 35-to-1, which is a 35-chip payoff, plus you'd still keep your original one-chip bet, so you end up with 36 chips. Now if the odds are stated as "for" that means you do not receive back your original bet. If the odds in your single number bet were 35-*for*-1 you would still receive a 35-chip payoff but the casino would keep your original one-chip bet so you would only end up with 35 chips. The only place in a casino where the odds are always stated as "for" is in video poker. You might also come across it on a couple of craps bets where the odds are stated as "for-one" rather than "to-one" in order to give the casino a slightly better edge.

Now, getting back to our roulette examples, let's look at all of the outside bets that you can make and keep in mind that the house edge on all of these outside bets is...do you remember the number?...that's right...5.26%.

There are three bets you can make that will pay you even money, or 1-to-1, which means that if you win, you will get back one dollar for every dollar you bet:

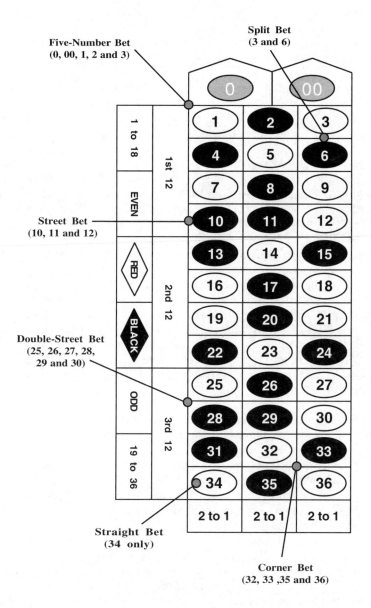

Typical felt layout for placing bets on American double-zero roulette wheel

Red or black - If you put a chip on red then a red number must come up in order for you to win. If the ball lands on a black number, 0 or 00 - you lose. The same thing goes for black - you lose if it comes in red, 0 or 00 and you win if the ball lands on a black number.

Odd or even - If you put a chip on odd then the ball must land on an odd number in order for you to win. If it lands on 0, 00, or an even number - you lose. If you bet on even, you win if an even number shows up and lose if the ball lands on 0, 00 or an odd number.

1 through 18 and 19 through 36 - If you bet on 1 through 18, then you win if a number from 1 through 18 comes in and you lose if the ball lands on 0, 00 or a number higher than 18. Similarly, if you bet on 19 through 36, you win if one of those numbers comes in and you lose on 0, 00 or any number lower than 19.

The only other bets left are the *dozens* and columns bets. If you look at the roulette betting layout you can see three areas that each correspond to 12-number sections on the table. The one marked 1st 12 covers the numbers from 1 to 12, the one marked 2nd 12 covers the numbers from 13 to 24 and the other one that's marked 3rd 12 covers the last section of numbers from 25 to 36. If you bet on the 1st 12 you would win if a number from 1 to 12 came in and you would lose if anything else came in, including 0 or 00. The same principle holds true for each of the other dozen bets where you would win if a number in that section came in and you would lose if anything else showed up. All dozens bets pay 2-to-1.

 The last bet to look at is the *column* bet and that is also a bet that pays 2-to-1. There are three possible column bets you can make and you'll notice that each area corresponds to the numbers in the column directly above it. So, if you put a chip under the first column you will win if any of the numbers in that column come in and you will lose if any other number, including 0 or 00 shows up. Once again, the same rule is in effect for each of the other columns where you would win if the number appears in the column above your bet and you would lose if it doesn't.

All right, now you know all the possible bets and you know how to make them at the table. So, the next question is "How do you win?" and the answer to that is very simple - You have to get lucky! And that's the ONLY way you can win at roulette. As you found out earlier, every bet, except for the 5-number bet, which I'm sure you'll never make, has a house edge of?...that's right...5.26%. So, feel free to put your chips all over the table and then just hope that you're lucky enough to have one of your numbers come up. You see, it just doesn't matter what you do because you'll always have that same house edge of 5.26% working against you on every bet you make.

Now, you may have heard of a system for roulette where you should place your bets only on the numbers that are evenly spaced out around the wheel. For example, if you wanted to play only four numbers, you could bet on 1,2,31 and 32 because when you looked at a roulette wheel, you would notice that if you divided it into four equal parts, you would have a number that appears in each of the four sections. So, is this a good system? Well, actually it's no better and no worse than any other roulette system. The fact is that it's purely a matter of chance where the ball happens to land and it makes no difference whether the numbers you choose are right next to each other or evenly spaced out on the wheel. Each number has an equal chance to occur on every spin of the wheel and the house edge always remains at 5.26%.

You can probably tell that I wouldn't recommend roulette as a good game to play because there are other games that offer much better odds, but if you really insist on playing the game I have three good suggestions for you. #1 - Go to Atlantic City! In Atlantic City if you make an even-money outside bet, like red or black, odd or even, 1 through 18 or 19 through 36 and if 0 or 00 come up, the state gaming regulations allow the casino to take only half of your bet. Because you only lose half of your bet this also lowers the casino edge on these outside bets in half to 2.63%. This rule is only in effect for even-money bets so keep in mind that on all other bets the house edge still remains at that very high 5.26%.

The second suggestion I have for you also involves some travel and here it is: Go to Europe! The game of roulette began in Europe and many casinos over there use a single-zero wheel which makes it a much better game because the house edge on a single-zero roulette wheel is only 2.70%. To make it even better, they have a rule called "en prison" which is similar to the Atlantic City casino rule. If you make an even-money outside bet and the ball lands on 0 you don't lose right away. Instead, your bet is "imprisoned" and you have to let it ride on the next spin. Then, if your bet wins, you can remove it from the table. Because of this rule, the casino edge on this bet is cut in half to 1.35% which makes it one of the best bets in the casino and almost four times better than the same bet when it's made on a standard double-zero roulette wheel in the United States.

Now, if you're not into traveling and you don't think you can make it to Atlantic City or Europe, then you'll just have to settle for suggestion #3 which is: Win quickly! Naturally, this is easier said than done, but in reality, if you want to win at roulette the best suggestion I can give you is that you try to win quickly and then walk away from the table because the longer you continue to bet the longer that big 5.26% house edge will keep eating away at your bankroll. One major principle of gambling is that in order to win you must only play the games that have the lowest casino edge and, unfortunately, roulette is not one of them.

Before closing out this look at roulette, let's take a minute to examine one of the most famous betting systems of all time and the one that many people frequently like to use on roulette. It's called the Martingale system and it is basically a simple system of doubling your bet whenever you lose. The theory behind it is that sooner or later you'll have to win and thus, you will always come out ahead. As an example, let's say you're playing roulette and you bet $1 on red, if you lose you double your next bet to $2 and if you lose that then you double your next bet to $4 and if you lose that you double your next bet to $8 and so forth until you eventually win. Now, when you finally do win you will end up with a profit equal to your original bet, which in this case is $1. If you started the same system with a $5 bet, you would have to bet $10 after your first loss, $20 after your second loss and so forth, but whenever you won you would end up with a $5 profit.

In theory, this sounds like a good idea but in reality it's a terrible system because eventually you will be forced to risk a great amount of money for a very small profit. Let's face it, even if you only wanted to make a $1 profit on each spin of the wheel, sooner or later you will hit a major losing streak where you will have to bet an awful lot of money just to make that $1 profit. For example, if you go eight spins without a winner, you would have to bet $256 on the next spin and if that lost then you'd have to bet $512. Would you really want to risk that kind of money just to make $1? I don't think so. You may think that the odds are highly unlikely that you would lose that many bets in a row, but eventually it will happen and when it does you will suffer some astronomical losses. One other problem with this system is that eventually you won't be able to double your bet because you will have reached the casino maximum, which in most casinos is $500 on roulette. Just keep in mind that the Martingale system works best when it's played for fun on paper and not for real money in a casino. If it was truly a winning system it would have bankrupted the world's casinos years ago.

Baccarat

by Steve Bourie

When you think of Baccarat you probably think of a game that's played by the casino's wealthiest players who sit at a private table and can afford to bet tens of thousands of dollars on the flip of a card and you know what? You're right! The game of Baccarat has always had a reputation as being for the richest gamblers and that usually scared off the average player, but nowadays more and more people are discovering that Baccarat is really a good game for the small stakes player because 1. It has a relatively small advantage for the casino and 2. It's very simple to play.

The mini-Baccarat table is the kind of Baccarat table you're most likely to find in the standard American casino and the game is played pretty much the same as regular Baccarat except that in the mini version all of the hands are dealt out by the dealer and the players never touch the cards. Other than that, the rules are virtually the same. Oh yes, one other difference you'll find is that the betting minimums will always be lower on mini-Baccarat and it's usually pretty easy to find a table with a $5 minimum.

Now, as noted before, the game of Baccarat is very simple to play and that's because the only decision you have to make is what bet you want to make from the three that are available: player, banker or tie. After the players make their bets the game begins and two 2-card hands are dealt from a shoe that contains 8 decks of cards. One hand is dealt for the banker and another hand is dealt for the player. The values of the two cards in each hand are added together and the object of the game is to have a total as close to 9 as possible. After the values of the first two cards in each hand are totaled, a third card can be drawn by either the player, the banker or both. But, the decision as to whether or not a third card should be drawn is not decided by the dealer or the players - it is only decided by the rules of the game.

Actually the name Baccarat comes from the Italian word for zero and as you'll see there are lots of zeros in this game because when you add the cards together all of the 10's and all of the face cards are counted as zeros, while all of the other cards from ace though 9 are counted at their face value. So, a hand of Jack, 6 has a total of 6; 10,4 has a total of 4; king, 7 has a total of 7; and ace, queen which would be a great hand in blackjack, only has a total of 1. The other thing about adding the cards together is that no total can be higher than 9. So, if a total is 10 or higher you have to subtract 10 to determine its value. For example, 8,8 totals 16 but you subtract 10 and your total is 6; 9,5 has a total of 4; 8,3 has a total of 1; and 5,5 has a total of 0.

Once again, the object of the game of Baccarat is to have a total as close to 9 as possible, so after the first two cards are dealt if either the player or banker hand has a total of 9 then that's called a "natural" and that hand is the winner. If neither hand has a total of 9 then the next best possible hand is a total of 8 (which is also called a "natural") and that hand would be the winner. If both the player and the banker end up with the same total then it's a tie and neither hand wins.

Now, if neither hand has an 8 or a 9 then the rules of the game have to be consulted to decide whether or not a third card is drawn. Once that's done, the values of the cards are added together again and whichever hand is closest to a total of 9 is the winner. If both hands end up with the same total then it's a tie and neither hand wins.

If you want to bet on the player hand just put your money in the area marked "player" and if you win you'll be paid off at even-money, or $1 for every $1 you bet. The casino advantage on the player bet is 1.36%. If you want to bet on the banker hand you would place your bet in the area marked "banker" and if you win, you'll also be paid off at even-money, but you'll have to pay a 5% commission on the amount you win. So, if you won $10 on your bet, you would owe a 50¢ commission to the house. The 5% commission is only required if you win and not if you lose. The dealer will keep track of the amount you owe by putting an equal amount in a small area on the table that corresponds to your seat number at the table. So, if you're sitting at seat #3 and won $10 on the bank hand the dealer would pay you $10 and then put 50¢ in the #3 box. This lets him know how much you owe the casino in commissions and when you get up to leave the table you'll have to pay the dealer whatever amount is in that box. After adjusting for that 5% commission the casino advantage on the banker bet is 1.17%

Finally, if you want to bet on a tie you would place your bet in the area marked "tie" and if you win you'll be paid off at 8-to-1, or $8 for every $1 you bet. The big payoff sounds nice but actually this is a terrible bet because the casino advantage is a very high 14.1% and this bet should never be made.

As you've seen, the casino advantage in Baccarat is very low (except for the tie bet) and the rules are set in advance so no decisions are made by either the players or the dealer about how to play the cards. This means that, unlike blackjack where you have to decide whether or not you want another card, you have no decisions to make and no skill is involved. This also means that Baccarat is purely a guessing game, so even if you've never played the game before you can sit at a table and play just as well as anyone who's played the game for 20 years! This is the only game in the casino where this can happen and that's why I tell people that Baccarat is an especially good game for the beginning player because you need no special knowledge to take advantage of those low casino edge bets.

The only part of Baccarat that gets a little confusing is trying to understand the rules concerning the draw of a third card, but remember, the rules are always the same at every table and they'll usually have a printed copy of the rules at

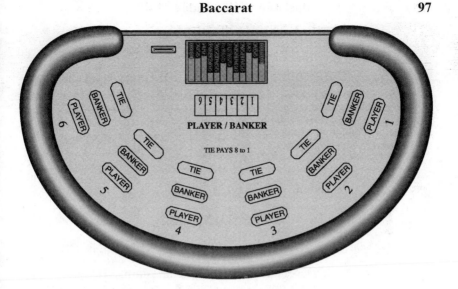

A Sample Mini-Baccarat Table Layout

the table and will give you a copy if you ask for it. After playing the game for awhile you'll start to remember the rules on your own, but until then here's a rundown on how it works:

As noted before, if the first two cards in either hand total 8 or 9, then the game is over and the highest total wins. If the totals are both 8 or both 9 then it's a tie and neither hand wins. For any other total the rules have to be consulted and it's always the player hand that goes first. If the player hand has a total of 6 or 7, it must stand. The only other totals it can possibly have are 0,1,2,3,4 or 5 and for all of those totals it must draw a card.

PLAYER HAND RULES

8,9	STANDS (Natural)
6,7	STANDS
0,1,2,3,4,5	DRAWS

There, that wasn't too hard to understand was it? If the player hand has a total of 6 or 7 it stands and for anything else it has to draw a card. Well, that was the easy part because now it gets a little complicated.

After the player hand is finished the banker hand must take its turn and if its first 2 cards total 0,1 or 2 it must draw a card. If its two cards total 7 it must stand and if the total is 6 it will stand, but only if the player hand did not take a card.

BANK HAND RULES

8,9	STANDS (Natural)
0,1,2	DRAWS
6	STANDS (If player took no card)
7	STANDS

The only other possible totals the bank can have are 3,4,5 or 6 and the decision as to whether or not a 3rd card is drawn depends on the 3rd card that was drawn by the player hand.

When the banker hand has a total of 3 it must stand if the player's 3rd card was an 8 and it must draw if the player's 3rd card was any other card.

IF BANK HAS 3 and
Player's third card is 8 - BANK STANDS
Player's third card is 1,2,3,4,5,6,7,9,10 - BANK DRAWS

When the banker hand has a total of 4 it must stand if the player's 3rd card was a 1,8,9, or 10 and it must draw if the player's 3rd card was any other card.

IF BANK HAS 4 and
Player's third card is 1,8,9,10 - BANK STANDS
Player's third card is 2,3,4,5,6,7 - BANK DRAWS

When the banker hand has a total of 5 it must draw if the player's 3rd card was a 4,5,6 or 7 and it must stand if the player's 3rd card was any other card.

IF BANK HAS 5 and
Player's third card is 1,2,3,8,9,10 - BANK STANDS
Player's third card is 4,5,6,7 - BANK DRAWS

When the banker hand has a total of 6 it must draw if the player's 3rd card was a 6 or 7 and it must stand if the player's 3rd card was any other card.

IF BANK HAS 6 and
Player's third card is 1,2,3,4,5,8,9,10 - BANK STANDS
Player's third card is 6 or 7 - BANK DRAWS

There you have it - those are the rules of Baccarat concerning the draw of a third card. As you saw they were a little complicated, but remember that you don't have to memorize the rules yourself because the dealer will know them and play each hand by those rules, but you can always ask for a copy of the rules at the table to follow along.

Now let's try some sample hands: The player hand has queen,9 for a total of 9 and the banker hand has 4,4 for a total of 8. Which hand wins? Both hands are naturals, but the player hand total of 9 is higher than the banker hand total of 8, so the player hand is the winner.

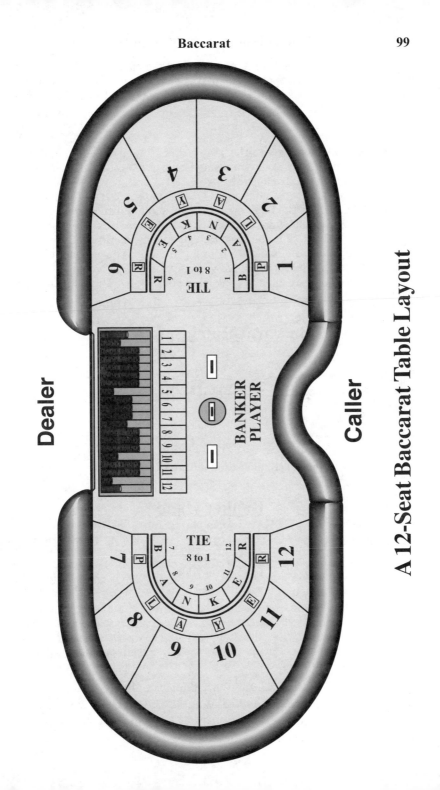

Dealer

Caller

A 12-Seat Baccarat Table Layout

If the player hand has 4,2 for a total of 6 and the banker hand has ace, jack which totals 1, what happens? The player hand must stand on its 6 and the banker hand must always draw when it has a total of 0,1 or 2. Let's say the bank draws a 7 and wins 8 to 6.

What happens when the player hand has king, 5 and the bank hand has 2,4? The player hand must draw and let's say it gets a 7 for a total of 2. The banker hand has a total of 6 and if it could stand on that total it would win because its 6 is higher than the 2 held by the player. Of course, if you were betting on banker that's exactly what you would want to happen but, unfortunately for you, the rules require the bank hand to draw another card whenever its first two cards total 6 and the third card drawn by the player is a 7. So now, instead of having a winning hand you have to hope that the card you draw isn't a 5, which would give you a total of 1 making you a loser. You also wouldn't want to draw a 6 because that would give you a total of 2 which would give you a tie. In this case let's say that the bank hand goes on to draw an 8 which gives it a total of 3 and it wins 4 to 2.

Baccarat Rules Summary

Player Hand

When the first two cards total	
0-1-2-3-4-5	Draws
6-7	Stands
8-9	Natural (Banker cannot draw)

Banker Hand

When the first two cards total	DRAWS when player's third card is	STANDS when player's third card is
0-1-2	Always Draws	
3	1-2-3-4-5-6-7-9-0	8
4	2-3-4-5-6-7	1-8-9-0
5	4-5-6-7	1-2-3-8-9-0
6	6-7	1-2-3-4-5-8-9-0
7		Stands
8-9		Stands (Natural)

**If the Player's hand does not draw a third card,
then the Banker's hand stands on a total of 6 or more.**

If the player hand has 3, ace for a total of 4 and the banker hand has 8,7 for a total of 5, what happens? The player hand must draw and say it gets a 9 for a total of 3. Once again, the banker hand would like to stand on its total because it would win, but the rules have to be consulted first and in this case when the banker's first 2 cards total 5 and the player's third card drawn is a 9 the banker hand must stand, so the banker hand wins 5 to 3.

Finally, let's say the player hand has 4,3 for a total of 7 and the banker hand has 6,10 for a total of 6. The player hand must always stand on totals of 6 or 7 and the banker hand must also stand on its total of 6 because the player hand didn't take a third card. The player hand wins this one 7 to 6.

All right, now that you know how to play Baccarat we come to the important question which is - how do you win? Well, as I said before, if you bet on player you'll only be giving the casino a 1.36% edge and if you bet on banker you'll be giving the casino an even more modest edge of just 1.17%. While both of these are pretty low edges to give the casino you're still stuck with the fact that the casino will always have an edge over you and in the long run the game of Baccarat is unbeatable. So, if that's the case then how do you win? Well, the answer to that is very simple - You have to get lucky! And that's the ONLY way you can win at Baccarat. Of course, this is easier said than done, but fortunately, in the game of Baccarat, you have the option of making two bets that require no skill and both offer the casino a very low edge especially when you compare them to roulette where the house has a 5.26% advantage on a double-zero wheel and slot machines where the edge is about 5% to 15% I always stress the point that when you gamble in a casino you have to play the games that have the lowest casino edge in order to have the best chance of winning and with that in mind you can see that Baccarat is not that bad a game to play for the recreational gambler.

Now let's take a quick look at one of the most common systems for betting on Baccarat. One thing that many Baccarat players seem to have in common is a belief in streaks and the casinos accommodate these players by providing scorecards at the table that can be used to track the results of each hand. Many players like to bet on whatever won the last hand in the belief that it will continue to come in and they hope for a long streak.

The thinking for these players is that since Baccarat is purely a guessing game it's just like guessing the outcome of a coin toss and chances are that a coin won't alternately come up heads, tails, heads, tails, heads, tails but rather that there will be streaks where the same result will come in for awhile. So, is this a good system? Well, actually, it's no better and no worse than any other system because no matter what you do you'll still have the same casino edge going against you on every bet you make: 1.36% on the player and 1.17% on the banker. The one good thing about a system like this though is that you don't have to sit there and guess what you want to play each time. Instead, you go into the game knowing how you're going to play and you don't have to blame yourself if your guess is wrong, instead you get to blame it on your system!

Craps

by Steve Bourie

At first glance the game of craps looks a little intimidating because of all the various bets you can make but actually the game itself is very simple, so first let me explain the game without any reference to the betting.

Everyone at the craps table gets a turn to roll the dice, but you don't have to roll if you don't want to. The dice are passed around the table clockwise and if it's your turn to roll you simply take two dice and roll them to the opposite end of the table. This is your first roll of the dice which is also called the "come-out" roll. If you roll a 7 or 11 that's called a "natural" and you win, plus you get to roll again. If you roll a 2,3 or 12 those are all called "craps" and you lose, but you still get to roll again. The only other possible numbers you can roll are 4,5,6,8,9 or 10 and if one of those numbers shows up, then that number becomes your "point" and the object of the game is to roll that number again before you roll a 7.

If a 7 shows up before your "point" number does then you lose and the dice move on to the next shooter. If your "point" number shows up before a 7 does, then you have made a "pass." You then win your bet and you get to roll again. That's all there is to the game of craps.

Now that you know how to play the game, let's find out about the different kinds of bets you can make. Two of the best bets you'll find on the craps table are in the areas marked "pass" and "don't pass". When you bet on the "pass" line you're betting that the shooter will win. To make a pass line bet you put your bet right in front of you on the pass line. Pass line bets are paid even-money and the house edge on a pass line bet is 1.41% You can also bet on the "don't pass" line in which case you're betting that the shooter will lose. To make a don't pass bet you put your bet in front of you in the don't pass area. Don't pass bets are also paid even-money and the house edge on them is 1.40%.

In reality, the odds are always 1.41% against the shooter and in favor of the "don't pass" bettor by that same amount. Of course, if you're a "don't pass" bettor the casinos don't want to give you a bet where you have an edge so they have a rule in effect on "don't pass" bets where on the come out roll if the shooter throws a 12, you don't win. You don't lose either, the bet is just considered a "push," or tie, and nothing happens. In some casinos they may make 2 instead of 12 the number that's a push. Just look on the don't pass line and you'll you see the word "bar" and then the number that the casino considers a push. In our illustration it says bar 12, so in this casino your bet on the don't pass line will be a push if the come-out roll is a 12. This rule is what gives the casino its advantage on don't pass bets and it doesn't matter whether the casino bars the 2 or 12 the result is the same 1.40% advantage for the house.

All right, let's say you put $10 on the pass line and you roll the dice. If you roll 7 or 11 you win $10 and if you roll 2,3 or 12 you lose $10. So, what happens if you roll any of the other numbers? Well, as I said before, that number becomes your point and you have to roll that number again before you roll a 7 in order to win your pass line bet.

Once your point is established the dealer at each end of the table will move a marker into the box that corresponds to your point number to let everyone at the table know what your point is. The marker that's used has two different sides. One side is black with the word "off" and the other side is white with the word "on." Before any point is established the marker is kept in the Don't Come box with the black side facing up until you roll a point number and then the dealer turns it over to the white side and moves it inside the box that contains your point number.

For example let's say your come-out roll is a 4. The dealer simply turns the marker over to the white side that says "on" and places it in the 4 box. This lets everyone know that 4 is your point and that you will continue to roll the dice, no matter how long it takes, until you roll a 4, which will make you a winner, or a 7, which will make you a loser.

Now, keep in mind that once your point is established you can't remove your pass line bet until you either win, by throwing your point, or lose, by rolling a 7. The reason for this is that on the come out roll the pass line bettor has the advantage because there are 8 ways to win (by rolling a 7 or 11) and only 4 ways to lose (by rolling a 2, 3 or 12). If a point number is rolled, no matter what number it is, there are then more ways to lose than to win and that's why the bet can't be removed. If you were allowed to remove your bet everyone would just wait for the come-out roll and if they didn't win they would take their bet back which would give them a big advantage over the house and, as you know, casinos don't like that, so that's why you can't remove your bet.

As previously noted, the pass line is one of the best bets you'll find, but there is a way to make it even better because once your point number is established the casino will allow you to make another bet that will be paid off at the true odds. This is a very good bet to make because the casino has no advantage on this bet.

In this instance, since your point was 4, the true odds are 2-to-1 and that's what your bet will be paid off at: $2 for every $1 you bet. This is called an "odds bet," "taking the free odds" or "betting behind the line" and to make this bet you simply put your chips directly behind your pass line bet. There is a limit to how much you're allowed to bet and for many years most casinos allowed a maximum of 2 times the amount of your pass line bet. Nowadays, however, many casinos offer 5 times odds and some casinos are even allowing up to 100 times odds. In the U.S. the Horseshoe casinos offer 100X odds at all of their locations.

Because the casino has no advantage on these bets you are effectively lowering the house edge on your total pass line bet by taking advantage of these free odds bets. For example, the normal house edge on a pass line bet is 1.41% but if you also make a single odds bet along with your pass line bet you will lower the house edge on your total pass line bets to .85%. If the casino offers double odds then the edge on your bets is lowered to .61%. With triple odds the edge is lowered to .47% and if you were to play in a casino that allowed 10 times odds the edge would be lowered to only .18% which means that, statistically speaking, over time, that casino would only make 18¢ out of every $100 you bet on that table. As you can see, the more the casino allows you to bet behind the line, the more it lowers their edge, so it's always a good idea to take advantage of this bet. By the way, free odds bets, unlike regular pass line bets, can be removed or reduced, at any time.

All right, let's make our free odds bet on our point number of 4 by putting $20 behind the line. Then we continue to roll until we either roll a 4 or a 7. If a 4 came up we would get even money on the pass line bet, plus 2-to-1 on the free odds bet, for a total win of $50. But, if we rolled a 7, we would lose both the pass line bet and the free odds bet for a total loss of $30.

In this example we used 4 as our point number, but there are 5 other numbers that could appear and here are the true odds for all of the possible point numbers: the 4 and 10 are 2-to-1; the 5 and 9 are 3-to-2; and the 6 and 8 are 6-to-5. You'll notice that the numbers appear in pairs and that's because each paired combination has the same probability of occurring.

7 = 6 ways	1+6,6+1,2+5,5+2,3+4,4+3
6 = 5 ways	1+5,5+1,2+4,4+2,3+3
8 = 5 ways	2+6,6+2,3+5,5+3,4+4

As you can see there are 6 ways to make a 7 and only 5 ways to make a 6 or 8. Therefore, the true odds are 6-to-5.

7 = 6 ways	1+6,6+1,2+5,5+2,3+4,4+3
4 = 3 ways	1+3,3+1,2+2
10 = 3 ways	4+6,6+4,5+5

There are 6 ways to make a 7 and only 3 ways to make a 4 or 10, so the true odds are 6-to-3, which is the same as 2-to-1;

7 = 6 ways	1+6,6+1,2+5,5+2,3+4,4+3
5 = 4 ways	1+4,4+1,2+3,3+2
9 = 4 ways	3+6,6+3,4+5,5+4

and finally, there are 6 ways to make a 7, but just 4 ways to make a 5 or 9, so the true odds here are 6-to-4 which is the same as 3-to-2.

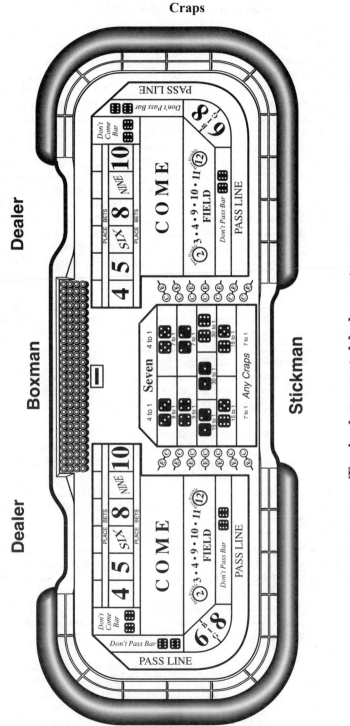

Typical craps table layout

It's important that you remember these numbers, because 1.You want to make sure that you're paid the right amount when you do win and 2. You want to make sure that when you make your odds bets you make them in amounts that are paid off evenly.

As an example, if your point is 5 and you have $5 on the pass line, you wouldn't want to bet $5 behind the line because at 3-to-2 odds the casino would have to pay you $7.50 and they don't deal in change. When making the odds bet on the 5 or 9 you should always bet in even amounts and in the situation just mentioned most casinos would allow you to add an extra $1 so you would have $6 out and they could pay you $9, if you won. The only other situation where this occurs is on the 6 and 8 where the payoff is 6-to-5. So, in that instance you want to make your bets in multiples of $5. Also, if your pass line bet is $15, most casinos will allow you to bet $25 behind the line because, if you win, it's quicker for them to pay you $30, rather than dealing in $1 chips to give you $18 for $15. When situations like this exist, it's good to take advantage of them and bet the full amount you're allowed because that helps to lower the casino edge even more.

We've spent all this time talking about pass line betting, so what about don't pass betting? Well, everything applied to pass line betting works pretty much just the opposite for don't pass betting. If you put $10 on don't pass you would win on the come out roll if the shooter rolled a 2 or 3, you would tie if the shooter rolled a 12, and you would lose if the shooter rolled a 7 or 11. If any other number comes up then that becomes the shooter's point number and if he rolls a 7 before he rolls that same point number, you will win. If he rolls his point number before he rolls a 7, you will lose.

Don't pass bettors are also allowed to make free odds bets to back up their original bets, however, because the odds are in their favor they must lay odds rather than take odds. This means that if the point is 4 or 10, the don't pass bettor must lay 2-to-1, or bet $10 to win $5; on 5 or 9 he must lay 3-to-2, or bet $6 to win $4; and on 6 or 8 he must lay 6-to-5, or bet $6 to win $5. By taking advantage of these free odds bets the casino advantage is slightly lowered on the total don't pass bets to .68% with single odds; .46% with double odds; .34% with triple odds and .12% with 10 times odds. If you want to you can remove, or reduce the amount of your free odds, bet at any time. To make a free odds bet on don't pass you should place your odds bet right next to your original bet and then put a chip on top to connect the two bets. Keep in mind that when you make a free odds bet on don't pass the casino will allow you to make your bet based on the payoff, rather than the original amount of your don't pass bet. In other words, if the casino offered double odds, the point was 4 and you had $10 on don't pass, you would be allowed to bet $40 because you would only win $20 which was double the amount of your original $10 bet. Since you have to put out more money than you'll be getting back, laying odds is not very popular at the craps table and you'll find that the vast majority of craps players would rather bet with the shooter and take the odds. Statistically speaking, it makes no difference whether you are laying or taking the odds because they both have a zero advantage for the house.

One last point about don't pass betting is that once the point is established, the casino will allow you to remove your don't pass bet if you want to - but don't do it! As noted before, on the come out roll the pass line bettor has the advantage because there are 8 rolls that can win and only 4 that can lose, but once the point is established, there are more ways the shooter can lose than win, so at that point the don't pass bettor has the advantage and it would be foolish to remove your bet.

Now, let's take a look at the area marked come and don't come. Since you already know how to bet pass and don't pass, you should easily understand come and don't come because they're the exact same bets as pass and don't pass, except for the fact that you bet them after the point has already been established.

Let's say that the shooter's point is 6 and you make a come bet by putting a $5 chip anywhere in the come box. Well, that's just like making a pass line bet, except that the shooter's next roll becomes the come-out roll for your bet. If the shooter rolls a 7 or 11, you win. If a 2,3, or 12 is rolled you lose, and if anything else comes up then that becomes your point and the shooter must roll that number again before rolling a 7 in order for you to win. In this example if the shooter rolled a 4 the dealer would move your $5 come bet up into the center of the 4 box and it would stay there until either a 4 was rolled, which would make you a winner, or a 7 was rolled which would make you a loser. The house edge on a come bet is the same 1.41% as on a pass line bet. You are allowed free odds on your come bet and you make that bet by giving your chips to the dealer and telling him you want to take the odds. The dealer will then place those chips slightly off center on top of your come bet to show that it's a free odds bet. By the way, if you win, the dealer will put your winnings back in the come bet area so be sure to pick them up off the table or else it will be considered a new come bet.

One other point to note here is that when you make a come bet your bet is always working on every roll, even a come-out roll. However, when you take the odds on your come bets they are never working on the come-out roll. That may sound a little confusing, but here's what it means. In our example the shooter's initial point was 6 and then we made a $5 come bet. The shooter then rolled a 4 which became the point for our come bet. The dealer then moved our $5 come bet to the middle of the 4 box at the top of the table. We then gave $10 to the dealer and said we wanted to take the odds on the 4. On the next roll the shooter rolls a 6 which means he made a pass by rolling his original point number. The next roll will then become the shooter's come-out roll and the odds bet on our 4 will not be working. If the shooter rolls a 7 the pass line bettors will win and we will lose our $5 come bet because he rolled a 7 before rolling a 4. The dealer will then return our $10 odds bet because it wasn't working on the come-out roll. Now, if you want to, you can request that your odds bet be working on the come-out roll by telling the dealer. Then he'll put a marker on top of your bet to show that your odds bet is in effect on the come-out roll.

Naturally, don't come betting is the same as don't pass betting, except again for the fact that the bet isn't made until after the point is established. In this case let's say the point is 5 and you make a don't come bet by placing a $5 chip in the don't come box. Well, once again, that's just like making a don't pass bet except that the shooter's next roll becomes the come-out roll for your bet. If the shooter rolls a 2 or 3, you win. If a 7 or 11 is rolled, you lose. If a 12 is rolled it's a standoff and if anything else comes up then that becomes your point and the shooter must seven-out, or roll a 7, before rolling that point number again in order for you to win. In this example if the shooter rolled a 10 the dealer would move your $5 don't come bet into the upper part of the 10 box and it would stay there until either a 7 was rolled, which would make you a winner, or a 10 was rolled which would make you a loser. The house edge on a don't come bet is the same 1.40% as on a don't pass bet and you can make a free odds bet on your don't come bet by giving your chips to the dealer and telling him you want to lay the odds. The dealer will then place those chips next to and on top of your don't come bet to show that it's a free odds bet. The final point to note here is that don't come bets, as well as the free odds bets on them, are always working - even on the come-out roll.

Now let's talk about place betting and that refers to the 6 numbers you see in the area at the top of the table: 4,5,6,8,9 and 10. Anytime during a roll you can make a bet that one of those numbers will appear before a 7 and if it does you will receive a payoff that is slightly less than the true odds. For example: the true odds are 2-to-1 that a 4 or 10 will appear before a 7. However, if you make a place bet on the 4 or 10 you will only be paid off at 9-to-5 and that works out to a casino advantage of 6.67%.

The true odds of a 5 or 9 appearing before a 7 are 3-to-2, but on a place bet you would only receive a payoff of 7-to-5 which works out to a casino edge of 4.0%. Finally, on the 6 and 8 the true odds are 6-to-5 that one of those numbers will appear before a 7, but on a place bet you would only be paid off at 7-to-6 which means the casino would have an edge of 1.52% on this bet.

As you can see, making a place bet on the 6 or 8 gives the casino its lowest edge and this means that a place bet on the 6 or 8 is one of the best bets you will find on the craps table.

When you want to make a place bet you aren't allowed to put the bet down yourself, you have to let the dealer do it for you. To do this you would just drop your chips down onto the table and tell the dealer what bet you wanted to make. For example you could put three $5 chips down and say "Place the 4,5 and 9." The dealer would then put $5 on the edge of the 4 box, $5 on the edge of the 5 box and $5 on the edge of the 9 box. You'll notice that when the dealer puts your bets on the edge of the boxes they will always be placed in an area that corresponds to where you're standing at the table and this helps the dealer to remember who placed that bet.

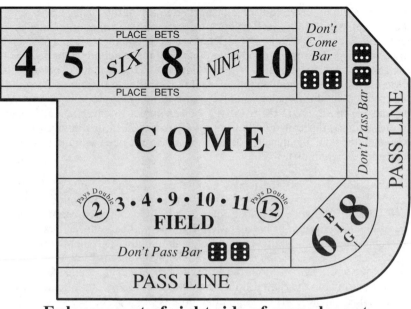

Enlargement of right side of craps layout

When making a place bet you don't have to bet more than one number and you don't have to bet the same amount on each number. You should, however, make sure that you always bet in multiples of $5 whenever you bet on the 4,5,9 or 10 and in multiples of $6 whenever you bet the 6 and 8. This will allow you to always get the full payoff on your bet. If, for example, you bet $3 on the 6 and you won you would only get back even-money, or $3, rather than the $3.50 which your bet should have paid and this results in an even bigger advantage for the casino. Another thing about place bets is that, unlike pass line bets, you can remove your place bets at any time and you do that by telling the dealer you want your bet down and he will take your chips off the table and return them to you. You could also tell the dealer that you didn't want your bet to be working on any particular roll or rolls and you do this by saying for example "off on the 5." The dealer would then put a little button on top of your bet that said "off" and he would remove it when you told him you wanted that number working again.

When we spoke about come bets before I mentioned that come bets are always working on every roll, but that's not the case with place bets because place bets are never working on the come-out roll. If you wanted to, however, you could ask for your place bet to be working on the come out roll by telling the dealer you wanted it working and he would place a button on top of your bet that said "on" to show that your bet was working on the come-out roll.

One last point about place bets is that when you win the dealer will want to know what you want to do for your next bet and you have three choices: if you want to make the same bet just say "same bet" and the dealer will give you your winning chips and leave your original place bet on the table. If you don't want to bet again, just say "take it down" and the dealer will return your place bet along with your winnings. And if you want to double your bet just say "press it" and the dealer will add your winning chips to your other place bet and return any extra chips to you. For example, if you won a $10 place bet on the 5 the dealer would have to give you back $14 in winning chips. If you said "press it" the dealer would add $10 to your place bet and return the remaining $4 in chips to you.

Besides, place betting there is also another way to bet that one of the point numbers will show up before a 7 does and that's called buying a number. A buy bet is basically the same as a place bet except you have to pay a commission of 5% of the amount of your bet and then if you win, the casino will pay you at the true odds. When making a buy bet you should always remember to bet at least $20 because 5% of $20 is $1 and that's the minimum amount the casino will charge you. The reason for the $1 minimum is because that's the smallest denomination chip they have at the craps table and they won't make change for anything under $1. The casino edge on any buy bet for $20 works out to 4.76% so let's take a look at a chart that shows the difference between buying and placing the point numbers.

Point Number	Casino Edge Buy Bet	Casino Edge Place Bet
4 or 10	4.76%	6.67%
5 or 9	4.76%	4.00%
6 or 8	4.76%	1.52%

As you can see the only numbers that you would want to buy rather than place are the 4 and 10 because the 4.76% edge on a buy bet is lower than the 6.67% edge on a place bet. For 5 and 9 the 4.76% edge on a buy bet is slightly worse than the 4.00% edge on a place bet and for the 6 and 8 the 4.76% is a hefty three times higher than the 1.52% edge on the place bet.

To buy the 4 or 10 you would just put your chips down on the layout and tell the dealer what bet you wanted to make. For example, if you put down $21 and said "buy the 10." The dealer will then keep the $1 chip for the house and put your $20 in the same area as the place bets but he'll put a button on top that says "buy" to let him know that you bought the number rather than placed it. Buy bets, just like place bets, can be removed at any time and are always off on the come-out roll. Also, if you do remove your buy bet you will get your 5% commission back.

Besides buy bets where you're betting with the shooter and hoping that a point number will appear before a 7 does, there are also lay bets where you're doing just the opposite - you're betting against the shooter and hoping that a 7 will appear before a point number does.

Lay bets are also paid at the true odds and you have to pay a 5% a commission of the amount you will win rather than the amount you're betting. Once again, when making a lay bet you should always remember to make them based on a minimum payoff of $20 because 5% of $20 is $1 and that's the minimum amount the casino will charge you.

Lay Number	Payoff	Casino Edge
4 or 10	$40 for $20	2.44%
5 or 9	$30 for $20	3.23%
6 or 8	$24 for $20	4.00%

For 4 and 10 you'll have to lay $40 to win $20 and the casino edge is 2.44%; for the 5 and 9 you'll have to lay $30 to win $20 and the casino edge is 3.23%; and for the 6 and 8 you'll have to lay $24 to win $20. The casino edge on that bet is 4.00%.

To make a lay bet you would just put your chips down on the layout and tell the dealer what you wanted to bet. For example, if you put down $41 and said "lay the 10." The dealer would then keep the $1 chip for the house and put your $40 in the same area as the don't come bets but he'll put a button on top that says "buy" to let him know that it's a lay bet. Lay bets, unlike buy bets, are always working on come-out rolls. Lay bets are, however, similar to buy bets in that they can be removed at any time and if you do remove your lay bet you will also receive your 5% commission back.

There are only a few other bets left located on the ends of the table to discuss and two of them are the big 6 and the big 8 which are both very bad bets. To bet the big 6 you place a chip in the big 6 box and then if the shooter rolls a 6 before rolling a 7 you win even money, or $1 for every $1 you bet. To bet the big 8 the same rules would apply: you put your bet in the box and then hope that the shooter rolls an 8 before rolling a 7 so you could win even money on your bet. The big 6 and big 8 can both be bet at any time and both are always working, even on the come-out roll. The casino edge on both the big 6 and the big 8 is 9.1%, which is the biggest edge we've seen so far. But, if you think back about some of the other bets we discussed doesn't this bet sound familiar? It should. This bet is the exact same as a place bet on the 6 or 8, but instead of getting paid off at 7-to-6 we're only getting paid off at even-money! Why would you want to bet the big 6 or big 8 at a house edge of more than 9% instead of making a place bet on the 6 or 8 at a house edge of only 1.5%? The answer is you wouldn't - so don't ever make this bet because it's a sucker bet that's only for people who don't know what they're doing.

The last bet we have to discuss on the player's side of the table is the field bet which is a one-roll bet that will pay even money if a 3,4,9,10 or 11 is rolled and 2-to-1 if a 2 or 12 is rolled. To make a field bet you would just place your chip anywhere in the field box and at first glance it doesn't seem like a bad bet. After all, there are 7 numbers you can win on and only 4 numbers you can lose on! The only problem is that there are 20 ways to roll the 4 losing numbers and only 16 ways to roll the 7 winning numbers and even after factoring in the double payoff for the 2 and 12 the casino winds up with a hefty 5.6% advantage. In some casinos they pay 3-to-1 on the 2 (or the 12) which cuts the casino edge in half to a more manageable 2.8%, but as you've seen there are still much better bets you can make. By the way, if you win on a field bet the dealer will put your winning chips right next to your bet so it's your responsibility to pick them up, or else they'll be considered a new bet!

Now, let's take a look at some of the long-shots, or proposition bets in the center of the table. When you look at these bets one of the first things you'll notice is that, unlike the bets on the other side of the table, the winning payoffs are clearly labeled. The reason they do that is so you can see those big payoffs and want to bet them, but as you'll see, although the payoffs are high, so are the casino advantages.

All of the proposition bets are controlled by the stickman and he is the person who must make those bets for you. So, if you wanted to make a $1 bet on "any craps" you would throw a $1 chip to the center of the table and say "$1 any craps" and the stickmen would place that bet in the proper area for you. Then if you won, the stickman would tell the dealer at your end of the table to pay you. You should also be aware that they will only pay you your winnings and keep your original bet in place. If you don't want to make the same bet again, you should tell the stickman that you want your bet down and it will be returned to you.

There are only four proposition bets that are not one-roll bets and they are known as the "hardways." They are the hard 4, hard 6, hard 8 and hard 10. To roll a number the hardway means that the number must be rolled as doubles. For example 3 and 3 is a hard 6, but a roll of 4-2, or 5-1 are both called an easy 6, because they are easier to roll than double 3's.

To win a bet on hard 10 the shooter has to roll two 5's before rolling a 7 or an easy 10 such as 6-4 or 4-6. To win a bet on hard 4 the shooter has to roll two 2's before rolling a 7 or an easy 4 such as 3-1 or 1-3. The true odds of rolling a hard 4 or hard 10 are 8-to-1, but the casino will only pay you 7-to-1 which works out to a casino advantage of 11.1% on both of these bets.

To win a bet on hard 6 the shooter must roll two 3's before rolling a 7 or an easy 6 such as 5-1, 1-5; or 4-2, 2-4. To win a bet on hard 8 the shooter must roll two 4's before rolling a 7 or an easy 8 such as 6-2, 2-6 or 5-3, 3-5. The true odds of rolling a hard 6 or hard 8 are 10-to-1, but the casino will only pay you 9-to-1 which works out to a casino advantage of 9.1% on both of these bets.

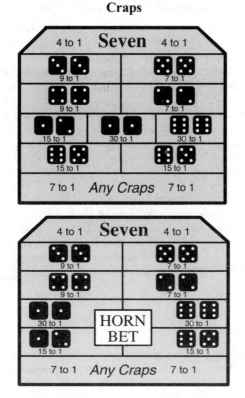

Two different types of proposition bets layouts

As noted before, all of the other proposition bets are one-roll bets which means that the next roll of the dice will decide whether you win or lose. As you'll see, the house edge on all of these bets is very high and they should all be avoided.

For the any craps bet you will win if a 2,3,or 12 is thrown on the next roll and lose if any other number comes up. The true odds are 8-to-1 but the casino will only pay you at 7-to-1 which gives them an edge of 11.1% on this bet and you'll notice that the stickman can put your bet either in the any craps box or, more likely, he'll put it on the circled marked "C" which stands for craps. The reason your bet will be placed in the "C" circle is that it's put in the circle that corresponds to where you're standing at the table and it makes it easier for the stickman to know who that bet belongs to.

For a craps 2 bet you win if the next roll is a 2 and lose if any other number shows up. The true odds are 35-to-1 but the casino will only pay you 30-to-1 which means that the edge on this bet is 13.9% In some casinos the odds for this bet will be shown as 30-for-1 which is actually the same as 29-to-1 and this results in an even bigger edge of 16.7% for the casino.

A craps 12 bet works the same as a craps 2 bet, except that now you will only win if a 12 is thrown. Again, the true odds are 35-to-1 but you will only be paid at 30-to-1 which means the casino edge on this bet is the same 13.9% as in the last craps 2 bet. Also if the bet is shown on the layout as 30-for-1 the casino edge is raised to 16.7%.

For a craps 3 bet you will only win if the next throw is a 3. The true odds are 17-to-1, but the casino will only pay you 15-to-1 which results in a casino advantage of 11.1% Once again, in some casinos the payoff will be shown as 15-for-1 which is the same as 14-to-1 and the house edge in that casino is an even higher 16.7%.

The 11 bet is similar to the craps 3 bet, except that now the only number you can win on is 11. The true odds of rolling an 11 are 17-to-1, but the casino will only pay you 15-to-1 which gives them an 11.1% advantage. Additionally, if the payoff is shown on the layout as 15-for-1 rather than 15-to-1 the casino edge will be even higher at 16.7%. By the way, because 11 sounds so much like 7 you will always hear 11 referred to at the table as "yo" or "yo-leven" to eliminate any confusion as to what number you are referring to. So, if you wanted to bet $5 on 11 you would throw a $5 chip to the stickman and say "$5 yo" and then he will either place it in the 11 box or place it on top of the "E" circle that corresponds to where you're standing at the table.

With a horn bet you are betting on the 2,3,11 and 12 all at once. A horn bet has to be made in multiples of $4 because you're making 4 bets at one time and you'll win if any one of those 4 numbers shows up on the next roll. You'll be paid off at the odds for the number that came in and you'll lose the rest of your chips. For example, if you make an $8 horn bet, this is the same as betting $2 on the 2, $2 on the 3, $2 on the 11 and $2 on the 12. If the number 2 came in you would get paid off at 30-to-1 so you would get back $60 in winnings and the casino would keep the $6 that you lost for the three $2 bets on the 3,11 and 12. The only advantage of a horn bet is that it allows you to make 4 bad bets at once rather than one at a time.

The last proposition bet we have to look at is also the worst bet on the craps table and it's the any 7 bet. With this bet you win if a 7 is rolled and lose if any other number comes up. The true odds are 5-to-1, but the casino will only pay you at 4-to-1 which gives them an edge of 16.7%

So there you have it! We've gone over all the possible bets you can make and now it's time to tell you how to win at the game of craps. Unfortunately, as you've seen, craps is a negative expectation game which means that every bet you make has a built-in advantage for the house. Actually, there is one bet that the casino has no advantage on and do you remember the name of that one? That's right it's the free odds bet and it's great that the casino has no advantage on that bet but the only way you're allowed to make that bet is to first make a negative expectation bet on pass/don't pass or come/don't come, so in essence, there are no bets you can make where you have an advantage over the house and in the long run the game of craps is unbeatable.

So, if that's the case then how do you win? Well, in reality there is only one way to win in craps and that way is to get lucky! Of course, this is easier said than done, but you will find it much easier to come out a winner if you only stick to the bets that offer the casino its lowest edge and those are the only bets you should ever make.

If you want to bet with the shooter I suggest you make a pass line bet, back it up with the free odds and then make a maximum of two come bets that are also both backed up with free odds. For example if double odds are allowed, you could start with a $5 pass line bet and say a 4 is rolled. You would then put $10 behind the line on your 4 and make a $5 come bet. If the shooter then rolled an 8 you would take $10 in odds on your come bet on the 8 and make another $5 come bet. If the shooter then rolled a 5 you would take $10 in odds on your come bet on the 5 and then stop betting. The idea here is that you always want to have a maximum of three numbers working and once you do, you shouldn't make anymore bets until one of your come numbers hits, in which case you would make another come bet, or if your pass line bet wins and then you would follow that up with another pass line bet. The important thing to remember is not to make more than two come bets because you don't want to have too much out on the table if the shooter rolls a 7. By using this betting system you'll only be giving the casino an edge of around .60% on all of your bets and with just a little bit of luck you can easily walk away a winner.

If you wanted to be a little more aggressive with this betting system there are some modifications you could make such as making a maximum of three come bets rather than two, or you could add place bets on the 6 and 8. Remember that a place bet on either the 6 or 8 only gives the casino a 1.52% advantage and that makes them both the next best bets after pass/don't pass and come/don't come. To add the place bets you would start off the same as before, but after you've made your second come bet you would look at the 6 and 8 and if they weren't covered you would then make a $6 place bet on whichever one was open or on both. By adding the place bets on the 6 and 8 you would always have at least three numbers in action and you could have as many as five covered at one time.

One final option with this system is to gradually increase the amount of your pass line and come bets by 50%, or by doubling them, and then backing them up with full odds, but I would only suggest you do this if you've been winning for a while because it could get very expensive if the table was cold and no one was rolling many numbers. Of course, if the table got real cold you could always change your strategy by betting against the shooter and the strategy for that is basically just the opposite of the one I just told you about.

To bet against the shooter you would start with a $5 don't pass bet which you would back up with single free odds and then bet a maximum of two don't come bets that are both backed up with single odds. The reason you don't want to back up your bets with double odds is because when you're betting against the shooter you have to lay the odds which means you're putting up more money than you'll be getting back and, once again, it could get very expensive if a shooter got on a hot roll and made quite a few passes.

For an example of this system let's say you start with a $5 don't pass bet and a 4 is rolled. You would then lay the odds by putting $10 next to your $5 don't pass bet and then make a $5 don't come bet. If the shooter then rolled an 8 you would lay $6 in odds on your don't come bet on the 8 and make another $5 don't come bet. If the shooter then rolled a 5 you would lay $9 in odds on your come bet on the 5 and then stop betting. The idea here is that you always want to have a maximum of three numbers working and once you do that, you shouldn't make anymore bets until, hopefully, the shooter sevens out and all of your bets win. If that does happen, then you would start all over again with a new don't pass bet. Once again, the important thing to remember is not to make more than two don't come bets because you don't want to have too much out on the table if the shooter gets hot and starts to roll a lot of numbers. With this system you'll always have a maximum of three numbers in action and you'll only be giving the casino an edge of about .80% on all of your bets. Some options to bet more aggressively with this system are to increase your free odds bets to double odds rather than single odds and also to make three don't come bets, rather than stopping at two. The choice is up to you but remember that because you must lay the odds and put out more money than you'll be getting back you could lose a substantial amount rather quickly if the roller got hot and made a lot of point numbers.

Now, one last point I want to make about betting craps is that the bankroll you'll need is going to be much bigger than the bankroll you'll need for playing any other casino game. If you're betting with the shooter you'll have one $5 pass line bet with double odds and two come bets with double odds which means that you could have as much as $45 on the table that could be wiped out with the roll of a 7. If you're betting against the shooter you'll have $5 on don't pass with single odds and two don't come bets with single odds which means you could have as much as $44 on the table that could be wiped out if the shooter got on a "hot" roll and made a lot of numbers. As I said before, you need to have an adequate bankroll to be able to ride out the losing streaks that will eventually occur and you need to be able to hold on until things turn around and you start to win.

So how much of a bankroll is enough? Well, I would say about 7 times the maximum amount of money you'll have out on the table is adequate and 10 times would be even better. In both of our examples then you should have a bankroll of at least $300. If you don't have that much money to put out on the table then you might want to consider having less money out on the table by making only one come or don't come bet rather than two or maybe even just limiting your bets to pass and don't pass along with the free odds.

Just remember that it doesn't matter whether you want to bet with the shooter or against the shooter - both of these systems will give you the best chance of winning because they allow the casino only the slightest edge and with a little bit of luck you can easily come out a winner. Good luck!

A Few Last Words

by Steve Bourie

When I sit down to put this book together each year I try to make sure that everything in here will help to make you a better and more knowledgeable gambler when you go to a casino.

I try to include stories that will help you understand how casinos operate, how to choose the best casino games and also how to play those games in the best way possible.

My philosophy with this book is that gambling in a casino is a fun activity and, according to research studies, for about 98% of the people who visit casinos this statement is true. The vast majority of people who gamble in casinos are recreational players who enjoy the fun and excitement of gambling. They know that they won't always win and they also realize that over the long term they will most likely have more losing sessions than winning ones. They also understand that any losses they incur will be the price they pay for their fun and they only gamble with money they can afford to lose. In other words, they realize that casino gambling is a form of entertainment, just like going to a movie or an amusement park, and they are willing to pay a price for that entertainment. Unfortunately, there are also some people who go to casinos and become problem gamblers.

According to Gamblers Anonymous you may be a problem gambler if you answer yes to at least seven of the following 20 questions:

1. Do you lose time from work due to gambling?
2. Does gambling make your home life unhappy?
3. Does gambling affect your reputation?
4. Do you ever feel remorse after gambling?
5. Do you ever gamble to get money with which to pay debts or to otherwise solve financial difficulties?
6. Does gambling cause a decrease in your ambition or efficiency?
7. After losing, do you feel you must return as soon as possible and win back your losses?
8. After a win, do you have a strong urge to return and win more?
9. Do you often gamble until your last dollar is gone?
10. Do you ever borrow to finance your gambling?
11. Do you ever sell anything to finance your gambling?
12. Are you reluctant to use your "gambling money" for other expenses?
13. Does gambling make you careless about the welfare of your family?
14. Do you ever gamble longer than you planned?

15. Do you ever gamble to escape worry or trouble?
16. Do you ever commit, or consider committing, an illegal act to finance your gambling?
17. Does gambling cause you to have difficulty sleeping?
18. Do arguments, disappointments, or frustrations create within you an urge to gamble?
19. Do you have an urge to celebrate good fortune by a few hours of gambling?
20. Do you ever consider self-destruction as a result of your gambling?

If you believe you might have a gambling problem you should be aware that help is available from The National Council on Problem Gambling, Inc. It is the foremost advocacy organization in the country for problem gamblers and is headquartered in Washington, D.C. It was formed in 1972 as a non-profit agency to promote public education and awareness about gambling problems and operates a 24-hour nationwide help line at (800) 522-4700, plus a website at www.ncpgambling.org. Anyone contacting that organization will be provided with the appropriate referral resources for help with their gambling problem.

Another good source for anyone seeking help with a gambling problem is Gambler's Anonymous. They have chapters in many cities throughout the U.S. as well as in most major cities throughout the world. You can see a list of all those cities on their website at www.gamblersanonymous.org or contact them by telephone at (213) 386-8789.

A third program, Gam-Anon, specializes in helping the spouse, family and close friends of compulsive gamblers rather than the gamblers themselves. If you are adversely affected by a loved one who is a compulsive gambler, then Gam-Anon is an organization that may benefit you. They have a website at www.gam-anon.org that lists the cities which host meetings. They can also be contacted by telephone at (718) 352-1671.

I sincerely hope that none of you reading this book will ever have a need to contact any of these worthwhile organizations, but it was an issue that I felt should be addressed.

ALABAMA

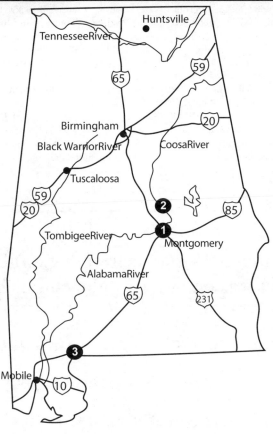

Alabama has three Indian casinos that offer Class II video gaming machines.

Class II video gaming devices look like slot machines, but are actually bingo games and the spinning reels are for "entertainment purposes only." No public information is available concerning the payback percentages on any gaming machines in Alabama.

The minimum gambling age is 21 and all of the casinos are open 24 hours. For Alabama tourism information call (800) 252-2262, or go to: www.alabama.travel.

Creek Casino Montgomery
1801 Eddie Tullis Drive
Montgomery, Alabama 36117
(334) 273-9003
Website: www.creekcasinomontgomery.com
Map: **#1**

Toll Free: (888) 772-9946
Casino Size: 21,000 Square feet
Restaurants: 3 snack bar
Overnight RV Parking: Free
Senior discount: Various on Mon if 55+.

Wind Creek Casino & Hotel - Atmore
303 Poarch Road
Atmore, Alabama 36502
(251) 446-4200
Website: www.windcreekcasino.com
Map: **#3** (55 miles NE. of Mobile)

Room Reservations: (866) 946-3360
Rooms: 236 Price Range: $99-$139
Casino Size: 80,000 Square Feet
Restaurants: 4 (1 open 24 hours) Valet: Free
Buffets: B-$10 (Mon)/$14.95 (Sat)/$24.95 (Sun)
 L-$9.95/$14.95 (Tue/Sat)/$24.95 (Sun)
 D-$12.95/ $14.95 (Tue/Thu)/
 $24.95 (Fri-Sun)
Overnight RV Parking: Free

Wind Creek Casino & Hotel - Wetumpka
100 River Oaks Drive
Wetumpka, Alabama 36092-3084
(334) 514-0469
Website: www.windcreekwetumpka.com
Map: **#2** (20 miles N. of Montgomery)

Toll Free: (888) 772-9946
Rooms: 270 Price Range: $109-$158
Suites: 13 Price Range: $179-$289
Casino Size: 39,000 Square Feet
Restaurants: 2
Buffets: B-$10 (Thu)/$14.95 (Sat/Sun)
 L-$9.95/$14.95 (Sat/Sun)
 D-$14.95/$24.95 (Fri-Sun)
Overnight RV Parking: Free

ARIZONA

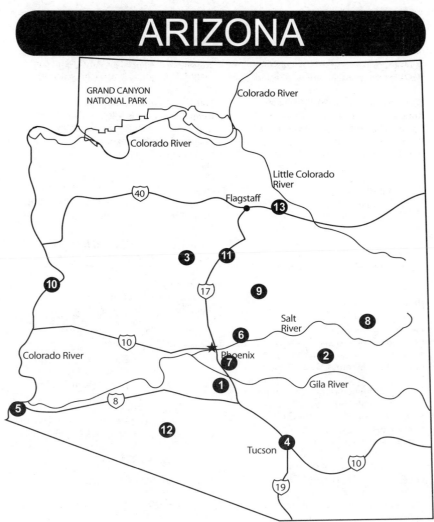

All Arizona casinos are located on Indian reservations and all of them offer slot machines, video poker and video keno. Optional games include: blackjack (BJ), Spanish 21 (S21), let it ride (LIR), casino war (CW), pai gow poker (PGP), three card poker (TCP), Mississippi stud (MS), poker (P), live keno (K), and bingo (BG).

Arizona tribes aren't required to release information on their slot machine percentage paybacks, however, according to the Arizona Department of Gaming, the terms of the compact require each tribes' machines to return the following minimum and maximum paybacks: video poker and video blackjack - 83% to 100%, slot machines - 80% to 100%, keno - 75% to 100%. Each tribe is free to set its machines to pay back anywhere within those limits.

The minimum gambling age is 21 and all casinos are open 24 hours. For more information on visiting Arizona call the state's Office of Tourism at (866) 275-5816 or visit their website at: www.azot.com

Apache Gold Casino Resort
Highway 70 Mile Post 258
San Carlos, Arizona 85501
(928) 475-7800
Map: **#2** (90 miles E. of Phoenix)
Website: www.apache-gold-casino.com

Toll-Free Number: (800) 272-2438
Rooms: 146 Price Range: $79-$114
Suites: 10   Price Range: $119-$179
Restaurants: 2 Liquor: Yes
Buffets: L/D-$7.00/$10.00 (Mon)/$12 (Thu-Sat)
Casino Size: 10,000 Square Feet
Other Games: BJ, BG, P
Overnight RV Parking: Yes
Senior Discount: 15% food and room
          discount if 55+.
Special Features: Hotel is off-property
and is Best Western. 18-hole golf course.
Convenience store. 60-space RV Park ($25
per night) w/full hookups and dump station.

Blue Water Casino
11300 Resort Drive
Parker, Arizona 85344
(928) 669-7000
Website: www.bluewaterfun.com
Map: **#10** (160 miles W. of Phoenix)

Toll-Free Number: (888) 243-3360
Rooms: 200 Price Range: $79-$154
Suites: 25 Price Range: $99-$199
Restaurants: 4 Liquor: Yes
Buffet: B- $7.95
      L-$9.95
      D-$11.95/$15.95 (Sat)
Other Games: BJ, TCP, P, BG
Casino Size: 30,000 Square Feet
Overnight RV Parking: Free (only 1 night)
          RV Dump: No
Senior Discount: Various buffet discounts.
Special Features: 100-slip marina with
Wakeboard park.

Bucky's Casino & Resort
530 E. Merritt
Prescott, Arizona 86301
(928) 776-1666
Website: www.buckyscasino.com
Map: **#3** (91 miles S.W. of Flagstaff)

Toll-Free Number: (800) 756-8744
Room Reservations: (800) 967-4637
Rooms: 81 Price Range: $89-$209
Suites: 80 Price Range: $129-$239
Restaurants: 3 Liquor: Yes
Other Games: BJ, P, BG
Casino Size: 24,000 Square Feet
Overnight RV Parking: No
Special Features: Located in Prescott Resort
Hotel. Free on-site shuttle service.

Casino Arizona 101 & McKellips
524 N. 92nd Street
Scottsdale, Arizona 85256
(480) 850-7777
Website: www.casinoarizona.com
Map: **#6** (15 miles N.E. of Phoenix)

Toll-Free Number: (877) 724-4687
Restaurants: 5 Liquor: Yes
Buffets: B-$17.50(Sun)
      L-$9.95/$17.50 (Sun)
      D-$14.50/$17.50 (Wed/Thu)/
          $19.50 (Fri/Sat)
Casino Size: 40,000 Square Feet
Other Games: BJ, LIR, TCP, K, PGP, CW, BG
Overnight RV Parking: Check in with Security
          /RV Dump: No
Special Features: 500-seat showroom.

Casino Del Sol
5655 W. Valencia
Tucson, Arizona 85757
(520) 883-1700
Website: www.casinodelsol.com
Map: **#4**

Toll-Free Number: (800) 344-9435
Rooms: 200 Price Range: $105- $190
Suites: 15 Price Range: $148-$408
Restaurants: 5 Liquor: Yes
Buffets: B-$9.00/$25.00 (Sun)
      L-$15.99/$25.00 (Sun)
      D $19.00/$28.00 (Thu)
Casino Size: 22,500 Square Feet
Other Games: BJ, P, BG, TCP, S21, PGP, CW
Overnight RV Parking: Free/RV Dump: No
Special Features: 4,400-seat amphitheater.

Casino of the Sun

7406 S. Camino De Oeste
Tucson, Arizona 85757
(520) 883-1700
Website: www.solcasinos.com
Map: **#4**

Toll-Free Number: (800) 344-9435
Restaurants: 2 Liquor: No
Overnight RV Parking: Free/RV Dump: No
Special Features: Smoke shop. Gift shop.

Cliff Castle Casino Hotel

555 Middle Verde Road
Camp Verde, Arizona 86322
(928) 567-7999
Website: www.cliffcastlecasino.net
Map: **#11** (50 miles S. of Flagstaff)

Toll-Free Number: (800) 381-7568
Room Reservation Number: (800) 524-6343
Rooms: 82 Price Range: $80-$100
Suites: 2 Price Range: $105-$135
Restaurants: 7 Liquor: Yes
Buffet: B- $7.00 L- $11.00
        D- $13.00/$15.00 (Sat)
Casino Size: 14,000 Square Feet
Other Games: BJ, P
Overnight RV Parking: Free/RV Dump: No
Special Features: Casino is in Cliff Castle
Lodge. Bowling alley. Kids Quest childcare
facility.

Cocopah Resort

15136 S. Avenue B
Somerton, Arizona 85350
(928) 726-8066
Map: **#5** (13 miles S.W. of Yuma)
Website: www.cocopahresort.com

Toll-Free Number: (800) 237-5687
Rooms: 101 Price Range: $87- $107
Suites: 7 Price Range: $127-$187
Restaurants: 2 Liquor: Yes
buffet: B- $8.99 D- $15.95 (Fri only)
Other Games: BJ, BG
Overnight RV Parking: No
Special Features: 18-hole golf course.

Desert Diamond Casino - I-19

1100 West Pima Mine Road
Sahuarita, Arizona 85629
(520) 294-7777
Website: www.desertdiamondcasino.com
Map: **#4**

Toll-Free Number: (866) 332-9467
Restaurants: 2 Liquor: Yes
Buffets: L - $9.99/$16.99 (Sun)
        D - $12.99/$19.99 (Fri/Sat)
Casino Size: 15,000 Square Feet
Other Games: BJ, P, S21, K
Overnight RV Parking: Free/RV Dump: No
Special Features: 2,500-seat event center.

Desert Diamond Casino - Nogales

7350 S. Nogales Highway
Tucson, Arizona 85706
(520) 294-7777
Website: www.desertdiamondcasino.com
Map: **#4**

Toll-Free Number: (866) 332-9467
Rooms: 140 Rates: $86-$196
Suites: 8 Rates: $266-$350
Restaurants: 3 Liquor: Yes
Buffets: L - $9.99/$16.99 (Sun)
        D - $12.99/$19.99 (Fri)/$16.99 (Sat)
Casino Size: 15,000 Square Feet
Other Games: BJ, P, TCP, PGP, K, BG, S21
Overnight RV Parking: Free/RV Dump: No

Desert Diamond Casino - Why

Highway 86 Mile Post 55
Ajo, Arizona 85321
(520) 547-4306
Website: www.desertdiamondcasino.com
Map: **#12** (125 miles S.W. of Phoenix)

Toll-Free Number: (866) 332-9467
Restaurants: 1 Snack Bar
Hours: 10am-12am Daily
Other Games: Only machines
Overnight RV Parking: No
Special Features: Located on State Highway
86 at mile post 55 near Why, Arizona.

Fort McDowell Casino
10424 North Fort McDowell Road
Fountain Hills, Arizona 85264
(480) 837-1424
Website: www.fortmcdowellcasino.com
Map: **#6** (25 miles N.E. of Phoenix)

Toll-Free Number: (800) 843-3678
Rooms: 238 Rates: $99-$229
Suites: 8 Rates: $219-$375
Restaurants: 6 Liquor: Yes
Buffets: L- $9.50/$14.50 (Sun)
        D- $9.50 (Mon)/$14.95 (Tue/Fri/Sun)/
        $15.95 (Wed/Thu)
Other Games: BJ, P, K, BG
Overnight RV Parking: No
Special Features: Free local shuttle. Gift shop.

Harrah's Ak Chin Casino Resort
15406 Maricopa Road
Maricopa, Arizona 85239
(480) 802-5000
Website: www.harrahsakchin.com
Map: **#1** (25 miles S. of Phoenix)

Toll-Free Number: (800) 427-7247
Rooms: 142 Price Range: $109-$299
Suites: 4 Price Range: Casino Use Only
Restaurants: 4 Liquor: Yes
Buffets: L- $13.99/$19.99 (Sun)
        D- $17.99/$25.99 (Fri/Sat)
Casino Size: 43,000 Square Feet
Other Games: BJ, P, K, BG, MS,
        TCP, LIR, PGP
Overnight RV Parking: Free/RV Dump: No
Senior Discount: Various Mon/Thu if 50+
Special Features: Free local shuttle.

Hon-Dah Resort Casino
777 Highway 260
Pinetop, Arizona 85935
(928) 369-0299
Website: www.hon-dah.com
Map: **#8** (190 miles N.E. of Phoenix)

Toll-Free Number: (800) 929-8744
Rooms: 126 Price Range: $99-$119
Suites: 2 Price Range: $160-$190
Restaurants: 1 Liquor: Yes
Buffets: B/L/D-$13.95/$22.95 (Fri-Sun)
Casino Size: 20,000 Square Feet
Overnight RV Parking: Must use RV park
Other Games: P
Special Features: 258-space RV park ($29.20 per night). Convenience store. Gas station.

Lone Butte Casino
1077 South Kyrene Road
Chandler, Arizona 85226
(520) 796-7777
Website: www.wingilariver.com
Map: **#7** (10 miles S.W. of Phoenix)

Toll-Free Number: (800) 946-4452
Restaurants: 3 Liquor: Yes
Casino Size: 10,000 Square Feet
Other Games: BJ, BG, PGP, TCP
Overnight RV Parking: Free 4 day max/
        RV Dump: No

Mazatzal Hotel & Casino
Highway 87 Mile Post 251
Payson, Arizona 85541
(928) 474-6044
Website: www.777play.com
Map: **#9** (90 miles N.E. of Phoenix)

Toll-Free Number: (800) 777-7529
Suites: 40 Prices: $112-$165
Restaurants: 2 Liquor: Yes
Buffets: Brunch- $16.95 (Sun Only)
        L-$8.95 (Mon-Sat)
        D-$10.95(Fri)
Casino Size: 35,000 Square Feet
Other Games: BJ, P, K, BG (Mon-Thu)
Overnight RV Parking: Free/RV Dump: No
Special Features: Offers Stay & Play packages (Sun-Thu) with local motels. Free shuttle.

Paradise Casino Arizona
450 Quechan Drive
Yuma, Arizona 85364
(760) 572-7777
Website: www.paradise-casinos.com
Map: **#5** (244 miles W. of Tucson)

Toll-Free Number: (888) 777-4946
Restaurants: 1 Liquor: Yes
Other Games: BG
Overnight RV Parking: Free/RV Dump: No
Special Features: Part of casino is located across the state border in California. Poker offered in CA casino. 10% food discount with players club card.

Spirit Mountain Casino
8555 South Highway 95
Mohave Valley, Arizona 86440
(928) 346-2000
Map: **#12** (15 miles S. of Bullhead City)

Toll-Free Number: (888) 837-4030
RV Reservations: (928) 346-1225
Restaurants: 1 Snack Bar Liquor: Yes
Casino Size: 12,000 Square Feet
Other Games: Only Machines
Overnight RV Parking: Must use RV park.
Special Features: Adjacent to 82-space
Spirit Mountain RV park ($25 per night).
Convenience store. Gas station.

Talking Stick Resort
9700 E. Indian Bend
Scottsdale, Arizona 85256
(480) 850-7777
Website: www.talkingstickresort.com
Map: **#6** (15 miles N.E. of Phoenix)

Toll-Free Number: (866) 877-9897
Rooms: 470 Prices: $100-$189
Suites: 27   Prices: $449-$799
Restaurants: 2 Liquor: Yes
Buffet Prices: B-$9.95/ $27.95 (Sun)
        L-$13.95 D-$20.95/ $26.95 (Fri/Sat)
Other Games: BJ, P, TCP, LIR,
        CW, K, PGP, BG
Overnight RV Parking: Free 3 day max/RV Dump: No

Twin Arrows Navajo Casino Resort
22181 Resort Blvd
Twin Arrows, Arizona 86004
(928) 856-7200
Website: www.twinarrows.com
Map: **#13** (40 miles E. of Flagstaff)

Toll-Free Number: (855) 946-8946
Rooms: 85 Price Range: $159-$189
Suites: 5 Price Range: $379-$489
Restaurants: 4
Other Games: BJ, TCP, PGP
Special Features: Located at Twin Arrows
exit of Interstate 40. Alcohol is only served
in dining areas.

Vee Quiva Hotel & Casino
15091 S. Komatke Lane
Laveen, Arizona 85339
(520) 796-7777
Website: www.wingilariver.com
Map: **#7** (10 miles S.W. of Phoenix)

Toll-Free Number: (800) 946-4452
Restaurants: 2 Liquor: Yes
Casino Size: 15,000 Square Feet
Other Games: BJ, P, BG, TCP, PGP, MS
Overnight RV Parking: Free 4 day max/
        RV Dump: No

Wild Horse Pass Hotel & Casino
5040 Wild Horse Pass Blvd
Chandler, Arizona 85226
(520) 796-7727
Website: www.wingilariver.com
Map: **#7** (25 miles S.E. of Phoenix)

Toll-Free Number: (800) 946-4452
Rooms: 223 Rates: $99-$299
Suites: 19 Rates: $169-$369
Restaurants: 3 Liquor: Yes
Casino Size: 100,000 Square Feet
Other Games: BJ, PGP, LIR, TCP, P
Overnight RV Parking: Free 4 day max/
        RV Dump: No
Senior Discount: Various Mon if 50+.
Special Features: 1,400-seat showroom.

Yavapai Casino
1501 E. Highway 69
Prescott, Arizona 86301
(928) 445-5767
Website: www.buckyscasino.com
Map: **#3** (91 miles S.W. of Flagstaff)

Toll-Free Number: (800) 756-8744
Casino Size: 6,000 Square Feet
Restaurants: 1 Snack Bar Liquor: Yes
Overnight RV Parking: No
Special Features: Located across the street
from Bucky's Casino. Free local-area shuttle
bus.

ARKANSAS

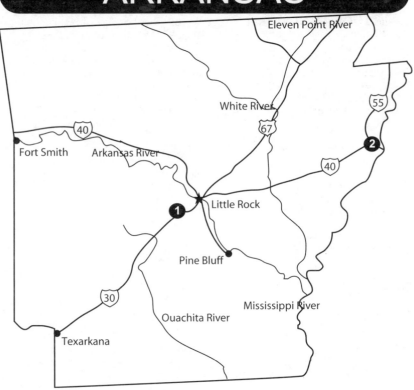

Arkansas has two pari-mutuel facilities featuring "electronic games of skill," which are defined as "games played through any electronic device or machine that affords an opportunity for the exercise of skill or judgment where the outcome is not completely controlled by chance alone."

The games offered are video poker, video blackjack, and "skill" slots where you have two opportunities to spin the reels. The "skill" factor comes into play because after seeing the results of your first spin you then have to decide whether to keep none, one, two, or all three of the symbols on each reel before you spin them again.

Table games offered include: poker (P), let it ride (LIR) and three card poker (TCP).

Gaming regulations require that all of the electronic games of skill must return a minimum of 83%.

For the one year period from July 2013 through June 2014, the average gaming machine's return at Oaklawn was 93.96% and at Southland it was 93.20%

The minimum gambling age is 21 for slots and 18 for pari-mutuel wagering. For more information on visiting Arkansas call the state's tourism office at (800) 628-8725 or visit their website at: www.arkansas.com.

Oaklawn Racing and Gaming
2705 Central Avenue
Hot Springs, Arkansas 71901
(501) 623-4411
Website: www.oaklawn.com
Map: **#1** (55 miles S.W.. of Little Rock)

Toll-Free Number: (800) 625-5296
Restaurants: 3
Hours: 10am-3am /5am(Fri/Sat)
Other Games: P
Admission: Free Parking: Free
Overnight RV Parking: No
Special Features: Live throroughbred racing Mid-January through Mid-April. Daily simulcasting of horse racing.

Southland Park Gaming & Racing
1550 North Ingram Boulevard
West Memphis, Arkansas 72301
(870) 735-3670
Website: www.southlandgreyhound.com
Map: **#2** (130 miles E. of Little Rock)

Toll-Free Number: (800) 467-6182
Restaurants: 4
Other Games: P, LIR, TCP
Admission: Free Parking: Free
Preferred Parking: $3/Valet Parking: Free
Buffets: B- $5.99/$9.99 (Sat/Sun)
        L/D-$12.99/$14.99 (Tue/Thu/Sun)/
        /$24.99(Fri/Sat)
Overnight RV Parking: No
Special Features: Live greyhound racing Mon/Wed-Sat. Daily simulcasting of greyhound and horse racing. Buffet discount for players club members. Electronic table games.

CALIFORNIA

All California casinos are located on Indian reservations and all are legally allowed to offer electronic gaming machines, blackjack, and other house-banked card games. The games of craps and roulette are not permitted. However, some casinos do offer modified versions of craps and roulette that are played with cards rather than dice or roulette wheels.

Most California card rooms also offer some form of player-banked blackjack, but because they are prohibited by law from playing blackjack, the game is usually played to 22 rather than 21. Additionally, players must pay a commission to the house on every hand they play. The amount will vary depending on the rules of the house but, generally, it's about two to five percent of the total amount bet. There are about 90 card rooms in California and you can see a listing of them on the Internet at: *http://www.cgcc.ca.gov.*

California's tribes aren't required to release information on their slot machine percentage paybacks and the state of California does not require any minimum returns.

Unless otherwise noted, all California casinos are open 24 hours and offer: slots, video poker, and video keno. Optional games offered include: baccarat (B), blackjack (BJ), Spanish 21 (S21), mini-baccarat (MB), poker (P), pai gow poker (PGP), Caribbean stud poker (CSP), let it ride (LIR), three card poker (TCP), four card poker (FCP) bingo (BG), casino war (CW), Mississippi stud (MS) and off track betting (OTB).

The minimum gambling age is not uniform at all casinos; it is 21 at some casinos and 18 at others.

Although most of the casinos have toll-free numbers be aware that some of those numbers will only work for calls made within California. Also, many of the casinos are in out-of-the-way locations, so it is advisable to call ahead for directions, especially if you will be driving at night.

For more information on visiting California contact the state's department of tourism at (800) 862-2543 or www.visitcalifornia.com.

Agua Caliente Casino
32-250 Bob Hope Drive
Rancho Mirage, California 92270
(760) 321-2000
Website: www.hotwatercasino.com
Map: **#3** (115 miles E. of L. A.)

Toll-Free Number: (888) 999-1995
Gambling Age: 21
Rooms: 340 Price Range: $98-$219
Suites: 22 Price Range $289-$429
Restaurants: 4 Liquor: Yes
Buffets: B-$9.99/$24.99 (Sun) L- $14.99
        D-$19.99/$24.99 (Fri-Sat)
Other Games: BJ, MB, CSP, TCP,
        S21, LIR, P, PGP
Overnight RV Parking: Only offered at
        adjacent Flying J truck stop
Special Features: Associated with Spa Casino.
Offers card version of craps.

Augustine Casino
84001 Avenue 54
Coachella, California 92236
(760) 391-9500
Website: www.augustinecasino.com
Map: **#8** (125 miles E. of L. A.)

Toll-Free Number: (888) 752-9294
Gambling Age: 21
Restaurants: 2 Liquor: Yes
Buffets: B-$8.95
        D-$11.95 (Mon-Thu)/$27.50 (Sat)
Other Games: BJ, TCP, S21
Overnight RV Parking: No

Barona Valley Ranch Resort and Casino
1932 Wildcat Canyon Road
Lakeside, California 92040
(619) 443-2300
Website: www.barona.com
Map: **#1** (15 miles N.E. of San Diego)

Toll-Free Number: (888) 722-7662
Room Reservations: (877) 287-2624
Gambling Age: 18
Rooms: 397 Price Range: $119-$189
Suites: 9 Price Range: Private Use Only
Restaurants: 8 Liquor: Yes
Buffets: B/L/D-$26.99

Other Games: BJ, B, MB, P, CSP, PGP, MS, TCP, LIR, CW, OTB, FCP
Overnight RV Parking: Free 3 day Max/ RV Dump: No
Special Features: Offers card versions of roulette and craps. Food court. Wedding chapel. 18-hole golf course. Buffet discounts for players club members.

Bear River Casino Hotel
11 Bear Paws Way
Loleta, California 95551
(707) 733-9644
Website: www.bearrivercasino.com
Map: **#38** (10 miles S. of Eureka)

Toll-Free Number: (800) 761-2327
Gambling Age: 21
Rooms: 105 Prices: $80-$119
Restaurants: 2 Liquor: Yes
Buffet: B- $14.95 (Sun)
Casino Size: 31,000 Square Feet
Other Games: BJ, S21, P, PGP, TCP
Overnight RV Parking: Yes. Check in with security first

Black Oak Casino
19400 Tuolumne Road North
Tuolumne, California 95379
(209) 928-9300
Website: www.blackoakcasino.com
Map: **#5** (100 miles S.E. of Sacramento)

Toll-Free Number: (877) 747-8777
Gambling Age: 21
Restaurants: 6 Liquor: Yes
Buffet: B-$7.99 (Sat)/$14.99 (Sun)
    L- $7.99/$14.99 (Sat/Sun)
    D-$12.99/$14.99 (Tue/Wed)/$22.99 (Fri)/
        $18.99 (Sat)
Casino Size: 22,000 Square Feet
Other Games: BJ, TCP, LIR, PGP,
        S21, FCP, MB, P
Overnight RV Parking: No

Blue Lake Casino & Hotel
777 Casino Way
Blue Lake, California 95525
(707) 668-9770
Website: www.bluelakecasino.com
Map: **#34** (10 miles N. of Eureka)

Toll-Free Number: (877) 252-2946
Gambling Age: 21
 Rooms: 102 Rates: $100-$150
Suites: 12 Rates: $200-$335
Restaurants: 2 Liquor: Yes
Other Games: BJ, S21, P, TCP, FCP,
        PGP, BG (Mon/Tue)
Overnight RV Parking: Free/RV Dump: No

Cache Creek Indian Bingo & Casino
14455 Highway 16
Brooks, California 95606
(530) 796-3118
Website: www.cachecreek.com
Map: **#2** (35 miles N.W. of Sacramento)

Toll-Free Number: (800) 452-8181
Gambling Age: 21
Room Reservations: (888) 772-2243
Rooms: 173 Prices: $159-$309
Suites: 27 Prices: $159-$349
Restaurants: 9   Liquor: Yes
Buffets: L/D-$12.99/$22.99 (Sat)
Casino Size: 18,000 Square Feet
Other Games: BJ, P, CSP, LIR, PGP, MS,
        TCP, B, MB, FCP, CW
Overnight RV Parking: Free/RV Dump: No
Special Features: Offers card versions of craps and roulette. Full-service spa. No buffet Wed or Thu. $3 buffet discount for players club members.

Cahuilla Casino
52702 Highway 371
Anza, California 92539
(951) 763-1200
Website: www.cahuillacasino.com
Map: **#19** (30 miles S. of Palm Springs)

Toll-Free Number: (888) 371-2692
Gambling Age: 21
Restaurants: 2 Liquor: Yes
Overnight RV Parking: Free/RV Dump: No
Senior Discount: Various Wed if 55+

Casino Pauma
777 Pauma Reservation Road
Pauma Valley, California 92061
(760) 742-2177
Website: www.casinopauma.com
Map: **#20** (35 miles N.E. of San Diego)

Toll-Free Number: (877) 687-2862
Gambling Age: 18
Restaurants: 1 Liquor: Yes
Buffets: L-$8.95/$12.95 (Sat/Sun)
        D-$12.95
Casino Size: 35,000 Square Feet
Other Games: BJ, P, PGP, TCP, LIR, MB
Overnight RV Parking: Free/RV Dump: No
Senior Discount: Various Thu if 55+
Special Features: Offers card versions of craps and roulette.

Cherae Heights Casino
27 Scenic Drive
Trinidad, California 95570
(707) 677-3611
Website: www.cheraeheightscasino.com
Map: #4 (25 miles N. of Eureka)

Toll-Free Number: (800) 684-2464
Gambling Age: 21
Restaurants: 3 Liquor: Yes
Other Games: BJ, S21, P, PGP, TCP, BG
Overnight RV Parking: Free/RV Dump: No

Chicken Ranch Bingo
16929 Chicken Ranch Road
Jamestown, California 95327
(209) 984-3000
Website: www.chickenranchcasino.com
Map: #5 (100 miles S.E. of Sacramento)

Toll-Free Number: (800) 752-4646
Gambling Age: 18
Restaurants: 1 Snack Bar Liquor: No
Buffet: B/L- $4.50 (Tue)
Hours: 9am-1am (Mon-Wed)
24 hours (Thu-Sun)
Casino Size: 30,000 Square Feet
Other Games: Slots only, BG (Thu-Sun)
Overnight RV Parking: No

Chukchansi Gold Resort & Casino
711 Lucky Lane
Coarsegold, California 93614
(559) 692-5200
Website: www.chukchansigold.com
Map: #25 (35 miles N. of Fresno)

Toll-Free Number: (866) 794-6946
Gambling Age: 21
Rooms: 190 Prices: $99-$199
Suites: 6 Prices: Casino Use Only
Restaurants: 7 Liquor: Yes
Buffets: B- $12.00 (Sat)/ $14.00 (Sun)
L-$12.00/$14.00 (Sun)
D-$12.00/$14.00 (Wed)/$20.00(Fri/Sat)
Other Games: BJ, S21, TCP, P,
PGP, LIR, FCP
Overnight RV Parking: Free/RV Dump: No
Senior Discount: $5.99 lunch buffet if 55+

Chumash Casino Resort
3400 East Highway 246
Santa Ynez, California 93460
(805) 686-0855
Website: www.chumashcasino.com
Map: #13 (40 miles N.W. of Santa Barbara)

Toll-Free Number: (800) 728-9997
Gambling Age: 18
Room Reservations: (800) 248-6274
Rooms: 89 Prices: $195-$350
Suites: 17 Prices: $380-$550
Restaurants: 3 Liquor: No
Buffets: L-$17.95
D-$21.95/$25.95(Thu-Sun)
Casino Size: 94,000 Square Feet
Other Games: S21, BJ, P, BG (Sun-Wed),
TCP, FCP, LIR, MB, MS
Overnight RV Parking: No
Special Features: Spa.

Colusa Casino Resort
3770 Highway 45
Colusa, California 95932
(530) 458-8844
Website: www.colusacasino.com
Map: #6 (75 miles N. of Sacramento)

Toll-Free Number: (800) 655-8946
Gambling Age: 21
Room Reservations: (877) 869-7829
Rooms: 50 Prices: $119-$139
Suites: 10 Prices: $199-$219
Restaurants: 3 Liquor: Yes
Buffets: B- $12.95 (Sat/Sun) L-$9.95
D-$13.95/ $24.95 (Fri)/$19.95 (Sat)
Other Games: BJ, MB, P, TCP, PGP,
BG (Sat-Wed)
Overnight RV Parking: Free/RV Dump: No

Coyote Valley Casino
7751 N. State Street
Redwood Valley, California 95470
(707) 485-0700
Website: www.coyotevalleycasino.com
Map: #23 (115 miles N. of San Francisco)

Toll-Free Number: (800) 332-9683
Gambling Age: 21
Restaurants: 1 Cafe Liquor: Yes
Other Games: BJ, PGP, P
Overnight RV Parking: Free/RV Dump: No

Desert Rose Casino
901 County Road 56
Alturas, California 96101
(530) 233-3141
Website: www.desertrosecasino.net
Map: **#27** (250 miles N.E. of Sacramento)

Gambling Age: 21
Restaurants: 1 Snack Bar Liquor: Yes
Hours: 10am-12am/2am (Fri/Sat)
Casino Size: 5,000 Square Feet
Overnight RV Parking: Free/RV Dump: No
Senior Discount: Monday specials from
10am to 6pm if 55 or older.

Diamond Mountain Casino and Hotel
900 Skyline Drive
Susanville, California 96130
(530) 252-1100
Website: www.diamondmountaincasino.com
Map: **#31** (160 Miles N.E. of Sacramento)

Toll-Free Number: (877) 319-8514
Gambling Age: 21
Rooms: 63 Prices: $79-$109
Suites: 7 Prices: $119-$189
Restaurants: 2 Liquor: Yes
Casino Size: 26,000 Square Feet
Other Games: BJ, BG (Tue/Sun)
Overnight RV Parking: Free/RV Dump: No
Senior Discount: 50% off in lava cafe for 55+
from 2-5 pm.

Eagle Mountain Casino
681 South Tule Road
Porterville, California 93257
(559) 788-6220
Website: www.eaglemtncasino.com
Map: **#21** (60 miles S.E. of Fresno)

Toll-Free Number: (800) 903-3353
Gambling Age: 18
Hours: 11am-4am/ 24 hours (Fri/Sat)
Restaurants: 2 Liquor: No
Buffets: L-$10.00 (Tue/Thu)/$12.00 (Fri-Sun)
D-$16.00(Fri/Sat)
Casino Size: 9,600 Square Feet
Other Games: BJ, P
Overnight RV Parking: Free/RV Dump: No
Special Features: Food court with four fast
food stations.

Elk Valley Casino
2500 Howland Hill Road
Crescent City, California 95531
(707) 464-1020
Website: www.elkvalleycasino.com
Map: **#7** (84 miles N. of Eureka)

Toll-Free Number: (888) 574-2744
Gambling Age: 21
Restaurants: 1 Liquor: Yes
Casino Size: 23,000 Square Feet
Other Games: BJ, P, BG (Sun-Tue/Fri)
Overnight RV Parking: No
Senior Discount: $3.95 lunches on Tuesdays.

Fantasy Springs Casino
82-245 Indio Springs Drive
Indio, California 92203
(760) 342-5000
Website: www.fantasyspringsresort.com
Map: **#8** (125 miles E. of Los Angeles)

Toll-Free Number: (800) 827-2946
Gambling Age: 21
Rooms: 250 Prices: $99-$209
Suites: 11 Prices: $350-$599
Restaurants: 6 Liquor: Yes
Buffets: L-$13.99/$22.99 (Sun)
D-$18.99/$23.99 (Sat)
Casino Size: 95,000 Square Feet
Other Games: BJ, S21, MB, LIR, PGP,
TCP, FCP, BG, OTB
Overnight RV Parking: Free/RV Dump: No
Special Features: 24-lane bowling center.
5,000-seat special events center. Card version
of craps. Golf course.

Feather Falls Casino
3 Alverda Drive
Oroville, California 95966
(530) 533-3885
Website: www.featherfallscasino.com
Map: **#22** (100 miles N. of Sacramento)

Toll-Free Number: (877) 652-4646
Gambling Age: 21
Rooms: 74 Prices: $79-$89
Suites: 10 Prices: $180-$280
Restaurants: 2 Liquor: Yes
Buffets: B-$6.95/$10.95 (Sat/Sun)
L-$8.95 D-$12.95/$15.95 (Fri/Sat)
Casino Size: 38,000 Square Feet
Other Games: BJ, P
Overnight RV Parking: No
Senior Discount: Various on Mon/Wed if 55+

Gold Country Casino
4020 Olive Highway
Oroville, California 95966
(530) 538-4560
Website: www.goldcountrycasino.com
Map: **#22** (100 miles N. of Sacramento)

Toll-Free Number: (800) 334-9400
Gambling Age: 21
Rooms: 87 Prices: $59-$139
Restaurants: 3 Liquor: Yes
Buffets: L-$9.99/$11.99 (Sat/Sun)
        D-$12.99/$14.99 (Thu)/
            $19.99 (Fri/Sat)/$11.99 (Sun)
Other Games: BJ, P, TCP,
        PGP, FCP, BG (Wed-Sun)
Overnight RV Parking: Free/RV Dump: No
Senior discount: 10% off buffet if 55+.
Special Features: 1,200-seat showroom.

Golden Acorn Casino and Travel Center
1800 Golden Acorn Way
Campo, California 91906
(619) 938-6000
Website: www.goldenacorncasino.com
Map: **#33** (40 miles S.E. of San Diego)

Toll-Free Number: (866) 794-6244
Gambling Age: 18
Restaurants: 2 Liquor: Yes
Other Games: BJ, TCP
Overnight RV Parking: Free/RV Dump: No
Special Features: 33-acre auto/truck stop and
convenience store.

Graton Resort & Casino
630 Park Court
Rohnert Park, California 94928
Website: www.gratonresortcasino.com
Map: **#42** (50 miles N. of San Francisco)

Gambling age: 21
Restaurants: 4 Liquor: Yes
Casino Size: 18,000 Square Feet
Other Games: BJ, PGP, TCP, B, FCP
Overnight RV Parking: Free/RV Dump: No
Special Features: Food court with eight fast
food outlets.

Harrah's Resort Southern California
33750 Valley Center Road
Valley Center, California 92082
(760) 751-3100
Website: harrahsresortsoutherncalifornia.com
Map: **#20** (35 miles N.E. of San Diego)

Toll-Free Number: (877) 777-2457
Gambling Age: 21
Rooms: 552 Prices: $89-$409
Suites: 101 Prices: $129-$609
Restaurants: 7 Liquor: Yes
Buffets: B-$22.99 (Sat/Sun) L-$19.99
        D-$24.99/$29.99 (Fri/Sat)
Casino Size: 55,000 Square Feet
Other Games: BJ, PGP, MB, P, MS,
            TCP, LIR, FCP
Overnight RV Parking: Free/RV Dump: No
Special Features: Card version of craps and
roulette.

Havasu Landing Resort & Casino
5 Main Street
Havasu Lake, California 92363
(760) 858-4593
Website: www.havasulanding.com
Map: **#18** (200 miles E. of L. A.)

Toll Free Number: (800) 307-3610
Gambling Age: 21
Restaurants: 1 Liquor: Yes
Hours: 8:30am-12:30am/2:30am (Fri/Sat)
Other Games: BJ, TCP
Overnight RV Parking: Must use RV park
Casino Size: 6,000 Square Feet
Special Features: Tables open 11:30 am/
12:30 pm (Mon-Thu). Marina, RV park ($27-
$32 per night), campground rentals. Mobile
homes available for daily rental.

Hopland Sho-Ka-Wah Casino
13101 Nakomis Road
Hopland, California 95449
(707) 744-1395
Website: www.shokawah.com
Map: **#32** (100 miles N. of San Francisco)

Toll Free Number: (888) 746-5292
Gambling Age: 21
Restaurants: 2 Liquor: Yes
Buffets: L-$9.95 (Mon) D-$9.99 (Thu)
Other Games: BJ, PGP, BG
Overnight RV Parking: Free/RV Dump: No

Jackson Rancheria Casino & Hotel
12222 New York Ranch Road
Jackson, California 95642
(209) 223-1677
Website: www.jacksoncasino.com
Map: **#9** (60 miles S.E. of Sacramento)

Toll-Free Number: (800) 822-9466
Gambling Age: 18
Rooms: 77 Price Range: $89-$149
Suites: 9 Price Range: $199-$399
Restaurants: 2 Liquor: No
Buffets: L-$10.00 (Mon-Fri)
            D-$16.95/$24.95 (Fri/Sat)
Other Games: BJ, PGP, LIR, TCP, CW,
            FCP, MB, P
Overnight RV Parking: No
Special Features: Offers card versions of craps
and roulette. 805-seat showroom. 100-space
RV park ($40-$55 per night).

Konocti Vista Casino Resort & Marina
2755 Mission Rancheria Road
Lakeport, California 95453
(707) 262-1900
Website: www.knocti-vista-casino.com
Map: **#11** (120 miles N. of San Francisco)

Toll-Free Number: (800) 386-1950
Gambling Age: 21
Rooms: 80 Prices: $89-$139
Restaurants: 1 Liquor: Yes
Other Games: BJ, PGP
Overnight RV Parking: Must use RV park
RV Dump: Free
Special Features: Marina with 80 slips.
74-space RV park ($19-$25 per night).

Lucky Bear Casino
12510 Highway 96
Hoopa, California 95546
(530) 625-5198
Map: **#24** (30 miles N.E. of Eureka)

Gambling Age: 18
Restaurants: 1 Snack Bar Liquor: No
Hours: 10am-12am/1am (Fri/Sat)
Other Games: BJ, BG
Overnight RV Parking: No
Special Features: Non-smoking casino.

Lucky 7 Casino
350 N. Indian Road
Smith River, California 95567
(707) 487-7777
Website: www.lucky7casino.com
Map: **#7** (100 miles N. of Eureka)

Toll-Free Number: (866) 777-7170
Gambling Age: 21
Restaurants: 1 Liquor: Yes
Casino Size: 24,000 Square Feet
Other Games: BJ, BG (Sun/Tue/Wed), P
Overnight RV Parking: Free/RV Dump: No

Mono Wind Casino
37302 Rancheria Lane
Auberry, California 93602
(559) 855-4350
Website: www.monowind.com
Map: **#25** (30 miles N.E. of Fresno)

Gambling Age: 18
Restaurants: 1 Liquor: Yes
Casino Size: 10,000 Square Feet
Overnight RV Parking: Free/RV Dump: No

Morongo Casino Resort and Spa
49750 Seminole Drive
Cabazon, California 92230
(951) 849-3080
Website: www.morongocasinoresort.com
Map: **#3** (90 miles E. of L. A.)

Toll-Free Number: (800) 252-4499
Gambling Age: 18
Rooms: 310 Prices: $109-$299
Suites: 32 Prices: $229-$499
Restaurants: 5 Liquor: Yes
Buffets: B- $23.95 (Sun)
         L-$12.95/$17.95 (Thu)/$14.95 (Sat)
         D-$14.95 (Mon/Fri)/
            $17.95 (Tue/Wed)/$21.95 (Thu)/
            $23.95 (Sat/Sun)
Casino Size: 145,000 Square Feet
Other Games: BJ, P, TCP, FCP, MS,
            LIR, MB, PGP, BG
Overnight RV Parking: Free/RV Dump: No
Special Features: Card version of craps.

Paiute Palace Casino
2742 N. Sierra Highway
Bishop, California 93514
(760) 873-4150
Website: www.paiutepalace.com
Map: **#26** (130 miles N.E. of Fresno)

Toll-Free Number: (888) 372-4883
Gambling Age: 21
Restaurants: 1 Liquor: Yes
Other Games: BJ, P
Overnight RV Parking: $15/RV Dump: No
Senior Discount: 10% off in restaurant if 50+
Special Features: 24-hour gas station and convenience store.

Pala Casino Spa and Resort
11154 Highway 76
Pala, California 92059
(760) 510-5100
Website: www.palacasino.com
Map: **#20** (35 miles N.E. of San Diego)

Toll-Free Number: (877) 946-7252
Gambling Age: 21
Room Reservations: (877) 725-2766
Rooms: 425 Prices: $129-$219
Suites: 82 Prices: $159-$360
Restaurants: 9 Liquor: Yes
Buffets: B-$30.74 (Sat/Sun)
          L-$23.74
          D-$30.74/$35.74 (Fri/Sat)
Other Games: BJ, B, MB, TCP, PGP,
          MS, LIR, P
Overnight RV Parking: Free (park in west lot)
          RV Dump: No
Special Features: Offers card versions of craps and roulette. Fitness center and spa. Discount on buffet if players club member.

Pechanga Resort and Casino
45000 Pechanga Parkway
Temecula, California 92592
(951) 693-1819
Website: www.pechanga.com
Map: **#28** (50 miles N. of San Diego)

Toll-Free Number: (877) 711-2946
Gambling Age: 21
Room Reservations: (888) 732-4264
Rooms: 458 Price Range: $109-$349
Suites: 64 Price Range: $179-$750
Restaurants: 8 Liquor: Yes
Buffets: B-$19.99 (Sat/Sun) L-$16.99
          D- $21.99/$26.99 (Fri/Sat)
Other Games: BJ, MB, P, PGP, LIR, TCP
Overnight RV Parking: Must use RV park
RV Dump: $14.00 charge to use
Casino Size: 88,000 Square Feet
Special Features: 168-space RV park ($45 per night/$55 Fri-Sat). Offers card version of craps.

Pit River Casino
20265 Tamarack Avenue
Burney, California 96013
(530) 335-2334
Website: www.pitrivercasino.com
Map: **#29** (190 miles N. of Sacramento)

Toll-Free Number: (888) 245-2992
Gambling Age: 18
Restaurants: 1 Snack Bar Liquor: No
Casino Hours: 9am-12am/2am (Fri/Sat)
Other Games: BJ, P
Overnight RV Parking: Free/RV Dump: No
Senior Discount: $5 match play and lunch special on Mondays if 55+.
Special Features: Tables open at 4pm/2pm (Sun).

Quechan Casino Resort
525 Algodones Road
Winterhaven, California 92283
(760) 572-3900
Website: www.playqcr.net
Map: **#37** (170 miles E. of San Diego)

Toll-Free Number: (877) 783-2426
Rooms: 158 Price Range: $89-$119
Suites: 8 Price Range: $159-$299
Gambling Age: 21
Restaurants: 2 Liquor: Yes
Other Games: BJ, P, PGP, TCP
Overnight RV Parking: Free/RV Dump: No
Special Features: Part of casino is located across the state border in Arizona. Offers video versions of craps and roulette. 10% off food with players club card.

Red Earth Casino
3089 Norm Niver Road
Salton City, California 92274
(760) 395-1700
Website: www.redearthcasino.com
Map: **#39** (114 miles S.E. of Riverside)

Gambling Age: 21
Restaurants: 1 Liquor: Yes
Casino Size: 10,000 Square Feet
Overnight RV Parking: Free/RV Dump: No

Red Fox Casino
300 Cahto Drive
Laytonville, California 95454
(760) 395-1200
Website: www.redfoxcasino.net
Map: **#30** (150 miles N.W. of Sacramento)

Toll-Free Number: (888) 473-3369
Gambling Age: 18
Restaurants: 1 Snack Bar Liquor: No
Hours: 10am-12am
Overnight RV Parking: Free/RV Dump: No
Senior Discount: 50% off meals if 55+

Red Hawk Casino
5250 Honpie Road
Placerville, California 95667
(530) 677-7000
Website: www.redhawkcasino.com
Map: **#40** (40 miles E of Sacramento)

Toll-Free Number: (888) 573-3495
Gambling Age: 21
Restaurants: 6 Liquor: Yes
Buffets: B- $11.99 (Sat)/$18.99 (Sun)
　　　L-$10.50
　　　D- $14.50/$25.99 (Fri/Sat)/
　　　　$15.99 (Sun)
Other Games: BJ, P, PGP, TCP, LIR, MB, FCP, B
Special Features: Childcare facility. Shopping arcade. Offers a card version of craps and roulette.

River Rock Casino
3250 Hwy 128 East
Geyserville, California 95441
(707) 857-2777
Website: www.riverrockcasino.com
Map: **#32** (75 miles N. of San Fran.)

Gambling Age: 21
Restaurants: 2 Liquor: Yes
Other Games: BJ, MB, PGP, TCP
Overnight RV Parking: No
Senior discount: 10% off buffet Tue if 55+

Robinson Rancheria Resort & Casino
1545 East Highway 20
Nice, California 95464
(707) 275-9000
Website: www.rrrc.com
Map: **#11** (115 miles N.W. of Sacramento)

Toll-Free Number: (800) 809-3636
Gambling Age: 21
Rooms: 49 Price Range: $79-$109
Suites: 2 Price Range: $119-$295
Restaurants: 2 Liquor: Yes
Buffets: D-$15.95 (Thu)/$17.95 (Fri/Sat)
Casino Size: 37,500 Square Feet
Other Games: BJ, P, PGP, LIR, TCP,
       BG (Wed-Sun)
Overnight RV Parking: Free (one night only)
RV Dump: No
Senior Discount: Various on Wed if 55+.
Special Features: 60-site RV park ($18/$25 per night), 2.5 miles from casino.

Rolling Hills Casino
2655 Barham Avenue
Corning, California 96021
(530) 528-3500
Website: www.rollinghillscasino.com
Map: **#36** (115 miles N. of Sacramento)

Toll-Free Number: (888) 331-6400
Gambling Age: 21
Rooms: 90 Price Range: $109-$169
Suites: 21 Price Range: $159-$215
Restaurants: 2 Liquor: Yes
Buffet: B-$8.95 L-$10.95
       D-$15.95/$19.95 (Fri)
Casino Size: 60,000 Square Feet
Other Games: BJ, PGP, TCP
Overnight RV Parking: Free in truck lot
RV Dump: Only for those staying in RV Park
Senior Discount: Various Tue/Thu if 50+.
Special Features: 72-space RV park ($28 per night).

Running Creek Casino
635 East Highway 20
Upper Lake, California 95485
(707) 275-9209
Website: www.runningcreekcasino.com
Map: **#11** (120 miles N.W. of Sacramento)

Gambling Age: 21
Restaurants: 1 Liquor: Yes
Other Games: BJ
Casino Size: 33,000 Square Feet

San Manuel Indian Bingo & Casino
5797 North Victoria Avenue
Highland, California 92346
(909) 864-5050
Website: www.sanmanuel.com
Map: **#12** (65 miles E. of L. A.)

Toll-Free Number: (800) 359-2464
Gambling Age: 21
Restaurants: 6 Liquor: Yes
Buffet: L-$11.95/ $18.95 (Sun)
       D-$15.95/$22.95(Wed)/
       $19.95 (Fri/Sun)/$24.95 (Sat)
Casino Size: 75,000 Square Feet
Other Games: BJ, MB, P, PGP, LIR, TCP,
       FCP, BG
Overnight RV Parking: Free/RV Dump: No
Senior Discount: Special bingo price Fri if 55+.
Special Features: Food court with 3 fast food dining stations. Offers a card version of craps and roulette.

San Pablo Lytton Casino
13255 San Pablo Avenue
San Pablo, California 94806
(510) 215-7888
Website: www.sanpablolytton.com
Map: **#41** (15 miles N of Oakland)

Gambling Age: 21
Restaurants: 2
Other Games: BJ, TCP, B, PGP
Special Features: All machines are Class-II gaming machines based on bingo. All table game players must place $1 ante for every $100 bet.

Sherwood Valley Rancheria Casino
100 Kawi Place
Willits, California 95490
(707) 459-7330
Website: www.svrcasino.com
Map: **#11** (130 miles N. of San Francisco)

Gambling Age: 18
Restaurants: 1 Deli Liquor: No
Casino Size: 6,000 Square Feet
Other Games: Slots Only
Overnight RV Parking: Free/RV Dump: No

Soboba Casino
23333 Soboba Road
San Jacinto, California 92583
(909) 654-2883
Website: www.soboba.net
Map: **#3** (90 miles E. of L. A.)

Toll-Free Number: (866) 476-2622
Gambling Age: 21
Restaurants: 1 Liquor: Yes
Casino Size: 52,000 Square Feet
Other Games: BJ, S21, P, PGP, LIR,
    TCP, FCP, BG
Overnight RV Parking: Free/RV Dump: No
Special Features: Offers card version of
roulette.

Spa Resort Casino
140 N. Indian Canyon Drive
Palm Springs, California 92262
(760) 323-5865
Website: www.sparesortcasino.com
Map: **#3** (115 miles E. of L. A.)

Toll-Free Number: (800) 258-2946
Gambling Age: 21
Restaurants: 5 (1 open 24 hours) Liquor: Yes
Buffets: B-$9.99 (Sat/Sun)
    L-$14.99/$23.99 (Sun)
    D-$15.99/$23.99 (Fri-Sat)
Casino Size: 15,000 Square Feet
Other Games: BJ, MB, PGP, TCP, LIR
Overnight RV Parking: No
Special Features: Offers card version of
roulette.

Spotlight 29 Casino
46200 Harrison Place
Coachella, California 92236
(760) 775-5566
Website: www.spotlight29.com
Map: **#8** (130 miles E. of L. A.)

Toll-Free Number: (866) 377-6829
Gambling Age: 21
Restaurants: 2 Liquor: Yes
Buffets: L-$10.95/$12.95 (Sat/Sun)
    D-$15.95/$19.95 (Fri)/$17.99 (Sat)
Other Games: BJ, S21, P, PGP, TCP
Overnight RV Parking: Free/RV Dump: No
Special Features: Three fast-food outlets
including McDonald's. 2,200-seat showroom.
Special breakfast buffet for players club
members.

Sycuan Resort & Casino
5469 Casino Way
El Cajon, California 92019
(619) 445-6002
Website: www.sycuan.com
Map: **#14** (10 miles E. of San Diego)

Toll-Free Number: (800) 279-2826
Gambling Age: 21
Room Reservations: (800) 457-5568
Rooms: 103 Price Range: $129-$169
Suites: 14 Price Range: $249-$599
Restaurants: 5 Liquor: Yes
Buffets: L-$25.95 (Sat/Sun)
    D-$25.95
Casino Size: 73,000 Square Feet
Other Games: BJ, S21, P, BG, CW, TCP,
    CSP, FCP, OTB, PGP
Overnight RV Parking: Free/RV Dump: No
Senior Discount: Various Wed 7am-7pm if 55+.
Special Features: Offers card/tile versions of
roulette and craps. Hotel is three miles from
casino with free shuttle service. Three 18-hole
golf courses. 500-seat showroom.

Table Mountain Casino & Bingo
8184 Table Mountain Road
Friant, California 93626
(559) 822-2485
Website: www.tmcasino.com
Map: #15 (15 miles N. of Fresno)

Toll-Free Number: (800) 541-3637
Gambling Age: 18
Restaurants: 3 Liquor: No
Buffet: D-$11.99/$21.99 (Tue)/$13.99 (Fri-Sun)
Other Games: BJ, S21, P, PGP, TCP,
          BG, CW
Overnight RV Parking: Free/RV Dump: No
Senior Discount: Buffet discount Mon-Fri
if 55+.

Tachi Palace Hotel and Casino
17225 Jersey Avenue
Lemoore, California 93245
(559) 924-7751
Website: www.tachipalace.com
Map: #10 (50 miles S. of Fresno)

Toll-Free Number: (800) 942-6886
Gambling Age: 18
Room Reservations: (800) 615-8030
Rooms: 215 Price Range: $79-$159
Suites: 40 Price Range: $149-$259
Restaurants: 8 Liquor: Yes
Buffets: B-$14.99 (Sat)/$16.99 (Sun)
     L- $11.99
     D- $16.99/$19.99 (Thu)/$17.99 (Fri)/
        $15.99 (Sat)/$16.99 (Sun)
Casino Size: 50,000 Square Feet
Other Games: BJ, P, PGP, TCP, S21,
          FCP, MB, BG
Overnight RV Parking: Free/RV Dump: No
Senior Discount: $5.99 lunch buffet if 55+.
Special Features: Offers a card-based version
of roulette.

Thunder Valley Casino
1200 Athens Ave
Lincoln, California 95648
(916) 408-7777
Website: www.thundervalleyresort.com
Map: #35 (35 miles N.E. of Sacramento)

Toll-Free Number: (877) 468-8777
Gambling Age: 21
Rooms: 297 Price Range: $115-$189
Suites: 40 Price Range: $300-$399
Restaurants: 4 Liquor: Yes
Buffets: B/L-$11.49/$16.95 (Sun)
     D-$15.49/$28.95 (Fri)/ $26.99 (Sat)
Other Games: BJ, MB, PGP, P, MS,
          LIR, TCP, FCP
Overnight RV Parking: No
Special Features: Affiliated with Station
Casinos of Las Vegas. Five fast-food outlets.
Buffet discount with players club card. Card
versions of craps and roulette.

Tortoise Rock Casino
Baseline Road
Twentynine Palms, California 92277
(760) 367-9759
Website: www.tortiserockcasino.com
Map: #8 (125 miles E. of L. A.)

Restaurants: 1
Casino Size: 30,000 Square Feet
Other Games: P, S21, TCP
Overnight RV Parking: Free/RV Dump: No

Twin Pine Casino & Hotel
22223 Highway 29 at Rancheria Road
Middletown, California 95461
(707) 987-0197
Website: www.twinpine.com
Map: #32 (100 miles N. of San Francisco)

Toll-Free Number: (800) 564-4872
Rooms: 57 Price Range: $89-$109
Suites: 3 Price Range: $149-$250
Gambling Age: 21
Restaurants: 1 Liquor: No
Other Games: BJ, P, TCP
Overnight RV Parking: No/RV Dump: No
Senior Discount: Various Tue/Thu mornings
8:30 am-11:00 am if 55+.

Valley View Casino Resort
16300 Nyemii Pass Road
Valley Center, California 92082
(760) 291-5500
Website: www.valleyviewcasino.com
Map: **#20** (35 miles N.E. of San Diego)

Toll-Free Number: (866) 843-9946
Gambling Age: 21
Rooms: 100 Price Range: $119-$239
Suites: 8 Price Range: $299-$439
Restaurants: 2 Liquor: Yes
Buffets:B- $22.99 (Sat-Sun)
        L-$19.99/$26.99 (Sat/Sun)
        D-$32.99
Other Games: BJ, PGP, TCP, MB
Overnight RV Parking: Free/RV Dump: No
Special Features: Players club members
receive $3 off buffets. Offers card-based
version of roulette.

Viejas Casino
5000 Willows Road
Alpine, California 91901
(619) 445-5400
Website: www.viejas.com
Map: **#16** (25 miles E. of San Diego)

Toll-Free Number: (800) 847-6537
Rooms: 99 Price Range: $129-$289
Suites: 29 Price Range: $260-$500
Gambling Age: 18
Restaurants: 7 Liquor: Yes
Buffets: B- $25.95 (Fri-Sun)
        L-$15.95 D-$25.95
Other Games: BJ, B, MB, P, LIR, TCP
            FCP, CW, PGP, BG, OTB
Overnight RV Parking: Free/RV Dump: No
Special Features: 51-store factory outlet
shopping center. Buffet discounts for players
club members. Card-based versions of craps
and roulette.

Win-River Casino
2100 Redding Rancheria Road
Redding, California 96001
(530) 243-3377
Website: www.winrivercasino.com
Map: **#17** (163 miles N. of Sacramento)

Toll-Free Number: (800) 280-8946
Gambling Age: 21
Restaurants: 1 Liquor: Yes
Buffets: B- $24.95 (Sun)
Casino Size: 37,000 Square Feet
Other Games: BJ,TCP, PGP, FCP,
            P, BG (Sun-Wed)
Overnight RV Parking: Free/RV Dump: No
Special Features: Comedy club. Food
discounts for players club members. 1,000-
seat showroom.

COLORADO

Colorado casinos can be found in the mountain towns of Black Hawk, Central City and Cripple Creek. There are also two Indian casinos (which abide by Colorado's limited gaming rules) in Ignacio and Towaoc.

When casino gambling was initially introduced in 1991 it was limited in that only electronic games (including slots, video poker, video blackjack and video keno) and the table games of poker, blackjack, let it ride and three-card poker were allowed. Plus, a single wager could not exceed $5.

All that changed, however, on July 2, 2009 when the maximum bet was raised to $100, plus the games of craps and roulette were added to the mix. Additionally, the casinos were allowed to stay open for 24 hours, rather than having to be closed between 2 a.m. and 8 a.m.

Here's information, as supplied by Colorado's Division of Gaming, showing the slot machine payback percentages for each city's casinos for the one-year period from July 1, 2013 through June 30, 2014:

	Black Hawk	Central City	Cripple Creek
1¢ Slots	89.91%	90.42%	**91.64%**
5¢ Slots	93.25%	**94.54%**	93.45%
25¢ Slots	93.83%	94.34%	**95.06%**
$1 Slots	94.51%	**95.34%**	94.98%
$5 Slots	94.55%	92.36%	**95.19%**
All	92.65%	92.61%	**93.58%**

These numbers reflect the percentage of money returned on each denomination of machine and encompass all electronic machines including video poker and video keno. The best returns for each category are highlighted in bold print.

The minimum gambling age at all Colorado casinos is 21, including Indian casinos.

For information on visiting Central City, call (303) 582-5251 or visit their website at: www.centralcitycolorado.us.

For information on visiting Black Hawk, call (303) 582-5221, or visit their website at: www.cityofblackhawk.org.

All casinos offer electronic games (slots, video poker, video blackjack and video keno). Some casinos also offer: blackjack (BJ), craps (C), roulette (R), poker (P), let it ride (LIR), Mississippi stud (MS) and three card poker (TCP).

Black Hawk

Map Location: **#1** (35 miles west of Denver. Take U.S. 6 through Golden to Hwy 119. Take Hwy 119 to Black Hawk. Another route is I-70 West to exit 244. Turn right onto Hwy. 6. Take Hwy 6 to 119 and into Black Hawk.)

The casinos in Black Hawk and Central City are located one mile apart. The Black Hawk Shuttle Service provides free transportation throughout Black Hawk and Central City.

Ameristar Black Hawk
111 Richman Street
Black Hawk, Colorado 80422
(720) 946-4000
Website: www.ameristar.com

Toll-Free Number (866) 667-3386
Rooms: 472 Price Range: $109-$209
Suites: 64 Price Range: $309-$549
Restaurants: 6
Buffets: B- $17.99 (Sat/Sun)
L-$12.99 D-$16.99/$21.99 (Fri/Sat)
Casino Size: 46,534 Square feet
Other Games: BJ, P, C, R, MS

Black Hawk Station
141 Gregory Street
Black Hawk, Colorado 80422
(303) 582-5582
Website: www.blackhawkstationcasino.net

Casino Size: 1,827 Square feet
Restaurants: 1 (snack bar)
Casino Hours: 8am-2am
Special Features: Includes **Sasquatch Casino**.

Bull Durham Saloon & Casino
110 Main Street
Black Hawk, Colorado 80422
(303) 582-0810
Website: www.bulldurhamcasino.com

Restaurants: 1 (snack bar)
Casino Size: 2,579 Square Feet

Canyon Casino
131 Main Street
Black Hawk, Colorado 80422
(303) 777-1111
Website: www.canyoncasino.com

Restaurants: 1
Casino Size: 8,456 Square Feet (Canyon)
Casino Size: 2,428 Square Feet (Grand Plateau)
Other Games: BJ, C, R
Special Features: Connected to **Grand Plateau Casino**.

Gilpin Hotel Casino
111 Main Street
Black Hawk, Colorado 80422
(303) 582-1133
Website: www.thegilpincasino.com

Restaurants: 2
Other Games: BJ, C, R
Casino Size: 11,087 Square Feet
Senior Discount: Specials on Tue if 50+.

Golden Gates Casino
261 Main Street
Black Hawk, Colorado 80422
(303) 582-1650
Website: www.thegoldengatescasino.com

Restaurants: 5
Casino Size: 8,004 Square Feet (Golden Gates)
Casino Size: 3,440 Square Feet (Golden Gulch)
Other Games: P, BJ
Special Features: Connected to **Golden Gulch Casino**.

Golden Mardi Gras Casino
333 Main Street
Black Hawk, Colorado 80422
(303) 582-5600
Website: www.goldenmardigras.com

Restaurants: 1
Casino Size: 17,888 Square Feet
Other Games: BJ, C, R, TCP
Special Features: Skybridge to **The Lodge Casino.**

Isle of Capri Casino - Black Hawk
401 Main Street
Black Hawk, Colorado 80422
(303) 998-7777
Website: www.isleofcapricasinos.com

Toll-Free Number (800) 843-4753
Rooms: 107 Price Range: $99-$229
Suites: 130 Price Range: $129-$179
Restaurants: 3
Buffets: B-$9.99/$19.99 (Sat/Sun) L-$12.99
          D-$19.99/$24.99 (Fri-Sun)
Casino Size: 27,611 Square Feet
Other Games: BJ, TCP, LIR, C, R, MS

Lady Luck Casino
340 Main Street
Black Hawk, Colorado 80422
(303) 582-3000
Website: www.isleofcapricasinos.com

Toll-Free Number (888) 523-9582
Rooms: 140 Price Range: $79-$206
Suites: 24 Price Range: $174-$215
Restaurants: 2   Valet parking: Free
Casino Size: 17,726 Square Feet
Other Games: BJ, P, C, R, TCP
Senior Discount: Various Wed/Fri if 40+.
Special Features: Affiliated with Isle of Capri.

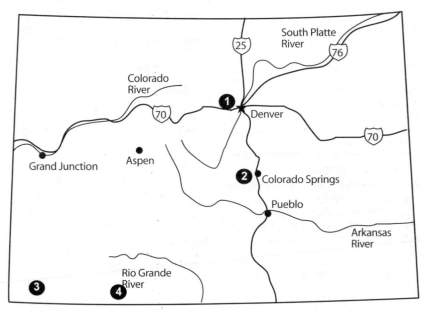

The Lodge Casino at Black Hawk
240 Main Street
Black Hawk, Colorado 80422
(303) 582-1771
Website: www.thelodgecasino.com

Rooms: 47 Price Range: $119-$165
Suites: 3 Price Range: Casino Use Only
Restaurants: 3
Buffets: B-$7.49 L-$11.49/$16.99 (Sat/Sun)
      D-$16.99/$21.49 (Fri/Sat)
Casino Size: 23,951 Square Feet
OtherGames: BJ, P, C, R, TCP, MS
Senior Discount: 50% off breakfast and lunch
      buffets Mon/Tue if 50+.
Special Features: Skybridge to **Golden Mardi Gras Casino**. Free valet parking.

Monarch Casino Black Hawk
444 Main Street
Black Hawk, Colorado 80422
(303) 582-1000
Website: www.monarchblackhawk.com

Restaurants: 1
Buffet: B-$5.99 L-$8.99/$13.99 (Sat-Sun)
      D-$17.99
Casino Size: 25,860 Square Feet
Other Games: BJ, TCP, R, C, FCP
Senior Discount: 50% off buffet Mon if 50+.

Red Dolly Casino
530 Gregory Street
Black Hawk, Colorado 80422
Website: www.reddollycasino.net
(303) 582-1100

Restaurants: 1 (snack bar)
Casino Size: 1,992 Square Feet

Saratoga Casino
101 Main Street
Black Hawk, Colorado 80422
(303) 582-6162
Website: www.saratogacasinobh.com

Toll-Free Number: (800) 538-5825
Restaurants: 2
Casino Size: 17,129 Square Feet
Other Games: BJ, C, R, TCP

Wild Card Saloon & Casino
112 Main Street
Black Hawk, Colorado 80422
Website: www.thewildcardsaloon.com
(303) 582-3412

Restaurants: 1
Casino Size: 2,750 Square Feet
Special Features: Grocery store.

Z Casino
101 Gregory Street
Black Hawk, Colorado 80422
(303) 271-2500
Website: www.bullwhackers.com

Toll-Free Number: (800) 426-2855
Restaurants: 2
Casino Size: 10,471 Square Feet
Senior Discount: Specials on Tue if 55+.
Special Features: Bakery.

Central City

Map location: **#1** (same as Black Hawk).
Central City is located one mile from Black
Hawk. Turn left at the third stoplight on Hwy.
119 and proceed up Gregory Street.

Century Casino & Hotel - Central City
102 Main Street
Central City, Colorado 80427
(303) 582-5050
Website: www.cnty.com

Toll-Free Number: (888) 507-5050
Rooms: 22 Price Range $119-$159
Restaurants: 2
Casino Size: 13,899 Square Feet
Other Games: BJ, P, TCP, C, R

Dostal Alley Saloon & Gaming Emporium
1 Dostal Alley
Central City, Colorado 80427
(303) 582-1610
Website: www.dostalalley.net

Restaurants: 1 Snack Bar
Casino Size: 1,041 Square Feet

Famous Bonanza/Easy Street
107 Main Street
Central City, Colorado 80427
(303) 582-5914
Website: www.famousbonanza.com

Toll-Free Number: (866) 339-5825
Restaurants: 1
Casino Size: 5,056 Square Feet (F. Bonanza)
Casino Size: 4,289 Square Feet (Easy Street)
Other Games: BJ, TCP, R

Johnny Z's Casino
132 Lawrence Street
Central City, Colorado 80427
(303) 582-5623
Website: www.johnnyzscasino.com

Restaurants: 1
Casino Size: 35,000 Square Feet
Games Offered: BJ, C, TCP
Overnight RV Parking: Free/RV Dump: No

Reserve Casino Hotel
321 Gregory Street
Central City, Colorado 80427
(303) 582-0800
Website: www.reservecasinohotel.com

Toll-Free Number: (800) 924-6646
Room Reservations: (866) 924-6646
Rooms: 118 .Price Range $119-$169
Suites: 6 Price Range $159-$219
Restaurants: 2
Buffets: B/L-$13.99 (Sat/Sun)
           D-$19.99 (Fri)/$17.99 (Sat/Sun)
Casino Size: 31,695 Square Feet
Other Games: BJ, P, TCP, C, R
Special Features: Tony Roma's restaurant.
Covered parking garage.

Cripple Creek

Map Location: **#2** (47 miles west of Colorado
Springs. Take exit 141 at Colorado Springs
off I-25. Go west on Hwy. 24 to the town of
Divide. Turn left onto Hwy. 67 and go 18 miles
to Cripple Creek.)

All casinos offer electronic games (slots, video
poker, video blackjack and video keno). Some
casinos also offer: blackjack (BJ), poker (P),
let it ride (LIR) and three card poker (TCP).

Big Jim's Casino
279 E Bennett Avenue
Cripple Creek, Colorado 80813
(719) 689-2601
Website: www.bigjimscasino.com

Restaurants: 1 snack bar
Hours: 8am-4am daily
Other Games: BJ

Brass Ass Casino
264 E. Bennett Avenue
Cripple Creek, Colorado 80813
(719) 689-2104
Website: www.triplecrowncasinos.com

Restaurants: 1 (snack bar)
Casino Size: 7,486 Square Feet
Other Games: BJ, TCP, C, R
Special Features: Free hot dogs and popcorn for players. Connected to **Midnight Rose** and **J.P. McGill's**. Covered parking garage.

Bronco Billy's Casino
233 E. Bennett Avenue
Cripple Creek, Colorado 80813
(719) 689-2142
Website: www.broncobillyscasino.com

Toll Free Number: (877) 989-2142
Restaurants: 3
Other Games: BJ, TCP, C, R
Casino Size: 6,086 Square Feet (Bronco's)
Casino Size: 5,991 Square Feet (Buffalo's)
Casino Size: 1,300 Square Feet (Billy's)
Senior Discount: Specials Mon/Fri 8am-6pm.
Special Features: Includes **Buffalo Billy's Casino** & **Billy's Casino**. Free popcorn. Free cookies on weekends. Free donuts Mon-Thu. 49¢ breakfast.

Century Casino - Cripple Creek
200-220 E. Bennett Avenue
Cripple Creek, Colorado 80813
(719) 689-0333
Website: www.cnty.com

Toll-Free Number: (888) 966-2257
Rooms: 21 Price Range: $89-$99
Suites: 3 Price Range: $119
Restaurants: 1
Casino Size: 5,609 Square Feet
Other Games: BJ, P, R
Special Features: Rooms for club members only.

Colorado Grande Casino
300 E. Bennett Avenue
Cripple Creek, Colorado 80813
(719) 689-3517
Website: www.coloradogrande.com

Toll Free Number: (877) 244-9469
Rooms: 7 Prices: $59-$119
Restaurants: 1
Casino Size: 2,569 Square Feet
Senior Discount: Dining discounts if 50+
Special Features: Free cookies on weekends. Covered parking garage.

Double Eagle Hotel & Casino
442 E. Bennett Avenue
Cripple Creek, Colorado 80813
(719) 689-5000
Website: www.decasino.com

Toll-Free Reservations: (800) 711-7234
Rooms: 146 Price Range: $89-$139
Suites: 12 Price Range: $159-$500
Restaurants: 3
Casino Size: 14,631 Square Feet (Double Eagle)
Casino Size: 6,018 Square Feet (Gold Creek)
Other Games: BJ, P, R, TCP
Special Features: Connected to **Gold Creek** casino. Starbucks. Players club members get room discount. Covered parking garage. 48-space RV park ($15/$40 with hookups).

Johnny Nolon's Casino
301 E. Bennett Avenue
Cripple Creek, Colorado 80813
(719) 689-2080
Website: www.johnnynolons.com

Restaurants: 2
Casino Size: 3,505 Square Feet
Senior Discount: Free lunch Mondays 11:30am-1pm with AARP card.

J.P. McGill's Hotel & Casino
232 E. Bennett Avenue
Cripple Creek, Colorado 80813
(719) 689-2446
Website: www.triplecrowncasinos.com

Toll-Free Number: (888) 461-7529
Rooms: 36 Price Range: $80-$115
Suites: 5 Price Range: $180-$240
Restaurants: 1
Casino Size: 7,386 Square Feet
Special Features: Connected to **Midnight Rose** and **Brass Ass**. 10% room/food discount for slot club members. Free popcorn for players. Covered parking garage.

Midnight Rose Hotel & Casino
256 E. Bennett Avenue
Cripple Creek, Colorado 80813
(719) 689-2865
Website: www.triplecrowncasinos.com

Toll-Free Number: (800) 635-5825
Rooms: 19 Price Range: $90-$120
Restaurants: 2
Buffets: D-$24.99 (Thu-Sun)
Casino Size: 9,590 Square Feet
Other Games: P
Special Features: Connected to **Brass Ass** and **J.P. McGill's**. 10% room/food discount for players club members. Covered parking garage.

Wildwood Casino At Cripple Creek
119 Carbonate Sreet
Cripple Creek, Colorado 80813
(719) 689-2814
Website: www.playwildwood.com

Toll-Free Number: (877) 945-3963
Valet Parking: Free
Restaurants: 3
Buffet: D-$23.95 (Fri/Sat)
Casino Size: 18,965 Square Feet
Other Games: BJ, P, C, R
Senior Discount: Various Thu if 50+
Special Features: Covered parking garage.

Indian Casinos

Sky Ute Casino and Lodge
14826 Highway 172 N.
Ignacio, Colorado 81137
(970) 563-3000
Website: www.skyutecasino.com
Map Location: **#4** (345 miles S.W. of Denver, 20 miles S.E. of Durango)

Toll-Free Number: (888) 842-4180
Room Reservations: (800) 876-7017
Rooms: 36 Price Range: $90-$150
Restaurants: 2 Liquor: No
Hours: 24 Hours Daily
Other Games: BJ, TCP, LIR, C, R
           Bingo (Wed/Thu/Fri/Sun)
Overnight RV Parking: Must use RV Park
Senior Discount: 10% off room/food if 55+.
Special Features: 24-space RV park on property ($45/$55 per night). Southern Ute Cultural Center and Museum. Free local shuttle.

Ute Mountain Casino & RV Park
3 Weeminuche Drive
Towaoc, Colorado 81334
(970) 565-8800
Website: www.utemountaincasino.com
Map Location: **#3** (425 miles S.W. of Denver, 11 miles S. of Cortez on Hwys. 160/166)

Toll-Free Number: (800) 258-8007
Hotel Reservations: (888) 565-8837
RV Reservations: (800) 889-5072
Rooms: 70 Price Range: $75-$109
Suites: 20 Price Range: $126-$155
Restaurants: 1 Liquor: No
Buffets: D-$22.99 (Thu-Sat)
Casino Size: 32,000 Square Feet
Other Games: BJ, C, R, P, PGP, TCP
           Keno, Bingo (Fri-Tue)
Overnight RV Parking: Must use RV park
Senior Discount: 15% off non-buffet food
           if 55+
Special Features: 84-space RV Park ($30-$34 per night). Ute Tribal Park tours available.

CONNECTICUT

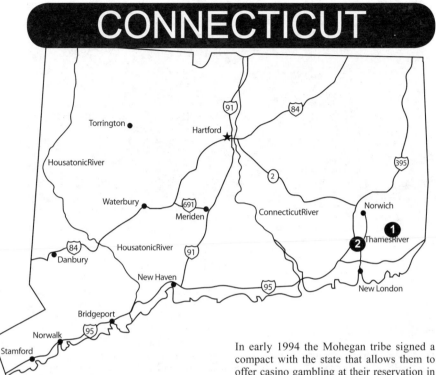

Foxwoods was New England's first casino and it is now the second largest casino in the world.

The Mashantucket Pequot Tribe which operates Foxwoods had to sue the state to allow the casino to open. They argued that since the state legally permitted "Las Vegas Nights," where low-stakes casino games were operated to benefit charities, then the tribe should be entitled to do the same. Eventually, they won their case before the U.S. Supreme Court and begun construction of their casino which was financed by a Malaysian conglomerate (after 22 U.S. lenders turned down their loan requests).

When the casino first opened in February 1992, slot machines were not permitted. In January 1993 a deal was made between Governor Weicker and the Pequots which gave the tribe the exclusive right to offer slot machines in return for a yearly payment of 25% of the gross slot revenue. The agreement was subject to cancellation, however, if the state allowed slot machines anywhere else in Connecticut.

In early 1994 the Mohegan tribe signed a compact with the state that allows them to offer casino gambling at their reservation in Uncasville (map location #2). The Pequots gave permission for the Mohegans to have slot machines in their casino. The same 25% of the gross slot revenue payment schedule also applies to the Mohegans. The payment schedules are subject to cancellation, however, if the state legalizes any other form of casino gambling. The Mohegan casino opened in October 1996.

The minimum gambling age at both properties is 18 for bingo and 21 for the casino. Both casinos are open 24 hours. For information on visiting Connecticut call the state's Vacation Center at (800) 282-6863 or visit their website at www.ctbound.org.

The games offered at Foxwoods are: blackjack, craps, roulette, baccarat, mini-baccarat, midi baccarat, big six (money wheel), pai gow poker, pai gow tiles, Caribbean stud poker, sic bo, let it ride, casino war, Spanish 21, three-card poker, Crazy 4 poker and poker; in addition to bingo, keno and pull tabs. There is also a Race Book offering off-track betting on horses, greyhounds and jai-alai.

Foxwoods Resort Casino, North America's largest casino, has over 300,000 square feet of gaming space. The property features three hotels, over 30 food and beverage outlets, 24 retail shops, 6 casinos, Ultimate Race Book, various high limit gaming areas, a 3,200-seat bingo room, a state of the art, smoke-free World Poker Room™ and more than 6,800 electronic gaming machines.

Foxwoods Resort Casino
350 Trolley Line Boulevard
Mashantucket, Connecticut 06338
(860) 312-3000
Website: www.foxwoods.com
Map Location: **#1** (45 miles S.E. of Hartford; 12 miles N. of I-95 at Mystic). From I-95 take exit 92 to Rt. 2-West, casino is 7 miles ahead. From I-395 take exit 79A to Rt. 2A follow to Rt. 2-East, casino is 2 miles ahead.

Hotel Reservations: (800) 369-9663
Rooms: 1,398 Price Range: $119-$599
Suites: 209 Price Range: $208-$1,500
Restaurants: 28 (3 open 24 hours)
Buffets: B- $11.99 L-$17.99
        D-$19.99/$21.99 (Fri-Sun)
Casino Size: 323,376 Square Feet
Overnight RV Parking: Free (self-contained only) RV Dump: No
Special Features: Three hotels with pool, Grand Pequot Tower hotel spa and beauty salon, golf. Headliner entertainment, The Club and Atrium Lounge. Gift shops. Dream Card Mega Store. Hard Rock Cafe. Dream Card members earn complimentaries at table games, slots, poker and race book. 10% room discount for AAA and AARP members. Two Rees Jones designed golf courses. $1 buffet discount for Dream Card members.

In May, 2008 a new casino was added at Foxwoods. Originally called the MGM Grand at Foxwoods, in 2013 it was renamed the Fox Tower. It is connected to the Foxwoods Casino Resort by a covered, moving, walkway.

The property has its own casino offering electronic gaming machines, plus the following games: blackjack, craps, roulette, Spanish 21, and three-card Poker.

The following information is from Connecticut's Division of Special Revenue regarding Foxwoods' slot payback percentages:

Denomination	Payback %
1¢	89.39
2¢	90.85
5¢	90.51
25¢	91.92
50¢	90.54
$1.00	93.24
$5.00	93.79
$10.00	95.16
$25.00	95.36
$100.00	94.82
Average	**91.67**

These figures reflect the total percentages returned by each denomination of slot machine from July 1, 2013 through June 30, 2014.

The games offered at Mohegan Sun are: blackjack, craps, roulette, baccarat, mini-baccarat, pai gow, wheel of fortune, bingo, pai gow poker, Caribbean stud poker, let it ride, Spanish 21, casino war, Mississippi stud, sic bo and keno. There is also a race book offering off-track betting on horses, greyhounds and jai-alai.

Mohegan Sun Casino
1 Mohegan Sun Boulevard
Uncasville, Connecticut 06382
(860) 862-8000
Website: www.mohegansun.com
Map Location: **#2** (Take I-95 Exit 76/I-395 North. Take Exit 79A (Route 2A) East. Less than 1 mile to Mohegan Sun Boulevard)

Toll-Free Number: (888) 226-7711
Room Reservations: (888) 777-7922
Rooms: 1,020 Price Range: $199-$699
Suites: 180 Price Range: $299-$1,300
Restaurants: 29 (3 open 24 hours)
Buffets (Seasons): B-$12.50 L-$21.00
D-$25.00
Casino Size: 295,000 Square Feet
Overnight RV Parking: Free/RV Dump: No
Special Features: Food court with specialty food outlets. Kids Quest supervised children's activity center. On-site gas station. 30-store shopping arcade.

Here's information from Connecticut's Division of Special Revenue regarding Mohegan Sun's slot payback percentages:

Denomination	Payback %
1/4¢	86.42
1/2¢	85.98
1¢	89.26
2¢	89.28
5¢	88.66
25¢	91.65
50¢	91.21
$1.00	93.27
$5.00	94.11
$10.00	96.05
$25.00	95.30
$100.00	95.18
Average	**91.91**

These figures reflect the total percentages returned by each denomination of slot machine from July 1, 2013 through June 30, 2014.

DELAWARE

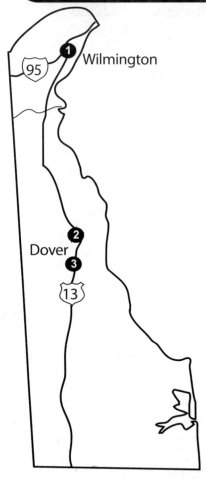

According to figures from the Delaware Lottery for the one-year period from July 25, 2013 through June 26, 2014 the average VLT return at Delaware Park was 92.53%, at Dover Downs it was 92.31% and at Harrington Raceway it was 91.87%.

In mid-2009 the state legalized sports betting for Delaware's three casinos. You can bet on professional and college sporting events, but not on single games-only on multiple games as seen on parlay cards.

In January 2010 the Delaware legislature approved the addition of table games for the state's casinos. All Delaware casinos offer: blackjack, roulette, craps, slots and video poker. Some casinos also offer: mini-baccarat (MB), poker (P), pai gow poker (PGP), Caribbean stud poker (CSP), let it ride (LIR), big 6 (B6), bingo (BG), keno (K), three card poker (TCP), Mississippi stud (MS), casino war (CW), four card poker (FCP) and Spanish 21 (S21).

All casinos are open 24 hours, but they are also closed on Easter and Christmas.

If you want to order a drink while playing, be aware that Delaware gaming regulations do not allow casinos to provide free alcoholic beverages. The minimum gambling age is 21 for slots and 18 for horse racing.

For more information on visiting Delaware call the state's tourism office at (800) 441-8846 or visit their website at: www.visitdelaware.com.

Delaware's three pari-mutuel facilities all feature slot machines. Technically, the machines are video lottery terminals (VLT's) because they are operated in conjunction with the Delaware Lottery. Unlike VLT's in other states, however, Delaware's machines pay out in cash. The VLT's also play other games including: video poker, video keno and video blackjack.

By law, all video lottery games must return between 87% and 95% of all wagers on an annual basis. Games can return above 95% but only with the Lottery Director's approval.

Delaware Park Racetrack & Slots
777 Delaware Park Boulevard
Wilmington, Delaware 19804
(302) 994-2521
Website: www.delawarepark.com
Map: **#1**

Toll-Free Number: (800) 417-5687
Restaurants: 8
Admission: Free Parking: Free
Valet Parking: $4
Other Games: P, K, TCP, FCP, PGP, MS
Overnight RV Parking: Free/RV Dump: No
Special Features: Live thoroughbred
racing late-April to early-November. Daily
simulcasting of horse racing. Ask for Delaware
Park discounted hotel rate at Christiana Hilton
(800-348-3133).

Dover Downs Hotel Casino
1131 N. DuPont Highway
Dover, Delaware 19901
(302) 674-4600
Website: www.doverdowns.com
Map: **#2**

Toll-Free Number: (800) 711-5882
Rooms: 206 Price Range: $125-$250
Suites: 26 Price Range: $195-$805
Restaurants: 9
Buffets: B-$11.50/$15.50 (Sat/Sun)
        L-$15.50 D-$18.50/$19.50 (Thu/Fri)
Admission: Free Parking: Free
Valet Parking: $4
Casino Size: 91,000 Square Feet
Other Games: S21, TCP, PGP, B, LIR, FCP
Overnight RV Parking: Free/RV Dump: Free
        (Not free during NASCAR events)
Special Features: Casino is non-smoking. Live
harness racing November through April. Daily
simulcasting of horse racing. Comedy Club.
Motorsports speedway with NASCAR racing.
$2 buffet discount for players club members.

Harrington Raceway & Casino
Delaware State Fairgrounds
U.S. 13 South
Harrington, Delaware 19952
(302) 398-4920
Website: www.harringtonraceway.com
Map: **#3** (20 miles S. of Dover)

Toll-Free Number: (888) 887-5687
Restaurants: 3
Buffets: B-$9.95 (Tue/Sat)
        L-$13.95/$16.95 (Sun) D- $16.95
Admission: Free
Parking: Free Valet Parking: $2
Other Games: MB, P, PGP, TCP, B6, MS,
        FCP, LIR, CW, S21
Overnight RV Parking: Free/RV Dump: No
Special Features: Live harness racing April-
June and August-October. Daily simulcasting
of horse racing. Table games open 9am-
2am/24-hours (Fri/Sat).

FLORIDA

Florida has three forms of casino gambling: casino boats, Indian casinos and gaming machines at pari-mutuels in two south Florida counties.

The casino boats offer gamblers the opportunity to board ships that cruise offshore where casino gambling is legal. From the west coast the boats travel nine miles out into the Gulf of Mexico. From the East coast they travel three miles out into the Atlantic Ocean.

Unless otherwise noted, all Florida casino boats offer: blackjack, craps, roulette, slots and video poker. Some casinos also offer: mini-baccarat (MB), poker (P), pai gow poker (PGP), three-card poker (TCP), Caribbean stud poker (CSP), let it ride (LIR), big 6 wheel (B6) bingo (BG) and sports book (SB).

Due to security restrictions, you must present a photo ID at all casino boats or you will not be allowed to board.

For Florida visitor information call (888) 735-2872 or visit their website at: www.visitflorida.com.

Cape Canaveral

Map: **#9** (60 miles S.E. of Orlando)

Victory Casino Cruises - Cape Canaveral
180 Christopher Columbus Drive
Cape Canaveral, Florida 32920
(321) 799-0021
Website: www.victorycasinocruises.com

Toll-Free Number: (855) 468-4286
Gambling Age: 18
Food Service: A la Carte
Schedule: 11am-4pm (Mon-Sat)
            12pm-6pm (Sun)
            7pm-12am (Sun-Thu)
            7pm-12:30am (Fri/Sat)
Price: $10
Buffet Price: $15/$20 (Fri-Sun)
Port Charges: Included   Parking: Free
Other Games: MB, TCP, SB, LIR, BG
Special Features: 1,200-passenger *Victory I* departs from Port Canaveral. 6-hour cruise on Sundays.

Fort Myers Beach

Map: **#5** (40 miles N. of Naples)

Big "M" Casino
450 Harbor Court
Fort Myers Beach, Florida 33931
(239) 765-7529
Website: www.bigmcasino.com

Toll-Free Number: (888) 373-3521
Gambling Age: 21   Ship's Registry: U.S.A.
Schedule: 10:30am - 4:30pm (Wed-Sun)
              6:00pm - 11:45pm (Fri/Sat)
Prices: $10
With Buffet: $23.73/$30.09 (night cuise)
Port Charges: Included
Parking: Free (Valet also free)
Other Games: LIR, TCP
Special Features: 400-passenger *Big M* sails from Moss Marina next to Snug Harbor on Fort Myers Beach. Closed Mondays unless a major holiday. Must be 21 or older to board. A la carte menu also available. Cashback for slot play.

Jacksonville

Map: **#8**

Victory Casino Cruises - Jacksonville
4378 Ocean Street
Jacksonville, Florida 32233
(855) 468-4286
Website: www.victoryjax.com

Toll-Free Number: (855) 468-4286
Gambling Age: 18
Food Service: A la Carte/buffet
Schedule: 11am-4:30pm (Mon-Sat)
            11am-5pm (Sun)
            7pm-12am (Sun-Thurs)
            7pm-1am (Fri/Sat)
Price: $10
Buffet Price: $15 (Wed/Thurs)/$20 (Fri-Sun)
Port Charges: Included Parking: Free
Games Offered: MB,TCP, SB, BG, LIR
Special Features: 1,200-passenger *Victory II* departs from historic Mayport. 6-hour cruise on Sundays, no buffet on Sunday AM cruise.

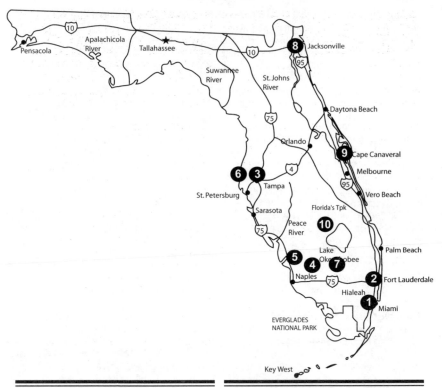

Port Richey

Map: **#6** (37 miles N.W. of Tampa)

SunCruz Casino - Port Richey
7917 Bayview Street
Port Richey, Florida 34668
(727) 848-3423
Website: www.portricheycasino.com

Toll-Free Number: (800) 464-3423
Gambling Age: 18
Food Service: A la Carte
Shuttle Schedule:
Departs: 11am/3:30pm/7pm
Returns: 5:30pm/9pm/12:00am
Price: $8 includes meal and $5 freeplay or
$10 matchplay.
Port Charges: Included   Parking: Free
Other Games: LIR, TCP
Special Features: 465-passenger *Royal Casino 1* stays offshore and a water taxi shuttles passengers back and forth according to above schedule. Shuttle departs from dock on Pithlachascotee River off of US 19 in Port Richey.

Indian Casinos

Florida has eight Indian gaming locations. The Seminole Tribe has seven and the eighth is on the Miccosukee Tribe's reservation.

The Seminoles signed a compact with the state that allows them to offer traditional Class III gaming machines. As part of their compact, five Seminole casinos are also allowed to offer blackjack (BJ), baccarat (B), mini-baccarat (MB), Mississippi stud (MS), three card poker (TCP), let it ride (LIR) and pai gow poker (PGP).

The Miccosukee Tribe has not signed a compact and they only offer Class II gaming machines at their casino.

Class II video gaming devices look like slot machines, but are actually bingo games and the spinning reels are for "entertainment purposes only." No public information is available concerning the payback percentages on any gaming machines in Florida's Indian casinos.

All of the casinos are open 24 hours (except Big Cypress) and the minimum gambling age is 18 at all Indian casinos for bingo or poker and 21 for electronic gaming machines and table games.

Miccosukee Resort & Gaming
500 S.W. 177 Avenue
Miami, Florida 33194
(305) 222-4600
Website: www.miccosukee.com
Map: #1

Toll-Free Number: (800) 741-4600
Room Reservations: (877) 242-6464
Rooms: 256 Price Range: $149-$149
Suites: 46 Price Range: $179-$189
Restaurants: 6 Liquor: Yes
Other Games: BG, P
Buffets: B-$8.99 L/D-$11.95/$19.95 (Fri)
Overnight RV Parking: Free/RV Dump: No

Seminole Casino Big Cypress
30000 Gator Tail Trail
Clewiston, Florida 33440
(863) 983-7245
Website: www.seminolebigcypresscasino.com

Map: #7 (60 miles N.W. of Fort Lauderdale)

Hours: 10am-6pm/11pm (Fri/Sat)
Restaurants: Snack Bar

Seminole Casino Brighton
17735 Reservation Road
Okeechobee, Florida 34974
(863) 467-9998
Website: www.seminolecasinobrighton.com
Map: #10 (75 miles N.W. of West Palm Beach)

Toll-Free Number: (866) 222-7466
Hours: 24 hours
Restaurants: 2 Liquor: Yes
Casino Size: 24,400 Square Feet
Other Games: BG (Wed-Sun)
Overnight RV Parking: No
Senior discount: 15% off food Sun if 50+.

Seminole Casino Coconut Creek
5550 NW 40th Street
Coconut Creek, Florida 33073
(954) 977-6700
Website: www.seminolecoconutcreekcasino.com
Map: #2

Toll-Free Number: (866) 222-7466
Restaurants: 2 Liquor: Yes
Buffet: B-$7.95/$27.95 (Sun)
          L-$14.95 D- $27.95 (Fri/Sat)
Casino Size: 30,000 Square Feet
Other Games: BJ, MB, TCP, PGP, MS,
          LIR, CW, S21
Overnight RV Parking: Call ahead.

Seminole Casino Immokalee
506 South 1st Street
Immokalee, Florida 33934
(941) 658-1313
Website: www.seminoleimmokaleecasino.com
Map: #4 (35 miles N.E. of Naples)

Toll-Free Number: (800) 218-0007
Restaurants: 4 Liquor: Yes
Casino Size: 22,000 Square Feet
Other Games: BJ, MB, TCP, PGP, LIR, P, S21
Overnight RV Parking: Yes

Seminole Classic Casino
4150 N. State Road 7
Hollywood, Florida 33021
(954) 961-3220
Website: www.seminolehollywoodcasino.com
Map: #2 (1 miles S. of Fort Lauderdale)

Toll-Free Number: (800) 323-5452
Restaurants: 3 Liquor: Yes
Casino Size: 73,500 Square Feet
Other Games: BJ, MB, TCP, PGP, MS,
          LIR, BG, S21, CW
Overnight RV Parking: Free/RV Dump: No
Special Features: Located one block south of Hard Rock Hotel & Casino.

The Seminole Hard Rock Hotel & Casino in Hollywood features a 130,000-square-foot casino, including a poker room, plus a 500-room hotel with a European-style spa. There is also an adjacent complex featuring 24 retail shops, 17 restaurants, 10 nightclubs and a 5,500-seat Hard Rock Live entertainment venue.

Seminole Hard Rock
Hotel & Casino - Hollywood
1 Seminole Way
Hollywood, Florida 33314
(954) 327-7625
www.seminolehardrockhollywood.com
Map: **#2** (1 mile S. of Fort Lauderdale)

Toll-Free Number: (866) 502-7529
Room Reservations: (800) 937-0010
Rooms: 437 Price Range: $159-$399
Suites: 63 Price Range: $299-$449
Valet Parking: $7 ($4 with players Card)
Restaurants: 17   Liquor: Yes
Buffets: Brunch-$64.95 (Sun)
Casino Size: 130,000 Square Feet
Other Games: BJ, MB, TCP, PGP, LIR, MS
Overnight RV Parking: No
Special Features: Food court. Lagoon-style pool. Health spa. Shopping mall with 20 stores.

Seminole Hard Rock
Hotel & Casino - Tampa
5223 N. Orient Road
Tampa, Florida 33610
(813) 627-7625
www.hardrockhotelcasinotampa.com
Map: **#3**

Toll-Free Number: (800) 282-7016
Room Reservations: (800) 937-0010
Rooms: 204 Price Range: $209-$369
Suites: 46 Price Range: $359-$459
Restaurants: 2 (1 open 24 hours) Liquor: Yes
Buffets: B-$20 (Sun) L-$20 D- $27/$40 (Fri)
Casino Size: 90,000 Square Feet
Other Games: BJ, MB, TCP, PGP, LIR, MS
Overnight RV Parking: Call ahead.
Special Features: Food court. Health club.

Pari-Mutuels

Broward County (home county of Fort Lauderdale) and Miami-Dade County both have four pari-mutuel facilities that each offer electronic gaming machines, but no table games.

Florida gaming regulations require a minimum payback of 85% on all gaming machines. From July 1, 2013 through June 30, 2014, the gaming machines at Gulfstream returned 92.62%, the return was 91.77% at Mardi Gras Gaming, 92.88% at The Isle, 93.86% at Magic City, 93.05% at Miami Jai Alai, 90.91% at Calder and 93.59% at Hialeah Park.

South Florida's pari-mutuel facilities (as well as most pari-mutuels throughout the state), also offer poker. Admission to all casinos is free and they are allowed to be open a maximum of 18 hours per day during the week and 24 hours on the weekends and some holidays.

If you want to order a drink while playing, be aware that Florida gaming regulations do not allow pari-mutuel casinos to provide free alcoholic beverages.

The minimum gambling age is 18 for pari-mutuel betting or poker and 21 for gaming machines.

Calder Casino & Race Course
21001 N. W. 27th Avenue
Miami Gardens, Florida 33056
(305) 625-1311
Website: www.calderracecourse.com
Map: #1

Toll Free: (800) 333-3227
Parking: Free Valet: $5
Hours: 9am-3am/24 hours (Fri/Sat)
Restaurants: 3
Buffets: L-$10.99 D-$17.99
Other Games: P
Special Features: Live horse racing Thu-Sun at 12:40pm from late April through early Jan. Daily simulcasting of thoroughbred racing.

Casino Miami Jai-Alai
3500 N.W. 37th Avenue
Miami Florida 33142
(305) 633-6400
Website: www.casinomiamijaialai.com
Map: #1

General Admission: $1
Parking: Free Valet: $3
Restaurants: 1
Special Features: Live jai-alai Wed-Mon at noon and Fri/Sat at 7pm. Daily simulcasting of jai-alai and harness racing. Electronic versions of roulette and blackjack.

Dania Casino & Jai-Alai
301 E. Dania Beach Boulevard
Dania Beach, Florida 33004
(954) 920-1511
Website: www.dania-jai-alai.com
Map: #2

Self-Parking: Free Valet: $3
Restaurants: 1
Other Games: P
Overnight RV Parking: No
Special Features: Live jai-alai games Tue-Sat eves and Tue/Sat/Sun afternoons. Daily simulcasting of thoroughbred/harness racing and jai-alai. **THIS CASINO IS TEMPORARILY CLOSED AND EXPECTED TO REOPEN LATE-2015.**

Gulfstream Park Racing & Casino
901 S. Federal Highway
Hallandale Beach, Florida 33009
(954) 454-7000
Website: www.gulfstreampark.com
Map: #2

Track Admission: $3/$5 (Fri-Sat)
Parking: Free Valet: $6
Hours: 9am-3am/ 24 Hours (Fri/Sat)
Restaurants: 3
Overnight RV Parking: No
Special Features: Live thoroughbred racing Wed-Sun from January through April. Daily simulcasting of thoroughbred racing. Outdoor shopping area with over 20 shops and restaurants.

Hialeah Park Casino
2200 East 4th Avenue
Hialeah, Florida 33013
(305) 885-8000
Website: www.hialeahparkracing.com
Map: #1

Restaurants: 4 Valet Parking: $5
Casino Hours: 9am-3am/24 hours (Fri/Sat)
Special Features: Electronic versions of blackjack and roulette

Magic City Casino
401 NW 38th Court
Miami, Florida 33126
305-649-3000
Website: www.magiccitycasino.com
Map: #1

Toll-free Number: (888) 566-2442
Parking: Free
Hours: 10am-4am/5am (Fri/Sat)
Restaurants: 2
Other Games: P
Buffet: L-$10.95 (Sat/Sun)
        D- $15.95 (Sat/Sun)
Special Features: Live dog racing Tue/Thu-Sun at 1pm. Daily simulcasting of dog and harness racing. $2 off buffet with players club card.

Mardi Gras Racetrack and Gaming Center
831 N. Federal Highway
Hallandale Beach, Florida 33009
(954) 924-3200
Website: www.playmardigras.com
Map: #2

Toll-Free Number: (877) 557-5687
Track Admission: Free
Parking: Free Valet: $7
Hours: 9am-3am/24 Hours (Fri/Sat)
Restaurants: 2
Overnight RV Parking: No
Special Features: Live dog racing daily November through May. Daily simulcasting of dog, thoroughbred and harness races. Poker room is open 24 hours.

Isle Casino Racing Pompano Park
777 Isle of Capri Circle
Pompano Beach, Florida 33069
(954) 972-2000
Website: www.theislepompanopark.com
Map: #2

Toll-Free Number: (800) 843-4753
Track Admission: Free
Self-Parking: Free Valet: Free
Hours: 9am-3am/24 hours (Fri/Sat)
Restaurants: 6
Buffet: B- $20.99 (Sun) L- $14.99
        D- $24.99/ $29.99 (Fri-Sat)
Overnight RV Parking: No
Special Features: Live harness racing various evenings (see website for schedules). Daily simulcasting of thoroughbred/harness racing and jai-alai.

GEORGIA

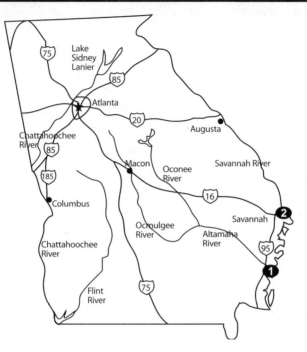

There are two casino boats in Georgia which sail three miles out into international waters where casino gambling is permitted.

The boats offer blackjack, craps, roulette, poker, slots and video poker. Due to security restrictions, you must present a photo ID or you will not be allowed to board.

For information on visiting Georgia call the state's tourism department at (800) 847-4842 or visit their website at www.georgia.org.

Emerald Princess II Casino
1 Gisco Point Drive
Brunswick, Georgia 31523
(912) 265-3558
Website: www.emeraldprincesscasino.com
Map Location: **#1** (75 miles S. of Savannah)

Reservation Number: (800) 842-0115
Gambling Age: 18   Parking: Free
Schedule
11:00am - 4:00pm (Fri/Sat)
 1:00pm - 6:00pm (Sun)
 7:00pm - 12:00am (Mon-Thu)
 7:00pm - 1:00am (Fri/Sat)
Price: $10   Port Charges: Included
Special Features: 400-passenger *Emerald Princess II* sails from Gisco Point, at the southern end of the Sidney Lanier Bridge. Soup, salad and sandwich included with cruise. Reservations are required for all cruises. Packages with hotel accommodations are available. No one under 18 permitted to board.

Trade Winds Casino Cruise - Savannah
810 East US Highway 80
Savannah, Georgia 31410
(912) 265-3558
Website: www.emeraldprincesscasino.com
Map Location: **#1** (75 miles S. of Savannah)

Reservation Number: (844) 752-2576
Gambling Age: 18   Parking: Free
Schedule:
11:00am - 4:30pm (Fri/Sat)
 1:00pm - 7:00pm (Sun)
 7:00pm - 12:30am (Mon-Thu)
 7:00pm - 1:30am (Fri/Sat)
Price: $14.95   Port Charges: Included
Senior Discount: Board for $10 and receive
$10 Matchplay if 55+ on Friday/Saturday.
Special Features: 500-passenger *Escapade*
sails from Savannah, Georgia, Light meal
included with entry fee. No cruises Monday.

Visit our website:
americancasinoguide.com

• Casino News
• Casino Travel Info
• Casino Promotions
• U.S. Casino Directory
• Casino Discussion Forum
• Money-saving Casino Offers
• FREE Educational Gambling Videos

IDAHO

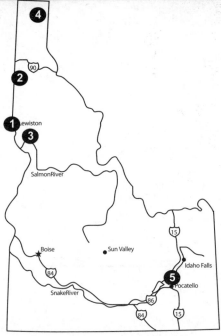

Idaho has seven Indian casinos that offer electronic pull-tab machines and other video games. The machines don't pay out in cash. Instead they print out a receipt which must be cashed by a floor attendant or taken to the cashier's cage. Some casinos also offer bingo (BG), off-track betting (OTB) and poker (P).

The terms of the compact between the tribes and the state do not require any minimum payback percentage that the gaming machines must return to the public.

The minimum gambling age at all casinos is 18 and they are all open 24 hours. For Idaho tourism information call (800) 635-7820 or visit their website: www.visitid.org.

Bannock Peak Casino
1707 W. Country Road
Pocatello, Idaho 83204
(208) 235-1308
Website: www.shobangaming.com
Map: **#5** (5 miles N. of Pocatello)

Restaurants: 1 Snack Bar Liquor: No
Hours: 10am-12am/1am (Fri/Sat)
Casino Size: 5,000 Square Feet
Other Games: Only gaming machines
Overnight RV Parking: Free/RV Dump: No

Clearwater River Casino
17500 Nez Perce Road
Lewiston, Idaho 83501
(208) 746-5733
Website: www.crcasino.com
Map: **#1** (250 miles N. of Boise)

Toll-Free Number: (877) 678-7423
Rooms: 47 Price Range: $89-$99
Suites: 3 Price Range $189-$199
Restaurants: 1   Liquor: No
Casino Size: 30,000 Square Feet
Other Games: K, BG (Mon/Thu/Fri/Sun)
Overnight RV Parking: Free/RV Dump: No
Special Features: 33-space RV park ($27 per night).

Coeur D'Alene Casino Resort Hotel
37914 South Nukwalqw
Worley, Idaho 83876
(208) 686-5106
Website: www.cdacasino.com
Map: **#2** (350 miles N. of Boise)

Toll-Free Number: (800) 523-2464
Rooms: 202 Price Range: $65-$200
Suites: 8 Price Range $150-$450
Restaurants: 7   Liquor: Yes Valet Parking: Free
Buffet: B-$9.99/$12.99 (Sat/Sun) L-$12.99
        D-$16.99/$24.99 (Fri/Sat)
Casino Size: 30,000 Square Feet
Other Games: BG (Fri/Sat), OTB, P
Overnight RV Parking: Free/RV Dump: No
Special Features: 18-hole golf course.

Fort Hall Casino
Ross Fork Road
Fort Hall, Idaho 83203
(208) 237-8778
Website: www.shobangaming.com
Map: **#5** (14 miles N. of Pocatello)

Toll-Free Number: (800) 497-4231
Restaurants: 1 Snack Bar Liquor: No
Casino Size: 15,000 Square Feet
Other Games: BG (Wed-Sun)
Overnight RV Parking: Must use RV Park
Special Features: 47-space RV park ($27 per night).

It'Se-Ye-Ye Casino
419 Third Street
Kamiah, Idaho 83536
(208) 935-7860
Website: www.crcasino.com
Map: **#3** (225 miles N. of Boise)

Restaurants: 1 Liquor: No
Hours: 7am-12am/24 hours (Fri/Sat)
Casino Size: 2,300 Square Feet
Overnight RV Parking: Free/RV Dump: No

Kootenai River Inn Casino and Spa
7169 Plaza Street
Bonners Ferry, Idaho 83805
(208) 267 8511
Website: www.kootenairiverinn.com
Map: **#4** (450 miles N. of Boise)

Toll-Free Number: (800) 346-5668
Rooms: 47 Price Range: $115-$160
Suites: 4 Price Range $150-$375
Restaurants: 1 Liquor: Yes
Casino Size: 30,000 Square Feet
Other Games: BG (1st and 3rd Wed)
Overnight RV Parking: Free/RV Dump: No
Special Features: Hotel is Best Western. Spa.

Sage Hill Casino
2 North Eagle Road
Blackfoot, Idaho 83221
Map: **#5** (14 miles N. of Pocatello)
Website: www.shobangaming.com
(208) 237-4998

Restaurants: 1
Casino Hours: 6:30am-2am/24 hours (Fri/Sat)
Casino Size: 13,200 Square Feet
Other Games: Only gaming machines

ILLINOIS

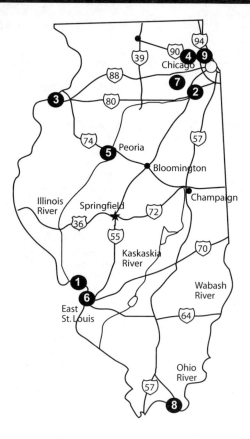

Illinois was the second state to legalize riverboat casinos. Riverboat casinos began operating there in September 1991 with the launching of the first boat: the Alton Belle.

All Illinois riverboats remain dockside and do not cruise. Unlike Mississippi, however, the casinos are not open 24 hours and state law limits the number of gaming licenses to 10.

Here's information from the Illinois Gaming Board showing each casino's average slot payback percentage for the one-year period from July 1, 2013 through June 30, 2014:

CASINO	PAYBACK %
Casino Queen	92.75
Harrah's Joliet	91.36
Hollywood - Aurora	91.97
Argosy Alton	91.91
Hollywood - Joliet	91.36
Jumer's	91.25
Grand Victoria	91.25
Par-A-Dice	91.07
Rivers Casino	89.78
Harrah's Metropolis	88.92

These figures reflect the total percentages returned by each casino for all of their electronic machines.

Admission is free to all Illinois casinos. All casinos are non-smoking and, unless otherwise noted, all casinos offer: slots, video poker, blackjack, craps, roulette and three card poker. Some casinos also offer: let it ride (LIR), baccarat (B), mini-baccarat (MB), poker (P), Texas hold em bonus (THB), Caribbean stud poker (CSP), Mississippi stud (MS), pai gow poker (PGP) and four card poker (FCP).

If you want to order a drink while playing, be aware that Illinois gaming regulations do not allow casinos to provide free alcoholic beverages. The minimum gambling age is 21.

For more information on visiting Illinois contact the state's Bureau of Tourism at (800) 226-6632 or www.enjoyillinois.com

Argosy Casino Alton
1 Front Street
Alton, Illinois 62002
(618) 474-7500
Website: www.argosyalton.com
Map: **#1** (260 miles S.W. of Chicago, 25 miles N. of St. Louis, MO)

Toll-Free Number: (800) 711-4263
Restaurants: 3
Buffets: L-$14.99/$19.99 (Sun)
        D-$17.99/$19.99 (Sat)
Valet Parking: $5 (Free for players club members)
Casino Hours: 8am-6am Daily
Casino Size: 23,000 Square Feet
Other Games: MS
Overnight RV Parking: Yes
Special Features: Casino features a 1,200-passenger modern yacht and a barge docked on the Mississippi River. Table games open at 10am daily. 10% off buffets for players club members.

Casino Queen
200 S. Front Street
E. St. Louis, Illinois 62201
(618) 874-5000
Website: www.casinoqueen.com
Map: **#6** (290 miles S.W. of Chicago)

Toll-Free Number: (800) 777-0777
Rooms: 150 Price Range: $89-$149
Suites: 7 Price Range: $149-$699
Buffets: B-$8.95/$11.95 (Sat)/$15.95 (Sun)
        L-$11.95/$15.95 (Sun)
        D-$14.95 (Tue-Thu)/$20.95(Fri/Sat)
Valet Parking: $5
Casino Hours: 8am-6am Daily
Casino Size: 40,000 Square Feet
Other Games: MB, CSP, MS
Senior Discount: Various Tue 9am-12am if 50+
Overnight RV Parking: Must use RV park
Special Features: Land-based casino. 140-space RV park ($53 per night). Sports Bar. No dinner buffet Sun/Mon. MetroLink light-rail station at doorstep.

Grand Victoria Casino
250 S. Grove Avenue
Elgin, Illinois 60120
(847) 468-7000
Website: www.grandvictoriacasino.com
Map: **#4** (41 miles N.W. of Chicago)

Toll Free Number: (888) 508-1900
Restaurants: 4
Buffets: L-$15.99/$19.99 (Sat/Sun)
        D-$19.99/$18.99 (Thu)/$32.99(Fri/Sat)
Valet Parking: $5
Casino Hours: 8:30am-6:30am Daily
Casino Size: 29,850 Square Feet
Other Games: MB, THB, P, MS
Overnight RV Parking: Yes
Senior Discount: $1 off buffets if 65+
Special Features: 1,200-passenger paddle wheeler-replica docked on the Fox River.

The Best Places To Play In The Chicago Area

by John Grochowski

Gambling in the Chicago area has gone through an unusual period of stability in the last few years – at least in regards to casinos. The last new casino to open was Rivers in Des Plaines, Illinois, in 2011, and the intervening years have brought no buyouts, mergers or new themes. The biggest change has been a remodeling at Grand Victoria Casino in Elgin, Illinois, which has had its interior look updated with modern lighting, new carpeting, wider aisles a big buffet upgrade and a menu freshening in its steakhouse. There are as many games as there were before the property re-think, but it somehow feels airier, more open and easy to navigate.

Still, while Grand Victoria is an oasis of change in a mostly stable, mature market, there has been a major expansion in opportunity to play slots and video poker. That's because operation of video gaming machines in Illinois bars and licenses has been picking up steam since a central monitoring system has been selected and installed. Illinois law allows bars, restaurants, truck stops and service organizations such as the Elks and VFW to operate up to five video gaming machines. Some communities, including the City of Chicago, have opted out, but even so, by mid-2014 there were more than 17,000 machines in operation at such facilities across the state. That's more slots than there are in Illinois' 10 casinos combined.

Each site is limited to five gaming terminals, and the terminals include both slot and video poker games. They are games with random number generators, and work just like casino slots, except there are some restrictions. Credit denominations must range between 5 cents and 25 cents, the maximum wager is $2, and the maximum payout for a single play is $500. A quarter video poker game can't pay the $1,000 jackpot players are used to on quarter machines.

Those provisions have meant slot manufacturers have had to rework the math on their games, and pay table changes go far deeper than just halving the royal flush payback. On one made-for-Illinois-video-gaming version of 7-5 Double Double Bonus Poker, Bally Technologies devised a game with an eight-quarter maximum bet that paid a max of $500 on either a royal flush or four Aces with a low-card kicker. Both are short of player expectations, so Bally raised paybacks on straight flushes. For a five-coin bet, a straight flush pays the same 250 coins you'd get in a casino. But then it jumps to 600 coins for a six-coin bet, 1,000 for seven and 1,500 for eight. The result is a 96.2 percent game with expert play, similar to the 95.7 you'd get on a casino version of DDB.

Away from the bars and restaurants and into the casinos, there are eight in the metropolitan Chicago area that straddles the Illinois-Indiana border, or nine if you count the two boats at Majestic Star in Gary separately. Still, the market is a real mixed bag.

There are a number of dividing lines. To start with, there's Illinois vs. Indiana. For many years, the casinos closest to downtown Chicago were those in Indiana, though the Rivers opening changed that. Today, you can flip a coin, with Rivers being about 16 miles from the North Loop, and Horseshoe Casino in Hammond, Indiana, being about 16 miles from the South Loop. The other Indiana casinos closest to Chicago --- Ameristar in East Chicago and Majestic Star I and II in Gary, are less than 10 miles east of Horseshoe. On the Illinois side, Hollywood Casinos in Aurora and Joliet, Harrah's in Joliet and Grand Victoria in Elgin all are between 40 and 50 miles from the Loop.

A little outside the Chicago area, but within easy drives of about an hour and a half, are Blue Chip Casino in Michigan City, Indiana, Four Winds Casino in New Buffalo, Michigan, Potawatomi Bingo Casino in Milwaukee. Increase the range to a three-hour drive, and that brings in a couple of Illinois casinos, Par-A-Dice casino in Peoria and Jumer's Casino Rock Island.

There remain differences in the markets, though the riverboat cruises that once were required in Illinois and the simulated cruise times on the stationary Indiana vessels are a thing of the past. Players used to pay up to $28 for the privilege of boarding a boat and risking their money. The boarding fees are gone with the times, thank goodness.

In Illinois, which has a limit of 1,200 gaming positions per license, the typical mix consists of about 1,100 slots and video poker machines, along with about 30 table games. Rivers is an exception, with 48 tables and 1,044 slots as it caters to big players. The only limit in Indiana is that the games must fit on a boat, so the casinos there are much larger --- the largest facility, Horseshoe Hammond's barge, has more than 3,000 electronic games and 140-plus table games. One consequence is that there is a much larger selection of new table games in Indiana. If you want to try Blackjack Switch or Boston Stud, you're more likely to find it in Indiana.

In Indiana, casinos are permitted to remain open 24 hours a day, and they do. In Illinois, 24-hour gaming has never been approved. And Illinois has a smoking ban, while Indiana does not.

There's another division between high-end properties and the rest of the market. The two casinos closest to Chicago, Rivers and Horseshoe, have positioned themselves as high-end properties, with premium dining and other amenities, and correspondingly high minimum wagers. Even with the restriction on gaming positions, Rivers earns more than $30 million in gaming revenue each month, and sometimes tops $40 million. The other four Illinois casinos in the area each take in less than $20 million a month. On the Indiana side, Horseshoe in Hammond regularly reports monthly gaming revenue of more than $40 million, while Ameristar usually checks in at just under $20 million, and the two Majestic Stars combined do a bit less than that.

Back in the casinos, Chicago area players have little these days that resembles its video poker hey-day of the mid-2000s. Then, Chicagoans used to the volume of 99-percenters close to home were often shocked to find pay tables that didn't match up when they visited the Las Vegas Strip. Alas, the video poker oasis has dried up, though there remain some good plays on high-denomination and multi-hand games.

VIDEO POKER: There are no 100 percent-plus games in the Chicago area, the last having disappeared in 2003 when Empress Joliet moved from its old boats onto the current Hollywood barge. For nearly a decade, Empress had 10-7 Double Bonus poker, a 100.17-percent game with expert play, and even added a progressive jackpot on dollar games. Empress bought new gaming equipment for the barge, and in putting video poker on IGT's new game platform, Empress had to get each game re-approved by the Illinois Gaming Board. The board found that 10-7 Double Bonus did not meet its standard that no game may pay more than 100 percent in the long run.

Poof! The best deal in the Chicago area was gone.

The scenario repeated itself in 2009 when Jumer's Casino Rock Island, on the Mississippi River in northwest Illinois, moved onto its new boat. Long a staple on the old Jumer's boat, quarter 10-7 Double Bonus had to be scaled back for the move to meet state licensing standards. With five-coins wagered, the 250-coin pays on four 5s through Kings or on straight flushes have been scaled back to 239 coins. That leaves a 99.8 percent game with expert play.

The one oasis of high-paying video poker for players with moderate budgets is Majestic Star II in Gary. In its video poker room, a bank of quarter machines includes a 99.8-percent version of Triple Bonus Poker Plus; Not So Ugly Deuces Wild (99.7); 9-6 Jacks or Better (99.5); 8-5 ACES Bonus Poker (99.4) and more. The one downside is that it takes $100 in play to earn one rewards point on these machines, as opposed to $10 per point on other machines, but the upgrade in payback at the machines is well worth it.

For bigger players, the closest to 100-percent games in the Chicago market today is 8-5 Super Aces with a 60-for-1 straight flush. It's a 99.94 percent game, one of several good plays on $5-$10-$25 multidenomination games at Horseshoe Hammond. Also available on the same multigame units are 9-6 Bonus Poker Deluxe (99.6), 9-7 Triple Double Bonus (99.6) and other goodies. There are even more high payers if on Triple Play/Five Play/Ten Play games starting at $2 denominations. But with a max-coin bet, that's $30 on Triple Play, $75 on Five Play and $150 on Ten Play. It's not for the faint of heart or short of bankroll.

What about games for those of more modest means? There's not much for quarter single-hand players, though there are a couple of good plays on one lone Spin Poker game at Hollywood Joliet. There, NSU Deuces (99.7), 9-6 Jacks or Better (99.5) and other high-payers are available. Spin Poker has a 45-coin max bet, but you can play one hand at a time and get the full pay table.

At dollar level, one go-to game for Chicago area operators is 9-6 Double Double Bonus Poker (98.98 percent), with a progressive jackpot. Hollywood (nee Empress) Joliet, Harrah's Joliet and Ameristar East Chicago all have $1 progressives, with the two Joliet casinos both offering three-way progressives --- progressive jackpots on royal flushes, four Aces with a low card kicker, and four Aces without the kicker.

Other than that, most high-paying games on the Illinois side of the border either are at $5 denomination on up, or multihand machines of at least $1 denomination.

CRAPS: The addition of Rivers gave the Chicago area a second casino catering to big craps players. Rivers offers 100x odds --- the same as Horseshoe in Hammond. Horseshoe had dramatically changed the face of Chicago area craps after Jack Binion bought the former Empress in 1999. Bringing in 100x odds and $10,000 maximums was a radical change for Chicago, which had been a double-odds kind of town through the mid-1990s.

Now 20x odds have become common among competitors, while Rivers, which hired many of its key gaming personnel from Horseshoe, makes it a 100x odds duo.

BLACKJACK: Most games in the Chicago area use either six or eight decks. Table minimums are high, especially in Illinois where anything under $15 a hand is rare treat for a midweek morning. In Indiana, you can still find $5 tables at Majestic Star. Tables that use continuous shufflers are six decks, dealer hits soft 17, double after split permitted, house edge vs. a basic strategy player 0.63 percent. At $25 tables without the continuous shufflers, you can find the same game with late surrender, reducing the house edge to 0.33 percent. There are a few double-deck games, but with tougher rules, including double down only on two-card 10s and no resplitting of pairs.

Until recent years, the only casinos in the area that had dealers hit soft 17 were Hollywood Aurora and Grand Victoria in Elgin. That's changed. Every casino in the area now hits soft 17 on what passes for low-limit tables here. Hitting soft 17 adds about two-tenths of a percent to the house edge, so basic strategy players who could easily find six-deck games with house edges of 0.41 percent a couple of years ago now are facing edges of 0.6 percent or more. There are no stand-on-all-17s games for less than $25 minimums in the area, and at the five Illinois casinos, the stand/hit soft 17 divider is at $50 minimums.

The Majestic Star $25 game with late surrender has the lowest house edge in the region, but others are close. At Harrrah's Joliet, and Hollywood Joliet, you can not only double down after splitting pairs but also resplit Aces in a six-deck game. That brings a house edge against a basic strategy player of 0.34 percent. If you want to play at lower limits, the lowest house edge at regular blackjack is the 0.56 percent at $10 tables at Hollywood Joliet, a six-deck game where the dealer hits soft 17, but you can double after splits.

OTHER TABLE GAMES: You'll find the lowest minimum bets in Indiana. At Majestic Star, $5 tables remain a big part of the mix. For the high rollers, Horseshoe in Indiana and Rivers in Illinois both have what you're looking for, including max bets of $100,000 a hand at baccarat.

With bigger table pits, Indiana casinos offer much more variety than the Illinois competition. In addition to blackjack and craps, Illinois operations tend to stick with roulette and Caribbean Stud, with a little mini-baccarat, Let It Ride or Three Card Poker in the mix at some casinos. In Indiana, most operators have all those games, and also pick and choose from among pai-gow poker, Spanish 21, 3-5-7 Poker, Four Card Poker, Boston Stud, Bonus Six, Play Four --- if there's a promising new game, someone in Indiana is likely to try it.

SLOT MACHINES: Along with the rest of the country, Chicago has seen a great expansion in video bonusing slot games, with the hottest trend being toward lower and lower coin denominations. All Chicago area casinos now penny slots. Horseshoe had been reluctant to join the penny trend, but the nationwide growth and popularity of the games have even casinos that cater to big players clamoring for copper.

Traditional three-reel games remain a big part of the mix at dollars and above, with Majestic Star having the largest selection of quarter three-reelers.

All slot machines in the area have gone TITO --- ticket in, ticket out for easy payouts with no delays for hopper fills or hopper jams.

One thing you'll not find in Illinois or Indiana is million-dollar jackpots. Wide-area progressives such as Megabucks that link several different properties to the same jackpot are illegal in Illinois and Indiana. If you're a jackpot chaser, you'll need to go to Potawatomi in Milwaukee or Four Winds in New Buffalo, which both are on the national Native American link.

Slot payouts tend to be higher in Illinois than in Indiana, from quarters on up, but the Indiana casinos pay as much or more than the Illinois operations in nickels and below. Illinois averages tend to hover around 95 percent on dollars, 93 percent on quarters and 88 percent on nickels, 85 percent on pennies while Indiana returns, are around 94 percent on dollars, 92 percent on quarters and 89 percent on nickels and 86 percent on pennies --- with variations from casino to casino, of course.

Harrah's Joliet
150 N. Joliet Street
Joliet, Illinois 60432
(815) 740-7800
Website: www.harrahsjoliet.com
Map: **#2** (43 miles S.W. of Chicago)

Toll-Free Number: (800) 427-7247
Rooms: 200 Price Range: $92-$235
Suites: 4 Price Range: Casino Use Only
Restaurants: 4
Valet Parking: $5/Free if hotel guest
Casino Hours: 8am-6am Daily
Casino Size: 39,000 Square Feet
Other Games: MB, LIR, FCP, P, MS
Overnight RV Parking: No
Special Features: Casino is on a barge docked on the Des Plaines River.

Harrah's Metropolis
100 E. Front Street
Metropolis, Illinois 62960
(618) 524-2628
Website: www.harrahsmetropolis.com
Map: **#8** (Across from Paducah, KY.)

Toll-Free Number: (800) 929-5905
Rooms: 252 Price Range: $55-$229
Suites: 6 Price Range: Casino Use Only
Restaurants: 4 Valet Parking: Free
Buffets: L-$10.99/$15.99 (Sat/Sun)
D-$14.99/$18.99 (Sat/Sun)
Hours: 9am-5am/7am (Fri/Sat)
Other Games: LIR, MB, P
Casino Size: 30,985 Square Feet
Overnight RV Parking: Free/RV Dump: No
Special Features: 1,300-passenger sidewheeler-replica docked on the Ohio River.

Hollywood Casino - Aurora

1 New York Street Bridge
Aurora, Illinois 60506
(630) 801-7000
Website: www.hollywoodcasinoaurora.com
Map: **#7** (41 miles W. of Chicago)

Toll Free Number: (800) 888-7777
Restaurants: 3
Buffets: L-$12.99/$19.99 (Sun)
     D-$16.99/$28.99 (Fri)/$19.99 (Sat-Sun)
Valet Parking: $5
Casino Hours: 8:30am-4:30am/6:30 (Fri/Sat)
Casino Size: 41,384 Square Feet
Other Games: MB, P, MS
Overnight RV Parking: No
Special Features: Casino is on a barge docked on the Fox River. $3 buffet discount for players club members.

Hollywood Casino - Joliet

777 Hollywood Blvd
Joliet, Illinois 60436
(815) 744-9400
Website: www.hollywoodcasinojoliet.com
Map: **#2** (43 miles S.W. of Chicago)

Toll-Free Number: (888) 436-7737
Rooms: 85 Price Range: $79-$120
Suites: 17 Price Range: $109-$129
Casino Hours: 8:30am-6:30am Daily
Restaurants: 4
Buffets: B-$16.99 (Sun)
     L-$13.99
     D-$17.99/$34.99 (Fri)/$22.99 (Sat)
Valet Parking: Free
Casino Size: 50,000 square feet
Other Games: MB, CSP, P, MS
Overnight RV Parking: Must use RV park
Special Features: 2,500-passenger barge docked on the Des Plaines River. Rooms are at on-property Empress Hotel. 80-space RV park ($35-$45 per night).

Jumer's Casino & Hotel Rock Island

777 Jumer Drive
Rock Island, Illinois 61201
(309) 756-4600
Website: www.jumerscri.com
Map: **#3** (170 miles W. of Chicago)

Toll-Free Number: (800) 477-7747
Rooms: 205 Price Range: $99-$209
Suites: 7 Price Range: $159-$599
Restaurants: 4 Valet Parking: Free
Buffets: B-$9.99 (Sun) L/D-$14.99
Casino Hours: 7am-5am Daily
Casino Size: 42,000 Square Feet
Other games: THB, PGP, MS, P
Overnight RV Parking: Free/Dump: No

Par-A-Dice Hotel Casino

21 Blackjack Boulevard
East Peoria, Illinois 61611
(309) 698-7711
Website: www.paradicecasino.com
Map: **#5** (170 miles S.W. of Chicago)

Toll-Free Number: (800) 727-2342
Room Reservations: (800) 547-0711
Rooms: 195 Price Range: $105-$155
Suites 13 Price Range: $175-$500
Restaurants: 4 Valet Parking: $5
Buffets: B-$7.95 L-$10.99
     D-$13.99/$17.99 (Sat/Sun)
Casino Hours: 8am-6am
Casino Size: 26,116 Square Feet
Other Games: MB, LIR, CSP, P, MS
Overnight RV Parking: Free/RV Dump: No
Senior Discount: Various Wed if 55+
Special Features: 1,600-passenger modern boat docked on the Illinois River.

Rivers Casino

3000 S River Road
Des Plaines, Illinois 60018
(847) 795-0777
Website: www.playrivers.com
Map: **#9** (20 miles N.W. of Chicago)

Toll Free Number: (888) 307-0777
Restaurants: 6
Buffet Prices: B-$22.00 (Sun) L-$19.50
     D-$27.00/$35.00 (Wed)
Casino Hours: 9am-7am Daily
Casino Size: 43,687 Square Feet
Other Games: B, MB, CSP, FCP, MS, S21, PGP
Overnight RV Parking: No
Special features: Closest casino to O'Hare airport. Free lounge entertainment nightly.

INDIANA

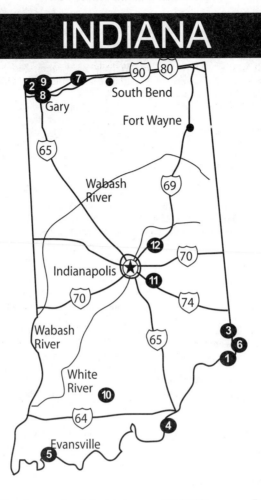

In June 1993 Indiana became the sixth state to legalize riverboat gambling. All of the state's riverboat casinos offer dockside gambling and, unless otherwise noted, are open 24 hours. The minimum gambling age is 21.

Following is information from the Indiana Gaming Commission regarding average slot payout percentages for the one-year period from July 1, 2013 through June 30, 2014:

CASINO	PAYBACK %
Rising Star	91.61
Hoosier Park	91.58
Blue Chip	91.49
French Lick	91.45
Belterra	91.18
Hollywood	91.18
Indiana Grand	91.08
Majestic Star	90.40
Ameristar	90.31
Tropicana	90.25
Majestic Star II	90.15
Horseshoe SI	90.15
Horseshoe Hammond	89.83

These figures reflect the average percentage returned by each casino for all of their electronic machines including slot machines, video poker, video keno, etc.

Unless otherwise noted, all casinos offer: blackjack, craps, roulette, slots, video poker, video keno and Caribbean stud poker. Optional games include: baccarat (B), mini-baccarat (MB), poker (P), pai gow poker (PGP), three card poker (TCP), Mississippi stud (MS), pai gow (PG), four card poker (FCP), Spanish 21 (S21), big 6 wheel (B6) and let it ride (LIR).

If you want to order a drink while playing, be aware that Indiana gaming regulations do not allow casinos to provide free alcoholic beverages.

NOTE: If you happen to win a jackpot of $1,200 or more in Indiana, the casino will withhold 3.4% of your winnings for the Indiana Department of Revenue. You may, however, be able to get *some* of that money refunded by filing a state income tax return. The $1,200 threshold also applies to any cash prizes won in casino drawings or tournaments.

For more information on visiting Indiana call (800) 289-6646 or visit their website at www.enjoyindiana.com.

Ameristar East Chicago
777 Ameristar Boulevard
East Chicago, Indiana 46312
(219) 378-3000
Website: www.ameristarcasinos.com
Map: **#9** (12 miles E. of Chicago)

Toll-Free Number: (877) 496-1777
Hotel Reservations: (866) 711-7799
Rooms: 286 Prices: $149-$219
Suites: 7 Prices: Casino Use Only
Restaurants: 5
Buffets: B-$9.99/ $13.99 (Sat/Sun) L-$13.99
        D-$15.99/$26.99 (Fri)/$21.99 (Sat)
Valet Parking: $5/ Discount for club members
Casino Size: 53,000 Square Feet
Other Games: B, MB, PGP, TCP, LIR, MS
Overnight RV Parking: No
Special Features: 3,750-passenger modern yacht docked on Lake Michigan.

Belterra Casino Resort and Spa
777 Belterra Drive
Florence, Indiana 47020
(812) 427-7777
Website: www.belterracasino.com
Map: **#1** (35 miles S.W. of Cincinnati, Ohio)

Toll-Free Number: (888) 235-8377
Rooms: 600 Price Range: $109-$249
Suites: 8 Price Range: $249-$499
Restaurants: 7 Valet Parking: Free
Buffets: B-$14.99/$20.99 (Sun) L-$16.99
        D-$20.99/$31.99(Fri/Sat)
Casino Size: 38,000 Square Feet
Other Games: P, PGP, TCP, LIR, MB, MS
Overnight RV Parking: Free (must park in back rows of parking lot)/RV Dump: No
Special Features: 2,600-passenger sidewheeler docked on the Ohio River. Health club and spa. 18-hole golf course. 1,500-seat showroom. 10x odds on craps.

Blue Chip Casino & Hotel
2 Easy Street
Michigan City, Indiana 46360
(219) 879-7711
Website: www.bluechip-casino.com
Map: **#7** (40 miles E. of Chicago)

Toll-Free Number: (888) 879-7711
Rooms: 180 Price Range: $109-$275
Suites: Casino Use Only
Restaurants: 4 Valet Parking: Free
Buffets: B-$11.99/$7.77 (Fri)/$16.99 (Sat/Sun)
        L-$13.99
        D- $19.99/$13.99 (Wed)/
        $26.99 (Fri)/$28.99 (Sat)
Casino Size: 25,000 Square Feet
Other Games: MB, LIR, P, TCP, FCP, MS
Overnight RV Parking: Free/RV Dump: No
Senior Discount: Various Mon if 50+.
Special Features: 2,000-passenger modern yacht docked in a man-made canal.

The 5,000-passenger *Horseshoe Southern Indiana* is the world's largest riverboat casino.

French Lick Springs Resort & Casino
8670 West State Road 56
French Lick, Indiana 47432
(812) 936-9300
Website: www.frenchlick.com
Map: **#10** (108 miles S. of Indianapolis)

Toll-Free Number: (888) 936-9360
Rooms: 442 Price Range: $159-$239
Restaurants: 12   Valet Parking: Free
Buffets: D-$19.95/$24.95 (Fri)
Casino Size: 84,000 Square Feet
Other Games: MB, TCP, P, PGP, MS, LIR, MS
Overnight RV Parking: Free/RV Dump: No
Special Features: Two 18-hole golf courses. Full-service spa. Six-lane bowling alley. Located on a 3,500-passenger barge in a man-made moat. 10% off buffet for players club members.

Hollywood Casino & Hotel - Lawrenceburg
777 Hollywood Boulevard
Lawrenceburg, Indiana 47025
(812) 539-8000
Website: www.hollywoodindiana.com
Map: **#3** (95 miles S.E. of Indianapolis)

Toll-Free Number: (888) 274-6797
Rooms: 440 Price Range: $79-$249
Restaurants: 5   Valet Parking: $3
Buffets: B-$17.99 (Sat/Sun) L-$11.99
    D-$20.99/$26.99 (Fri)/$23.99 (Sat)
Casino Size: 80,000 Square Feet
Other Games: B6, MB, LIR, P, TCP, PGP,
    FCP, B, MS
Overnight RV Parking: Free (only in lot across the street from the casino)/RV Dump: No
Special Features: 4,000-passenger modern yacht docked on the Ohio River.

Horseshoe Casino Hotel Southern Indiana
11999 Casino Center Drive SE
Elizabeth, Indiana 47117
(812) 969-6000
Website: www.horseshoe-indiana.com
Map: **#4** (20 miles S. of New Albany)

Toll-Free Number: (866) 676-7463
Reservation Number: (877) 237-6626
Rooms: 503 Prices: Price Range: $99-$229
Restaurants: 9   Valet Parking: Free
Buffets: B-$23.99 (Sat/Sun)
        L-$20.99 D-$20.99/$34.99 (Fri/Sat)
Casino Size: 93,000 Square Feet
Other Games: S21, B, MB, CSP, MS,
        P, PGP, LIR, TCP
Overnight RV Parking: Free/RV Dump: No
Special Features: 5,000-passenger sidewheeler
docked on the Ohio River. 18-hole golf course.

Horseshoe Casino Hammond
777 Casino Center Drive
Hammond, Indiana 46320
(219) 473-7000
Website: www.chicagohorseshoe.com
Map: **#2** (10 miles E. of Chicago)

Toll-Free Number: (866) 711-7463
Restaurants: 5
Buffets: B-$21.99 (Sat/Sun)
        L-$16.99 D-$21.99
Valet Parking: $5/$3 with Total Rewards Card
Casino Size: 43,000 Square Feet
Other Games: MB, TCP, LIR, P,
        B6, PG, B, MS
Overnight RV Parking: Free/RV Dump: No
Special Features: 4,000-passenger barge
docked on Lake Michigan.

Majestic Star Casinos & Hotel
1 Buffington Harbor Drive
Gary, Indiana 46406
(219) 977-7777
Website: www.majesticstarcasino.com
Map: **#8** (15 miles E. of Chicago)

Toll-Free Number: (888) 225-8259
Rooms: 300 Price Range: $69-$129
Restaurants: 6
Buffets: B-$8.99 L-$10.99/$13.99 (Sun)
        D-$13.99/$22.99 (Fri/Sat)
Valet Parking: Free
Casino Size: 43,000 Square Feet
Other Games: S21, B, MB, MS, CSP,
        PGP, TCP, LIR, P, MS
Overnight RV Parking: Free/RV Dump: No
Special Features: Two boats: 1,300-passenger
and 2,300-passenger modern yachts docked on
Lake Michigan.

Rising Star Casino Resort
777 Rising Star Drive
Rising Sun, Indiana 47040
(812) 438-1234
Website: www.risingstarcasino.com
Map: **#6** (40 miles S.W. of Cincinnati)

Toll-Free Number: (800) 472-6311
Rooms: 294 Price Range: $109-$169
Restaurants: 5   Valet Parking: Free
Buffets: B-$15.95 (Sun) L-$12.95
        D-$17.95/$25.95 (Thu-Sat)
Casino Size: 40,000 Square Feet
Other Games: TCP, B6, S21, MS,
        CSP, TCP, LIR
Overnight RV Parking: Free/RV Dump: No
Senior Discount: Various discounts Tue if 55+
Special Features: 3,000-passenger paddle
wheeler docked on Ohio River. Hotel is Hyatt.
18-hole golf course. 1,100-seat showroom.
10x odds on craps.

Tropicana Evansville
421 N.W. Riverside Drive
Evansville, Indiana 47708
(812) 433-4000
Website: www.tropevansville.com
Map: **#5** (168 miles S.W. of Indianapolis)

Toll-Free Number: (800) 342-5386
Rooms: 240 Price Range: $119-$149
Suites: 10 Price Range: $159-$239
Restaurants: 9 Valet Parking: $5
Buffets: B/L-$11.95 (Sat/Sun)
Casino Size: 47,863 Square Feet
Other Games: S21, P, TCP, LIR, MS
Overnight RV Parking: No
Senior Discount: Join Club 55, if 55+
Special Features: 2,700-passenger old fashioned paddlewheeler docked on the Ohio River.

Indiana Grand Casino
4200 N. Michigan Road
Shelbyville, Indiana 46176
(317) 421-0000
Website: www.indianagrand.com
Map: **#11** (32 miles S.E. of Indianapolis)

Toll-Free Number: (877) 386-4463
Restaurants: 4
Buffets: L-$11.95/$17.95 (Sun)
       D-$18.95/$26.95 (Fri)/$19.95 (Sat)
Casino Size: 70,000 Square Feet
Other Games: Only Gaming Machines
Special Features: Thoroughbred horse racing late April through early July. Harness racing mid-July through early November. Year-round simulcasting of thoroughbred and harness racing.

Pari-Mutuels

In April 2007, the Indiana state legislature authorized the state's two horse tracks to have up to 2,000 electronic gaming machines.

Both casinos are open 24 hours and the minimum gambling age is 21. The minimum age for pari-mutuel betting is 18.

Hoosier Park
4500 Dan Patch Circle
Anderson, Indiana 46013
(765) 642-7223
Website: www.hoosierpark.com
Map: **#12** (45 miles N.E. of Indianapolis)

Toll-Free Number: (800) 526-7223
Restaurants: 7
Buffets: B-$22.95 (Sun)
      L-$9.95/$12.95 (Sat)
      D-$15.95/$24.95 (Fri/Sat)
Other Games: Only Gaming Machines
Casino Size: 92,000 Square Feet
Special Features: Thoroughbred horse racing August through October. Harness racing Late March through May. Year-round simulcasting of thoroughbred and harness racing.

IOWA

Iowa was the first state to legalize riverboat gambling. The boats began operating on April Fools Day in 1991 and passengers were originally limited to $5 per bet with a maximum loss of $200 per person, per cruise.

In early 1994 the Iowa legislature voted to eliminate the gambling restrictions. Additionally, gaming machines were legalized at three of the state's four pari-mutuel facilities. In mid-2004 a provision was added to allow table games at those three tracks. That same year the state also legalized casinos on moored barges that float in man-made basins of water and no longer required the casinos to be on boats. Iowa also has three Indian casinos.

Here's information, as supplied by the Iowa Racing and Gaming Commission, showing the electronic gaming machine payback percentages for all non-Indian locations for the one-year period from July 1, 2013 through June 30, 2014:

LOCATION	PAYBACK%
Prairie Meadows	91.76
Wild Rose - Emmetsburg	91.74
Isle of Capri - Waterloo	91.02
Rhythm City	91.07
Isle of Capri - Bettendorf	90.98
Lady Luck - Marquette	91.04
Wild Rose - Clinton	91.24
Riverside	91.00
Catfish Bend	90.74
Mystique Casino	90.55
Ameristar	90.61
Diamond Jo Dubuque	90.74
Diamond Jo Worth	90.59
Lakeside	90.19
Grand Falls	90.51
Horsehoe Council Bluffs	89.49
Harrah's	89.26

These figures reflect the total percentages returned by each riverboat casino or pari-mutuel facility for all of its electronic machines including: slots, video poker, video keno, etc.

Admission to all Iowa casinos is free and, unless otherwise noted, all casinos are open 24 hours.

All Iowa casinos offer: blackjack, roulette, craps, slots and video poker. Some casinos also offer: mini-baccarat (MB), poker (P), pai gow poker (PGP), Caribbean stud poker (CSP), let it ride (LIR), big 6 (B6), bingo (BG), keno (K), Mississippi stud (MS), three card poker (TCP), four card poker (FCP) and Spanish 21 (S21). The minimum gambling age is 21.

NOTE: If you happen to win a jackpot of $1,200 or more in Iowa, the casino will withhold 5% of your winnings for the Iowa Department of Revenue. If you want to try and get that money refunded, you will be required to file a state income tax return and, depending on the details of your return, you *may* get some of the money returned to you. The $1,200 threshold would also apply to any cash prizes won in casino drawings or tournaments.

For more information on visiting Iowa call the state's tourism department at (800) 345-4692 or visit their website at www.traveliowa.com.

Ameristar Casino Council Bluffs
2200 River Road
Council Bluffs, Iowa 51501
(712) 328-8888
Website: www.ameristarcasinos.com
Map: **#8**

Toll-Free Number: (877) 462-7827
Rooms: 152 Price Range: $120-$265
Suites: 8 Price Range: $240-$300
Restaurants: 5 Valet Parking: Free
Buffets: B-$13.99 (Sat)/$16.99 (Sun)
　　　　　L-$12.99
　　　　　D-$16.99/$26.99 (Fri)/$18.99 (Sat/Sun)
Casino Size: 38,500 Square Feet
Other Games: S21, PGP, TCP, MS
Overnight RV Parking: No
Senior Discount: Various discounts if 55+
Special Features: 2,700-passenger sidewheeler replica on the Missouri River. Kids Quest supervised children's center.

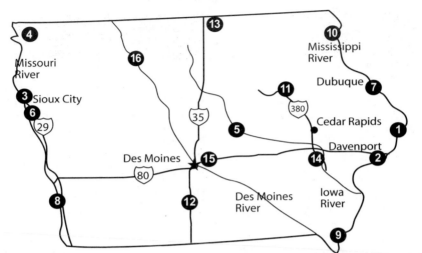

Catfish Bend Casino - Burlington
3001 Wine Gard Ave
Burlington, Iowa 52601
(319) 753-2946
Website: www.catfishbendcasino.com
Map: **#9** (180 miles S.E. of Des Moines)

Toll Free Number: (800) 372-2946
Rooms: 20 Price Range: $99-$149
Suites: 20 Price Range: $169-$269
Restaurants: 4 (1 open 24 hours)
Hours: 8am-3am/24 hours (Fri/Sat)
Casino Size: 23,000 Square Feet
Other Games: S21, P, PGP,
　　　　　　TCP, FCP, MB, MS
Overnight RV Parking: Free/RV Dump: No
Special features: Land-based casino.

Diamond Jo Casino Dubuque
400 E. Third Street
Dubuque, Iowa 52001
(563) 690-2100
Website: www.diamondjodubuque.com
Map: **#7**

Toll-Free Number: (800) 582-5956
Restaurants: 3   Valet Parking: Free
Buffets: B-$12.95 (Sat/Sun) L-$9.95
　　　　D-$14.95
Casino Size: 36,683 Square Feet
Other Games: LIR, PGP, TCP, MS
Overnight RV Parking: Free RV Dump: No
Special features: Land-based casino.

Diamond Jo Casino Worth
777 Diamond Jo Lane
Northwood, Iowa 50459
(641) 323-7777
Website: www.diamondjoworth.com
Map: **#13** (140 miles N. of Des Moines)

Toll-Free Number: (877) 323-5566
Rooms: 100 Price Range: $120-$160
Restaurants: 4   Valet Parking: Free
Buffets: B/L-$12.99 (Sat/Sun)
　　　　D-$14.99/$17.99 (Fri)/$16.99 (Sat)
Casino Size: 36,363 Square Feet
Other Games: TCP, P, PGP, MS
Overnight RV Parking: Free/RV Dump: No
Special features: Land-based casino. Burger
King and Starbucks.

Grand Falls Casino Resort
1415 Grand Falls Boulevard
Larchwood, Iowa 51241
(712) 777-7777
Website: www.grandfallscasinoresort.com
Map: **#4** (17 Miles SE of Sioux Falls, SD)

Toll-Free number: (877)511-4386
Rooms: 88 Price Range: $115-$195
Suites: 10 Price Range: $210-$480
Restaurants: 3 Valet Parking: Free
Buffets: B-$8.99 L-$10.99/$16.99 (Sun)
　　　　D-$17.99/$18.99 (Fri)
Casino Size: 37,810
Other Games: P, FCP, PGP, MS
Overnight RV Parking: No
Special features: 1,200-seat event center.
14-space RV park ($20-$40 per night).

Hard Rock Hotel & Casino Sioux City
111 3rd Street
Sioux City, Iowa 51101
(712) 226-76000
Website: www.hardrockcasinosiouxcity.com
Map: **#8**

Rooms: 50 Price Range: $149-$179
Suites: 4 Price Range: $209-$279
Restaurants: 4 Liquor: Yes
Buffets: B-$15.99 (Sat/Sun)
        L-$12.99/$15.99 (Sat/Sun)
        D-$16.99/$18.99 (Fri/Sat)
Casino Size: 20,000 Square Feet
Overnight RV Parking: Yes
Other Games: TCP, LIR, PGP, MS

Harrah's Council Bluffs
One Harrah's Boulevard
Council Bluffs, Iowa 51501
(712) 329-6000
Website: www.harrahscouncilbluffs.com
Map: **#8**

Toll Free Number: (800) 472-7247
Rooms: 240 Price Range: $111-$295
Suites: 11 Price Range: $250-$325
Restaurants: 5 Valet Parking: Free
Buffets: B-$16.99 (Sat-Sun)
        L-$13.99
        D-$16.99/$19.99 (Fri/Sat)
Casino Size: 33,406 Square Feet
Other Games: S21, TCP, LIR, PGP, MS
Overnight RV Parking: Free/RV Dump: No
Special Features: 25,000 square foot land-based casino. Buffet discount for players club members.

Isle Casino Hotel - Bettendorf
1821 State Street
Bettendorf, Iowa 52722
(563) 359-7280
Website: www.isleofcapricasino.com
Map: **#2**

Toll-Free Number: (800) 724-5825
Rooms: 220 Price Range: $90-$260
Suites: 36 Price Range $155-$525
Restaurants: 4 Valet Parking: Free
Buffets: B-$6.99/$8.99 (Sat/Sun)
        L-$8.99/$10.99 (Sat/Sun)
        D-$13.99/$15.99 (Fri-Sun)
Other Games: P, PGP, TCP, MS
Casino Size: 28,976 Square Feet
Overnight RV Parking: Free/RV Dump: No
Senior Discount: Various on Tue if 50+
Special Features: 2,500-passenger old-fashioned paddle wheeler on the Mississippi River. 53-slip marina.

Isle Casino Hotel - Waterloo
777 Isle of Capri Boulevard
Waterloo, Iowa 52701
(319)833-4753
Website: www.theislewaterloo.com
Map: **#11** (90 miles W. of Dubuque)

Toll-Free Number: (800) 843-4753
Rooms: 170 Price Range: $90-$200
Suites: 27 Price Range: $160-$280
Restaurants: 3
Buffets: B-$8.99/$14.99 (Sun) L-$10.99
        D-$15.99/$16.99 (Fri/Sat)
Other Games: P, TCP, PGP, MB, MS
Casino Size: 43,142 Square Feet
Overnight RV Parking: Free/RV Dump: No
Senior Discount: Various Tue/Thu if 50+
        and always $1 off buffet if 50+.
Special features: Land-based casino.

Lady Luck Casino - Marquette
100 Anti Monopoly Street
Marquette, Iowa 52158
(563) 873-3531
Website: www.isleofcapricasino.com
Map: **#10** (60 miles N. of Dubuque)

Toll-Free Number: (800) 496-8238
Rooms: 22 Price Range: $142-$155
Suites: 3 Price Range: $150-$175
Restaurants: 2   Valet Parking: Free
Buffets: B-$8.99 (Sat)/$13.99 (Sun)
        L-$9.99
        D-$13.99/$16.99 (Fri/Sat)
Hours: 9am-2am/24 Hours (Fri/Sat)
Other Games: P, TCP, MS, no roulette
Casino Size: 17,925 Square Feet
Overnight RV Parking: Free/RV Dump: No
Senior Discount: Various Tue/Thu if 50+
        and always 10% off buffet if 55+.
Special Features: 1,200-passenger paddle
wheeler on the Mississippi River.

Lakeside Casino
777 Casino Drive
Osceola, Iowa 50213
(641) 342-9511
Website: www.terribleslakeside.com
Map: **#12** (50 miles S. of Des Moines)

Toll-Free Number: (877) 477-5253
Suites: 63   Price: $110-$170
Restaurants: 2   Valet Parking: Free
Buffets: B-$7.99 (Sat)/$16.99 (Sun)
        L-$8.99/ $12.99 (Sun)
        D-$11.99/$14.99 (Sun)/
            $16.99 (Thu/Sat)/$18.99 (Fri)
Casino Size: 36,200 Square Feet
Other Games: P, PGP, TCP
Overnight RV Parking: Free with players club card/
        RV Dump: No
Senior Discount: Various on Mon/Wed if 50+.
Special Features: Casino is on a barge.
47-space RV park ($20 per night). Fishing/
boating dock.

Riverside Casino & Golf Resort
3184 Highway 22
Riverside, Iowa 52327
(319) 648-1234
Website: www.riversidecasinoandresort.com
Map: **#14** (81 miles W. of Davenport)

Toll-Free Number: (877) 677-3456
Rooms: 200 Price Range: $90-$135
Restaurants: 4   Valet Parking: Free
Buffets: B-$8.99 L-$10.99/$16.99 (Sat/Sun)
        D-$16.99
Casino Size: 56,400 Square Feet
Overnight RV Parking: Free/RV Dump: No
Other Games: P, PGP, TCP, MS
Special features: Land-based casino. 18-hole
golf course. 1,200-seat showroom.

Rhythm City Casino
101 West River Drive
Davenport, Iowa 52801
(319) 328-8000
Website: www.rhythmcitycasino.com
Map: **#2** (80 miles S.E. of Cedar Rapids)

Toll-Free Number: (800) 262-8711
Restaurants: 1   Valet Parking: Free
Buffets: B-$5.00/$9.00 (Sun) L-$7.00
        D-$9.00/$11.00 (Fri/Sat)
Casino Size: 29,692 Square Feet
Other Games: PGP, TCP, P, MS
Overnight RV Parking: No
Senior Discount: Various Mon/Wed if 50+
Special Features: 2,200-passenger riverboat
on the Mississippi River. Affiliated with Isle
of Capri Casinos.

Wild Rose Casino - Clinton
777 Wild Rose Drive
Clinton, Iowa 52733
(563) 243-9000
Website: www.wildroseresorts.com
Map: **#1** (90 miles E. of Cedar Rapids)

Toll-Free Number: (800) 457-9975
Rooms: 60 Price Range: $79-$109
Suites: 6 Price Range: $129-$149
Restaurants: 2 Valet Parking: Free
Buffets: D-$12.99 (Fri/Sat)
Hours: 8am-2am/4am (Fri/Sat)
Casino Size: 19,681 Square Feet
Additional Games: PGP, LIR, P
Overnight RV Parking: Free/RV Dump: No
Special Features: Land-based casino.

Wild Rose Casino - Emmetsberg
777 Main Street
Emmetsburg, Iowa 50536
(712) 852-3400
Website: www.wildroseresorts.com
Map: **#16** (120 miles N.E. of Sioux City)

Toll-Free Number: (877) 720-7673
Rooms: 62 Price Range: $60-$100
Suites: 8 Price Range: $170-$200
Restaurants: 2   Valet Parking: Free
Buffets: B-$3.99 L-$8.99
        Brunch -$10.99 (Sun)
        D-$8.99(Sun)/$10.95 (Mon/Tue)
        $10.99 (Tue)/$12.95 (Fri)/$13.95(Sat)
Hours: 8am-2am/24 Hours (Fri/Sat)
Casino Size: 16,357 Square Feet
Other Games: P, PGP
Senior Discount: Various Tue if 55+
Overnight RV Parking: Must use RV park
Special features: Land-based casino. $2 off
buffets for players club members. 68-space
RV park ($15 per night).

Indian Casinos

Blackbird Bend Casino
1 Blackbird Bend Blvd
Onawa, Iowa 51040
(712) 423-9646
Website: www.blackbirdbendcasinoomaha.com
Map: **#4** (40 miles S. of Sioux City)

Hours: 8am-3am/24 hours (Fri/Sat)
Casino Size: 6,800 Square Feet
Other Games: Slots Only
Overnight RV Parking: No
Special features: Land-based casino.

Meskwaki Bingo Casino Hotel
1504 305th Street
Tama, Iowa 52339
(641) 484-2108
Website: www.meskwaki.com
Map: **#5** (40 miles W. of Cedar Rapids)

Toll-Free Number: (800) 728-4263
Rooms: 390 Price Range: $95-$200
Suites: 14 Price Range: $280-$345
Restaurants: 5 Liquor: Yes   Valet Park: Free
Buffets: B-$8.95 L-$9.95
        D-$12.95/$20.95 (Fri/Sat)
Other Games: S21, MB, P, PGP, LIR, TCP
        MS, K, BG, Off-Track Betting
Overnight RV Parking: Must Use RV Park
Senior Discount: $1 off buffet if 55+
Special Features: 50-space RV park ($19 per
night). Spa.

WinnaVegas Casino
1500 330th Street
Sloan, Iowa 51055
(712) 428-9466
Website: www.winnavegas.biz
Map: **#6** (20 miles S. of Sioux City)

Toll-Free Number: (800) 468-9466
Rooms: 52 Price Range: $95-$120
Restaurants: 1 Liquor: Yes   Valet Park: Free
Buffets: B- $8.99 (Sat/Sun) L-$8.99
        D-$12.49/$15.99 (Thu/Sat)/$18.99 (Fri)
Other Games: P, BG, TCP, P
Overnight RV Parking: Free/RV Dump: No
Special Features: 20-space RV park ($10/night).

Pari-Mutuels

Horseshoe Casino - Council Bluffs
2701 23rd Avenue
Council Bluffs, Iowa 51501
(712) 323-2500
Website: horseshoecouncilbluffs.com
Map: **#8** (102 miles S. of Sioux City)

Toll-Free Number: (877) 771-7463
Rooms: 158 Price Range: $149-$300
Restaurants: 3   Valet Parking: Free
Buffets: L-$13.99/$17.99 (Sun)
　　　D-$18.99/$21.99 (Fri/Sat)
Casino Size: 78,810 Square Feet
Other Games: P, PGP, MB, S21, TCP, FCP, MS
Overnight RV Parking: Free/RV Dump: No
Special Features: Live dog racing (Tue-Sun). Daily horse and greyhound race simulcasting. Free shuttle service from local hotels. Affiliated with Harrah's. 100x odds on craps.

Mystique Casino
1855 Greyhound Park Road
Dubuque, Iowa 52001
(563) 582-3647
Website: www.mystiquedbq.com
Map: **#7**

Toll-Free Number: (800) 373-3647
Restaurants: 4   Valet Parking: Free
Buffets: L-$11.95
　　　D- $12.95/$19.95 (Fri)/$14.95 (Sat)
Hours: 8am-3am/24 Hours (Fri/Sat)
Casino Size: 47,067 Square Feet
Other Games: TCP, FCP, P, PGP, MS
Overnight RV Parking: Free/RV Dump: No
Senior Discount: Various specials Wed if 55+.
Special Features: Live greyhound racing (Wed-Sun) from late-April through October. Greyhound, harness and thoroughbred simulcasting all year.

Prairie Meadows Racetrack & Casino
1 Prairie Meadows Drive
Altoona, Iowa 50009
(515) 967-1000
Website: www.prairiemeadows.com
Map: **#15** (5 miles E. of Des Moines)

Toll-Free Number: (800) 325-9015
Restaurants: 3   Valet Parking: Free
Buffets: B- $6.95/ $11.95 (Sat/Sun) L- $8.95
　　　D-$11.95/$14.95 (Wed)/ $16.95 (Fri/Sat)
Casino Size: 85,680 Square Feet
Other Games: MB, P, PGP, TCP, MS
Overnight RV Parking: Yes
Senior Discount: Various specials if 55+
Special Features: Live thoroughbred and quarter-horse racing April through October. Daily simulcasting of dog and horse racing.

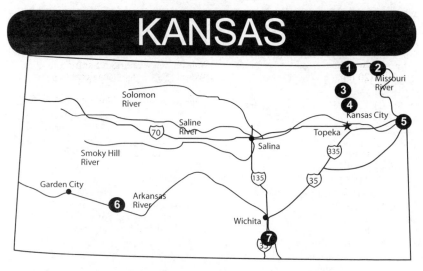

KANSAS

Kansas has three casinos that are state owned and operated. Additionally, there are five Indian casinos in Kansas.

The Kansas Racing & Gaming Commission does not release information about the payback percentages on electronic gaming machines at their casinos. However, gaming regulations require that all machines return no less than 87%.

Unless otherwise noted, all state-run casinos are open 24 hours and offer the following games: slot machines, video poker, video keno, blackjack, craps and roulette. Other games include: poker (P), Caribbean stud poker (CSP), let it ride (LIR), Mississippi stud (MS), three card poker (TCP) and bingo (BG). The minimum gambling age is 21.

For information on visiting Kansas call the state's tourism department at (785) 296-2009 or visit their website at www.travelks.com

Boot Hill Casino & Resort
4000 W Comanche Street
Dodge City, Kansas 67801
(620) 682-7777
Website: www.boothillcasino.com
Map: **#6** (155 miles W of Wichita)

Toll-free Number: (877) 906-0777
Restaurants: 1 Valet Parking: Free
Buffets: L-$19.99 (Sat/Sun)
Other Games: P, TCP, MS
Overnight RV Parking: Free/RV Dump: No
Special Features: Hampton Inn adjacent to casino.

Hollywood Casino at Kansas Speedway
777 Hollywood Casino Boulevard
Kansas City, Kansas 66111
(913) 288-9300
Website: hollywoodcasinokansas.com
Map: **#5**

Restaurants: 2   Valet Parking: $5
Buffets: L-$13.99
   D-$16.99/$29.99 (Wed/Thu)/$19.99 (Fri/Sat)
Casino Size: 80,000 Square Feet
Other Games: P, MB, MS
Overnight RV Parking: Free/RV Dump: No

Kansas Star Casino
108 West Main St.
Mulvane, Kansas 67110
(316) 719-5000
Website: www.kansasstarcasino.com
Map: **#7** (20 miles S of Wichita)

Restaurants: 3 Valet Parking: No
Buffets: L-$9.99/$11.99 (Sun)
          D-$11.99/$14.99 (Fri/Sat)
Casino Size: 21,000 Square Feet
Other Games: BG, P, TCP, LIR, MS, No roulette
Overnight RV Parking: Free/RV Dump: No

Indian Casinos

There are five Indian casinos in Kansas and they are not required to release information on their slot machine payback percentages. However, according to officials at the Kansas State Gaming Agency, which is responsible for overseeing the tribal-state compacts, "the minimum payback percentage for electronic gaming devices is 80%."

Unless otherwise noted, all Kansas Indian casinos are open 24 hours and offer the following games: blackjack, craps, roulette, slots and video poker. Other games include: poker (P), Caribbean stud poker (CSP), mini-baccarat (MB), let it ride (LIR), pai gow poker (PGP), Mississippi stud (MS), three card poker (TCP) and bingo (BG). The minimum gambling age is 21.

Casino White Cloud
777 Jackpot Drive
White Cloud, Kansas 66094
(785) 595-3430
Website: www.casinowhitecloud.org
Map: **#2** (70 miles N.E. of Topeka)

Toll-Free Number: (877) 652-6115
Restaurants: 2 Liquor: Yes Valet Parking: No
Buffets: L-$10.00 D-$11.00
Casino Size: 21,000 Square Feet
Casino Hours: 9am-1am/3am (Fri/Sat)
Other Games: BG, TCP, No Roulette
Overnight RV Parking: Free/RV Dump: No

Golden Eagle Casino
1121 Goldfinch Road
Horton, Kansas 66439
(785) 486-6601
Map: **#3** (45 miles N. of Topeka)
Website: www.goldeneaglecasino.com

Toll-Free Number: (888) 464-5825
Restaurants: 2 Liquor: No Valet Parking: No
Buffets: L-$7.95/$5.00 (Mon)
 D-$14.95/$17.95 (Thu)/$10.95(Sun/Fri)
Other Games: P, TCP, BG (Wed-Sun)
Overnight RV Parking: Free/RV Dump: No
Senior Discount: Various Tue if 50+
Special Features: RV hookups available ($10 per night).

Prairie Band Casino & Resort
12305 150th Road
Mayetta, Kansas 66509
(785) 966-7777
Website: www.pbpgaming.com
Map: **#4** (17 miles N. of Topeka)

Toll-Free Number: (888) 727-4946
Rooms: 297 Price Range: $100-$150
Suites: 8 Price Range: Casino Use Only
Restaurants: 3 Liquor: Yes Valet Parking: Free
Buffets: B-$7.99 L-$9.99/$14.99 (Sun)
          D-$15.99/$21.99 (Mon)/
             $19.99 (Tue)/$22.99 (Fri)
Casino Size: 33,000 Square Feet
Other Games: MB, P, PGP, LIR, TCP, MS
Overnight RV Parking: Must use RV park.
Special Features: 67-space RV park ($21-$32 per night).

Sac & Fox Casino
1322 U.S. Highway 75
Powhattan, Kansas 66527
(785) 467-8000
Map: **#1** (60 miles N. of Topeka)
Website: www.sacandfoxcasino.com

Toll-Free Number: (800) 990-2946
Restaurant: 3 Liquor: Yes Valet Parking: No
Buffets: L-$7.99/$11.99 (Sun)
       D-$9.99/$15.99 (Fri/Sat)
Casino Size: 40,000 Square Feet
Other Games: TCP
Overnight RV Parking: Free/RV Dump: No
Senior Discount: $1 off meals if 55 or older
Special Features: 24-hour truck stop. Golf driving range. 12-space RV park ($10 per night).

7th Street Casino
803 North 7th Street
Kansas City, Kansas 66101
(913) 371-3500
Website: www.7th-streetcasino.com
Map: **#5**

Restaurant: 2 Liquor: Yes Valet Parking: No
Casino Size: 20,000 Square Feet
Other Games: Only Gaming Machines
Overnight RV Parking: No/RV Dump: No

LOUISIANA

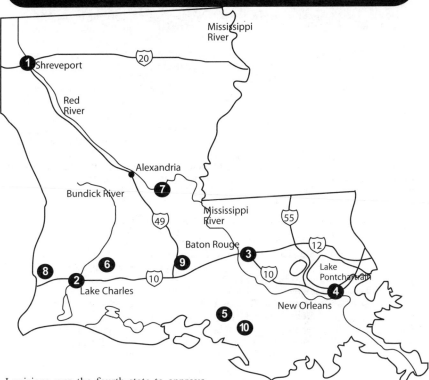

Louisiana was the fourth state to approve riverboat casino gambling and its 1991 gambling law allows a maximum of 15 boats statewide. In 1992 a provision was added for one land-based casino in New Orleans.

The state also has three land-based Indian casinos and four slot machine-only (no video poker or video keno) casinos located at pari-mutuel facilities. Additionally, video poker is permitted at Louisiana truck stops, OTB's and bars/taverns in 31 of the state's 64 parishes (counties). All riverboat casinos in Louisiana are required to remain dockside and all are open 24 hours.

Gaming regulations require that gaming machines in casinos be programmed to pay back no less than 80% and no more than 99.9%. For video gaming machines at locations other than casinos the law requires a minimum return of 80% and a maximum return of 94%.

Louisiana gaming statistics are not broken down by individual properties. Rather, they are classified by region: Baton Rouge (BR), Lake Charles (LC), New Orleans (NO) and Shreveport/Bossier City (SB).

The Baton Rouge casinos consist of the Belle of Baton Rouge, Hollywood Casino, L'Auberge and Evangeline Downs. The Lake Charles casinos include: Isle of Capri, L'Auberge Resort and Delta Downs. New Orleans area casinos are: Amelia Belle, Boomtown, Harrah's (landbased), Treasure Chest and Fairgrounds Raceway. The Shreveport/Bossier city casinos include: Boomtown, Diamond Jack's, Sam's Town, Eldorado, Horseshoe and Harrah's Louisiana Downs.

Here's information, as supplied by the Louisiana State Police-Riverboat Gaming Section, showing the average electronic machine payback percentages for each area's casinos for the 12-month period from June, 2013 through May, 2014:

	BR	**LC**	**NO**	**SB**
1¢	88.7%	88.6%	88.5%	**88.9%**
5¢	93.0%	91.5%	**93.4%**	90.7%
25¢	**92.9%**	92.5%	92.7%	91.7%
$1	**93.5%**	**93.5%**	93.0%	92.7%
$5	**94.5%**	93.8%	**94.5%**	93.0%
All	90.8%	**91.3%**	90.2%	90.7%

These numbers reflect the percentage of money returned on each denomination of machine and encompass all electronic machines including video poker and video keno. The best returns for each category are highlighted in bold print.

NOTE: If you happen to win a jackpot of $1,200 or more in Louisiana, the casino will withhold 6% of your winnings for the Louisiana Department of Revenue. If you want to try and get that money refunded, you will be required to file a state income tax return and, depending on the details of your return, you *may* get some of the money returned to you. The $1,200 threshold would also apply to any cash prizes won in casino drawings or tournaments.

All casinos offer: blackjack, craps, roulette, slots, video poker, three card poker and Mississippi stud. Optional games include: Spanish 21 (S21), baccarat (B), mini-baccarat (MB), poker (P), Caribbean stud poker (CSP), pai gow poker (PGP), let it ride (LIR), casino war (CW), four card (FCP), big 6 wheel (B6), keno (K), Texas hold 'em Bonus (THB), ultimate texas hold em (UTH) and bingo (BG). The minimum gambling age is 21 for casino gaming and 18 for pari-mutuel betting.

For more information on visiting Louisiana call the state's tourism department at (800) 633-6970 or visit www.louisianatravel.com

Amelia Belle Casino
500 Lake Palourde Road
Amelia, Louisiana 70340
(985) 631-1777
Website: www.ameliabellecasino.com
Map: **#10**   (75 miles S. of Baton Rouge)

Restaurants: 2
Buffets: L- $13.95/$17.95 (Fri)/$13.50 (Sat)/
$12.50 (Sun)
D- $14.95/$19.95 (Fri)/$17.50 (Sat)/
$13.50 (Sun)
Casino Size: 27,928 Square Feet
Other Games: P, B, MB, TCP
Overnight RV Parking: Free (Must park in employee lot)
Special Features: 1,200-passenger paddle wheeler on Bayou Boeuf.

Belle of Baton Rouge
103 France Street
Baton Rouge, Louisiana 70802
(225) 378-6000
Website: www.belleofbatonrouge.com
Map: **#3**

Toll-Free Number: (800) 676-4847
Rooms: 100 Price Range: $100-$135
Suites: 88 Price Range: $155-$195
Restaurants: 5   Valet Parking: $10
Buffets: B- $12.99 (Sat/Sun)
D- $27.99 (Fri)/$23.99 (Sat)
Casino Size: 28,500 Square Feet
Other Games: MB, P, PGP
Overnight RV Parking: Yes/RV dump: No
Special Features: 1,500-passenger paddle wheeler on the Mississippi River. 300-room Sheraton Hotel is adjacent to casino (800-325-3535). 10% off food/drink for players club members.

Boomtown Casino & Hotel Bossier City
300 Riverside Drive
Bossier City, Louisiana 71171
(318) 746-0711
Website: www.boomtownbossier.com
Map: **#1** (across the Red River From Shreveport)

Toll-Free Number: (866) 462-8696
Rooms: 100 Price Range: $90-$185
Suites: 88 Price Range: $119-$219
Restaurants: 4   Valet Parking: Free
Buffets: B-$8.49/$9.99 (Sat/Sun)
        L-$11.99/$14.99 (Sun)
        D-$19.99/26.99 (Fri/Sat)
Casino Size: 25,635 Square Feet
Overnight RV Parking: No
Senior Discount: $4.99 breakfast if 55+.
Special Features: 1,925-passenger paddle wheeler on the Red River. $1 off buffets for players club members.

Boomtown Casino New Orleans
4132 Peters Road
Harvey, Louisiana 70058
(504) 366-7711
Website: www.boomtownneworleans.com
Map: **#4** (a suburb of New Orleans)

Toll-Free Number: (800) 366-7711
Restaurants: 5   Valet Parking: Free
Buffets: B-$19.99 (Sun)
        L-$12.99
        D-$15.99/$29.99 (Fri/Sat)
Casino Size: 29,027 Square Feet
Other Games: MB, P, PGP
Overnight RV Parking: Free/RV Dump: No
Senior Discount: $2 off buffets if players
            club member.
Special Features: 1,600-passenger paddle wheeler on the Harvey Canal. Family arcade.

Diamond Jacks Casino - Bossier City
711 DiamondJacks Boulevard
Bossier City, Louisiana 71111
(318) 678-7777
Website: www.diamondjacks.com
Map: **#1** (across the Red River from Shreveport)

Toll-Free Number: (866) 552-9629
Suites: 570 Price Range: $119-$159
Restaurants: 3   Valet Parking: Free
Buffets: B-$10.99 /$14.99 (Sun)
        L-$13.99
        D-$17.99/$22.99(Fri/Sat)
Casino Size: 29,921 Square Feet
Other Games: S21, FCP, LIR, MS, UTH
Overnight RV Parking: Must use RV park
Senior Discount: 50% off buffet if 50+
Special Features: 1,650-passenger paddle wheeler on the Red River. 32-space RV park ($25/$30 Fri-Sat). Supervised childcare center. 1,200-seat showroom. Buffet discount for players club members.

Eldorado Casino Shreveport
451 Clyde Fant Parkway
Shreveport, Louisiana 71101
(318) 220-0981
Website: www.eldoradoshreveport.com
Map: **#1**

Hotel Reservations: (877) 602-0711
Suites: 403 Price Range: $110-$220
Restaurants: 4   Valet Parking: Free
Buffet: B-$15.99 (Sat/Sun) L-$12.99
        D-$17.99/$23.99 (Thu)/$22.99 (Fri)
Casino Size: 28,226 Square Feet
Other Games: CW, CSP, LIR,
            PGP, P, MB, UTH
Overnight RV Parking: Free (Weekdays only)
Special Features: 1,500-passenger paddle wheeler on the Red River.

Golden Nugget Casino - Lake Charles
2550 Golden Nugget Blvd
Lake Charles, Louisiana 70601
Website: www.goldennuggetlc.com

Expected to open in early 2015.
Rooms: 739
Restaurants: 8

Harrah's New Orleans
8 Canal Street
New Orleans, Louisiana 70130
(504) 533-6000
Website: www.harrahs.com
Map: **#4**

Toll-Free Number: (800) 847-5299
Suites: 450 Price Range: $180-$335
Restaurants: 4
Buffet: B-$15.99 L-$16.99/$33.99 (Sun)
        D-$33.99
Valet Parking: $10 first two hours/$5 for each
        additional two hours/$40 maximum
   (Free for Diamond and Platinum members)
Casino Size: 125,119 Square Feet
Other Games: MB, PGP, CSP, LIR,
        B, FCP, B6, UTH
Overnight RV Parking: No
Special Features: Landbased casino. Five
themed gaming areas. Fast food court. Daily
live jazz music. Self-parking costs $5 to $25
depending on length of stay. Players club
members playing for minimum of 30 minutes
can get validated for up to 24 hours of free
parking.

Hollywood Casino - Baton Rouge
1717 River Road North
Baton Rouge, Louisiana 70802
(225) 381-7777
Website: www.hollywoodbr.com
Map: **#3**

Toll-Free Number: (800) 447-6843
Restaurants: 3   Valet Parking: Free
Buffets: L-$13.95/$17.95 (Sun)
        D-$28.95(Thu)/$22.95(Fri/Sat)
Casino Size: 27,900 Square Feet
Overnight RV Parking: Free/RV Dump: No
Special Features: 1,500-passenger paddle
wheeler on the Mississippi River.

Horseshoe Casino Hotel - Bossier City
711 Horseshoe Boulevard
Bossier City, Louisiana 71111
(318) 742-0711
Website: www.horseshoebossiercity.com
Map: **#1** (across the Red River from Shreveport)

Toll-Free Number: (800) 895-0711
Suites: 606 Price Range: $100-$555
Restaurants: 3   Valet Parking: Free
Buffets: L-$15.99/$23.99(Fri)
        D-$20.99/$25.99 (Fri)
Casino Size: 28,095 Square Feet
Other Games: MB, P, CSP, TCP, B, FCP, LIR
Overnight RV Parking: Free/RV Dump: No
Senior Discount: 10% buffet discount if 55+.
Special Features: 2,930-passenger paddle
wheeler on the Red River.

Isle of Capri Casino - Lake Charles
100 Westlake Avenue
Westlake, Louisiana 70669
(337) 430-0711
Website: www.isleofcapricasino.com
Map: **#2** (220 miles W. of New Orleans)

Toll-Free Number: (800) 843-4753
Inn Rooms: 241 Price Range: $80-$195
Suite Rooms: 252 Price Range: $140-$295
Restaurants: 4   Valet Parking: Free
Buffets: B-$10.99 (Sun) L-$10.99
        D-$14.99/$25.99 (Fri/Sat)
Casino Size: 51,569 Square Feet
Other Games: LIR, PGP, FCP, MB, UTH, P
Overnight RV Parking: Must use RV park
Senior Discount: Various Tue if 50+
Special Features: Two 1,200-passenger paddle
wheelers on Lake Charles. 8-space RV park
($20 per night).

L'Auberge Casino Hotel Baton Rouge
777 L'Auberge Avenue
Baton Rouge, Louisiana 70820
(225) 215-7777
Website: www.lbatonrouge.com
Map: #3

Toll-Free Number: (866) 261-7777
Rooms: 200 Price Range: $150-$330
Suites: 6 Price Range: $550-$850
Restaurants: 5 Valet Parking: Free
Buffet: B-$12.99
    L-$14.99/$19.99 (Sun)
    D-$19.99/$24.99 (Thu)/ $29.99 (Fri/Sat)
Casino Size: 29,876 Square Feet
Games Offered: P, LIR, MB, B,
        TCP, FCP, PGP
Overnight RV Parking: No
Special Features: 1,600-seat event center

L'Auberge Casino Resort Lake Charles
3202 Nelson Road
Lake Charles, Louisiana 70601
(337) 475-2900
Website: www.llakecharles.com
Map: #2 (220 miles W. of New Orleans)

Toll-Free Number: (866) 580-7444
Rooms: 636 Price Range: $189-$289
Suites: 99 Price Range: $599-$849
Restaurants: 8 Valet Parking: Free
Buffet: B-$10.99/$21.99 (Sat/Sun)
    L-$14.99
    D-$24.99/$29.99 (Tue/Thu-Sat)
Casino Size: 27,000 Square Feet
Other Games: MB, B, PGP, LIR, P,
        TCP, FCP, THB, MS
Overnight RV Parking: Must use RV park.
Special Features: 18-hole golf course. Spa.
Pool with lazy river ride. 1,500-seat event
center. 13-space RV park ($35 per night).

Margaritaville Resort Casino - Bossier City
777 Margaritaville Way
Bossier City, Louisiana 71111
(855) 346-2489
Website: www.margaritavillebossiercity.com
Map: #1 (across the Red River from Shreveport)

Rooms: 354 Price Range: $89-$219
Suites: 36 Price Range: $319-$589
Restaurants: 5 Liquor: Yes
Buffets: B- $9.95 L- $25.95 (Sat/Sun)
    D- $25.95
Casino Size: 26,624
Other Games: MB, B, FCP, MS
Overnight RV Parking: Yes/RV Dump: No

Sam's Town Hotel & Casino Shreveport
315 Clyde Fant Parkway
Shreveport, Louisiana 71101
(318) 424-7777
Website: www.samstownshreveport.com
Map: #1

Toll-Free Number: (866) 861-0711
Rooms: 514 Price Range: $76-$180
Restaurants: 4 Valet Parking: Free
Buffet: B-$14.99 (Sat/Sun) L-$11.99
    D-$16.99/$22.99 (Fri/Sat)
Casino Size: 29,194 Square Feet
Other Games: MB, LIR, TCP, MS
Overnight RV Parking: No
Special Features: 1,650-passenger paddle
wheeler on the Red River.

Treasure Chest Casino
5050 Williams Boulevard
Kenner, Louisiana 70065
(504) 443-8000
Website: www.treasurechest.com
Map: #4 (a suburb of New Orleans)

Toll-Free Number: (800) 298-0711
Restaurants: 4 Valet Parking: $5
Buffet: L-$11.99/$21.99 (Sat/Sun)
    D- $17.99/$19.99 (Tue/Thu)/
        $25.99 (Wed/Fri/Sat)
Casino Hours: 8am-3am/24 hours (Fri/Sat)
Casino Size: 23,680 Square Feet
Other Games: MB, PGP, TCP, LIR, FCP, MS
Overnight RV Parking: No
Special Features: 1,900-passenger paddle
wheeler on Lake Pontchartrain. Hilton Garden
Inn located next to casino (504-712-0504).

Indian Casinos

Coushatta Casino Resort
777 Coushatta Drive
Kinder, Louisiana 70648
(800) 584-7263
Website: www.coushattacasinoresort.com
Map: **#6** (35 miles N.E. of Lake Charles)

Room Reservations: (888) 774-7263
Hotel Rooms: 118 Price Range: $130-$215
Suites: 90 Price Range: Casino Use Only
Inn Rooms: 195 Price Range: $99-$149
Lodge Rooms: 92 Price Range: $89-$109
Restaurants: 6 Liquor: Yes Valet Park: Free
Buffets: B-$10.00 L-$12.00/$15.00 (Sat/Sun)
           D-$22.00/$24.00 (Thu)/32.00 (Fri)
Casino Size: 105,000 Square Feet
Other Games: MB, P, PGP, LIR,
           TCP, FCP, THB, MS
Overnight RV Parking: No
Special Features: Land-based casino.
100-space RV park ($19/$24 Fri-Sat). Video
arcade. Kids Quest childcare center. 18-hole
golf course.

Cypress Bayou Casino
832 Martin Luther King Road
Charenton, Louisiana 70523
(318) 923-7284
Website: www.cypressbayou.com
Map: **#5** (75 miles S. of Baton Rouge)

Toll-Free Number: (800) 284-4386
Restaurants: 8 Liquor: Yes Valet Parking: Free
Casino Size: 27,900 Square Feet
Other Games: PGP, LIR, B, OTB, FCP, BG
Overnight RV Parking: Free/RV Dump: No
Special Features: Land-based casino. Gift
shop. Cigar bar. 12-space RV park ($10-$22
per night; $55 on holidays).

Jena Choctaw Pines Casino
21160 Highway 167
Dry Prong, Louisiana 71423
(318) 648-7773
Website: www.jenachoctawpinescasino.com
Map: **#5** (75 miles S. of Baton Rouge)

Toll-Free Number: (855) 638-5825
Restaurants: 2 Liquor: Yes
Buffets: L-$9.50/$11.50 (Sun)
          D- $13.50/$15.50 (Wed)/$17.50 (Fri/Sat)
Other Games: P
Overnight RV Parking: Yes

Paragon Casino Resort
711 Paragon Place
Marksville, Louisiana 71351
(318) 253-1946
Website: www.paragoncasinoresort.com
Map: **#7** (30 miles S.E. of Alexandria)

Toll-Free Number: (800) 946-1946
Rooms: 335 Price Range: $95-$235
Suites: 57 Price Range: $155-$355
Restaurants: 6 Liquor: Yes Valet Parking: Free
Buffets: B-$7.99 L-$9.99/$12.99 (Sun)
           D-$16.99/ $18.99 (Wed/Thu)/
           $24.99 (Fri/Sat)
Casino Size: 103,520 Square Feet
Other Games: MB, LIR, OTB, TCP, PGP
Overnight RV Parking: Must use RV park
Special Features: Land-based casino.
185-space RV Park ($17/$22 Fri-Sat). Video
arcade. Kids Quest childcare center. 18-hole
golf course.

Pari-Mutuels

Delta Downs Racetrack & Casino
2717 Highway 3063
Vinton, Louisiana 70668
(337) 589-7441
Website: www.deltadowns.com
Map: **#8** (20 miles W. of Lake Charles)

Toll-Free Number: (800) 589-7441
Room Reservations: (888) 332-7829
Rooms: 203 Price Range: $120-$285
Suites: 33 Price Range: Casino use only
Restaurants: 4 Valet Parking: Free
Buffets: B- $14.99 (Sat/Sun)
          L-$11.99 D-$14.99/
                $24.99 (Fri/Sat)/$15.99 (Sun)
Casino Size: 14,901 Square Feet
Other Games: Only slots, no video poker
Overnight RV Parking: Free/RV Dump: No
Special Features: Live thoroughbred and
quarter-horse racing (Wed-Sat) early October
through mid-July. Daily simulcasting of horse
racing.

Evangeline Downs Racetrack & Casino
2235 Creswell Lane Extension
Opelousas, Louisiana 70570
(337) 896-7223
Website: www.evangelinedowns.com
Map: **#9** (30 miles W. of Baton Rouge)

Toll-Free Number: (866) 472-2466
Restaurants: 3 Valet Parking: Free
Buffets: L-$11.99/$14.99 (Sat/Sun)
        D-$16.99/$27.99 (Fri)
Casino Size: 14,619 Square Feet
Other Games: Only slots, no video poker
Overnight RV Parking: Free/RV Dump: No
Senior Discount: Various Tue if 50 or older
Special Features: Live thoroughbred and
quarter-horse racing (Wed-Sat) April through
November. Daily simulcasting of horse racing.

Fair Grounds Racecourse & Slots
1751 Gentilly Boulevard
New Orleans, Louisiana 70119
(504) 944-5515
Website: www.fairgroundsracecourse.com
Map: **#4**

Restaurants: 1 Valet Parking: $20
Other Size: 15,000 Square Feet
Other Games: Only slots, no video poker
Casino Hours: 9am-12am/10am-12am (Sun)
Overnight RV Parking: No
Special Features: Live thoroughbred racing
November through March.

Harrah's Louisiana Downs
8000 E. Texas Street
Bossier City, Louisiana 71111
(318) 742-5555
Website: www.harrahslouisianadows.com
Map: **#1**

Toll-Free Number: (800) 427-7247
Restaurants: 5 Valet Parking: Free
Buffets: B-$16.99 (Sun)
         L-$14.99 (Thu/Fri)/$20.99 (Sat)
         D-$18.99/$19.99 (Fri)/$24.99 (Sat)
Casino Size: 12,855 Square Feet
Other Games: Only slots, no video poker
Overnight RV Parking: Free/RV Dump: No
Senior Discount: Various Tue if 50 or older
Special Features: Live thoroughbred racing
(Thu-Sun) May through early October.
Live quarter-horse racing racing (Sat-Wed)
late October through November. Daily
simulcasting of horse racing.

MAINE

For more information on visiting Maine call their Office of Tourism at (888) 624-6345 or visit their website at www.visitmaine.com.

Hollywood Slots Hotel & Raceway
500 Main Street
Bangor, Maine 04402
(207) 262-6146
Website: www.hollywoodslotsatbangor.com
Map: **#1**

Toll-Free Number: (877) 779-7771
Rooms: 90 Price Range: $149-$219
Admission: Free Parking: Free
Restaurants: 1
Buffets: B-$12.99 (Sun)
         L-$10.99
         D-$15.99/$16.99 (Sat)
Hours: 8am-3am
Other Games: LIR, P
Special Features: Live harness racing day and evenings from early May through late July and mid-October through mid-November. Daily simulcasting of horse and harness racing.

Oxford Casino
777 Casino Way
Oxford, Maine 04270
(207) 539-6700
Website: www.oxfordcasino.com
Map: **#2** (55 miles S.W. of Agusta)

Restaurants: 1
Buffet: D-$9.95 (Thu)
Other Games: No Blackjack
Overnight RV Parking: Free (limit 24 hours)/ RV Dump: No

Maine has two racetrack casinos (racinos) that offer electronic gaming machines, as well as live table games.

State gaming regulations require a minimum return of 89% on all machines and during the 6-month period from January 2014 through June 2014, the average return on gaming machines was 91.11% at Oxford casino and 89.05% at Hollywood casino.

Unless otherwise noted, all casinos offer: slots, video poker, video keno, craps, blackjack, roulette, three card poker and Mississippi Stud. Optional games include: let it ride (LIR) and Poker (P).

The minimum gambling age is 21 for slots and 18 for pari-mutuel wagering.

MARYLAND

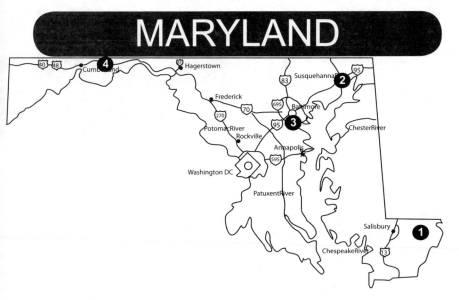

Maryland has five casinos that are allowed to offer electronic gaming machines, as well as live table games. However, as of August 2013, the Casino at Ocean Downs had no table games and did not have any plans to install them.

No public information is available about the actual payback percentages on gaming machines in Maryland. However, gaming regulations require a minimum payback of 87%

All casinos are open 24 hours and, unless otherwise noted, offer: slots, video poker, video keno, craps, blackjack, roulette and three card poker. Optional games include: let it ride (LIR), Pai Gow Poker (PGP), baccarat (B),Ultimate Texas Hold'em (UTH), Mississippi Stud (MS), Poker (P), Four Card Poker (FCP) and Texas Hold'em Bonus (THB).

If you want to order a drink while playing, be aware that Illinois gaming regulations do not allow casinos to provide free alcoholic beverages. The minimum gambling age is 21 for casinos and 18 for pari-mutuel wagering.

For Maryland tourism information, call (800) 543-1036, or visit their website at www.visitmaryland.com

Casino at Ocean Downs
10218 Racetrack Road
Berlin, Maryland 21811
(410) 641-0600
Website: www.oceandowns.com
Map: **#1** (110 miles SE of Annapolis)

Track Admission: Free
Self-Parking: Free Valet: No
Restaurants: 2
Overnight RV Parking: No
Special Features: Live harness racing Sun/Wed/Thu/Sat eves mid-June through late August. Daily simulcasting of thoroughbred and harness racing. Electronic versions of table games only.

Hollywood Casino - Perryville
1201 Chesapeake Overlook Parkway
Perryville, Maryland 29103
(410) 378-8500
Website: hollywoodcasinoperryville.com
Map: **#2** (30 miles NE of Baltimore)

Self-Parking: Free Valet Parking: $3
Restaurants: 2
Other Games: P, FCP
Casino Size: 35,000 Square Feet
Overnight RV Parking: No

Horseshoe Casino Baltimore
1525 Russell Street
Baltimore, Maryland 21230
(443) 931-4200

Toll-Free Number: (844) 777-7463
Restaurants: 4
Games offered: B, PGP, FCP, MS
Casino Size: 122,000 square feet
Special Features: 100x odds on craps.

Maryland Live! Casino
7000 Arundel Mills Cir #7777
Handover, Maryland 21076
(443) 842-7000
Website: www.marylandlivecasino.com

Map: **#3** (10 miles SW of Baltimore)

Toll-free Number: (855) 563-5483
Restaurants: 5
Self-Parking: Free Valet: $10
Buffets: L-$14.99/$17.99 (Sun)
          D-$17.99/$34.99 (Fri/Sat)
Casino Size: 160,000 Square Feet
Other Games: MS
Hours: 8am-2am/4am (Fri/Sat)
Overnight RV Parking: No
Special Features: Ram's Head Center Stage
entertainment venue.

Rocky Gap Casino Resort
Exit 50 off Interstate 68
Flintstone, Maryland 21530
(301) 784-8400
Website: www.rockygapresort.com

Map: **#4** (125 miles NW of Baltimore)

Rooms: 195 Price Range: $165-$175
Suites: 5 Price Range: $224-$265
Buffets: D-$19.99 (Wed/Thu/Sun)/
               $25.99 (Fri/Sat)
Restaurants: 4
Other Games: P
Self-Parking: Free Valet: Free
Overnight RV Parking: No

MASSACHUSETTS

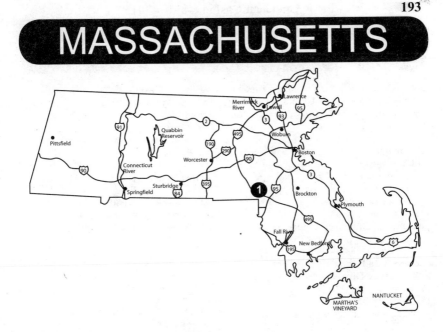

Massachusetts Governor Deval Patrick signed a bill in late 2011 that legalized casinos. The law allows three casinos, in three different geographic regions, plus one slot parlor.

As of August 2014, the slot parlor location had been chosen, Plainridge Race Course, a harness racing track located about 35 miles southwest of Boston. The Plainridge Park Casino is currently under construction and is expected to open in June 2015.

The first resort-casino license in Region B (Western Massachusetts) was awarded to MGM Springfield on June 13, 2014. The Massachusetts Gaming Commission was expected to award the resort-casino license for Region A (Eastern Massachusetts) by September, 2014. They also expected to award the final resort-casino license for Region C (Southeastern Massachusetts) by Spring, 2015. Early 2016 is the earliest any of those casino/resorts are expected to open.

For information on visiting Massachusetts call (800) 447-6277 or visit their web site at www.massvacation.com

Planridge Park Casino
301 Washington Street
Plainville, Massachusetts 02762
(508) 643-2500

Map: **#1** (40 miles SW of Boston)

Toll-Free Number: (866) 946-5463
Set to open June 2015

MICHIGAN

One of Michigan's most popular casinos is actually in Canada. It's Casino Windsor in Ontario which is just across the river from downtown Detroit.

All winnings are paid in Canadian currency and the minimum gambling age is 19. The casino is open 24 hours and offers the following games: blackjack, Spanish 21, craps, roulette, poker, baccarat, mini-baccarat, big six wheel, pai-gow poker, Caribbean stud poker, three-card poker and let it ride.

Caesars Windsor
377 Riverside Drive East
Windsor, Ontario N9A 7H7
(519) 258-7878
Website: www.caesarswindsor.com
Map: **#12**

PRICES ARE IN CANADIAN DOLLARS
Toll-Free Number: (800) 991-7777
Room Reservations: (800) 991-8888
Rooms: 349 Price Range: $130-$260
Suites: 40 Price Range: $190-$760
Restaurants: 6 (1 open 24 hours)
Buffets: L-$18.99/$22.99 (Sun)
          D-$24.99/$27.99(Fri/Sat)
Valet Parking: Free
Casino Size: 100,000 Square Feet
Overnight RV Parking: Check with security/
                      RV Dump: No
Special Features: Entire casino is non-smoking. Buffet discount with slot club card.

The only casinos in Michigan not on indian reservations are located in downtown Detroit. All three are open 24 hours and offer the following games: blackjack, craps, roulette, baccarat, mini-baccarat, Caribbean stud poker, three-card poker, pai gow poker, let it ride, big 6 wheel, Spanish 21, Mississippi stud and casino war. No public information is available about the payback percentages on Detroit's gaming machines.

The minimum gambling age at all Detroit casinos is 21 and all three casinos offer free valet parking.

Greektown Casino
555 E. Lafayette Boulevard
Detroit, Michigan 48226
(313) 223-2999
Website: www.greektowncasino.com
Map: **#12**

Toll free Number: (888) 771-4386
Rooms: 400 Price Range: $150-$250
Restaurants: 2 Valet Parking: Free
Casino Size: 75,000 Square Feet
Other Games: Poker, no Spanish 21

MGM Grand Detroit Casino
1777 Third Avenue
Detroit, Michigan 48226
(313) 393-7777
Website: www.mgmgranddetroit.com
Map: **#12**

Toll-Free Number: (877) 888-2121
Room Reservations: (800) 991-8888
Rooms: 335 Price Range: $250-$345
Suites: 65 Price Range: $450-$2,000
Restaurants: 6 (1 open 24 hrs) Valet Parking: Free
Buffets: B-$28.00 (Sun)
         L-$22.00
         D-$28.00/$39.00 (Wed)/$32.00 (Thu)
Casino Size: 75,000 Square Feet
Overnight RV Parking: No

MotorCity Casino and Hotel
2901 Grand River Avenue
Detroit, Michigan 48201
(313) 237-7711
Website: www.motorcitycasino.com
Map: **#12**

Toll-Free Number: (877) 777-0711
Rooms: 359 Price Range: $179-$289
Suites: 41 Price Range: $439-$799
Restaurants: 7 (1 open 24 hours)
Buffets: B-$14.00 (Sat/Sun) L-$23.00
         D-$28.00/$39.00 (Mon)
Casino Size: 75,000 Square Feet
Overnight RV Parking: Free/RV Dump: No

Indian Casinos

Indian casinos in Michigan are not required to release information on their slot machine payback percentages. However, according to officials at the Michigan Gaming Control Board, which is responsible for overseeing the tribal-state compacts, "the machines must meet the minimum standards for machines in Nevada or New Jersey." In Nevada the minimum return is 75% and in New Jersey it's 83%. Therefore, Michigan's Indian casinos must return at least 75% in order to comply with the law.

Unless otherwise noted, all Indian casinos in Michigan are open 24 hours and offer the following games: blackjack, craps, roulette, slots and video poker. Other games offered include: Spanish 21 (S21), craps (C), roulette (R), baccarat (B), mini-baccarat (MB), poker (P), Caribbean stud poker (CSP), let it ride (LIR), three-card poker (TCP), four-card poker (FCP), Mississippi stud (MS), keno (K) and bingo (BG).

The minimum gambling age is 19 at all five Kewadin casinos, plus the Odawa casino resort in Petoskey. It is 21 at all other Indian casinos except for the following seven where it's 18: Leelanau Sands, Turtle Creek, Island Resort, Ojibwa, Ojibwa II, Lac Vieux and Soaring Eagle. Valet parking is free at all casinos.

For more information on visiting Michigan call the state's department of tourism at (800) 543-2937 or go to www.michigan.org.

Bay Mills Resort & Casino
11386 Lakeshore Drive
Brimley, Michigan 49715
(906) 248-3715
Website: www.4baymills.com
Map: **#3** (12 miles S.W. of Sault Ste. Marie)

Toll-Free Number: (888) 422-9645
Rooms: 142 Price Range: $56-$169
Suites: 4 Price Range: $150-$220
Restaurants: 5 (1 open 24 hours) Liquor: Yes
Buffets: B-$8.99 L- $10.99/$11.49 (Sun)
      D-$13.99/$24.99 (Tue/Fri)
Casino Size: 15,000 Square Feet
Other Games: P, CSP, LIR, TCP, BG
Overnight RV Parking: Must use RV park
Special Features: 76-space RV park ($21/$29 with hookups). 18-hole golf course.

FireKeepers Casino
11177 East Michigan Ave
Battle Creek, Michigan 49014
(269) 962-0000
Website: www.firekeeperscasino.com
Map: **#18**

Toll-Free Number: (877) 352-8777
Valet Parking: $3/Free for slot club members
Restaurants: 5 Liquor: Yes
Buffets: L-$15.95 D-$19.95/$24.95 (Fri-Sun)
Casino Size: 107,000 Square Feet
Other Games: MB, TCP, LIR, PGP, P, BG, MS
Overnight RV Parking: Free/RV Dump: No
Special Features: Sports bar. Dance club. Food court. Buffet discount with players club card.

Four Winds Dowagiac
580100 M-51
Dowagiac, Michigan 49047
(269) 926-4500
Website: www.fourwindscasino.com
Map: **#21** (110 miles E. of Chicago)

Toll-Free Number: (866) 494-6371
Rooms: 242 Price Range: $180-$210
Restaurants: 1 Liquor: Yes Valet Parking: Free
Other Games: MS
Overnight RV Parking: Free/RV Dump: No

Four Winds Hartford
68600 Red Arrow Highway
Hartford, Michigan 49057
(269) 926-4500
Website: www.fourwindscasino.com
Map: **#21** (110 miles E. of Chicago)

Toll-Free Number: (866) 494-6371
Restaurants: 1 Liquor: Yes Valet Parking: Free
Casino Size: 52,000 Square Feet
Other Games: No craps, MB, TCP, MS
Overnight RV Parking: Free/RV Dump: No

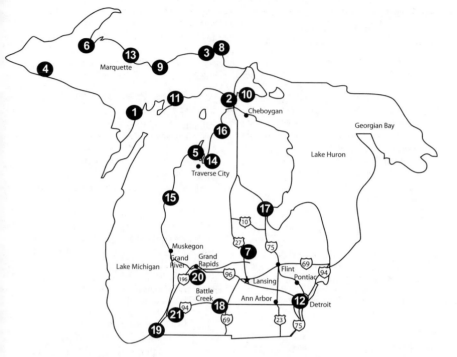

Four Winds New Buffalo
11111 Wilson Rd.
New Buffalo, Michigan 49117
(269) 926-4500
Website: www.fourwindscasino.com
Map: **#19** (60 miles E. of Chicago)

Toll-Free Number: (866) 494-6371
Rooms: 415 Price Range: $179-$349
Suites: 36 Price Range: $199-$549
Restaurants: 5   Liquor: Yes
Buffets: B-$22.00 (Sat/Sun)
      L- $18.00 D-$22.00/$28.00 (Thu/Fri)/
          $34.00 (Sat)
Casino Size: 135,000 Square Feet
Other Games: B, MB, P, LIR, MS,
        TCP, FCP, PGP
Overnight RV Parking: Free/RV Dump: No

Gun Lake Casino
1123 129th Ave
Wayland, Michigan 49348
(269) 792-7777
Website: www.gunlakecasino.com

Map: **#20** (23 miles S of Grand Rapids)

Toll-free Number: (866) 398-7111
Restaurants: 1 Liquor: Yes Valet Parking: Free
Casino Size: 30,000 Square Feet
Other Games: B, LIR, FCP, MS
Overnight RV Parking: Free/RV Dump: No
Special Features: Food court with four fast food outlets.

Island Resort & Casino
W399 US Highway 2 and US Highway 41
Harris, Michigan 49845
(906) 466-2941
Website: www.islandresortandcasino.com
Map: **#1** (13 miles W. of Escanaba on Hwy. 41)

Toll-Free Number: (800) 682-6040
Rooms: 102 Price Range: $79-$119
Suites: 11 Price Range: $129-$379
Restaurants: 3 Liquor: Yes
Casino Size: 135,000 Square Feet
Overnight RV Parking: Must use RV park
Other Games: S21, P, TCP, FCP, LIR, BG
Special Features: 53-space RV park ($20 per night). RV Park Opened seasonally May 1- Nov 31.

Kewadin Casino - Christmas
N7761 Candy Cane Lane
Munising, Michigan 49862
(906) 387-5475
Website: www.kewadin.com
Map: **#9** (40 miles E. of Marquette)

Toll-Free Number: (800) 539-2346
Restaurants: 1 Liquor: Yes
Hours: 9am-1am/3am (Fri/Sat)
Valet Parking: Not offered
Casino Size: 3,060 Square Feet
Other Games: LIR, TCP, No craps/roulette
Overnight RV Parking: Free/RV Dump: No
Special Features: Free local-area shuttle service.

Kewadin Casino - Hessel
3 Mile Road
Hessel, Michigan 49745
(906) 484-2903
Website: www.kewadin.com
Map: **#10** (20 miles N.E. of St. Ignace)

Toll-Free Number: (800) 539-2346
Restaurants: 1 Deli Liquor: Yes
Valet Parking: Not offered
Hours: 9am-11pm/Midnight (Fri/Sat)
Casino Size: 6,500 Square Feet
Other Games: Only gaming machines
Overnight RV Parking: Must use RV Park
Special Features: 40-space RV park open May-October ($5/$10 with hook-ups per night).

Kewadin Casino - Manistique
US 2 East, Rte 1
Manistique, Michigan 49854
(906) 341-5510
Website: www.kewadin.com
Map: **#11** (95 miles S.E. of Marquette)

Toll-Free Number: (800) 539-2346
Restaurants: 1 Deli Liquor: Yes
Valet Parking: Not offered
Hours: 9am-1am/3am (Fri/Sat)
Casino Size: 25,000 Square Feet
Other Games: LIR, TCP, No Craps
Overnight RV Parking: Free/RV Dump: No
Special Features: Free shuttle service from local motels. No table games Mon/Tue.

Kewadin Casino Hotel - Sault Ste. Marie
2186 Shunk Road
Sault Ste. Marie, Michigan 49783
(906) 632-0530
Website: www.kewadin.com
Map: **#8**

Toll-Free Number: (800) 539-2346
Rooms: 300 Price Range: $85-$105
Suites: 20 Price Range: $115-$130
Restaurants: 2 Liquor: Yes
Buffets: B-$8.49/$11.99 (Sun) L-$9.99
D-$14.99/$24.95 (Sat)
Casino Size: 85,123 Square Feet
Other Games: P, LIR, TCP, K, BG
Overnight RV Parking: Must use RV park
Senior Discount: Various Thu 7am-7pm if 50+.
Special Features: Free shuttle service to local motels and airport. 75-space RV park ($10-$12 per night).

Kewadin Casino - St. Ignace
3039 Mackinaw Trail
St. Ignace, Michigan 49781
(906) 643-7071
Website: www.kewadin.com
Map: **#2** (50 miles S. of Sault Ste. Marie)

Toll-Free Number: (800) 539-2346
Rooms: 81 Prices: $105-$120
Suites: 11 Prices: $135-$160
Restaurants: 1 Deli Liquor: Yes
Buffets: B-$8.49 (Sat/Sun) L-$11.99
        D-$14.99/$19.99 (Fri)/$24.99 (Sat)
Casino Size: 56,168 Square Feet
Other Games: P, LIR, TCP, FCP, K
Overnight RV Parking: Must use RV Park.
Senior Discount: Various Thu 7am-7pm if 50+.
Special Features: Local motels/hotels offer packages with free shuttle service. Sports bar. 21-space RV park ($10 per night).

Kings Club Casino
12140 W. Lakeshore Drive
Brimley, Michigan 49715
(906) 248-3700
Website: www.4baymills.com
Map: **#3** (12 miles S.W. of Sault Ste. Marie)

Toll-Free Number: (888) 422-9645
Restaurants: 3 Liquor: Yes
Valet Parking: Not offered
Casino Size: 6,500 Square Feet
Other Games: BG, no blackjack, craps or roulette
Overnight RV Parking: Must use RV park
Senior Discount: Various Tue 10am-10pm if 50+.
Special Features: Two miles from, and affiliated with, Bay Mills Resort & Casino. 75-space RV park ($21/$29 w/hookup) at Bay Mills.

Lac Vieux Desert Casino
N 5384 US 45 North
Watersmeet, Michigan 49969
(906) 358-4226
Website: www.lvdcasino.com
Map: **#4** (49 miles S.E. of Ironwood)

Toll-Free Number: (800) 583-3599
Room Reservations: (800) 895-2505
Rooms: 107 Price Range: $65-$75
Suites: 25 Price Range: $105-$115
Restaurants: 1 Liquor: Yes
Valet Parking: Not offered
Buffets: L/D-$8.95/$14.99 (Fri/Sat)
Casino Size: 25,000 Square Feet
Other Games: P, BG
Overnight RV Parking: Must use RV park
Senior Discount: 10% off in restaurant if 55+
Special Features: 9-hole golf course. 14-space RV park ($15 per night).

Leelanau Sands Casino & Lodge
2521 N.W. Bayshore Drive
Peshawbestown, Michigan 49682
(231) 534-8100
Website: www.casino2win.com
Map: **#5** (4 miles N. of Sutton's Bay)

Toll-Free Number: (800) 922-2946
Room Reservations: (800) 930-3008
Rooms: 51 Price Range: $120-$160
Suites: 2 Price Range: $160-$180
Restaurants: 2 Liquor: Yes
Buffets: B-$7.95/$11.95 (Sun)
        L-$11.95
Casino Size: 29,000 Square Feet
Hours: 8am-2am Daily
Other Games: TCP, LIR, BG (Sun/Wed-Fri)
Overnight RV Parking: Free/RV Dump: No
Senior Discount: Various on Thu if 55+.
Special Features: RV hook-ups available for $7 per night.

Little River Casino Resort
2700 Orchard Drive
Manistee, Michigan 49660
(231) 723-1535
Website: www.lrcr.com
Map: **#15** (60 miles S.W of Traverse City)

Toll-Free Number: (888) 568-2244
Rooms: 271 Price Range: $130-$160
Suites: 20 Price Range: $250-$260
Restaurants: 3 Liquor: Yes
Buffets: B-$9.99 L-$11.99
    D-$13.99/$24.99 (Fri/Sat)
Casino Size: 75,000 Square Feet
Other Games: LIR, TCP, MS, BG (Sun-Wed).
Overnight RV Parking: Free/RV Dump: Free
Special Features: 95-space RV park open
April-November ($16-$36 per night).

Odawa Casino Resort
1760 Lears Road
Petoskey, Michigan 49770
(231) 439-9100
Website: www.odawacasino.com
Map: **#16** (50 miles S.W of Cheboygan)

Toll-Free Number: (877) 442-6464
Rooms: 127 Price Range: $89-$139
Suites: 10 Price Range- $119-$169
Restaurants: 4 Liquor: Yes
Buffets: B-$10.95 (Sun)
    L-$10.95/$15.95 (Sun)
    D-$18.95/$25.95 (Thu)
Casino Size: 33,000 Square Feet
Other Games: LIR, P, TCP
Overnight RV Parking: Free/RV Dump: No
Senior Discount: Various Wed/Sun 8am-8pm
    if 55+
Special Features: Hotel is 1/4-mile from
casino and rooms offer views of Little
Traverse Bay. Free shuttle service to/from
local hotels.

Ojibwa Casino Resort - Baraga
797 Michigan Avenue
Baraga, Michigan 49908
(906) 353-6333
Website: www.ojibwacasino.com
Map: **#6** (30 miles S. of Houghton)

Toll-Free Number: (800) 323-8045
Rooms: 78 Price Range: $69-$89
Suites: 2 Price Range: $79-$99
Restaurants: 1 Liquor: Yes
Casino Size: 17,000 Square Feet
Other Games: TCP, LIR, BG (Tue/Thu)
Overnight RV Parking: Must use RV park
Senior Discount: Various Mon 11am-2pm if 55+.
Special Features: 12-space RV Park ($20 per
night). 8-lane bowling alley. Table games open
Friday-Sunday.

Ojibwa Casino - Marquette
105 Acre Trail
Marquette, Michigan 49855
(906) 249-4200
Website: www.ojibwacasino.com
Map: **#13**

Toll-Free Number: (888) 560-9905
Restaurants: 1 Snack Bar Liquor: Yes
Valet Parking: Not offered
Other Games: P
Overnight RV Parking: Free/RV Dump: Yes
Senior Discount: Various Mon 10-5 if 55+
Special features: 7-space RV Park (Free).
Table games open 2pm-2am/4am (Fri/Sat).

Saganing Eagles Landing Casino
2690 Worth Road
Standish, Michigan 48658
(888) 732-4537
Website: www.saganing-eagleslanding.com
Map: #**#17**

Casino Size: 32,000 Square Feet
Restaurants: 7 Valet Parking: Free
Overnight RV Parking: Must stay in RV park
Special Features: Subway restaurant.
Electronic versions of blackjack and roulette.
50-space RV park ($15 per night).

Soaring Eagle Casino & Resort
6800 E Soaring Eagle Boulevard
Mount Pleasant, Michigan 48858
(517) 775-5777
Website: www.soaringeaglecasino.com
Map: **#7** (65 miles N. of Lansing)

Toll-Free Number: (888) 732-4537
Room Reservations: (877) 232-4532
Rooms: 491 Price Range: $180-$385
Suites: 21 Price Range: $199-$449
Restaurants: 5   Liquor: Yes
Buffets: L-$17.75 D-$19.75
Casino Size: 150,000 Square Feet
Other Games: P, MB, CSP, LIR, TCP, FCP,
          BG (Wed-Mon), B6, K, MS
Overnight RV Parking: Free/RV Dump: No
Special Features: Casino is in two separate
buildings. Kids Quest childcare center. Video
arcade. Gift shop. Art gallery. Off property
RV park with free shuttle ($47-$72 per night).

Turtle Creek Casino
7741 M-72 East
Williamsburg, Michigan 49690
(231) 534-8888
Website: www.turtlecreekcasino.com
Map: **#14** (8 miles E. of Traverse City)

Toll-Free Number: (888) 777-8946
Rooms: 127 Price Range: $180-$230
Suites: 10 Price Range: $350-$400
Restaurants: 2 Liquor: Yes Valet Parking: Free
Buffets: B-$8.95 D-$18.95/$27.95 (Mon/Wed)
Casino Size: 72,000 Square Feet
Other Games: CSP, LIR, P, TCP, FCP,
          BG (Wed/Thu/Fri/Sun)
Overnight RV Parking: Free/RV Dump: No

MINNESOTA

All Minnesota casinos are located on Indian reservations and under a compact reached with the state the only table games permitted are card games such as blackjack and poker. Additionally, the only kind of slot machines allowed are the electronic video variety. Therefore, you will not find any mechanical slots that have traditional reels - only video screens.

According to the terms of the compact between the state and the tribes, however, the minimum and maximum payouts are regulated as follows: video poker and video blackjack - 83% to 98%, slot machines - 80% to 95%, keno - 75% to 95%. Each tribe is free to set its machines to pay back anywhere within those limits and the tribes do not not release any information regarding their slot machine percentage paybacks.

The hours of operation are listed for those casinos that are not open on a 24-hour basis. Unless otherwise noted, all casinos offer: video slots, video poker, video keno and blackjack. Optional games include: poker (P), Caribbean stud poker (CSP), pai gow poker (PGP), three-card poker (TCP), Mississippi stud (MS), let it ride (LIR) and bingo (BG).

The minimum gambling age is 18 at all casinos. Valet parking is free at all casinos except Jackpot Junction and Mystic Lake.

For more information on visiting Minnesota call the state's office of tourism at (800) 657-3700 or go to www.exploreminnesota.com.

Black Bear Casino Resort
1785 Highway 210
Carlton, Minnesota 55718
(218) 878-2327
Website: www.blackbearcasinoresort.com
Map: **#1** (130 miles N. of Twin Cities)

Toll-Free Number: (888) 771-0777
Reservation Number: (800) 553-0022
Rooms: 158 Price Range: $50-$110
Suites: 60 Price Range: $60-$150
Restaurants: 2 (open 24 hours) Liquor: Yes
Buffets: B-$8.99 L-$7.99 D-$11.99/
    $17.99 (Thu)/$14.99 (Fri)/$12.99 (Sat)
Casino Size: 65,000 Square Feet
Other Games: P, BG
Overnight RV Parking: Free/RV Dump: No
Senior Discount: Various Mon if 52+
Special Features: Golf Course. Arcade.

Fond-du-Luth Casino
129 E. Superior Street
Duluth, Minnesota 55802
(218) 722-0280
Website: www.fondduluthcasino.com
Map: **#3** (150 miles N.E. of Twin Cities)

Toll-Free Number: (800) 873-0280
Restaurants: 2 Snack Bars Liquor: Yes
Casino Size: 20,000 Square Feet
Other Games: Only Blackjack and Slots
Overnight RV Parking: No
Senior Discount: Various Tue 10am-5pm if 55+
Special Features: One hour free parking in lot adjacent to casino (must be validated in casino). Free shuttle to/from Black Bear Casino.

Fortune Bay Resort/Casino
1430 Bois Forte Road
Tower, Minnesota 55790
(218) 753-6400
Website: www.fortunebay.com
Map: **#4** (150 miles N.E. of Twin Cities. 24 miles N.E. of Virginia, MN on the S. shore of Lake Vermilion)

Toll-Free Number: (800) 992-7529
Hotel Reservations: (800) 555-1714
Rooms: 83 Price Range: $85-$155
Suites: 33 Price Range: $95-$350
Restaurants: 4 Liquor: Yes Valet: Free
Buffets: B-$8.95/$15.95 (Sat/Sun) L-$9.95
      D-$16.95/$25.95(Fri/Sat)
Casino Size: 17,000 Square Feet
Other Games: MS, BG (Wed/Fri-Sun)
Overnight RV Parking: Must use RV park
Senior Discount: Specials Mon/Thu if 55+.
Special Features: Located on S.E. shore of Lake Vermilion. 84-slip marina. 36-space RV Park ($25-$30 per night). Snowmobile and hiking trails. 18-hole golf course.

Grand Casino Hinckley
777 Lady Luck Drive
Hinckley, Minnesota 55037
(320) 384-7777
Website: www.grandcasinomn.com
Map: **#5** (75 miles N. of Twin Cities. One mile E. of I-35's Hinckley exit on Hwy. 48)

Toll-Free Number: (800) 472-6321
Hotel/RV/Chalet Reservations: (800) 995-4726
Rooms: 485 Price Range: $80-$150 (Hotel)
      Price Range: $50-$100 (Inn)
      Price Range: $80-$120 (Chalet)
Suites: 52 Price Range: $99-$202
Restaurants: 6 Liquor: Yes Valet: Free
Buffets: B-$11.99 (Sat/Sun) L-$9.99
    D-$13.99/$15.99 (Wed)/$23.99 (Thu)/
    $16.99(Fri/Sat)
Casino Size: 54,800 Square Feet
Other Games: P, BG (Thu-Mon)
Overnight RV Parking: Must use RV park
Special Features: 222-space RV park ($27 per night/$35 Fri/Sat). Kids Quest childcare center. 18-hole golf course. Free pet kennel.

Grand Casino Mille Lacs
777 Grand Avenue
Onamia, Minnesota 56359
(320) 532-7777
Website: www.grandcasinomn.com
Map: **#6** (90 miles N. of Twin Cities. On Highway 169 on the W. shore of Lake Mille Lacs)

Toll-Free Number: (800) 626-5825
Room Reservations: (800) 468-3517
Rooms: 284 Price Range: $49-$155
Suites: 14 Price Range: $89-$389
Restaurants: 4 Liquor: No Valet Parking: Free
Buffets: Brunch-$10.99 (Sat/Sun) L-$8.99
   D-$12.99/$14.99 (Wed)/$22.99 (Fri)
   $15.99(Sat)/$19.99 (Sun)
Casino Size: 42,000 Square Feet
Other Games: P, BG, MS
Overnight RV Parking: Free/RV Dump: No
Special Features: Resort has two hotels (one is off-property). Kids Quest childcare center. Free pet kennel.

Grand Portage Lodge & Casino
70 Casino Drive
Grand Portage, Minnesota 55605
(218) 475-2401
Website: www.grandportage.com
Map: **#7** (N.E. tip of Minnesota. 300 miles N. of Twin Cities. On Highway 61, five miles from the Canadian border)

Reservation Number: (800) 543-1384
Rooms: 90 Price Range: $49-$129
Suites: 10 Price Range: $125-$205
Restaurants: 2 Liquor: Yes
Valet Parking: Not Offered
Casino Size: 15,268 Square Feet
Other Games: BG (Tue/Fri), No Blackjack
Overnight RV Parking: Must use RV park
Special Features: On shore of Lake Superior. Hiking, skiing and snowmobile trails. Gift shop. Marina. 10-space RV park open June-Sept ($30 per night). Free shuttle service to/from Thunder Bay, Ontario.

Jackpot Junction Casino Hotel
39375 County Highway 24
Morton, Minnesota 56270
(507) 697-8000
Website: www.jackpotjunction.com
Map: **#8** (110 miles S.W. of Twin Cities)

Toll-Free Number: (800) 946-2274
Rooms: 253 Price Range: $49-$89
Suites: 23 Price Range: $95-$135
Restaurants: 4 (1 open 24 hours) Liquor: Yes
Buffets: B-$8.99/$13.00(Sun) L-$9.25
   D-$12.25/$13.25 (Sat)
Valet Parking: Not Offered
Other Games: P, TCP, BG
Senior Discount: Various Wed if 50+
Overnight RV Parking: Must use RV park.
Special Features: 70-space RV park ($25-$35 per night). Kids Quest childcare center. 18-hole golf course. Gift shop. No bingo on Wednesdays.

Little Six Casino
2354 Sioux Trail N.W.
Prior Lake, Minnesota 55372
(952) 445-9000 (Mystic Lake)
Website: www.littlesixcasino.com
Map: **#10** (25 miles S.W. of Twin Cities. On County Road 83)

Toll-Free: (800) 262-7799 (Mystic Lake)
Restaurants: 1 Liquor: No
Special Features: 1/4-mile north of Mystic Lake Casino.

Mystic Lake Casino Hotel
2400 Mystic Lake Boulevard
Prior Lake, Minnesota 55372
(952) 445-9000
Website: www.mysticlake.com
Map: **#10** (25 miles S.W. of Twin Cities. On
County Road 83, 3 miles S. of Hwy 169)

Toll-Free Number: (800) 262-7799
Hotel Reservations: (800) 813-7349
RV Reservations: (800) 653-2267
Rooms: 400 Price Range: $95-$189
Suites: 16 Price Range: $179-$400
Restaurants: 6 Liquor: Yes
Buffets: L-$11.95/$15.95 (Sat)/$19.95 (Sun)
    D-$16.95/$29.95 (Wed)/$22.95 (Fri)/
    $18.95(Sat)
Valet Parking: Free
Casino Size: 102,000 Square Feet
Other Games: BG
Overnight RV Parking: Must use RV Park
Senior Discount: Various Thu 8-11am if 55+
Special Features: Free shuttle bus service from
Twin Cities area. Also has a second casino -
Dakota Country with 45,000-square-feet of
gaming space. 122-space RV park ($33 per
night spring/summer, $21 fall/winter). Health
club. Childcare facility.

Northern Lights Casino & Hotel
6800 Y Frontage Rd NW
Walker, Minnesota 56484
(218) 547-2744
Website: www.northernlightscasino.com
Map: **#11** (175 miles N. of the Twin Cities.
Near the S. shore of Lake Leech four miles S.
of Walker, MN at the junction of Highways
371 & 200)

Toll-Free Number: (800) 252-7529
Room Reservations: (866) 652-4683
Rooms: 105 Price Range: $100-$120
Suites: 4 Price Range: $120-$190
Restaurants: 2 Liquor: Yes Valet Parking: Free
Buffets: L-$8.50/$9.95 (Sat/Sun)
    D-$11.50/$24.95 (Thu)/
    $13.95 (Sun)
Casino Size: 40,000 Square Feet
Other Games: P
Overnight RV Parking: Free/RV Dump: No
Senior Discount: Various Mon 8am-12am if 50+
Special Features: 90-foot dome simulates star
constellations. 20% room discount for players
club members.

Palace Casino & Hotel
6280 Upper Cass Frontage Rd NW
Cass Lake, Minnesota 56633
(218) 335-7000
Website: www.palacecasinohotel.com
Map: **#12** (220 miles N.W. of Twin Cities)

Toll-Free Number: (877) 972-5223
Room Reservations: (800) 442-3910
Rooms: 64 Price Range: $73-$102
Suites: 16 Price Range $92-$121
Restaurants: 2 Liquor: No
Buffet: L-$8.25 D-$13.95/$14.99 (Fri)/
    $16.99 (Sat)
Casino Size: 30,000 Square Feet
Other Games: BG
Overnight RV Parking: Free/RV Dump: Free
Senior Discount: Various Tue 8am-mid if 50+
Special Features: 15-space RV park offers free
parking and hookup.

Prairie's Edge Casino Resort
5616 Prairie's Edge Lane
Granite Falls, Minnesota 56241
(320) 564-2121
Website: www.prairiesedgecasino.com
Map: **#2** (110 miles W. of Twin Cities. Five
miles S.E. of Granite Falls on Highway 67 E.)

Toll-Free Number: (866) 293-2121
Rooms: 79 Price Range: $59-$89
Suites: 10 Price Range: $129-$159
Restaurants: 2 Liquor: Yes
Buffets: B-$12.95 (Sun)
    D-$11.95/$12.95 (Sat)
Valet Parking: Not Offered
Casino Size: 36,000 Square Feet
Other Games: P
Overnight RV Parking: Must use RV Park
Special Features: 55-space RV park ($16 per
night/$24 with hookups). Convenience store.
Non-smoking slot area. No buffet Mon/Tue.

Seven Clans Casino Red Lake
10200 Route 89
Red Lake, Minnesota 56671
(218) 679-2500
Web: www.sevenclanscasino.com
Map: **#16** (200 miles N.W. of Duluth)

Toll-Free Number: (888) 679-2501
Rooms: 40 Prices: $100-$120
Restaurants: 1 Liquor: No
Casino Size: 40,000 Square Feet
Other Games: P
Overnight RV Parking: Free/RV Dump: No
Senior Discount: Special Mon 10am-7pm
if 55+.

Seven Clans Casino Thief River Falls
20595 Center Street East
Thief River Falls, Minnesota 56701
(218) 681-4062
Website: www.sevenclanscasino.com
Map: **#15** (275 miles N.W. of Minneapolis)

Toll-Free Number: (800) 881-0712
Room Reservations: (866) 255-7848
Suites: 151 Price Range: $90-$120
Restaurants: 1 Liquor: No
Buffets: B-$8.95 L/D-$10.95
Valet Parking: Not Offered
Casino Size: 16,000 Square Feet
Other Games: P
Overnight RV Parking: Free/RV Dump: No
Senior Discount: 10% off food if 55+ .
Special features: Indoor water park. Malt shop.

Seven Clans Casino Warroad
1012 E. Lake Street
Warroad, Minnesota 56763
(218) 386-3381
Website: www.sevenclanscasino.com
Map: **#9** (400 miles N.W. of Twin Cities)

Toll-Free Number: (800) 815-8293
Room Reservations: (888) 714-5514
Rooms: 34 Price Range: $55-$90
Suites: 7 Price Range: $70-$120
Restaurants: 1 Liquor: No
Casino Size: 13,608 Square Feet
Other Games: P
Overnight RV Parking: Free/RV Dump: No
Senior Discount: Various Tue 8am-6pm if 55+
Special Features: Hotel is Super 8 located
one mile from casino with free shuttle service
provided.

Shooting Star Casino Hotel
777 Casino Boulevard
Mahnomen, Minnesota 56557
(218) 935-2701
Website: www.starcasino.com
Map: **#13** (250 miles N.W. of Twin Cities)

Room Reservations: (800) 453-7827
Rooms: 360 Price Range: $79-$95
Suites: 30 Price Range: $110-$120
Restaurants: 4 Liquor: Yes
Buffets: B-$7.99 L-$10.50
    D-$12.50/$14.99(Thu)/19.99 (Fri)/
    $16.99 (Sat)
Other Games: P, BG
Overnight RV Parking: Must use RV park
Senior Discount: Various 1st Thu of month if 50+
Special Features: 47-space RV park ($20 per
night). Childcare facility for children up to
12 years of age.

Treasure Island Resort & Casino
5734 Sturgeon Lake Road
Red Wing, Minnesota 55066
(651) 388-6300
Website: www.treasureislandcasino.com
Map: **#14** (40 miles S.E. of Twin Cities.
Halfway between Hastings and Red Wing, off
Highway 61 on County Road 18)

Toll-Free Number: (800) 222-7077
Room/RV Reservations: (888) 867-7829
Restaurants: 4 Liquor: Yes
Rooms: 250 Price Range: $89-$129
Suites: 28 Price Range: $179-$239
Buffets: B-$14.75 (Sat/Sun) L-$10.99
    D-$14.49/$25.00 (Thu)/$16.95 (Fri/Sat)
Valet Parking: $3
Casino Size: 110,000 Square Feet
Other Games: P, PGP, TCP, FCP, BG
Overnight RV Parking: Must use RV Park
Senior Discount: Wed 8am-8pm if 55+.
Special Features: 95-space RV park open
April-October ($27 per night/13 amp $35 per
night/50amp). 137-slip marina. Dinner and
sightseeing cruises. Childcare facility for
children up to 12 years of age.

White Oak Casino
45830 US Hwy 2
Deer River, Minnesota 56636
(218) 246-9600
Website: www.whiteoakcasino.com
Map: **#17** (5 miles N.W. of Grand Rapids)

Toll-Free Number: (800) 653-2412
Restaurants: 1 Snack Bar Liquor: Yes
Casino Size: 11,000 Square Feet
Overnight RV Parking: Free/RV Dump: No
Senior Discount: Various Tue 10am-6pm if 50+

Pari-Mutuels

Minnesota has two racetracks that offer the card games of blackjack, poker, pai gow poker, let it ride, Mississippi stud, Caribbean stud poker, three card poker and four card poker.

The completely nonsmoking card rooms are open 24 hours and admission is free. Players must pay a commission to the card room on each hand played for all games except regular poker, where a rake is taken from each pot. The minimum gambling age is 18.

Canterbury Park
1100 Canterbury Road
Shakopee, Minnesota 55379
(952) 445-7223
Website: www.canterburypark.com
Map: **#10** (22 miles S.W. of Twin Cities)

Horse Track Toll-Free: (800) 340-6361
Card Room Toll-Free: (866) 667-6537
Admission: $5 (for horse racing)
Admission: Free (for card room)
Self-Parking: Free   Valet Parking: $6
Restaurants: 2
Casino Size: 18,000 Square Feet
Overnight RV Parking: Free/RV Dump: No
Special Features: Live horse racing Mid-May through August. Daily simulcasting. Free shuttle service to/from Mall of America.

Running Aces
15201 Zurich Street NE
Columbus, Minnesota 55372
(651) 925-4600
Website: www.runningacesharness.com
Map: **#10** (25 miles S.W. of Twin Cities. On County Road 83)

Toll-Free: (877) 786-2237
Admission: Free
Self Parking: Free   Valet: $4 (Fri-Sun)
Restaurants: 1
Buffets: B-$18.95 (Sun)
               D-$22.95 (Fri)
Other Games: No Caribbean Stud Poker or Let it Ride
Special Features: Live Horse racing mid-May through mid-August.

MISSISSIPPI

Mississippi was the third state to legalize riverboat gambling when it was approved by that state's legislature in 1990. The law restricts casinos to coast waters (including the Bay of St. Louis and the Back Bay of Biloxi) along the Mississippi River and in navigable waters of counties that border the river.

Mississippi law also requires that riverboats be permanently moored at the dock and they are not permitted to cruise. This allows the riverboats to offer 24-hour dockside gambling. The Isle of Capri in Biloxi was the first casino to open on August 1, 1992 followed one month later by The President.

Since the law does not require that the floating vessel actually resemble a boat, almost all of the casinos are built on barges. This gives them the appearance of a land-based building, rather than a riverboat.

Due to the destruction caused by Hurricane Katrina in August 2005, the Mississippi legislature allowed the state's gulf coast casinos to be rebuilt on land within 800-feet of the shoreline and some casinos have been rebuilt in that manner.

The Mississippi Gaming Commission does not break down its slot statistics by individual properties. Rather, they are classified by region. The **Coastal** region includes Biloxi, Gulfport and Bay Saint Louis. The **North** region includes Tunica, Greenville and Lula. The **Central** region includes Vicksburg and Natchez.

With that in mind here's information, as supplied by the Mississippi Gaming Commission, showing the machine payback percentages for each area's casinos for the one-year period from June 1, 2013 through May 31, 2014:

These numbers reflect the percentage of money returned on each denomination of machine and encompass all electronic machines including video poker and video keno. The best returns for each category are highlighted in bold print and you can see that all of the gaming areas offer rather similar returns on their machines.

Unless otherwise noted, all casinos are open 24 hours and offer: slots, video poker, blackjack, craps, roulette and three card poker. Other game listings include: Spanish 21 (S21), baccarat (B), mini-baccarat (MB), poker (P), pai gow poker (PGP), let it ride (LIR), Caribbean stud poker (CSP) Mississippi stud (MS), big six wheel (B6), casino war (CW) and keno (K). The minimum gambling age is 21.

NOTE: If you happen to win a jackpot of $1,200 or more in Mississippi, the casino will deduct 3% of your winnings and pay it to the Mississippi Tax Commission as a gambling tax. The tax is nonrefundable and the $1,200 threshold would also apply to any cash prizes won in casino drawings or tournaments.

For more information on visiting Mississippi call the state's tourism department at (866) 733-6477 or go to: www.visitmississippi.org

For Biloxi tourism information call (800) 237-9493 or go to: www.gulfcoast.org. For Tunica tourism information call (888) 488-6422 or go to: www.tunicatravel.com.

	Coastal	North	Central
1¢ Slots	**91.50%**	91.42%	91.23%
5¢ Slots	94.57%	94.48%	**94.90%**
25¢ Slots	**94.67%**	93.55%	93.68%
$1 Slots	94.06%	**94.77%**	94.45%
$5 Slots	95.06%	95.49%	**95.59%**
All	**92.78%**	92.47%	92.28%

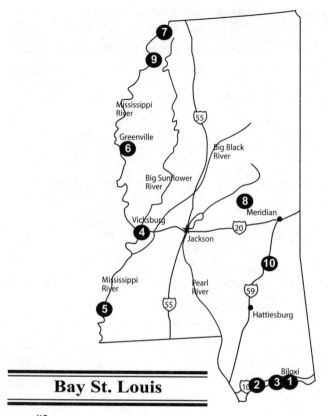

Bay St. Louis

Map: **#2** (on St. Louis Bay, 60 miles E. of New Orleans)

Hollywood Casino Bay St. Louis
711 Hollywood Boulevard
Bay St. Louis, Mississippi 39520
(228) 467-9257
Website: www.hollywoodcasinobsl.com

Toll-Free Number: (866) 758-2591
Rooms: 498 Price Range: $99-$179
Suites: 78 Price Range: Casino Use Only
Restaurants: 4 (1 open 24 hours)
Buffets: B- $9.99 (Sat/Sun)
        L-$12.99/$24.99 (Sat/Sun)
        D-$20.99/$24.99 (Thu-Sun)
Casino Size: 56,300 Square Feet
Other games: PGP, P, MB, MS
Overnight RV Parking: Must use RV park
Special Features: 100-space RV Park ($35/$45 per night). 18-hole golf course.

Silver Slipper Casino
5000 South Beach Boulevard
Bay St. Louis, Mississippi 39520
(228) 469-2777
Website: www.silverslipper-ms.com

Toll-Free Number: (866) 775-4773
Restaurants: 3 (1 open 24 hours)
Buffets: L-$13.95/ $26.95 (Sun)
        D-$14.95/$26.95 (Thu-Sun)
Casino Size: 36,826 Square Feet
Other Games: K, P, PGP, MB, MS
Overnight RV Parking: Must use RV park.
Special Features: Land-based casino. 24-space RV park ($25-$35 per night) $2 buffet discount for players club members.

Biloxi

Map: **#1** (On the Gulf of Mexico, 90 miles E. of New Orleans)

Beau Rivage Resort & Casino
875 Beach Boulevard
Biloxi, Mississippi 39530
(228) 386-7111
Website: www.beaurivageresort.com

Toll-Free Number: (888) 750-7111
Room Reservations: (888) 567-6667
Rooms: 1,740 Price Range: $120-$300
Suites: 95 Price Range: $220-$450
Restaurants: 10 (1 open 24 hours)
Buffets: B- $11.99 L-$14.99/$20.99(Sat/Sun)
        D- $21.99/$24.99 (Thu)/$29.99 (Fri/Sat)
Casino Size: 75,744 Square Feet
Other Games: MB, PGP, P, CSP, LIR
Overnight RV Parking: No
Special Features: Casino is on a barge. 18-hole golf course. Spa. Beauty salon. 13-store shopping arcade.

Boomtown Casino - Biloxi
676 Bayview Avenue
Biloxi, Mississippi 39530
(228) 435-7000
Website: www.boomtownbiloxi.com

Toll-Free Number: (800) 627-0777
Restaurants: 4 (1 open 24 hours)
Buffets: L-$12.99/$24.99 (Sat/Sun)
        D-$18.99/$13.99 (Wed)/
        $21.95 (Thu)/$24.95 (Fri-Sun)
Casino Size: 51,665 Square Feet
Other Games: MS, PGP
Overnight RV Parking: Free/RV Dump: No
Special Features: Casino is on a barge.

Golden Nugget - Biloxi
151 Beach Boulevard
Biloxi, Mississippi 39530
(228) 435-5400
Website: www.goldennugget.com/Biloxi

Toll-Free Number: (800) 777-7568
Rooms: 541 Price Range: $99-$219
Suites: 200 Price Range: $119-$279
Restaurants: 4 (1 open 24 hours)
Buffets: B-$9.99
        L-$17.99/$22.99 (Sun)
        D-$19.99/$27.99 (Thu-Sun)
Casino Size: 54,728 Square Feet
Other Games: P, MS, MG, PGP
Overnight RV Parking: Free/RV Dump: No
Senior Discount: Various Sun/Mon/Thu if 50+
Special Features: Land-based casino. Spa. Beauty salon. Golf packages offered. Food court with several fast food outlets.

Hard Rock Hotel & Casino - Biloxi
777 Beach Boulevard
Biloxi, Mississippi 39530
(228) 374-7625
Website: www.hardrockbiloxi.com

Toll-Free Number: (877) 877-6256
Rooms: 306 Prices: $99-$450
Suites: 64 Prices: $229-$629
Restaurants: 4 (1 open 24 hours)
Buffets: B-$11.99 L-$12.99
        D-$21.99/$24.99 (Fri/Sat)
Casino Size: 53,800 Square Feet
Other Games: MB, P, PGP, MS
Overnight RV Parking: No
Special Features: Casino is on a barge. Spa. Nightclub. Collection of rock and roll memorabilia on display.

Harrah's Gulf Coast
265 Beach Boulevard
Biloxi, Mississippi 39530
(228) 436-2946
Website: www.harrahsgulfcoast.com

Toll-Free Number: (800) 946-2946
Rooms: 500 Price Range: $80-$220
Suites: 40 Price Range: $239-$509
Restaurants: 8 (1 open 24 hours)
Buffets: B-$9.99/$14.99 (Sat/Sun) L-$12.99
          D-$19.99/$28.99 (Fri/Sat)/$23.99 (Sun)
Casino Size: 31,275 Square Feet
Other Games: MB, PGP, LIR, MS
Overnight RV Parking: Free/RV Dump: No
Special Features: Land-based casino. 18-hole
golf course. Spa. Beauty salon. Starbucks.

IP Casino Resort Spa
850 Bayview Avenue
Biloxi, Mississippi 39530
(228) 436-3000
Website: www.ipbiloxi.com

Toll-Free Number: (888) 946-2847
Rooms: 1,088 Price Range: $100-$400
Suites: 14 Price Range: $200-$600
Restaurants: 8 (1 open 24 hours)
Buffets: B-$12.00/$18.00 (Sat/Sun) L-$15.00
          D-$22.00/ $29.00 (Fri/Sat)/
          $24.00 (Sun)
Casino Size: 81,733 Square Feet
Other Games: MB, PGP, LIR, MS, P
Overnight RV Parking: Free (Check in with
          security first)/RV Dump: No
Special Features: Casino is on a barge.

Palace Casino Resort
158 Howard Avenue
Biloxi, Mississippi 39530
(228) 432-8888
Website: www.palacecasinoresort.com

Toll-Free Number: (800) 925-2239
Rooms: 234 Price Range: $89-$249
Suites: 14 Price Range: $500-$525
Restaurants: 3 (1 open 24 hours)
Buffets: B-$9.99 L-$14.99/$21.99 (Sun)
          D-$21.99/$28.99 (Sat)
Casino Size: 38,000 Square Feet
Other Games: PGP, MS
Overnight RV Parking: No
Special Features: Land-based casino. 10-slip
marina. 100% smoke-free casino.

Treasure Bay Casino and Hotel
1980 Beach Boulevard
Biloxi, Mississippi 39531
(228) 385-6000
Website: www.treasurebay.com

Toll-Free Number: (800) 747-2839
Rooms: 234 Price Range: $89-$179
Suites: 14 Price Range: $229-$259
Restaurants: 5 (1 open 24 hours)
Buffets: B-$8.99 L-$11.99 D-$24.99
Casino Size: 28,140 Square Feet
Other Games: PGP, CSP, LIR, MS
Overnight RV Parking: No
Special Features: Land-based casino.

Greenville

Map: **#6** (On the Mississippi River, 121 miles
N.W. of Jackson)

Harlow's Casino Resort
4250 Highway 82 West
Greenville, Mississippi 38701
(228) 436-4753
Website: www.harlowscasino.com

Toll-Free Number: (866) 524-5825
Rooms: 105 Price Range: $99-$165
Suites: 45 Price Range: $149-$210
Restaurants: 4 (1 open 24 hours)
Buffets: B-$12.99 (Sat/Sun) L-$11.49
          D-$14.99/$24.99 (Fri/Sat)
Casino Size: 33,000 Square Feet
Other Games: P, MS, no Three Card Poker
Overnight RV Parking: Free/RV Dump: No
Special Features: Land-based casino.

Trop Casino Greenville
240 S Walnut Street
Greenville, Mississippi 38701
(662) 334-7711
Website: www.tropgreenville.com

Toll-Free Number: (800) 878-1777
Hotel Reservations: (800) 228-2800
Restaurants: 1   Valet Parking: No
Casino Size: 21,318 Square Feet
Other Games: No roulette
Overnight RV Parking: Free/RV Dump: No
Senior Discount: Various Thursdays if 50+
Special Features: Casino is on an actual
paddlewheel boat.

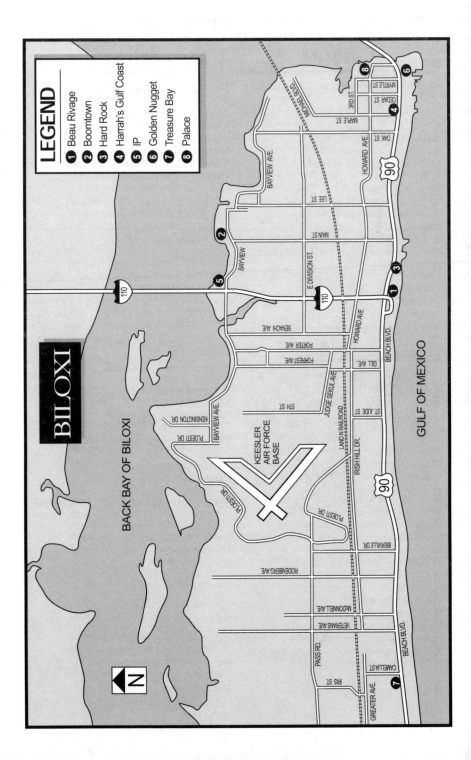

Gulfport

Map: **#3** (On the Gulf of Mexico, 80 miles E. of New Orleans)

Island View Casino Resort
3300 W. Beach Boulevard
Gulfport, Mississippi 39501
(228) 314-2100
Website: www.islandviewcasino.com

Toll-Free Number: (800) 817-9089
Rooms: 600 Price Range: $109-$199
Restaurants: 3 (1 open 24 hours) Valet: Free
Buffets: B-$10.99 L-$12.99/$14.99(Sun)
D-$23.99
Casino Size: 82,935 Square Feet
Other Games: LIR, PGP, MS, MB
Overnight RV Parking: Free/RV Dump: No
Special Features: Land-based casino.

Lula

Map **#9** (On the Mississippi River, 70 miles S. of Memphis, TN)

Isle of Capri Casino & Hotel - Lula
777 Isle of Capri Parkway
Lula, Mississippi 38644
(662) 363-4600
Website: www.isleofcapricasino.com

Toll-Free Number: (800) 789-5825
Toll-Free Number: (800) 843-4753
Rooms: 485 Price Range: $59-$299
Suites: 40 Price Range: Casino Use Only
Restaurants: 3
Buffets: B-$8.99 (Sat/Sun) L-$10.99
D-$15.99/$22.99 (Fri)/$23.99 (Sat)
Casino Size: 63,500 Square Feet
Other Games: MS
Overnight RV Parking: $16.30 per night.
Senior Discount: Various on Wed if 50+.
Special Features: 28-space RV Park ($15 per night. First night free if staying two or more) Video arcade. Fitness center.

Natchez

Map: **#5** (on the Mississippi River, 102 miles S.W. of Jackson)

Isle of Capri Casino & Hotel - Natchez
53 Silver Street
Natchez, Mississippi 39120
(601) 445-0605
Website: www.isleofcapricasino.com

Toll-Free Number: (800) 722-5825
Rooms: 138 Price Range: $59-$129
Suites: 5 Price Range: Casino Use Only
Restaurants: 1
Buffets: L-$7.99 D-$11.99/$14.99 (Fri/Sat)
Casino Size: 17,634 Square Feet
Other Games: No roulette
Overnight RV Parking: No
Senior Discount: Various if 50+.
Special Features: Casino is built on barge that resembles 1860s paddlewheeler. Hotel is across street with free shuttle service to/ from casino.

Magnolia Bluffs Casino
521 Main Street
Natchez, Mississippi 39120
(601) 442-2220
Website: www.magnoliabluffscasino.com

Toll-Free Number: (888) 505-5777
Casino Size: 16,032 Square Feet
Restaurants: 3
Buffets: L-$11.00 D-$14.00/$15.00 (Fri/Sat)

The Best Places To Play On The Gulf Coast
(Biloxi and Gulfport Only)

Roulette - The house edge on a single-zero wheel cuts the house edge from 5.26% down to a more reasonable 2.70%. Unfortunately, there are no casinos on the Gulf Coast that offer single-zero roulette.

Craps - IP and Boomtown are the most liberal of all gulf coast casinos by offering 20X odds on their craps games. All other casinos offer 10X odds.

Blackjack - Gulf Coast casinos offer some decent blackjack games with liberal rules, but all of the casinos hit soft 17, except for Treasure Bay. Hitting soft 17 results in an extra mathematical advantage of .20% for the house. All of the recommendations in this section apply to players using perfect basic strategy for each particular game.

The best single-deck game can be found at the Isle of Capri where the dealer hits on soft 17 and doubling down is only allowed totals of 10 or more. The casino advantage in this game is .48%. Five other casinos also offer a single-deck game, but all should be avoided because they all pay 6-to-5 rather than the standard 3-to-2 for winning blackjacks. The casino edge in all of these games is more than 1.40%.

Treasure Bay is the best double-deck game, with the following rules: stand on soft 17, double down on any first two cards, re-split any pair (including aces) and doubling allowed after splitting. This works out to a casino edge of just .14%. Next best is Harrah's which has similar rules, except they hit soft 17, which brings the casino edge up to .34%. A similar game is offered at the Palace, except they only allow doubling on first two-card totals of 9, 10 or 11 and that brings the casino edge up to .47%.

Beau Rivage, Boomtown, Golden Nugget, Hard Rock, IP and Island View have the same rules as Harrah's, but they do not allow re-splitting of aces and that game has a casino edge of .40%.

For six-deck shoe games the best place to play is Treasure Bay, which stands on soft 17, allows doubling down on any first two cards, doubling after splitting and re-splitting of aces. The casino advantage in this game is .34%.

The Golden Nugget, Grand, Hard Rock, IP, Island View and Palace offer an identical game, except they hit soft 17 and that brings the casino edge up to .56%. Beau Rivage has a similar game, except they add late surrender to the mix and that lowers the edge slightly to .46%.

Video Poker - Some of the best video poker games on the Gulf Coast for lower limit players are 9/6 Double Double Bonus (98.98%), 9/6 Jacks or Better (99.54%), 8/5 Bonus Poker (99.17%) and a version of Deuces Wild called Illinois Deuces (98.9%).

Island View has 9/6 Jacks or Better for quarters, 50-cent and $1 denominations, all with progressive jackpots. They also have the same denominations of games, including progressive jackpots, for 9/6 Double Double Bonus.

The Golden Nugget offers a $1 version of 8/5 Bonus, plus 25-cent, 50-cent and $1 9/6 Double Double Bonus games.

The Palace has 8/5 Bonus for quarters in 10-play.

The IP offers 9/6 Jacks for quarters, 50 cents and $1. They also offer $1 and $2 8/5 Bonus Poker with a progressive jackpot. There is also 25-cent, 50-cent and $1 9/6 Double Double Bonus. Illinois Deuces is also offered in denominations ranging from 25-cents through $25.

Treasure Bay has 50-cent and $1 8/5 Bonus as well as 50-cent and $1 9/6 Jacks or Better.

Tunica

Map: **#7** (on the Mississippi River, 28 miles S. of Memphis, TN)

Bally's Tunica
1450 Bally's Boulevard
Robinsonville, Mississippi 38664
(662) 357-1500
Website: www.ballystunica.com

Toll-Free Number: (800) 382-2559
Rooms: 235 Price Range: $39-$119
Suites: 8 Price Range: Casino Use Only
Restaurants: 3
Buffets: L-$8.99 D-$14.99
Casino Size: 46,536 Square Feet
Other Games: MS
Overnight RV Parking: Free/RV Dump: No
Special Features: Refrigerators in every room.

Fitz Casino/Hotel
711 Lucky Lane
Robinsonville, Mississippi 38664
(662) 363-5825
Website: www.fitzgeraldstunica.com

Toll-Free Number: (800) 766-5825
Room Reservations: (888) 766-5825
Rooms: 507 Price Range: $35-$119
Suites: 70 Price Range: $59-$129
Restaurants: 3   Valet Parking: Free
Buffets: B- $8.99 L- $9.99/$15.99 (Sun)
          D- $15.99/$21.99 (Fri/Sat)
Casino Size: 38,457 Square Feet
Other Games: MS
Overnight RV Parking: Free/RV Dump: No
Special Features: Indoor pool and spa. Sports pub.

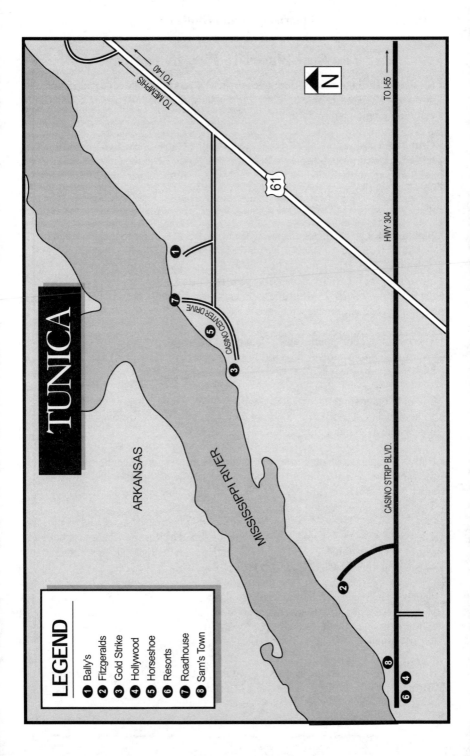

The Best Places To Play in Tunica

Roulette - The house edge on a single-zero wheel cuts the house edge from 5.26% down to a more reasonable 2.70%. Unfortunately, there are no casinos in Tunica that offer single-zero roulette

Craps - All casinos offer 20X odds, except for the Horseshoe which offers 100X odds. Four casinos pay triple (rather than double) on 12 in the field, which cuts the house edge on this bet in half from 5.6 percent to 2.8 percent. The casinos offering this slightly better field bet are: Hollywood, Horseshoe, Gold Strike and Sam's Town.

Blackjack - The blackjack games in Tunica are most similar to those offered in downtown Las Vegas. Most casinos offer both single and double-deck games, as well as six-deck shoe games. That's good. The bad part, however, is that dealers hit soft 17 at all casinos, except for Resorts. This results in an extra advantage for the house of .20%. All of the following recommendations apply to players using perfect basic strategy for each particular game.

The best one-deck game can be found at Fitzgeralds which allows doubling down on any two cards and re-splitting any pair (including aces) which results in a casino advantage of just .15%

The only other single-deck game can be found at Sam's Town where they offer a game identical to the above except they won't allow you to re-split aces and this results in a slightly higher house edge of .18%.

Bally's, Fitzgeralds, Gold Strike, Hollywood, Horseshoe and Roadhouse all offer the same double-deck games which have the following rules: double down on any first two cards, re-split any pair (including aces), and double down after split. This works out to a casino edge of .35%.

The best double-deck game. however, can be found at Resorts where the above same rules are offered, except the dealer stands on soft 17 and the re-splitting of aces is not allowed. This lowers the house edge to only .19%.

The six-deck games found at Bally's, Fitzgeralds, Gold Strike, Hollywood, Horseshoe and Roadhouse all have rules identical to their two-deck games which results in a casino advantage of .56%. Sam's Town has a game simialr, but with a slightly higher casino edge of .63% because they won't allow you to re-split aces.

Resorts, however, has the best six-deck game because it is the same as at Sam's Town, except the dealer stands on soft 17 and that lowers the house edge to only .43%.

Video Poker - Some of the best video poker games in Tunica for lower limit players are 9/7 Double Bonus (99.1%), 9/6 Jacks or Better (99.5%), 8/5 Bonus Poker (99.2%) and a version of Deuces Wild called Illinois Deuces (98.9%).

Bally's has Illinois Deuces for quarters.

Roadhouse has 9/6 Jacks in a 100-coin penny game with a progressive and also the same game with an Illinois Deuces pay table.

Fitz has 9/6 Jacks for quarters, plus 8/5 Bonus for quarters through $5 and Illinois Deuces for quarters.

Sam's Town offers 9/6 Jacks for quarters, 50-cents and $1.

Gold Strike Casino Resort
100 Casino Center Drive
Robinsonville, Mississippi 38664
(662) 357-1111
Website: www.goldstrikemississippi.com

Toll-Free Number: (888) 245-7529
Room Reservations: (866) 245-7511
Rooms: 1,130 Price Range: $79-$159
Suites: 70 Price Range: $175-$229
Restaurants: 3
Buffets: B-$11.99/$21.99 (Sun) L-$16.99
          D-$21.99/$2.99 (Fri/Sat)
Casino Size: 50,486 Square Feet
Other Games: MB, P, CSP, LIR, FCP, MS
Overnight RV Parking: Free/RV Dump: No
Special Features: Food court with three fast-food restaurants. Health spa. Starbucks. Suites only available through casino host on Fri/Sat.

Hollywood Casino Tunica
1150 Casino Strip Boulevard
Robinsonville, Mississippi 38664
(662) 357-7700
Website: www.hollywoodtunica.com

Toll-Free Number: (800) 871-0711
Rooms: 437 Price Range: $59-$199
Suites: 57 Price Range: $149-$369
Restaurants: 3
Buffets: B-$9.99 L-$10.99/$14.99 (Sun)
          D-$16.99/$19.99 (Fri/Sat)
Casino Size: 55,000 Square Feet
Other Games: P, MS
Overnight RV Parking: Must use RV park
Special Features: Casino features a collection of Hollywood memorabilia. 123-space RV park ($18 per night). Indoor pool and jacuzzi. 18-hole golf course.

Horseshoe Casino & Hotel
1021 Casino Center Drive
Robinsonville, Mississippi 38664
(662) 357-5500
Website: www.horseshoetunica.com

Toll-Free Number: (800) 303-7463
Rooms: 200 Price Range: $50-$32580
Suites: 311 Price Range: $129-$479
Restaurants: 5
Buffets: B-$19.99 (Sat/Sun)
        L-$13.99 D-$20.99/$26.99 (Fri/Sat)
Casino Size: 63,000 Square Feet
Other Games: B, MB, P, LIR, CSP, MS
Overnight RV Parking: Free/RV Dump: No
Special Features: Bluesville Nightclub.

Resorts Casino Tunica
1100 Casino Strip Boulevard
Tunica Resorts, Mississippi 38664
(662) 363-7777
Website: www.resortstunica.com

Reservation Number: (866) 676-7070
Rooms: 182 Price Range: $49-$149
Suites: 19 Price Range: Casino Use Only
Restaurants: 4
Buffets: B-$13.99 (Sat/Sun) L-$9.99
        D-$15.99/$20.99 (Fri/Sat)
Casino Size: 42,902 Square Feet
Overnight RV Parking: Free/RV Dump: Free
Special Features: 18-hole River Bend Links
golf course is adjacent to property.

Sam's Town Tunica
1477 Casino Strip Boulevard
Robinsonville, Mississippi 38664
(662) 363-0711
Website: www.samstowntunica.com

Toll-Free Number: (800) 456-0711
Room Reservations: (800) 946-0711
Rooms: 850 Price Range: $59-$149
Suites: 44 Price Range: $99-$199
Restaurants: 4
Buffets: B-$8.99 L-$9.99
        D-$15.99/$21.99 (Fri/Sat)
Casino Size: 66,000 Square Feet
Other Games: MS, LIR
Overnight RV Parking: Free/RV Dump: No
Special Features: 18-hole golf course.
100-space RV park ($12.99 per night).

Tunica Roadhouse Casino and Hotel
1107 Casino Center Drive
Robinsonville, Mississippi 38664
(662) 363-4900
Website: www.tunica-roadhouse.com

Toll-Free Number: (800) 391-3777
Suites: 140 Price Range: $85-$330
Restaurants: 3
Casino Size: 31,000 Square Feet
Other Games: CSP, P
Overnight RV Parking: Free/RV Dump: No
Special Features: All suite hotel with jacuzzi
in every room. Spa and fitness center.

Vicksburg

Map: **#4** (on the Mississippi River, 44 miles
W. of Jackson)

Vicksburg is one of the most historic cities in
the South and is most famous for its National
Military Park where 17,000 Union soldiers are
buried. The Park is America's best-preserved
Civil War battlefield and you can take a 16-
mile drive through the 1,858-acre Park on a
self-guided tour. In the Park you can also see
the U.S.S. Cairo, the only salvaged Union
Ironclad. Admission to the Park is $8 per car
and allows unlimited returns for seven days.

There are about 12 historic homes in Vicksburg
that are open to the public for narrated tours.
Admission prices are $6 for adults and $4 for
children 12 and under. Some of the homes also
function as Bed and Breakfasts and rooms can
be rented for overnight stays.

For more information on visiting Vicksburg
call the city's Convention and Visitors Bureau
at (800) 221-3536, or visit their website at:
www.vicksburgcvb.org

Ameristar Casino Hotel - Vicksburg
4146 Washington Street
Vicksburg, Mississippi 39180
(601) 638-1000
Website: www.ameristarcasino.com

Reservation Number: (800) 700-7770
Rooms: 146 Price Range: $89-$179
Suites: 4 Price Range: $131-$209
Restaurants: 3
Buffets: B-$15.99 (Sun) L-$10.99
          D-$15.99/$25.99 (Fri/Sat)
Casino Size: 72,210 Square Feet
Other Games: P, LIR, MS
Overnight RV Parking: Must use RV park.
Special features: 67 space RV park ($22.50-
$27 per night).

DiamondJacks Casino - Vicksburg
3990 Washington Street
Vicksburg, Mississippi 39180
(601) 636-5700
Website: www.diamondjacks.com

Toll-Free Number: (877) 711-0677
Rooms: 60 Price Range: $49-$79
Suites: 62 Price Range: $129-$200
Restaurants: 3
Buffets: L-$9.99
          D-$12.99/$23.99 (Fri/Sat)
Casino Size: 28,000 Square Feet
Other Games: MS
Overnight RV Parking: No

Lady Luck Casino Vicksburg
1380 Warrenton Road
Vicksburg, Mississippi 39182
(601) 636-7575
Website: www.rainbowcasino.com

Toll-Free Number: (800) 503-3777
Room Reservations: (800) 434-5800
Rooms: 82 Price Range: $89-$120
Suites: 7 Price Range: $149-$219
Restaurants: 1
Buffets: L-$9.99
          D-$13.99/$16.99 (Thu)/$23.99 (Fri/Sat)
Casino Size: 25,000 Square Feet
Other Games: No Three Card Poker
Overnight RV Parking: Yes
Special Features: Affiliated with Isle of Capri
Casinos

Riverwalk Casino & Hotel
1046 Warrington Road
Vicksburg, Mississippi 39180
(601) 634-0100
Website: www.riverwalkvicksburg.com

Toll-Free Number: (866) 615-9125
Room Reservations: (601) 634-0100
Rooms: 80 Price Range: $49-$99
Suites: 4 Price Range: $109-$129
Restaurants: 2
Buffets: L- $9.99/$15.99 (Sun)
          D- $14.99/$19.99(Thu)/
            $26.99 (Fri/Sat)/$15.99 (Sun)
Casino Size: 25,000 square feet
Other Games: MS

Indian Casinos

Bok Homa Casino
1 Choctaw Road
Heidelberg, Mississippi 39439
Website: www.bokhomacasino.com

Toll-Free Number: (866) 447-3275
Restaurants: 1 (open 24 hours)
Casino Size: 27,000 Square Feet
Overnight RV Parking: Free/RV Dump: No

Pearl River Resort
Highway 16 West
Philadelphia, Mississippi 39350
(601) 650-1234
Website: www.pearlriverresort.com
Map: **#8** (81 miles N.E. of Jackson)

Toll-Free Number: (800) 557-0711
Room Reservations (866) 447-3275
Silver Star Rooms: 420 Prices: $79-$259
Silver Star Suites: 75 Prices: $199-$780
Golden Moon Rooms: 427 Prices: $99-$299
Golden Moon Suites: 145 Prices: $329-$879
Restaurants: 12 Liquor: Yes
Buffet: L-$10.99/$15.99 (Sat/Sun)
        D-$14.99/$23.99 (Sat)
Silver Star Casino Size: 90,000 Square Feet
Other Games: MB, P, CSP, B6
Overnight RV Parking: Free/RV Dump: No
Special Features: Two separate hotels across
the street from each other. Golden Moon has
a 9,000-seat events arena, plus a slots-only
casino that is only open Fridays and Saturdays.
18-hole golf course. 15-acre water park.
Health spa. Beauty salon. Shopping arcade
with nine stores.

MISSOURI

In November, 1992 Missouri voters approved a state-wide referendum to allow riverboat gambling. That made Missouri the fifth state to approve this form of gambling.

Since Missouri riverboats are not required to cruise, almost all casinos are built on a barge which gives them the appearance of a land-based building, rather than a riverboat.

When Missouri's riverboat casinos first began operating they were required to cruise and they all conducted two-hour gaming sessions with a $500 loss-limit on each session. In early 2000 the law was changed to allow continuous boardings and cruising was no longer required. In November 2008 the state's $500 loss limit provision was eliminated as the result of a state-wide referendum.

Unlike dockside gaming in Mississippi, most Missouri casinos are not open 24 hours and the hours of operation are listed for each casino.

Here's information from the Missouri Gaming Commission regarding the payback percentages for each casino's electronic machines for the 12-month period from July 1, 2013 through June 30, 2014:

Unless otherwise noted, all casinos offer: slots, video poker, craps, blackjack, roulette, and three card poker. Optional games include: baccarat (B), mini-baccarat (MB), caribbean stud poker (CSP), poker (P), pai gow poker (PGP), let it ride (LIR), Spanish 21 (S21), Mississippi stud (MS), ultimate Texas hold em (UTH) and four card poker (FCP).

If you want to order a drink while playing, be aware that Missouri gaming regulations do not allow casinos to provide free alcoholic beverages. The minimum gambling age is 21.

NOTE: If you happen to win a jackpot of $1,200 or more in Missouri, the casino will withhold 4% of your winnings for the Missouri Department of Revenue. If you want to try and get that money refunded, you will be required to file a state income tax return and, depending on the details of your return, you may get some of the money returned to you. The $1,200 threshold would also apply to any cash prizes won in casino drawings or tournaments.

For more information on visiting Missouri call the state's Travel Center at (800) 877-1234 or go to: www.visitmo.com.

CASINO	PAYBACK %
Isle of Capri - Boonville	91.2
River City	91.1
Ameristar-K.C.	91.0
Lumiere Place	90.8
Isle - Cape Girardeau	90.7
Mark Twain	90.7
Terrible's St. Jo	90.7
Ameristar-St. Charles	90.6
Harrah's N.K.C.	90.5
Hollywood	90.5
Argosy	90.3
Isle of Capri K.C.	90.3
Lady Luck	89.2

These figures reflect the total percentages returned by each casino for all of their electronic machines including slot machines, video poker, video keno, etc.

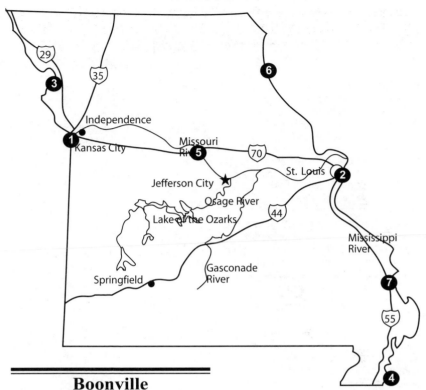

Boonville

Map: **#5** (100 miles E. of Kansas City)

Isle of Capri Casino - Boonville
100 Isle of Capri Boulevard
Boonville, Missouri 65233
(660) 882-1200
Website: www.isleofcapricasino.com

Toll-Free Number: (800) 843-4753
Rooms: 114 Price Range: $79-$169
Suites: 27 Price Range: $119-$209
Restaurants: 3   Valet Parking: $2
Buffets: B-$8.99/$14.99 (Sun)
            L-$10.99/$14.99 (Sun)
            D-$15.99/$18.99 (Fri/Sat)
Hours: 8am-5am/24 Hours (Fri/Sat)
Casino Size: 28,000 Square Feet
Other Games: LIR, MS, no three card poker
Overnight RV Parking: Free (in West lot.)
                /RV Dump: No
Senior Discount: Various on Tue/Thu if 50+
Special Features: 600-passenger barge on the
Missouri River.

Cape Girardeau

Map: **#7** (115 miles S. of St. Louis)

Isle of Capri Casino - Cape Girardeau
338 Broadway Street
Cape Girardeau, Missouri 63701
(573)730-7777
Website: www.isleofcapricasino.com

Toll-Free Number (800) 843-4753
Restaurants: 4
Buffets: B-$6.95/$15.95 (Sun)
            L-$10.95/$15.95 (Sun)
            D-$15.95/$23.95 (Fri/Sat)
Hours: 8am-5am/24 Hours (Fri/Sat)
Casino Size: 38,304 Square Feet
Other Games: P, B6, MB, MS
Overnight RV Parking: Free (in West lot.)
                /RV Dump: No
Senior Discount: Various on Tue/Thu if 50+
Special Features: 600-passenger barge on the
Missouri River. 750-seat event center.

Caruthersville

Map: **#4** (200 miles S. of St. Louis)

Lady Luck Caruthersville
777 East Third Street
Caruthersville, Missouri 63830
(573) 333-6000
Website: www.ladyluckcaruthersville.com

Toll-Free Number: (800) 679-4945
Restaurants: 4   Valet Parking: Free
Hours: 9am-3am/24 hours (Fri/Sat)
Casino Size: 21,400 Square Feet
Other Games: LIR, P, MS
Overnight RV Parking: Free/RV Dump: Free
Special Features: 875-passenger sternwheeler on the Mississippi River. 27-space RV park ($20 per night). 3,000-seat amphitheater.

Kansas City

Map: **#1**

Ameristar Casino Hotel Kansas City
3200 North Ameristar Drive
Kansas City, Missouri 64161
(816) 414-7000
Website: www.ameristar.com

Toll-Free Number: (800) 499-4961
Rooms: 142 Price Range: $149-$229
Suites: 42 Price Range: $169-$529
Restaurants: 14   Valet Parking: $5
Buffets: L-$12.99/$16.99 (Sat/Sun)
        D-$15.99/$27.95 (Fri)/$19.99 (Sat)
Casino Size: 140,000 Square Feet
Other Games: MB, P, LIR, FCP, PGP, MS
Overnight RV Parking: Free/RV Dump: No
Special Features: 4,000-passenger barge adjacent to the Missouri River. 41-screen Sports Pub. 18-screen movie theater complex. Burger King. 1,384-seat event center.

Argosy Casino Hotel & Spa
777 N.W. Argosy Parkway
Riverside, Missouri 64150
(816) 746-3100
Website: www.argosykansascity.com

Toll-Free Number: (800) 270-7711
Rooms: 250 Price Range: $139-$199
Suites: 8 Price Range: $650
Restaurants: 5   Valet Parking: $4
Buffets: B-$12.99/$14.99 (Sat/Sun)
        L-$13.99
        D-$19.99/$32.99 (Fri/Sat)/
        $20.99 (Sun)
Hours: 8am-5am/24 Hours (Sat/Sun)
Casino Size: 62,000 Square Feet
Other Games: S21, PGP, LIR, MS, UTH
Overnight RV Parking: No
Special Features: 4,675-passenger single-deck Mediterranean-themed barge adjacent to the Missouri River.

Harrah's North Kansas City
One Riverboat Drive
N. Kansas City, Missouri 64116
(816) 472-7777
Website: www.harrahs.com

Toll-Free Number: (800) 427-7247
Rooms: 350 Price Range: $89-$249
Suites: 42 Price Range: $119-$279
Restaurants: 5   Valet Parking: $5
Buffets: B-$11.99/$17.99 (Sun) L-$13.99
        D-$18.99/$24.99(Fri)/
        $29.99(Sat)/$20.99 (Sun)
Casino Size: 63,300 Square Feet
Other Games: MB, P, PGP, LIR, MS, UTH
Senior Discount: Various if 50+.
Overnight RV Parking: Free/RV Dump: No
Special Features: 1,700-passenger two-deck barge adjacent to the Missouri River. Closed 5am-8am Wednesdays.

The Best Places To Play Blackjack in Kansas City

All Missouri casinos "hit" soft 17. This is slightly more advantageous for the casino than "standing" on soft 17 and it adds an extra .20% to the casino's mathematical edge in all blackjack games.

The only single-deck blackjack games in Kansas City are offered at the Isle of Capri and Harrah's, but since blackjacks pay 6-to-5, rather than the traditional 3-to-2 (7.5-to-5), this results in an overall casino advantage of almost 1.5% and it's best to avoid these games.

The Isle of Capri offers the best two-deck game. It has a .35% casino advantage against a basic strategy player and the rules are: dealer hits soft 17 (ace and six), double down on any two cards, split and re-split any pair (including aces), and double allowed after splitting. Next best are Argosy, Ameristar and Harrah's which all offer the same game, with the exception of allowing aces to be re-split. The casino advantage in this game is .40%.

Ameristar, Argosy, Harrah's and The Isle all offer an identical six-deck blackjack game with the following rules: dealer hits soft 17 (ace and six), double down on any two cards, split and re-split any pair (including aces), and double allowed after splitting. The casino's mathematical edge against a perfect basic strategy player in this game is .56%.

Isle of Capri Casino - Kansas City
1800 E. Front Street
Kansas City, Missouri 64120
(816) 855-7777
Website: www.isleofcapricasinos.com

Toll-Free Number: (800) 843-4753
Restaurants: 4   Valet Parking: Free
Buffets: B-$7.99/$14.99 (Sun) L-$10.99
        D-$13.99/$24.99 (Fri/Sat)
Casino Size: 30,000 Square Feet
Other Games: UTH, MS, no three card poker
Overnight RV Parking: Free/RV Dump: No
Senior Discount: Various Tue/Thu if 50+
Special Features: 2,000-passenger two-deck Caribbean-themed barge docked in a man-made lake fed by the Missouri River. Closed 5am-6am Wednesdays.

La Grange

Map: **#6** (150 miles N.W. of St. Louis)

Mark Twain Casino
104 Pierce Street
La Grange, Missouri 63448
(573) 655-4770
Website: www.marktwaincasinolagrange.com

Toll-Free Number: (866) 454-5825
Restaurants: 1   Valet Parking: Not Offered
Hours: 8am-2am/4am (Fri/Sat)
Casino Size: 18,000 Square Feet
Other Games: FCP, UTH
Overnight RV Parking: Must use RV park
Special Features: 600-passenger barge on the Mississippi River. 8-space RV park ($25 per night). Gift shop.

St. Joseph

Map: **#3** (55 miles N. of Kansas City)

St. Jo Frontier Casino
77 Francis Street
St. Joseph, Missouri 64501
(816) 279-5514
Website: www.stjofrontiercasino.com

Toll-Free Number: (800) 888-2946
Restaurants: 3   Valet Parking: Not Offered
Buffets: B-$8.49/$11.49 (Sun) L-$9.49
            D-$12.99/$19.99 (Tue)/
            $14.99(Wed)/$16.99 (Thu)
Hours: 8am-1:30am/3:30am (Fri/Sat)
Casino Size: 18,000 Square Feet
Overnight RV Parking: Free/RV Dump: No
Senior Discount: 50% off breakfast buffet
                Mon/Tue if 55+.
Special Features: 1,146-passenger paddlewheel
boat adjacent to the Missouri River. Gift shop.

St. Louis

Map: **#2**

In addition to the five St. Louis-area casinos
listed below, the Casino Queen in E. St. Louis,
Illinois is also a nearby casino. It is located
on the other side of the Mississippi river from
downtown St. Louis. Additionally, the Alton
Belle in Alton, Illinois is about 25 miles north
of St. Louis.

Ameristar Casino St. Charles
1 Ameristar Boulevard
St. Charles, Missouri 63301
(314) 949-4300
Website: www.ameristarcasinos.com

Toll-Free Number: (800) 325-7777
Rooms: 400 Price Range: $149-$269
Restaurants: 7   Valet Parking: $5
Buffets: L-$15.99/$19.99 (Sat/Sun)
        D-$17.99/$19.99 (Fri/Sat)
Casino Size: 130,000 Square Feet
Other Games: P, LIR, FCP, MB, MS
Overnight RV Parking: No
Senior Discount: Various Wed if 55+
Special Features: 2,000-passenger barge on
the Missouri River.

Hollywood Casino St. Louis
777 Casino Center Drive
Maryland Heights, Missouri 63043
(314) 770-8100
Website: www.hollywoodcasinostlouis.com

Toll-Free Number: (866) 758-2591
Rooms: 455 Price Range: $139-$309
Suites: 47 Price Range: $289-$469
Restaurants: 7 Valet Parking: $5
Buffets: L-$13.99/$15.99 (Sat/Sun)
            D-$17.99/$31.99 (Fri)/$25.99 (Sat)
Hours: 8am-5am/24 Hours (Fri-Sun)
Casino Size: 120,000 Square Feet Total
Other Games: B, MB, P, PGP, MS,
                LIR, FCP, CSP, UTH
Overnight RV Parking: Free/RV Dump: No
Senior Discount: Various Tue/Fri if 50+.
Special Features: Two 3,200-passenger
barges on the Missouri River. Ben & Jerry's
Ice cream.

Lumière Place Casino Resort
999 North Second Street
St. Louis, Missouri 63102
(314) 450-5000
Website: www.lumiereplace.com

Toll-Free Number: (877) 450-7711
Suites: 300 Price Range: $159-$299
Restaurants: 5   Valet Parking: Free
Buffets: B-$10.99 (Thu-Sat)/$22.99 (Sun)
        L-$14.99
        D-$18.99/$19.99 (Tue)/
            $34.99 (Fri)/$24.99 (Sat)
Hours: 24 Hours (closed 6am-8am Wed)
Casino Size: 75,000 Square Feet
Other Games: MB, P, LIR, B,
                FCP, PGP, UTH
Special Features: 2,500-passenger barge
floating in a man-made canal 700 feet from
the Mississippi River. Property also features
200-room Four Seasons Hotel.

The Best Places To Play Blackjack in St. Louis

All Missouri casinos "hit" soft 17. This is slightly more advantageous for the casino than "standing" on soft 17 and it adds an extra .20% to the casino's mathematical edge in all blackjack games.

The best two-deck games are offered at Ameristar and River City with these rules: double down on any two cards, split and re-split any pair (except aces), and double allowed after splitting. The casino advantage is .40%. A similar game is offered by Hollywood with two rule changes: no doubling after splitting and doubling down is limited to two-card totals of 9 or more. The casino advantage is .65%. Lumiere Place has a game similar to Hollywood, but they don't allow re-splits and the advantage there is .68%.

All four St. Louis casinos: Ameristar, Hollywood, Lumiere Place and River City offer an identical six-deck blackjack game with the following rules: double down on any two cards, split and re-split any pair (including aces), and double allowed after splitting. The casino's mathematical edge against a perfect basic strategy player in these games is .56%.

The same game is offered at the Casino Queen in nearby E. St. Louis, Illinois but the house stands on soft 17 in that game and it lowers the casino advantage to only .35%.

River City Casino
777 River City Casino Boulevard
St. Louis, Missouri 63125
(314)388-7777
Website: www.rivercity.com

Toll-Free Number: (888) 578-7289
Restaurants: 4 Liquor: Yes
Buffets:B-$19.99 (Sat/Sun) L-$15.50
　　　　D-$21.99/$19.99(Tue/Thu)/
　　　　$29.99 (Wed)/$26.99 (Fri/Sat)/
　　　　$18.99 (Sun)
Casino Size: 90,000 Square Feet
Hours: 8am-5am/24 hours (Fri/Sat)
Other Games: P, FCP, LIR, MB, B6, MS, PGP
Overnight RV Parking: No

MONTANA

Montana law permits bars and taverns to have up to 20 video gaming devices that play video poker, video keno, or video bingo. These machines are operated in partnership with the state and are not permitted to pay out in cash; instead, they print out a receipt which must be taken to a cashier.

The maximum bet on these machines is $2 and the maximum payout is limited to $800. Montana gaming regulations require these machines to return a minimum of 80%.

All of Montana's Indian casinos offer Class II video gaming devices that look like slot machines, but are actually bingo games and the spinning reels are for "entertainment purposes only."

The maximum bet on the machines in Indian casinos is $5 and the maximum payout is capped at $1,500. According to Montana's Gambling Control Division, there are no minimum payback percentages required for gaming machines on Indian reservations. The minimum gambling age is 18.

For Montana tourism information call (800) 847-4868 or go to: www.visitmt.com

Apsaalooke Nights Casino
71 Heritage Road
Crow Agency, Montana 59022
(406) 638-4440
Website: www.apsaalookenightscasino.com
Map: **#2** (65 miles S.E. of Billings)

Casino Size: 4,000-square feet
Hours: 8am-2am

Bear Paw Casino
426 Laredo Road
Box Elder, Montana 59521
(406) 395-4863
Map: **#1** (90 miles N.E. of Great Falls)

Restaurants: 1 Liquor: No
Overnight RV Parking: No/RV Dump: No

Charging Horse Casino
P.O. Box 1259
Lame Deer, Montana 59043
(406) 477-6677
Map: **#3** (90 miles S.E. of Billings on Hwy. 212)

Restaurants: 1 Liquor: No
Hours: 8am-2am Daily
Other Games: Bingo (Thu-Sat)
Overnight RV Parking: Free/RV Dump: No

Fort Belknap Casino
104 Assiniboine Avenue
Harlem, Montana 59526
(406) 353-2235
Map: **#8** (155 miles N.E of Great Falls)

Hours: 10am - 2am/9am - 3am (Sat/Sun)

Glacier Peaks Casino
416 W Central Avenue
Browning, Montana 59417
(406) 338-2274
Website: www.glacierpeakscasino.com
Map: **#6** (140 miles N.W of Great Falls)

Toll-Free: (877) 238-9946
Rooms: 86 Price Range: $170-$185
Suites:14 Price Range: $198-$210
Restaurants: 1 Snack Bar Liquor: No
Hours: 8am-2am Daily
Other Games: Poker, Bingo (Wed-Fri)
Overnight RV Parking: Free, check in with security first/RV Dump: Free

Gray Wolf Peak Casino
27050 US Highway 93 North
Missoula, Montana 59808
(406) 726-3778
Map: **#7**

Hours: 8am- 2am
Restaurants: 1
Overnight RV Parking: Free/RV Dump: Free

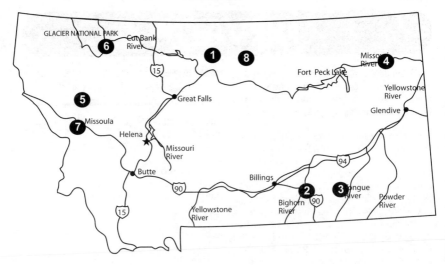

KwaTaqNuk Casino Resort
303 Highway 93
E. Polson, Montana 59860
(406) 883-3636
Website: www.kwataqnuk.com
Map: **#5** (65 miles N. Of Missoula)

Room Reservations: (800) 882-6363
Rooms: 112 Price Range: $54-$145
Restaurants: 1 Liquor: Yes
Hours: 24 Hours Daily
Overnight RV Parking: Free/RV Dump: Free
Special Features: Hotel is Best Western. Two
casinos, one is nonsmoking.

Northern Winz Casino
11275 US Highway 87
Box Elder, Montana 59521
(406) 395-5420
Map: **#1** (90 miles N.E. of Great Falls)

Restaurants: 2 Liquor: No
Overnight RV Parking: No

Silver Wolf Casino
300 Highway 25 East
Wolf Point, Montana 59201
(406) 653-3476
Map: **#4** (180 miles N.E of Billings)

Restaurants: 1 Snack Bar Liquor: No
Hours: 10am-12am/2am (Fri/Sat)/12am (Sun)
Other Games: Bingo
Overnight RV Parking: Free/RV Dump: No

NEVADA

All Nevada casinos are open 24 hours and, unless otherwise noted, offer: slots, video poker, craps, blackjack, and roulette. The minimum gambling age is 21.

For Nevada tourism information call (800) 237-0774 or go to: www.travelnevada.com.

Other games in the casino listings include: sports book (SB), race book (RB), Spanish 21 (S21), baccarat (B), mini-baccarat (MB), pai gow (PG), poker (P), pai gow poker (PGP), Caribbean stud poker (CSP), let it ride (LIR), three-card poker (TCP), Mississippi stud (MS), four card poker (FCP), sic bo (SIC), keno (K), big 6 wheel (B6) and bingo (BG).

Amargosa Valley

Map Location: **#8** (91 miles N.W. of Las Vegas on Hwy. 95)

Longstreet Inn Casino & RV Resort
4400 South Highway 373
Amargosa Valley, Nevada 89020
(775) 372-1777
Website: www.longstreetcasino.com

Rooms: 59 Price Range: $69-$119
Restaurants: 1
Other Games: No table games
Overnight RV Parking: No
Senior Discount: 10% off food if 55 or older
Special Features: 51-space RV Park ($18 per night). 24-hour convenience store.

Battle Mountain

Map Location: **#9** (215 mile N.E. of Reno on I-80)

Nevada Club
8 E. Front Street
Battle Mountain, Nevada 89820
(775) 635-2453

Restaurants: 1
Casino Size: 840 Square Feet
Other Games: No table games
Overnight RV Parking: No

Beatty

Map Location: **#10** (120 miles N.W. of Las Vegas on Hwy. 95)

Stagecoach Hotel & Casino
900 East Highway 95
Beatty, Nevada 89003
(775) 553-2419

Reservation Number: (800) 424-4946
Rooms: 50 Price Range: $35-$59
Restaurants: 2 (1 open 24 hours)
Casino Size: 8,820 Square Feet
Other Games: SB, RB, P, B6, no roulette
Overnight RV Parking: Free/RV Dump: No
Special Features: Swimming pool and Jacuzzi. Seven miles from Rhyolite ghost town.

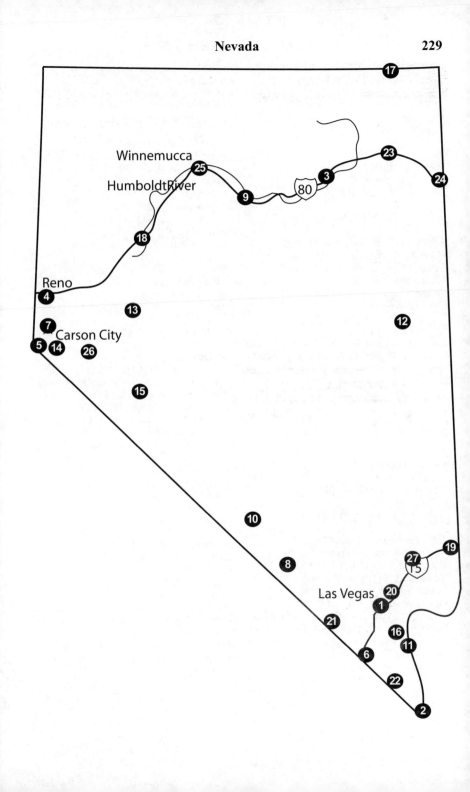

Boulder City

Map Location: **#11** (22 miles S.E. of Las Vegas on Hwy. 93)

Hacienda Hotel & Casino
1843 US Highway 93
Boulder City, Nevada 89005
(702) 293-5000
Website: www.haciendaonline.com

Reservation Number: (800) 245-6380
Rooms: 360 Price Range: $40-$100
Suites: 18 Price Range: $90-$160
Restaurants: 3 (1 open 24 hours)
Casino Size: 17,276 Square Feet
Other Games: SB, RB, P, TCP
Senior Discount: $6.95 Thu Buffet if 55+
Overnight RV Parking: No
Currently closed for remodeling and will re-open as Hoover Dam Lodge in late-2015

Carson City

Map Location: **#7** (32 miles S. of Reno on Hwy. 395)

Carson Nugget
507 N. Carson Street
Carson City, Nevada 89701
(775) 882-1626
Website: www.ccnugget.com

Toll-Free Number: (800) 426-5239
Reservation Number: (800) 338-7760
Rooms: 82 Price Range: $53-$72
Restaurants: 5 (1 open 24 hours)
Casino Size: 28,930 Square Feet
Other Games: SB, RB, P, TCP, K
Overnight RV Parking: Free/RV Dump: No
Special Features: Rare gold display. Free supervised childcare center. Rooms are one block away from casino.

Carson Station Hotel Casino
900 S. Carson Street
Carson City, Nevada 89702
(775) 883-0900
Website: www.carsonstation.com

Toll-Free Number: (800) 501-2929
Rooms: 92 Price Range: $64-$84
Suites: 3 Price Range: $99-$119
Restaurants: 2
Casino Size: 12,750 Square Feet
Other Games: SB, RB, TCP,
                    K, No Roulette
Overnight RV Parking: No
Special Features: Hotel is Best Western.

Casino Fandango
3800 S. Carson Street
Carson City, Nevada 89005
(775) 885-7000
Website: www.casinofandango.com

Restaurants: 3
Casino Size: 40,891 Square Feet
Buffets: L-$11.99 (Wed-Fri)/$15.99 (Sat/Sun)
   D-$11.99 (Wed/Thu/Sun)/$19.99 (Fri/Sat)
Other Games: SB, RB, P, PGP, TCP, K
Overnight RV Parking: Free/RV Dump: No
Senior Discount: Buffet discount if 55+

Gold Dust West - Carson City
2171 Highway 50 East
Carson City, Nevada 89701
(775) 885-9000
Website: www.gdwcasino.com

Toll-Free Number: (877) 519-5567
Rooms: 148 Price Range: $75-$125
Suites: 22 Price Range: $105-$175
Restaurants: 2 (1 open 24 hours)
Casino Size: 12,000 Square Feet
Other Games: SB, RB, TCP, P, no roulette
Overnight RV Parking: Must use RV park
Senior Discount: Various Wed if 50+
Special Features: Hotel is Best Western. 48-space RV park ($30-$33). 32-lane bowling center.

Elko

Map Location: **#3** (289 miles N.E. of Reno on I-80)

Commercial Casino
345 4th Street
Elko, Nevada 89801
(775) 738-3181
Website: www.northernstarcasinos.com

Toll-Free Number: (800) 648-2345
Restaurants: 2 (1 open 24 hours)
Casino Size: 8,441 Square Feet
Other Games: No table games
Overnight RV Parking: Yes/RV Dump: No
Senior Discount: Various Tue if 55+
Special Features: Oldest continually operating casino in Nevada. 10-foot-tall stuffed polar bear in casino. Large gunfighter art collection.

Gold Dust West - Elko
1660 Mountain City Highway
Elko, Nevada 89801
(775) 777-7500
Website: www.gdwcasino.com

Restaurants: 2
Casino Size: 12,544
Other Games: TCP
Senior Discount: Various Tue if 50+

Red Lion Hotel & Casino
2065 Idaho Street
Elko, Nevada 89801
(775) 738-2111
Website: www.redlioncasino.com

Reservation Number: (800) 545-0044
Rooms: 223 Price Range: $75-$119
Suites: 2 Price Range: $259
Restaurants: 3 (1 open 24 hours)
Casino Size: 16,850 Square Feet
Other Games: P, TCP, SB, RB
Overnight RV Parking: No

Stockmen's Hotel & Casino
340 Commercial Street
Elko, Nevada 89801
(775) 738-5141
Website: www.northernstarcasinos.com

Reservation Number: (800) 648-2345
Rooms: 141 Price Range: $45-$75
Restaurants: 2
Casino Size: 6,744 Square Feet
Other Games: SB, RB, TCP, No roulette
Overnight RV Parking: Free/RV Dump: No
Special Features: 24-hour shuttle service.

Ely

Map Location: **#12** (317 miles E. of Reno on Hwy. 50)

Hotel Nevada & Gambling Hall
501 Aultman Street
Ely, Nevada 89301
(775) 289-6665
Website: www.hotelnevada.com

Reservation Number: (888) 406-3055
Rooms: 45 Price Range: $35-$125
Restaurants: 1 (open 24 hours)
Casino Size: 3,730 Square Feet
Other Games: SB, RB, P, TCP,
          No craps or roulette
Overnight RV Parking: Free RV Dump: No
Special Features: Historical display of mining, ranching and railroad artifacts.

Fallon

Map Location: **#13** (61 miles E. of Reno on Hwy. 50)

Bonanza Inn & Casino
855 W. Williams Avenue
Fallon, Nevada 89406
(775) 423-6031

Rooms: 74 Price Range: $50-$65
Restaurants: 1
Casino Size: 5,830 Square Feet
Other Games: SB, RB, K, No table games
Overnight RV Parking: $15 per night

Stockman's Casino
1560 W. Williams Avenue
Fallon, Nevada 89406
(775) 423-2117
Website: www.stockmanscasino.com

Holiday Inn Reservations: (888) 465-4329
Rooms: 98 Price Range: $79-$99
Suites: 8 Price Range: $99-$139
Restaurants: 2 (1 open 24 hours)
Casino Size: 8,614 Square Feet
Other Games: SB, RB, K, No roulette or craps
Senior Discount: 1st/3rd Tue free lunch if 55+
Overnight RV Parking: No
Special Features: Hotel is Holiday Inn Express.

Gardnerville

Map Location: **#14** (45 miles S. of Reno on Hwy. 395)

Sharkey's Casino
1440 Highway 395N
Gardnerville, Nevada 89410
(775) 782-3133
Website: www.sharkeyscasino.net

Restaurants: 1
Casino Size: 4,650 Square Feet
Other Games: SB, RB, No table games
Overnight RV Parking: No
Senior Discount: 10% off food if 50+

Topaz Lodge & Casino
1979 Highway 395 South
Gardnerville, Nevada 89410
(775) 266-3338
Website: www.topazlodge.com

RV/Room Reservations: (800) 962-0732
Rooms: 59 Price Range: $72-$85
Restaurants: 3 (1 open 24 hours)
Casino Size: 12,800 Square Feet
Other Games: SB, RB, BG, K,
                    TCP, No roulette
Overnight RV Parking: Must use RV park
Special Features: 60-space RV park ($20 per night).

Hawthorne

Map Location: **#15** (138 miles S.E. of Reno on Hwy. 95)

El Capitan Resort Casino
540 F Street
Hawthorne, Nevada 89415
(775) 945-3321
Website: www.northernstarcasinos.com

Toll Free: (800) 922-2311
Rooms: 103 Price Range: $50-$78
Restaurants: 1 (open 24 hours)
Casino Size: 12,860 Square Feet
Other Games: SB, RB, No table Games
Overnight RV Parking: Free/RV Dump: Free

Henderson

Map Location: **#16** (15 miles S.E. of Las Vegas on Hwy. 93)

Club Fortune Casino
725 S Racetrack Drive
Henderson, Nevada 89015
(702) 566-5555
Website: www.clubfortunecasino.com

Restaurants: 1
Casino Size: 11,953
Other Games: P
Special Features: $1.49 breakfast special every day from 6am-11am.

Eldorado Casino
140 Water Street
Henderson, Nevada 89015
(702) 564-1811
Website: www.eldoradocasino.com

Restaurants: 3
Casino Size: 17,756 Square Feet
Other Games: SB, K, BG, TCP, No craps
Overnight RV Parking: No

Emerald Island Casino
120 Market Street
Henderson, Nevada 89015
(702) 567-9160
Website: www.emeraldislandcasino.com

Restaurants: 1
Casino Size: 9,300 Square Feet
Other Games: No table games
Overnight RV Parking: No.

Fiesta Henderson Casino Hotel
777 West Lake Mead Drive
Henderson, Nevada 89015
(702) 558-7000
Website: www.fiestahendersonlasvegas.com

Toll-Free Number: (866) 469-7666
Rooms: 224 Price Range: $20-$100
Suites: 8 Price Range: $135-$259
Restaurants: 4 (1 open 24 hours)
Buffets: B-$11.99 (Sun) L-$8.99
          D-$11.99
Casino Size: 73,450 Square Feet
Other Games: SB, RB, PGP, B, MB, K, BG
Overnight RV Parking: No
Senior Discount: Join Fun Club if 50+
Special Features: Buffet discount with players club card.

Green Valley Ranch Resort Spa Casino
2300 Paseo Verde Drive
Henderson, Nevada 89012
(702) 617-7777
Website: www.greenvalleyranchresort.com

Room Reservations: (866) 782-9487
Rooms: 200 Price Range: $128-$330
Suites: 45 Price Range: $310-$3,000
Restaurants: 8 (1 open 24 hours)
Buffets: B-$8.99/$18.99 (Sun) L-$10.99
          D-$18.99/$29.99 (Fri)
Casino Size: 144,568 Square Feet
Other Games: SB, RB, B, MB, MS, BG,
              P, CSP, PGP, LIR, TCP
Overnight RV Parking: No
Senior Discount: Various Wed if 55+

Jokers Wild
920 N. Boulder Highway
Henderson, Nevada 89015
(702) 564-8100
Website: www.jokerswildcasino.com

Restaurants: 2 (1 open 24 hours)
Casino Size: 23,698 Square Feet
Other Games: SB, K
Overnight RV Parking: No
Senior Discount: Various Tue/Wed if 55+

M Resort • Spa • Casino
12300 Las Vegas Blvd South
Henderson, Nevada 89044
(702) 797-1000
Website: www.themresort.com

Toll-free Number: (877) 673-7678
Rooms: 355 Price Range: $89-$199
Suites: 35 Price Range: $129-$409
Restaurants: 7 (1 open 24 hours)
Buffet: B- $39.99 (Sat-Sun) L- $15.99
         D- $23.99/$39.99 (Fri-Sun)
Casino Size: 93,061 Square Feet
Other Games: RB, SB, PGP, MS,
              MB, LIR, TCP

Railroad Pass Hotel & Casino
2800 S. Boulder Highway
Henderson, Nevada 89015
(702) 294-5000
Website: www.railroadpass.com

Toll-Free Number: (800) 654-0877
Rooms: 100 Price Range: $39-$69
Suites: 20 Price Range: $59-$99
Restaurants: 3 (1 open 24 hours)
Buffets: B-$6.99/$8.99 (Sun) L-$6.99
          D-$8.49/$10.99 (Fri/Sat)
Casino Size: 12,803 Square Feet
Other Games: SB, RB, PGP
Overnight RV Parking: No
Senior Discount: Various Tue if 55+

Skyline Restaurant & Casino
1741 N. Boulder Highway
Henderson, Nevada 89015
(702) 565-9116
Website:www.skylinerestaurantandcasino.com

Restaurants: 1
Casino Size: 4,000 Square Feet
Other Games: SB, RB, P, No craps or roulette
Overnight RV Parking: No

Sunset Station Hotel and Casino
1301 W. Sunset Road
Henderson, Nevada 89014
(702) 547-7777
Website: www.sunsetstation.com

Toll-Free Number: (888) 319-4655
Reservation Number: (888) 786-7389
Rooms: 448 Price Range: $39-$149
Suites: 18 Price Range: $69-$189
Restaurants: 7 (1 open 24 hours)
Buffets: B-$8.99/$14.99 (Sun) L-$10.99
        D-$14.99
Casino Size: 93,703 Square Feet
Other Games: SB, RB, MB, PGP,
        LIR, TCP, K, BG
Overnight RV Parking: No
Senior Discount: Various Wed if 50+
Special Features: 13-screen movie theater.
Kids Quest childcare center. Hooters sports
bar. Food Court with eight fast food stations.
Bowling Alley. Buffet discount for players
club members.

Jackpot

Map Location: **#17** (Just S. of the Idaho
border on Hwy. 93)

Barton's Club 93
1002 Highway 93
Jackpot, Nevada 89825
(775) 755-2341
Website: www.bartonsclub93.com

Toll-Free Number: (800) 258-2937
Rooms: 98 Price Range: $35-$85
Suites: 4 Price Range: $81-$151
Restaurants: 2
Buffets: B-$9.99 (Sat/Sun) D-$16.99 (Fri/Sat)
Casino Size: 12,550 Square Feet
Other Games: PGP, LIR
Overnight RV Parking: No

Cactus Pete's Resort Casino
1385 Highway 93
Jackpot, Nevada 89825
(775) 755-2321
Website: www.ameristarcasinos.com

Reservation Number: (800) 821-1103
Rooms: 272 Price Range: $79-$129
Suites: 28 Price Range: $159-$209
Restaurants: 4 (1 open 24 hours)
Buffets: Brunch-$16.99 (Sun)
        D-$13.99/$22.99 (Fri/Sat)
Casino Size: 24,727 Square Feet
Other Games: SB, RB, P, PGP, TCP, LIR, K
Overnight RV Parking: Must use RV park
Special Features: 91-space RV park ($18-
$24 per night). Every Wed 5pm-11pm two
restaurants are 2-for-1. 18-hole golf course.
Beauty Salon. Ampitheatre and tennis courts.

Horseshu Hotel & Casino
1220 Highway 93
Jackpot, Nevada 89825
(702) 755-7777
Website: www.ameristarcasinos.com

Reservation Number: (800) 432-0051
Rooms: 110 Price Range: $59-$99
Suites: 10 Price Range: $79-$129
Restaurants: 1
Casino Size: 3,377 Square Feet
Other Games: No roulette or craps
Overnight RV Parking: No

Jean

Map Location: **#6** (22 miles S.W. of Las Vegas on I-15; 12 miles from the California border)

Gold Strike Hotel & Gambling Hall
1 Main Street
Jean, Nevada 89019
(702) 477-5000
Website: www.stopatjean.com

Reservation Number: (800) 634-1359
Rooms: 800 Price Range: $30-$66
Suites: 13 Price Range: $59-$119
Restaurants: 3 (1 open 24 hours)
Buffets: B-$12.95 (Sat/Sun) L-$8.99
        D-$12.99/$13.99 (Sat/Sun)
Casino Size: 37,006 Square Feet
Other Games: SB, RB
Overnight RV Parking: No
Special Features: Burger King. Table games open 11am-3am.

Lake Tahoe

Map Location: **#5** (directly on the Nevada/California border; 98 miles northeast of Sacramento and 58 miles southwest of Reno).

The area is best known for its many recreational activities with skiing in the winter and water sports in the summer. Lake Tahoe Airport is located at the south end of the basin. The next closest airport is in Reno with regularly scheduled shuttle service by bus. Incline Village and Crystal Bay are on the north shore of Lake Tahoe, while Stateline is located on the south shore. For South Lake Tahoe information call the Lake Tahoe Visitors Authority at (800) 288-2463 and for North Lake Tahoe information call the Incline Village/Crystal Bay Convention & Visitors Authority at (800) 468-2463.

Here's information, as supplied by Nevada's State Gaming Control Board, showing the slot machine payback percentages for all of the south shore casinos for the fiscal year beginning July 1, 2013 and ending June 30, 2014:

Denomination	Payback %
1¢ Slots	88.75
5¢ Slots	N/A
25¢ Slots	92.15
$1 Slots	93.44
All Slots	93.79

And here's that same information for the north shore casinos:

Denomination	Payback %
1¢ Slots	92.56
5¢ Slots	N/A
25¢ Slots	88.59
$1 Slots	94.84
All Slots	94.52

These numbers reflect the percentage of money returned to the players on each denomination of machine. All electronic machines including slots, video poker and video keno are included in these numbers.

Optional games in the casino listings include: sports book (SB), race book (RB), Spanish 21 (S21), baccarat (B), mini-baccarat (MB), poker (P), pai gow poker (PGP), Caribbean stud poker (CSP), let it ride (LIR), three-card poker (TCP), four card poker (FCP), Mississippi stud (MS), keno (K) and bingo (BG).

Cal-Neva Resort Spa & Casino
2 Stateline Road
Crystal Bay, Nevada 89402
(775) 832-4000
Website: www.calnevaresort.com

Reservation Number: (800) 225-6382
Rooms: 199 Price Range: $108-$179
Suites: 18 Price Range: $243-$269
Restaurants: 1
Casino Size: 500 Square Feet
Other Games: Machines only
Overnight RV Parking: No
Special Features: Straddles California/Nevada state line on north shore of Lake Tahoe. European Spa. Three wedding chapels. Florist. Photo studio. Bridal boutique. Gift shop. Airport shuttle. Internet cafe. **TEMPORARILY CLOSED FOR RENOVATIONS EXPECTED TO REOPEN MID-2015**

Crystal Bay Club Casino
14 State Route 28
Crystal Bay, Nevada 89402
(775) 833-6333
Website: www.crystalbaycasino.com

Restaurants 2 (1 open 24 hours)
Casino Size: 14,020 Square Feet
Other Games: RB, SB, P
Overnight RV Parking: No

Harrah's Lake Tahoe
18 Lake Tahoe Boulevard
Stateline, Nevada 89449
(775) 588-6611
Website: www.harrahslaketahoe.com

Reservation Number: (800) 427-7247
Rooms: 463 Price Range: $109-$359
Suites: 62 Price Range: $199-$800
Restaurants: 9
Buffets: Brunch-$17.99 (Sat)/$21.99 (Sun)
     D-$21.99/$29.99 (Fri-Sun)
Casino Size: 89,244 Sq Ft (including Harvey's)
Other Games: SB, B, MB, P, PG, PGP, MS,
     CSP, LIR, TCP, B6, K
Overnight RV Parking: No
Special Features: On south shore of Lake
Tahoe. Health club. Pet kennel.

Harveys Resort Hotel/Casino - Lake Tahoe
18 Lake Tahoe Boulevard
Stateline, Nevada 89449
(775) 588-2411
Website: www.harveys.com

Toll-Free Number: (800) 553-1022
Reservation Number: (800) 427-8397
Rooms: 704 Price Range: $79-$249
Suites: 36 Price Range: $199-$679
Restaurants: 5 (1 open 24 hours)
Casino Size: 89,244 Sq Ft (including Harrah's)
Other Games: SB, RB, B, MB, P, PG, PGP,
     CSP, LIR, TCP, B6, K
Overnight RV Parking: No
Special Features: On south shore of Lake
Tahoe. 2,000-seat amphitheater. Hard Rock
Cafe. Owned by Harrah's. Lake cruises.

Hyatt Regency Lake Tahoe
Resort & Casino
111 Country Club Drive
Incline Village, Nevada 89451
(775) 832-1234
Website: www.laketahoehyatt.com

Toll-Free Number: (800) 553-3288
Hyatt Reservations: (800) 233-1234
Rooms: 412 Price Range: $210-$435
Suites: 48 Price Range: $540-$1,400
Restaurants: 4 (1 open 24 hours)
Buffets: B-$21.00 (Sat/Sun) D-$32.00 (Fri)/
     $28.00 (Sat/Sun)
Casino Size: 18,900 Square Feet
Other Games: SB, RB, P, LIR, TCP
Overnight RV Parking: No
Senior Discount: Food/room discounts if 62+
Special Features: On north shore of Lake
Tahoe. Two Robert Trent Jones golf courses.

Lakeside Inn and Casino
168 Highway 50
Stateline, Nevada 89449
(775) 588-7777
Website: www.lakesideinn.com

Toll-Free Number: (800) 523-1291
Room Reservations: (800) 624-7980
Rooms: 124 Price Range: $69-$159
Suites: 8   Price Range: $109-$299
Restaurants: 4 (1 open 24 hours)
Casino Size: 17,852 Square Feet
Other Games: SB, RB, P, K
Overnight RV Parking: No
Senior Discount: Various if 55+
Special Features: On south shore of Lake
Tahoe. $4.99 breakfast 11pm-11am. $10.50
prime rib dinner 4pm-10pm. Numerous
specials for birthday celebrants. $2 drinks at
all times.

Montbleu Resort Casino & Spa
55 Highway 50
Stateline, Nevada 89449
(775) 588-3515
Website: www.montbleuresort.com

Toll-Free Number: (888) 829-7630
Reservation Number: (800) 648-3353
Rooms: 403 Price Range: $89-$299
Suites: 37 Price Range: $229-$999
Restaurants: 6 (1 open 24 hours)
Buffets: B- $10.95 (Sat/Sun)
        D-$12.99
Casino Size: 45,000 Square Feet
Other Games: SB, RB, P, LIR, TCP, PGP
Overnight RV Parking: No
Special Features: On south shore of Lake Tahoe. Health spa. No buffet Tue/Wed.

Tahoe Biltmore Lodge & Casino
#5 Highway 28
Crystal Bay, Nevada 89402
(775) 831-0660
Website: www.tahoebiltmore.com

Reservation Number: (800) 245-8667
Rooms: 92 Price Range: $69-$129
Suites: 7 Price Range: $139-$189
Restaurants: 2 (1 open 24 hours)
Buffets: B- $14.99 (Sun)
Casino Size: 10,398 Square Feet
Other Games: SB, RB, P
Overnight RV Parking: Free/RV Dump: No
Senior Discount: Various if 55 or older.
Special Features: On north shore of Lake Tahoe. $9.95 prime rib dinner Tuesdays.

See page 269 for a story on "The Best Places to Gamble in Reno/Tahoe"

Las Vegas

Map Location: **#1**

Las Vegas is truly the casino capital of the world! While many years ago the city may have had a reputation as an "adult playground" run by "shady characters," today's Las Vegas features many world-class facilities run by some of America's most familiar corporate names.

Las Vegas has more motel/hotel rooms - 150,000 - than any other city in the U.S. and it attracts more than 39 million visitors each year. The abundance of casinos in Las Vegas forces them to compete for customers in a variety of ways and thus, there are always great bargains to be had, but only if you know where to look.

H. Scot Krause is 20 year Las Vegas Vereran. He is a freelance writer, gaming industry analyst and researcher who writes the weekly Vegas Values column that appears on the American Casino Guide website.

Here are Scot's picks for the best deals available to the Las Vegas visitor.

Best Appetizer Bargain
Golden Gate Shrimp Cocktail, $3.99
Skyline Casino $1.49

While the price continues to sneak up over the years (99 cents for many years, up to $1.99, then $2.99 and now $3.99) it's still hard to beat the quality and price of downtown's Golden Gate Shrimp Cocktail for $3.99 compared to most restaurants in Las Vegas. "Las Vegas' Original Shrimp Cocktail" is featured in Du-Par's and boasts a heap of ocean shrimp in a classic "tulip" sundae glass, served with their "secret cocktail sauce" and a wedge of fresh lemon. If you don't mind venturing off the Strip a bit, try the Skyline Casino in Henderson for their bargain $1.49 Shrimp Cocktail.

Best Steak Deal
Ellis Island, $7.99

Mentioned elsewhere, you may find other steak deals in Las Vegas, but the steak special at Ellis Island Casino & Brewery still remains the leader in steak bargain. It's not on the menu but available for the asking 24 hours a day, 7 days a week. For $8.99 you get a generous cut of tenderloin cooked to your liking, bread, salad, vegetable of the day, choice of potato and a beer (or root beer) from the microbrewery. But with your Passport Player's Card you can get it down to $7.99 if you play $1 through any machine and then print out a coupon from a Passport Central kiosk for the $1 discount. This is not a menu item! Ask your server for the special and they will be happy to take care of you!

Best Place to Play Slots
Palms
Downtown

Subjective, of course, but the Palms openly shares/shared and boasted the payback percentages on all of their slot machines. Numbers are among the best paybacks in Las Vegas, if not the best. Few seem to have challenged them or the numbers, but luck can happen anywhere. Your mileage may vary, but if you're a slot player, I'd try the Palms. For a little less noise and commotion hit the casino during the daytime rather than evenings when it fills up with the "younger" bar crowds. (Unless you like that sort of thing!) Downtown Las Vegas is also a hotbed of activity for slot players and generally the downtown casinos yield a higher payback percentage overall than the Strip. The El Cortez and Rampart Casino released their slot paybacks as similar to The Palms. The nice thing about downtown is that you can pop in and out of all of the casinos with ease until you find your lucky casino or machine! You'll even find a few old coin droppers still left downtown for that "old-time" Vegas feel.

Best Video Poker
South Point

South Point's gaming amenities include more than 2,563 of the most popular slot and video poker machines featuring ticket-in, ticket-out technology. They (arguably) offer the most video poker machines with paybacks over 99% of any casino in the city. Combine that with slot club benefits and year round good promotions and you've got a winning play! Generally if a casino offers good video poker it follows that the slots may be set to higher payouts too. They want your business, so both tend to be better.

Best Bargain Show(s)
Mac King, Harrah's

The plaid-suited magician is hilarious and talented and cheap enough to take the whole family. Normally priced around $27, tickets can usually be found for far less using coupons, including FREE tickets (usually with the price of a drink.) Check this year's American Casino Guide book for that very coupon! Great afternoon bargain show! See him again for the first time!

Best Free Attraction
Bellagio Fountains and Conservatory

Everyone has their favorite free attraction but the water show at Bellagio is by far a fan favorite for tourists as well as locals. It's quite a dazzling display. Some call it "romantic." While you're there, don't miss the Conservatory inside the hotel. Beautiful displays of flowers, gardens and scenery are changed four times a year depicting the seasons. Often breathtaking and definitely aromatic!

Hard Rock Hotel & Casino

My personal favorite? I really enjoy the artifacts, photographs and showcases of various rock and rollers from years past and present at the Hard Rock Hotel & Casino. Check the side halls and alcoves for displays you might ordinarily miss. I also find the free aquarium attraction at the Silverton Casino to be up-close, relaxing and intriguing.

Best Buffet(s)

Generally, the "best buffets" are not exactly "bargains." Usually considered to be among the best (but also pricey) by popular opinion are the buffets at Caesars Palace, Wynn, Bellagio, Cosmopolitan and Planet Hollywood. For a locals casino, Red Rock Resort keeps the prices down and gets high praises. And although they all seem to be constantly changing prices and food selections, for good value, variety, consistency and quality, for my money (or comps) I would give Seasons Buffet (great made-to-order pastas!) at Silverton and Studio B Buffet at M Resort a try. A downtown favorite among tourists and as well as locals is Main Street Station. Perhaps, surprisingly, we find the little Festival Buffet at Fiesta Rancho a top notch favorite for the Mongolian·Grill cooking station. The selection of vegetables is great, always cut fresh and sized well.

Unlike New Jersey, the Nevada Gaming Control Board does not break down its slot statistics by individual properties. Rather, they are classified by area.

The annual gaming revenue report breaks the Las Vegas market down into two major tourist areas: the Strip and downtown. There is also a very large locals market in Las Vegas and those casinos are shown in the gaming revenue report as the Boulder Strip and North Las Vegas areas.

When choosing where to do your slot gambling, you may want to keep in mind the following slot payback percentages for Nevada's fiscal year beginning July 1, 2013 and ending June 30, 2014:

1¢ Slot Machines
The Strip - 88.19%
Downtown - 88.83%
Boulder Strip - 89.14%
N. Las Vegas - 90.72%

5¢ Slot Machines
The Strip - 91.46%
Downtown - 91.30%
Boulder Strip - 96.42%
N. Las Vegas - 95.45%

25¢ Slot Machines
The Strip - 91.52%
Downtown - 94.76%
Boulder Strip - 96.71%
N. Las Vegas - 96.61%

$1 Slot Machines
The Strip - 93.37%
Downtown - 95.20%
Boulder Strip - 96.08%
N. Las Vegas - 96.03%

$1 Megabucks Machines
The Strip - 87.89%
Downtown - 88.45%
Boulder Strip - 87.15%
N. Las Vegas - 88.30%

All Slot Machines
The Strip - 92.50%
Downtown - 93.36%
Boulder Strip - 93.75%
N. Las Vegas - 93.77%

These numbers reflect the percentage of money returned to the players on each denomination of machine. All electronic machines including slots, video poker and video keno are included in these numbers and the highest-paying returns are shown in bold print.

As you can see, the machines in downtown Las Vegas pay out more than those located on the Las Vegas Strip.

Returns even better than the downtown casinos can be found at some of the other locals casinos along Boulder Highway such as Sam's Town and also in the North Las Vegas area. Not only are those numbers among the best returns in the Las Vegas area, they are among the best payback percentages for anywhere in the United States.

This information is pretty well known by the locals and that's why most of them do their slot gambling away from the Strip unless they are drawn by a special players club benefit or promotion.

If you are driving an RV to Las Vegas and want to stay overnight for free in a casino parking lot the only casino that will allow you to do that is Bally's.

Other games in the casino listings include: sports book (SB), race book (RB), Spanish 21 (S21), baccarat (B), mini-baccarat (MB), pai gow (PG), poker (P), pai gow poker (PGP), Caribbean stud poker (CSP), let it ride (LIR), three-card poker (TCP), Mississippi stud (MS), four card poker (FCP), big 6 wheel (B6), sic bo (SIC), keno (K) and bingo (BG).

The Alamo Casino
8050 Dean Martin Drive
Las Vegas, Nevada 89139
(702) 361-1176
Website: www.thealamo.com

Other Games: SB, no craps/roulette
Casino Size: 3,000 Square Feet
Special Features: Truck stop. Food court with fast food outlets.

Aria Resort & Casino
3730 Las Vegas Boulevard South
Las Vegas, Nevada 89109
(702) 590-7757
Website: www.arialasvegas.com

Reservation Number: (866) 359-7757
Rooms: 3,436 Price Range: $179-$799
Suites: 568 Price Range: $500-$7,500
Restaurants: 10
Buffet B-$19.99/$29.99 (Sat/Sun)
          L- $23.99/$29.99 (Thu/Fri)
          D-$34.99/$39.99 (Fri/Sat)
Casino Size: 150,000 Square Feet
Other Games: SB, RB, B, MB, P, PG, PGP,
          LIR, TCP, B6, FCP, CW
Special Features: Located within 76-acre City Center project. Adjacent to 500,000-square-foot Crystals shopping/entertainment complex. *Zarkana* Cirque du Soleil stage show. 80,000-square-foot Spa.

Arizona Charlie's - Boulder
4575 Boulder Highway
Las Vegas, Nevada 89121
(702) 951-9000
Website: www.arizonacharliesboulder.com

Reservation Number: (888) 236-9066
RV Reservations: (800) 970-7280
Rooms: 300 Price Range: $31-$85
Restaurants: 3 (1 open 24 hours)
Buffets: B-$7.49/$11.99 (Sun) L-$9.99
          D-$11.99/$12.99 (Tue/Fri-Sun)
Casino Size: 47,541 Square Feet
Other Games: SB, RB, PGP, BG
Special Features: 239-space RV park ($32 per night). Buffet discount with slot club card.

Arizona Charlie's - Decatur
740 S. Decatur Boulevard
Las Vegas, Nevada 89107
(702) 258-5200
Website: www.arizonacharliesdecatur.com

Reservation Number: (800) 342-2695
Rooms: 245 Price Range: $65-$99
Suites: 10 Price Range: $119-$169
Restaurants: 5 (1 open 24 hours)
Buffets: B- $9.99 (Fri/Sat)/12.99 (Sun)
     L- $10.99/$12.99 (Sun)
     D- $12.99/$17.99 (Fri/Sat)
Casino Size: 55,227 Square Feet
Other Games: SB, RB, P, PGP, K, BG, B
Special Features: Buffet discount with players club card.

Bally's Las Vegas
3645 Las Vegas Boulevard S.
Las Vegas, Nevada 89109
(702) 739-4111
Website: www.ballyslv.com

Toll-Free Number: (800) 722-5597
Reservation Number: (888) 215-1078
Rooms: 2,814 Price Range: $79-$219
Suites: 265 Price Range: $129-$449
Restaurants: 11 (1 open 24 hours)
Buffets: Brunch-$89.99 (Sun)
Casino Size: 66,187 Square Feet
Other Games: SB, RB, B, MB, P, CW, PG,
     PGP, CSP, LIR, TCP, K, B6, MS
Overnight RV Parking: Free/RV Dump: No
Senior Discount: Various if 55+
Special Features: 20 retail stores. *Jubilee* stage show.

Bellagio
3600 Las Vegas Boulevard S.
Las Vegas, Nevada 89109
(702) 693-7111
Website: www.bellagioresort.com

Reservation Number: (888) 987-6667
Rooms: 2,688 Price Range: $149-$499
Suites: 308 Price Range: $575-$5,500
Restaurants: 13 (2 open 24 hours)
Buffets: B- $18.99/$29.99 (Sat/Sun)
     L- $22.99/$29.99 (Sat/Sun)
     D- $33.99/$39.99 (Fri/Sat)
Casino Size: 156,000 Square Feet
Other Games: SB, RB, B, MB, P, PG, PGP,
     CSP, LIR, TCP, B6
Special Features: Lake with nightly light and water show. Shopping mall. Two wedding chapels. Beauty salon and spa. Cirque du Soleil's "O" stage show.

Binion's Gambling Hall and Hotel
128 E. Fremont Street
Las Vegas, Nevada 89101
(702) 382-1600
Website: www.binions.com

Toll-Free Number: (800) 937-6537
Restaurants: 4 (1 open 24 hours)
Casino Size: 77,800 Square Feet
Other Games: SB, RB, P, PGP, LIR,
     TCP, B6
Special Features: Steak House on 24th floor offers panoramic views of Las Vegas. Free souvenir photo taken in front of $1,000,000 cash.

Boulder Station Hotel & Casino
4111 Boulder Highway
Las Vegas, Nevada 89121
(702) 432-7777
Website: www.boulderstation.com

Toll-Free Number: (800) 981-5577
Reservation Number: (800) 683-7777
Rooms: 300 Price Range: $29-$139
Restaurants: 6 (1 open 24 hours)
Buffets: B-$7.99 L-$10.99/$14.99 (Sat/Sun)
        D-$14.99
Casino Size: 89,443 Square Feet
Other Games: SB, RB, MB, P, PGP,
        TCP, K, BG, B
Special Features: 11-screen movie complex.
Kids Quest childcare center. Buffet discount
for slot club members.

Caesars Palace
3570 Las Vegas Boulevard S.
Las Vegas, Nevada 89109
(702) 731-7110
Website: www.caesarspalace.com

Toll-Free Number: (800) 634-6001
Reservation Number: (800) 634-6661
Rooms: 3,349 Price Range: $109-$500
Petite Suites: 242 Price Range: $300-$600
Suites: 157 Price Range: $750-$4,400
Nobu Rooms Price Range: $159-$379
Nobu Suites Price Range: $609-$1,560
Restaurants: 12 (1 open 24 hours)
Buffets: B-$25.95
        L-$35.95
        D-$50.95
Casino Size: 139,229 Square Feet
Other Games: SB, RB, B, MB, PG, P, S21
        PGP, CSP, LIR, TCP, B6, K
Special Features: Health spa. Beauty salon.
Shopping mall with 125 stores and interactive
attractions. *Celine Dion* stage show.

California Hotel & Casino
12 Ogden Avenue
Las Vegas, Nevada 89101
(702) 385-1222
Website: www.thecal.com

Reservation Number: (800) 634-6505
Rooms: 781 Price Range: $36-$105
Suites: 74 Price Range: Casino Use Only
Restaurants: 4 (1 open 24 hours)
Casino Size: 35,848 Square Feet
Other Games: SB, PGP, LIR, TCP, K
Special Features: 93-space RV park ($14/$17
per night). Offers charter packages from
Hawaii.

Casino Royale Hotel & Casino
3411 Las Vegas Boulevard S.
Las Vegas, Nevada 89109
(702) 737-3500
Website: www.casinoroyalehotel.com

Toll-Free Number: (800) 854-7666
Rooms: 151 Price Range: $69-$89
Suites: 3 Price Range: $149-$189
Restaurants: 4 (1 open 24 hours)
Casino Size: 22,000 Square Feet
Other Games: TCP
Special Features: Outback, Denny's and
Subway. Refrigerator in every room. 20x
odds on craps.

Circus Circus Hotel & Casino
2880 Las Vegas Boulevard S.
Las Vegas, Nevada 89109
(702) 734-0410
Website: www.circuscircus.com

Room Reservations: (877) 224-7287
RV Reservations: (800) 562-7270
Rooms: 3,770 Price Range: $39-$119
Suites: 122 Price Range: $89-$269
Restaurants: 9 (2 open 24 hours)
Buffets: B- $14.99/$15.99 (Sat/Sun)
        L-$15.99/$16.99 (Sat/Sun)
        D- $17.99/$18.99(Fri/Sat)
Casino Size: 123,928 Square Feet
Other Games: SB, RB, P, PGP, MS,
        LIR, TCP, B6
Special Features: Free circus acts 11am-
midnight. Wedding chapel. Midway and
arcade games. Indoor theme park.

The Best Places To Play In Las Vegas

Roulette - There are 16 casinos in Las Vegas that offer single-zero roulette: Aria, Bellagio, Caesars Palace, Encore, M Resort, Mandalay Bay, MGM Grand, Mirage, Monte Carlo, Palazzo, Paris, Planet Hollywood, Riviera, Cosmopolitian, Venetian and Wynn. This game has a 2.70% edge as compared to the usual 5.26% edge on a double-zero roulette wheel. Be aware that all of these casinos offer single-zero wheels at just some of their roulette games and not all of them. The minimum bet is $25 at Aria, M, MGM Grand, Mirage, Monte Carlo and Venetian/Palazzo. It's $50 at Bellagio and $100 at all of the other casinos.

Craps - 20X odds is the highest offered in Las Vegas and there are three casinos offering that game: Casino Royale, Sam's Town and Main Street Station.

Blackjack- All recommendations in this section apply to basic strategy players. For single-deck games you should always look for casinos that pay the standard 3-to-2 for blackjacks. Many casinos only pay 6-to-5 for blackjack and this increases the casino edge to around 1.5% and they should be avoided. Many casinos also offer a blackjack game called Super Fun 21. This is another game that should be avoided as the casino advantage is around 1%.

The best single-deck game can be found at the El Cortez which offers the following rules: dealer hits soft 17, double down on any first two cards, split any pair, re-split any pair (except aces), and no doubling after splitting. The casino edge in this game is .18% and the minimum bet is $5.

There are 11 casinos with two-deck games offering the following rules: dealer stands on soft 17, double down on any first two cards, re-split any pair (except aces) and doubling allowed after splitting. The casinos that offer it are: Aria, Bellagio, Hard Rock, MGM Grand, Mandalay Bay, Mirage, Monte Carlo, New York New York, Palms, Treasure Island and Venetian (not at Palazzo). The casino edge in these games is .19% with minimum bets of $50 and up.

The best double-deck game, however, is offered at M Resort. This game has the same rules as the above games except it allows the re-splitting of aces and that brings the casino edge down to .14% The minimum bet at this game is $100.

The remaining best two-deckers in Las Vegas can be found at some "locals" casinos that have the same rules as above, with one exception: the dealer hits soft 17. The casino advantage is .35% and the game can be found at all of the Station casinos, plus Arizona Charlie's Boulder and Silverton. The minimum bet at these casinos is usually $5.

For six-deck shoe games the best casinos have these rules: dealer stands on soft 17, double after split allowed, late surrender offered and resplitting of aces allowed. The casino edge in this game works out to .26% and you can find it at many major casinos: Aria, Bellagio, Caesars Palace, Cosmopolitan, Hard Rock, M Resort, Mandalay Bay, MGM Grand, Monte Carlo, NYNY, Palms, SLS, Tropicana, Wynn and the Venetian/Palazzo. The minimum bet at these casinos is usually at least $25.

Almost all of these casinos also offer this same game with identical rules except that they will hit soft 17. The minimums in this game are lower ($5 or $10) but the casino's mathematical edge is raised to .46%.

Cosmopolitan, MGM Grand, Mirage, Monte Carlo and Venetian/Palazzo offer the best eight deck games. They have the same rules as the .26% six-deck game and the casino advantage is .49% with minimum bets of $5 or $10.

It should also be noted that there are many casino offering six and eight-deck shoe games that only pay 6-to-5 for blackjack, rather than 3-to-2. These games should definitely be avoided as they triple the casino advantage to as high as 2%.

Video Poker- Smart video poker players know that some of the best machines to look for are: 9/6 Jacks or Better (99.54% return), 8/5 Bonus Poker (99.17% return), 10/7 Double Bonus (100.17% return), full-pay Deuces Wild (100.76% return), 10/6 Double Double Bonus (100.07% return) and Not So Ugly Deuces (99.73% return). These games are very hard to find at Las Vegas Strip casinos, but they are usually widely available at "locals" casinos along Boulder Highway, or in Henderson or North Las Vegas.

Following is a list of casinos offering some of these better paying video poker games. The abbreviations used for each listing are JB (9/6 jacks or better), BP (8/5 bonus poker), DB (10/7 Double Bonus), DDB (10/6 double double bonus), FPDW (full-pay deuces wild) and NSUD (not so ugly deuces).

Strip-area Casinos
Circus Circus: BP - quarter to $1
Cosmopolitan: BP - dime to $25
Ellis Island: JB - quarter to $1; NSUD - nickel to $5; BP - quarter to $1
Excalibur: JB - $1 to $5; BP - $1 to $5
Gold Coast: JB - quarter to $5; NSUD - quarter to $2; BP - quarter to $10
Hard Rock: BP - quarter to $25
Luxor: JB - $1 to $10; BP - $1 to $10
Mandalay Bay: BP - $2 to $10
MGM Grand: JB - $1 to $25; BP - $1 to $100
NYNY: JB - quarter to $10; BP - quarter to $10 (note - these machines do not have a players club card reader on them so you will not be able to earn any comps or cashback).
Orleans: BP - quarter to $1; NSUD - quarter
Palace Station: JB- quarter to $1; DB - nickel to $1; DDB - nickel to $1; FPDW - nickel; NSUD - quarter to $1
Palms: JB -penny to $2; BP - quarter to $50; DB - quarter to fifty cents; DDB - quarter to fifty cents; FPDW - quarter; NSUD - quarter to $1
Silver Sevens: JB - nickel to $1; BP - nickel to $1; DB - nickel to quarter; FPDW - quarter
Treasure Island: JB - fifty cents to $10; BP - fifty cents to $10
Tropicana: BP - nickel to $25
Tuscany: BP - quarter to $1
Westgate: JB - nickel to $5; NSUD - quarter; BP - quarter to $10
Winn: JB - $5 to $100; BP - $5 to $100

Downtown Casinos
California: JB - quarter to $1; BP - nickel to $5; DB - quarter to $1; NSUD - nickel to fifty cent
The D: BP - dime to $5; DB- quarter; Loose Deuces (101.60% return) - nickel; NSUD - dime to $1
El Cortez: JB - dime to $1; DB - quarter to fifty cents; BP - dime to $5
Four Queens: JB - quarter to $1; DB - quarter and $1
Fremont: JB - $1; NSUD - quarter to $5; BP - quarter to $5
Golden Nugget: JB - $5 to $25; BP - quarter and $5

Locals Casinos - If you are looking for the best video poker in Las Vegas then you may want to make a side trip to some of the casinos along Boulder Highway, as well as in Henderson or North Las Vegas. Most of these casinos offer all of the games listed above in a variety of denominations. The casino company that operates the most locals properties is Station Casinos which owns: Sunset Station, Boulder Station, Texas Station, Santa Fe Station, Palace Station, Green Valley Ranch, Red Rock, Fiesta Henderson and Fiesta Rancho. The other major player is Boyd Gaming, which operates Sam's Town, Gold Coast, Orleans, Suncoast, California, Fremont and Main Street Station. All of these locals casinos will offer good video poker games, coupled with a good players club that will allow you to redeem your points at any of their company-owned casinos.

The Cosmopolitan of Las Vegas
3708 Las Vegas Boulevard South
Las Vegas, Nevada 89109
(702) 698-7000
Website: www.cosmopolitanlasvegas.com

Toll-free Number: (877) 551-7778
Rooms: 2,600 Price Range: $180-$480
Suites: 395 Price Range: $450-$1,500
Restaurants: 13
Buffets: L-$27.00/$33 (Sat/Sun)
       D-$38.00/$41.00 (Fri-Sun)
Casino Size: 63,628 Square Feet
Other games: RB, SB, LIR, B, MB,
       PGP, TCP, S21, B6, CW

The Cromwell Las Vegas
3595 Las Vegas Boulevard S.
Las Vegas, Nevada 89109
(855) 895-3002
Website: www.thecromwell.com

Formerly Known as Bill's Gamblin' Hall
Reservation Number: (844) 426-2766
Rooms: 624 Price Range: $159-$349
Suites: 14 Price Range: $609-$999
Restaurants: 1
Casino Size: 33,673 Square Feet
Other Games: P, PGP, MB
Special Features: Drai's beach club-nightclub.

The D Las Vegas
301 Fremont Street
Las Vegas, Nevada 89101
(702) 388-2400
Website: www.thed.com

Reservation Number: (800) 274-5825
Rooms: 624 Price Range: $29-$99
Suites: 14 Price Range: $109-$239
Restaurants: 2 (1 open 24 hours)
Casino Size: 33,673 Square Feet
Other Games: SB, RB, S21, LIR,
       PGP, TCP, K
Special Features: Fast food court with
McDonald's and Krispy Kreme.

Downtown Grand Casino
206 North 3rd Street
Las Vegas, Nevada 89101
(855) 384-7263
Website: www.downtowngrand.com

Rooms: 626 Price Range: $59-$179
Suites: 8 Price Range: Casino Use Only
Restaurants: 5
Casino Size: 35,000 Square Feet
Other Games: B, PGP, TCP, B6

Eastside Cannery
5255 Boulder Highway
Las Vegas, Nevada 89122
(702) 856-5300
Website: www.eastsidecannery.com

Reservation Number: (866) 999-4899
Rooms: 190 Price Range: $39-$99
Rooms: 20 Price Range: $90-$199
Restaurants: 5 (1 open 24 hours)
Buffets: L-$9.99/$12.99 (Sat/Sun)
       D-$12.99/$14.99 (Fri/Sat)
Casino Size: 62,479 Square Feet
Other Games: SB, RB, P, PGP, BG, TCP
Senior Discount: Food discounts if 55+
Special features: $2 buffet discount with
player's club card.

El Cortez Hotel & Casino
600 E. Fremont Street
Las Vegas, Nevada 89101
(702) 385-5200
Website: www.elcortezhotelcasino.com

Reservation Number: (800) 634-6703
Rooms: 299 Price Range: $29-$109
Suites: 10 Price Range: $60-$159
Restaurants: 2 (1 open 24 hours)
Casino Size: 45,300 Square Feet
Other Games: SB ,RB, MB, P, PGP, K
Special Features: Video arcade. Gift shop and
ice cream parlor. Barber shop. Beauty salon.

Ellis Island Casino & Brewery
4178 Koval Lane
Las Vegas, Nevada 89109
(702) 733-8901
Website: www.ellisislandcasino.com

Restaurants: 1 (open 24 hours)
Casino Size: 12,316 Square Feet
Other Games: SB, RB
Special Features: Super 8 Motel next door.
$7.99 steak dinner (not on menu, must ask for it). #1 Microbrewery in Nevada as voted by the state's Brewers Association.

Encore Las Vegas
3131 Las Vegas Boulevard S.
Las Vegas, Nevada 89109
(702) 770-7800
Website: www.encorelasvegas.com

Reservations Number: (888) 320-7125
Suites: 1,800 Price Range: $239-$769
Tower Suites: 234 Price Range $299-$2,500
Restaurants: 9 (1 open 24 hours)
Buffets: B- $21.99/$32.99 (Sat/Sun)
        L- $25.99
        D- $39.99/$40.99 (Fri/Sat)
Casino Size: 186,187 Sq. Ft. (Includes Wynn)
Other Games: SB, RB, B, MB, P, PG, CW,
        PGP, CSP, LIR, TCP, B6
Special Features: *Le Reve* stage show. Attached to Wynn Las Vegas.

Excalibur Hotel/Casino
3850 Las Vegas Boulevard S.
Las Vegas, Nevada 89109
(702) 597-7777
Website: www.excaliburcasino.com

Reservation Number: (800) 937-7777
Rooms: 4,008 Price Range: $33-$141
Suites: 46 Price Range: $160-$390
Restaurants: 5 (1 open 24 hours)
Buffets: B-$16.00 L-$17.00 D-$22.00
Casino Size: 98,628 Square Feet
Other Games: SB, RB, MB, P, PGP,
        LIR, CW, TCP, B6, K
Special Features: Canterbury wedding chapel. Strolling Renaissance entertainers. Video arcade and midway games. Nightly *Tournament of Kings* dinner show. Food Court with fast food outlets.

Flamingo Las Vegas
3555 Las Vegas Boulevard S.
Las Vegas, Nevada 89109
(702) 733-3111
Website: www.flamingolasvegas.com

Reservation Number: (800) 732-2111
Rooms: 3,545 Price Range: $50-$205
Suites: 215 Price Range: $205-$855
Restaurants: 8 (1 open 24 hours)
Buffets: B- $18.99 L- $20.99
        D- $24.99/$28.99 (Fri/Sat)
Casino Size: 72,279 Square Feet
Other Games: SB, RB, MB, P, PGP, MS
        LIR, TCP, B6, K, CSP
Special Features: Health Spa. Shopping arcade. Jimmy Buffet's Margaritaville restaurant.

Four Queens Hotel/Casino
202 Fremont Street
Las Vegas, Nevada 89101
(702) 385-4011
Website: www.fourqueens.com

Reservation Number: (800) 634-6045
Rooms: 690 Price Range: $39-$119
Suites: 48 Price Range: $149-$240
Restaurants: 3 (1 open 24 hours)
Casino Size: 27,269 Square Feet
Other Games: SB, RB, PGP, LIR, TCP, K, MS

Fremont Hotel & Casino
200 E. Fremont Street
Las Vegas, Nevada 89101
(702) 385-3232
Website: www.fremontcasino.com

Toll-Free Number: (800) 634-6460
Reservation Number: (800) 634-6182
Rooms: 428 Price Range: $36-$115
Suites: 24 Price Range: Casino Use Only
Restaurants: 4 (1 open 24 hours)
Buffets: B- $8.99/$14.99 (Sat/Sun)
        L- $9.99/$14.99 (Sat/Sun)
        D- $16.99/$22.99 (Tues/Fri)
Casino Size: 30,244 Square Feet
Other Games: SB, RB, PGP, LIR, TCP, K
Special Features: 99¢ shrimp cocktail at snack bar. Tony Roma's restaurant.

The Best Vegas Values
By H. Scot Krause

Welcome to "Vegas Values!" It's an exclusive weekly column found only at: Americancasinoguide. com, the companion website to this book. The column is updated weekly with some of the best casino promotions found throughout Las Vegas. Below are examples from the "Vegas Values" column. Remember, promotions are subject to change and may be cancelled at anytime. Call ahead to verify before making a special trip.

Arizona Charlie's Boulder and Decatur: You'll need your ace/PLAY card for the café's $2.99 skillet breakfast consisting of two eggs, hash browns and choice of bacon or sausage and toast or biscuit and gravy, or the $3.99 breakfast special of steak or ham, eggs, hash browns & toast. You must present your players card to your server and purchase a beverage.

Downtown Grand: Join "My Points" players club as a new member and receive a random amount of freeplay instantly, from $3 up to $1,000.

El Cortez: Have an IRS tax refund check you're ready to cash? Get a 5% free slot bonus for it. Cash your IRS check (or any government issued check) at the El Cortez main cage and you'll receive an extra 5% (up to $50) in FREE slot play money. The offer generally runs year round.

Ellis Island Casino & Brewery: Known for their off-the-menu-great steak special. For $8.99 you get a generous cut of tenderloin cooked to your liking, bread, salad, vegetable of the day, choice of potato and a beer (or root beer) from the microbrewery. But with your Passport Players Card you can get it down to $7.99 if you play $1 through any machine and then print out a coupon from a Passport Central kiosk for the $1 discount. It's not on the menu. Ask your server for it! Also: New members signing up for the "Passport Players Club" who play at least $1 coin in will receive a free play spin where they get anywhere from $10 free play to $500. Everyone is a winner.

Four Queens: New members signing up for the Royal Players Club receive a FREE t-shirt or canvas tote bag after earning 40 points within the first 24 hours of enrolling. (gifts may vary.) Also: Show a players card from any downtown Las Vegas casino at the Four Queens and they will give you $10 in free play (even if you already have their card!) Offer can be redeemed only one time per player per lifetime!

Gold Coast and Orleans: Birthday Promotion: During your birth month, after earning a minimum one point, swipe for a FREE prize at a kiosk. (Some active play is required to receive the kiosk swipe offer.)

Golden Nugget: New members signing up for the 24 Karat Club have a chance to win up to $1,000 in FREE Slot Play. This new promotion gives new 24 Karat Club members a FREE promotional slot machine spin instantly upon joining, awarding FREE Slot Play in denominations ranging from $5 to $1,000.

Hooters Casino Hotel: New members signing up for the "Rewards Club" receive a $5 food voucher for Hooters or Mad Onion, and a $5 matchplay voucher for table games. New members signing up can also receive up to $500 in free slot play. Receive $10 in free slot play for every 250 points earned up to a maximum of $500 with up to 48 hours to earn and redeem. Visit the Rewards Club for complete details.

Main Street Station: "Score with Four" promotion. Hit any four-of-a-kind, straight flush or royal flush and receive a scratch card for additional cash. Most cards are of the $2 to $5 variety, but they do offer cards valued at $20, $50 and $100, as well as the extremely rare $5,000 cards.

Sam's Town: Earn five points after becoming a new B Connected club member and play the "Money Madness" scratch card game. Every card wins an instant prize. You must provide an e-mail address to participate.

South Point: Birthday Promotion: Offers birthday guests 2,500 FREE points after earning your first point during your birthday month. A $6+ value.

Silver Sevens Casino (formerly Terrible's): Offers table game rebates. Ask for details in the table games pit area about a 5% loss rebate on losses of $500 and 10% on losses on $1,000. They offer $3 craps games with 3-5x odds and several double-deck blackjack games that pay 3-to-2 for blackjack.

Gold Coast Hotel & Casino
4000 W. Flamingo Road
Las Vegas, Nevada 89103
(702) 367-7111
Website: www.goldcoastcasino.com

Toll-Free Number: (888) 402-6278
Rooms: 750 Price Range: $34-$114
Suites: 27 Price Range: $165-$245
Restaurants: 6 (1 open 24 hours)
Buffets: B-$6.99/$12.99 (Sun) L-$8.99
  D- $12.99/$24.99 (Fri)
Casino Size: 88,915 Square Feet
Other Games: SB, RB, MB, PGP, TCP,
  K, BG, LIR
Special Features: 70-lane bowling center.
Showroom. Buffet discount with players
club card.

Golden Gate Hotel & Casino
One Fremont Street
Las Vegas, Nevada 89101
(702) 385-1906
Website: www.goldengatecasino.com

Reservation Number: (800) 426-1906
Rooms: 106 Price Range: $31-$84
Restaurants: 2 (2 open 24 hours)
Casino Size: 12,243 Square Feet
Other Games: SB, RB, TCP, LIR
Special Features: $3.99 shrimp cocktail.
Oldest hotel in Vegas (opened 1906).

The Golden Nugget
129 E. Fremont Street
Las Vegas, Nevada 89101
(702) 385-7111
Website: www.goldennugget.com

Toll-Free Number: (800) 634-3403
Reservation Number: (800) 634-3454
Rooms: 1,805 Price Range: $59-$149
Suites: 102 Price Range: $149-$750
Restaurants: 8 (1 open 24 hours)
Buffets: B-$11.99 /$19.99 (Sat/Sun)
  L- $13.99
  D-$19.99/$23.99 (Fri-Sun)
Casino Size: 47,796 Square Feet
Other Games: SB, RB, MB, P, PGP,
  LIR, TCP, B6, K
Special Features: World's largest gold nugget
(61 pounds) on display. Health spa. Swimming
pool with shark tank.

Hard Rock Hotel & Casino
4455 Paradise Road
Las Vegas, Nevada 89109
(702) 693-5000
Website: www.hardrockhotel.com

Toll-Free Number: (800) 473-7625
Rooms: 1,130 Price Range: $55-$420
Suites: 387 Price Range: $179-$529
Restaurants: 2 (1 open 24 hours)
Casino Size: 59,125 Square Feet
Other Games: SB, RB, B, MB, PGP, P,
  LIR, TCP, B6
Special Features: Rock and Roll memorabilia
display. Beach Club with cabanas and sandy
beaches. Lagoon with underwater music.

Harrah's Las Vegas
3475 Las Vegas Boulevard S.
Las Vegas, Nevada 89109
(702) 369-5000
Website: www.harrahslasvegas.com

Toll-Free Number: (800) 392-9002
Reservation Number: (800) 427-7247
Rooms: 2,672 Price Range: $35-$255
Suites: 94 Price Range: $110-$595
Restaurants: 10 (1 open 24 hours)
Buffets: B- $19.99/$24.99 (Sat/Sun)
  L- $20.99 D- $24.99
Casino Size: 90,637 Square Feet
Other Games: SB, RB, MB, P, PG, PGP,
  LIR, TCP, B6, K, MS
Special Features: Mardi Gras-themed casino.
Improv Comedy Club. *Mac King, Legends in
Concert* and *Defending the Caveman* stage
shows.

Hooters Casino Hotel
115 East Tropicana Avenue
Las Vegas, Nevada 89109
(702) 739-9000
Website: www.hooterscasinohotel.com

Toll-Free Number: (866) 584-6687
Rooms: 694 Price Range: $55-$195
Suites: 17 Price Range: $205-$500
Restaurants: 4 (1 open 24 hours)
Casino Size: 25,000 Square Feet
Other Games: SB, RB, LIR, P, PGP, TCP

Jerry's Nugget
See North Las Vegas section

Free Things To See In Las Vegas!

Conservatory at Bellagio

Looking for some greenery during your Las Vegas stay? The Bellagio Conservatory has got you covered and is completely free! Every season, the Bellagio's 140 expert horticulturists create a breathtaking new scene made up of intricate floral arrangements, gazebos, bridges, and ponds for guests to explore. The themes begin with the Chinese New Year in January and changes for summer, fall, and winter. The conservatory is located inside the Bellagio and is open 24 hours, with live music offered from 5-6pm daily in the south graden.

Las Vegas Club Hotel & Casino
18 E. Fremont Street
Las Vegas, Nevada 89101
(702) 385-1664
Website: www.vegasclubcasino.com

Reservation Number: (800) 634-6532
Rooms: 410 Price Range: $25-$110
Restaurants: 4 (1 open 24 hours)
Casino Size: 19,616 Square Feet
Other Games: PGP, TCP, BG
Special Features: Sports themed-casino with large collection of sports memorabilia.

The LINQ Hotel & Casino
3535 Las Vegas Boulevard S.
Las Vegas, Nevada 89109
(702) 731-3311
Website: www.thelinq.com

Toll-Free Number: (800) 351-7400
Reservation Number: (800) 634-6441
Rooms: 1,088 Price Range: $40-$125
Suites: 225 Price Range: $110-$285
Restaurants: 10 (1 open 24 hours)
Buffets: B/L-$12.99 D-$18.99
Casino Size: 28,361 Square Feet
Other Games: SB, RB, P, PGP, LIR,
MS, TCP, B6
Special Features: Auto museum (admission charge). Video arcade. Wedding chapel. Formerly known as The Quad.

Longhorn Casino
5288 Boulder Highway
Las Vegas, Nevada 89122
(702) 435-9170

Restaurants: 1 (open 24 hours)
Casino Size: 4,825 Square Feet
Other Games: SB, RB, no craps or roulette

Luxor Las Vegas
3900 Las Vegas Boulevard S.
Las Vegas, Nevada 89119
(702) 262-4000
Website: www.luxor.com

Reservation Number (800) 288-1000
Pyramid Rooms: 1,948 Price Range: $59-$249
Pyramid Suites 237 Price Range: $165-$375
Tower Rooms: 2,256 Price Range: $79-$269
Tower Suites 236 Price Range: $179-$509
Restaurants: 6 (1 open 24 hours)
Buffets: B-$16.00 L-$17.00 D-$22.00
Casino Size: 100,090 Square Feet
Other Games: SB, RB, MB, P, PGP,
LIR, TCP
Special Features: 30-story pyramid-shaped hotel with Egyptian theme. *Carrot Top* comedy show. Cirque Du soleil *Believe* Stage show. IMAX theater.

Main Street Station Hotel & Casino
200 N. Main Street
Las Vegas, Nevada 89101
(702) 387-1896
Website: www.mainstreetcasino.com

Toll-Free Number: (800) 713-8933
Reservation Number: (800) 465-0711
Rooms: 406 Price Range: $36-$109
Suites: 14 Price Range: Casino Use Only
Restaurants: 4 (1 open 24 hours)
Buffets: B- $8.99/$12.99 (Sat/Sun)
        L- $9.99 D- $12.99/
            $15.99 (Tues/Thu/Sat)/$22.99 (Fri)
Casino Size: 26,918 Square Feet
Other Games: PGP, LIR, TCP
Special Features: 99-space RV park ($14/$17 per night).
Special Features: Buffet discount for players club members.

Mandalay Bay
3950 Las Vegas Boulevard S.
Las Vegas, Nevada 89109
(702) 632-7777
Web Site: www.mandalaybay.com

Reservation Number: (877) 632-7000
Rooms: 3,220 Price Range: $89-$360
Suites: 424 Price Range: $130-$600
Restaurants: 16 (1 open 24 hours)
Buffets: B- $17.99/$25.99 (Sat/Sun)
        L- $21.99 D- $32.99
Casino Size: 160,344 Square Feet
Other Games: SB, RB, B, MB, P, PG, PGP,
        LIR, TCP, B6
Special Features: 424-room Four Seasons Hotel on 35th-39th floors. *House of Blues* restaurant. Sand and surf beach with lazy river ride. Shark Reef exhibit (admission charge). Spa. Michael Jackson *ONE* Cirque Du Soleil show

Max Casino at Westin Las Vegas
160 East Flamingo Road
Las Vegas, Nevada 89109
(702) 836-5900
Website: www.starwood.com

Westin Reservations: (800) 228-3000
Rooms: 816 Price Range: $99-$159
Suites: 10 Price Range: $289-$429
Restaurants: 1 (open 24 hours)
Buffets: B-$18.00
Casino Size: 13,500 Square Feet
Other Games: RB, SB, TCP

MGM Grand Hotel Casino
3799 Las Vegas Boulevard S.
Las Vegas, Nevada 89109
(702) 891-1111
Website: www.mgmgrand.com

Toll-Free Number: (800) 929-1111
Reservation Number: (800) 646-7787
Skyloft Reservations: (877) 646-5638
Rooms: 5,005 Price Range: $80-$280
Suites: 752 Price Range: $159-$899
Skylofts: 51 Price Range: $800-$10,000
Restaurants: 15 (1 open 24 hours)
Buffets: B-$17.99/$26.99 (Sat/Sun)
        L- $20.99 D-$29.99/$36.99 (Fri/Sat)
Casino Size: 156,023 Square Feet
Other Games: SB, RB, B, MB, PG, PGP,
        P, LIR, TCP, B6, CW
Special Features: Largest hotel in America. Comedy Club. Rainforest Cafe. Midway games and arcade. Free lion habitat exhibit. Cirque du Soleil *Ka* stage show.

Free Things To See In Las Vegas!

Fremont Street Experience

This $70 million computer-generated sound and light show takes place 90 feet in the sky over a pedestrian mall stretching four city blocks in downtown Las Vegas and in mid-2004 the entire system was upgraded with new LED modules to provide even crisper and clearer images. It's like watching the world's largest plasma TV with larger-than-life animations, integrated live video feeds, and synchronized music.

There are five differently themed shows nightly. Starting times vary, beginning at dusk, but then begin on the start of each hour through midnight.

The Mirage
3400 Las Vegas Boulevard S.
Las Vegas, Nevada 89109
(702) 791-7111
Website: www.themirage.com

Reservation Number: (800) 627-6667
Rooms: 3,044 Price Range: $89-$450
Suites: 281 Price Range: $299-$1,500
Restaurants: 12 (1 open 24 hours)
Buffets: B-$15.99/$25.99 (Sat/Sun)
      L-$22.99 D-$29.99
Casino Size: 97,550 Square Feet
Other Games: SB, RB, B, MB, PG, P, CW
      PGP, LIR, TCP, B6, MS
Special Features: Siegfried & Roy's Secret Garden and Dolphin Habitat (admission charge). Aquarium display at check-in desk. Simulated volcano with periodic "eruptions." *Terry Fator* and Cirque du Soleil's *Love* stage shows.

Monte Carlo Resort & Casino
3770 Las Vegas Boulevard S.
Las Vegas, Nevada 89109
(702) 730-7777
Website: www.montecarlo.com

Reservation Number: (800) 311-8999
Rooms: 3,002 Price Range: $60-$190
Suites: 259 Price Range: $139-$499
Restaurants: 7 (1 open 24 hours)
Buffets: B/L-$17.95/$21.95 (Fri-Sun)
      D- $23.95/$26.95 (Fri-Sun)
Casino Size: 101,983 Square Feet
Other Games: SB, RB, MB, B, P, PGP,
      FCP, CSP, LIR, TCP
Special Features: Food court. Microbrewery. Pool with lazy river ride. Health spa.

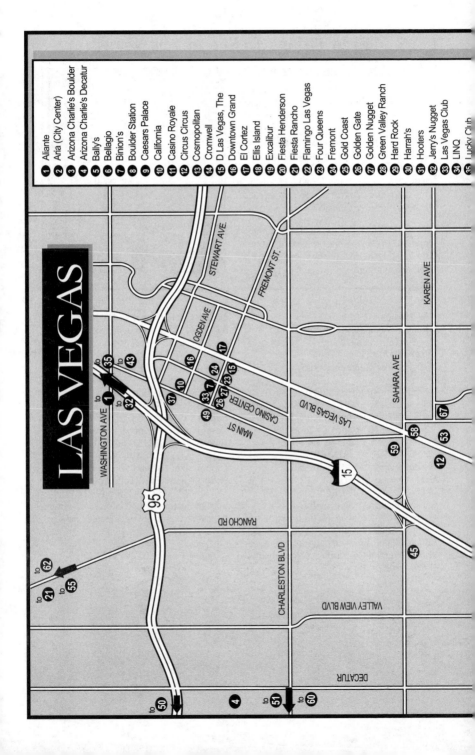

LAS VEGAS

1 Aliante
2 Aria (City Center)
3 Arizona Charlie's Boulder
4 Arizona Charlie's Decatur
5 Bally's
6 Bellagio
7 Binion's
8 Boulder Station
9 Caesars Palace
10 California
11 Casino Royale
12 Circus Circus
13 Cosmopolitan
14 Cromwell
15 D Las Vegas, The
16 Downtown Grand
17 El Cortez
18 Ellis Island
19 Excalibur
20 Fiesta Henderson
21 Fiesta Rancho
22 Flamingo Las Vegas
23 Four Queens
24 Fremont
25 Gold Coast
26 Golden Gate
27 Golden Nugget
28 Green Valley Ranch
29 Hard Rock
30 Harrah's
31 Hooters
32 Jerry's Nugget
33 Las Vegas Club
34 LINQ
35 Lucky Club

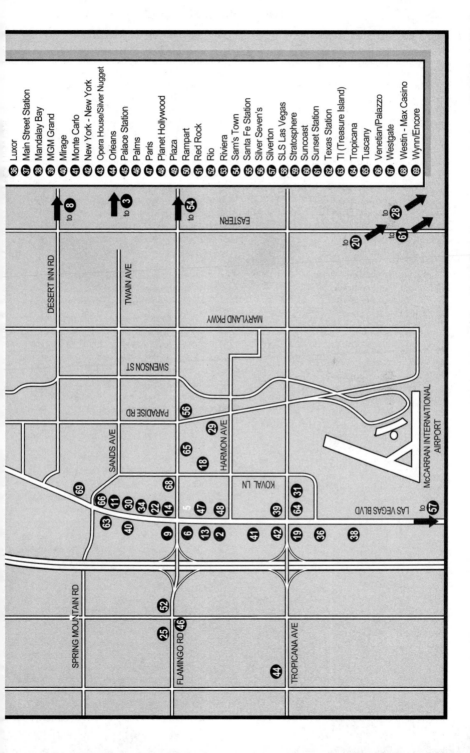

36 Luxor
37 Main Street Station
38 Mandalay Bay
39 MGM Grand
40 Mirage
41 Monte Carlo
42 New York - New York
43 Opera House/Silver Nugget
44 Orleans
45 Palace Station
46 Palms
47 Paris
48 Planet Hollywood
49 Plaza
50 Rampart
51 Red Rock
52 Rio
53 Riviera
54 Sam's Town
55 Santa Fe Station
56 Silver Seven's
57 Silverton
58 SLS Las Vegas
59 Stratosphere
60 Suncoast
61 Sunset Station
62 Texas Station
63 TI (Treasure Island)
64 Tropicana
65 Tuscany
66 Venetian/Palazzo
67 Westgate
68 Westin - Max Casino
69 Wynn/Encore

New York-New York Hotel & Casino
3790 Las Vegas Boulevard S.
Las Vegas, Nevada 89109
(702) 740-6969
Website: www.nynyhotelcasino.com

Reservation Number: (800) 693-6763
Rooms: 2,024 Price Range: $60-$260
Suites: 12 Price Range: Casino Use Only
Restaurants: 8 (1 open 24 hours)
Casino Size: 90,000 Square Feet
Other Games: SB, RB, MB, PGP, SIC
            CSP, LIR, TCP, B6, FCP
Special Features: Replica Statue of Liberty
and Empire State Building. *Manhattan
Express* roller coaster. Cirque du Soleil's
Zumanity stage show.

The Orleans Hotel & Casino
4500 West Tropicana Avenue
Las Vegas, Nevada 89103
(702) 365-7111
Website: www.orleanscasino.com

Reservation Number: (800) 675-3267
Rooms: 1,828 Price Range: $38-$165
Suites: 58 Price Range: $199-$499
Restaurants: 9 (1 open 24 hours)
Buffets: B- $8.99/$21.99 (Sun)
        L- $10.99
        D- $19.99/ $25.99 (Fri)/$21.99 (Sat)
Casino Size: 137,000 Square Feet
Other Games: SB, RB, MB, P,
            PGP, LIR, TCP, K
Special Features: 70-lane bowling center.
18-screen movie theater. Kids Tyme childcare.
9,000-seat arena. Free shuttle to Gold Coast
and Cromwell.

Palace Station Hotel & Casino
2411 West Sahara Avenue
Las Vegas, Nevada 89102
(702) 367-2411
Website: www.palacestation.com

Reservation Number: (800) 544-2411
Rooms: 949 Price Range: $25-$109
Suites: 82 Price Range: $75-$159
Restaurants: 6 (1 open 24 hours)
Buffets: B-$7.99/$14.99 (Sun) L-$9.99
        D-$14.99
Casino Size: 84,000 Square Feet
Other Games: SB, RB, B, MB, PG, P, PGP,
            TCP, K, BG
Special Features: Buffet discount with players
club card.

The Palms
4321 Flamingo Road
Las Vegas, Nevada 89103
(702) 942-7777
Website: www.palms.com

Toll Free Number: (866) 942-7777
Reservation Number: (866) 942-7770
Rooms: 447 Price Range: $109-$359
Suites: 60 Price Range: $149-$750
Specialty Suites: 9 Prices: $2,500-$40,000
Restaurants: 10 (1 open 24 hours)
Buffets: B-$8.99/$19.99 (Sun) L-$12.99
        D-$20.99/$25.99 (Fri/Sat)
Casino Size: 87,178 Square Feet
Other Games: SB, RB, MB, P, PGP,
            MS, TCP, B6, CW
Special Features: 14-theater cineplex. IMAX
theater. Tattoo shop. Kids Quest childcare
center. Recording studio. Playboy store.

Free Things To See In Las Vegas!

Welcome to Las Vegas Sign

Located on the Las Vegas Strip just south of Mandalay Bay is the historic "Welcome to Fabulous Las Vegas" sign. The sign, which was built in 1959 and has since become a well-known Vegas landmark, reads "Welcome to Fabulous Las Vegas, Nevada" on the front and "Drive Carefully" and "Come Back Soon" on the back.

The sign has its own 12-car parking lot and photos can be taken near the sign with ease. The parking lot also has room for two buses and there is access for individuals with disabilities. Parking is free and the sign can be accessed 24 hours a day.

In order to access the "Welcome to Las Vegas" sign parking lot, you must be heading south on Las Vegas Boulevard going away from Mandalay Bay and toward the Las Vegas Outlet Center.

Paris Casino Resort
3655 Las Vegas Boulevard S.
Las Vegas, Nevada 89109
(702) 946-7000
Website: www.parislasvegas.com

Reservation Number: (888) 266-5687
Rooms: 2,916 Price Range: $90-$340
Suites: 300 Price Range: $285-$870
Restaurants: 11 (1 open 24 hours)
Buffets: B- $21.99/$23.99 (Sat/Sun)
      L- $24.99/$30.99 (Sat/Sun)
      D- $30.99/$33.99 (Fri/Sat)
Casino Size: 95,263 Square Feet
Other Games: SB, RB, B, MB, TCP, MS, PG, PGP, LIR, K, B6
Special Features: Replicas of Paris landmarks. 50-story Eiffel Tower with restaurant/ observation deck. *Jersey Boys* and *Anthony Cools* stage shows

Planet Hollywood Resort & Casino
3667 Las Vegas Boulevard S.
Las Vegas, Nevada 89109
(702) 785-5555
Website: www.planethollywoodresort.com

Reservation Number: (877) 333-9474
Rooms: 1,878 Price Range: $89-$269
Parlor Rooms: 466 Price Range: $259-$369
Suites: 223 Price Range: $229-$689
Restaurants: 5 (1 open 24 hours)
Buffets: B- $21.99/$30.99 (Sat/Sun)
      L- $19.99 D- $29.99
Casino Size: 64,470 Square Feet
Other Games: SB, RB, B, MB, P, PGP, MS, LIR, TCP, B6
Special Features: 130-store retail mall. 7,000-seat Theater of the Performing Arts. Health spa and salon. Britney Spears *Piece of Me* stageshow. V-theater located in the Miracle Mile Shops offers a variety of stage shows.

Plaza Hotel & Casino
1 Main Street
Las Vegas, Nevada 89101
(702) 386-2110
Website: www.plazahotelcasino.com

Reservation Number: (800) 634-6575
Rooms: 1,037 Price Range: $49-$139
Suites: 60 Price Range: $69-$189
Restaurants: 5 (1 open 24 hours)
Casino Size: 51,436 Square Feet
Other Games: SB, RB, PGP, MB,
P, LIR, TCP, BG
Special Features: Oscar's Steakhouse offers
full view of Fremont Street Experience.

The Quad
This property was renamed The LINQ on
October 30, 2014. See its listing on page 249.

Rampart Casino
221 N. Rampart Boulevard
Las Vegas, Nevada 89128
(702) 507-5900
Website: www.rampartcasino.com

Toll-Free Number: (866) 999-4899
Reservation Number: (877) 869-8777
Rooms: 440 Price Range: $139-$229
Suites: 70 Price Range: $209-$399
Restaurants: 6 (1 open 24 hours)
Buffets: L-$9.99/$14.99 (Sat/Sun)
D- $15.99/$21.99 (Wed/Fri)/
$18.99 (Thu/Sat)
Casino Size: 47,330 Square Feet
Other Games: SB, RB, PGP, TCP, FCP
Special Features: Hotel is JW Marriott. Golf
course. Spa.

Red Rock Resort Spa Casino
10973 W. Charleston Boulevard
Las Vegas, Nevada 89135
(702) 797-7777
Website: www.redrocklasvegas.com

Rooms: 366 Price Range: $125-$360
Suites: 48 Price Range: $285-$520
Restaurants: 10 (1 open 24 hours)
Buffets: B-$8.99/$18.99 (Sun)
L-$11.99 D-$18.99/$21.99 (Sat)
Casino Size: 119,309 Square Feet
Other Games: SB, RB, MB, P, PGP, MS,
TCP, LIR, K, BG, B
Special Features: 16-screen movie complex.
Childcare center. Full-service spa.

Rio Suites Hotel & Casino
3700 W. Flamingo Road
Las Vegas, Nevada 89103
(702) 252-7777
Website: www.playrio.com

Toll-Free Number: (800) 752-9746
Reservation Number: (866) 746-7671
Suites: 2,563 Price Range: $99-$259
Restaurants: 18 (1 open 24 hours)
Buffets: B- $20.99/30.99 (Sat/Sun)
L-$22.99/30.99 (Sat/Sun) D- $30.99
Seafood Buffet: D-$44.99 (opens 3:30pm)
Casino Size: 117,330 Square Feet
Other Games: SB, RB, B, MB, P, PG,
MS, PGP, LIR, TCP, K
Overnight RV Parking: Free/RV Dump: No
Special Features: 20-store shopping mall.
Three wedding chapels. *Penn and Teller*
stage show.

Riviera Hotel & Casino
2901 Las Vegas Blvd. South
Las Vegas, Nevada 89109
(702) 734-5110
Website: www.rivierahotel.com

Toll-Free Number: (800) 634-3420
Reservation Number: (800) 634-6753
Rooms: 2,100 Price Range: $59-$159
Suites: 154 Price Range: $229-$329
Restaurants: 5 (1 open 24 hours)
Casino Size: 91,800 Square Feet
Other Games: SB, RB, MB, P, B6,
PGP, LIR, TCP
Special Features: Fast food court with 8
outlets. *Crazy Girls* stage show. Comedy Club.

Free Things To See In Las Vegas!

The Fountains at Bellagio

More than one thousand fountains dance in front of the Bellagio hotel, creating a union of water, music and light. The display spans more than 1,000 feet, with water soaring as high as 240 feet. The fountains are choreographed to music ranging from classical and operatic pieces to songs from Broadway shows.

Showtimes are every 30 minutes from 3 p.m (noon on Sat/Sun) until 7 p.m. After 7 p.m. the shows start every 15 minutes until midnight. A list of all musical selections is available on the Bellagio website at: www.bellagio.com.

Sam's Town Hotel & Gambling Hall
5111 Boulder Highway
Las Vegas, Nevada 89122
(702) 456-7777
Website: www.samstownlv.com

Toll-Free Number: (800) 897-8696
Reservation Number: (800) 634-6371
Rooms: 620 Price Range: $29-$99
Suites: 30 Price Range: $89-$209
Restaurants: 6 (1 open 24 hours)
Buffets: B-$7.99/$12.99 (Sat/Sun) L-$9.99
        D-$15.99/$24.99 (Fri)
Casino Size: 120,681 Square Feet
Other Games: SB, RB, MB, P, LIR,
        TCP, K, BG, PGP
Special Features: 500-space RV park ($18-$22 per night). Indoor promenade with free laser-light show. 24-hour 56-lane bowling center. 18-theater cinema complex. Childcare center. Buffet discount for players club members.

Santa Fe Station Hotel & Casino
4949 North Rancho Drive
Las Vegas, Nevada 89130
(702) 658-4900
Website: www.santafestationlasvegas.com

Toll Free Number: (866) 767-7770
Reservation Number: (866) 767-7771
Rooms: 200 Price Range: $29-$89
Restaurants: 3 (1 open 24 hours)
Buffets: B-$6.99/$12.99 (Sat/Sun)
        L-$9.99 D-$12.99/$17.99 (Sat)
Casino Size: 156,401 Square Feet
Other Games: SB, RB, MB, P, PGP,
        TCP, K, BG
Special Features: 60-lane bowling center. 16-screen cinema. Live entertainment. Kids Quest childcare center.

Silver Saddle Saloon
2501 E. Charleston Boulevard
Las Vegas, Nevada 89104
(702) 474-2900
Website: www.silversaddlesaloon.com

Restaurants: 1
Other Games: No craps or roulette.
Blackjack only played 10am-5am (Fri/Sat).

Silver Sevens Hotel and Casino
4100 Paradise Road
Las Vegas, Nevada 89156
(702) 733-7000
Website: www.silversevenscasino.com

Reservation Number: (800) 640-9777
Rooms: 370 Price Range: $45-$140
Restaurants: 2 (1 open 24 hours)
Buffets: B- $6.99/$11.99 (Sat/Sun)
　　　　L-$6.99 D-$9.99/$12.99 (Fri/Sat)
Casino Size: 27,225 Square Feet
Other Games: SB, RB, PGP, P, BG
Special features: 24-hour $9.99 dinner
specials.

Silverton Casino Hotel Lodge
3333 Blue Diamond Road
Las Vegas, Nevada 89139
(702) 263-7777
Website: www.silvertoncasino.com

Toll-Free Number: (800) 588-7711
Room/RV Reservations: (866) 946-4373
Rooms: 292 Price Range: $65-$95
Suites: 8 Price Range: $169-$369
Restaurants: 8 (1 open 24 hours)
Buffets: L- $10.99/$19.99 (Sat/Sun)
　　　　D- $15.99/$25.99 (Fri)/$21.95 (Sat)
Casino Size: 71,829 Square Feet
Other Games: SB, RB, PGP, TCP, K, BG
Special Features: Starbucks coffee house.

Slots-A-Fun Casino
2890 Las Vegas Boulevard S.
Las Vegas, Nevada 89109
(702) 734-0410

Toll-Free Number: (800) 354-1232
Restaurants: 1 Subway Sandwich Shop
Casino Size: 16,733 Square Feet
Other Games: No table games

SLS Hotel & Casino
2535 Las Vegas Boulevard S.
Las Vegas, Nevada 89109
(702) 737-2111
Website: www.slslasvegas.com

Reservation Number: (855) 761-7757
Rooms: 1,350 Price Range: $139-$359
Suites: 250 Price Range: $294-$799
Restaurants: 6
Casino Size: 60,000 Square Feet

South Point Hotel and Casino
9777 Las Vegas Boulevard S.
Las Vegas, Nevada 89123
(702) 796-7111
Website: www.southpointcasino.com

Toll-Free Number: (866) 796-7111
Rooms: 1,325 Price Range: $59-$150
Suites: 25 Price Range: $150-$950
Restaurants: 12 (1 open 24 hours)
Buffets: B- $9.95 L- $12.95/$19.95 (Sat/Sun)
　　　　D- $18.95/$27.95 (Fri/Sat)
Casino Size: 137,232 Square Feet
Other Games: SB, RB, MB, P,
　　　　　　　PGP, TCP, BG
Special Features: 16-screen movie complex.
Equestrian center with 4,400-seat arena and
1,200 stalls. 64-lane bowling center. Kids
Tyme childcare facility. Health spa.

Stratosphere Hotel & Casino
2000 Las Vegas Boulevard S.
Las Vegas, Nevada 89104
(702) 380-7777
Website: www.stratospherehotel.com

Reservation Number: (800) 998-6937
Rooms: 2,444 Price Range: $35-$149
Suites: 250 Price Range: $95-$219
Restaurants: 8 (1 open 24 hours)
Buffets: B/L-$14.99 D-$19.99
Casino Size: 80,000 Square Feet
Other Games: SB, RB, P, B6,
　　　　　　　PGP, LIR, TCP, CSP
Senior Discount: Tower discount if 55+
Special Features: 108/109 story Indoor/
Outdoor Observation Deck(admission charge).
Revolving restaurant at top of tower. 50 retail
stores. *Frank Moreno* and *Pinup* stage shows.

Free Things To See In Las Vegas!

Volcano at The Mirage

Another fun Vegas attraction that won't cost you anything is the iconic volcano at the Mirage. The volcano first opened in 1989, but received a $25 million update in 2008, making it anything but dated. The volcano's choreographed, fire eruptions occur nightly and feature an original soundtrack put together by Grateful Dead drummer Mickey Hart and Indian composer Zakir Hussain. This, combined with sounds from actual volcanic eruptions create a truly

thrilling experience. The volcano is located outside the Mirage (you can't miss it!) and eruptions being at 8pm nightly and occur every half-hour through midnight, with the exception of 8:30pm.

Suncoast Hotel and Casino
9090 Alta Drive
Las Vegas, Nevada 89145
(702) 636-7111
Website: www.suncoastcasino.com

Toll-Free Number: (866) 636-7111
Rooms: 432 Price Range: $49-$150
Suites: 40 Price Range: $165-$265
Restaurants: 9 (1 open 24 hours)
Buffets: B- $12.99/$17.99 (Sun) L- $13.99
    D- $17.99/$24.99 (Fri)/$24.99 (Sat)
Casino Size: 95,898 Square Feet
Other Games: SB, RB, MB, P, PGP, TCP, BG
Special Features: 64-lane bowling center.
16-screen movie theater. Kids Tyme childcare.
Seattle's Best Coffee. Free shuttles to airport,
Strip and other Coast properties.

Treasure Island (TI)
3300 Las Vegas Boulevard S.
Las Vegas, Nevada 89109
(702) 894-7111
Website: www.treasureisland.com

Reservation Number: (800) 944-7444
Rooms: 2,665 Price Range: $75-$229
Suites: 220 Price Range: $125-$999
Restaurants: 9 (2 open 24 hours)
Buffets: B- $17.95/$23.99 (Sat/Sun) L-$20.95
    D- $25.95/$28.95 (Fri-Sun)
Casino Size: 50,335 Square Feet
Other Games: SB, RB, B, MB, P, PG,
    PGP, LIR, TCP, B6, K
Special Features: Health spa/salon. Two
wedding chapels. Starbucks. Krispy Kreme.
Cirque du Soleil's *Mystere* stage show.

Tropicana Resort & Casino
3801 Las Vegas Boulevard S.
Las Vegas, Nevada 89109
(702) 739-2222
Website: www.troplv.com

Reservation Number: (888) 826-8767
Rooms: 1,877 Price Range: $74-$194
Suites: 115 Price Range: $199-$599
Restaurants: 5 (1 open 24 hours)
Buffets: B- $20.99/$25.99 (Sat/Sun)
    L- $17.99
Casino Size: 44,570 Square Feet
Other Games: SB, RB, MB, PGP, B6,
    LIR, TCP, P, UTH, UTH
Senior Discount: Various if 65+
Special Features: Wedding chapel.

Tuscany Suites & Casino
255 East Flamingo Road
Las Vegas, Nevada 89109
(702) 893-8933
Website: www.tuscanylv.com

Reservation Number: (877) 887-2261
Suites: 760 Price Range: $21-$199
Restaurants: 4 (1 open 24 hours)
Casino Size: 22,450 Square Feet
Other Games: SB, RB
Special Features: All suite hotel. Wedding chapel.

The Venetian Resort Hotel Casino
3355 Las Vegas Boulevard S.
Las Vegas, Nevada 89109
(702) 414-1000
Website: www.venetian.com

Reservation Number: (888) 283-6423
Suites: 4,046 Price Range: $149-$5,000
Restaurants: 17 (1 open 24 hours)
Casino Size: 138,684 Square Feet
Other Games: SB, RB, B, MB, P, PG, CW,
    PGP, CSP, LIR, TCP, B6, S21
Special Features: Recreates city of Venice with canals, gondoliers and replica Campanile Tower, St. Mark's Square, Doge's Palace and Rialto Bridge. 90 retail stores. Madame Tussaud's Wax Museum. Canyon Ranch Spa. *Human Nature* and *Rock of Ages* stage shows.

Westgate Las Vegas Resort & Casino
3000 Paradise Road
Las Vegas, Nevada 89109
(702) 732-5111
Website: www.thelvh.com

Reservation Number: (800) 732-7117
Rooms: 2,956 Price Range: $69-$129
Suites: 305 Price Range: $130-$1,750
Restaurants: 11 (1 open 24 hours)
Buffets: B- $19.99 (Sat/Sun only)
    L- $16.99 D- $21.99
Casino Size: 74,725 Square Feet
Other Games: SB, RB, B, MB, PGP,
    LIR, TCP, B6, P, CW
Special Features: World's largest race and sports book. Health club. Jogging track.

Wild Wild West Casino
3330 West Tropicana Avenue
Las Vegas, Nevada 89103
(702) 740-0000
Website: www.wwwesthotelcasino.com

Reservation Number: (800) 634-3488
Rooms: 262 Price Range: $39-$119
Restaurants: 1 (open 24 hours)
Casino Size: 11,250 Square Feet
Other Games: SB, RB
Special Features: Part of Station Casinos group. Discount smoke shop. 15-acre truck plaza.

Wynn Las Vegas
3145 Las Vegas Boulevard S.
Las Vegas, Nevada 89109
(702) 770-7000
Website: www.wynnlasvegas.com

Toll-Free Number: (888) 320-9966
Rooms: 2,359 Prices: $167-$639
Suites: 351 Prices: $450-$1,300
Restaurants: 18 (2 open 24 hours)
Buffets: B- $19.99/$31.99 (Sat/Sun) L- $25.99
    D- $38.99/$39.99 (Fri/Sat)
Casino Size: 186,187 Square Feet
Other Games: SB, RB, B, MB, P, PG,
    PGP, LIR, TCP, B6
Special Features: 150-foot man-made mountain with five-story waterfall. 18-hole golf course. Full-service Ferrari and Maserati dealership. *Le Reve* stage show. Spa and salon.

Laughlin

Map location: **#2** (on the Colorado River, 100 miles south of Las Vegas and directly across the river from Bullhead City, Arizona)

Laughlin is named after Don Laughlin, who owns the Riverside Hotel & Casino and originally settled there in 1966. The area offers many water sport activities on the Colorado River as well as at nearby Lake Mojave.

For Laughlin tourism information call: (800) 452-8445. You can also visit their Website at: www.visitlaughlin.com.

Here's information, as supplied by Nevada's State Gaming Control Board, showing the slot machine payback percentages for all of Laughlin's casinos for the fiscal year beginning July 1, 2013 and ending June 30, 2014:

Denomination	Payback %
1¢ Slots	88.97
5¢ Slots	92.75
25¢ Slots	94.73
$1 Slots	95.40
$1 Megabucks	88.80
$5 Slots	94.45
All Slots	92.67

These numbers reflect the percentage of money returned to the players on each denomination of machine. All electronic machines including slots, video poker and video keno are included in these numbers.

Optional games in the casino listings include: sports book (SB), race book (RB), Spanish 21 (S21), baccarat (B), mini-baccarat (MB), poker (P), pai gow poker (PGP), Caribbean stud poker (CSP), let it ride (LIR), three-card poker (TCP), four card poker (FCP), keno (K), sic bo (SIC), Mississippis stud (MS), big 6 wheel (B6) and bingo (BG).

Aquarius Casino Resort
1900 S. Casino Drive
Laughlin, Nevada 89029
(702) 298-5111
Website: www.aquariuscasinoresort.com

Reservation Number: (800) 435-8469
Rooms: 1,900 Price Range: $39-$89
Suites: 90 Price Range: $109-$299
Restaurants: 6 (1 open 24 hours)
Buffets: B/L-$14.99/$17.99 (Sun)
　　　D-$19.99/$28.99 (Fri)/$24.99 (Sat)
Casino Size: 57,070 Square Feet
Other Games: SB, RB, MB, P, FCP,
　　　　　　LIR, TCP, B6, K
Overnight RV Parking: No
Special Features: Fast Food court. Outback Steakhouse. 3,300-seat amphitheater.

Colorado Belle Hotel Casino & Microbrewery
2100 S. Casino Drive
Laughlin, Nevada 89029
(702) 298-4000
Website: www.coloradobelle.com

Reservation Number: (800) 477-4837
Rooms: 1,124 Price Range: $19-$70
Suites: 49 Price Range: $105-$175
Restaurants: 6 (1 opened 24 hours)
Casino Size: 44,953 Square Feet
Other Games: SB, RB, P, PGP,
　　　　　　TCP, LIR, K
Overnight RV Parking: No
Special Features: Video arcade. Microbrewery. Spa.

Don Laughlin's
Riverside Resort Hotel & Casino
1650 S. Casino Drive
Laughlin, Nevada 89029
(702) 298-2535
Website: www.riversideresort.com

Reservation Number: (800) 227-3849
Rooms: 1,405 Price Range: $45-$89
Executive Rooms: 93 Price Range: $79-$699
Restaurants: 7 (2 open 24 hours)
Buffets: B-$8.99 L-$8.49/$12.99 (Sun)
        D-$14.99/$17.99 (Fri)
Casino Size: 89,106 Square Feet
Other Games: SB, RB, P, LIR, PGP
        TCP, FCP, K, BG
Overnight RV Parking: Must use RV park
Special Features: 740-space RV park ($23-$27 per night). Six-screen cinema. Free classic car exhibit. 34-lane bowling center. Childcare center.

Edgewater Hotel Casino
2020 S. Casino Drive
Laughlin, Nevada 89029
(702) 298-2453
Website: www.edgewater-casino.com

Toll-Free Number: (800) 289-8777
Reservation Number: (800) 677-4837
Rooms: 1,420 Price Range: $20-$75
Suites: 23 Price Range: $95-$195
Restaurants: 3 (1 opened 24 hours)
Buffets: B- $7.99/$13.99 (Sun)
        L-$8.99/$12.99 (Sun)
        D- $12.99/$19.99 (Fri/Sat)
Casino Size: 45,927 Square Feet
Other Games: SB, RB, P, PGP, TCP, LIR
Overnight RV Parking: No

Golden Nugget Laughlin
2300 S. Casino Drive
Laughlin, Nevada 89029
(702) 298-7111
Website: www.goldennugget.com

Reservation Number: (800) 237-1739
Rooms: 300 Price Range: $24-$89
Suites: 4   Price Range: $150-$300
Restaurants: 5 (1 open 24 hours)
Casino Size: 32,600 Square Feet
Other Games: SB, RB, PGP, TCP,
        K, P, LIR
Overnight RV Parking: Free/RV Dump: No
Special Features: Suites must be booked through casino marketing.

Harrah's Laughlin Casino & Hotel
2900 S. Casino Drive
Laughlin, Nevada 89029
(702) 298-4600
Website: www.harrahslaughlin.com

Reservation Number: (800) 427-7247
Rooms: 1,451 Price Range: $19-$139
Suites: 115 Price Range: $114-$249
Restaurants: 4 (1 open 24 hours)
Buffets: B/L-$13.99/$14.99 (Sun)
        D-$18.99/$26.99 (Fri)/$22.99 (Sat)
Casino Size: 56,357 Square Feet
Other Games: SB, RB, P, PGP,
        TCP, LIR, K
Overnight RV Parking: No
Special Features: Salon and day spa. Beach and pools. 300-seat showroom. 3,000-seat amphitheater. McDonald's. Cinnabon. Starbucks.

Pioneer Hotel & Gambling Hall
2200 S. Casino Drive
Laughlin, Nevada 89029
(702) 298-2442
Website: www.pioneerlaughlin.com

Reservation Number: (800) 634-3469
Rooms: 416 Price Range: $25-$85
Suites: 20 Price Range: $60-$90
Restaurants: 2 (1 open 24 hours)
Buffets: B-$11.95 (Sun)
Casino Size: 16,300 Square Feet
Other Games: SB, RB, LIR, TCP
Overnight RV Parking: Free/RV Dump: No
Special Features: Western-themed casino. Western wear store. Liquor/cigarette store.

River Palms Resort Casino
2700 S. Casino Drive
Laughlin, Nevada 89029
(702) 298-2242
Website: www.river-palms.com

Toll-Free Number: (800) 835-7904
Reservation Number: (800) 835-7903
Rooms: 995 Price Range: $30-$65
Suites: 8 Price Range: $55-$295
Restaurants: 7 (1 open 24 hours)
Buffets: B-$8.99 (Sat/Sun)
         D-$9.99/$12.99 (Fri/Sat)
Casino Size: 29,488 Square Feet
Other Games: SB, RB, P, LIR, BG, TCP, PGP
Overnight RV Parking: Free/RV Dump: No
Special Features: Health spa.

Tropicana Laughlin
2121 S. Casino Drive
Laughlin, Nevada 89029
(702) 298-4200
Website: www.troplaughlin.com

Toll-Free Number: (800) 243-6846
Rooms: 1,501 Price Range: $39-$69
Suites: 55 Price Range: $79-$119
Restaurants: 5 (1 open 24 hours)
Buffets: B-$8.99/$14.99 (Sat/Sun)
         D-$10.99/$18.99 (Fri/Sat)
Casino Size: 52,840 Square Feet
Other Games: SB, RB, PGP, MS,
         TCP, LIR, MS
Overnight RV Parking: Free/RV Dump: No
Special Features: Display of railroad antiques
and memorabilia. Free train rides (Noon-10pm
Fri/Sat). Train-shaped swimming pool.

Lovelock

Map Location: **#18** (92 miles N.E. of Reno
on I-80)

Sturgeon's Inn and Casino
1420 Cornell Avenue
Lovelock, Nevada 89419
(775) 273-2971

Rooms: 74 Price Range: $59-$70
Spa Rooms: 2 Price Range: $89-$100
Restaurants: 1
Casino Size: 7,000 Square Feet
Other Games: SB, RB, No Table Games
Overnight RV Parking: Free/RV Dump: No
Special Features: Hotel is Ramada Inn.

Mesquite

Map Location: **#19** (77 miles N.E. of Las
Vegas on I-15 at the Arizona border)

Here's information, as supplied by Nevada's
State Gaming Control Board, showing the
slot machine payback percentages for all of
the Mesquite area casinos for the fiscal year
beginning July 1, 2013 and ending June 30,
2014:

Denomination	Payback %
1¢ Slots	90.72
5¢ Slots	95.98
25¢ Slots	95.88
$1 Slots	95.52
$1 Megabucks	87.60
All Slots	94.28

These numbers reflect the percentage of
money returned on each denomination
of machine and encompass all electronic
machines including slots, video poker and
video keno.

CasaBlanca Hotel-Casino-Golf-Spa
950 W. Mesquite Boulevard
Mesquite, Nevada 89027
(702) 346-7529
Website: www.casablancaresort.com

Reservation Number: (800) 459-7529
Rooms: 500 Price Range: $39-$109
Suites: 18 Price Range: $69-$229
Restaurants: 3 (1 open 24 hours)
Buffets: B-$7.99 (Sat/Sun)
         D-$15.99 (Fri)/$12.99 (Sat)
Casino Size: 27,000 Square Feet
Other Games: SB, RB, PGP, TCP, LIR, K
Overnight RV Parking: Must use RV park
Special Features: 45-space RV park ($20-$30
per night). 18-hole golf course. Health spa.

Eureka Casino & Hotel
275 Mesa Boulevard
Mesquite, Nevada 89027
(702) 346-4600
Website: www.eurekamesquite.com

Reservation Number: (800) 346-4611
Rooms: 192 Price Range: $49-$109
Suites: 18 Price Range: $99-$249
Restaurants: 2 (1 open 24 hours)
Buffets: B-$8.99/$12.99 (Sat)/$16.99 (Sun)
    L-$10.99 D-$14.99 /$21.99 (Fri/Sat)
Casino Size: 40,285 Square Feet
Other Games: SB, RB, P, PGP, TCP, LIR, BG
Overnight RV Parking: No
Special Features: $2 off buffet with players club card.

Virgin River Hotel/Casino/Bingo
100 Pioneer Boulevard
Mesquite, Nevada 89027
(702) 346-7777
Website: www.virginriver.com

Reservation Number: (800) 346-7721
Rooms: 720 Price Range: $25-$60
Suites: 2 Price Range: $250
Restaurants: 2 (1 open 24 hours)
Buffets: B-$6.99 L-$8.99/$10.99 (Sun)
    D-$12.99 /$13.99 (Tue/Thu)/
    $16.99 (Fri)/$14.99 (Sat)
Casino Size: 37,000 Square Feet
Other Games: SB, RB, PGP, TCP, K, BG
Overnight RV Parking: Must use RV park
Special Features: 24-lane bowling center. Four movie theaters.

Minden

Map Location: **#14** (42 miles S. of Reno on Hwy. 395)

Carson Valley Inn
1627 Highway 395 N.
Minden, Nevada 89423
(775) 782-9711
Website: www.cvinn.com

Reservation Number: (800) 321-6983
Hotel Rooms: 146 Price Range: $75-$115
Hotel Suites: 7 Price Range: $129-$189
Lodge Rooms: 75 Price Range: $69-$99
Lodge Suites: 5 Price Range: $89-$119
Restaurants: 4 (1 open 24 hours)
Casino Size: 22,800 Square Feet
Other Games: SB, RB, P,
    TCP, no roulette
Overnight RV Parking: Free/Dump: $5
Senior Discount: Various discounts if 50+
Special Features: 59-space RV park ($28-$38 per night). 24-hour convenience store. Wedding chapel. Childcare center.

N. Las Vegas

Map Location: **#20** (5 miles N.E. of the Las Vegas Strip on Las Vegas Blvd. N.)

Aliante Casino & Hotel
7300 Aliante Parkway
North Las Vegas, Nevada 89084
(702) 692-7777
Website: www.aliantecasinohotel.com

Toll-Free Number: (877) 477-7627
Rooms: 202 Price Range: $59-$129
Restaurants: 6
Buffets: B-$8.99/$14.99 (Sat/Sun) L- $11.99
    D- $14.99/$22.99 (Fri)/$18.99 (Sat)
Casino Size: 125,000 Square Feet
Other Games: SB, RB, P,
    TCP, PGP, BG
Overnight RV Parking: No
Special Features: 16-screen Regal Theater. Arcade.

Bighorn Casino
3016 E. Lake Mead Boulevard
N. Las Vegas, Nevada 89030
(702) 642-1940

Restaurants: 1
Casino Size: 3,740 Square Feet
Other Games: SB, RB, No craps or roulette
Overnight RV Parking: No

Cannery Hotel & Casino
2121 E Craig Road
N. Las Vegas, Nevada 89030
(702) 507-5700
Website: www.cannerycasino.com

Toll-Free Number: (866) 999-4899
Rooms: 201 Price Range: $39-$119
Restaurants: 5 (1 open 24 hours)
Buffets: B- $2.99 (Sat/Sun)
        L- $9.99
        D- $14.99/$15.99 (Tue/Thu)
Casino Size: 79,485 Square Feet
Other Games: RB, SB, P, PGP, BG
Overnight RV Parking: No
Special Features: Property is themed to
resemble a 1940's canning factory. Buffet
discount for players club members.

Fiesta Rancho Casino Hotel
2400 N. Rancho Drive
N. Las Vegas, Nevada 89130
(702) 631-7000
Website: www.fiestarancholasvegas.com

Reservation Number: (800) 731-7333
Rooms: 100 Price Range: $29-$119
Restaurants: 4 (1 open 24 hours)
Buffets: B- $12.99 (Sat/Sun)
        L- $9.99
        D- $12.99
Casino Size: 59,951 Square Feet
Other Games: SB, RB, B, MB, PGP, K, BG
Overnight RV Parking: Yes/Dump: No
Senior Discount: Join Fiesta 50 for discounts
Special Features: Ice skating arena. Coffee
bar. Smoke shop. Buffet discount for players
club members.

Jerry's Nugget
1821 Las Vegas Boulevard North
N. Las Vegas, Nevada 89030
(702) 399-3000
Website: www.jerrysnugget.com

Restaurants: 2
Casino Size: 32,511 Square Feet
Other Games: SB, RB, K, BG
Overnight RV Parking: No
Senior Discount: Various if 55+
Special Features: Bakery.

Lucky Club Casino
3227 Civic Center Drive
N. Las Vegas, Nevada 89030
(702) 399-3297
Website: www.luckyclublv.com

Reservation Number: (877) 333-9291
Rooms: 92 Price Range: $49-$99
Suites: 3 Price Range: $119-$129
Restaurants: 1 (open 24 hours)
Casino Size: 16,650 Square Feet
Other Games: SB, RB
Overnight RV Parking: No
Special Features: Closest hotel/casino to Las
Vegas Motor Speedway.

Opera House Saloon & Casino
2542 Las Vegas Blvd. North
N. Las Vegas, Nevada 89030
(702) 649-8801
Website: www.operahousecasino.com

Restaurants: 1
Casino Size: 15,100 Square Feet
Other Games: No table games, SB, RB, BG
Overnight RV Parking: No

The Poker Palace
2757 Las Vegas Blvd. North
N. Las Vegas, Nevada 89030
(702) 649-3799
Website: www.pokerpalace.net

Restaurants: 1
Casino Size: 25,900 Square Feet
Other Games: SB, RB, P, BG,
            No craps or roulette
Overnight RV Parking: No

Silver Nugget
2140 Las Vegas Boulevard North
N. Las Vegas, Nevada 89030
(702) 399-1111
Website: www.silvernuggetcasino.net

Restaurants: 1
Casino Size: 21,000 Square Feet
Other Games: SB, RB, BG, No roulette or craps
Overnight RV Parking: Must use RV park
Senior Discount: 10% off food if 55+
Special Features: 24-lane bowling center.

Texas Station
2101 Texas Star Lane
N. Las Vegas, Nevada 89032
(702) 631-1000
Website: www.texasstation.com

Toll-Free Number: (800) 654-8804
Reservation Number: (800) 654-8888
Rooms: 200 Price Range: $34-$194
Restaurants: 8 (1 open 24 hours)
Buffets: B-$8.99/$14.99 (Sun)
　　　　L-$11.99 D-$14.99
Casino Size: 123,045 Square Feet
Other Games: SB, RB, P, PGP,
　　　　TCP, K, BG
Overnight RV Parking: No
Senior Discount: Various if 50+
Special Features: 18-screen movie theater. 60-lane bowling center. Kids Quest childcare center. Food court. Wedding chapels. Video arcade. 2,000-seat events center. Buffet discount for players club members.

Pahrump

Map Location: **#21** (59 miles W. of Las Vegas on Hwy. 160)

Gold Town Casino
771 Frontage Road
Pahrump, Nevada 89048
(775) 751-7777
Website: www.gtowncasino.com

Toll Free Number: (888) 837-7425
Restaurants: 1
Casino Size: 12,000 Square Feet
Other Games: BG
Overnight RV Parking: Yes. Free/RV Dump: No
Special Features: General store and gas station.

Pahrump Nugget Hotel & Gambling Hall
681 S. Highway 160
Pahrump, Nevada 89048
(775) 751-6500
Website: www.pahrumpnugget.com

Toll Free Number: (866) 751-6500
Rooms: 69 Price Range: $69-$89
Suites: 1 Price Range: $110-$213
Restaurants: 3 (1 open 24 hours)
Buffet: D-$14.99 (Fri)
Casino Size: 17,400 Square Feet
Other Games: SB, RB, P, TCP, BG, UTH
Overnight RV Parking: No
Special Features: 24-lane bowling center. Video arcade. Non-smoking poker room. Supervised childcare center.

Saddle West Hotel/Casino & RV Park
1220 S. Highway 160
Pahrump, Nevada 89048
(775) 727-1111
Website: www.saddlewest.com

Reservation Number: (800) 433-3987
Rooms: 148 Price Range: $49-$115
Suites: 10 Price Range: $89-$129
Restaurants: 2 (1 open 24 hours)
Buffets: B- $6.45 L- $5.95/$12.95 (Sun)
　　　　D- $12.95/$11.95 (Wed)/
　　　　$13.95 (Tue/Sat)/$15.95 (Fri)
Casino Size: 15,496 Square Feet
Other Games: SB, RB, BG, No roulette
Overnight RV Parking: Free/RV Dump: No
Special Features: 80-space RV park ($25 per night). Closest casino to Death Valley Park.

Primm

Map Location: **#6** (25 miles S.W. of Las Vegas on I-15; 9 miles from the California border)

Buffalo Bill's Resort & Casino
31700 Las Vegas Boulevard S.
Primm, Nevada 89019
(702) 382-1212
Website: www.primmvalleyresorts.com

Toll-Free Number: (800) 386-7867
Rooms: 1,242 Price Range: $20-$85
Suites: 15 Price Range: $89-$125
Restaurants: 3 (1 open 24 hours)
Buffets: B-$10.99 (Fri/Sat)
        L-$12.99 (Fri/Sat) D-$15.99 (Fri/Sat)
Casino Size: 61,372 Square Feet
Other Games: SB, RB, P, PGP, LIR,
        TCP, B6
Overnight RV Parking: Free/RV Dump: No
Special Features: 3 Roller coasters. Flume ride. Two water slides. Movie theater. Video Arcade. 6,500-seat arena. Train shuttle connects to Whiskey Pete's and Primm Valley. Fast food court with 5 outlets.

Primm Valley Resort & Casino
31900 Las Vegas Boulevard S.
Primm, Nevada 89019
(702) 382-1212
Website: www.primmvalleyresorts.com

Reservation Number: (800) 386-7867
Rooms: 661 Price Range: $34-$99
Suites: 31 Price Range: $113-$178
Restaurants: 2 (1 open 24 hours)
Buffets: L-$11.99 D-$10.95
Casino Size: 35,279 Square Feet
Other Games: SB, RB, PGP
Overnight RV Parking: Free/RV Dump: No
Special Features: Free monorail to Whiskey Pete's. Al Capone's car and Bonnie & Clyde's "death" car on display. Free monorail service to Primm Valley.

Whiskey Pete's Hotel & Casino
100 W. Primm Boulevard
Primm, Nevada 89019
(702) 382-1212
Website: www.primmvalleyresorts.com

Reservation Number: (800) 386-7867
Rooms: 777 Price Range: $40-$99
Suites: 4 Price Range: $139-$219
Restaurants: 2 (1 open 24 hours)
Casino Size: 36,400 Square Feet
Other Games: SB, RB, P
Overnight RV Parking: Free/RV Dump: No

Reno

Map Location: **#4** (near the California border, 58 miles N.E. of Lake Tahoe and 32 miles N. of Carson City).

Reno may be best known for its neon arch on Virginia Street which welcomes visitors to "The Biggest Little City in the World." The current arch is actually the fourth one since the original arch was built in 1927. The area also houses the nation's largest car collection at the National Automobile Museum.

For Reno information call the Reno/Sparks Convention & Visitors Authority at (800) 367-7366 or go to: www.renolaketahoe.com.

Overnight parking of an RV in a casino parking lot is prohibited in Reno.

Here's information, as supplied by Nevada's State Gaming Control Board, showing the slot machine payback percentages for all of the Reno area casinos for the fiscal year beginning July 1, 2013 and ending June 30, 2014:

Denomination	Payback %
1¢ Slots	92.39
5¢ Slots	94.24
25¢ Slots	93.19
$1 Slots	96.09
$1 Megabucks	89.90
$5 Slots	95.64
All Slots	94.95

These numbers reflect the percentage of money returned on each denomination of machine and encompass all electronic machines including slots, video poker and video keno.

Optional games in the casino listings include: sports book (SB), race book (RB), Spanish 21 (S21), baccarat (B), mini-baccarat (MB), pai gow (PG), poker (P), pai gow poker (PGP), Caribbean stud poker (CSP), let it ride (LIR), three-card poker (TCP), four card poker (FCP), big 6 wheel (B6), keno (K) and bingo (BG).

Atlantis Casino Resort
3800 S. Virginia Street
Reno, Nevada 89502
(775) 825-4700
Website: www.atlantiscasino.com

Reservation Number: (800) 723-6500
Rooms: 975 Price Range: $49-$299
Suites: 120 Price Range: $79-$325
Restaurants: 8 (1 open 24 hours)
Buffets: B-$11.99/$14.99 (Sat)/$21.99 (Sun)
    L-$13.99/$15.99 (Sat) D-$18.99/
    $29.99 (Fri/Sat)
Casino Size: 64,814 Square Feet
Other Games: SB, RB, B, MB, P, PG,
    PGP, LIR, TCP, K
Senior Discount: 10% off buffet if 55+
Special Features: Health spa and salon.

Bonanza Casino
4720 N. Virginia Street
Reno, Nevada 89506
(775) 323-2724
Website: www.bonanzacasino.com

Restaurants: 2 (1 open 24 hours)
Buffets: Brunch-$9.95 (Sat/Sun)
    D-$9.95 (Fri/Sat)
Casino Size: 12,484 Square Feet
Other Games: SB, RB, no roulette

Circus Circus Hotel Casino/Reno
500 N. Sierra Street
Reno, Nevada 89503
(775) 329-0711
Website: www.circusreno.com

Toll-Free Number: (888) 682-0147
Reservation Number: (800) 648-5010
Rooms: 1,464 Price Range: $35-$109
Suites: 108   Price Range: $70-$210
Restaurants: 6 (1 open 24 hours)
Buffets: B/L-$8.99 (Fri)/$9.99 (Sat/Sun)
    D-$16.99 (Fri/Sat)
Casino Size: 66,679 Square Feet
Other Games: SB, RB, PGP, MS
    TCP, FCP, B6
Special Features: Free circus acts. Carnival games. 24-hour gift shop/liquor store. Buffet discount for players club members.

Club Cal-Neva/Virginian Hotel and Casino
38 E. Second Street
Reno, Nevada 89505
(775) 323-1046
Website: www.clubcalneva.com

Toll-Free Number (877) 777-7303
Rooms: 303 Price Range: $29-$129
Suites: 6 Price Range: $104-$194
Restaurants: 5 (1 open 24 hours)
Casino Size: 40,140 Square Feet
Other Games: SB, RB, P, PGP, LIR, TCP, K
Special Features: Hot dog and a beer for $3.75.

Eldorado Hotel Casino
345 N. Virginia Street
Reno, Nevada 89501
(775) 786-5700
Website: www.eldoradoreno.com

Toll-Free Number: (800) 648-4597
Reservation Number: (800) 648-5966
Rooms: 817 Price Range: $44-$129
Suites: 127 Price Range: $125-$399
Restaurants: 8 (1 open 24 hours)
Buffets: B- $9.99/$14.99 (Sat)/$16.99 (Sun)
    L- $10.99/$14.99 (Sat)/$16.99 (Sun)
    D- $14.99/$24.99 (Sat)/$16.99 (Sun)
Casino Size: 76,500 Square Feet
Other Games: SB, RB, MB, PG, PGP, P,
    LIR, TCP, K
Senior Discount: Food discounts if 60+
Special Features: In-house coffee roasting. Pasta shop. Microbrewery. Bakery. Butcher shop. Gelato factory. Buffet discount for players club members.

The Best Places To Play in Reno/Tahoe

Roulette- The house edge on a single-zero wheel cuts the house edge from 5.26% down to a more reasonable 2.70%. Unfortunately, there are no casinos in Reno/Tahoe that offer single-zero roulette

Craps- Almost all Reno/Tahoe area casino offer double odds on their crap games. The casino offering the highest odds is The Lakeside Inn in Lake Tahoe which offers 10X odds.

Blackjack - There's good news and bad news for blackjack players in Northern Nevada. The good news is that there is an abundance of single-deck and double-deck games available. The bad news is that all casinos in the Reno/Tahoe area hit soft 17. This results in a slightly higher advantage (.20%) for the casinos. Additionally, some casinos may also restrict your double-downs to two-card totals of 10 or 11 only. The following recommendations apply to basic strategy players.

For single-deck games you should always look for casinos that pay the standard 3-to-2 for blackjacks. A few casinos only pay 6-to-5 for blackjack and this increases the casino edge tremendously. The casino advantage in these games is around 1.5% and they should be avoided.

The best single-deck game is at the Alamo Travel Center in Sparks which has the following rules: double down on any first two cards, split any pair, resplit any pair, late surrender, and they will count a "six-card Charlie" as an automatic winner. The casino edge here is .10%.

Next best are four casinos that offer single-deck with the basic Northern Nevada rules: double down on any first two cards, split any pair and resplit any pair (except aces): Boomtown, John Ascuaga's Nugget, Rail City and Western Village. The casino edge here is .18%. (NOTE: There are numerous casinos that offer a game similar to this one except they will only allow you to double down on totals of 10 or more. This raises the casino edge in this game to .44%).

There are seven casinos that tie for best place to play double-deck blackjack: Atlantis, Club Cal-Neva, Eldorado, Grand Sierra, Peppermill, Siena and Silver Legacy. Their two-deck games have the following rules: double down on any first two cards, split any pair, and resplit any pair (except aces). This works out to a casino edge of .53%.

The best six-deck game can be found in Reno at the Silver Legacy The game's edge is .39% with these rules: double down on any two or more cards, split any pair, resplit any pair (except aces) and double allowed after split.

Next best is a game found at five Lake Tahoe casinos: Crystal Bay Club, Harrah's, Harvey's, Hyatt Regency and Lakeside Inn. The casino edge here is .56% with the following rules: double down on any two cards, split any pair, resplit any pair (including aces) and double allowed after split.

If you take away resplitting of aces from the previous game then you have a game with a casino edge of .63% which is offered in Reno at Atlantis, Circus Circus, Eldorado, Grand Sierra, John Ascuaga's Nugget, the Peppermill and Sands Regency.

Video Poker - Smart video poker players know that the five best varieties of machines to look for are: 8/5 Bonus Poker (99.17 % return), 9/6 Jacks or Better (99.54% return), 10/6 Double Double Bonus (100.07% return), 10/7 Double Bonus (100.17% return) and full-pay Deuces Wild (100.76% return).

All of these games are available in Northern Nevada, with the exception of full-pay Deuces Wild, which is hard to find. A slightly lesser-paying version, known as Not So Ugly Deuces (NSUD), which returns 99.73%, however, is widely available.

Following is a list of casinos offering the better paying video poker games. The abbreviations used for each listing are BP (8/5 Bonus Poker), JB (9/6 jacks or better), DDB (10/6 Double Double Bonus), DB (10/7 Double Bonus), FPDW (full-pay deuces wild) and NSUD (not so ugly deuces).

Reno/Sparks Casinos:
Atlantis: JB - penny to $100 (some with progressives); DB - nickel to $1 (some with progressives); DDB - nickel and quarter; BP - nickel to $1; FPDW - nickel
Circus Circus: JB - quarter to $5; BP - quarter and fifty-cent; NSUD - $1 to $5
Club Cal Neva: JB - fifty-cent and $1; BP - $1
Eldorado: JB - quarter to $5 (some with progressives); NSUD - quarter to $1; BP - quarter
Harrah's Reno: JB - quarter to $10; BP -quarter to $25
John Ascuaga's Nugget: JB - penny to $2; BP - quarter and $1; NSUD - penny to $2
Peppermill: JB - penny to $100; NSUD - two-cents to $100; BP - two-cents to $100
Rail City: JB - quarter and $1; DB - fifty-cent and dollar
Siena: JB - quarter to $5
Silver Legacy: JB - nickel to $1; FPDW - quarter; NSUD - $1; BP - quarter to $1
Western Village: JB - penny to $1; DB - nickel to $1; NSUD - penny to $1

Lake Tahoe Casinos:
Harrah's Lake Tahoe: JB - quarter to $100; BP - quarter to $100
Harvey's: JB - $5 to $100; BP - quarter to $100
Montbleu: JB - quarter to $1; BP - quarter to $1
Tahoe Biltmore: JB- quarter to $5; BP- quarter to $1; NSUD - quarter to $1

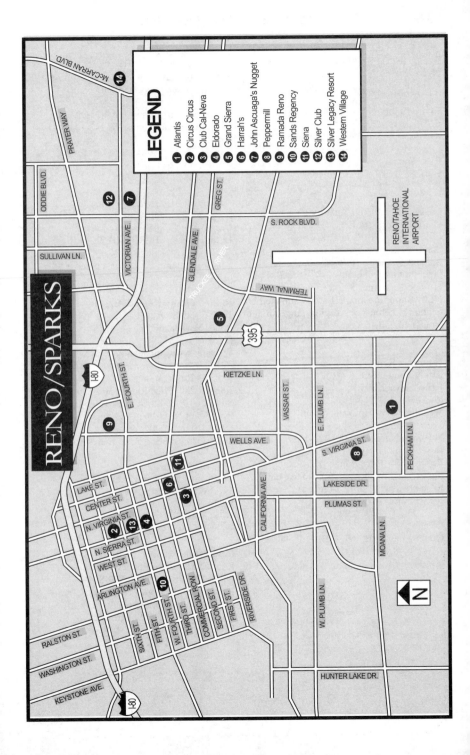

Grand Sierra Resort & Casino
2500 E. Second Street
Reno, Nevada 89595
(775) 789-2000
Website: www.grandsierraresort.com

Room Reservations: (800) 501-2651
RV Reservations: (888) 562-5698
Rooms: 1,847 Price Range: $79-$255
Suites: 154 Price Range: $149-$899
Restaurants: 10 (1 open 24 hours)
Buffets: B- $10.99/$15.99 (Sat)/$17.99 (Sat)
        L- $13.99/$15.99 (Sat)/$17.99 (Sat)
        D- $18.99/$21.99 (Fri/Sat)
Casino Size: 49,140 Square Feet
Other Games: SB, RB, MB, P, PG, PGP,
        LIR, TCP, K
Senior Discount: Various if 55+
Special Features: Two movie theaters. 50-lane bowling center. 174-space RV park ($40-$52 summer/$25-$35 winter). Health club. Shopping mall. Family amusement center. Laketop golf driving range. Indoor simulated golf.

Harrah's Reno
219 N. Center Street
Reno, Nevada 89501
(775) 786-3232
Website: www.harrahsreno.com

Toll-Free Number: (800) 423-1121
Reservation Number: (800) 427-7247
Rooms: 886 Price Range: $55-$200
Suites: 60 Price Range: Casino use only
Restaurants: 7 (1 open 24 hours)
Buffets: B/L-$17.99/ (Sun)
        D-$21.99/$26.99 (Fri/Sat)
Casino Size: 40,200 Square Feet
Other Games: SB, RB, MB, FCP, PG,
        PGP, LIR, TCP, K

Peppermill Hotel Casino Reno
2707 S. Virginia Street
Reno, Nevada 89502
(775) 826-2121
Website: www.peppermillreno.com

Toll-Free Number: (800) 648-6992
Reservation Number: (800) 282-2444
Rooms: 1,070 Price Range: $55-$135
Suites: 185 Price Range: $149-$209
Restaurants: 6 (1 open 24 hours)
Buffets: B-$13.99/$15.99 (Sat)/$21.99 (Sun)
        L-$14.99
        D-$19.99/$29.99 (Fri/Sat)/
        $20.99 (Sun)
Casino Size: 77,058 Square Feet
Other Games: SB, RB, MB, PG, P, PGP,
        LIR, TCP, K, FCP
Senior Discount: Various discounts if 55+

Ramada Reno Hotel & Casino
1000 E. 6th Street
Reno, Nevada 89512
(775) 786-5151
Website: www.ramadareno.com

Ramada Reservations: (888) 288-4982
Rooms: 280 Price Range: $69-$109
Suites: 6 Price Range: $89-$199
Restaurants: 2 (1 open 24 hours)
Casino Size: 8,000 Square Feet
Other Games: SB, RB, no roulette or craps

The Sands Regency Hotel Casino
345 North Arlington Avenue
Reno, Nevada 89501
(775) 348-2200
Website: www.sandsregency.com

Reservation Number: (800) 648-3553
Rooms: 811 Price Range: $39-$139
Suites: 27 Price Range: $99-$249
Restaurants: 4 (1 open 24 hours)
Buffets: L/D-$10.99/$12.99 (Fri/Sat)
Casino Size: 25,791 Square Feet
Other Games: SB, RB, P, LIR,
        PGP, TCP, BG

The arch in downtown Reno that welcomes visitors to
"The Biggest Little City in the World" is the city's most famous landmark.

Siena Hotel Spa Casino
1 S. Lake Street
Reno, Nevada 89501
(775) 327-4362
Website: www.sienareno.com

Toll-Free Number: (877) 743-6233
Rooms: 214 Price Range: $109-$259
Suites: 27 Price Range: $139-$649
Restaurants: 5 (1 open 24 hours)
Casino Size: 24,000 Square Feet
Other Games: SB, RB, PGP, K
Special Features: Health spa.

Silver Legacy Resort Casino
407 N. Virginia Street
Reno, Nevada 89501
(775) 325-7401
Website: www.silverlegacy.com

Toll-Free Number: (800) 687-7733
Reservation Number: (800) 687-8733
Rooms: 1,720 Price Range: $49-$175
Suites: 150 Price Range: $89-$200
Restaurants: 5 (1 open 24 hours)
Buffets: B-$8.99/$15.99 (Sat/Sun)
L-$10.49 D-$14.99/$23.99 (Fri/Sat)
Casino Size: 89,200 Square Feet
Other Games: SB, RB, MB, PG, PGP, P,
LIR, TCP, B6, K
Special Features: Simulated mining machine
above casino floor. Comedy club. Rum bar.
No buffet Mon/Tue.

Searchlight

Map Location: **#22** (58 miles S. of Las Vegas on Hwy. 95)

Searchlight Nugget Casino
100 N. Highway 95
Searchlight, Nevada 89046
(702) 297-1201
Website: www.searchlightnugget.com

Casino Size: 3,910 Square Feet
Other Games: P (Fri/Sat), no craps or roulette
Overnight RV Parking: Free/RV Dump: No
Special Features: Poker tables open at 6pm.

Sparks

Map Location: **#4** (Sparks is a suburb of Reno and is located one mile east of Reno on I-80)

Here's information, as supplied by Nevada's State Gaming Control Board, showing the slot machine payback percentages for all of the Sparks area casinos for the fiscal year beginning July 1, 2013 and ending June 30, 2014:

Denomination	Payback %
1¢ Slots	93.60
5¢ Slots	96.53
25¢ Slots	95.59
$1 Slots	96.38
$1 Megabucks	88.18
$5 Slots	96.44
All Slots	95.40

These numbers reflect the percentage of money returned on each denomination of machine and encompass all electronic machines including slots, video poker and video keno.

Alamo Casino & Travel Center
1959 East Greg Street
Sparks, Nevada 89431
(775) 355-8888
Website: www.thealamo.com

Super 8 Room Reservations: (800) 800-8000
Rooms: 64 Price Range: $79-$129
Suites: 7 Price Range: $104-$159
Restaurants: 1 (open 24 hours)
Casino Size: 7,150 Square Feet
Other Games: SB, RB, P, No roulette
Overnight RV Parking: Free/RV Dump: No
Special Features: Motel is Super 8. Truck stop. Video arcade. Post office and gas station.

John Ascuaga's Nugget
1100 Nugget Avenue
Sparks, Nevada 89431
(775) 356-3300
Website: www.janugget.com

Toll-Free Number: (800) 648-1177
Rooms: 1,450 Price Range: $85-$189
Suites: 150 Price Range: $109-$295
Restaurants: 8 (1 open 24 hours)
Buffets: B-$7.95/$13.95 (Sat)/$14.95 (Sun)
         D-$9.99/$22.95 (Fri/Sat)
Casino Size: 72,300 Square Feet
Overnight RV Parking: Free (3 day maximum)
         RV Dump: No
Other Games: SB, RB, P, PGP,
         LIR, TCP, K, BG
Special Features: Wedding chapel. Health club.

Rail City Casino
2121 Victorian Avenue
Sparks, Nevada 89431
(775) 359-9440
Website: www.railcity.com

Restaurants: 1
Buffets: B/L- $7.50
         D- $8.50/$10.95 (Fri)
Casino Size: 23,854 Square Feet
Other Games: SB, RB, P, K, no craps or roulette
Overnight RV Parking: No

Western Village Inn & Casino
815 Nichols Boulevard
Sparks, Nevada 89432
(775) 331-1069
Website: www.westernvillagesparks.com

Reservation Number: (800) 648-1170
Rooms: 147 Price Range: $55-$65
Suites: 4 Price Range: $155-$175
Restaurants: 3 (1 open 24 hours)
Casino Size: 26,452 Square Feet
Other Games: SB, RB
Overnight RV Parking: No/RV Dump: No
Senior Discount: Room discount if 55 or older

Verdi

Map Location: #4 (4 miles W. of Reno on I-80 at the California border)

Boomtown Hotel & Casino
2100 Garson Road
Verdi, Nevada 89439
(775) 345-6000
Website: www.boomtownreno.com

Toll-Free Number: (800) 648-3790
Room/RV Reservations: (877) 626-6686
Rooms: 318 Price Range: $69-$149
Suites: 20 Price Range: $105-$265
Restaurants: 4 (1 open 24 hours)
Buffets: B-$16.99(Sun)
        D-$33.99 (Fri-Sun)
Casino Size: 38,550 Square Feet
Other Games: SB, RB, P, PGP, TCP, K
Overnight RV Parking: Free (1 night only)/
        RV Dump: No
Special Features: 203-space RV park ($42 per night). 24-hour mini-mart. Indoor family fun center with rides and arcade games. Free shuttle to/from Reno. Buffet discount for players club members.

Gold Ranch Casino & RV Resort
350 Gold Ranch Road
Verdi, Nevada 89439
(775) 345-6789
Website: www.goldranchrvcasino.com

RV Reservations: (877) 927-6789
Restaurants: 2
Casino Size: 8,370 Square Feet
Other Games: SB, RB No Table Games
Overnight RV Parking: Must use RV park
Special Features: 105-space RV park ($32-$70 per night). 24-hour mini-mart.

Wells

Map Location: #23 (338 miles N.E. of Reno on I-80)

Alamo Casino Wells
1440 6th Street
Wells, Nevada 89835
(775) 752-3344

Restaurants: 1
Casino Size: 6,100 Square Feet
Other Games: No table games
Overnight RV Parking: Free/RV Dump: No

W. Wendover

Map Location: #24 (Just W. of the Utah border on I-80)

Here's information, as supplied by Nevada's State Gaming Control Board, showing the slot machine payback percentages for all of the Wendover area casinos for the fiscal year beginning July 1, 2013 and ending June 30, 2014:

Denomination	Payback %
1¢ Slots	93.48
5¢ Slots	94.49
25¢ Slots	93.65
$1 Slots	96.11
$5 Slots	96.31
All Slots	94.48

These numbers reflect the percentage of money returned on each denomination of machine and encompass all electronic machines including slots, video poker and video keno.

Montego Bay Casino Resort
100 Wendover Boulevard
W. Wendover, Nevada 89883
(775) 664-9100
Website: www.wendoverfun.com

Toll-Free Number: (877) 666-8346
Reservation Number: (800) 537-0207
Rooms: 437 Price Range: $54-$109
Suites: 75 Price Range: $94-$179
Restaurants: 2 (1 open 24 hours)
Buffets: B-$16.95 (Sat/Sun) L-$13.95
          D-$16.95/$27.95 (Fri)/$22.95 (Sat)
Casino Size: 49,400 Square Feet
Other Games: SB, RB, P, PGP, LIR,TCP
Overnight RV Parking: Free/RV Dump: No
Senior Discount: $2 buffet discount if 55+
Special Features: Connected by sky bridge
to Wendover Nugget. Liquor Store. Golf
packages.

Peppermill Inn & Casino
680 Wendover Boulevard
W. Wendover, Nevada 89883
(775) 664-2255
Website: www.wendoverfun.com

Reservation Number: (800) 648-9660
Rooms: 302 Price Range: $50-$170
Suites: 42 Price Range: $60-$205
Restaurants: 2 (1 open 24 hours)
Buffets: B- $14.95 (Sat/Sun) L- $10.95
          D- $14.95/$24.95 (Fri)/$19.95 (Sat)
Casino Size: 30,577 Square Feet
Other Games: SB, RB, PGP, LIR, TCP
Overnight RV Parking: Free/RV Dump: No
Senior Discount: $2 buffet discount if 55+

Rainbow Hotel Casino
1045 Wendover Boulevard
W. Wendover, Nevada 89883
(775) 664-4000
Website: www.wendoverfun.com

Toll-Free Number: (800) 217-0049
Rooms: 379 Price Range: $50-$150
Suites: 50 Price Range: $70-$205
Restaurants: 3 (1 open 24 hours)
Buffets: B-$16.95 (Sat/Sun) L-$13.95
          D-$16.95/$27.95 (Fri)/$22.95 (Sat)
Casino Size: 57,360 Square Feet
Other Games: SB, RB, P, PGP, LIR, TCP, BG
Overnight RV Parking: Free/RV Dump: No
Senior Discount: $2 buffet discount if 55+

Red Garter Hotel & Casino
1225 Wendover Boulevard
W. Wendover, Nevada 89883
(775) 664-2111
Website: www.redgartercasino.com

Toll-Free Number: (800) 982-2111
Rooms: 46 Price Range: $27-$65
Restaurants: 1 (open 24 hours)
Casino Size: 17,342 Square Feet
Other Games: SB, TCP, K
Overnight RV Parking: No

Wendover Nugget Hotel & Casino
101 Wendover Boulevard
W. Wendover, Nevada 89883
(775) 664-2221
Website: www.wendovernugget.com

Toll-Free Number: (800) 848-7300
Rooms: 500 Price Range: $50-$109
Suites: 60 Price Range: $75-$205
Restaurants: 3 (1 open 24 hours)
Buffets: B-$16.95 (Sat/Sun) L-$12.95
          D-$15.95/$27.95 (Fri)/$22.95 (Sat)
Casino Size: 37,074 Square Feet
Other Games: SB, RB, P, TCP,
          LIR, PGP, K,
Overnight RV Parking: Must use RV park
Senior Discount: Room/food discounts if 55+
Special Features: 56-space RV park ($35 per
night). Sky bridge to Montego Bay.

Winnemucca

Map Location: **#25** (164 miles N.E. of Reno
on I-80)

Model T Hotel/Casino/RV Park
1130 W. Winnemucca Boulevard
Winnemucca, Nevada 89446
(775) 623-2588
Website: www.modelt.com

Reservation Number: (800) 645-5658
Rooms: 75 Price Range: $80-$90
Restaurants: 2 (1 open 24 hours)
Casino Size: 7,053 Square Feet
Other Games: SB, RB, No table games
Overnight RV Parking: Free/RV Dump: No
Special Features: Hotel is Quality Inn.
58-space RV park ($33 per night).

Winnemucca Inn
741 W. Winnemucca Boulevard
Winnemucca, Nevada 89445
(775) 623-2565
    Website: www.winnemuccainn.com

Reservation Number: (800) 633-6435
Rooms: 105 Price Range: $69-$115
Suites: 6 Price Range: $109-$170
Restaurants: 1 (open 24 hours)
Casino Size: 3,000 Square Feet
Other Games: SB, RB, No craps or roulette
Overnight RV Parking: No

Winners Hotel/Casino
185 W. Winnemucca Boulevard
Winnemucca, Nevada 89445
(775) 623-2511
Website: www.winnerscasino.com

Reservation Number: (800) 648-4770
Rooms: 123 Price Range: $49-$70
Suites: 3 Price Range: $69-$99
Restaurants: 2 (1 open 24 hours)
Casino Size: 10,340 Square Feet
Other Games: SB, RB, BG (Wed/Fri/Sat),
        TCP, P
Overnight RV Parking: Free/ Dump: No
Senior Discount: Room discount if 55+

Yearington

Map Location: **#26** (60 miles S.E. of Reno
on Hwy. Alt. 95)

Casino West
11 N. Main Street
Yerington, Nevada 89447
(775) 463-2481

Reservation Number: (800) 227-4661
Rooms: 49 Price Range: $46-$50
Suites: 29 Price Range: $55-59
Restaurants: 1 (open 24 hours)
Buffets: D- $13.95 (Fri)/$8.95 (Sat/Sun)
Casino Size: 4,950 Square Feet
Other Games: P, No craps or roulette
Overnight RV Parking: Must use RV park
Senior Discount: Room discounts if 55+
Special Features: Hotel is Best Western.
5-space RV park ($15 per night). Movie
theater. 12-lane bowling alley.

Indian Casinos

Avi Resort & Casino
10000 Aha Macav Parkway
Laughlin, Nevada 89029
(702) 535-5555
Website: www.avicasino.com
Map Location: **#2**

Toll-Free Number: (800) 284-2946
Rooms: 426 Price Range: $35-$110
Suites: 29 Price Range: $51-$135
Restaurants: 4 (1 open 24 hours)
Buffets: B-$6.99/$19.99 (Sat/Sun)
        L-$8.99
        D-$11.99/$16.99 (Fri)/$14.99 (Sat)
Casino Size: 25,000 Square Feet
Other Games: SB, RB, P, TCP, PGP,
        LIR, K, BG
Overnight RV Parking: Free/RV Dump: No
Special Features: 260-space RV park ($18
May-Oct/$28 Nov-April). On Colorado River
with boat dock, launch and private beach. Fast
Food Court. 8-screen cinema. Smoke shop.
Kids Quest childcare center.

Moapa Tribal Casino
Interstate 15, Exit 75
Moapa, Nevada 89025-0340
(702) 864-2601
Website: www.moapapaiutes.com
Map Location: **#27** (65 miles N.E. of Las Vegas)

Other Games: Machines only
Overnight RV Parking: No

NEW JERSEY

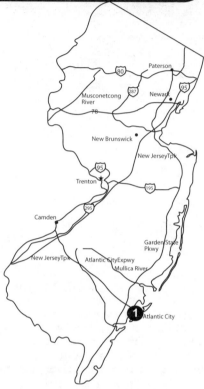

Map Location: #1 (on the Atlantic Ocean in southeast New Jersey, 130 miles south of New York City and 60 miles southeast of Philadelphia)

Once a major tourist destination that was world-famous for its steel pier and boardwalk attractions, Atlantic City gradually fell into decline and casino gambling was seen as its salvation when voters approved it there in 1976.

All Atlantic City casinos are located along the boardwalk, except for three: Borgata, Harrah's and Golden Nugget. Those three are located in the marina section.

Following is information from the New Jersey Casino Control Commission regarding average slot payout percentages for the 12-month period from July 1, 2013 through June 30, 2014:

CASINO	PAYBACK %
Borgata	91.6
Harrah's	91.6
Resorts	91.1
Bally's A.C.	90.9
Golden Nugget	90.8
Caesars	90.8
Trump Taj Mahal	90.7
Tropicana	90.6

These figures reflect the total percentages returned by each casino for all of their electronic machines which include slot machines, video poker, etc.

All Atlantic City casinos are open 24 hours and, unless otherwise noted, the games offered at every casino are: slots, video poker, craps, blackjack, Spanish 21, roulette, mini-baccarat, Caribbean stud poker, three card poker, four card poker, let it ride, pai gow tiles and pai gow poker. Additional games offered include: sic bo (SB), keno (K), baccarat (B), casino war (CW), poker (P), off-track betting (OTB), Texas hold'em bonus (THB), Mississippi stud (MS) and big six wheel (B6). The minimum gambling age is 21.

For more information on visiting New Jersey you can contact the state's Travel & Tourism Department at (800) 537-7397 or go to: www.visitnj.com.

For information only on Atlantic City call (800) 847-4865 or go to: www.atlanticcitynj.com.

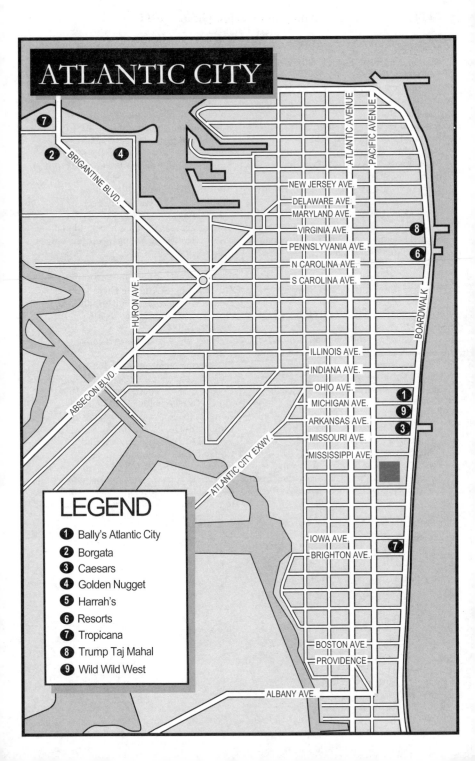

Bally's Atlantic City
1900 Pacific Avenue
Atlantic City, New Jersey 08401
(609) 340-2000
Website: www.ballysac.com

Toll-Free Number: (800) 772-7777
Reservation Number: (800) 225-5977
Rooms: 1,611 Price Range: $92-$389
Suites: 146   Price Range: $210-$620
Restaurants: 18   Valet Parking: $5
Buffets (W.W. West): B-$19.99 (Sat-Mon)
　　　　　L-$19.99/34.99 (Sun/Mon)
　　　　　D-$34.99/$39.99(Fri/Sat)
Casino Size 104,646 Square Feet
Other Games: B6, SB, K, P, THB
Special Features: Southern walkway connects to Wild Wild West casino.

Borgata Hotel Casino and Spa
One Borgata Way
Atlantic City, New Jersey 08401
(609) 317-1000
Website: www.theborgata.com

Toll-Free Number: (866) 692-6742
Rooms: 2,200 Prices Range: $119-$519
Suites: 600 Price Range: $299-$1,000
Restaurants: 13   Valet Parking: $5
Buffets: B-$15.95/$27.95 (Sun)
　　　　　L-$18.95 D-$30.95
Casino Size: 136,667 Square Feet
Other Games: B, B6, SB, CW, THB
Special Features: 3,700-seat events center. 1,000-seat music theater. Comedy club. Health spa. Barbershop. Hair and nail salon.

Caesars Atlantic City
2100 Pacific Avenue
Atlantic City, New Jersey 08401
(609) 348-4411
Website: www.caesarsac.com

Toll-Free Number: (800) 443-0104
Reservation Number: (800) 524-2867
Rooms: 979 Price Range: $125-$450
Suites: 198   Price Range: $195-$800
Restaurants: 12 Valet Park: $10/$20 (Fri-Sun)
Buffets: Brunch-$59.95 (Sun)
　　　　　L/D-$34.99/$39.99 (Sat)
Casino Size: 111,812 Square Feet
Other Games: B, SB, B6, THB, MS
Special Features: Roman themed hotel and casino. Health spa. Shopping arcade. Unisex beauty salon.

Golden Nugget Atlantic City
Huron Avenue & Brigantine Boulevard
Atlantic City, New Jersey 08401
(609) 441-2000
Website: www.goldennugget.com

Reservation Number: (800) 365-8786
Toll-Free Number (800) 777-8477
Rooms: 568 Price Range: $89-$359
Suites: 160 Price Range: $175-$650
Restaurants: 9   Valet Parking: $5
Buffets: B-$14.99 L-$16.99
　　　　　D-$20.99/$26.99 (Fri-Sun)
Casino Size: 70,250 Square Feet
Other Games: B6, P, MS
Special Features: Adjacent to marina with 640 slips. 3-acre recreation deck with pools, jogging track, tennis courts, miniature golf course and health club. 1,500-seat event center.

The Best Places To Play in Atlantic City

Blackjack: Some Atlantic City casinos offer a single-deck blackjack game. The problem is that these single-deck games only pay 6-to-5 when you get a blackjack rather than the standard 3-to-2 and this raises the casino advantage in this game to at least 1.58%. Bally's and Harrah's also offer an eight-deck game that only pays 6-to-5 for blackjack and the casino advantage in this game is around 2%. All off these are very bad games and should be avoided.

Other than those 6-to-5 variations, the blackjack games offered at Atlantic City casinos are pretty much all the same: eight-deck shoe games with double down on any first two cards, dealer hits soft 17, pairs can be split up to three times and doubling after splitting is allowed. This works out to a casino edge of .67% against a player using perfect basic strategy and every casino in Atlantic City offers this game, except for Borgata where the dealers stand on soft 17 on some of their games. This is the best eight-deck game in the city and the casino advantage advantage is .42%.

If you're willing to make higher minimum bets you can find slightly better games. All casinos offer six-deck games with minimum bets of $25, $50 or $100 per hand where the dealers stand on soft 17 and the casino edge in these games is lowered to .42%. It is offered at every casino in the city, except for Wild Wild West which only offers eight-deck games. Additionally, the Golden Nugget offers the city's best six-deck game because they add late surrender to the above rules, which brings their house advantage down to .34%. The minimum bet on this game is $50.

Roulette: When choosing roulette games it's usually best to play in a casino offering a single-zero wheel because the casino advantage is 2.70% versus a double-zero wheel which has a 5.26% advantage. However, that situation is somewhat different in Atlantic City because of certain gaming regulations. On double-zero wheels the casinos can only take one-half of a wager on even money bets (odd/even, red/black, 1-18/19-36) when zero or double-zero is the winning number. This lowers the casino edge on these particular bets to 2.63%, while the edge on all other bets remains at 5.26%. This rule is not in effect on single-zero wheels and virtually all bets on that game have a 2.70% house edge. There are five casinos that have single-zero roulette wheels: Harrah's, Bally's, Borgata, Trump Taj Mahal, Tropicana and Caesars. You should be aware, however, that almost all of these games are only open on weekends (or by special request) and they require $25-$100 minimum bets.

Craps: All Atlantic City casinos offer 5x odds.

Video Poker: There have been several changes in Atlantic City's video poker offerings in the past year, and most of them do not benefit the player. Some casinos have reduced or eliminated their full-pay inventory, at least for lower-end players, and others have made it more difficult to earn comps and other benefits on their better games. The most prominent example is the Caesars Entertainment properties (Caesars, Bally's and Harrah's), which added some full-pay machines, but require $50 of play ($25 at the dollar and up levels) to earn one Total Rewards Credit, as opposed to $10 per point on the short-pay games. (One Reward Credit equals a penny in comps.) There are no true advantage plays in Atlantic City, but a disciplined player can do well by combining expert play with promotions such as multiple-point days. But don't quit your day job.

The best widely available game in Atlantic City is 9/6 Jacks or Better (99.54%), which can be found in about half of the city's gaming halls. Borgata is the best place to find it in abundance and in multiple denominations, but they have reduced their inventory in recent months. Be sure to check the pay table before putting your cash into the bill acceptor, as many of the machines are short-pay.

Multi-Denomination Games – Most video poker games are found in multi-denominational machines, where the player can choose whether to play quarters, halves, dollars, or higher.

Borgata has 9/6 Jacks or Better in the B-bar (a smoking area with drinks comped for players), but the section gets noisy and crowded as the day progresses. There is a row of slant-top machines near the Amphora high-roller lounge, in a non-smoking section but adjacent to the smoking area. Several more machines are scattered around the casino.

Harrah's has three multi-game, multi-denomination machines with 9/6 Jacks or Better and 9/7 Double Bonus forming a triangle in the non-smoking section. Follow the path that leads from the parking garage escalator. There are also two carousels of about eight machines each with 9/6 Double Double Bonus near the Total Rewards club booth. Players on these games still earn one Reward Credit for every $10 played.

Bally's has a bank of four machines against the wall on the boardwalk side of the casino, with 9/6 Jacks or Better, 9/7 Double Bonus, 9/6 Double Double Bonus, and a couple of Aces & Faces versions of the games.

Golden Nugget has a bank of four slant tops in the back near the entrance to the high-limit slot room. They can be played in quarters, dollars, or $2, and have 9/6 Jacks or Better, 8/5 Bonus, 9/7 Double Bonus, 9/6 Double Bonus, and Aces & Faces games. Look for the black face glass.

The best place for 8/5 Bonus Poker is Resorts, and it can be found in multi-game machines scattered throughout the casino. Resorts recently lowered the amount of cashback and comp dollars awarded on these games, but it is still one of the better places in town to earn rewards on full-pay video-poker.

Quarter Games – The best quarter game in Atlantic City is in the Tropicana. A row of five full-pay (99.59%), Five- Joker progressive games can be found in an alcove just outside the Slot City Estates area. The seats are almost always filled, so unless you arrive in the wee hours of the morning, you'll probably have to wait for a chance to play. Look for Sigma machines with a purple face glass near the entrance to the women's restroom.

Caesars has a set of six slant-top progressive 9/6 Jacks or Better machines in the video-poker area near the center of the casino, but the jackpot rises slowly.

Another good quarter play can be found at Bally's, in the form of 8/5 Bonus triple-play progressives. There are two banks of the game, one with 14 machines in the video-poker area in the south corner of the casino on the boardwalk side. The other is a circle of six machines near the Noodle Village restaurant. If you come on a multiple-point day, be prepared to wait for a seat.

Dollar Games – Bally's has three multi-game machines with triple-play 9/6 Jacks or Better and 8/5 Bonus Poker in the high-limit area off the hotel lobby. There are also four dollar machines with 9/6 Jacks or Better in the video-poker area of the main casino.

The Diamond Cove high-limit area at Harrah's has a row of slant-top machines with 9/6 Jacks or better, 8/5 Bonus Poker, and 9/7 Double Bonus Poker at the $1 and $2 levels.

Trump Taj Mahal has three slant-top machines with 9/6 Jacks or Better in the Sultan's Palace area in dollars and higher.

Double Double Bonus players can find their favorite game in dollars at the Golden Nugget. They're at the bar near the entrance to the casino, but games at lower denominations are short-pay.

For higher-level players, 9/6 Jacks or Better, 8/5 Bonus Poker, and 9/6 Double Double Bonus can be found at the $5 and up levels in most high-limit slot rooms in town.

Harrah's Resort Atlantic City
777 Harrah's Boulevard
Atlantic City, New Jersey 08401
(609) 441-5000
Website: www.harrahs.com

Reservation Number: (800) 242-7724
Rooms: 2,010 Price Range: $89-$439
Suites: 616 Price Range: Casino Use Only
Restaurants: 8   Valet Parking: $5
Buffets: B-$26.99 (Sat)/$42.99 (Sun)
L-$36.99
D-$36.99/$39.99 (Sat)
Casino Size: 158,966 Square Feet
Other Games: B6, K, P, THB, MS
Special Features: 65-slip marina. Beauty salon. Miniature golf course (in season).

Resorts Casino Hotel
1133 Boardwalk
Atlantic City, New Jersey 08401
(609) 344-6000
Website: www.resortsac.com

Toll-Free Number: (800) 334-6378
Reservation Number: (800) 334-6378
Rooms: 879 Price Range: $79-$375
Suites: 79 Price Range: $250-$1,000
Restaurants: 10   Valet Park: $5/$15(Fri-Sat)
Buffets: L/D-$19.99
Casino Size: 97,707 Square Feet
Other games: B6, THB, MS
Special Features: Indoor/outdoor pools. Health spa. 1,350-seat theater. Comedy club. Beachfront Margaritaville bar & restaurant. Various buffet discounts for players club members. $5 valet discount with players club card. No buffet Thu/Fri.

Tropicana Casino & Resort
2831 Boardwalk
Atlantic City, New Jersey 08401
(609) 340-4000
Website: www.tropicana.net

Toll-Free Number: (800) 843-8767
Reservation Number: (800) 338-5553
Rooms: 1,426 Price Range: $79-$409
Suites: 340 Price Range: $155-$675
Restaurants: 16   Valet Park: $5/$10 (Fri-Sun)
Buffets: B-$18.95 L/D-$27.95
Casino Size: 132,896 Square Feet
Other Games: B6, P, THB
Special Features: Features "The Quarter," a dining/entertainment complex with 30 stores.

Trump Taj Mahal Casino Resort
1000 Boardwalk at Virginia Avenue
Atlantic City, New Jersey 08401
(609) 449-1000
Website: www.trumptaj.com

Reservation Number: (800) 825-8888
Rooms: 1,795 Price Range: $150-$450
Suites: 311 Price Range: $350-$600
Restaurants: 11   Valet Parking: $5
Buffets: B-$15.50 L/D- $23.95
Casino Size: 149,239 Square Feet
Other Games: B6, K, THB
Special Features: Health spa. Hard Rock cafe. 5,000-seat event center. 1,400-seat showroom.

NEW MEXICO

New Mexico's Indian casinos offer an assortment of table games and electronic gaming machines. Additionally, slot machines are allowed at the state's racetracks as well as at about 40 various fraternal and veterans clubs.

New Mexico gaming regulations require that electronic machines at racetracks and fraternal/veterans organizations return a minimum of 80% to a maximum of 96%.

New Mexico's Indian tribes do not make their slot machine payback percentages a matter of public record but the terms of the compact between the state and the tribes require all electronic gaming machines to return a minimum of 80%.

Unless otherwise noted, all New Mexico Indian casinos are open 24 hours and offer: blackjack, craps, roulette, video slots and video poker. Some casinos also offer: Spanish 21 (S21), mini-baccarat (MB), poker (P), pai gow poker (PGP), three card poker (TCP), four card poker (FCP), Caribbean stud poker (CSP), let it ride (LIR), Mississippi stud (MS), casino war (CW), big 6 wheel (B6), keno (K), bingo (BG) and off track betting (OTB). The minimum gambling age is 21 for the casinos and 18 for bingo or pari-mutuel betting.

Please note that all New Mexico casinos are prohibited from serving alcohol on the casino floor. If a casino serves alcohol it can only be consumed at the bar and not in the casino itself.

For information on visiting New Mexico call the state's tourism department at (800) 733-6396 or go to: www.newmexico.org.

Apache Nugget Travel Center and Casino
US Highway 550 and NM Highway 537
Dulce, New Mexico 87528
(575) 289-2486
Website: www.apachenugget.com
Map: **#15** (on Jicarilla reservation at intersection of Hwys 550 and 537 near Cuba)

Restaurants: 1 Liquor: No
Other Games: Only gaming machines
Casino Size: 12,000 Square Feet
Hours: 8am-12am/1am (Thu)/2am (Fri/Sat)
Overnight RV Parking: Free (check in with
　　　　　　　　security first)/RV Dump: No

Buffalo Thunder Resort & Casino
30 Buffalo Thunder Trail
Santa Fe, New Mexico 87506
(505) 455-5555
Website: www.buffalothunderresort.com
Map: **#2**

Room Reservations: (877) 848-6337
Rooms: 350 Price Range: $109-$229
Suites: 45 Price Range: $229-$279
Restaurants: 6 Liquor: Yes
Buffets: D- $15.95/$19.99 (Fri)/$17.99 (Sat)
Other Games: P, TCP
Casino Size: 61,000 Square Feet
Special Features: Hotel is Hilton. Health Spa. Retail shopping area. Native American art gallery. Buffet closed Mon/Tue.

Camel Rock Casino
17486-A Highway 84/285
Santa Fe, New Mexico 87504
(505) 984-8414
Website: www.camelrockcasino.com
Map: **#2**

Toll-Free Number: (800) 462-2635
Restaurants: 1   Liquor: No
Hours: 7am-3am/24 Hours (Thurs-Sat)
Casino Size: 60,000 Square Feet
Other Games: TCP
Overnight RV Parking: Free/RV Dump: No
Senior Discount: Various on Thursday if 55+

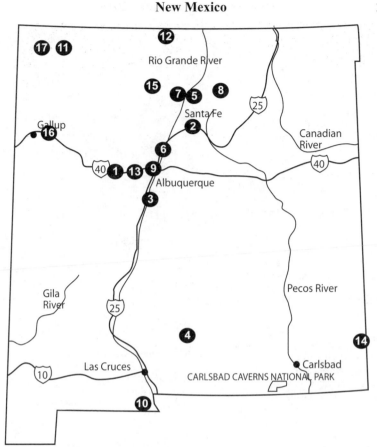

Casino Apache Travel Center
25845 U.S. Highway 70
Ruidoso, New Mexico 88340
(575) 464-7777
Map: **#4** (90 miles N.E. of Las Cruces)

Restaurants: 1 Liquor: Yes
Hours: 8am-4am/24 Hours (Thurs-Sun)
Other Games: No Craps, TCP
Casino Size: 10,000 Square Feet
Overnight RV Parking: Free/RV Dump: No
Special Features: Free shuttle service to Inn
of the Mountain Gods Casino. Truck stop.
Discount smoke shop.

Casino Express
14500 Central Avenue
Albuquerque, New Mexico 87120
(505) 552-7777
Map: **#3** (I-40 at exit 140)

Toll-Free Number: (866) 352-7866
Other Games: Only gaming machines
Overnight RV Parking: Free/RV Dump: No
Special Features: Adjacent to, and affiliated
with, Route 66 Casino.

Cities of Gold Casino Hotel
10-B Cities of Gold Road
Santa Fe, New Mexico 87501
(505) 455-3313
Website: www.citiesofgold.com
Map: **#2 (**Intersection of Hwys 84/285/502)

Toll-Free Number: (800) 455-3313
Room Reservations: (877) 455-0515
Rooms: 122 Price Range: $65-$109
Suites: 2 Price Range: $136
Restaurants: 3 Liquor: Yes
Buffets: B-$7.95/$11.95 (Sun)
　　　　L-$8.95 D-$10.99/$11.99 (Sat)/
　　　　　$19.99 (Sun)
Hours: 7am-3am/24 hours (Fri/Sat)
Casino Size: 40,000 Square Feet
Other Games: TCP, MS, BG (Wed-Sun)
Overnight RV Parking: No
Special Features: They also operate the Cities of Gold Sports Bar which is one block away from main casino. Liquor is served there but they only have slots and OTB - no table games. 27-hole golf course.

Dancing Eagle Casino and RV Park
Interstate 40, Exit 108
Casa Blanca, New Mexico 87007
(505) 552-1111
Website: www.dancingeaglecasino.com
Map: **#1** (40 miles W. of Albuquerque)

Toll-Free Number: (877) 440-9969
Restaurants: 1 Liquor: No
Hours: 8am-4am/24 hours (Fri/Sat)
Casino Size: 21,266 Square Feet
Other Games: No craps, BG (Sat/Sun)
Senior Discount: Various Mon-Thu if 50+
Overnight RV Parking: Free/RV Dump: No
Special Features: Located on I-40 at exit 108. Truck stop. 35-space RV park ($20 per night/$10 for players club members).

Fire Rock Navajo Casino
249 State Highway 118
Church Rock, New Mexico 87313
(505) 905-7100
Website: www.firerocknavajocasino.com
Map: **#16** (8 miles E of Gallup)

Toll-Free Number: (866) 941-2444
Restaurants: 1
Buffet: B- $9.99 (Sun) D-$21.99 (Thu)
Casino Size: 64,000 square Feet
Other Games: P, No Craps, BG, S21

Flowing Water Navajo Casino
2710 US Highway 64
Waterflow, New Mexico 87421
(505) 368-2300
Map: **#17** (105 miles N of Gallup)

Restaurants:1
Casino Size: 11,000 square Feet

Inn of the Mountain Gods Resort & Casino
277 Carrizo Canyon Road
Mescalero, New Mexico 88340
(575) 464-7777
Website: www.innofthemountaingods.com
Map: **#4** (90 miles N.E. of Las Cruces)

Toll-Free Number: (800) 545-9011
Rooms: 250 Price Range: $149-$199
Suites: 23 Price Range: $269-$399
Restaurants: 4 Liquor: Yes
Buffets: B-$8.99/$12.99 (Sat/Sun)
　　　　L-$9.99/$16.99 (Sat/Sun)
　　　　D-$10.99/$24.99 (Fri)/$18.99 (Sat/Sun)
Hours: 8am-4am/24 Hours (Fri/Sat)
Casino Size: 38,000 Square Feet
Other Games: MB, P, PGP, LIR,
　　　　　　TCP, FCP, MS
Overnight RV Parking: Free/RV Dump: No
Senior Discount: 20% off buffet if 55+
Special Features: 18-hole golf course.

Isleta Resort Casino
11000 Broadway S.E.
Albuquerque, New Mexico 87105
(505) 724-3800
Website: www.isleta.com
Map: **#3**

Toll-Free Number: (877) 475-3827
Restaurants: 6 Liquor: Yes
Hours: 8am-4am/24 Hours (Thu-Sun)
Casino Size: 30,000 Square Feet
Other Games: P, LIR, TCP, BG
Overnight RV Parking: Free/RV Dump: No
Special Features: Convenience store. Gas station. Three nine-hole golf courses. Alcohol is only served at sports bar in casino.

Northern Edge Navajo Casino
2732 Navajo Route 36
Farmington, New Mexico 87401
(505) 960-7000
Website: www.northernedgenavajocasino.com
Map: **#11** (150 miles N.W of Sante Fe)

Toll-free Number: (877) 241-7777
Rooms: 124 Price Range: $89-$209
Restaurants: 1 Liquor: Yes
Hours: 8am-4am/24 hours (Fri-Sun)
Casino Size: 36,000 square feet
Other Games: TCP, P, S21, MB
Overnight RV Parking: No
Special Features: 24 lane bowling alley. Food court with fast food outlets.

Ohkay Casino Resort
Highway 68
Ohkay Owingeh, New Mexico 87566
(575) 747-1668
Website: www.ohkay.com
Map: **#5** (24 miles N. of Santa Fe)

Toll-Free Number: (800) 752-9286
Room Reservation (877) 829-2865
Rooms: 101 Price Range: $84-$104
Suites: 24 Price Range: $114-$134
Restaurants: 2 Liquor: Yes
Buffets: B- $9.99 (Sun)
         D-$6.99/$9.99 (Sun)
Hours: 7am-3am/24 hrs (Fri-Sun)
Casino Size: 30,000 Square Feet
Overnight RV Parking: Free/RV Dump: No
Special Features: Hotel is Best Western. Sporting clays club.

Palace West Casino
1-74 State Road 45 Southwest
Albuquerque, New Mexico 87105
(505) 869-4102
Map: **#3** (at Coors & Isleta Road)

Hours: 9am-1am Daily
Other Games: Only gaming machines
Overnight RV Parking: Free/RV Dump: No
Special Features: Completely nonsmoking.

Route 66 Casino Hotel
14500 Central Avenue
Albuquerque, New Mexico 87121
(505) 352-7866
Website: www.rt66casino.com
Map: **#13** (20 miles W. of Albuquerque)

Toll-Free Number: (866) 352-7866
Rooms: 154 Rates: $79-$109
Restaurants: 2 Liquor: No
Buffets: L-$10.99/$13.99 (Sun)
         D-$10.99/$23.99 (Thu-Sat)
Hours: 8am-4am/24 Hours (Fri-Sun)
Other Games: P, PGP, TCP, BG
Overnight RV Parking: Free/RV Dump: No
Special Features: Johnny Rockets restaurant. Adjacent to, and affiliated with, Casino Express.

San Felipe Casino Hollywood
25 Hagan Road
Algodones, New Mexico 87001
(505) 867-6700
Website: www.sanfelipecasino.com
Map: **#6** (17 miles N. of Albuquerque)

Toll-Free Number: (877) 529-2946
Restaurants: 1 Liquor: No
Buffets: B/L-$7.95 D-$11.95
Hours: 8am-4am/24 Hours (Fri-Sat)
Other Games: P, TCP
Overnight RV Parking: Must use RV park
Special Features: 100-space RV park ($10 per night). Adjacent to Hollywood Hills Speedway.

Sandia Resort & Casino
30 Rainbow Road NE
Albuquerque, New Mexico 87113
(505) 796-7500
Website: www.sandiacasino.com
Map: **#9**

Toll-Free Number: (800) 526-9366
Rooms: 198 Price Range: $188-$226
Suites: 30 Price Range: $269-$339
Restaurants: 4   Liquor: Yes
Buffets: B-$8.95 L-$10.95/$14.95 (Sun)
      D-$13.50/$25.95 (Sat/Sun)
Hours: 8am-4am/24 Hours (Fri-Sun)
Casino Size: 65,000 Square feet
Other Games: P, CSP, LIR, TCP,
      PGP, BG, K, MB
Overnight RV Parking: Free/RV Dump: No
Senior Discount: Various Wed 10am-6pm
if 50+
Special Features: 4,200-seat amphitheater.
18-hole golf course. Smoke-free slot room.

Santa Ana Star Casino
54 Jemez Dam Canyon Road
Bernalillo, New Mexico 87004
(505) 867-0000
Website: www.santaanastar.com
Map: **#6** (17 miles N. of Albuquerque)

Restaurants: 5   Liquor: No
Buffets: B-$14.95 (Sun) L-$9.95
   D-$12.95/$9.95 (Thu)/$22.95 (Fri/Sat)
Hours: 8am-4am/24 Hours (Thurs-Sat)
Casino Size: 19,000 Square Feet
Other Games: P, LIR, FCP, PGP
Overnight RV Parking: Free/RV Dump: No
Senior Discount: Various Mondays if 50+
Special Features: 36-lane bowling alley. 18-
hole golf course. Spa. Smoke shop. 3,000-seat
event center. No buffet Tuesday or Wednesday.

Santa Claran Hotel Casino
460 North Riverside Drive
Espanola, New Mexico 87532-3470
(505) 367-4500
Website: www.santaclaran.com
Map: **#7** (25 miles N of Sante Fe)

Rooms: 124 Price Range: $89-$129
Suites: 19 Price Range: $169-$189
Restaurants: 4 Liquor: Yes
Hours: 8am-4am/24 hours (Fri/Sat)
Casino Size: 36,000 square feet
Other Games: TCP, P, MS
Overnight RV Parking: No
Special Features: 24 lane bowling alley.

Sky City Casino Hotel
Interstate 40, Exit 102
Acoma, New Mexico 87034
(505) 552-6017
Website: www.skycitycasino.com
Map: **#1** (50 miles W. of Albuquerque)

Toll-Free Number: (888) 759-2489
Rooms: 132 Price Range: $79-$99
Suites: 15 Price Range: $109-$129
Restaurants: 4 Liquor: No
Buffets: B-$6.99/$8.99 (Sat/Sun)
     L-$9.95 D-$12.99/$18.99 (Fri)/
     $14.99 (Sat)/$19.99 (Sun)
Hours: 8am-4am/24 Hours (Fri/Sat)
Casino Size: 30,000 Square Feet
Other Games: TCP, BG
Overnight RV Parking: Free/RV Dump: No
Senior Discount: various if 55+
Special Features: 42-space RV park ($25 per
night). No bingo Saturday.

Taos Mountain Casino
700 Veterans Highway
Taos, New Mexico 87571
(575) 737-0777
Website: www.taosmountaincasino.com
Map: **#8** (50 miles N.E. of Santa Fe)

Toll-Free Number: (888) 946-8267
Restaurants: 1 Deli   Liquor: No
Hours: 8am-1am/2am (Thu-Sat)
Other Games: No Roulette, TCP
Overnight RV Parking: No
Special Features: Entire casino is non-smoking.

Wild Horse Casino & Hotel
13603 US Highway 64
Dulce, New Mexico 87529
(575) 759-3663
Website: www.apachenugget.com
Map: **#12** (95 miles N.W. of Santa Fe)

Room Reservations: (800) 428-2627
Rooms: 43 Price Range: $75-$95
Restaurants: 1 Liquor: Yes
Hours: 11am-1am/
       9am-1am (Thu)/2am (Fri/Sat)/12am (Sun)

Pari-Mutuels

The Downs Racetrack and Casino
201 California Northeast
Albuquerque, New Mexico 87108
(505) 767-7171
Website: www.abqdowns.com
Map: **#9**

Restaurants: 1
Buffets: D- $21.95 (Wed)
Hours: 10am-1am/2am (Fri/Sat)
Other Games: Only gaming machines
Overnight RV Parking: No
Senior Discount: $2 off buffets if 55+
Special Features: Live horse racing August through October. Daily simulcasting of horse racing.

Ruidoso Downs & Billy The Kid Casino
1461 Highway 70 West
Ruidoso Downs, New Mexico 88346
(575) 378-4431
Website: www.ruidownsracing.com
Map: **#4** (90 miles N.E. of Las Cruces)

Restaurants: 2
Hours: 10am-Midnight/1am (Fri/Sat)
Other Games: Only gaming machines
Overnight RV Parking: No
Senior Discount: Various Wed 11am-9pm if 55+
Special Features: Live horse racing (Thu-Sun) late May through early September. Daily simulcasting of horse racing.

Sunland Park Racetrack & Casino
1200 Futurity Drive
Sunland Park, New Mexico 88063
(575) 874-5200
Website: www.sunland-park.com
Map: **#10** (5 miles W. of El Paso, TX)

Restaurants: 5
Hours: 10am-1am/2am (Thu)/4am (Fri/Sat)
Other Games: Only gaming machines
Overnight RV Parking: Free/$5 w/hookups
Special Features: Live thoroughbred and quarter-horse racing December through April. Daily simulcasting of horse racing.

SunRay Park and Casino
#39 Road 5568
Farmington, New Mexico 87401
(575) 566-1200
Website: www.sunraygaming.com
Map: **#11** (150 miles N.W. of Santa Fe)

Restaurants: 1
Hours: 11am-2am/3am (Thu)/4am (Fri)
       10-am-4am (Sat)/10am-2am (Sun)
Other Games: Only gaming machines
Overnight RV Parking: No
Special Features: Live horse racing (Thu-Sun) from mid-April through June. Daily simulcasting of horse racing.

Zia Park Race Track & Black Gold Casino
3901 W. Millen Drive
Hobbs, New Mexico 88240
(575) 492-7000
Website: www.blackgoldcasino.net
Map: **#14** (70 miles N.E. of Carlsbad)

Toll-Free Number: (888) 942-7275
Restaurants: 3
Hours: 10am-1am/4am (Fri/Sat)/2am (Sun)
Other Games: Only gaming machines
Overnight RV Parking: Free/RV Dump: No
Special Features: Live horse racing mid-September through early December. Daily simulcasting of horse racing. Buffet discount with players club card.

NEW YORK

Indian Casinos (Class III)

There are five Indian casinos located in upstate New York which offer traditional Class III casino gambling.

All of these casinos are open 24 hours and offer the following games: blackjack, craps, and roulette. Some casinos also offer: Spanish 21 (S21), baccarat (B), mini-baccarat (MB), big six wheel (B6), keno (K), poker (P), pai gow poker (PGP), let it ride (LIR), three-card poker (TCP), four-card poker (FCP), Mississippi stud (MS) and casino war (CW).

The minimum gambling age is 21 at the three Seneca casinos and 18 at the other two casinos. For more information on visiting New York call the state's travel information center at (800) 225-5697 or go to: www.iloveny.com.

Akwesasne Mohawk Casino Resort
873 State Route 37
Akwesasne, New York 13655
(518) 358-2222
Website: www.mohawkcasino.com
Map: **#2** (65 miles W. of Champlain)

Toll-Free Number: (888) 622-1155
Rooms: 145 Price Range: $119-$155
Suites: 5 Price Range: $175-$500
Restaurants: 2 Liquor: Yes Valet Park: Free
Buffets: B-$12.95 (Sat/Sun)
      L-$10.95/$23.95 (Sat/Sun)
      D-$17.95/$19.95 (Fri/Sat)
Casino Size: 40,000 Square Feet
Other Games: S21, P, LIR, TCP, MS,
      PGP, FCP, MB
Overnight RV Parking: Free/RV Dump: No

Seneca Allegany Casino & Hotel
777 Seneca Allegany Boulevard
Salamanca, New York 14779
(716) 945-9300
Website: www.senecaalleganycasino.com
Map: **#12** (65 miles S. of Buffalo)

Toll-Free Number: (877) 553-9500
Rooms: 189 Price Range: $115-$345
Suites: 23 Price Range: $215-$445
Restaurants: 6 (1 open 24 hours)
 Liquor: Yes Valet Park: Free
Buffets: L-$16.95 D-$21.95
Casino Size: 48,000 Square Feet
Other Games: TCP, LIR, S21, B6, MS
Overnight RV Parking: No
Special Features: Buffet discount for players club members.

Seneca Buffalo Creek Casino
1 Fulton Street
Buffalo, New York 14204
(716) 853-7576
www.senecabuffalocreekcasino.com
Map: **#3**

Restaurants: 2 Liquor: Yes
Valet Park: Free
Casino Size: 65,000 Square Feet
Games Offered: MS, S21, LIR, TCP, THB
Overnight RV Parking: No

Seneca Niagara Casino
310 Fourth Street
Niagara Falls, New York 14303
(716) 299-1100
Website: www.senecaniagaracasino.com
Map: **#4**

Toll-Free Number: (877) 873-6322
Rooms: 574 Price Range: $139-$265
Suites: 30 Price Range: $239-$305
Restaurants: 4 Liquor: Yes Valet Park: Free
Buffets: B-$12.99 (Sat/Sun) L- $16.99
      D-$21.99/ $30.99 (Fri/Sun)
Other Games: S21, B, MB, P, PGP, MS,
      TCP, LIR, FCP, K
Overnight RV Parking: No
Special Features: Buffet discount for players club members.

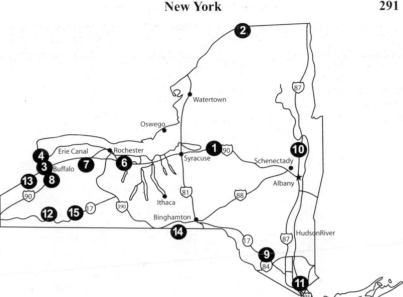

Turning Stone Casino Resort
5218 Patrick Road
Verona, New York 13478
(315) 361-7711
Website: www.turning-stone.com
Map: **#1** (adjacent to NY State Thruway exit 33 at Verona, off Route 365, 30 miles E. of Syracuse)

Toll-Free Number: (800) 771-7711
Rooms: 572 Price Range: $130-$229
Suites: 143 Price Range: $179-$595
Restaurants: 14 Liquor: No Valet Park: $5
Buffets: B-$9.95/$11.95 (Sat/Sun)
　　　　L-$13.95/ $15.95 (Sat)/$18.95 (Sun)
　　　　D-$17.95/$19.95 (Tue)/
　　　　　$22.95 (Fri/Sat)/$20.95 (Sun)
Casino Size: 122,000 Square Feet
Other Games: B, MB, P, LIR, PGP, BG,
　　　　　　TCP, FCP, K, CW, B6, S21
Overnight RV Parking: No
Special Features: Three golf courses. Gift shop. Discount smoke shop. 800-seat showroom. 175-space RV park ($40 per night/$55 weekends).

Indian Casinos (Class II)

There are some Indian casinos that offer Class II gambling which consist of electronic gaming machines which look like slot machines, but are actually games of bingo and the spinning video reels are for "entertainment purposes only." No public information is available concerning the payback percentages on the video gaming machines.

All of these casinos have a cashless system whereby you have to go to a cashier cage, or a kiosk, get a "smart" card and deposit money to that card's account. The machines will then deduct losses from, or credit wins to, your account.

Additionally, after playing don't forget to cash out because all remaining credits on cards will be forfeited at the end of the day.

Some of these casinos also offer high-stakes bingo and poker, as shown in the "Other Games" listings.

Mohawk Bingo Palace
202 State Route 37
Akwesasne, New York 13655
(518) 358-2246
Website: www.mohawkpalace.com
Map: **#2** (65 miles W. of Champlain)

Toll-Free Number: (866) 452-5768
Restaurants: 1 Liquor: No Valet Park: No
Other Games: Bingo
Overnight RV Parking: Free/RV Dump: No

Seneca Gaming - Irving
11099 Route 5
Irving, New York 14081
(716) 549-4389
Website: www.senecagames.com
Map: **#13** (38 miles S.W. of Buffalo)

Toll-Free Number: (800) 421-2464
Restaurants: 1 Liquor: No Valet Park: No
Hours: 9:30am-2am/4:30am (Fri/Sat)
Other Games: Bingo
Overnight RV Parking: Free (must check in
          with security first)/RV Dump: No
Special Features: Discount smoke shop.

Seneca Gaming - Oil Spring
5374 West Shore Road
Cuba, New York 14727
(716)968-9307
Website: www.senecagames.com
Map: **#15** (80 miles SW of Buffalo)

Hours: 9:30am-12am Daily
Other Games: Bingo, Poker
Overnight RV Parking: No/RV Dump: No

Seneca Gaming - Salamanca
768 Broad Street
Salamanca, New York 14779
(716) 549-4389
Website: www.senecagames.com
Map: **#12** (65 miles S. of Buffalo)

Toll-Free Number: (877) 860-5130
Restaurants: 1 Liquor: No Valet Park: No
Hours: 9:30am-1am/2am (Fri/Sat)
Other Games: Bingo, Poker
Overnight RV Parking: Free (must check in
          with security first)/RV Dump: No

Pari-Mutuels

In October 2001, legislation was passed to allow for the introduction of slot machine-type video lottery machines at New York racetracks. Officially referred to as Video Gaming Machines (VGM's), they are regulated by the New York Lottery.

All VGM's offer standard slot machine-type games, plus keno in denominations from five cents to $10. The machines all accept cash but do not pay out in cash. They print a receipt which must be taken to a cashier.

The VGM's do not operate like regular slot machines or video poker games. Instead, they are similar to scratch-off-type lottery tickets with a pre-determined number of winners. The legislation authorizing the VGM's states, "the specifications for video lottery gaming shall be designed in such a manner as to pay prizes that average no less than ninety percent of sales."

Here's information, as supplied by the New York Lottery, showing the video gaming machine payback percentages for each of the state's racetracks for the one-year period from July 1, 2013 through June 30, 2014:

LOCATION	PAYBACK %
Resorts World	94.94
Empire City	92.25
Monticello	91.91
Finger Lakes	91.68
Saratoga	91.58
Tioga Downs	91.45
Fairgrounds	91.21
Vernon Downs	91.05
Batavia Downs	91.01

All Video Gaming Machine facilities are alowed to be open for 20 hours a day, with varrying hours. Some are open 8am-4am, some are open 9am-5am, etc. and all are non-smoking. Please call to confirm hours if necessary. Admission is free to all facilities and the minimum gambling age is 18 for playing VGM's, as well as for pari-mutuel betting.

Batavia Downs Gaming
8315 Park Road
Batavia, New York 14020
(585) 343-3750
Website: www.batavia-downs.com
Map: #7 (35 miles E. of Buffalo)

Toll-Free: (800) 724-2000
Restaurants: 2   Valet Parking: No
Buffets: B- $11.95 (Sun)
Overnight RV Parking: No
Special Features: Live harness racing Tue/
Wed/Fri/Sat from early August through
early December. Daily simulcasting of
thoroughbred and harness racing.

Empire City at Yonkers Raceway
8100 Central Avenue
Yonkers, New York 10704
(914) 968-4200
Website: www.yonkersraceway.com
Map: #11 (20 miles N. of Manhattan)

Restaurants: 3
Valet: $10
Special Features: Year-round live harness
racing Mon/Tue/Thu-Sat evenings. Daily
simulcasting of thoroughbred and harness
racing. Electronic versions of roulette, craps
and baccarat.

Finger Lakes Gaming & Racetrack
5857 Route 96
Farmington, New York 14425
(585) 924-3232
Website: www.fingerlakesgaming.com
Map: #6 (25 miles S. of Rochester)

Restaurants: 3   Valet Parking: $3
Buffets: B-$16.95 (Sun) L-$16.95 D-$19.95
Casino Size: 28,267 Square Feet
Overnight RV Parking: Call for permission
Senior Discount: Various Tue if 50+
Special Features: Live thoroughbred
horse racing (Fri-Tue) mid-April through
December. Daily simulcasting of harness and
thoroughbred racing. No racing Sunday.

Hamburg Casino at The Fairgrounds
5820 South Park Avenue
Hamburg, New York 14075
(716) 649-1280
Website: www.the-fairgrounds.com
Map: #8 (15 miles S. of Buffalo)

Toll-Free: (800) 237-1205
Restaurants: 2   Valet Parking: No
Buffets: L - $14.99/$15.99 (Sat)/$18.99 (Sun)
D- $18.99/$22.99 (Sat)
Casino Size: 27,000 Square Feet
Overnight RV Parking: Yes
Special Features: Live harness racing Wed/Fri-
Sat from January through July. Simulcasting
Wed-Sun of thoroughbred and harness racing.

Monticello Gaming & Raceway
204 Route 17B
Monticello, New York 12701
(845) 794-4100
Website: monticellocasinoandraceway.com
Map: #9 (50 miles W. of Newburgh)

Toll-Free: (866) 777-4263
Admission: Free   Self-Parking: Free
Restaurants: 1   Valet Parking: $2
Buffets: L/D-$11.95/$15.95 (Thu-Sun)
Overnight RV Parking: Free/RV Dump: No
Senior Discount: Buffet discount Tue if 55+
Special Features: Year-round live harness
racing Mon-Thu. Daily simulcast of
thoroughbred and harness racing.

Resorts World New York
110-00 Rockaway Boulevard
Jamaica, New York 11417
(718) 215-2828
Website: www.rwnewyork.com
Map: #5 (15 miles E. of Manhattan)

Admission: Free   Clubhouse: $5
Valet: $5
Restaurants: 2
Special Features: Live thoroughbred racing
Wed-Sun. Daily simulcasting of thoroughbred
racing. Electronic versions of craps, blackjack,
roulette and baccarat.

Saratoga Gaming and Raceway
342 Jefferson Street
Saratoga Springs, New York 12866
(518) 584-2110
Website: www.saratogaraceway.com
Map: **#10** (25 miles N. of Schenectady)

Toll-Free: (800) 727-2990
Restaurants: 5   Valet Parking: $3
Buffets: L-$12.95 D-$14.95
Casino Size: 55,000 Square Feet
Overnight RV Parking: Free
Senior Discount: $6.95 buffet Tue if 50+
Special Features: Live harness racing Thu-Sat evenings from March through mid-December. Daily simulcasting of thoroughbred and harness racing. Buffet discount if players club member. Electronic version of craps.

Tioga Downs
2384 West River Road
Nichols, New York 13812
Website: www.tiogadowns.com
Map: **#14** (30 miles W. of Binghamton)

Toll-Free: (888) 946-8464
Restaurants: 2   Valet Parking: $3
Buffets: B-$17.00 (Sun) L-$10.00
       D-$12.00/$18.00 (Thu-Sat)/$17.00 (Sun)
Casino Size: 19,000 Square Feet
Overnight RV Parking: Free
Senior Discount: Various Wed if 50+
Special Features: Live harness racing on Fri-Sun from May through mid-September. Daily simulcasting of thoroughbred and harness racing.

Vernon Downs
4229 Stuhlman Rd
Vernon, New York 13476
(315) 829-2201
Website: www.vernondowns.com
Map: **#1** (30 miles E. of Syracuse)

Toll-Free Number: (877) 888-3766
Room Reservations: (866) 829-3400
Suites: 175 Price Range: $59-$159
Restaurants: 1   Valet Parking: $2
Buffets: B-$13.95 (Sun)
       L- $10.00/$12.99 (Fri-Sun)
       D-$10.00/$16.99 (Fri/Sun)/$21.99 (Sat)
Casino Size: 28,000 Square Feet
Overnight RV Parking: Free/RV Dump: No
Special Features: Live harness racing Thu-Sat evenings late mid-April through early-November. Daily simulcasting of thoroughbred and harness racing.

Canadian Casinos

If you are traveling to the Buffalo area there are two nearby Canadian casinos just across the border in Niagara Falls, Ontario.

All winnings are paid in Canadian currency and the minimum gambling age is 19. Both casinos are open 24 hours and offer the following games: blackjack, Spanish 21, craps, baccarat, mini-baccarat, pai-gow poker, three-card poker and let it ride.

Casino Niagara
5705 Falls Avenue
Niagara Falls, Ontario L2G 3K6
(905) 374-3589
Website: www.casinoniagara.com
Map: **#4**

PRICES ARE IN CANADIAN DOLLARS
Toll-Free Number: (888) 946-3255
Restaurants: 6   Valet Parking: $5
Buffets: L-$12.95 D-$18.95
Casino Size: 100,000 Square Feet
Other games: Poker
Overnight RV Parking: Free/RV Dump: No
Senior Discount: Various Wed if 55+

Fallsview Casino Resort
6380 Fallsview Boulevard
Niagara, Ontario L2G 7X5
(905) 358-3255
Website: www.fallsviewcasinoresort.com
Map: **#4**

PRICES ARE IN CANADIAN DOLLARS
Toll-Free Number: (888) 325-5788
Room Reservations: (888) 888-1089
Rooms: 340 Price Range: $249-$350
Suites: 28 Price Range: $359-$559
Restaurants: 10   Valet Parking: $20
Buffets: B-$13.00 L/D-$22.00
Other Games: Pai Gow (tiles), Casino War,
          Sic Bo, Poker
Casino Size: 180,000 Square Feet
Overnight RV Parking: No
Special Features: Spa/fitness center. 1,500-
seat theatre. Additional Hilton and Sheraton
hotels connected by walkway. Buffet discount
for players club members.

NORTH CAROLINA

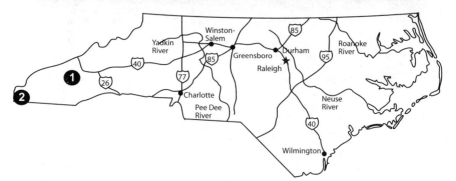

North Carolina has one Indian casino. In August, 1994 the state's Eastern Band of Cherokee Indians signed a compact with the governor to allow forms of video gambling. According to the terms of the compact, the video machines must be games of skill and they are required to return a minimum of 83% and a maximum of 98%.

Initially, no live table games were offered at the Cherokee Casino, only video slots, video poker, and digital versions of tables games such as blackjack. However, in 2012 an amended compact was signed to allow regular table games and the casino now offers live blackjack, craps, roulette and mini-baccarat. There is also a poker room.

Some of the slots offered are called "Lock N Roll" and are different than slots you will find in traditional casinos. With these "skill" slots you have two opportunities to spin the reels. The "skill" factor comes into play because after seeing the results of your first spin you then have to decide whether to keep none, one, two, or all three of the symbols on each reel before you spin them again.

The casino also offers more traditional looking slots, called "Cherokee Raffle Reels." However, once again, they operate differently from regular slot machines because you are actually being entered into a raffle drawing.

The casino is open 24 hours and the minimum gambling age is 21.

A new $100 million casino project is being built by Caesars Entertainment Corporation in conjunction with the Eastern Band of Cherokee Indians.

Located in Cherokee County, just outside the town of Murphy (map locations #2), the facility, known as Harrah's Cherokee Valley River Casino & Hotel, will feature a 60,000-square-foot casino, a 300-room hotel and a variety of dining options.

The property is expected to open by the summer of 2015.

For more information on visiting North Carolina call the state's division of travel & tourism at (800) 847-4862 or go to: www. visitnc.com.

Harrah's Cherokee Casino
777 Casino Drive
Cherokee, North Carolina 28719
(828) 497-7777
Website: www.harrahscherokee.com
Map: **#1** (55 miles S.W. of Asheville)

Toll-Free Number: (800) 427-7247
Rooms 1,108 Price Range: $119-$369
Suites: 107 Price Range: Casino Use Only
Restaurants: 5   Liquor: No
Valet Parking: $8
Buffets: B-$21.95 (Sat/Sun)
           D-$25.50/$31.95 (Sat/Sun)
Overnight RV Parking: No
Special Features: 1,500-seat entertainment pavilion.

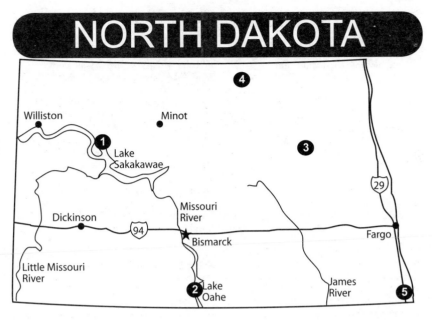

NORTH DAKOTA

North Dakota has more than 800 sites throughout the state that offer blackjack, with betting limits of $1-$25, for the benefit of charities.

There are also six Indian casinos which are limited by law to the following maximum bet limits: blackjack-$100 (two tables in a casino may have limits up to $250), craps-$60, roulette-$50, slots/video poker-$25 and poker-$50 per bet, per round with a maximum of three rounds.

The terms of the state's compact with the tribes require gaming machines to return a minimum of 80% and a maximum of 100%. However, if a machine is affected by skill, such as video poker or video blackjack, the machines must return a minimum of 83%.

All casinos are open 24 hours and offer: blackjack, craps, roulette, slots, video poker and video keno. Optional games include: Spanish 21 (S21), Caribbean stud poker (CSP), let it ride (LIR), poker (P), three-card poker (TCP), keno (K), bingo (BG), big-6 wheel (B6) and off-track betting (OTB). The minimum age requirement is 21 for casino gambling and 18 for bingo.

For information on visiting North Dakota call the state's tourism office at (800) 435-5663 or go to: www.ndtourism.com.

Dakota Magic Casino & Hotel
16849 102nd Street SE
Hankinson, North Dakota 58041
(701) 634-3000
Website: www.dakotamagic.com
Map: **#5** (50 miles S. of Fargo)

Toll-Free Number: (800) 325-6825
Rooms: 111 Price Range: $70-$110
Suites: 8 Price Range: $150-$240
Restaurants: 1 Liquor: Yes Valet Parking: No
Buffets: B-$11.99 (Sat/Sun) L-$9.95
    D-$14.99/$16.99 (Wed)/$18.99 (Fri)
Casino Size: 24,000 Square Feet
Other Games: P
Overnight RV Parking: Free/RV Dump: Fee
Senior Discount: Various on Mon if 55+
Special Features: 25-space RV park ($10 summer/$5 winter). 10% off rooms for seniors.

Four Bears Casino & Lodge
202 Frontage Road
New Town, North Dakota 58763
(701) 627-4018
Website: www.4bearscasino.com
Map: **#1** (150 miles N.W. of Bismarck)

Toll-Free Number: (800) 294-5454
Rooms: 97 Price Range: $95
Suites: 3 Price Range: $105
Restaurants: 2 Liquor: Yes Valet Parking: No
Buffets: B-$9.95 L-$10.95
          D-$19.95/$22.95 (Wed/Thu/Sat)
Other Games: P, TCP, LIR
Overnight RV Parking: Free/RV Dump: No
Senior Discount: Various Tue if 55+
Special Features: 85-space RV park ($25 per night). Nearby marina. 1,000-seat event center.

Prairie Knights Casino & Resort
7932 Highway 24
Fort Yates, North Dakota 58538
(701) 854-7777
Website: www.prairieknights.com
Map: **#2** (60 miles S. of Bismarck)

Toll-Free Number: (800) 425-8277
Rooms: 92 Price Range: $65-$90
Suites: 4 Price Range: $90-$150
Restaurants: 2 Liquor: Yes Valet Parking: No
Buffets: L/D-$9.95
Casino Size: 42,000 Square Feet
Other Games: TCP, LIR, No Roulette
Overnight RV Parking: Free/RV Dump: Free
Senior Discount: $7.95 buffet 11am -2pm
          (Mon-Fri) if 55+
Special Features: 12-space RV park ($15 per night) at casino. 32-space RV park ($15 per night) at marina. Free RV dump at marina. $50 rooms for players club members. Convenience store.

Sky Dancer Hotel & Casino
Highway 5 West
Belcourt, North Dakota 58316
(701) 244-2400
Website: www.skydancercasino.com
Map: **#4** (120 miles N.E. of Minot)

Toll-Free Number: (866) 244-9467
Rooms: 70 Price Range: $65-$90
Suites: 27 Price Range: $65-$90
Restaurants: 2 Liquor: Yes Valet Parking: No
Casino Size: 25,000 Square Feet
Buffets: B-$6.95 L-$7.95
          D-$9.95/$18.95 (Fri)/$16.95 (Sat)
Other Games: P, LIR, BG, OTB (Wed-Sun),
          FCP, No Craps
Overnight RV Parking: Free/RV Dump: Free
Special Features: Gift shop.

Spirit Lake Casino & Resort
Highway 57
Spirit Lake, North Dakota 58370
(701) 766-4747
Website: www.spiritlakecasino.com
Map: **#3** (6 miles S. of Devil's Lake)

Toll-Free Number: (800) 946-8238
Rooms: 108 Price Range: $69-$129
Suites: 16 Price Range: $109-$159
Restaurants: 3 Liquor: No Valet Parking: Free
Buffets: B-$5.50/$7.00 (Sun) L-$6.95
          D-$7.00/$20.00 (Wed)
Casino Size: 45,000 Square Feet
Other Games: P, BG, No roulette
Overnight RV Parking: Must use RV park
Senior Discount: Various on Monday if 55+
Special Features: 15-space RV park ($23.30 per night). Gift shop. Discount smoke shop. 32-slip marina. Players club members get 10% off rooms.

Turtle Mountain Chippewa Mini-Casino
1 Sailor Ave
Belcourt, North Dakota 58316
(701) 477-6438
Map: **#4** (120 miles N.E. of Minot)

Restaurants: 1 Liquor: Yes Valet Parking: No
Other Games: Only Machines - No Table Games
Casino Hours: 8am-11:30pm
Overnight RV Parking: Free/RV Dump: No
Special Features: Affiliated with and located four miles east of Sky Dancer Hotel and Casino.

OHIO

Ohio has casinos in four cities: Cleveland, Cincinnati, Columbus and Toledo. All of the casinos are non-smoking, open 24 hours and the minimum gambling age is 21.

Unless otherwise noted, all Ohio casinos offer: blackjack, craps, roulette, slots and video poker. Some casinos also offer: mini-baccarat (MB), baccarat (B), poker (P), pai gow poker (PGP), Mississippi stud (MS), let it ride (LIR), three card poker (TCP), fourcard poker (FCP) and bingo (BG).

If you want to order a drink while playing, be aware that Ohio gaming regulations do not allow casinos to provide free alcoholic beverages. Additionally, casinos are not allowed to serve any alcohol between the hours of 2 a.m. and 6 a.m.

NOTE: If you happen to win a jackpot of $1,200 or more in Ohio, the casino will withhold approximately 5% of your winnings for the Ohio Department of Taxation. The $1,200 threshold also applies to any cash prizes won in casino drawings or tournaments.

Additionally, the casino will withhold another approximate 2.5% of your winnings for city taxes in Columbus, Cleveland and Cincinatti. In Toledo, the city tax won't be withheld until you win $2,000, or more. The $1,200 and $2,000 thresholds would also apply to any cash prizes won in casino drawings or tournaments.

Here's information from the Ohio Casino Control Commission regarding the payback percentages for each casino's electronic machines for the 12-month period from July 1, 2013 through June 30, 2014:

CASINO	PAYBACK %
Horseshoe Cincinatti	92.03
Hollywood Columbus	91.73
Hollywood Toledo	90.92
Horseshoe Cleveland	92.01

For tourism information, call the Ohio Division of Travel and Tourism at (800) 282-5393, or visit their website at www.discoverohio.com

Hollywood Casino - Columbus
200 Georgesville Road
Columbus, Ohio 43228
(614) 308-3333
Website: www.hollywoodcasinocolumbus.com
Map: #**6**

Toll-Free Number: (855) 617-4206
Restaurants: 3 Valet Parking: Free
Buffets: L-$13.99 D-$19.99/$29.99 (Sat/Sun)
Casino Size: 120,000 Square Feet
Other games: TCP, FCP, MB, B6, PGP, MS
Overnight RV Parking: Free/RV Dump: No

Hollywood Casino - Toledo
777 Hollywood Blvd
Toledo, Ohio 43605
(419) 661-5200
Website: www.hollywoodcasinotoledo.com
Map: #**4**

Toll-Free Number: (877) 777-9579
Valet Parking: $5
Buffets: L-$15.99 D-$21.99/$29.99 (Fri/Sat)
Casino Size: 125,000 square feet
Other games: MB, LIR, P, B6, MS, FCP

Horseshoe Casino - Cincinatti
1000 Broadway
Cincinnati, Ohio 45202
(513) 252-0777
Website: www.horseshoecincinnati.com
Map: #**5**

Restaurants: 3 Valet Parking: Free
Buffets: L-$16.99/$23.99 (Sat/Sun)
        D-$23.99/$27.99 (Fri/Sat)
Casino Size: 100,000 Square Feet
Other games: TCP, FCP, LIR, MS
Senior Discount: Buffet discount Wed if 55+
Special features: 100x odds on craps.

Horseshoe Casino - Cleveland
100 Public Square
Cleveland, Ohio 44113
(216) 297-4777
Website: www.horseshoecleveland.com
Map: #**8**

Toll-free Number: (855) 746-3777
Restaurants: 3
Buffet: B-$11.99/$23.99 (Sun)
        L-$15.99 D-$25.99
Casino Size: 96,000 Square Feet
Games Offered: P, PGP, TCP, FCP, LIR
Special features: 100x odds on craps.

Pari-Mutuels

In Ohio, pari-mutuels are allowed to offer video lottery terminals that are regulated by the Ohio Lottery Commission.

All racetrack casinos (racinos) are open 24 hours and the minimum gambling age is 21. The minimum age for pari-mutuel betting is 18.

Belterra Park Gaming & Entertainment Center
6301 Kellogg Avenue
Cincinnati, Ohio 45230
(513) 232-8000
Website: www.belterrapark.com/
Map: #5
Restaurants: 4 Admission: Free
Buffets: L-$15.99/$21.99 (Sun)
        D-$16.99/$19.99 (Fri/Sat)
Special Features: Live racing May-October. Racing Thu-Sun. Daily simulcast.

Hard Rock Rocksino at Northfield Park
10705 Northfield Road
Northfield, Ohio 44067-1236
(330) 467-4101
Website: www.hrrocksinonorthfieldpark.com
Map: #**3** (10 miles SE. of Clevland)

Restaurants: 2
Buffets: L-$14.99/$19.99 (Sun)
      D-$16.99/$19.99 (Fri/Sat)
Admission: Free/$1.75 (Fri/Sat)
Clubhouse: $1.25 (Mon/Wed)/$3 (Fri/Sat)
Special Features: Daily Simulcast. Live racing
Mon/Tue/Fri/Sat.

Hollywood Gaming at Dayton Valley Raceway
3100 Needmore Rd
Dayton, Ohio 45414
(937) 329-9828
Website: www.hollywooddaytonraceway.com
Map: #**1** (10 miles SW. of Columbus)

Restaurants: 3

Hollywood Gaming at Mahoning Valley Race Course
655 North Canfield Niles Road
Austintown, Ohio 44515
(877) 788-3777
Website: www.hollywoodmahoningvalley.com

Restaurants: 4
Special Features: Live racing (schedule to be determined).

Miami Valley Gaming
6000 SR 63
Lebanon, Ohio 45036
(513) 934-7070
Website: www.miamivalleygaming.com

Toll Free (855) 946-6847
Restaurants: 3 Admission: Free
Buffets: L- $13.99/$14.99 (Sun)
      D- $18.99/$19.99 (Fri/Sat)
Special Features: Live Harness racing February-May. Daily simulcast.

OKLAHOMA

All Oklahoma Indian casinos are allowed to offer both Class II and Class III gaming machines.

Most casinos offer only Class II machines which look like slot machines, but are actually games of bingo and the spinning video reels are for "entertainment purposes only." Some casinos also offer traditional Class III slots.

In either case, the gaming machines are not allowed to accept or payout in coins. All payouts must be done by a printed receipt or via an electronic debit card. No public information is available concerning the payback percentages on gaming machines in Oklahoma.

Most, but not all, casinos with card games such as blackjack, let it ride or three-card poker, etc., offer a player-banked version where players must pay a commission to the house on every hand they play. The amount of the commission charged varies, depending on the rules of each casino, but it's usually 50 cents to $1 per hand played. Call the casino to see if they charge a commission. Roulette and dice games are not permitted in Oklahoma.

There are also two horse racing facilities in Oklahoma which feature Class II gaming machines.

All Oklahoma Indian casinos offer gaming machines. Other games include: blackjack (BJ), craps (C), roulette (R), mini-baccarat (MB), poker (P), three-card poker (TCP), pai gow poker (PGP), let it ride (LIR), Mississippi stud (MS), bingo (BG) and off-track betting (OTB).

Not all Oklahoma Indian casinos serve alcoholic beverages and the individual listings note which casinos do serve it. Unless otherwise noted, all casinos are open 24 hours. The minimum gambling age is 18 at some casinos and 21 at others.

For more information on visiting Oklahoma call the Oklahoma Tourism Department at (800) 652-6552 or go to: www.travelok.com

Ada Gaming Center
1500 North Country Club Road
Ada, Oklahoma 74820
Website: www.chickasaw.net
(580) 436-3740
Map: **#2** (85 miles S.E. of Oklahoma City)

Restaurants: 1   Liquor: No
Casino Size: 9,220 Square Feet
Other Games: BJ, P, MS
Overnight RV Parking: No
Special Features: Located in travel plaza with gas station and convenience store.

Ada Travel Plaza
201 Latta Road
Ada, Oklahoma 74820
(580) 310-0900
Website: www.chickasaw.net
Map: **#2** (85 miles S.E. of Oklahoma City)

Restaurants: 1 Snack Bar   Liquor: No
Overnight RV Parking: No
Special Features: Located in travel plaza with gas station and convenience store.

Apache Casino Hotel
2315 East Gore Boulevard
Lawton, Oklahoma 73502
(580) 248-5905
Website: www.apachecasinohotel.com
Map: **#17** (86 miles S.W. of Oklahoma City)

Rooms: 124 Price Range: $127-$187
Suites: 8 Price Range: Casino Use Only
Restaurants: 1 (2 snack bars)   Liquor: Yes
Casino Size: 7,700 Square Feet
Other games: BJ, TCP, C, BG
Overnight RV Parking: Free/RV Dump: No

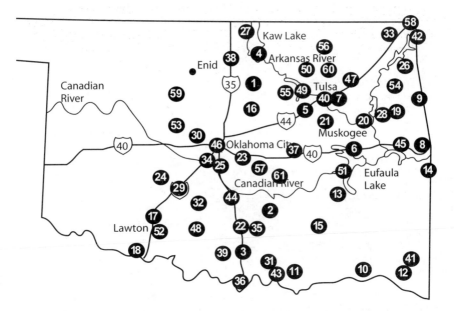

Black Gold Casino
288 Mulberry Lane (on Route 70)
Wilson, Oklahoma 73463
(580) 668-9248
Website: www.chickasaw.net
Map: **#39** (112 miles S. of Oklahoma City)

Casino Size: 3,744 Square Feet
Other Games: MS
Restaurants: 1 Snack Bar   Liquor: No
Overnight RV Parking: Free/RV Dump: No
Special Features: Located in travel plaza with gas station and convenience store.

Black Hawk Casino
42008 Westech Road
Shawnee, Oklahoma 74804
(405)275-4700
Website: www.theblackhawkcasino.com
Map: **#23** (40 Miles E. of Oaklhoma City)

Restaurants: 1   Liquor: Yes
Casino Size: 8,600 Sqaure Feet
Other Games: P, BJ, LIR, TCP
Overnight RV Parking: No

Bordertown Outpost Casino
67901 East 100 Road
Wyandotte, Oklahoma 74370
(918) 666-6770
Map: **#42** (90 miles N.E. of Tulsa)

Overnight RV Parking: Free/RV Dump: No

Buffalo Run Casino
1000 Buffalo Run Boulevard
Miami, Oklahoma 74354
(918) 542-7140
Website: www.buffalorun.com
Map: **#33** (89 miles N.E. of Tulsa)

Rooms: 88 Room Rates: $91-$109
Suites: 12 Room Rates: $111-$132
Restaurants: 1   Liquor: Yes
Other Games: BJ, TCP, FCP
Overnight RV Parking: Free/RV Dump: No
Senior Special: Free breakfast Mon 8am-10am if 55+
Special Features: 2,000-seat showroom.

Cash Springs Gaming Center
West First and Muskogee Streets
Sulphur, Oklahoma 73086
(580) 622-2156
Map: **#35** (84 miles S. of Oklahoma City)

Toll-Free Number: (866) 622-2156
Restaurants: 1   Liquor: No
Overnight RV Parking: Free

Checotah Indian Community Bingo
830 North Broadway
Checotah, Oklahoma 74426
(918) 473-5200
Map: **#6** (120 miles E. of Oklahoma City)

Restaurants: 1
Hours: 8am-6am
Casino Size: 8,000 Square Feet
Other Games: BG
Overnight RV Parking: No

Cherokee Casino - Ft. Gibson
US Highway 62
Ft. Gibson, Oklahoma 74338
(918) 207-3593
Website: www.cherokeecasino.com
Map: **#54** (80 miles E. of Tulsa)

Restaurants: 1 Deli   Liquor: No
Overnight RV Parking: No
Senior Discount: Various Thu if 55+

Cherokee Casino - Ramona
31501 US 75 Hwy
Ramona, Oklahoma 74061
(918) 535-3800
Website: www.cherokeecasino.com
Map: **#60** (30 miles N. of Tulsa)

Restaurants: 1

Cherokee Casino & Inn - Roland
Interstate 40 and Highway 64
Roland, Oklahoma 74954
(918) 427-7491
Website: www.cherokeecasino.com
Map: **#8** (175 miles E. of Oklahoma City)

Toll-Free Number: (800) 256-2338
Rooms: 45   Room Rates: $59-$119
Suites: 12 Room Rates: $89-$179
Restaurants: 1 Deli   Liquor: Beer Only
Casino Size: 28,000 Square Feet
Other Games: P, BJ, TCP
Overnight RV Parking: Free/RV Dump: No

Cherokee Casino - Sallisaw
1621 West Ruth Avenue
Sallisaw, Oklahoma 74955
(918) 774-1600
Website: www.cherokeecasino.com
Map: **#45** (160 miles E. of Oklahoma City)

Toll-Free Number: (800) 256-2338
Restaurants: 1   Liquor: Beer only
Casino Size: 22,000 Square Feet
Other Games: OTB
Overnight RV Parking: Free/RV Dump: No

Cherokee Casino - Tahlequah
16489 Highway 62
Tahlequah, Oklahoma 74464
(918) 207-3600
Website: www.cherokeecasino.com
Map: **#19** (83 miles S.E. of Tulsa)

Restaurants: 1 Snack Bar   Liquor: No
Overnight RV Parking: Free/RV Dump: No

Cherokee Casino - West Siloam Springs
7300 West US Highway 412
W. Siloam Springs, Oklahoma 74338
(918) 422-6301
Website: www.cherokeecasino.com
Map: **#9** (85 miles E. of Tulsa)

Toll-Free Number: (800) 754-4111
Restaurants: 2   Liquor: Yes
Buffets: L-$7.47 (Mon-Sat) D-$11.21
Other Games: BJ, P, OTB, FCP
Overnight RV Parking: Free/RV Dump: No

Chisholm Trail Casino
7807 N. Highway 81
Duncan, Oklahoma 73533
(580) 255-1668
Website: www.chilsomtrailcasino.com
Map: **#48** (79 miles S. of Oklahoma City)

Casino Size: 22,000 Square Feet
Restaurants: 1   Liquor: No
Overnight RV Parking: Free/RV Dump: No
Other Games: BJ, TCP

Choctaw Casino - Broken Bow
1790 South Park Drive
Broken Bow, Oklahoma 74728
(580) 584-5450
Website: www.choctawcasinos.com
Map: **#41** (235 miles S.E. of Oklahoma City)

Restaurants: 1 Snack Bar   Liquor: No
Overnight RV Parking: Free/ RV Dump: No

Choctaw Casino - Grant
US Highway 271
Grant, Oklahoma 74738
(580) 326-8397
Website: www.choctawcasinos.com
Map: **#10** (200 miles S. of Oklahoma City)

Restaurants: 1 Deli   Liquor: No
Rooms: 40 Price Range: $72-$102
Buffets: B- $8.99 (Sat)/$9.99 (Sun) L-$11.50
D-$12.50/$21.00 (Fri/Sat)
Other Games: BJ, P
Overnight RV Parking: No

Choctaw Casino - Idabel
1425 Southeast Washington Street
Idabel, Oklahoma 74745
(580) 286-5710
Website: www.choctawcasinos.com
Map: **#12** (240 miles S.E. of Oklahoma City)

Toll-Free Number: (800) 634-2582
Restaurants: 1   Liquor: No
Casino Size: 11,000 Square Feet
Overnight RV Parking: Must check-in at front desk/RV Dump: No

Choctaw Casino - McAlester
1638 South George Nigh Expressway
McAlester, Oklahoma 74501-7411
(918) 423-8161
Website: www.choctawcasinos.com
Map: **#13** (130 miles S.E. of Oklahoma City)

Toll-Free Number: (877) 904-8444
Restaurants: 1   Liquor: No
Other Games: BJ
Casino Size: 17,500 Square Feet
Overnight RV Parking: Free/RV Dump: No
Special Features: Blackjack games open at 4pm.

Choctaw Casino Hotel - Pocola
Interstate 540
Pocola, Oklahoma 74902
(918) 436-7761
Website: www.choctawcasinos.com
Map: **#14** (195 miles E. of Oklahoma City)

Toll-Free Number: (800) 590-5825
Rooms: 118 Price Range: $99-$119
Suites: 10 Price Range: $149-$279
Restaurants: 2   Liquor: No
Other Games: BJ, C, R, TCP, P
Overnight RV Parking: Free/RV Dump: No

Choctaw Casino Resort
4418 South Highway 69/75
Durant, Oklahoma 74701
(580) 920-0160
Website: www.choctawcasinos.com
Map: **#11** (150 miles S.E. of Oklahoma City)

Toll-Free Number: (800) 788-2464
Room Reservations: (580) 931-8340
Rooms: 40 Price Range: $99-$279
Suites: 4 Price Range: $209-$750
Restaurants: 2   Liquor: No
Buffets: B-$17.99 (Sun) L- $14.99
D-$18.99/$24.99 (Fri/Sat)
Casino Size: 36,000 Square Feet
Other Games: BJ, P, OTB, TCP, LIR,
MB, PGP, BG (Thu-Sun)
Senior Discount: Various Thu if 55+
Overnight RV Parking: Must use RV Park/ RV Dump: No
Special Features: Free shuttle buses from Dallas and Fort Worth. 75-space RV park ($40-$50 nightly).

Choctaw Casino - Stringtown
895 North Highway 69
Stringtown, Oklahoma 74569
(580) 346-7862
Website: www.choctawcasinos.com
Map: **#15** (163 miles S.E. of Oklahoma
City)

Restaurants: 2   Liquor: No
Overnight RV Parking: Free/RV Dump: No

Cimarron Casino
821 W. Freeman Avenue
Perkins, Oklahoma 74059
(405) 547-5352
Website: www.cimarroncasino.com
Map: **#16** (60 miles N. of Oklahoma City)

Restaurants: 1 Snack Bar   Liquor: Yes
Other Games: BJ
Overnight RV Parking: No

Comanche Nation Casino
402 South East Interstate Drive
Lawton, Oklahoma 73502
(580) 354-2000
Website: www.comanchenationcasinos.com
Map: **#17** (86 miles S.W. of Oklahoma City)

Toll-Free Number: (866) 354-2500
Restaurants: 1   Liquor: Yes
Other Games: BJ, TCP, P, OTB, BG
Senior Special: Various on Wed if 55+
Overnight RV Parking: Free, must get pass
from front desk first (with hook ups)/
RV Dump: No

Comanche Red River Casino
Highway 36 and Highway 70
Devol, Oklahoma 73531
(580) 299-3378
Website: www.comanchenationcasinos.com
Map: **#18** (125 miles S.W. of Oklahoma City)

Toll-Free Number: (866) 280-3261
Restaurants: 1   Liquor: Yes
Casino Size: 52,500 Square Feet
Other Games: BJ, TCP, MS
Overnight RV Parking: Check-in at front
desk (with hook ups)/RV Dump: No
Senior Special: Various Mon if 55+
Special Features: Drive-thru smoke shop.

Comanche Spur Casino
9047 US Highway 62
Eldon, Oklahoma 73538
(580) 492-5502
Website: www.comanchenationcasinos.com
Map: **#29** (75 miles S.W. of Oklahoma City)

Restaurants: 1   Liquor: No
Hours: 11am-12am/2am (Fri/Sat)
Senior Special: Various Wed if 55+
Overnight RV Parking: No
Special features: Smoke shop. Convenience
store.

Comanche Star Casino
Rt 3 and Hwy 53
Walters, Oklahoma 73572
(580) 875-2092
Website: www.comanchenationcasinos.com
Map: **#52** (25 miles S.E. of Lawton)

Restaurants: 1   Liquor: No
Hours: 12pm-11pm/1am (Fri/Sat)
Casino Size: 7,000 Square Feet
Overnight RV Parking: No

Creek Nation Casino - Bristow
121 West Lincoln
Bristow, Oklahoma 74010
(918) 367-9168
Website: www.creeknationbristow.com
Map: **#5** (60 miles N.E. of Oklahoma City)

Restaurants: 1 Snack Bar   Liquor: No
Hours: 8am-6am
Overnight RV Parking: No

Creek Nation Casino - Eufaula
806 Forest Avenue
Eufaula, Oklahoma 74432
(918) 689-9191
Map: **#51** (135 miles E. of Oklahoma City)

Restaurants: 1 Snack Bar   Liquor: No
Hours: 10am-3am/4am (Thu-Sat)
Overnight RV Parking: No

Creek Nation Casino - Holdenville
221 East Willow St.
Holdenville, Oklahoma 74848
(405) 379-3321
Map: **#61** (75 miles S.E. of Oklahoma City)

Hours: 12pm-12am/2am (Fri/Sat)/10pm (Sun)
Overnight RV Parking: No

Creek Nation Casino - Muscogee
3420 West Peak Boulevard
Muskogee, Oklahoma 74403
(918) 683-1825
Website: www.creeknationcasino.net
Map: **#20** (50 miles S.E. of Tulsa)

Restaurants: 1 Liquor: No
Other Games: BJ, P, BG
Casino Size: 22,500 Square Feet
Overnight RV Parking: Free/RV Dump: No

Creek Nation Casino - Okemah
1100 S. Woodie Guthrie
Okemah, Oklahoma 74859
(918) 623-0051
Map: **#37** (72 miles E. of Oklahoma City)

Restaurants: 1 Liquor: No
Overnight RV Parking: Free/RV Dump: No

Creek Nation Travel Plaza
Highway 75 and 56 Loop
Okmulgee, Oklahoma 74447
(918) 752-0090
Map: **#21** (45 miles S. of Tulsa)

Restaurants: 1 Snack Bar Liquor: No
Overnight RV Parking: Free/RV Dump: No
Special Features: Gas station and convenience
store. Burger King.

Davis Trading Post
Interstate 35 and Highway 7
Davis, Oklahoma 73030
(580) 369-5360
Website: www.chickasaw.net
Map: **#22** (75 miles S. of Oklahoma City)

Restaurants: 1 Liquor: No
Overnight RV Parking: Free/RV Dump: No

Downstream Casino Resort
69300 East Nee Road
Quapaw, Oklahoma 74363
(918) 919-6000
Website: www.downstreamcasino.com
Map: **#58** (On the border of OK, MO, and KS)

Toll-Free Number: (888) 396-7876
Rooms: 200 Price Range: $99-$199
Suites: 22 Price Range: $199-$399
Restaurants:5 Liquor: Yes
Buffet: B-$10.95 (Sun) L-$6.95
    D-$17.95/20.95(Tue)/$19.95 (Fri/Sat)
Gambling Age: 18
Casino size: 70,000 Square feet
Other Games: P, FCP, OTB, TCP
Special Features: Only casino/hotel in the
country located in three states: Oklahoma,
Missouri, and Kansas.

Duck Creek Casino
10085 Ferguson Road
Beggs, Oklahoma 74421
(918) 267-3468
Map: **#21** (35 miles S. of Tulsa)

Restaurants: 1 Snack Bar Liquor: No
Hours: 9am-7am Daily
Casino Size: 5,000 Square Feet
Overnight RV Parking: No

Feather Warrior Casino - Canton
301 NW Lake Road
Canton, Oklahoma 73724
(580) 886-2490
Website: www.featherwarrior.com
Map: **#59** (60 miles N. W. of Okla. City)

Restaurants: 1 Snack Bar Liquor: No
Hours: 11am-2am/10am-2am (Fri-Sun)
Casino Size: 2,200 Square Feet
Overnight RV Parking: Free/RV Dump: No

Feather Warrior Casino - Watonga
1407 S. Clarence Nash Boulevard
Watonga, Oklahoma 73772
(580) 623-7333
Website: www.featherwarrior.com
Map: **#53** (70 miles N. W. of Okla. City)

Restaurants: 1 Snack Bar Liquor: No
Hours: 11am-2am/10am-2am (Fri-Sun)
Casino Size: 2,200 Square Feet
Overnight RV Parking: Free/RV Dump: No

Fire Lake Casino
41207 Hardesty Road
Shawnee, Oklahoma 74801
(405) 273-2242
Website: www.winatfirelake.com
Map: **#23** (38 miles E. of Oklahoma City)

Restaurants: 1 Liquor: Yes
Buffets: B-$4.99 (Sat/Sun) L-$7.99/$9.99 (Fri)
       D- $10.99/$12.99 (Fri)
Other Games: BJ, P, BG, TCP
Overnight RV Parking: Free/RV Dump: No
Senior Discount: Various Sun if 55+

First Council Casino
12875 North Highway 77
Newkirk, Oklahoma 74647
(580) 448-3015
Website: www.myfirstwin.com
Map: **#27** (Just south of the Kansas state line)

Toll-Free: (877) 725-2670
Restaurants: 3   Liquor: Yes
Casino Size: 125,000 Square Feet
Other Games: BJ, BG, TCP
Overnight RV Parking: Free/RV Dump: No
Special Features: 3,000-seat event center.

Gold Mountain Casino
1410 Sam Noble Parkway
Ardmore, Oklahoma 73401
(580) 223-3301
Website: www.chickasaw.net
Map: **#3** (100 miles S. of Oklahoma City)

Restaurants: 1   Liquor: No
Casino Size: 8,620 Square Feet
Overnight RV Parking: No
Special Features: Tobacco shop.

Gold River Casino
Highway 281
Anadarko, Oklahoma 73005
(405) 247-6979
Website: www.goldriverok.com
Map: **#24** (60 miles S.W. of Oklahoma City)

Toll-Free Number: (800) 280-1018
Restaurants: 1   Liquor: No
Casino Size: 12,000 Square Feet
Casino Hours: 9am-4am/24 hrs (Fri/Sat)
Senior Discount: Various Tue if 55+
Overnight RV Parking: Free/RV Dump: No

Golden Pony Casino
Hwy. I-40, Exit 227 Clearview Road
Okemah, Oklahoma 74859
(918) 560-6199
Website: www.goldenponycasino.com
Map: **#37** (72 miles E. of Oklahoma City)

Toll-free Number: (877) 623-0072
Restaurants: Snack Bar   Liquor: No
Overnight RV Parking: Free/RV Dump: No

Goldsby Gaming Center
1038 West Sycamore Road
Norman, Oklahoma 73072
(405) 329-5447
Website: www.chickasaw.net
Map: **#25** (21 miles S. of Oklahoma City)

Restaurants: 1   Liquor: No
Other Games: BG (Wed-Sun)
Casino Size: 23,007 Square Feet
Overnight RV Parking: No

Grand Casino Hotel & Resort
777 Grand Casino Boulevard
Shawnee, Oklahoma 74851
(405) 964-7263
Website: www.grabdresortok.com
Map: **#23** (38 miles E. of Oklahoma City)

Room Reservations: (405) 964-7777
Rooms: 242 Price Range: $129-$149
Suites: 20 Price Range: $149-$179
Restaurants: 3   Liquor: Yes
Buffets: B-$12.95 (Sun) L-$9.95/$12.95 (Sun)
       D-$12.95/ $26.95 (Fri/Sat)
Casino Size: 125,000 Square Feet
Other Games: BJ, P, K, TCP
Overnight RV Parking: $50 per night
Special Features: 3,000-seat event center.

Grand Lake Casino
24701 S. 655th Road
Grove, Oklahoma 74344
(918) 786-8528
Website: grandlakecasino.com
Map: **#26** (80 miles N.E. of Tulsa)

Toll-Free Number: (800) 426-4640
Restaurants: 1   Liquor: Yes
Other Games: BJ, P, TCP
Casino Size: 45,000 Square Feet
Overnight RV Parking: No

Hard Rock Hotel & Casino Tulsa
770 W Cherokee Street
Catoosa, Oklahoma 74015
(918) 384-7800
Website: www.hardrockcasinotulsa.com
Map: **#7** (a suburb of Tulsa)

Toll-Free Number: (800) 760-6700
Rooms: 130 Price Range: $59-$149
Suites: 20 Price Range: $160-$515
Restaurants: 4   Liquor: Yes
Buffets: B-$8.95/$10.95 (Sat/Sun)
        L-$10.95 D-$17.95/$23.99 (Fri/Sat)
Casino Size: 80,000 Square Feet
Other Games: BJ, P, TCP
Overnight RV Parking: Free/RV Dump: No

High Winds Casino
61475 E. 100 Road
Miami, Oklahoma 74354
(918) 541-9463
Website: www.highwindscasino.com
Map: **#33** (89 miles N.E. of Tulsa)

Restaurants: 2 Liquor: Yes
Overnight RV Parking: Free/RV Dump: No

Indigo Sky Casino
70220 East US Highway 60
Wyandotte, Oklahoma 74370
Website: www.indigoskycasino.com
Map: **#26** (90 miles N.E. of Tulsa)

Toll-Free: (888) 992-7591
Rooms: 117 Room Rates:$99-$109
Restaurants: 2
Other Games: BJ, TCP, FCP, LIR, P, OTB, BG
Overnight RV Parking: Must use RV park
Special Features: 45-space RV Park ($10 per
night)

Kickapoo Casino
25230 East Highway 62
Harrah, Oklahoma 73045
(405) 964-4444
Website: www.kickapoo-casino.com
Map: **#23** (31 miles E. of Oklahoma City)

Restaurants: 1   Liquor: No
Other Games: BJ, MB
Senior Special: Various on Tue if 55+
Overnight RV Parking: Free/RV Dump: No

Kiowa Casino
County Road 1980
Devol, Oklahoma 73531
(580)299-3333
Website:www.kiowacasino.com
Map: **#18** (125 miles S.W. of Oklahoma
City)

Toll-Free Number: (866) 370-4077
Restaurants: 3   Liquor: Beer Only
Buffets: B-$11.50 (Sat/Sun)
        L-$9.50/
        D-$11.50/$21.00 (Fri/Sat)
Other Games: BJ, TCP
Overnight RV Parking: Free/RV Dump: No
Special Features: No table games Monday.

Lucky Star Casino - Clinton
101 N. Indian Hospital Road
Clinton, Oklahoma 73601
(580) 323-6599
Website: www.luckystarcasino.org
Map: **#29** (85 miles W. of Oklahoma City)

Restaurants: 1   Liquor: No
Other Games: BJ, MS
Overnight RV Parking: Free/RV Dump: No

Lucky Star Casino - Concho
7777 North Highway 81
Concho, Oklahoma 73022
(405) 262-7612
Website: www.luckystarcasino.org
Map: **#30** (35 miles N.W. of Oklahoma City)

Restaurants: 1   Liquor: Yes
Other Games: BJ, P, MS
Casino Size: 40,000 Square Feet
Overnight RV Parking: Free/RV Dump: Free
Special Features: Free RV hookups (must
register first).

Lucky Turtle Casino
64499 East Highway 60
Wyandotte, Oklahoma 74370
(918) 678-3767
Map: **#42** (90 miles N.E. of Tulsa)

Restaurants: 1   Liquor: No
Casino Size: 4,000 Square Feet
Overnight RV Parking: No
Special Features: Convenience store.

Madill Gaming Center
902 South First Street
Madill, Oklahoma 73446
(580) 795-7301
Website: www.chickasaw.net
Map: **#31** (122 miles S. of Oklahoma City)

Restaurants: 1   Liquor: No
Casino Size: 2,071 Square Feet
Overnight RV Parking: No

Native Lights Casino
12375 N. Highway 77
Newkirk, Oklahoma 74647
(580) 448-3100
Website: www.nativelightscasino.com
Map: **#27** (106 miles N. of Oklahoma City)

Toll-Free Number: (877) 468-3100
Restaurants: 1   Liquor: Yes
Hours: 10am-12am/3am (Fri/Sat)
Overnight RV Parking: Free/RV Dump: No

Newcastle Gaming Center
2457 Highway 62 Service Road
Newcastle, Oklahoma 73065
(405) 387-6013
Website: www.mynewcastlecasino.com
Map: **#34** (19 miles S. of Oklahoma City)

Restaurants: 1   Liquor: Yes
Casino Size: 44,622 Sqaure Feet
Other Games: BJ, K, TCP
Overnight RV Parking: Free/RV Dump: No

One Fire Casino
1901 North Wood Drive
Okmulgee, Oklahoma 74447
(918) 756-8400
Website: www.onefirecasino.com
Map: **#21** (45 miles S. of Tulsa)

Restaurants: 1   Liquor: No
Casino Size: 10,000 Square Feet
Overnight RV Parking: Free/RV Dump: No

Osage Casino - Bartlesville
222 Allen Road
Bartlesville, Oklahoma 74003
(918) 335-7519
Website: www.osagecasinos.com
Map: **#56** (50 miles N. of Tulsa)

Restaurants: 2   Liquor: No
Buffet: B-$7.00 (Mon) L-$12.00 (Sun)
        D-$12.00 (Thu)/$24.00 (Sat/Sun)
Other Games: BJ, P
Senior Discount: Various Mon-Wed if 50+
Overnight RV Parking: No

Osage Casino - Hominy
Highway 99
Hominy, Oklahoma 74035
(918) 885-2990
Website: www.osagecasinos.com
Map: **#49** (44 miles N.W. of Tulsa)

Restaurants: 1   Liquor: No
Hours: 10am-2am/4am (Wed-Sat)
Other Games: P
Senior Discount: Various Sun/Wed/Thu if 50+
Overnight RV Parking: Free/RV Dump:No

Osage Casino - Pawhuska
201 N.W. 15th Street (at Highway 99)
Pawhuska, Oklahoma 74056
(918) 287-1072
Website: www.osagecasinos.com
Map: **#50** (a suburb of Tulsa)

Restaurants: 1   Liquor: No
Hours: 10am-12:00am / 2:00am (Thurs)/
        10:00am-3:00am (Fri/Sat)
Senior Discount: Various Mon/Tue if 50+
Overnight RV Parking: Free/RV Dump: No

Osage Casino - Ponca City
73 N City View Road
Ponca City, Oklahoma 74601
(918) 335-7519
Website: www.osagecasinos.com
Map: **#5** (50 miles N.W. of Tulsa)

Rooms: 46 Price Range: $129-$219
Suites: 2 Price Range: Casino USe Only
Restaurants: 2 Liquor: No
Other Games: BJ
Senior Discount: Various Mon-Thu if 50+
Overnight RV Parking: No

Osage Casino - Sand Springs
301 Blackjack Drive (on Highway 97T)
Sand Springs, Oklahoma 74063
(918) 699-7727
Website: www.osagecasinos.com
Map: **#40** (a suburb of Tulsa)

Toll-Free Number: (877) 246-8777
Restaurants: 2 Liquor: Yes
Senior Discount: Various Mon-Thu if 50+
Overnight RV Parking: No

Osage Casino - Skiatook
6455 West Rogers Boulevard
Skiatook, Oklahoma 74070
(918) 396-2626
Website: www.osagecasinos.com

Other Games: BJ
Overnight RV Parking: No

Osage Casino - Tulsa
951 W. 36th Street North
Tulsa, Oklahoma 74127
(918) 699-7740
Website: www.osagecasinos.com
Map: **#40**

Toll-Free Number: (877) 246-8777
Restaurants: 1 Liquor: Yes
Casino Size: 47,000 Square Feet
Other Games: BJ, P, TCP
Senior Discount: Various Mon/Tue if 50+
Overnight RV Parking: Free/RV Dump: No

Peoria Gaming Center
8520 S. Hwy 69A
Miami, Oklahoma 74354
(918) 540-0303
Map: **#33** (89 miles N.E. of Tulsa)

Restaurants: 1 Snack Bar Liquor: No
Hours: 10am-Midnight/2am (Fri-Sat)
Overnight RV Parking: No
Special features: Adjacent to Buffalo Run
Casino which allows overnight RV parking.

Prarie Moon Casino
202 South 8 Tribes Trail
Miami, Oklahoma 74354
(918) 542-8670
Website: www.miaminationcasinos.com
Map: **#33** (89 miles N.E. of Tulsa)

Restaurants: 1 Liquor: No
Overnight RV Parking: No

Quapaw Casino
58100 E. 66th Road
Miami, Oklahoma 74355
(918) 540-9100
Website: www.quapawcasino.com
Map: **#33** (89 miles N.E. of Tulsa)

Restaurants: 1 Liquor: Yes
Other Games: BJ, TCP, FCP
Overnight RV Parking: Free up to 3 days/
RV Dump: No
Senior Discount: Various Wed if 55+

River Mist Casino
Hwy 65 and Hwy 99
Konowa, Oklahoma 74849
(580) 925-3994
Map: **#2** (75 miles S.E. of Oklahoma City)

Restaurants: 1
Hours: 10am-12am/2am (Fri/Sat)

River Spirit Casino
1616 East 81st Street
Tulsa, Oklahoma 74137
(918) 299-8518
Website: www.riverspirittulsa.com
Map: **#40**

Toll-Free Number: (800) 299-2738
Restaurants: 5   Liquor: No
Buffets: B-$9.95/$21.95 (Sun) L-$9.99
    D-$12.49/$27.49 (Thu/Sat)/$24.99 (Fri)
Casino Size: 81,000 Square Feet
Other Games: BJ, P, TCP
Senior Disc: Buffet discount Mon/Tue if 50+
Overnight RV Parking: Free/RV Dump: No
Special Features: Separate non-smoking casino. Free shuttle to/from local hotels.

Riverwind Casino
1544 W. State Highway 9
Norman, Oklahoma 73072
(405) 364-7171
Website: www.riverwind.com
Map: **#25** (21 miles S. of Oklahoma City)

Toll-Free Number: (888) 440-1880
Rooms: 100 Price Range: $109-$249
Restaurants: 2   Liquor: Yes
Buffets: B-$8.99/$17.99 (Sat)/$13.99 (Sun)
    L-$10.99
    D-$16.99/$18.99 (Thu)/$29.99 (Fri)/
    $17.99 (Sat)
Casino Size: 60,000 Square Feet
Other Games: BJ, P, OTB, TCP, B
Senior Discount: Breakfast special Wed
Overnight RV Parking: Free/RV Dump: No
Special Features: 1,500-seat showroom.

Sac and Fox Casino - Stroud
356120 E 926 Road
Stroud, Oklahoma 74079
(918) 968-2540
Website: www.sandfcasino.com
Map: **#5** (60 miles N.E. of Oklahoma City)

Restaurants: 1   Liquor: Yes
Casino Size: 8,600 Sqaure Feet
Overnight RV Parking: No

Salt Creek Casino
1600 Highway 81
Pocasset, Oklahoma 73079
(405) 459-4000
Website: www.saltcreekcasino.com
Map: **#34** (50 miles S.W. of Oklahoma City)

Restaurants: 2
Overnight RV Parking: No
Other Games: TCP

Seminole Nation Casino
11277 Hwy 99
Seminole, Oklahoma 74868
(405) 382-3218
Map: **#57** (60 miles S.E of Oklahoma City)

Restaurants: 1 Snack Bar   Liquor:No
Other Games: BG
Overnight RV Parking: No

Seminole Nation Trading Post
US 59 and US 270
Wewoka, Oklahoma 74884
(405) 257-2010
Map: **#57** (60 miles E. of Oklahoma City)

Toll-Free Number: (866) 723-4005
Restaurants: 1   Liquor: Yes
Casino Size: 3,424 Square Feet
Overnight RV Parking: No
Special Features: Convenience store.

Seven Clans Paradise Casino
7500 Highway 177
Red Rock, Oklahoma 74651
(580) 723-4005
Website: www.okparadisecasino.com
Map: **#1** (82 miles N. of Oklahoma City)

Toll-Free Number: (866) 723-4005
Restaurants: 1   Liquor: Yes
Casino Size: 23,000 Square Feet
Other Games: BJ
Overnight RV Parking: Must use RV park
Senior Discount: Various Thu if 55+
Special Features: 7-space RV park ($10 per night). Convenience store and gas station.

SouthWind Casino - Kaw City
746 Grandview Drive
Kaw City, Oklahoma 74641
(580) 269-1260

Toll-Free Number: (855) 368-2480
Restaurants: 1 Liquor: No
Hours: 10am-10pm/2am (Thurs-Sat)
Overnight RV Parking: Free/RV Dump: No
Special Features: Oklahoma's only non-smoking casino

Southwind Casino - Newkirk
5640 North LaCann Drive
Newkirk, Oklahoma 74647
(580) 362-2578
Website: www.southwindcasino.com
Map: **#27** (106 miles N. of Oklahoma City)

Toll-Free Number: (866) 529-2464
Restaurants: 1   Liquor: No
Other Games: BJ, BG, OTB
Casino Hours: 8am-2am/24 hours (Fri/Sat)
Senior Discount: Various Mon if 55+
Overnight RV Parking: Free/RV Dump: No

Stone Wolf Casino & Grill
54251 S 349 Road
Pawnee, Oklahoma 74058
(918) 454-7777
Website: www.stonewolfcasino.com
Map: **#55** (57 miles N.W. of Tulsa)

Hours: 8am-2am/8am-2am (Thu)/24hrs (Fri-Sun)
Senior Discount: Various Thu if 55+

The Stables Casino
530 H Street Southeast
Miami, Oklahoma 74354
(918) 542-7884
Website: www.the-stables.com
Map: **#33** (89 miles N.E. of Tulsa)

Toll-Free Number: (877) 774-7884
Restaurants: 1   Liquor: Yes
Other Games: BJ
Overnight RV Parking: No

Sugar Creek Casino
4200 N. Broadway
Hinton, Oklahoma 73047
(405) 542-2946
Website: www.sugarcreekcasino.net

Other Games: BJ
Buffet: L-$6.99 D-$7.99/$9.99 (Wed-Sat)
Overnight RV Parking: No

Texoma Gaming Center
1795 Highway 70 East
Kingston, Oklahoma 73439
(580) 564-6000
Website: www.chickasaw.net
Map: **#43** (130 miles S. of Oklahoma City)

Restaurants: 1   Liquor: No
Overnight RV Parking: No
Special Features: Convenience store and KFC.

Thackerville Gaming Center
I-35 exit 1
Thackerville, Oklahoma 73459
(580)276-1727
Map: **#36** (124 miles S. of Oklahoma City)

Overnight RV Parking: Free/RV Dump: No

Thackerville Travel Gaming
Interstate 35, Exit 1
Thackerville, Oklahoma 73459
(580) 276-4706
Website: www.chickasaw.net
Map: **#36** (124 miles S. of Oklahoma City)

Restaurants: 1 Snack Bar   Liquor: No
Casino Hours: 9am - 6am
Overnight RV Parking: Free/RV Dump: No

Thunderbird Casino - Norman
15700 East State Highway 9
Norman, Oklahoma 73026
(405) 360-9270
Website: www.thunderbirdcasino.net
Map: **#25** (21 miles S. of Oklahoma City)

Toll-Free Number: (800) 259-5825
Restaurants: 1   Liquor: Yes
Other Games: BJ, TCP
Casino Size: 40,000 Square Feet
Overnight RV Parking: Free

Thunderbird Casino - Shawnee
2051 S. Gordon Cooper Dr
Shawnee, Oklahoma 73026
(405) 360-9270
Website: www.thunderbirdcasino.net
Map: **#23** (38 miles E. of Oklahoma City)

Toll-Free Number: (800) 259-5825

Tonkawa Casino
1000 Allen Drive
Tonkawa, Oklahoma 74653
(580) 628-2624
Website: www.tonkawacasino.com
Map: **#38** (91 miles N. of Oklahoma City)

Restaurants: 1 Snack Bar   Liquor: No
Other Games: BJ, LIR
Hours: 10am-2am
Overnight RV Parking: Free/RV Dump: No

Trading Post Casino
291 Agency Road
Pawnee, Oklahoma 74058
(918) 762-4466
Map: **#55** (57 miles N.W. of Tulsa)

Restaurants: 1   Liquor: No
Casino Size: 3,600 Square Feet
Overnight RV Parking: No
Special Features: Convenience store/gas station.

Treasure Valley Casino
I-35, Exit 55 (Highway 7)
Davis, Oklahoma 73030
(580) 369-2895
Website: www.treasurevalleycasino.com
Map: **#22** (75 miles S. of Oklahoma City)

Rooms: 55 Price Range: $75-$105
Suites: 4 Price Range: $159-$208
Restaurants: 2   Liquor: No
Casino Size: 19,666 Square Feet
Other Games: BJ, TCP
Overnight RV Parking: Free/RV Dump: No

Two Rivers Casino
101 White Eagle Dr
Ponca City, Oklahoma 74601
(580) 762-3901
Website: www.tworiverscasinook.com
Map: **#5** (50 miles N.W. of Tulsa)

Restaurants: 1
Hours: 8am-2am/24 hours (Fri/Sat)
Other Games: BG
Overnight RV Parking: Free/RV Dump: No

Washita Gaming Center
535 Oklahoma 145
Paoli, Oklahoma 73074
(405) 484-7777
Website: www.chickasaw.net
Map: **#44** (52 miles S. of Oklahoma City)

Restaurants: 1   Liquor: No
Casino Size: 6,335 Square Feet
Overnight RV Parking: No
Special Features: Convenience store.

Wilson Travel Plaza
354 Route 1
Wilson, Oklahoma 73463
(580) 668-9248
Map: **#39** (112 miles S. of Oklahoma City)

Restaurants: 1   Liquor: No
Overnight RV Parking: Free/RV Dump: No

WinStar Casino
Interstate 35, Exit 1
Thackerville, Oklahoma 73459
(580) 276-4229
Website: www.winstarworldcasino.com
Map: **#36** (124 miles S. of Oklahoma City)

Toll-Free Number: (800) 622-6317
Rooms: 395 price range: $79-$109
Suites: 40 price range:$89-$179
Restaurants: 5   Liquor: No
Buffet: B-$11.99 L-$14.99 D-$18.99
Other Games: BJ, P, BG, MS, MB,
                TCP, PGP, OTB, K
Casino Size: 169,824 Square Feet
Overnight RV Parking: Free/RV Dump: No
Senior Discount: $1 off buffets and
                various Wed if 55+
Special Features: 152-space RV ($25 per night)

Wyandotte Nation Casino
100 Jackpot Place
Wyandotte, Oklahoma 74370
(918) 678-4946
Website: www.wyandottecasinos.com
Map: **#26** (90 miles N.E. of Tulsa)

Toll-Free Number: (866) 447-4946
Restaurants: 2   Liquor: Yes
Other Games: BJ, TCP
Overnight RV Parking: No

Pari-Mutuels

Oklahoma has two horse tracks which offer Class II electronic video gaming machines as well as pari-mutuel betting on horse races. Admission is free to the casinos, but there is an admission charge for horse racing. The minimum gambling age is 18.

Cherokee Casino Will Rogers Downs
20900 S. 4200 Road
Claremore, Oklahoma 74017
(918) 283-8800
Map: **#47** (30 miles N.E. of Tulsa)
Website: www.cherokeestarrewards.com

Hours: 11am-1am/4am (Fri)/
       10am-4am(Sat)/ 1am (Sun)
Self-Parking: Free
Restaurants: 1
Overnight RV Parking: Must use RV park
Special Features: Live horse racing Feb-May. Daily simulcasting of horse racing. 400-space RV park ($32 per night/$10 without hookups).

Remington Park Racing • Casino
One Remington Place
Oklahoma City, Oklahoma 73111
(405) 424-1000
Website: www.remingtonpark.com
Map: **#46**

Toll-Free Number: (800) 456-4244
Hours: 10:30am-12am/
       2am (Thu)/3am (Fri/Sat)
Self-Parking: Free   Valet Parking: Free
Restaurants: 2
Buffet: D- $16.99 (Thu)
Overnight RV Parking: No
Senior Discount: Various Tue if 55+
Special Features: Live horse racing Thu-Sun. Daily simulcasting of horse racing. Buffet dicount for players club members.

OREGON

Oregon law permits bars and taverns to have up to six video lottery terminals that offer various versions of video poker. Racetracks are allowed to have no more than 10 machines. The maximum bet allowed is $2 and the maximum payout on any machine is capped at $600.

These machines are the same as regular video gaming devices but are called lottery terminals because they are regulated by the state's lottery commission which receives a share of each machine's revenue. The machines accept cash but do not pay out in cash; instead, they print out a receipt which must be taken to a cashier.

According to figures from the Oregon Lottery, during its fiscal year from July 1, 2013 through June 30, 2014, the VLT's had an approximate return of 92.23%.

There are nine Indian casinos in operation in Oregon. According to the governor's office which regulates the Tribe's compacts, "there is no minimum payback percentage required on the Tribe's machines. Each Tribe is free to set their own limits on their machines."

All casinos offer blackjack, slots and video poker. Some casinos also offer: craps (C), roulette (R), poker (P), Pai Gow Poker (PGP), Spanish 21 (S21), let it ride (LIR), three card poker (TCP), four card poker (FCP), big 6 wheel (B6), bingo (BG), keno (K) and off track betting (OTB). Unless otherwise noted, all casinos are open 24 hours and the minimum gambling age is 21 (18 for bingo).

For Oregon tourism information call (800) 547-7842 or go to: www.traveloregon.com.

Chinook Winds Casino Resort
1777 N.W. 44th Street
Lincoln City, Oregon 97367
(541) 996-5825
Website: www.chinookwindscasino.com
Map: **#4** (45 miles W. of Salem)

Toll-Free Number: (888) 244-6665
RV Reservations: (877) 564-2678
Room Reservations: (877) 423-2241
Rooms: 227 Price Range: $89-$184
Suites: 81 Price Range: $184-$264
Restaurants: 4 Liquor: Yes
Buffets: B-$10.95/$19.95 (Sun) L-$11.95
       D-$17.95/$21.95 (Fri)/$20.95 (Sat)
Other Games: C, R, P, LIR, TCP, PGP, K, BG
Overnight RV Parking: Free/RV Dump: No
Senior Discount: Meal discounts if 55+
Special Features: 51-space RV Park ($32/$45 per night). Childcare center. Video arcade. 18-hole golf course. RV park is off property.

Indian Head Casino
3636 Highway 26
Warm Springs, Oregon 97761
(541) 460-7777
Website: www.indianheadgaming.com
Map: **#5** (100 miles E. of Portland)

Restaurants: 2 Liquor: Yes
Buffets: D-$22.95 (Fri)
Casino Size: 25,000 Square Feet
Overnight RV Parking: Free/RV Dump: No

Kla-Mo-Ya Casino
34333 Hwy 97 North
Chiloquin, Oregon 97624
(541) 783-7529
Website: www.klamoyacasino.com
Map: **#7** (20 miles N. of Klamath Falls)

Toll-Free Number: (888) 552-6692
Restaurants: 2 Liquor: No
Overnight RV Parking: Free/RV Dump: No
Senior Discount: Various on Mondays if 55+

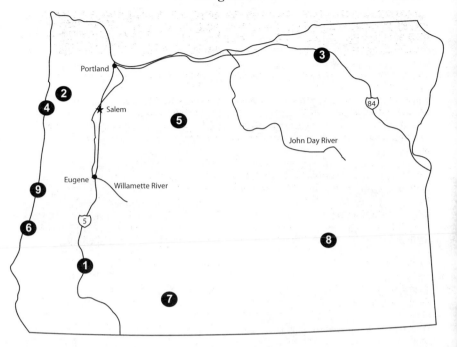

The Mill Casino Hotel
3201 Tremont Avenue
North Bend, Oregon 97459
(541) 756-8800
Website: www.themillcasino.com
Map: **#6** (75 miles S.W. of Eugene)

Toll-Free Number: (800) 953-4800
Rooms: 109 Price Range: $89-$136
Suites: 3 Price Range: $149-$239
Restaurants: 4 Liquor: Yes
Buffets: B-$8.95 (Mon/Tue)
   L-$10.95 (Mon/Tue)
   D-$14.95 (Mon/Tue)
Other Games: C, R, S21, PG, TCP
Overnight RV Parking: Free/RV Dump: No
Senior Discount: 10% off food if 55+
Special Features: 65-space RV park ($37-$72 per night spring/summer; $25-$35 fall/winter). Free local shuttle. Room and food discounts for players club members.

Seven Feathers Hotel & Casino Resort
146 Chief Miwaleta Lane
Canyonville, Oregon 97417
(541) 839-1111
Website: www.sevenfeathers.com
Map: **#1** (80 miles S. of Eugene)

Toll-Free Number: (800) 548-8461
Room Reservations: (888) 677-7771
Rooms: 146 Price Range: $69-$109
Restaurants: 4 Liquor: Yes
Buffets: B-$20.00 (Sun) D-$11.99/
   $22.99 (Thu)/$17.99 (Fri/Sat)/
   $16.99 (Sun)
Casino Size: 27,300 Square Feet
Other Games: C, R, P, LIR, PGP,
   TCP, FCP, K, BG
Senior Discount: $2 off buffet if 50+
Overnight RV Parking: Free/RV Dump: No
Special Features: 191-space RV park ($36-$44 per night). 18-hole golf course.

Spirit Mountain Casino
27100 Salmon River Highway
Grand Ronde, Oregon 97347
(503) 879-2350
Website: www.spiritmountain.com
Map: **#2** (85 miles S.W. of Portland)

Toll-Free Number: (800) 760-7977
Reservation Number: (888) 668-7366
Rooms: 94 Price Range: $89-$169
Suites: 6 Price Range: $169-$219
Restaurants: 5 Liquor: Yes
Buffets: B-$9.95 L-$10.95/$16.95 (Sun)
        D-$15.95/$19.95 (Fri/Sat)/$16.95 (Sun)
Other Games: C, R, P, PGP, LIR, TCP, K, BG
Overnight RV Parking: Free/RV Dump: Free
Special Features: Childcare center. Video
arcade. Players club members receive a $20
room discount.

Wildhorse Resort & Casino
72777 Highway 331
Pendleton, Oregon 97801
(541) 278-2274
Website: www.wildhorseresort.com
Map: **#3** (211 miles E. of Portland)

Toll-Free Number: (800) 654-9453
Rooms: 100 Price Range: $70-$100
Suites: 5 Price Range: $129- $149
Restaurants: 4 Liquor: Yes
Buffets: D-$14.95
Casino Size: 80,000 Square Feet
Other Games: C, R, P, TCP, K, BG
Overnight RV Parking: Free/RV Dump: No
Senior Discount: Various on Tue if 55+
Special Features: 100-space RV park ($28/$33
per night). Cultural Institute. 18-hole golf
course. Health spa. Child care center.

Three Rivers Casino & Hotel
5647 US Highway 126
Florence, Oregon 97439
(541) 997-7529
Website: www.threeriverscasino.com
Map: **#9** (61 miles W. of Eugene)

Toll-Free Number: (877) 374-8377
Rooms: 90 Price Range: $89-$139
Suites: 4 Price Range: $190- $250
Restaurants: 5 Liquor: Yes
Buffets: B-$9.99 (Sun) L-$9.99
        D-$14.99/$17.99 (Fri/Sat)
Other Games: C, R, P, K, BG, LIR, PGP
Overnight RV Parking: Free/RV Dump: No
Senior Discount: $2 off buffet Mon if 55+

PENNSYLVANIA

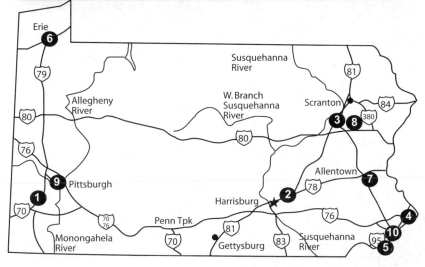

In July 2004 the Pennsylvania legislature authorized the legalization of slot machines at 14 locations throughout the state: seven racinos, five stand-alone casinos, and two hotel resorts.

All casinos can have up to 5,000 machines, except the resort licensees, which are allowed up to 600. As of August 2014, 12 of the casinos had opened. One license for a racino had not yet been awarded, plus a license which originally been awarded to Foxwoods Casino in Philadelphia was revoked, but it may be awarded to another casino in the future.

In January 2010 the Pennsylvania legislature approved the addition of table games, including live poker, for all casinos.

Unless otherwise noted, all casinos offer: slots, video poker, craps, blackjack, roulette, three card poker, mini-baccarat and Pai-gow poker. Optional games include: baccarat (B), poker (P), let it ride (LIR), pai gow (PG), big 6 wheel (B6), Spanish 21 (S21), four card poker (FCP), Sic-Bo (SIC), Mississippi stud (MS) and casino war (CW).

Pennsylvania gaming regulations require that gaming machines return a minimum of 85%. Following is information from the Pennsylvania Gaming Control Board regarding average slot payout percentages for the one-year period from July 1, 2013 through June 30, 2014:

CASINO	PAYBACK %
The Meadows	92.26
Sands Bethelem	89.78
Parx Casino	90.72
Presque Isle	89.45
Mount Airy	90.21
Valley Forge	89.84
The Rivers	89.70
Harrah's Philadelphia	89.73
Sugar House	89.45
Hollywood Casino at PN	89.20
Mohegan Sun at PD	89.81
Lady Luck Nemacolin	90.24

The minimum gambling age is 18 for pari-mutuel betting and 21 at casinos. All casinos are open 24 hours and admission is free. However, the casinos at the two hotel resorts are not open to the general public. You must be a guest of the resort in order to play at their casinos. However, you can buy a guest pass for temporary admission.

For more information on visiting Pennsylvania call their Office of Tourism at (800) 237-4363 or visit their website at www.visitpa.com.

Lady Luck Nemacolin
1001 Lafayette Drive
Farmington, Pennsylvania 15437
724.329.8555
Website: www.nemacolin.com
Map: **#11** (60 miles S.E. of Pittsburgh)

Room Reservations: (800) 422-2736
Rooms: 300 Price Range: $269-$789
Suites: 27 Price Range: $359-$2,999
Other Games: P, MS
Restaurants: 9
Special Features: Located at Nemacolin Woodlands Resort. Casino is affiliated with Isle of Capri Casinos. 20-space RV park open 4/27 through 11/26 with nightly rate of $90-$165. All room/RV rates do not include $20 daily resort fee. You must be a guest of the resort for admittance to the casino, or buy a $10 gift card to get access for a 24-hour period. You can also buy an annual membership for $45 which allows unlimited admission for two people, plus discounts on various amenities.

Mount Airy Resort & Casino
44 Woodland Road
Mount Pocono, Pennsylvania 18344
(570) 243-4800
Website: www.mounttairycasino.com
Map: **#8** (30 miles S.E. of Scranton)

Toll-Free Number: (877) 682-4791
Rooms: 175 Price Range: $159-$269
Suites: 25 Price Range: $259-$349
Restaurants: 3
Buffets: B-$9.99/$24.99 (Sun) L-$15.99
          D-$18.99/$24.99 (Fri)
Casino Size: 68,000 Square Feet
Other Games: P, LIR, B, PG, FCP, S21, MS
Special Features: 18-hole golf course. Spa.

Rivers Casino
777 Casino Drive
Pittsburgh, Pennsylvania 15212
(412) 231-7777
Website: www.theriverscasino.com
Map: **#9**

Toll-free Number: (877) 558-0777
Parking: $3 Valet Parking: $6/$12 (Fri-Sun)
Restaurants: 4
Buffets: L-$14.99/$21.99 (Sun) D-$21.99
Other Games: P, CW, B6, FCP, LIR, MS
Special Features: Free parking for players club members who play and put points on card.

Sands Casino Resort Bethlehem
77 Sands Boulevard
Bethlehem, Pennsylvania 18015
Website: www.pasands.com
Map: **#7** (60 miles N of Philadelphia)

Toll-Free number: (877) SANDS-77
Rooms: 288 Price Range: $129-$239
Suites: 22 Price Range: $249-$349
Restaurants: 6
Buffets: L-$15.95/$18.95 (Thu/Fri)/
              $20.94 (Sat)/$23.95 (Sun)
          D-$18.95/$20.95 (Thu)/$29.95 (Fri)/
              $59.95 (Sat)/$23.95 (Sun)
Other Games: B, PG, P, B6, LIR,
                CSP, TCP, CW, SB
Special Features: Food court with Nathan's Hot Dogs.

Sugar House Casino
1080 N Delaware Avenue
Philadelphia, Pennsylvania 19125
(267) 232-2000
Website: www.sugarhousecasino.com
Map: **#10**

Restaurants: 3
Casino Size: 45,000 Square Feet
Other Games: P, B, PG, S21, MB, MS

Valley Forge Convention Center Casino
1210 First Avenue
King of Prussia, Pennsylvania 19406
(610) 354-8212
Website: www.vfcasino.com
Map: **#10** (15 miles N.w of Philadelphia)

Room Reservations: Radisson Hotel Valley Forge, (800) 395-7046
Room Reservations: Valley Forge Scanticon Hotel (610) 265-1500
Restaurants: 3
Casino Size: 33,000 Square Feet
Other Games: LIR, B, MB, PG, PGP, S21
Special Features: Two hotels attached to convention center: Radisson Hotel Valley Forge www.radissonvalleyforge.com and the Valley Forge Scanticon Hotel www.scanticonvalleyforge.com You must be a guest of one of the hotels for admittance to the casino, or buy a $10 gift card to get access for a 24-hour period. You can also buy a three-month membership for $20 which allows unlimited admission for two people, plus a 10% discount in the restaurants.

Pari-Mutuels

Harrah's Philadelphia Casino & Racetrack
35 E. 5th Street
Chester, Pennsylvania 19013
(484) 490-2207
Website: www.harrahschester.com
Map: **#5** (8 miles S. of Philadelphia airport)

Toll-Free Number: (800) 480-8020
Valet Parking: $10
Restaurants: 6
Other Games: P, PG, FCP, LIR, B, B6, MS
Special Features: Live harness racing from mid-April through November. Daily simulcast of harness and thoroughbred racing.

Hollywood Casino at Penn National
720 Bow Creek Road
Grantville, Pennsylvania 17028
(717) 469-2211
Website: www.hollywoodpnrc.com
Map: #2 (16 miles N.E. of Harrisburg)

Restaurants: 1
Buffets: B-$19.99 (Sun) L-$14.99
 D-$14.99/$24.99 (Fri/Sat)
Casino Size: 45,000 Square Feet
Other Games: LIR, FCP, P, S21, B6
Special Features: Live thoroughbred horse racing Wed-Sat evenings all year long. Daily simulcast of harness and thoroughbred racing. No buffet Monday or Tuesday.

The Meadows Racetrack & Casino
210 Racetrack Road
Washington, Pennsylvania 15301
(724) 225-9300
Website: www.meadowsgaming.com
Map: **#1** (25 miles S.W. of Pittsburgh)

Valet Parking: $3
Restaurants: 3
Other Games: P, LIR, FCP, B, B6, PG, MS
Special Features: Live harness racing various evenings all year long. Daily simulcast of harness and thoroughbred racing.

Mohegan Sun at Pocono Downs
1280 Highway 315
Wilkes-Barre, Pennsylvania 18702
(570) 831-2100
Website: www.mohegansunpocono.com
Map: **#3** (20 miles S.W. of Scranton)

Valet Parking: Not Offered
Restaurants: 11
Buffets: B-$9.95 (Mon)/$17.99 (Sat/Sun)
 L-$13.99 D-$17.99/$22.99 (Fri/Sat)
Other Games: LIR, S21, P, B6, PG, MS
Special Features: Live harness racing various evenings early April through mid-November Daily simulcast of harness and thoroughbred racing.

Parx Casino and Racing
3001 Street Road
Bensalem, Pennsylvania 19020
(215) 639-9000
Website: www.parxcasino.com
Map: **#4** (18 miles N.E. of Philadelphia)

Toll-Free Number: (888) 588-7279
Valet Parking: $5
Restaurants: 3
Other Games: P, FCP, B6, B, SIC, PGP, PG, MS
Special Features: Thoroughbred horse racing Sat-Tue afternoons all year long. Friday racing added January and February. Daily simulcast of harness and thoroughbred racing.

Presque Isle Downs & Casino
8199 Perry Highway
Erie, Pennsylvania 16509
Website: www.presqueisledowns.com
Map: **#6**

Toll-Free Number: (866) 374-3386
Valet Parking: $3
Restaurants: 4
Buffets: B-$5.95 (Sat/Sun)
  L-$14.95/$17.95 (Sun)
  D-$17.95
Other Games: LIR, P, MS
Special Features: Live thoroughbred horse racing Wed-Sun May-September. Daily simulcast of harness and thoroughbred racing.

RHODE ISLAND

Rhode Island has two pari-mutuel facilities which both feature video lottery terminals (VLT's). These machines are the same as regular video gaming devices but are called lottery terminals because they are regulated by the state's lottery commission which receives a share of each machine's revenue. The machines accept cash but don't pay out in cash; instead, they print out a receipt which must be taken to a cashier.

All VLT's are programmed to play at least six different games: blackjack, keno, slots and three versions of poker (jacks or better, joker poker and deuces wild).

According to figures from the Rhode Island Lottery for the one-year period from August 1, 2013 through July 31, 2014 the average VLT return at Twin River was 90.99% and at Newport Grand it was 91.11%.

In early 2014 the Twin River Casino began offering live table games because it was approved in a referendum by local voters. Newport Grand Slots does not offer live table games because the voters in that jurisdiction did not pass a similar referendum.

The minimum gambling age in Rhode Island is 18. For information on visiting Rhode Island call the state's tourism division at (800) 556-2484 or go to: www.visitrhodeisland.com.

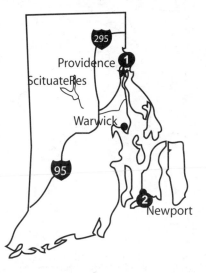

The games offered at Twin River are blackjack, craps, roulette, Spanish 21, pai gow poker, three card poker, let it ride and big 6 wheel.

Twin River Casino
1600 Louisquisset Pike
Lincoln, Rhode Island 02865
(401) 723-3200
Website: www.twinriver.com
Map: **#1** (10 miles N. of Providence)

Toll-Free Number: (877) 827-4837
Restaurants: 4   Valet Parking: Free
Admission: Free
Overnight RV Parking: No
Special Features: Daily (except Tuesday and Sunday) simulcasting of horse and dog racing.

Newport Grand Slots
150 Admiral Kalbfus Road
Newport, Rhode Island 02840
(401) 849-5000
Website: www.newportgrand.com
Map: **#2**

Toll-Free Number: (800) 451-2500
Restaurants: 1   Valet Parking: $2.50
Hours: 10am-1am/ 2am (Fri/Sat)
Admission: Free
Overnight RV Parking: No
Special Features: Daily simulcasting of horse racing, dog racing and jai-alai. Digital versions of blackjack and roulette.

SOUTH CAROLINA

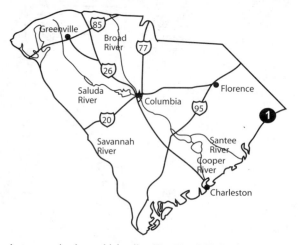

South Carolina has one casino boat which sails three miles out into international waters where casino gambling is permitted.

Big M Casino offers: blackjack, craps, roulette, three card poker, slots and video poker. Due to security restrictions, you must present a photo ID or you will not be allowed to board.

For more information on visiting South Carolina go to: www.discoversouthcarolina. com or call their tourism department at (800) 872-3505.

The Big "M" Casino
4491 Waterfront Avenue
Little River, South Carolina 29566
(843) 249-9811
Website: www.bigmcasino.com
Map Location: **#1** (35 miles N. of Myrtle Beach)

Reservation Number: (877) 250-5825
Ship's Registry: U.S.   Gambling Age: 21
Buffet: $10 am cruise/ $15 pm cruise
Schedule:

10:45am - 4:15pm	(Tue-Fri)
11:45am - 5:15pm	(Sat/Sun)
6:45pm - 11:45pm	(Sun-Thu)
6:45pm - 12:15am	(Fri/Sat)

Price: $25
Port Charges: None   Parking: Free
Other Games: Craps, Let it Ride
Special Features: 600-passenger *Diamond Girl II* sails from Little River waterfront. Free shuttle available from Myrtle Beach. Must be 18 or older to board. No cruises Monday.

SOUTH DAKOTA

South Dakota's bars and taverns are allowed to have up to 10 video lottery terminals (VLT's) that offer the following games: poker, keno, blackjack and bingo.

These machines are the same as regular video gaming devices but are called lottery terminals because they are regulated by the state's lottery commission which receives a share of each machine's revenue.

The machines accept cash but don't pay out in cash; instead, they print out a receipt which must be taken to a cashier. The maximum bet is $2 and the maximum payout allowed is $1,000.

Slot machines, as well as blackjack and poker are only permitted at Indian casinos and in Deadwood.

Deadwood was once most famous for being the home of Wild Bill Hickok who was shot to death while playing cards in the No. 10 Saloon. The hand he held was two pairs: black aces and black eights, which is now commonly referred to as a "dead man's hand." Wild Bill is buried in the local cemetery along with another local celebrity: Calamity Jane.

The first casinos in Deadwood opened on November 1, 1989. All of the buildings in the downtown area are required to conform with the city's authentic 1880's architecture. Many of the casinos are located in historic structures but there are also some new structures which were designed to be compatible with the historic theme of the town. The old No. 10 Saloon is still operating and you can actually gamble in the same spot where old Wild Bill bit the dust!

South Dakota law limits each casino licensee to a maximum of 30 slot machines and no one person is allowed to hold more than three licenses. Some operators combine licenses with other operators to form a cooperative which may look like one casino but in reality it's actually several licensees operating under one name.

The state's gaming laws originally limited blackjack, poker, let it ride and three-card poker bets to a maximum of $5, however, in July 2012 the law was changed to allow maximum bets of $1,000.

In addition to the Deadwood casinos, there are also nine Indian casinos in South Dakota. These casinos are also subject to the $1,000 maximum bet restrictions.

Here are statistics from the South Dakota Commission on Gaming for the payback percentages on all of Deadwood's slot machines for the one-year period from July 1, 2013 through June 30, 2014:

Denomination	Payback %
1¢ Slots	90.90
5¢ Slots	90.77
25¢ Slots	90.73
$1 Slots	92.54
$5 Slots	92.79

Unless otherwise noted, all casinos are opened 24 hours.

The Deadwood Trolly runs a scheduled shuttle service to all of the casinos that operates from 7 am to 1am weekdays and 7 am to 3 am on weekends. The cost is $1 per ride.

Unless otherwise noted, all casinos offer slot machines and video poker. Some casinos also offer: blackjack (BJ), let it ride (LIR), three-card poker (TCP), Caribbean stud poker (CSP), Mississippi stud (MS) and poker (P). Most of the Indian casinos also offer bingo (BG).

The minimum gambling age is 21 at all Deadwood and Indian casinos (18 for bingo at Indian casinos). South Dakota's casinos have very liberal rules about allowing minors in casinos and virtually all of the casinos will allow children to enter with their parents until about 8 p.m. Additionally, South Dakota is the only jurisdiction that will allow children to stand next to their parents while they are gambling.

For South Dakota tourism information call (800) 732-5682. For information on visiting Deadwood call the city's Chamber of Commerce at (800) 999-1876, or visit their website at www.deadwood.org.

Deadwood

Map: **#1** (in the Black Hills, 41 miles N.W. of Rapid City. Take I-90 W. Get off at the second Sturges exit and take Hwy. 14-A into Deadwood)

Best Western Hickok House
137 Charles Street
Deadwood, South Dakota 57732
(605) 578-1611
Website: www.bestwestern.com

Best Western Reservations: (800) 837-8174
Rooms: 38   Price Range: $50-$120
Restaurants: 1
Special Features: Hot tub and sauna.

Buffalo-Bodega Gaming Complex
658 Main Street
Deadwood, South Dakota 57732
Website: www.buffalobodega.com
(605) 578-1162

Restaurants: 1
Special Features: Oldest bar in Deadwood. Steakhouse restaurant. Ice cream parlor.

Bullock Hotel
633 Main Street
Deadwood, South Dakota 57732
(605) 578-1745
Website: www.historicbullock.com

Reservation Number: (800) 336-1876
Rooms: 26   Price Range: $75-$100
Suites: 2 Price Range: $130-$160
Restaurants: 1
Special Features: Deadwood's oldest hotel.

Nestled in the Black Hills of South Dakota, the entire city of Deadwood has been designated a national historic landmark. Free historic walking tours are offered daily.

Cadillac Jack's Gaming Resort
360 Main Street
Deadwood, South Dakota 57732
(605) 578-1500
Website: www.cadillacjacksgaming.com

Toll Free Number: (866) 332-3966
Rooms: 92 Price Range: $75-$175
Suites: 11 Price Range: $199-$309
Restaurants: 1
Hours: 24 Hours Daily
Casino Size: 10,000 Square Feet
Other Games: BJ, P
Special Features: Hotel is AmericInn. 15% off rooms for players club members. Free valet parking.

Celebrity Hotel & Casino
629 Main Street
Deadwood, South Dakota 57732
(605) 578-1909
Website: www.celebritycasinos.com

Toll-Free Number: (888) 399-1886
Rooms: 9 Price Range: $69-$129
Suites: 3 Price Range: $99-$159
Special Features: Car and motorcycle museum. Free to hotel guests, otherwise admission charge.

Deadwood Dick's Saloon and Gaming Hall
51 Sherman Street
Deadwood, South Dakota 57732
(605) 578-3224
Website: www.deadwooddicks.com

Toll Free Number: (877) 882-4990
Rooms: 5 Price Range: $80-$125
Suites: 6 Price Range: $125-$450
Restaurants: 1
Other Games: BJ, P
Special Features: Antique mall with 30 dealers.

Deadwood Gulch Gaming Resort
304 Cliff Street
Deadwood, South Dakota 57732
(605) 578-1294
Website: www.deadwoodgulch.com

Reservation Number: (800) 695-1876
Rooms: 95 Price Range: $79-$119
Restaurants: 1
Casino Size: 7,500 Square Feet
Other Games: BJ
Special Features: Free breakfast for hotel guests.

Deadwood Gulch Saloon
560 Main Street
Deadwood, South Dakota 57732
(605) 578-1207

Deadwood Mountain Grand
1906 Deadwood Mountain Dr.
Deadwood, South Dakota 57732
(605) 559-0386
Website: www.deadwoodmountaingrand.com

Toll-free Number: (877) 907-4726
Rooms: 90   Price Range: $129-$179
Suites: 8   Price Range: Casino Use only
Restaurants: 3
Casino Size: 7,500 Square Feet
Other Games: BJ, TCP
Special Features: 2,500-seat entertainment center.

Deadwood Station Bunkhouse and Gambling Hall
68 Main St
Deadwood, South Dakota 57732
(605) 578-3476
www.deadwoodstation.com

Toll-Free Number: (855) 366-6405
Rooms: 28 Price Range: $75-$105
Restaurants: 1

First Gold Hotel & Gaming
270 Main Street
Deadwood, South Dakota 57732
(605) 578-9777
Website: www.firstgold.com

Reservation Number: (800) 274-1876
Rooms: 101   Price Range: $59-$119
Suites: 1   Price Range: $99-$219
Restaurants: 2
Buffets: B/L- $10.95 D- $16.95/$24.95 (Fri/Sat)
Casino Size: 11,000 Square Feet
Other Games: BJ, TCP, MS
Senior Discount: 10% off room if 55+
Special Features: RV park located next door. Includes **Blackjack** and **Horseshoe** casinos.

Four Aces
531 Main Street
Deadwood, South Dakota 57732
(605) 578-2323
Website: www.fouracescasino.org

Toll Free Number: (800) 834-4384
Rooms: 59 Price Range: $55-$109
Suites: 5 Price Range: $89-$199
Restaurants: 1
Buffets: B/L-$9.99 D-$14.99/$23.99 (Fri/Sat)
Casino Size: 24,000 Square Feet
Other Games: BJ, TCP, LIR
Senior Discount: Room/food discounts if 55+
Special Features: Hotel is Hampton Inn.

Gold Dust Gaming & Entertainment Complex
688 Main Street
Deadwood, South Dakota 57732
(605) 578-2100
Website: www.golddustgaming.com

Toll-Free Number: (800) 456-0533
Rooms: 56 Price Range: $149-$209
Suites: 22 Price Range: $159-$219
Restaurants: 1
Casino Size: 30,000 Square Feet
Other Games: BJ, TCP
Special Features: Hotel is Holiday Inn Express. Largest gaming complex in Deadwood with eleven casinos. Free continental breakfast for hotel guests, indoor pool, gym, whirlpool, arcade. Includes **French Quarter**, **Legends** and **Silver Dollar** casinos.

Gulches of Fun
225 Cliff Street
Deadwood, South Dakota 57732
(605) 578-7550
Website: www.gulchesoffun.com

Reservation Number: (800) 961-3096
Rooms: 66 Price Range: $80-$130
Suites: 5 Price Range: $90-$149
Restaurants: 1
Special Features: Hotel is Comfort Inn. Family amusement center with rides and mini-golf.

Hickok's Hotel and Casino
685 Main Street
Deadwood, South Dakota 57732
(605) 578-2222
Website: www.hickoks.com

Rooms: 18 Price Range: $99-$179
Suites: 4 Price Range: $139-$189
Special Features: Video arcade. Includes **B.B. Cody's.**

Iron Horse Inn
27 Deadwood Street
Deadwood, South Dakota 57732
(605) 578-7700
Website: www.ironhorseinndeadwood.com

Toll Free Number: (877) 815-7974
Rooms: 19 Price Range: $79-$159
Suites: 4 Price Range: $149-$209
Casino Size: 1,000 Square Feet

The Lodge at Deadwood
100 Pine Crest Lane
Deadwood, South Dakota 57732
(605) 571-2132
Website: www.deadwoodlodge.com

Toll-Free Number: (877) 393-5634
Rooms: 100 Price Range: $109-$269
Suites: 40 Price Range: $99-$299
Restaurants: 2
Casino Size: 11,000 Square Feet
Other Games: BJ, TCP, P, FCP, CW, MS
Special Features: Electronic version of roulette.

Lucky 8 Gaming Hall/Super 8 Motel
196 Cliff Street
Deadwood, South Dakota 57732
(605) 578-2535
Website: www.deadwoodsuper8.com

Reservation Number: (800) 800-8000
Rooms: 47 Price Range: $40-$75
Suites: 4 Price Range: $95-$135
Restaurants: 1
Special Features: Video arcade. Free continental breakfast for hotel guests.

Martin & Mason Hotel
33 Deadwood Street
Deadwood, South Dakota 57732
(605) 578-1555
Website: www.martinmasonhotel.com

Rooms: 6 Prices: $110-$180
Suites: 2 Prices: $230-$375

Midnight Star
677 Main Street
Deadwood, South Dakota 57732
(605) 578-1555
Website: www.themidnightstar.com

Toll-Free Number: (800) 999-6482
Restaurants: 2
Other Games: BJ, TCP, LIR
Special Features: Sports bar & grill.

Mineral Palace Hotel & Gaming Complex
601 Main Street
Deadwood, South Dakota 57732
(605) 578-2036
Website: www.mineralpalace.com

Reservation Number: (800) 847-2522
Rooms: 63 Price Range: $109-$179
Suites: 4 Price Range: $129-$389
Restaurants: 1
Other Games: BJ, TCP
Special Features: Cappuccino/espresso bar. Liquor store.

Mustang Sally's
634 Main Street
Deadwood, South Dakota 57732
(605) 578-2025

Restaurants: 1

Old Style Saloon #10
657 Main Street
Deadwood, South Dakota 57732
(605) 578-3346
Website: www.saloon10.com

Toll-Free Number: (800) 952-9398
Restaurants: 1
Casino Size: 4,000 Square Feet
Other Games: BJ, P, TCP
Hours: 8am-2am
Special Features: August-September there is a reenactment of the "Shooting of Wild Bill Hickok" at 1, 3, 5 and 7 p.m. Wild Bill's chair and other old west artifacts on display. Italian restaurant. Includes **The Utter Place** card room.

Oyster Bay/Fairmont Hotel
628 Main Street
Deadwood, South Dakota 57732
(605) 578-2205

Restaurants: 1
Special Features: Historic restoration of 1895 brothel, spa and underground jail cell. Oyster bar.

Silverado - Franklin Historic Hotel & Gaming Complex
700-709 Main Street
Deadwood, South Dakota 57732
(605) 578-3670
Website: www.silveradocasino.com

Toll-Free Number: (800) 584-7005
Reservation Number: (800) 688-1876
Rooms: 80   Price Range: $89-$129
Suites: 15   Price Range: $159-$209
Restaurants: 1
Buffets: B/L-$10.95/$15.95 (Sun)
       D-$17.95/$22.95 (Fri/Sat)
Casino Size: 20,000 Square Feet
Other Games: BJ, P, LIR, TCP, CSP, FCP
Senior Discount: 30% off buffets if 50+

Tin Lizzie Gaming
555 Main Street
Deadwood, South Dakota 57732
(605) 578-1715
Website: www.tinlizzie.com

Toll-Free Number: (800) 643-4490
Restaurants: 1
Buffets: B-$4.99
Casino Size: 8,300 Square Feet
Other Games: BJ, TCP
Senior Discount: Various if 50+

Veterans of Foreign War
10 Pine Street
Deadwood, South Dakota 57732
(605) 722-9914

Hours: 9:30am-12am Daily

Wooden Nickel
9 Lee Street
Deadwood, South Dakota 57732
(605) 578-1952

Special Features: Includes **Lee Street Station** casino.

Indian Casinos

Dakota Connection
46102 County Highway 10
Sisseton, South Dakota 57262
(605) 698-4273
Website: www.dakotaconnection.com
Map: **#10** (165 miles N. of Sioux Falls)

Toll-Free Number: (800) 542-2876
Restaurants: 1   Liquor: No
Buffets: B-$6.99 (Sat)/$17.99 (Sun)
       L-$17.99 (Sun)
Other Games: BG
Overnight RV Parking: Free must register at players club/RV Dump: No

Dakota Sioux Casino
16415 Sioux Conifer Road
Watertown, South Dakota 57201
(605) 882-2051
Website: www.dakotasioux.com
Map: **#2** (104 miles N. of Sioux Falls)

Toll-Free Number: (800) 658-4717
Rooms: 88 Price Range: $59-$99
Suites: 12 Price Range: $109-$199
Restaurants: 1 Liquor: Yes
Buffets: B-$7.00 (Mon/Sat/Sun)
    L-$7.00 (Mon/Sun)
    D-$7.00 (Mon)/ $15.95 (Sat)
Other Games: BJ, P
Overnight RV Parking: Free/RV Dump: Free
Senior Discount: Specials on Mon if 55+
Special Features: 9-space RV park (Free, including hookups). $10 room discount for players club members.

Fort Randall Casino Hotel
38538 East Highway 46
Pickstown, South Dakota 57367
(605) 487-7871
Website: www.ftrandallcasino.com
Map: **#3** (100 miles S.W. of Sioux Falls)

Room Reservations: (800) 362-6333
Rooms: 57 Price Range: $59-$89
Suites: 2 Price Range: $79-$109
Restaurants: 1 Liquor: Yes
Buffets: B-$8.95 (Sat/Sun) L-$9.95
    D-$8.95/$24.95 (Sat)
Other Games: BJ, P, BG (Wed-Sun)
Overnight RV Parking: Free/RV Dump: Free
Senior Discount: Specials on Wed if 50+
Special Features: 20-space RV park (Free, including hookups).

Golden Buffalo Casino
321 Sitting Bull Street
Lower Brule, South Dakota 57548
(605) 473-5577
Map: **#4** (45 miles S.E. of Pierre)

Room Reservations: (605) 473-5506
Rooms: 38 Price Range: $45-$60
Restaurants: 1 Liquor: Yes
Hours: 8am-12:30am/2am (Fri/Sat)
Casino Size: 9,000 Square Feet
Other Games: BG (Wed/Sun), No blackjack
Overnight RV Parking: Free/RV Dump: Free
Senior Discount: Specials on Mon if 50+

Grand River Casino and Resort
2 U.S. 12
Mobridge, South Dakota 57601
(605) 845-7104
Website: www.grandrivercasino.com
Map: **#7** (240 miles N.E. of Rapid City)

Toll-Free Number: (800) 475-3321
Rooms: 38 Price Range: $60-$80
Suites: 2 Price Range: $150-$200
Restaurants: 1 Liquor: Yes
Buffets: B-$6.95 (Sun)
    D-$9.50/$14.95 (Sun)
Other Games: BJ, P (Thu)
Overnight RV Parking: Free/RV Dump: No
Special Features: 10-space RV park ($10 per night).

Lode Star Casino & Hotel
1003 Sd Highway 47
Fort Thompson, South Dakota 57339
(605) 245-6000
Map: **#6** (150 miles N.W. of Sioux Falls)

Room Reservations: (888) 268-1360
Restaurants: 1 Liquor: Yes
Rooms: 50 Price Range: $50-$75
Hours: 7am-2am/4am (Thu-Sat)
Other Games: BJ, P (Mon/Thu/Sat)
Overnight RV Parking: Free/RV Dump: No

Prairie Wind Casino & Hotel
U.S. 18
Pine Ridge, South Dakota 57770
(605) 867-6300
Website: www.prairiewindcasino.com
Map: **#9** (85 miles S.E. of Rapid City)

Toll-Free Number: (800) 705-9463
Rooms: 78 Price Range: $60-$99
Suites: 6 Price Range: $116-$156
Restaurants: 1 Liquor: No
Buffets: B-$9.95 (Sat/Sun)
    D-$12.95/$18.95 (Thu)/$16.95 (Fri)
Other Games: BJ, TCP, BG, P
Overnight RV Parking: Free/RV Dump: No
Special Features: Casino is located 12 miles East of Oelrichs off Hwy. 385 and 8 miles West of Oglala on Hwy. 18.

Rosebud Casino
Highway 83 (on SD/NE stateline)
Mission, South Dakota 57555
(605) 378-3800
Website: www.rosebudcasino.com
Map: **#8** (22 miles S. of Mission)

Toll-Free Number: (800) 786-7673
Room Reservations: (877) 521-9913
Rooms: 58 Price Range: $89-$109
Suites: 2 Price Range: $99-$129
Restaurants: 2 Liquor: Yes
Buffets: B-$13.99 (Sun) D-$13.99 (Thu-Sun)
Other Games: BJ, P (Sun/Thu), BG (Tue-Thu)
Overnight RV Parking: Free/RV Dump: No
Senior Discount: Various if 55+
Special Features: Hotel is Quality Inn. Located 22 miles S. of Mission, SD and 9 miles N. of Valentine, NE.

Royal River Casino & Hotel
607 S. Veterans Street
Flandreau, South Dakota 57028
(605) 997-3746
Website: www.royalrivercasino.com
Map: **#5** (35 miles N. of Sioux Falls on I-29)

Toll-Free Number: (800) 833-8666
Rooms: 108 Price Range: $60-$80
Suites: 12 Price Range: $90-$105
Restaurants: 2 Liquor: Yes
Buffets: B-$4.99 (Sat)/$9.99 (Sun)
    L-$7.99
    D-$19.99/$15.99 (Fri)/
        $13.99 (Sat)/$6.99 (Sun)
Casino Size: 17,000 Square Feet
Other Games: BJ, R, P (Thu-Sun)
Overnight RV Parking: Free/RV Dump: No
Special Features: 21-space RV park ($10 per night).

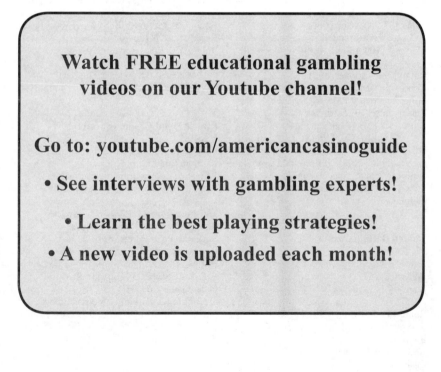

TEXAS

Texas has one Indian casino which offers class II gaming machines based on bingo. It also offers pull tab machines, bingo, poker and a player-banked blackjack game where each player must pay a commission to the house for each bet that is made. The commission is 50¢ for $3-$50 bets and $1 for bets over $50. The minimum gambling age is 21 and the casino is open 24 hours daily.

Class II video gaming devices look like slot machines, but are actually bingo games and the spinning reels are for "entertainment purposes only." No public information is available concerning the payback percentages on any gaming machines in Texas' Indian casino.

For more information on visiting Texas call (800) 888-8839 or go to: www.traveltex.com.

Kickapoo Lucky Eagle Casino Hotel
794 Lucky Eagle Drive
Eagle Pass, Texas 78852
(830) 758-1936
Website: www.luckyeagletexas.com
Map: **#1** (140 miles S.W. of San Antonio)

Toll-Free Number: (888) 255-8259
Rooms: 240 rates: $119-129
Restaurants: 1 Liquor: Yes Valet Parking: No
Buffets: L/D- $14.95
Casino Size: 16,000 Square Feet
Overnight RV Parking: Free/RV Dump: Free
Special Features: 20-space RV park ($15 per night).

WASHINGTON

The Indian casinos operating in Washington all have compacts with the state allowing them to offer table games, as well as electronic 'scratch' ticket games which use a finite number of tickets with a predetermined number of winners and losers.

These video gaming machines have a maximum bet of $20.

The Tribes are not required to release information on their slot machine percentage paybacks. However, according to the terms of the compact between the Tribes and the state, the minimum prize payout for electronic 'scratch' ticket games is 75%.

Most Washington casinos are open on a 24-hour basis. The hours of operation are noted in each casino's listing for those not open 24 hours.

All casinos offer blackjack, craps, roulette, slots, video poker and pull tabs. Optional games offered include: baccarat (B), mini-baccarat (MB), poker (P), pai gow poker (PGP), Caribbean stud poker (CSP), three-card poker (TCP), four card poker (FCP), Spanish 21 (S21), big 6 wheel (B6), keno (K), Off-Track Betting (OTB) and bingo (BG). The minimum gambling age is 21 at most casinos (at some it's 18) and 18 for bingo or pari-mutuel betting. Look in the "Special Features" listing for each casino to see which allow gambling at 18 years of age.

Although most of the casinos have toll-free numbers be aware that some of these numbers will only work for calls made within Washington.

For more information on visiting Washington call their tourism department at (800) 544-1800 or go to: www.experiencewashington.com.

Angel of the Winds Casino
3438 Stoluckquamish Lane
Arlington, Washington 98223
(360) 474-9740
Website: www.angelofthewinds.com
Map: **#22** (50 miles N. of Seattle)

Restaurants: 1 Liquor: Yes Valet Parking: Free
Buffets: L-$9.99/$15.99 (Sat/Sun)
         D-$15.99/$22.99 (Fri/Sat)
Other Games: P, TCP, FCP, PGP, K
Overnight RV Parking: Free/RV Dump: No
Special Features: **Hotel to Open Mid 2015**

BJ's Bingo
4411 Pacific Highway East
Fife, Washington 98424
(253) 922-0430
Website: www.bjs-bingo.com
Map: **#15** (a suburb of Tacoma)

Restaurants: 1
Other games: BG
Overnight RV Parking: Call ahead

Chewelah Casino
2555 Smith Road
Chewelah, Washington 99109
(509) 935-6167
Website: www.chewelahcasino.com
Map: **#13** (50 miles N. of Spokane)

Toll-Free Number: (800) 322-2788
Restaurants: 1 Liquor: No Valet Parking: No
Buffets: B- 7.99 (Sat)/$11.99 (Sun)
      L-$9.99 D-$12.99 (Thu)/$26.99 (Fri)
Hours: 8am-2am
Casino Size: 22,000 Square Feet
Other Games: S21, P
Overnight RV Parking: Free/RV Dump: No
Senior Discount: Various Wed if 55+
Special Features: One block from Double Eagle Casino. 20-space RV park ($15 per night). Gambling age is 18.

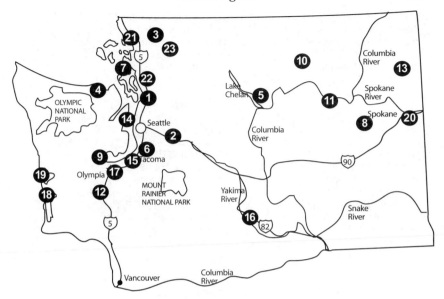

Coulee Dam Casino
515 Birch Street
Coulee Dam, Washington 99155
(509) 633-0766
Website: www.colvillecasinos.com
Map: **#11** (190 miles E. of Seattle)

Toll-Free Number: (800) 556-7492
Restaurants: 1 Deli Liquor: Yes
Hours: 10am-3am/24 Hours (Fri/Sat)
Other Games: Only gaming machines
Overnight RV Parking: Free/RV Dump: No
Special Features: Gambling age is 18.

Elwha River Casino
631 Stratton Road
Port Angeles, Washington 98363
(360) 452-3005
Website: www.elwharivercasino.com
Map: **#4** (70 miles N.W. of Seattle via ferry)

Restaurants: 1 Liquor: No Valet: Not offered
Other Games: Only gaming machines/keno
Hours: 10am-midnight/2am (Fri/Sat)

Emerald Queen Hotel & Casino at Fife
5700 Pacific Highway East
Fife, Washington 98424
(206) 594-7777
Website: www.emeraldqueen.com
Map: **#15** (a suburb of Tacoma)

Toll-Free Number: (888) 820-3555
Rooms: 130 Price Range: $89-$109
Suites: 10 Price Range: $179-$229
Restaurants: 1 Liquor: Yes Valet Parking: No
Buffets: L-$13.95/$19.95 (Sun) D-$24.95
Other Games: Only gaming machines/keno
Overnight RV Parking: No

Emerald Queen Casino at I-5
2024 East 29th Street
Tacoma, Washington 98404
(206) 383-1572
Website: www.emeraldqueen.com
Map: **#15** (a suburb of Tacoma)

Toll-Free Number: (888) 831-7655
Restaurants: 3 Liquor: Yes Valet Parking: Free
Buffets: L-$13.95/$24.95 (Sun) D-$24.95
Other Games: S21, PGP, CSP,
                         LIR, TCP, FCP, B6
Senior Discount: Buffet discount if 60+
Overnight RV Parking: Free/RV Dump: No
Special Features: Sports bar.

Little Creek Casino Resort
91 West Highway 108
Shelton, Washington 98584
(360) 427-7711
Website: www.little-creek.com
Map: **#9** (23 miles N. of Olympia off Hwy 101/108 interchange)

Toll-Free Number: (800) 667-7711
Rooms: 92 Price Range: $95-$219
Suites: 6 Price Range: $219-$575
Restaurants: 2 Liquor: Yes
Valet Parking: Free
Buffets: B-$8.95/$16.95 (Sun) L-$12.95/
D-$16.95/$24.95 (Fri/Sat)
Casino Size: 30,000 Square Feet
Other Games: S21, P, PGP, K, BG, FCP
Overnight RV Parking: Free/RV Dump: No
Senior Discount: Various Mon-Wed if 50+
Special Features: Indoor pool. Gift shop.

Lucky Dog Casino
19330 N. Highway 101
Shelton, Washington 98584
(360) 877-5656
Website: www.myluckydogcasino.com
Map: **#9** (23 miles N. of Olympia)

Toll-Free Number: (877) 582-5948
Restaurants: 1 Liquor: Yes Valet Parking: No
Hours: 8am-1am/2am (Fri-Sat)
Casino Size: 2,500 Square Feet
Overnight RV Parking: Call Ahead/RV Dump: No
Senior Discount: Various Mon if 50+
Special Features: Will reimburse up to two days of RV parking fees at participating RV parks. Call for details.

Lucky Eagle Casino
12888 188th Avenue SW
Rochester, Washington 98579
(360) 273-2000
Website: www.luckyeagle.com
Map: **#12** (26 miles S. of Olympia)

Toll-Free Number: (800) 720-1788
Rooms: 65 Price Range: $99-$135
Suites: 4 Price Range: $138-$265
Restaurants: 5 Liquor: Yes Valet Parking: No
Buffets: L-$10.95/$14.95 (Sun)
D-$14.95/$22.95 (Fri/Sat)
Hours: 8am-4am/6am (Fri/Sat)
Casino Size: 75,000 Square Feet
Other Games: P, PGP, TCP, K, BG
Overnight RV Parking: No
Senior Discount: Various specials Mon if 55+
Special Features: 20-space RV park ($25 per night).

Mill Bay Casino
455 Wapato Lake Road
Manson, Washington 98841
(509) 687-2102
Website: www.colvillecasinos.com
Map: **#5** (200 miles N.E. of Seattle on the N. shore of Lake Chelan)

Toll-Free Number: (800) 648-2946
Restaurants: 1 Liquor: Yes Valet Parking: No
Other Games: S21, PGP, P, TCP, FCP
Overnight RV Parking: Free/RV Dump: No
Senior Discount: Various Mon/Thu if 55+
Special Features: Gambling age is 18.

Muckleshoot Casino
2402 Auburn Way South
Auburn, Washington 98002
(253) 804-4444
Website: www.muckleshootcasino.com
Map: **#6** (20 miles S. of Seattle)

Toll-Free Number (800) 804-4944
Restaurants: 5 Liquor: Yes Valet Parking: Free
Buffets: B-$9.95 L-$14.95/$17.95 (Sat/Sun)
D-$19.95/$24.95 (Fri/Sat/Sun)
Other Games: S21, B, MB, P, PGP, CSP,
TCP, BG, FCP
Overnight RV Parking: Free/RV Dump: No
Senior Discount: Various on Tue if 55+
Special Features: Two casinos in separate buildings, one is non-smoking.

Nooksack Northwood Casino

9750 Northwood Road
Lynden, Washington 98264
(360) 734-5101
Website: www.northwood-casino.com
Map: **#3** (14 miles N. of Bellingham)

Toll-Free Number (877) 777-9847
Restaurants: 2 Liquor: Yes Valet Parking: No
Buffets: L/D-$11.95 (Tue)/$14.95 (Wed/Thu)/
$16.95 (Fri/Sat)
Hours: 9am-2am
Casino Size: 20,000 Square Feet
Other Games: Only Gaming Machines
Overnight RV Parking: Free/RV Dump: No
Senior Discount: Various Wed/Thu if 50+
Special Features: RV hook-ups available for
$15 per night.

Nooksack River Casino

5048 Mt. Baker Highway
Deming, Washington 98244
(360) 592-5472
Website: www.nooksackcasino.com
Map: **#23** (14 miles E. of Bellingham)

Toll-Free Number (877) 935-9300
Restaurants: 4 Liquor: Yes Valet Parking: Free
Buffets: B-$15.95 (Sun)
L-$11.95 /$4.99 (Thu)
D-$11.95/$22.99 (Fri)/$15.95 (Sat)
Hours: 10am-1am/3am (Fri/Sat)
Casino Size: 21,500 Square Feet
Other Games: S21, MB, P, PGP, TCP
Overnight RV Parking: Free/RV Dump: No
Senior Discount: Various on Wed/Thu if 55+
Special Features: 6-space RV park ($10 per
night).

Northern Quest Resort & Casino

100 N Hayford Road
Airway Heights, Washington 99001
(509) 242-7000
Website: www.northernquest.com
Map: **#20** (10 miles W. of Spokane)

Toll-Free Number (888) 603-7051
Rooms: 200 Prices $149-$199
Suites: 50 Prices: $239-$539
Restaurants: 4 Liquor: Yes Valet Parking: Free
Buffets: B/L-$12.95/$16.95 (Sun)
D-$16.95/$26.95 (Fri)/$21.95 (Sat)
Casino Size: 21,500 Square Feet
Other Games: S21, PGP, TCP,
K, OTB, P
Overnight RV Parking: Free/RV Dump: No
Senior Discount: $2 buffet discounts if 55+

Okanogan Casino

41 Appleway Road
Okanogan, Washington 98840
Website: www.colvillecasinos.com
(509) 422-4646
Map: **#10** (165 miles E. of Seattle)

Toll-Free Number: (800) 559-4643
Restaurants: 1 Liquor: Yes
Hours: 8am-4am/24 Hours (Fri/Sat)
Other Games: Only machines, P (Tue/Thu-Sat)
Overnight RV Parking: Free/RV Dump: No
Senior Discount: Discount breakfast & lunch if 55+
Special Features: Gambling age is 18.

The Point Casino

7989 Salish Lane NE
Kingston, Washington 98346
(360) 297-0070
Website: www.the-point-casino.com
Map: **#14** (18 miles W. of Seattle via
Bainbridge Ferry)

Toll-Free Number (866) 547-6468
Restaurants: 1 Liquor: Yes Valet Parking: No
Buffets: L-$9.95/$12.95 (Sat/Sun)
D-$15.95/$19.95 (Fri)/$23.95 (Sat)
Casino Size: 18,500 Square Feet
Other Games: S21, PGP, P
Overnight RV Parking: Free/RV Dump: No
Senior Discount: Various on Sun if 55+

Quil Ceda Creek Nightclub & Casino
6410 33rd Avenue N.E.
Tulalip, Washington 98271
(360) 551-1111
Website: www.quilcedacreekcasino.com
Map: **#1** (30 miles N. of Seattle)

Toll-Free Number: (888) 272-1111
Restaurants: 1 Liquor: Yes Valet Parking: No
Buffets: D- $16.95 (Wed)/$27.95 (Thu)
Casino Size: 52,000 Square Feet
Other Games: S21, PGP, TCP
Overnight RV Parking: Free/RV Dump: No
Special Features: One mile from Tulalip
Casino.

Quinault Beach Resort and Casino
78 Route 115
Ocean Shores, Washington 98569
(360) 289-9466
Website: www.quinaultbeachresort.com
Map: **#19** (90 miles W. of Tacoma)

Toll-Free Number: (888) 461-2214
Rooms: 159 Price Range: $116-$189
Suite: 9 Price Range: $289-$449
Restaurants: 2 Liquor: Yes Valet Parking: Free
Buffets: B-$14.95 (Sun)
        D-$16.95/$27.95 (Fri)
Casino Size: 16,000 Square Feet
Other Games: S21, P, PGP, LIR, TCP
Overnight RV Parking: Free (must register
        first at front desk)/RV Dump: No
Senior Discount: Various Wed if 55+

Red Wind Casino
12819 Yelm Highway
Olympia, Washington 98513
(360) 412-5000
Website: www.redwindcasino.com
Map: **#17**

Toll-Free Number: (866) 946-2444
Restaurants: 1 Liquor: Yes
Buffets: B-$10.00/$13.00 (Sat)/$20.00 (Sun)
        L-$15.00
        D-$19.00/$25.00 (Fri/Sat)/$20.00 (Sun)
Hours: 8am-5am/24 hrs (Fri/Sat/Sun)
Casino Size: 12,000 Square Feet
Other Games: S21, PGP, TCP, LIR, K, FCP
Overnight RV Parking: Free/RV Dump: No
Senior Discount: Various Mon-Fri if 55+

7 Cedars Casino
270756 Highway 101
Sequim, Washington 98382
(360) 683-7777
Website: www.7cedarscasino.com
Map: **#4** (70 miles N.W. of Seattle via ferry)

Toll-Free Number: (800) 458-2597
Restaurants: 2 Liquor: Yes
Buffets: L-$13.95
        D-$13.95/$21.95 (Fri/Sat)
Hours: 9am-3am/4am (Fri/Sat)
Other Games: S21, P, PGP, LIR, TCP, K,
        BG, OTB (Wed-Mon)
Overnight RV Parking: Free (Must check-in
        first)/RV Dump: No

Shoalwater Bay Casino
4112 Highway 105
Tokeland, Washington 98590
(360) 267-2048
Website: www.shoalwaterbaycasino.com
Map: **#18** (75 miles S.W. of Olympia)

Toll-Free Number: (888) 332-2048
Restaurants: 1 Liquor: No Valet Parking: No
Buffets: B-$6.95 (Sun) L-$7.95 D-$11.95/
        $16.95 (Fri/Sat)/$7.95 (Sun)
Hours: 10am-Midnight/2am (Fri/Sat)
Casino Size: 10,000 Square Feet
Other Games: S21, PGP, TCP, No C or R
Overnight RV Parking: No
Senior Discount: Various on Tue if 55+
Special Features: Table games open Thu-Sun
at 2pm. 15-space RV park across the street
($7/$15 with hook ups per night).

Silver Reef Hotel • Casino • Spa
4876 Haxton Way
Ferndale, Washington 98248
(360) 383-0777
Website: www.silverreefcasino.com
Map: **#21** (7 miles N. of Bellingham)

Toll-Free Number: (866) 383-0777
Rooms: 105 Price Range: $129-$169
Suites: 4 Price Range: $279-$299
Restaurants: 4 Liquor: Yes Valet Parking: No
Buffets: L-$12.95/$16.95 (Thu-Sun)
        D-$18.95/$27.95 (Thu/Fri)/$25.95(Sat)
Casino Size: 48,000 Square Feet
Other Games: S21, PGP, TCP, FCP
Overnight RV Parking: Free/RV Dump: No

Skagit Valley Casino Resort
5984 N. Darrk Lane
Bow, Washington 98232
(360) 724-7777
Website: www.theskagit.com
Map: **#7** (75 miles N. of Seattle)

Toll-Free Number: (877) 275-2448
Room Reservations: (800) 895-3423
Rooms: 74 Price Range: $99-$139
Suites: 29 Price Range: $179-$219
Restaurants: 3 Liquor: Yes Valet Parking: No
Buffets: B-$13.99 (Sun)
L-$7.99 D-$12.99/$21.50 (Fri/Sat)
Hours: 9am-3am/5am (Fri/Sat)
Casino Size: 26,075 Square Feet
Other Games: P, PGP, S21, K
Overnight RV Parking: No
Senior Discount: Various on Mon if 55+
Special Features: Two 18-hole golf courses.
2,700-seat outdoor events center. Health spa.

Snoqualmie Casino
37500 SE North Bend Way
Snoqualmie, Washington 98065
(425) 888-1234
Website: www.snocasino.com
Map: **#2** (30 miles E. of Seattle)

Restaurants: 5 Liquor: Yes
Buffets: L-$15.95/$18.95 (Sat/Sun)
D-$29.95/$36.95 (Tue)/$27.95 (Wed)/
$28.95 (Fri)
Other Games: S21, B, PGP, P, TCP

Suquamish Clearwater Casino Resort
15347 Suquamish Way Northeast
Suquamish, Washington 98392
(360) 598-8700
Website: www.clearwatercasino.com
Map: **#14** (15 miles W. of Seattle via Bainbridge Ferry)

Toll-Free Number: (800) 375-6073
Room Reservations: (866) 609-8700
Rooms:70 Room Rates: $79-$139
Suites: 15 Room Rates: $109-$169
Restaurants: 4 Liquor: Yes Valet Parking: Free
Buffets: B-$14.95 (Sun) L-$11.25
D-$15.95/$23.95 (Fri/Sat)
Casino Size: 22,000 Square Feet
Other Games: P, PGP, TCP, LIR, K
Overnight RV Parking: Free/RV Dump: No
Senior Discount: Various 1st Mon of month if 55+
Special features: Seattle and Edmonds Ferries fee reimbursed with qualified play. Gambling age is 18.

Swinomish Casino & Lodge
12885 Casino Drive
Anacortes, Washington 98221
(360) 293-2691
Website: www.swinomishcasino.com
Map: **#7** (70 miles N. of Seattle, between I-5 and Anacortes on Hwy. 20)

Toll-Free Number: (888) 288-8883
Restaurants: 2 Liquor: Yes Valet Parking: Free
Buffets: B-$22.95 (Sun)
L-$10.95 D-$10.95/$24.95 (Fri)/
$18.95 (Sat/Sun)
Casino Size: 23,000 Square Feet
Other Games: P, PGP, TCP, FCP,
BG, K, OTB, S21
Overnight RV Parking: Must use RV park
Senior Discount: Buffet discount if 55+
Special Features: 35-space RV park ($22/$25 per night). Gift shop.

Tulalip Casino
10200 Quil Ceda Boulevard
Tulalip, Washington 98271
(360) 651-1111
Website: www.tulalipcasino.com
Map: **#1** (30 miles N. of Seattle)

Toll-Free Number: (888) 272-1111
Rooms: 370 Room Rates: $105-$195
Suites: 23 Room Rates: $235-$325
Restaurants: 4 Liquor: Yes Valet Parking: Free
Buffets: B-$11.95 L-$13.95/$17.95 (Sun)
D-$20.95/$25.95 (Tue)
Casino Size: 45,000 Square Feet
Other Games: S21, B, MB, P, PGP, CSP,
TCP, FCP LIR, K, BG
Overnight RV Parking: Free/RV Dump: No
Senior Discount: Various on Tue if 50+
Special Features: 2,300-seat amphitheatre.
One mile from Quil Ceda Creek Casino.

Two Rivers Casino & Resort
6828-B Highway 25 South
Davenport, Washington 99122
(509) 722-4000
Website: www.two-rivers-casino.com
Map: **#8** (60 miles W. of Spokane)

Toll-Free Number: (800) 722-4031
Restaurants: 1 Liquor: No Valet Parking: No
Hours: 8am-10pm/12am (Fri/Sat)
Casino Size: 10,000 Square Feet
Overnight RV Parking: Must use RV park
Special Features: Regular slots. 100-space
RV park ($35 per night). 260-slip marina and
beach. Gambling age is 18.

Yakama Nation Legends Casino
580 Fort Road
Toppenish, Washington 98948
(509) 865-8800
Website: www.yakamalegends.com
Map: **#16** (20 miles S. of Yakima)

Toll-Free Number: (877) 726-6311
Restaurants: 2 Liquor: No Valet Parking: No
Buffets: B-$12.99 (Sun)
L-$9.99/$19.99 (Thu/Sat)
D-$9.99/$27.99 (Thu)/
$19.95 (Fri/Sat)/$12.99 (Sun)
Hours: 9am-4am/24 hours (Sat/Sun)
Casino Size: 45,000 Square Feet
Other Games: S21, P, PGP, TCP, LIR, K
Overnight RV Parking: Free/RV Dump: No
Senior Discount: Various on Tue if 55+
Special Features: Childcare center. Indoor
waterfall. Gambling age is 18.

Card Rooms

Card rooms have been legal in Washington
since 1974. Initially limited to just five tables
per location, the law was changed in 1996
to allow up to 15 tables. One year later, a
provision was added to allow house-banked
games. Permissible games include: blackjack,
Caribbean stud poker, pai gow poker, let it
ride, casino war and numerous other card
games. Baccarat, craps, roulette and keno are
not allowed.

The maximum bet at each card room is
dependent on certain licensing requirements
and is capped at either $25 or $100.
Additionally, the rooms can be open no more
than 20 hours per day. These card rooms are
now commonly called "mini-casinos." The
minimum gambling age in a card room is 18.

Each city and county has the option to ban
the card rooms so they are not found in every
major city (Seattle has none). Due to space
limitations we don't list all of the Washington
card rooms in this book.

For a list of card rooms, we suggest that
you contact the Washington State Gambling
Commission at (360) 486-3581, or visit their
website at: www.wsgc.wa.gov

WEST VIRGINIA

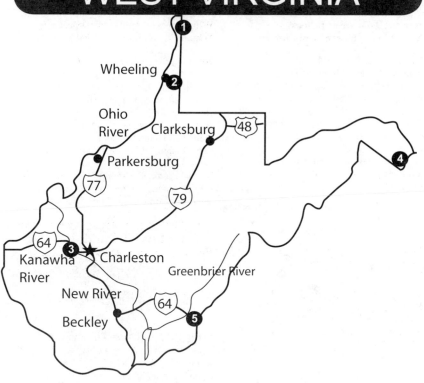

West Virginia has four pari-mutuel facilities and one resort hotel that feature video lottery terminals. The VLT's are the same as regular video gaming devices but are called lottery terminals because they are regulated by the state's lottery commission which receives a share of each machine's revenue.

West Virginia law requires that VLT's return a minimum of 80% to a maximum of 95%. VLT games include: slots, blackjack, keno and numerous versions of poker. The minimum gambling age is 21.

For the one-year period from July 1, 2013 through June 30, 2014 the average return on VLT's was: 89.29% at Mountaineer Park, 90.63% at Tri-State Park, 89.82% at Wheeling Island and 89.75% at Charles Town Races.

West Virginia law also allows bars, as well as restaurants that serve alcohol, to have up to five VLT's. Fraternal organizations are also allowed to have up to 10 VLT's. All of these machines are identical to the machines found at the racetracks, except they only print out tickets and do not pay out in cash.

All West Virgina casinos also offer the following table games: blackjack, craps, roulette, three card poker, four card poker and let it ride. Optional games offered include: poker (P), pai gow poker (PGP), Caribbean stud poker (CSP), Spanish 21 (S21), Mississippi stud (MS) and big 6 wheel (B6).

For West Virginia tourism information call (800) 225-5982 or go to: www.callwva.com.

The Casino Club at The Greenbrier
300 W. Main Street
White Sulphur Springs, West Virginia 24986
(304) 536-1110
Website: www.greenbrier.com
Map: **#5** (120 miles S.E. of Charleston)

Toll-free Number: (800) 453-4858
Rooms: 238 Price Range: $319-$545
Casino Hours: 11am-3am/11am-4am (Fri/Sat)
Casino Size: 75,000 square Feet
Other Games: B, MB
Special Features: Casino only open to hotel guests, sporting club or golf/tennis club members, or convention/event attendees. Dress code enforced. Men required to wear jackets after 7 p.m.

Hollywood Casino at Charles Town Races
750 Hollywood Drive
Charles Town, West Virginia 25414
(304) 725-7001
Website: www.ctownraces.com
Map: **#4** (320 miles N.E. of Charleston)

Toll-Free Number: (800) 795-7001
Rooms: 132 Price Range: $109-$189
Suites: 18 Price Range: $219-$289
Restaurants: 4 Valet Parking: $4/$6 (Fri-Sun)
Buffets: L-$13.99/$15.99 (Sat)/$17.99 (Sun)
        D-$17.99/$34.99 (Fri)/$24.99 (Sat)
Other Games: MB, MS, B6, PGP
Overnight RV Parking: Free/RV Dump: No
Special Features: Live thoroughbred racing Wed-Sun. Daily simulcasting of horse and dog racing. Food court with five fast-food outlets. No buffet Mon/Tue

Mardi Gras Casino & Resort
1 Greyhound Drive
Cross Lanes, West Virginia 25313
(304) 776-1000
Website: www.mardigrascasinowv.com
Map: **#3** (10 miles N.W. of Charleston)

Toll-Free Number: (800) 224-9683
Rooms: 132 Price Range: $169-$189
Suites: 21 Price Range: Casino Use Only
Restaurants: 5 Valet Parking: $3
Buffets: D-$9.99
Casino Size: 30,000 Square Feet
Other Games: B6, MB, P, MS
Overnight RV Parking: Free/RV Dump: No
Special Features: Live dog racing Wed-Mon. Daily simulcasting of horse and dog racing.

Mountaineer Casino Racetrack & Resort
1000 Washington Street
Newell, West Vigninia 26050
(304) 387-2400
Website: www.moreatmountaineer.com
Map: **#1** (35 miles N. of Wheeling)

Toll-Free Number: (800) 804-0468
Room Reservations: (800) 489-8192
Rooms: 238 Price Range: $117-$179
Suites: 20 Price Range: $165-$229
Restaurants: 8 Valet Parking: $5
Buffets: L-$8.99 D-$14.99
Hours: 24 Hours Daily
Other Games: P, B6, MB, PGP, S21, MS
Overnight RV Parking: Free/RV Dump: No
Special Features: 18-hole golf course. Spa and fitness center. Live thoroughbred racing Sat-Tue. Daily simulcasting of horse/dog racing.

Wheeling Island
Racetrack & Gaming Center
1 S. Stone Street
Wheeling, West Virginia 26003
(304) 232-5050
Website: www.wheelingisland.com
Map: **#2**

Toll-Free Number: (877) 946-4373
Room Reservations: (877) 943-3546
Rooms: 142 Price Range: $135-$165
Suites: 9 Price Range: $169-$250
Restaurants: 4 Valet Parking: $5
Buffets: B-$9.95 L-$13.95/$24.99 (Fri)/
        $18.95 (Sat)/$17.95 (Sun)
        D-$16.95/$24.95 (Fri)/$18.95 (Sat)
Hours: 24 Hours Daily
Casino Size: 50,000 Square Feet
Other Games: P, MS
Overnight RV Parking: Free/RV Dump: No
Senior Discount: Various on Wed if 50+
Special Features: Live dog racing daily except Tue/Thu. Daily simulcasting of horse and dog racing.

WISCONSIN

All Wisconsin casinos are located on Indian reservations.

The Tribes are not required to release information on their slot machine percentage paybacks, but according to the terms of the compact between the state and the tribes "for games not affected by player skill, such as slot machines, the machine is required to return a minimum of 80% and a maximum of 100% of the amount wagered."

All casinos offer blackjack, slots and video poker. Some casinos also offer: craps (C), roulette (R), mini baccarat (MB), poker (P), Pai Gow Poker (PGP), three card poker (TCP), four card poker (FCP), let it ride (LIR), big 6 wheel (B6), bingo (BG), keno (K) and off-track betting (OTB). Unless otherwise noted, all casinos are open 24 hours and the minimum gambling age is 21 (18 for bingo).

For visitor information contact the state's department of tourism at (800) 432-8747 or their website at: www.travelwisconsin.com.

Bad River Lodge Casino
U.S. Highway 2
Odanah, Wisconsin 54861
(715) 682-7121
Website: www.badriver.com
Map: **#1** (halfway between Ironwood, MI and Ashland, WI; 45 miles east of Duluth, MN on US 2)

Toll-Free Number: (800) 777-7449
Lodge Reservations: (800) 795-7121
Rooms: 42 Price Range: $40-$65
Suites: 8 Price Range: $60-$75
Restaurants: 2 Liquor: Yes
Casino Size: 19,200 Square Feet
Hours: 8am-2am Daily
Other Games: R, P, TCP, LIR
Overnight RV Parking: Free/RV Dump: Free
Senior Discount: Various dining specials throughout the week if 55+.
Special Features: 20-space RV park ($10/$20 per night). Gas station. Grocery store.

Ho-Chunk Gaming Black River Falls
W9010 Highway 54 East
Black River Falls, Wisconsin 54615
(715) 284-9098
Website: www.ho-chunkgaming.com
Map: **#8** (110 miles M.W. of Madison on Hwy. 54, 4 miles E. of I-94)

Toll-Free Number: (800) 657-4621
Rooms: 60 Price Range: $49-$88
Suites: 6 Price Range: $88-$125
Restaurants: 2 Liquor: Yes
Buffets: L-$8.98/$10.95 (Fri/Sat)/$11.95 (Sun)
        D-$12.50/$14.98 (Thu/Sun)/
        $19.98 (Fri/Sat)
Open 24 hours daily Memorial to Labor Day
Size: 35,000 Square Feet
Other Games: R, BG, TCP
Overnight RV Parking: Free/RV Dump: No
Senior Discount: $5 off bingo Sundays if 55+
Special Features: 10% off food/hotel for players club members.

Ho-Chunk Gaming Madison
4002 Evan Acres Rd.
Madison, Wisconsin 53718
(608)223-9576
Website: www.ho-chunkgaming.com
Map: **#17**

Toll-Free Number: (888) 248-1777
Restaurants: 1 Liquor: No
Casino Size: 22,000 Square Feet
Other Games: No blackack, P
Senior Discount: $5 free play on Wed if 55+

Ho-Chunk Gaming Nekoosa
949 County Road G
Nekoosa, Wisconsin 54457
(715) 886-4560
Website: www.ho-chunkgaming.com
Map: #15 (50 miles S. of Wausau)

Toll-Free Number: (800) 782-4560
Restaurants: 2 Liquor: Yes
Other Games: R, P, LIR, TCP
Overnight RV Parking: Free (must check-in
    first with security)/RV Dump: No
Senior Discount: Specials on Thu if 55+
Special Features: Smoke and gift shop.
Convenience store. Electronic versions of
roulette and craps.

Ho-Chunk Gaming Tomah
27867 Highway 21
Tomah, Wisconsin 54660
(608) 372-3721
Website: www.ho-chunkgaming.com
Map: #16 (3 miles E. of Tomah on Hwy 21)

Restaurants: 1 Snack Bar Liquor: No
Hours: 8am-Midnight/2am (Fri/Sat)
Casino Size: 2,000 Square Feet
Other Games: Only Gaming Machines
Special Features: Convenience store. Open
24 hours Fri-Sat during the summer.

Ho-Chunk Gaming Wisconsin Dells
S3214 Highway 12
Baraboo, Wisconsin 53913
(608) 356-6210
Website: www.ho-chunkgaming.com
Map: #4 (40 miles N. of Madison.)

Toll-Free Number: (800) 746-2486
Room Reservations: (800) 446-5550
Rooms: 295 Price Range: $79-$140
Suites: 20 Price Range: $130-$240
Restaurants: 4 Liquor: Yes
Buffets: B-$7.99 (Sat-Sun)
        L-$9.99/$11.99 (Sat/Sun)
        D-$12.99/$23.99 (Wed)/ $21.99 (Sat)
Casino Size: 90,000 Square Feet
Other Games: C, R, P, TCP, B, FCP
        OTB, BG (Tue-Sun)
Overnight RV Parking: Free/RV Dump: No
Special Features: Smoke shop. Free local
shuttle. Kids Quest childcare center.

Ho-Chunk Gaming Wittenberg
N7214 US Hwy 45
Wittenberg, Wisconsin 54499
(608) 372-3721
Website: www.ho-chunkgaming.com
Map: #18 (3 miles E. of Tomah on Hwy 21)

Restaurants: 1 Snack Bar Liquor: No
Casino Size: 2,000 Square Feet
Other Games: Only Gaming Machines
Special Features: Convenience store.

Hwy. 54 Casino
W180 State Hwy. 54
Oneida, Wisconsin 54155
(920) 869-6294
Map: #12 (Suburb of Green Bay)

Hours: 8am-11pm/12am (Fri/Sat)
Overnight RV Parking: Call ahead

IMAC Casino/Bingo
2100 Airport Drive
Green Bay, Wisconsin 54313
(800) 238-4263
Website: www.oneidabingoandcasino.net
Map: #12 (across from Austin Straubel
Airport, take Interstate 43 to Highway 172)

Other Games: BG, OTB
Hours: 8am-12am/2am (Fri/Sat)
Restaurants: 1 Liqur: Yes
Overnight RV Parking: $15 per night
Special features: Free shuttle service to
Oneida's Main Casino and Mason Street
Casino.

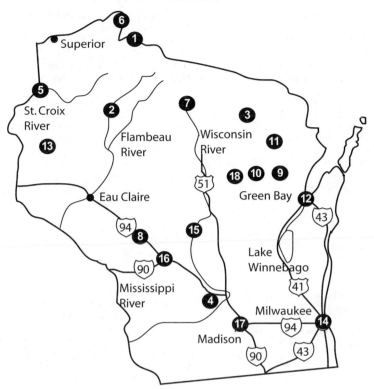

Lake of the Torches Resort Casino
510 Old Abe Road
Lac du Flambeau, Wisconsin 54538
(715) 588-7070
Website: www.lakeofthetorches.com
Map: **#7** (160 miles N.W. of Green Bay.
Heading N. on Hwy. 51, go left on Hwy. 47,
12 miles to casino)

Toll-Free Number: (800) 258-6724
Room Reservations: (888) 599-9200
Rooms: 88 Price Range: $95-$155
Suites: 13 Price Range: $150-$195
Restaurants: 2 Liquor: Yes
Buffets: B-$7.50 L-$8.75/$12.95 (Sat/Sun)
          D-$14.95/$19.95 (Fri/Sat)(Fri)
Other Games: P, BG (Wed-Sun)
Overnight RV Parking: Free/RV Dump: No
Special Features: Players club members get
20% off room and other discounts.

LCO Casino, Lodge & Convention Center
13767 W County Road B
Hayward, Wisconsin 54843
(715) 634-5643
Website: www.lcocasino.com
Map: **#2** (55 miles S.E. of Duluth, MN. 3 miles
N.E. of Hayward on county trunk B)

Toll-Free Number: (800) 526-2274
Room Reservations: (800) 526-5634
Rooms: 53 Price Range: $59-$89
Suites: 22 Price Range: $80-$130
Restaurants: 2 Liquor: Yes
Buffets:B-$8.95 (Sat/Sun)
          L-$10.95//$14.95 (Sun)
          D-$11.95/$12.95 (Fri/Sat)/
            $14.95 (Sun)
Casino Size: 35,000 Square Feet
Other Games: C, R, P, LIR, BG (Wed)
Overnight RV Parking: Free (must register
first at customer service)/RV Dump: No
Special Features: Nearby 8-space RV park
(Free). Sports lounge. Gift shop. No bingo
Mon/Sat.

Legendary Waters Resort & Casino
37600 Onigaming Drive
Red Cliff, Wisconsin 54814
(715) 779-3712
Website: www.legendarywaters.com
Map: #6 (70 miles E. of Duluth, MN on Hwy. 13)

Toll-Free Number: (800) 226-8478
RV Reservations: (715) 779-3743
Rooms: 50 Price Range: $75-$99
Suites: 7 Price Range: $109-$199
Restaurants: 1 Liquor: Yes
Buffets: B-$11.99 (Sun) D- $14.99 (Fri/Sat)
Other Games: P, BG (Fri/Sat/Sun)
Overnight RV Parking: Must use RV park
Special Features: Campground and 30-space RV park ($35 per night). 34-slip marina.

Menominee Casino Resort
N277 Highway 47/55
Keshena, Wisconsin 54135
(715) 799-3600
Website: www.menomineecasinoresort.com
Map: #9 (40 miles N.W. of Green Bay on Hwy. 47)

Toll-Free Number: (800) 343-7778
Rooms: 100 Price Range: $60-$90
Suites: 8 Price Range: $100-$145
Restaurants: 1 Liquor: Yes
Buffets: B-$12.99 (Sun)
         D-$9.99 (Fri)/$17.99 (Sat)/$12.99 (Sun)
Casino Size: 33,000 Square Feet
Other Games: C, R, P, LIR, TCP, BG
Overnight RV Parking: Free/RV Dump: No
Special Features: 60-space RV park ($21 per night). Gift shop. Smoke shop. No bingo Tues.

Mole Lake Casino & Lodge
3084 Wisconsin 55
Mole Lake, Wisconsin 54520
(715) 478-5290
Website: www.molelake.com
Map: #3 (100 miles N.W. of Green Bay)

Toll-Free Number: (800) 236-9466
Motel Reservations: (800) 457-4312
Motel Rooms: 25 Rates: $55-$75
Lodge Rooms: 65 Price Range: $71-$93
Lodge Suites: 10 Price Range: $81-$136
Restaurants: 2 Liquor: Yes
Hours: 7am-2am/3 am (Fri/Sat)
Other Games: BG (Fri-Tue)
Overnight RV Parking: Free/RV Dump: No
Special Features: Motel is two blocks from casino.

North Star Mohican Casino Resort
W12180 County Road A
Bowler, Wisconsin 54416
(715) 787-3110
Website: www.northstarcasinoresort.com
Map: #10 (50 miles N.W. of Green Bay)

Toll-Free Number: (800) 775-2274
Restaurants: 2   Liquor: Yes
Casino Size: 66,000 square Feet
Other Games: C, R, LIR, TCP, P,
                BG (Sun/Mon/Wed/Fri)
Overnight RV Parking: Free/RV Dump: Fee
Special Features: 57-space RV park ($25/$28 per night). Smoke shop. $10 freeplay with stay at RV park.

Oneida Bingo & Casino
2020 Airport Drive
Green Bay, Wisconsin 54313
(920) 494-4500
Website: www.oneidacasino.net
Map: #12 (across from Austin Straubel Airport, take Interstate 43 to Highway 172)

Toll-Free Number: (800) 238-4263
Reservation Number: (800) 333-3333
Rooms: 408 Price Range: $105-$159
Suites: 40 Price Range: $195-$449
Restaurants: 3   Liquor: Yes
Hours: 10am-4am (Tables)/24 Hours (Slots)
Other Games: C, R, P, LIR, MB,
                TCP, FCP, BG, OTB
Overnight RV Parking: Free/RV Dump: No
Special Features: Two casinos. One is connected to Radisson Inn where hotel rooms are located. Free local shuttle. Smoke shop.

Oneida Casino - Mason Street
2522 W. Mason Street
Green Bay, Wisconsin 54313
(920) 494-4500
Website: www.oneidacasino.net
Map: #12

Restaurant: 1
Casino Size: 38,000 square feet
Overnight RV Parking: Free/RV Dump: No

Oneida Casino Travel Center
5939 Old 29 Drive
Green Bay, Wisconsin 54313
(920) 865-7919
Website: www.oneidacasino.net
Map: #12

Restaurant: 1
Casino Size: 5,800 Square Feet
Overnight RV Parking: Free/RV Dump: No

Potawatomi Hotel & Casino
1721 W. Canal Street
Milwaukee, Wisconsin 53233
(414) 645-6888
Website: www.paysbig.com
Map: #14

Toll-Free Number: (800) 729-7244
Rooms: 381 Price Range: $189-$259
Suites: 17 Price Range: Casino Use Only
Restaurants: 6 Liquor: Yes
Buffets: B-$18.00 (Sun)
L-$14.00
D-$18.00/$14.00 (Tue/Thu)/
$36.00 (Wed/Fri)/$24.00 (Sat)
Casino Size: 38,400 Square Feet
Other Games: S21, C, R, P, PGP, TCP,
CW, B, LIR, FCP, BG, OTB
Overnight RV Parking: Free/RV Dump: No
Special Features: Smoke-free casino on 2nd
floor. No dinner buffet Sunday or Monday.

Potawatomi Carter Casino and Hotel
616 Highway 32
Carter, Wisconsin 54566
(715) 473-2021
Website: www.cartercasino.com
Map: #11 (85 miles N. of Green Bay on
Hwy. 32)

Toll-Free Number: (800) 487-9522
Lodge Reservations: (800) 777-1640
Rooms: 70 Price Range: $75-$95
Suites: 29 Price Range: $85-$150
Restaurants: 2 Liquor: Yes
Casino Size: 25,000 Square Feet
Other Games: C, R, LIR, TCP, BG (Wed-Sun)
Overnight RV Parking: Must use RV park
Senior Discount: Specials on Thu if 55+
Special Features: 10-space RV park ($15 per
night). 24-hour gas station and convenience
store. Craps/roulette open 6pm Sat/Sun.

St. Croix Casino Danbury
Highways 35 & 77
Danbury, Wisconsin 54830
(715) 656-3444
Website: www.stcroixcasino.com
Map: #5 (26 miles E. of Hinckley, MN)

Toll-Free Number: (800) 238-8946
Rooms: 45 Price Range: $60-$65
Suites: 1 Price Range: $80
Restaurants: 1 Liquor: Yes
Buffets: B-$8.99 (Sat/Sun)
L-$7.99 D-$11.99/$14.99 (Sat)
Casino Size: 22,500 Square Feet
Other Games: C, R, P
Overnight RV Parking: Must use RV park
Special Features: Craps and roulette only
offered on weekends. 35-space RV park ($15
per night). $10 off room for players club
members.

St. Croix Casino - Hertel Express
4384 State Road 70
Webster, Wisconsin 54893
(715) 349-5658
Map: #5 (26 miles E. of Hinckley, MN)

Restaraunts: 1
Other Games: Machines only
Overnight RV Parking: Call ahead

St. Croix Casino & Hotel
777 US Highway 8
Turtle Lake, Wisconsin 54889
(715) 986-4777
Website: www.stcroixcasino.com
Map: #13 (105 miles S. of Duluth, MN on
Hwy. 8)

Toll-Free Number: (800) 846-8946
Room Reservations: (800) 782-9987
Rooms: 145 Price Range: $55-$73
Suites: 8 Price Range: $95-$135
Restaurants: 2 Liquor: Yes
Buffets: B-$9.99 (Sat/Sun) L-$9.99
D-$12.99/$21.99(Sat)
Casino Size: 95,000 Square Feet
Other Games: MB, C, R, P, TCP, FCP, PGP
Overnight RV Parking: Must use RV park
Special Features: 20% off rooms for players
club members. 18-space RV park ($15/$25 for
electricity & water per night).

WYOMING

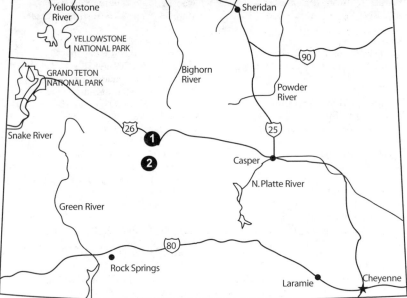

Wyoming's Indian casinos offer Class II bingo-type gaming machines, plus traditional Class III slot machines. Two of the casinos also offers some card-based table games.

The machines don't pay out in cash. Instead they print out a receipt which must be cashed by a floor attendant or taken to the cashier's cage. You can also make bets via a cashless system whereby you get a "smart" card and deposit money to that card's account. The machines will then deducts losses from, or credit wins to, your account.

No public information is available regarding the payback percentages on Wyoming's gaming machines. Unless otherwise noted, the casinos are open 24 hours and the minimum gambling age is 18.

For Wyoming tourism information call (800) 225-5996 or visit their website at: www.wyomingtourism.org

Little Wind Casino
693 Blue Sky Highway 132
Ethete, Wyoming 82520
(307) 438-7000
Map: **#2** (140 miles W. of Casper)

Restaurants: 1 Liquor: No Valet Parking: No
Casino Size: 1,920 Square Feet
Overnight RV Parking: Free/RV Dump: No
Senior Discount: Various on Tue if 55+
Special Features: Convenience store. Gas station.

Shoshone Rose Casino
5690 U.S. Highway 287
Lander, Wyoming 82520
(307) 335-7529
Website: www.thesrcasino.com
Map: **#2** (140 miles W. of Casper)

Restaurants: 1 Liquor: No Valet Parking: No
Casino Size: 7,000 Square Feet
Other games: Blackjack, Three Card Poker
Overnight RV Parking: No

789 Casino
10369 Highway 789
Riverton, Wyoming 82501
(307) 335-7529
Website: www.play789casino.com

Map: **#1** (125 miles W. of Casper)
Restaurants: 1 Liquor: No Valet Parking: No
Casino Size: 7,000 Square Feet
Overnight RV Parking: No

Wind River Hotel and Casino
10269 Highway 789
Riverton, Wyoming 82501
(307) 856-3964
Website: www.windrivercasino.com
Map: **#1** (125 miles W. of Casper)

Toll-Free Number: (866) 657-1604
Rooms: 80   Price Range: $109-$139
Suites: 10 Price Range: $250-$300
Restaurants: 2 Liquor: No Valet Parking: No
Other Games: Blackjack, Three Card Poker,
                Poker
Casino Size: 8,000 Square Feet
Senior Discount: Various Tue if 55+
Special Features: Smoke shop with 80 slot
machines. Gas station.

Casino Index

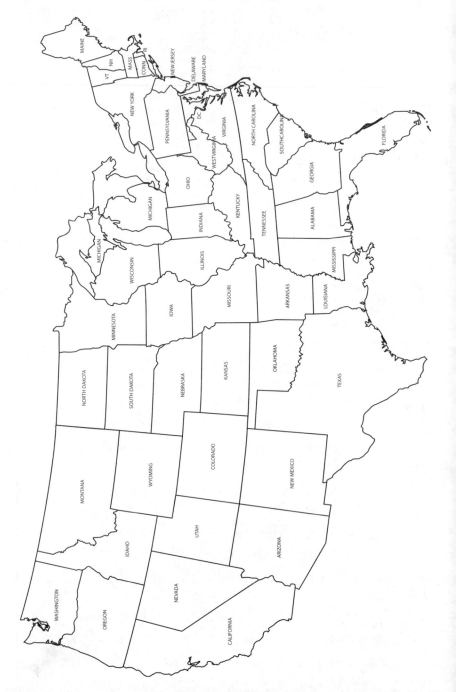

Reference Map Of U.S.

Coupon Directory

COUPON CHANGES

**Coupon offers can change without notice.
To see a list of any coupon changes, go to:
americancasinoguide.com/coupon-changes.html**

We will list any coupon changes on that page.

Notice

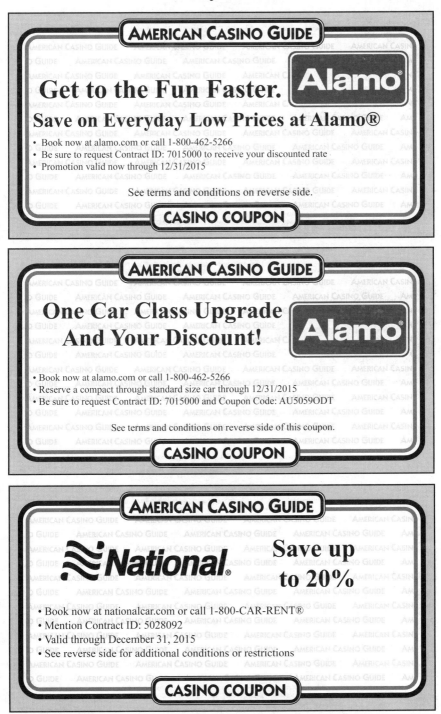

AMERICAN CASINO GUIDE

Get to the Fun Faster. **Alamo®**

Save on Everyday Low Prices at Alamo®

- Book now at alamo.com or call 1-800-462-5266
- Be sure to request Contract ID: 7015000 to receive your discounted rate
- Promotion valid now through 12/31/2015

See terms and conditions on reverse side.

CASINO COUPON

AMERICAN CASINO GUIDE

One Car Class Upgrade And Your Discount! **Alamo®**

- Book now at alamo.com or call 1-800-462-5266
- Reserve a compact through standard size car through 12/31/2015
- Be sure to request Contract ID: 7015000 and Coupon Code: AU5059ODT

See terms and conditions on reverse side of this coupon.

CASINO COUPON

AMERICAN CASINO GUIDE

National®   # Save up to 20%

- Book now at nationalcar.com or call 1-800-CAR-RENT®
- Mention Contract ID: 5028092
- Valid through December 31, 2015
- See reverse side for additional conditions or restrictions

CASINO COUPON

Terms and Conditions

Must present original coupon at time of rental. This promotional offer is not valid with any other discount/promotion. Discount applies to base rate only and is valid at participating Alamo locations in the U.S. and Canada through 12/31/15. Discount varies by rental date, location and vehicle type. Taxes, other governmentally authorized or imposed surcharges (including GST/ VAT), license and concession recoupment fees, airport and airport facility fees, fuel, one-way rental charge, and optional items (such as CDW up to US $30 per day) are extra. In the U.S. check your insurance and/or credit card for rental vehicle coverage. Renter and additional driver(s) must meet standard age, driver and credit requirements. 24-hour advance reservation is required. Availability is limited. Subject to change without notice. Blackout dates may apply. Void where prohibited. Alamo and Drive Happy are trademarks of Alamo Rent A Car. ©2014 Alamo Rent A Car. All rights reserved.

Terms and Conditions

Must present original coupon at time of rental. This promotional offer is not valid with any other discount/ promotion. Discount applies to base rate only and is valid at participating Alamo locations in the U.S. and Canada through 12/31/15. Discount varies by rental date, location and vehicle type. Taxes, other governmentally authorized or imposed surcharges (including GST/ VAT), license and concession recoupment fees, airport and airport facility fees, fuel, one-way rental charge, and optional items (such as CDW up to US $30 per day) are extra. In the U.S. check your insurance and/or credit card for rental vehicle coverage. Renter and additional driver(s) must meet standard age, driver and credit requirements. 24-hour advance reservation is required. Availability is limited. Subject to change without notice. Blackout dates may apply. Void where prohibited. ONE CAR CLASS UPGRADE: Offer valid when reserving a compact through standard vehicle in the U.S. and Canada. Valid through 12/31/2015. One coupon per Alamo rental and void once redeemed. Offer is subject to standard rental conditions. Blackout dates may apply. 24-hour advance reservation is required. Not valid with any other discount or promotional rate, except your American Casino Guide discount. Coupons are limited by pickup date, location and car type. Subject to availability and valid only at participating U.S. and Canada Alamo locations. Coupon VOID if bought, bartered or sold for cash. Void where prohibited. Alamo and Drive Happy are trademarks of Alamo Rent A Car. ©2014 Alamo Rent A Car. All rights reserved.

Terms and Conditions

Original coupon must be presented at time of rental. Up to 20% discount applies to base rate at participating National locations, through December 31, 2015. Taxes, other governmentally-authorized or imposed surcharges (including GST/VAT), license and concession recoupment fees, airport and airport facility fees, fuel, additional driver fee, one-way rental charge and optional items such as CDW up to US $30 per day are extra. In the U.S. check your insurance and/or credit card for rental vehicle coverage. Renter must meet standard age, driver and credit requirements. 24-hour advance reservation required. Availability is limited. Subject to change without notice. Blackout dates may apply. Void where prohibited. National, National Car Rental, and the "flag" are trademarks of Vanguard Trademark Holdings USA LLC. © 2014 National Car Rental. All rights reserved.

AMERICAN CASINO GUIDE

≋National®

$20 Off And Your Discount

- Book now at nationalcar.com or call 1-800-CAR-RENT®
- Mention Contract ID: 5028092 and Coupon Code: ND4410JDAF
- Promotion valid now through December 31, 2015
- Original coupon must be presented at time of rental
- See reverse side for additional conditions or restrictions

CASINO COUPON

AMERICAN CASINO GUIDE

≋National®

One Car Class Upgrade And Your Discount!

- Book online at nationalcar.com or call 1-800-CAR-RENT®
- Mention Contract ID: 5028092 and Coupon Code: NU25093JDB
- Promotion valid now through December 31, 2015
- See reverse side for additional conditions or restrictions

CASINO COUPON

AMERICAN CASINO GUIDE

GAMBLERS GENERAL STORE
THE WORLD'S LARGEST GAMBLING SUPERSTORE! OPEN 7 DAYS A WEEK!

**PERSONALIZED POKER CHIPS • SLOTS • ROULETTE • BLACKJACK • CRAPS
GAMBLING TABLES • RAFFLE DRUMS • AWARD WHEELS • BOOKS • VIDEOS**

10% Off Your Purchase!

Save 10% on your order from the largest Gambling Superstore in the world! We are located in Las Vegas, Nevada and offer genuine casino quality gaming products that can be used in casinos, homes, offices or parties.

CASINO COUPON

Terms and Conditions

Discount: Original coupon must be presented at time of rental. Up to 20% off discount applies to base rate only and valid at participating U.S. and Canada National locations. Discount varies by rental date, location and vehicle type. Taxes, other governmentally-authorized or imposed surcharges (including GST/VAT), license and concession recoupment fees, airport and airport facility fees, fuel, one-way rental charge and optional items (such as CDW up to U.S. $30 per day) are extra. In the U.S. check your insurance and/or credit card for rental vehicle coverage. Renter and additional driver(s) must meet standard age, driver and credit requirements. 24-hour advance reservation required. Availability is limited. Subject to change without notice. Blackout dates may apply. Void where prohibited. $20 OFF: Rent any size vehicle for a minimum of three (3) days with a Saturday night required. Valid through December 31, 2015. Offer subject to availability and valid only at participating U.S. and Canada National locations. One coupon per National rental and void once redeemed. Discount applies to base rate, which does not include taxes (including GST), other governmentally-authorized or imposed surcharges, license recoupment/air tax recovery and concession recoupment fees, airport and airport facility fees, fuel, additional driver fee, one-way rental charge, or optional items. Offer is subject to standard rental conditions. Blackout dates may apply. 24-hour advance reservation required. Not valid with any other discount or promotional rate, except your American Casino Guide discount. Coupon VOID if bought, bartered or sold for cash. Void where prohibited. National, National Car Rental, and the "flag" are trademarks of Vanguard Trademark Holdings USA LLC. © 2014 National Car Rental. All rights reserved.

Terms and Conditions

Discount: Original coupon must be presented at time of rental. Up to 20% off discount applies to base rate only and is valid at participating National locations. Discount varies by rental date, location and vehicle type. Taxes, other governmentally authorized or imposed surcharges (including GST/VAT), license and concession recoupment fees, airport and airport facility fees, fuel, one-way rental charge, and optional items (such as CDW up to US $30 per day) are extra. In the U.S. check your insurance and/or credit card for rental vehicle coverage. Renter and additional driver(s) must meet standard age, driver and credit requirements. 24-hour advance reservation is required. Availability is limited. Subject to change without notice. Blackout dates may apply. Void where prohibited. FREE UPGRADE: Rent a compact through Standard vehicle in the U.S. or Canada. Valid through December 31, 2015. One coupon per National rental and void once redeemed. Offer is subject to standard rental conditions. Blackout dates may apply. 24-hour advance reservation is required. Not valid with any other discount or promotional rate, except your American Casino Guide discount. Subject to availability and valid only at participating U.S. and Canada National locations. Coupon VOID if bought, bartered or sold for cash. In the U.S., offer valid for a one-car-class upgrade applied at the time of reservation. Void where prohibited. National, National Car Rental, and the "flag" are trademarks of Vanguard Trademark Holdings USA LLC. © 2014 National Car Rental. All rights reserved.

9:00AM-6:00PM Monday-Friday 9:00AM-5:00PM Sunday

CALL: (702) 382-9903 or (800) 322-2447
800 SOUTH MAIN STREET, LAS VEGAS, NEVADA 89101
Email: store@ggslv.com   Web: gamblersgeneralstore.com

Limit one coupon per order. Not valid with any other offer. Must present coupon at store, or mention code "ACG" when ordering by telephone or on our website. Valid through 12/31/15.

AMERICAN CASINO GUIDE

Buy 1 Hour, Get 1 Hour FREE

Hourly child care activity center
Caring for children 6 weeks to 12 years old.

kidsquest.com

Kids Quest activity center offers infant and toddler care, a Techno Quest video and arcade games area, a Karaoke Star Stage, gym, creative play activities, and an indoor playground, iPad Station, and birthday parties. (activities vary by center). Shoe-free, socks required.

CASINO COUPON

AMERICAN CASINO GUIDE

SLOTPLAY *Coupons*.com

5%Off Slot Play Discounts

Save an additional 5% off already discounted slot play at casinos all over the country from SlotPlayCoupons.com. See reverse for full details.

CASINO COUPON

AMERICAN CASINO GUIDE

DOUBLE EAGLE
HOTEL & CASINO
CRIPPLE CREEK, CO

GOLD CREEK CASINO
CRIPPLE CREEK, CO

Play $30 Get $10 FREE!

Play $30 and receive $10 in CasinoPlay. Must be a Premier Club member. Offer expires December 31, 2015.
See reverse for full details.

A current American Casino Guide Discount Card must be presented when redeeming this coupon, or offer is void

Present this coupon when you check in at any Kids Quest and receive the second hour of child care FREE with any purchase of the first hour. A photo ID required. Limit one coupon per family per visit. Not valid with any other offer. Non-transferable. Management reserves all rights. No cash value. No money back for unused time. Offer expires 12/31/15.

Valid at all Kids Quest locations. Las Vegas centers include Boulder Station, Red Rock Casino, Santa Fe Station, Sunset Station and Texas Station.

Am Cas Guide

For additional locations visit: www.kidsquest.com

Go to SlotPlayCoupons.com and enter the following promotion code, in your shopping cart, for the corresponding month in 2015 in which you are trying to redeem the coupon.

Jan - PNQ7KVWE	**July - H449M5XZ**
Feb - RWPH5SWF	**Aug - SWNHGJQV**
Mar - 82SVK4EY	**Sept - GJ5HY5WM**
April - ZN57XH9M	**Oct - F6T2QJT5**
May - 7PMX6R8N	**Nov - 8NRNVQ6X**
June - Q942Y47N	**Dec - EF9MRHJQ**

americancasinoguide.com

GOLD CREEK
CRIPPLE CREEK, CO

Gold Creek Casino
400 E. Bennett Avenue
Cripple Creek, CO 80813

(800) 711-7234
(719) 689-5000
www.decasino.com

DOUBLE EAGLE
HOTEL & CASINO
CRIPPLE CREEK, CO

Double Eagle Casino
442 E. Bennett Avenue
Cripple Creek, CO 80813

Must present coupon. Limit one coupon per customer per day. Not valid for use with any other coupons, ads or promotions. Must be 21 years of age and a Premier Club Member. Membership in Premier Club is free. Management reserves the right to cancel or change this promotion at any time. Valid through December 31, 2015

Offer void if coupon is copied or sold

AMERICAN CASINO GUIDE

2-4-1 Breakfast or Lunch buffet

MONARCH
CASINO • BLACK HAWK

Present this coupon with your Club Monarch card to the cashier at The Buffet and receive one *free* breakfast or lunch buffet with the purchase of a second buffet at the regular price. *See back for details.*

A current American Casino Guide Discount Card must be presented when redeeming this coupon, or offer is void

---

AMERICAN CASINO GUIDE

GET $25 FREE SLOT PLAY
SIGN UP TODAY!

Offer good for new Fan Club® members only.
Valid November 1, 2014 - December 30, 2015

A current American Casino Guide Discount Card must be presented when redeeming this coupon, or offer is void

---

AMERICAN CASINO GUIDE

MARDI GRAS CASINO

FREE Dessert with purchase of an Entrée

Present this coupon at The French Quarter Restaurant located on the 3rd floor to receive one dessert free when an entrée is purchased at regular menu price. See reverse for details.

A current American Casino Guide Discount Card must be presented when redeeming this coupon, or offer is void

MONARCH

CASINO • BLACK HAWK

P.O. Box 9 | 444 Main St.
Black Hawk, CO 80422 | 303.582.1000

Expires December 30, 2015. Valid daily.
Excludes holidays or special events. No cash
value. Gratuity not included. Must be 21. Not
valid in combination with any other offer.
Non-transferable. Management reserves all
rights. Must be a Club Monarch member.
*Not a member? Join today! It's fun, it's easy,
it's free.*

Club Member #_____

A C G 2 0 1 5 C 1

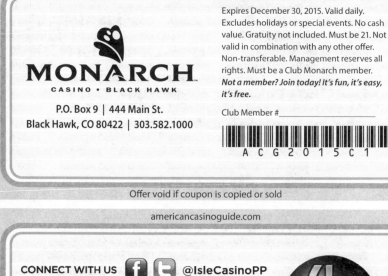

CONNECT WITH US @IsleCasinoPP

**777 ISLE OF CAPRI CIRCLE
POMPANO BEACH, FL 33069**

1-877-ISLE-2WIN
www.theislepompanopark.com

© 2013 Isle of Capri Casinos, Inc. Excluding holidays.
Cannot be combined with any other offer. Must be 21.
Gambling problem? Call 1-888-ADMIT-IT

Get Winning!
POMPANO PARK

MARDI GRAS CASINO

**831 N. Federal Highway
Hallandale Beach, FL 33009
(877) 557-5687
(954) 924-3200**

Must be 21 years of age to purchase & consume alcohol. Not valid on any other offer
or special. Limit one coupon per person. Cannot be combined with any other offer.

Original coupon must be presented (no photocopies). Tax and gratuity not included.
Management reserves the right to cancel or alter this coupon without prior notice.
Offer expires 12/30/15.

When gambling is no longer a game...call 1-888-ADMIT-IT.

AMERICAN CASINO GUIDE

MARDI GRAS CASINO

Receive $10 Bonus Play

Present this coupon at the Mardi Gras Casino Players' Club to receive $10 free bonus play. See reverse for details.

A current American Casino Guide Discount Card must be presented when redeeming this coupon, or offer is void

---

AMERICAN CASINO GUIDE

MARDI GRAS CASINO

Buy One Entrée, Get One FREE

Present this coupon at the French Quarter Restaurant and Bar to receive one entrée free when an entrée is purchased at regular menu price. See reverse for details.

A current American Casino Guide Discount Card must be presented when redeeming this coupon, or offer is void

---

AMERICAN CASINO GUIDE

Harrah's JOLIET

Buy One Buffet Get One FREE

Present this coupon at Flavors The Buffet, along with you Total Rewards® card, to receive one FREE buffet with the purchase of one buffet. All ages welcome. See reverse for full details.

A current American Casino Guide Discount Card must be presented when redeeming this coupon, or offer is void

MARDI GRAS CASINO

831 N. Federal Highway
Hallandale Beach, FL 33009
(877) 557-5687
(954) 924-3200

Must be 21 years of age or older and a Players' Club Member. Membership is free. Cannot be redeemed for cash. No reproduction allowed. Bonus play is not transferable into or out of the State of Florida.

Bonus play will be downloaded onto your Players' Club card. Management reserves the right to modify, amend or cancel this coupon at any time. Offer expires 12/30/15 and is valid once per year. The State of Florida assumes no liability. Limit one coupon per account per year. When gambling is no longer a game... call 1-888-ADMIT-IT.

MARDI GRAS CASINO

831 N. Federal Highway
Hallandale Beach, FL 33009
(877) 557-5687
(954) 924-3200

Must be 21 years of age to purchase & consume alcohol. Free entrée must be of equal or lesser value than purchased entrée. Not valid on any other offer or special. Cannot be combined with any other offer.

Limit one coupon per person. Original coupon must be presented (no photocopies). Tax and gratuity not included. Management reserves the right to cancel or alter this coupon without prior notice. Offer expires 12/30/15. When gambling is no longer a game… call 1-888-ADMIT-IT.

Harrah's
JOLIET

151 N. Joliet Street
Joliet, IL 60432
(815) 740-7800
harrahsjoliet.com

Offer valid on cash purchases only. Valid for dine in only. Alcohol and gratuity not included. Some restrictions apply. Not valid at any other outlet. See Total Rewards for complete details. Valid Total Rewards card required. In some cases a valid government issued picture ID may also be required. Subject to rules available at venue. This offer is non-transferable, non-negotiable, subject to availability, cannot be combined with any other discount, promotion or complimentary offer. Alteration, duplication or unauthorized use voids this offer. Some blackout dates may apply. Harrah's reserves the right to change or cancel this program at any time upon IGB approval. Harrah's employees and their immediate families are not eligible. Must be 21 years or older to gamble. Know When Stop Before You Start® If you or someone you know has a gambling problem, crisis counseling and referral services can be accessed by calling 1-800-GAMBLER (1-800-426-2537). ©2014, Caesars License Company, LLC. All rights reserved. Offer expires 12/30/15.

PAR·A·DICE

HOTEL·CASINO
EAST PEORIA, ILLINOIS

2-For-1 Buffet

Buy one Options Buffet and get the second buffet free. Coupon has
no cash value, must be 21 years of age or older. Present this coupon along
with B Connected Card and state identification to the Options Buffet.
See reverse for full details.

A current American Casino Guide Discount Card must be
presented when redeeming this coupon, or offer is void

PAR·A·DICE

HOTEL·CASINO
EAST PEORIA, ILLINOIS

$69 Room Rate

Sunday-Thursday

Present coupon at check-in. Blackout dates may apply. Subject to
availability. Valid for one day only. See reverse for full details.

A current American Casino Guide Discount Card must be
presented when redeeming this coupon, or offer is void

PAR·A·DICE

HOTEL·CASINO
EAST PEORIA, ILLINOIS

$10 in Free Slot Dollars For New Members

Present coupon and valid government issued photo ID to the
B Connected Club when enrolling as a new member of the
B Connected Club and receive $10 in slot play. Downloadable
slot play will be added to new account. See reverse for full details.

A current American Casino Guide Discount Card must be
presented when redeeming this coupon, or offer is void

americancasinoguide.com

21 Blackjack Blvd
East Peoria, IL 61611
(309) 699-7711
paradicecasino.com

Not valid with other offers or on Holidays. One coupon per person per valid dates. Non-transferable. Gratuity not included. Coupons not replaced if lost or stolen. Must be 21. Valid Military I.D., Passport, Driver's License, or State I.D. Card required. Other restrictions may apply. Valid through 12/30/2015. If you or someone you know has a gambling problem, crisis counseling and referral services can be accessed by calling 1-800-GAMBLER (1-800-426-2537)

Offer void if coupon is copied or sold

americancasinoguide.com

21 Blackjack Blvd
East Peoria, IL 61611
(309) 699-7711
paradicecasino.com

No holidays. Valid one day only. Not valid with other offers. Subject to availability. Non-transferable. Must be 21. Valid Military I.D., Passport, Driver's License, or State I.D. Card required. Room deposit required upon check-in. Hotel stays limited to 7 consecutive nights. Other restrictions may apply. Valid through 10/31/2015. If you or someone you know has a gambling problem, crisis counseling and referral services can be accessed by calling 1-800-GAMBLER (1-800-426-2537)

Offer void if coupon is copied or sold

americancasinoguide.com

21 Blackjack Blvd
East Peoria, IL 61611
(309) 699-7711
paradicecasino.com

Slot Dollars are non-transferable and non-cashable. See B Connected Club for more information. All downloaded Slot Dollars must be played off of machine and are valid until the end of the gaming day earned. Unauthorized use or alteration of coupons voids its use. Valid for new sign ups only. Valid through 12/30/2015. If you or someone you know has a gambling problem, crisis counseling and referral services can be accessed by calling 1-800-GAMBLER (1-800-426-2537)

Offer void if coupon is copied or sold

AMERICAN CASINO GUIDE

DELTA DOWNS®
RACETRACK ◆ CASINO ◆ HOTEL
2-For-1 Buffet

Buy one buffet and get a second one FREE. Coupon has no cash value, must be 21 years of age or older. Must be a B Connected member to redeem. See reverse for full details.

Offer Code: CBFAAPAK6

A current American Casino Guide Discount Card must be presented when redeeming this coupon, or offer is void

AMERICAN CASINO GUIDE

DELTA DOWNS®
RACETRACK ◆ CASINO ◆ HOTEL
Get 2,000 Points or a Free T-Shirt

Present this coupon to the B connected Club and receive 2,000 points or a free T-Shirt. Valid for New Card Members only. See reverse for more details.

A current American Casino Guide Discount Card must be presented when redeeming this coupon, or offer is void

AMERICAN CASINO GUIDE

TREASURE CHEST CASINO
KENNER, LOUISIANA

2-For-1
Buffet
(or 50% off when dining alone)

Present this coupon along with B Connected Card and state identification to the Treasure Island Buffet to get two lunch or dinner buffets for the price of one (or 50% off when dining alone). Coupon has no cash value, must be 21 years of age or older. See reverse for full details.

A current American Casino Guide Discount Card must be presented when redeeming this coupon, or offer is void

americancasinoguide.com

2717 Delta Downs Drive
Vinton, LA 70668
(800) 589-7441
www.deltadowns.com

Gratuities not included. Offer has no cash value. Valid only at Delta Downs. This offer cannot be used with any other offer. Offers are made at the sole discretion of Delta Downs and are subject to change or cancellation without prior notice. Valid state or government issued photo ID may be required for redemption. Unauthorized use or alteration of coupon voids its use. Original coupon (no photocopies) must be presented at the time of purchase. Delta Downs is not responsible for lost, misplaced or stolen coupons. Employees of Delta Downs are ineligible to participate in these offers. Disregard if prohibited from visiting Louisiana casinos. Management reserves all rights. Offer expires December 23, 2015

Offer void if coupon is copied or sold

americancasinoguide.com

2717 Delta Downs Drive
Vinton, LA 70668
(800) 589-7441
www.deltadowns.com

Valid only at Delta Downs. This offer cannot be used with any other offer and has no cash value. Offers are made at the sole discretion of Delta Downs and are subject to change or cancellation without prior notice. Valid state or government issued photo ID may be required for redemption. Unauthorized use or alteration of coupon voids its use. Original coupon (no photocopies) must be presented at the time of purchase. Delta Downs is not responsible for lost, misplaced or stolen coupons. Employees of Delta Downs are ineligible to participate in these offers. Disregard if prohibited from visiting Louisiana casinos. Management reserves all rights. While supplies last. Offer expires December 23, 2015

Offer void if coupon is copied or sold

americancasinoguide.com

KENNER, LOUISIANA

5050 Williams Boulevard
Kenner, LA, 70065
(800) 298-0711
www.treasurechest.com

Must be 21 or older and member of B Connected. Not valid on holidays or special priced buffet days. Cannot be combined with other offers. Limit one per person. Valid one time only. Management reserves the rights to change or cancel this offer at any time. Other restrictions apply. Expires 12/30/2015. Gambling Problem? Call 1-877-770-STOP (7867).

Offer Code: **85-400**

Offer void if coupon is copied or sold

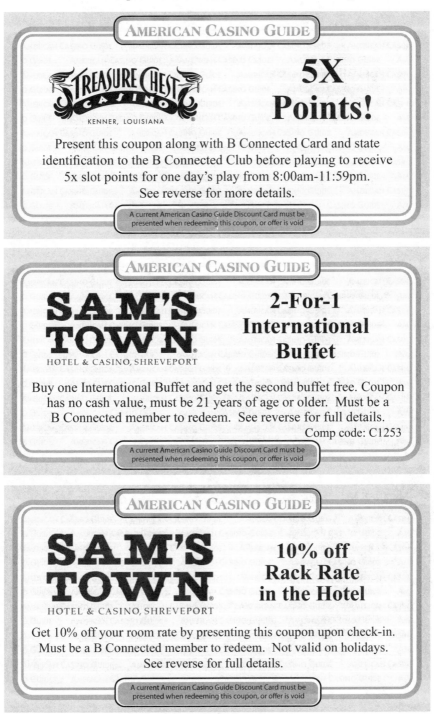

AMERICAN CASINO GUIDE

KENNER, LOUISIANA

5X Points!

Present this coupon along with B Connected Card and state identification to the B Connected Club before playing to receive 5x slot points for one day's play from 8:00am-11:59pm.
See reverse for more details.

A current American Casino Guide Discount Card must be presented when redeeming this coupon, or offer is void

---

AMERICAN CASINO GUIDE

SAM'S TOWN
HOTEL & CASINO, SHREVEPORT

2-For-1 International Buffet

Buy one International Buffet and get the second buffet free. Coupon has no cash value, must be 21 years of age or older. Must be a B Connected member to redeem. See reverse for full details.

Comp code: C1253

A current American Casino Guide Discount Card must be presented when redeeming this coupon, or offer is void

---

AMERICAN CASINO GUIDE

SAM'S TOWN
HOTEL & CASINO, SHREVEPORT

10% off Rack Rate in the Hotel

Get 10% off your room rate by presenting this coupon upon check-in.
Must be a B Connected member to redeem. Not valid on holidays.
See reverse for full details.

A current American Casino Guide Discount Card must be presented when redeeming this coupon, or offer is void

KENNER, LOUISIANA

**5050 Williams Boulevard
Kenner, LA, 70065
(800) 298-0711
www.treasurechest.com**

Must be 21 or older and member of B Connected. Multiplier valid up to 6,000 slot points for a maximum of 30,000 slot points. Not valid with other point offers. Valid from 8am-midnight. Valid one time only. One offer per person. Please allow up to 48 hours for points to be added to B Connected account. Management reserves the rights to change or cancel this offer at any time. Other restrictions apply. Expires 12/30/2015. Gambling Problem? Call 1-877-770-STOP (7867).

**315 Clyde Fant Parkway
Shreveport, Louisiana 71101
(318) 429-0711 • (877) 429-0711
www.samstownshreveport.com**

Must present the actual coupon to receive this offer. Online printed copies not valid. Valid at International Buffet Only. Gratuity not included. Valid at Sam's Town Shreveport only. Must be 21 years of age or older to redeem this offer. Offer is non-transferrable. One discount per person per coupon. This coupon good for one visit only; unredeemed balance not available for later use. No cash value. Not valid on holidays. Valid Photo I.D. and B Connected card required. Certain blackout dates may apply. Management reserves all rights. Expires 12/24/15. Gambling problem? Call (877) 770-7867.

**315 Clyde Fant Parkway
Shreveport, Louisiana 71101
(318) 429-0711 • (877) 429-0711
www.samstownshreveport.com**

Valid at Sam's Town Shreveport only. Offer cannot be combined with any other promotion, coupon, special event or discount. Must be 21 years of age or older to redeem this offer. Present this coupon and a valid ID upon check-in. Subject to availability. Room types not guaranteed. Not valid on holidays. A refundable deposit of $50 is due upon check-in. Nights must be consecutive. Credit Card will be charged first night's room/tax at time of reservation. Cancellation must be made 24 hours in advance to receive full refund. Certain blackout dates may apply. Boyd Gaming is not responsible for typographical errors. Expires 12/24/15. Gambling problem? Call 1-877-770-7867.

SAM'S TOWN
HOTEL & CASINO, SHREVEPORT

$5 in Free Slot Dollars For New Members

Present coupon and valid government issued photo ID to the
B Connected Club when enrolling as a new member of the
B Connected Club and receive $5 in slot play. Downloadable
slot play will be added to new account. See reverse for full details.

A current American Casino Guide Discount Card must be
presented when redeeming this coupon, or offer is void

SILVER SLIPPER

Buy One Buffet Get One Free!
(or 50% off when dining alone)

Buy one lunch or dinner at Jubilee Buffet
and get one free (or 50% off when
dining alone). See reverse for details.

A current American Casino Guide Discount Card must be
presented when redeeming this coupon, or offer is void

Coast

25% off at Coast Restaurant

Present this coupon to your server at Coast Restaurant during lunch or dinner
before ordering to receive 25% off your bill. See reverse for full details.

A current American Casino Guide Discount Card must be
presented when redeeming this coupon, or offer is void

AMERICAN CASINO GUIDE

25% off
Back Bay Buffet

Redeem at the Back Bay Buffet to
receive 25% OFF admission. Must be
21 years of age or older. Must be a
B Connected member to redeem.
See reverse for full details.

Casino • Resort • Spa
BILOXI, MISSISSIPPI

GL# 45-870-7020

A current American Casino Guide Discount Card must be
presented when redeeming this coupon, or offer is void

AMERICAN CASINO GUIDE

10% off
Prevailing Rate
in the Hotel

Get 10% off your room rate by calling
(888) 946-2847 to reserve and mention
offer code IPACG15. Must be 21 and
a B Connected Member. Not valid on
holidays and subject to availability. See
reverse for full details.

Casino • Resort • Spa
BILOXI, MISSISSIPPI

A current American Casino Guide Discount Card must be
presented when redeeming this coupon, or offer is void

AMERICAN CASINO GUIDE

HOLLYWOOD
Casino®
TUNICA, MS

Buy One
Epic Buffet and
Get One Free!

Enjoy two buffets for the price of one at Hollywood's Epic Buffet!
Dine and play among movie memorabilia in an authentic
Hollywood atmosphere 7 days a week! See reverse for details.

Exp: 12/31/15

#87005

A current American Casino Guide Discount Card must be
presented when redeeming this coupon, or offer is void

americancasinoguide.com

Casino • Resort • Spa

BILOXI, MISSISSIPPI

850 Bayview Ave
Biloxi, MS 39530
(888) 946-2847
www.ipbiloxi.com

Present this coupon, your B Connected Card and a valid photo ID to the cashier. Valid only at Back Bay Buffet at IP Casino Resort Spa in Biloxi, MS. Valid on cash or credit card purchases only. Not valid with any other offer. Management reserves all rights. Limit one coupon per person per day. Limit one transaction per coupon. Gratuity not included. No cash value. Valid through 12/29/2015. Don't Let The Game Get Out Of Hand. Gambling Problem? Call 1-888-777-9696.

Offer void if coupon is copied or sold

americancasinoguide.com

Casino • Resort • Spa

BILOXI, MISSISSIPPI

850 Bayview Ave
Biloxi, MS 39530
(888) 946-2847
www.ipbiloxi.com

Valid photo ID, coupon and credit card required at check-in. Not valid with any other coupon for back to back stays. Advance reservations and credit card upon booking required to guarantee room. Guest must be 21 or older and a B Connected member. Check-in time is 4:00PM. Valid for one standard room. Limit two people. Limit one coupon per person. Limited based on availability.Reservations not cancelled at least 24 hours in advance will result in total room rate (one day plus tax) being charged to credit card. Blackout dates apply. Offer is non-refundable. Not valid with any other promotion, group, or convention. Valid only at IP Casino Resort Spa in Biloxi, MS. Management reserves all rights. A resort fee of $5.00 plus tax, per night, will be applied. Valid through 12/29/2015. Don't Let The Game Get Out Of Hand. Gambling Problem? Call 1-888-777-9696.

Offer void if coupon is copied or sold

americancasinoguide.com

Sign up for a Marquee Rewards® card at the Player Services Counter. Marquee Rewards cards are free with valid, state issued ID. Then present this coupon at the Epic Buffet along with your Marquee Rewards card to receive your buy-one-get-one-free Epic Buffet® offer. Must be 21 years of age or older to redeem.

Hollywood Casino Tunica reserves the right to modify or cancel this promotion at anytime without prior notice. Offer not valid on Friday or Saturday. This coupon cannot be combined with any other promotion. Valid only at Hollywood Casino Tunica. Not transferable. One coupon per Player account. Offer void if sold. Offer expires 12/31/15.

TUNICA, MS
1150 Casino Strip Resorts Blvd.
Tunica Resorts, MS 38664
(800) 871-0711
(662) 357-7700

hollywoodcasinotunica.com

Offer void if coupon is copied or sold

AMERICAN CASINO GUIDE

HOLLYWOOD Casino®

TUNICA, MS

Room Rates From $59 (Sun-Thu)

Special packages available! Call 1-800-871-0711 for reservations. See reverse for details.

Exp: 12/31/15

A current American Casino Guide Discount Card must be presented when redeeming this coupon, or offer is void

---

AMERICAN CASINO GUIDE

GOLD STRIKE
HOTEL & GAMBLING HALL®

2-for-1 Buffet for Club Members!

Buy one buffet at Gold Strike and get a second buffet FREE! See reverse for details.

Settle to: 1895

A current American Casino Guide Discount Card must be presented when redeeming this coupon, or offer is void

---

AMERICAN CASINO GUIDE

GRAND LODGE CASINO
AT HYATT REGENCY LAKE TAHOE

$10 FREE Slot Play or $10 Matchplay!

New members only, present this coupon at the Players Advantage Club® booth, sign up for card and receive $10 in FREE slot play or a $10 table games matchplay. See reverse for more details.

A current American Casino Guide Discount Card must be presented when redeeming this coupon, or offer is void

Offer valid for American Casino Guide readers. Must be 21 years of age or older. Subject to availability. Valid for one night only, must present coupon.

Offer subject to change or cancellation at any time without prior notice. Valid only at Hollywood Casino Tunica. Not transferable. One coupon per Player account. Offer void if sold. Offer expires 12/31/15.

TUNICA, MS
**1150 Casino Strip Resorts Blvd.
Tunica Resorts, MS 38664
(800) 871-0711
(662) 357-7700**

hollywoodcasinotunica.com

**1 Main Street
Jean, NV 89019
(800) 634-1359
www.stopatjean.com**

To Redeem: 1) present this coupon with card (or join club) at the hotel front desk or table games manager to receive a validation slip. 2) Present this coupon and validation slip to the buffet cashier.

Must be at least 21 years of age and a member of, or join, Gold Strike's Cash & Comp Club. Offer may not be combined with any other offers or programs. Limit one redemption per club account. Offer not valid to employees of Gold Strike. Management reserves all rights. Offer expires 12/30/15.

**Jean is located at Exit 12 off I-15
Just 20 minutes south of the world famous Las Vegas Strip.**

**111 Country Club Drive
Incline Village, NV 89451
(775) 832-1234
(800) 327-3910**

Must be 21 years of age, or older. New accounts only. One offer per account. Management reserves the right to alter or change promotion at any time. Expires 12/31/15.

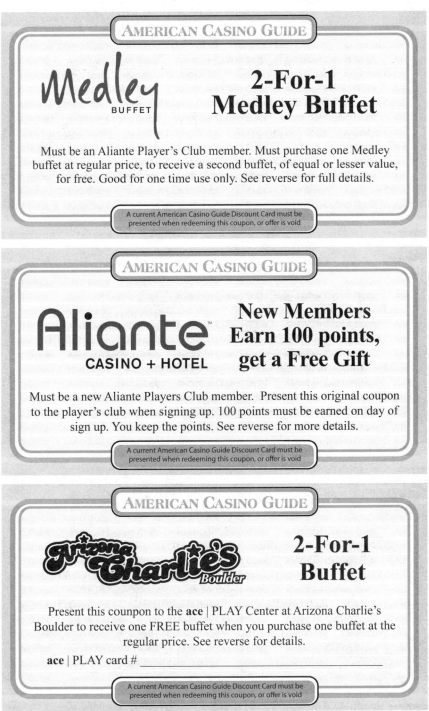

AMERICAN CASINO GUIDE

Medley BUFFET

2-For-1 Medley Buffet

Must be an Aliante Player's Club member. Must purchase one Medley buffet at regular price, to receive a second buffet, of equal or lesser value, for free. Good for one time use only. See reverse for full details.

A current American Casino Guide Discount Card must be presented when redeeming this coupon, or offer is void

AMERICAN CASINO GUIDE

Aliante CASINO + HOTEL

New Members Earn 100 points, get a Free Gift

Must be a new Aliante Players Club member. Present this original coupon to the player's club when signing up. 100 points must be earned on day of sign up. You keep the points. See reverse for more details.

A current American Casino Guide Discount Card must be presented when redeeming this coupon, or offer is void

AMERICAN CASINO GUIDE

Arizona Charlie's Boulder

2-For-1 Buffet

Present this counpon to the **ace | PLAY** Center at Arizona Charlie's Boulder to receive one FREE buffet when you purchase one buffet at the regular price. See reverse for details.

ace | PLAY card # _____

A current American Casino Guide Discount Card must be presented when redeeming this coupon, or offer is void

americancasinoguide.com

Aliante™
CASINO + HOTEL

7300 N Aliante Pkwy
North Las Vegas, NV 89084
www.aliantegaming.com
702-692-7777

Present this coupon at the Rewards Center to receive one coupon for a buy one get one free buffet at Medley Buffet. Must be an Aliante Players Club member. Membership is free. Gratuity not included. No cash value. Not valid with any other offer. Must be 21 years of age or older to redeem. Not valid with any other offer. Management reserves all rights. Not valid on holidays. Expires 12/30/2015. Settle to 49640

Offer void if coupon is copied or sold

americancasinoguide.com

Aliante™
CASINO + HOTEL

7300 N Aliante Pkwy
North Las Vegas, NV 89084
www.aliantegaming.com
702-692-7777

New members only. Must sign up for an Aliante Players Club card. Earn 100 points and present this coupon at the Rewards Center to receive a free gift. 100 points must be earned on day of sign up. Must be 21 years of age or older. Not valid with any other offer. Management reserves all rights. Expires 12/31/2015.

Offer void if coupon is copied or sold

americancasinoguide.com

4575 Boulder Highway
Las Vegas, NV 89121
702.951.5800
800.362.4040
ArizonaCharliesBoulder.com

Must be 21 years of age or older. Must present **ace | PLAY** card and surrender the original coupon (no photocopies) to the **ace | PLAY** Center representative for a voucher. Resale prohibited. No cash value. Maximum two people per coupon. Tax and tip are not included. Not valid for takeout. Management reserves the right to change or cancel this promotion at any time without notice. Valid through December 19, 2015.

Offer void if coupon is copied or sold

Here is your
American Casino Guide
Discount Card.

Cut out this card
and carry it with you!

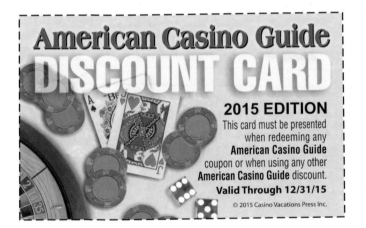

You **must** present this card to a
merchant whenever you redeem an
American Casino Guide coupon.

Do not lose this card.
No replacements will be given.

This card identifies you as the purchaser of an *American Casino Guide* and it entitles you to all of the benefits offered through our coupon program.

Print Name

Valid through December 31, 2015

This card **must be presented** when redeeming any *American Casino Guide* coupon or when using any other *American Casino Guide* discount.

…

AMERICAN CASINO GUIDE

2-For-1 Buffet

Present this counpon to the **ace** | PLAY Center at Arizona Charlie's Decatur to receive one FREE buffet when you purchase one buffet at the regular price. See reverse for details.

ace | PLAY card # _____

AMERICAN CASINO GUIDE

the SPA at BALLY'S   20% OFF   THE salon at BALLY'S

Redeem at the Bally's Spa or Salon for 20% off any service. See reverse for details.

AMERICAN CASINO GUIDE

BALLY'S LAS VEGAS

20% OFF ONE ITEM

Redeem at select Bally's stores for 20% off your purchase of one item. See reverse for details.

Offer code: GUIDE CPN

740 S. Decatur Boulevard
Las Vegas, NV 89107
702.258.5200
800.342.2695
ArizonaCharliesDecatur.com

Must be 21 years of age or older. Must present **ace | PLAY** card and surrender the original coupon (no photocopies) to the **ace | PLAY** Center representative for a voucher. Resale prohibited. No cash value. Maximum two people per coupon. Tax and tip are not included. Not valid for takeout. Management reserves the right to change or cancel this promotion at any time without notice. Valid through December 19, 2015.

3645 Las Vegas Blvd. S.
Las Vegas, NV 89109
702-967-4111
BallysLasVegas.com

Limit 1 coupon per guest. No cash value. Not valid on previously purchased services. Cannot be combined with any other offer. Subject to availability. Blackout dates may apply. Management reserves all rights. Offer subject to change or cancellation without notification. Offer expires 12/30/15.

3645 Las Vegas Blvd. S.
Las Vegas, NV 89109
702-967-4111
BallysLasVegas.com

Valid at Bally's Avenue Shop, Signatures Shop, Splashes Pool Shop (Seasonal), Les Elements Shop and The Strip. Not valid on previous purchases. Limit 1 coupon per guest. No cash value. Not valid on previously purchased tickets. Cannot be combined with any other offer. Subject to availability. Blackout dates may apply. Management reserves all rights. Offer subject to change or cancellation without notification. Offer Expires 12/30/15.

$5 Blackjack Matchplay

Present this coupon at any blackjack table, along with your Bigshot Players Club card, prior to the start of a hand and we'll match your bet of $5 if you win. See reverse for details.

A current American Casino Guide Discount Card must be presented when redeeming this coupon, or offer is void

2-for-1 Lunch or Dinner Entrée

Buy one lunch or dinner entrée in our restaurant and get one entrée of equal or lesser value FREE! Present to server before ordering. See reverse for more details.

A current American Casino Guide Discount Card must be presented when redeeming this coupon, or offer is void

2,000 Slot Club Points For New Members

Present this coupon at the Bigshot Players Club booth to receive 2,000 FREE slot club points when you join as a new member. See reverse for more details.

A current American Casino Guide Discount Card must be presented when redeeming this coupon, or offer is void

3016 E. Lake Mead Blvd.
N. Las Vegas, NV 89030
(702) 642-1940

Limit: one coupon per person, per month. Cannot be redeemed for cash. Must be 21 or older. Cannot be combined with any other offer or promotion. Non-transferable. Offer void if sold.

Must present original coupon (no photocopies). Not responsible for lost or stolen coupon. Management reserves all rights. Offer may be changed or discontinued at anytime at the discretion of management. Offer expires December 30, 2015.

3016 E. Lake Mead Blvd.
N. Las Vegas, NV 89030
(702) 642-1940

Limit one coupon per person. Must be 21 years or older. Purchase one lunch or dinner entrée to receive the second one of equal or lesser value free. Not valid on take out orders. Coupon is void if altered or duplicated. Must present original coupon (no photocopies).

Tax, beverages and gratuity are not included. Not valid with any other offers or discounts. Management reserves the right to cancel or modify offer at any time. Coupon has no cash value. Offer expires December 30, 2015.

3016 E. Lake Mead Blvd.
N. Las Vegas, NV 89030
(702) 642-1940

Valid for new accounts only. Must be 21 or older. Cannot be combined with any other offer or promotion. Non-transferable. Offer void if sold. Please allow up to 72 hours for points to reflect on account balance.

Must present original coupon (no photocopies). Not responsible for lost or stolen coupon. Management reserves all rights. Offer may be changed or discontinued at anytime at the discretion of management. Offer expires December 30, 2015.

Downtown Las Vegas Since 1951

Binion's

Gambling Hall & Hotel

**Double Points
(Up to 500)
for members of
Club Binion's**

Double your Club Binion's points (up to 500)
with this coupon! See reverse for more details.

Downtown Las Vegas Since 1951

Binion's

Gambling Hall & Hotel

**2-for-1 Binion's
Famous Hamburger
at Binion's Café**

Buy one of Binion's famous hamburgers at Binion's Café
and get one FREE! See reverse for more details.

**Bonanno's
NEW YORK PIZZERIA
Buy One Pizza Get One Free**

Present this coupon at Bonanno's New York Pizzeria, purchase a whole
pizza and get a second whole pizza free! See reverse for details.

Downtown Las Vegas Since 1951

Binion's

Gambling Hall & Hotel

128 East Fremont St.
Las Vegas, NV 89101
800.937.6537 • 702.382.1600
www.binions.com

Strictly limited to one coupon per person per 12 month period. Coupon has no cash value. Must be 21 years or older. Points must be earned on day of redemption. Offer valid for Club Binion's members only. Double points will be added to account within 48 hours. Management reserves the right to cancel or modify offer at any time without notice. Coupon is void if altered or duplicated. Offer expires December 27, 2015.

Downtown Las Vegas Since 1951

Binion's

Gambling Hall & Hotel

128 East Fremont St.
Las Vegas, NV 89101
800.937.6537 • 702.382.1600
www.binions.com

Strictly limited to one coupon per person per 12 month period. Must be 21 years or older. Must redeem coupon at Club Binion's to receive voucher for Binion's Café. Purchase one hamburger to receive the second one free. Offer valid only at Binion's Café. Coupon is void if altered or duplicated. Tax, alcoholic beverages and gratuity are not included. Not valid with any other offers or discounts. Management reserves the right to cancel or modify offer at any time. Coupon has no cash value. Offer expires December 27, 2015.

Palace Station Food Court
MGM Grand Food Court
Luxor Food Court
Flamingo Food Court
Mandalay Bay Food Court

Must present coupon to cashier prior to ordering. Offer has no cash value. Not valid with any other offer. One coupon per person. Subject to change or cancellation without prior notice. Offer valid through December 31, 2015.

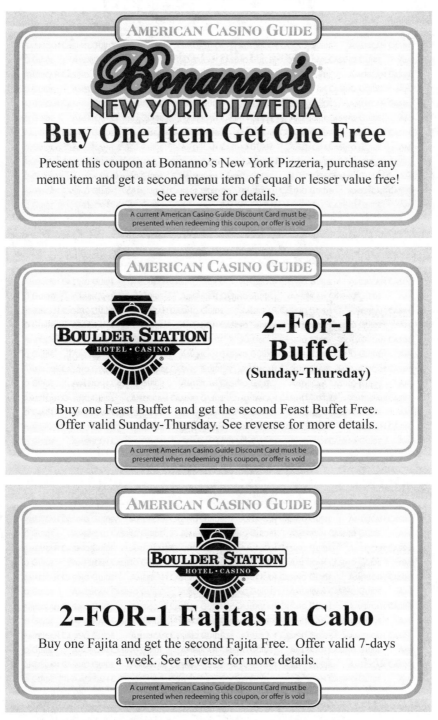

Bonanno's
NEW YORK PIZZERIA
Buy One Item Get One Free

Present this coupon at Bonanno's New York Pizzeria, purchase any
menu item and get a second menu item of equal or lesser value free!
See reverse for details.

A current American Casino Guide Discount Card must be
presented when redeeming this coupon, or offer is void

BOULDER STATION
HOTEL · CASINO

2-For-1
Buffet
(Sunday-Thursday)

Buy one Feast Buffet and get the second Feast Buffet Free.
Offer valid Sunday-Thursday. See reverse for more details.

A current American Casino Guide Discount Card must be
presented when redeeming this coupon, or offer is void

BOULDER STATION
HOTEL · CASINO

2-FOR-1 Fajitas in Cabo

Buy one Fajita and get the second Fajita Free. Offer valid 7-days
a week. See reverse for more details.

A current American Casino Guide Discount Card must be
presented when redeeming this coupon, or offer is void

americancasinoguide.com

Palace Station Food Court
MGM Grand Food Court
Luxor Food Court
Flamingo Food Court
Mandalay Bay Food Court

Must present coupon to cashier prior to ordering. Offer has no cash value. Not valid with any other offer. One coupon per person. Subject to change or cancellation without prior notice. Offer valid through December 31, 2015.

americancasinoguide.com

4111 Boulder Hwy
Las Vegas, NV 89121
(702) 432-7777
www.boulderstation.com

This voucher entitles bearer to one free breakfast, lunch or dinner in the Feast Buffet when accompanied by a cash paying guest. Tax and gratuity not included. One voucher per person/subscriber. Voucher must be presented to cashier. Vouchers are not transferable and are not redeemable for cash. Must be 21 or older. Not a line pass. Not valid on holidays, Not valid with any other offer. Offer may be changed or discontinued at any time at the discretion of management. Original vouchers only. Offer is void if sold. Offer expires 12/23/15. Settle to: #88-942

americancasinoguide.com

4111 Boulder Hwy
Las Vegas, NV 89121
(702) 432-7777
www.boulderstation.com

Tax and gratuity not included. One voucher per person/subscriber. Voucher must be presented to cashier. Vouchers are not transferable and are not redeemable for cash. Must be 21 or older. Not a line pass. Not valid on holidays, Not valid with any other offer. Offer may be changed or discontinued at any time at the discretion of managemnt. Original vouchers only. Offer is void if sold. Offer expires December 23, 2015. Settle To: #82-824

3570 Las Vegas Blvd. S
Las Vegas, NV 89109
702-731-7110
CaesarsPalace.com

Present coupon at time of purchase to redeem. Limit 2 per coupon. No cash value. Not valid on previously purchased tickets. Cannot be combined with any other offer. Subject to availability. Blackout dates may apply. Management reserves all rights. Offer subject to change or cancellation without notification. Offer Expires 12/30/15.

12 East Ogden Avenue
Las Vegas, NV 89101
(800) 634-6505
www.thecal.com

Must be 21 or older and have an active B Connected card. Not valid on holidays. Earn 250 base points playing slots on the same day original coupon is presented to the B Connected Club for redemption. Limit one coupon per person. Excludes dinner and specialty night buffets. Coupon has no cash value, cannot be combined with any other offer, or used more than once. Reproduction, sale, barter, or transfer are prohibited and render this coupon void. Management reserves all rights to change or discontinue this offer without notice. Expires 12/30/2015. Offer Code: BYCA0ZZK6

12 East Ogden Avenue
Las Vegas, NV 89101
(800) 634-6505
www.thecal.com

This voucher entitles the bearer to one free room night at the California Hotel and Casino, with the purchase of two room nights at the prevailing rate. Advance reservations required. Voucher must be presented upon check-in. Offer is not valid in conjunction with any other offer. Management reserves all rights to cancel this promotion without notification. Credit card required at the time of reservation and at check in. Guest is responsible for all incidental charges. Must be 21 or older. One free room per person. Offer expires December 28, 2015. This voucher has no cash value, cannot be combined with any other offer or used more than once.

CALIFORNIA
HOTEL · CASINO · LAS VEGAS

FREMONT
HOTEL & CASINO

MAIN STREET STATION
CASINO · BREWERY · HOTEL

New Members Play $25 Get $10

Present this coupon when signing up for a new B Connected
card to be eligible for Play $25 and Get $10 slot play.
See reverse for full details.

A current American Casino Guide Discount Card must be
presented when redeeming this coupon, or offer is void

the **D** LAS VEGAS

Get out of Blackjack Hand for Free
(push your bet on 22)

Redeem this coupon at player's club and have your bet pushed when you
get a 22. Maximum $25 bet. See reverse side for full details.

A current American Casino Guide Discount Card must be
presented when redeeming this coupon, or offer is void

the **D** LAS VEGAS

$25 Match Play for New Members

Bet $25 on any even-money bet and we'll pay you $50 if you win. Present
this coupon at Club D to receive your FREE $25 match play. Offer valid for
new members only. See reverse side for full details.

A current American Casino Guide Discount Card must be
presented when redeeming this coupon, or offer is void

California Hotel Casino	Fremont Hotel & Casino	Main Street Station
12 East Ogden Avenue	200 Fremont St	200 North Main Street
Las Vegas, NV 89101	Las Vegas, NV 89101	Las Vegas, NV 89101
(800) 634-6505	(800) 634-6460	(800) 713-8933
www.thecal.com	www.fremontcasino.com	www.mainstreetcasino.com

Present this coupon when signing up for a new B Connected card at your choice of casinos - the California, Fremont, or Main Street Station to be eligible for the Play & Get slot play. One Play & Get offer per new B Connected account. Slot play refers to non-cashable downloadable machine credits and will be uploaded to your B Connected account, pin number is required. Slot play is non-transferable and cannot be used with any other offer. You must be 21 or over to participate. Slot play will expire 24 hrs after coupon redemption. Management reserves the right to modify or cancel this promotion without prior notice. See the B Connected Club for additional details. Expires 12/30/2015. Offer code: TYFA0Z0K6

301 E. Fremont Street
Las Vegas, NV 89101
(702) 388-2400
www.TheD.com

Voucher must be redeemed at Club D prior to play. Offer valid for blackjack only (not valid on Super Fun 21). Bonus is not paid on double downs or pair splits. Limit one offer per account per calendar year. Maximum bonus payout not to exceed $25. A minimum buy-in of $100 is required.

Valid government issued ID required to join Club D. Must be 21 or older. Membership is free. Management reserves all rights. No cash value. Offer expires December 29, 2015.

301 E. Fremont Street
Las Vegas, NV 89101
(702) 388-2400
www.TheD.com

Offer valid for new members only. Voucher must be surrendered to Club D at time of sign-up to receive free match play offer. Good for one bet only, win or lose, (pushes play again). Limit one offer per account per calendar year.

Valid government issued ID required to join Club D. Must be 21 or older. Membership is free. Management reserves all rights. No cash value. Offer expires December 29, 2015.

the**D** LAS VEGAS

Up to $100
Free Play

Earn $5 in free play for every 50 points earned on slots or video poker.
Maximum bonus of $100. See reverse side for full details.

DOWNTOWN
GRAND
- LAS VEGAS -
HOTEL & CASINO

Free Deck
of Cards For
New Members

Present this coupon at Player Services and receive a
FREE deck of cards. See reverse for more details.

DOWNTOWN
GRAND
- LAS VEGAS -
HOTEL & CASINO

$10 Match Play for
Any Even-Money
Table Game Bet

Make a $10 even-money bet at blackjack, craps or roulette with this
coupon and your My Points Downtown Grand Card and receive a
FREE $10 Match Bet! See reverse for full details.

**301 E. Fremont Street
Las Vegas, NV 89101
(702) 388-2400
www.TheD.com**

Voucher must be redeemed at Club D prior to play. Receive $5 free slot play for every 50 points earned up to a $100 maximum bonus. Bonus must be redeemed within the first 24-hours after signup. Player keeps points earned. Limit one offer per account per calendar year.

Valid government issued ID required to join Club D. Must be 21 or older. Membership is free. Management reserves all rights. No cash value. Offer expires December 29, 2015.

**(702) 719-5100
206 N 3rd Street
Las Vegas, Nevada 89101
DowntownGrand.com**

Must be a new My Points Downtown Grand member to qualify. Available while supplies lasts. Offer is non-transferable and has no cash value. Management reserves all rights. Offer may be amended or cancelled at any time. Offer valid 11/1/14 - 12/31/15.

DOWNTOWN GRAND
- LAS VEGAS -
HOTEL & CASINO

**(702) 719-5100
206 N 3rd Street
Las Vegas, Nevada 89101
DowntownGrand.com**

Must be a My Points Downtown Grand member and 21, or older, to redeem. Must match with cash or Downtown Grand Las Vegas live chip. Cannot be combined with any other offer. Even money bets only. Maximum of one coupon per My Points Downtown Grand member. Management reserves all rights. Offer may be amended or cancelled at any time. Offer valid 11/1/14 - 12/31/15.

Play $10 and get up to $100 free play

(with your Passport Players Club Card)

Play $10 on slots or video poker and get up to $100 free play. Upon playing $10 through any Ellis Island slot or video poker machine, you will be enrolled into the Spin and Win promotion. See reverse for details.

Name_____ PPC_____

Earn 200 Points get a Free Entrée

While playing slots or video poker, earn 200 base points and earn a FREE entrée at either the BBQ or café. Present this coupon, at the Passport Players Club, then earn points and swipe at any kiosk. See reverse for more details.

Name_____ PPC_____

$5 Match Play for Any Even-Money Table Game Bet

Present this coupon, along with your Passport Players Club Card, to the promotions booth to receive your $5 Match Play coupon. See reverse for more details.

Name_____ PPC_____

400   **American Casino Guide - 2015**

4178 Koval Lane
Las Vegas, NV 89169
(702) 733-8901
www.ellisislandscasino.com

Must be playing with Passport Player's Club card, membership is free. Upon playing $10 through any slot or video poker machine, present this coupon at the Passport Players Club, you will be "Enrolled" into the spin and win promotion at the passport Central Kiosk. Participate in the promotional game where you can win $10 - $100 in Slot free play. Free play will automatically post in your account same day. Free play must be played through once to cash out. Limit one voucher per customer. One time only. No cash value. Not valid in conjunction with any other offer. Must be 21 years or older to redeem. Management reserves the right to cancel or change this offer at any time. Offer expires December 30, 2015.

Offer void if coupon is copied or sold

4178 Koval Lane
Las Vegas, NV 89169
(702) 733-8901
www.ellisislandscasino.com

Present this original coupon (no photocopies) to the Passport Players Club Card to enroll in this promotion. Earn 200 points then visit the club to be enrolled and swipe your Passport Players Club Card at any kiosk to print out your coupon for one free entree. Limit: one coupon per customer. No cash value. Must be 21 years of age or older. Tax and gratuity not included. Membership in Passport Players Club must be in good standing. Resale prohibited. Management reserves all rights. Offer expires 12/30/15.

Offer void if coupon is copied or sold

4178 Koval Lane
Las Vegas, NV 89169
(702) 733-8901
www.ellisislandscasino.com

Must be 21 years of age or older. Original coupon must be presented (no photocopies) along with your Passport Players Club Card. Membership in Passport Players Club must be in good standing. Resale prohibited. Limit one offer per calendar year per person. Management reserves the right to cancel or alter this coupon without prior notice. Offer expires 12/30/15.

Offer void if coupon is copied or sold

EMERALD ISLAND Casino
The Jewel of Henderson

2 FOR 1 ENTRÉE

Emerald Island Grille

Come in and enjoy the luck of the Irish! Buy one entrée
and get the second entrée of equal or lesser value of FREE!*

Settle to #635

DICK'S LAST RESORT
"The Shame O' The Strip"
EXCALIBUR

20% Off Your Bill

Present this coupon to your server before
ordering at Dick's Last Resort at Excalibur
to receive 20% off your check, excluding
alcohol. See reverse for more details.

FAT FATBURGER BAR

2-for-1 Drink

Present this coupon at the Fat Bar Las Vegas to
receive two well drinks or two select draft beers
for the price of one. See reverse for details.

402

American Casino Guide - 2015

**120 Market Street
Henderson, NV 89015
(702) 567-9160
The *Jewel* of Henderson**

NEVADA'S **ONLY** ALL PENNY CASINO!

Redeem this coupon at Emerald Rewards Center prior to dining. Must be 21 years of age and an Emerald Rewards Member. Limit one coupon per member. Steak Entrees & Daily Specials Excluded. Coupon has no cash value. Copies are not accepted Offer Valid to December 31, 2015.

emeraldislandcasino.com

"The Shame O' The Strip"
EXCALIBUR

**3850 Las Vegas Blvd. S
Las Vegas, NV 89109
(702) 597-7777
www.excalibur.com**

Present this original coupon (no photocopies) to your server at Dick's Last Resort to receive 20% off your check, excluding alcohol. Limit: one coupon per check. No cash value. Must be 21 years of age or older. Tax and gratuity not included. Resale prohibited. Management reserves all rights. To book special events, birthdays, bachelor/bachelorette and holiday parties, please call (702) 597-7991. (Coupon not valid with any offer or holidays or special events) Offer expires 12/23/15.

**3763 Las Vegas Blvd S
Las Vegas, NV 89109
(702) 736-4733
FatBurger.com**

This coupon is good for two (2) well drinks or two (2) select draft beers for the price of one (1) at Fat Bar located in front of Fatburger on the Las Vegas Strip. Minimum $7 purchase required. Must present coupon when ordering. Limit of one coupon per person. No cash value. Management reserves all rights. Offer not valid 12/31/14. Offer expires 12/30/15.

2-For-1 Buffet
(Sunday-Thursday)

Royal Flush Capital of the World.

Buy one Festival Buffet and get the second Festival Buffet free. Offer valid Sunday-Thursday. See reverse for more details.

Royal Flush Capital of the World.

$10 Dining Credit

Present this coupon to your server at Cafe Fiesta for a $10 dining credit good towards a purchase of $20 or more. See reverse for more details.

2-For-1 Buffet
(Sunday-Thursday)

Royal Flush Capital of the World.

Buy one Festival Buffet and get the second Festival Buffet free. Offer valid Sunday-Thursday. See reverse for more details.

americancasinoguide.com

Royal Flush Capital of the World.

777 W Lake Mead Pkwy
Henderson, NV 89015
(702) 558-7000
www.fiestahenderson.sclv.com

This voucher entitles bearer to one free lunch or dinner in the Festival Buffet when accompanied by a cash paying guest. Tax and gratuity not included. One voucher per person/subscriber. Voucher must be presented to cashier. Vouchers are not transferable and are not redeemable for cash. Must be 21 or older. Not a line pass. Not valid on holidays, Not valid with any other offer. Offer may be changed or discontinued at any time at the discretion of management. Original vouchers only. Offer is void if sold. Offer expires 12/23/15. Settle to: #88-942

Offer void if coupon is copied or sold

americancasinoguide.com

Royal Flush Capital of the World.

777 W Lake Mead Pkwy
Henderson, NV 89015
(702) 558-7000
www.fiestahenderson.sclv.com

This voucher entitles bearer to a $10 dining credit applied to a minimum check total of $20 or more (excluding alcohol). Gratuity not included. Offer valid for dine in only and valid 7 days per week. Limit one offer per check. Voucher is not transferable and is not redeemable for cash. Must be 21 or older. Not a line pass. Not valid on holidays. Not valid with any other offer. Offer may change or be discontinued at any time at the discretion of management. Original vouchers only. Offer is void if sold. Offer expires December 23, 2015. Settle To: #41-334

Offer void if coupon is copied or sold

americancasinoguide.com

Royal Flush Capital of the World.

2400 N Rancho Dr
N. Las Vegas, NV 89130
(702) 631-7000
www.fiestarancho.sclv.com

This voucher entitles bearer to one free lunch or dinner in the Festival Buffet when accompanied by a cash paying guest. Tax and gratuity not included. One voucher per person/subscriber. Voucher must be presented to cashier. Vouchers are not transferable and are not redeemable for cash. Must be 21 or older. Not a line pass. Not valid on holidays, Not valid with any other offer. Offer may be changed or discontinued at any time at the discretion of management. Original vouchers only. Offer is void if sold. Offer expires 12/23/15. Settle to: #88-942

Offer void if coupon is copied or sold

AMERICAN CASINO GUIDE

FIESTA RANCHO

Royal Flush Capital of the World.

$10 Dining Credit
(Sunday-Thursday)

Present this coupon to your server at Garduno's for a $10 dining credit good towards a purchase of $20 or more. See reverse for more details.

A current American Casino Guide Discount Card must be presented when redeeming this coupon, or offer is void

AMERICAN CASINO GUIDE

Burlesque

2-FOR-1 TICKETS

Redeem at the Flamingo Box Office for 2-for-1 tickets to X-Burlesque. See reverse for details.

Offer code: XBACG

A current American Casino Guide Discount Card must be presented when redeeming this coupon, or offer is void

AMERICAN CASINO GUIDE

X BURLESQUE UNIVERSITY
XBU

2-FOR-1 CLASSES

Redeem at the Flamingo Box Office for 2-for-1 admission to X-Burlesque University. See reverse for details.

Offer code: XBUACG

A current American Casino Guide Discount Card must be presented when redeeming this coupon, or offer is void

Royal Flush Capital of the World.

**2400 N Rancho Dr
N. Las Vegas, NV 89130
(702) 631-7000**
www.fiestarancho.sclv.com

This voucher entitles bearer to a $10 dining credit applied to a minimum check total of $20 or more (excluding alcohol). Gratuity not included. Offer valid for dine in only and valid 7 days per week. Limit one offer per check. Voucher is not transferable and are not redeemable for cash. Must be 21 or older. Not a line pass. Not valid on holidays. Not valid with any other offer. Offer may change or be discontinued at any time at the discretion of management. Original vouchers only. Offer is void if sold. Offer expires December 23, 2015. Settle To: #33-877

**3555 Las Vegas Blvd. S.
Las Vegas, NV 89109
702-733-3111
Flamingo.com**

Present coupon at time of purchase to redeem. Must be 18. Limit 4 per coupon. No cash value. Not valid on previously purchased tickets. Cannot be combined with any other offer. Subject to availability. Blackout dates may apply. Management reserves all rights. Offer subject to change or cancellation without notification. Offer expires 12/30/15.

**3555 Las Vegas Blvd. S.
Las Vegas, NV 89109
702-733-3111
Flamingo.com**

Present coupon at time of purchase to redeem. Limit 4 per coupon. Must be 18 years of age to attend. No cash value. Not valid on previously purchased tickets. Cannot be combined with any other offer. Subject to availability. Blackout dates may apply. Management reserves all rights. Offer subject to change or cancellation without notification. Offer Expires 12/30/15.

4 QUEENS
HOTEL • CASINO
LAS VEGAS

Double Points (Up to 500) for members of the Royal Players Club™

Double your Royal Players Club™ points (up to 500) with this coupon! See reverse for more details.

A current American Casino Guide Discount Card must be presented when redeeming this coupon, or offer is void

4 QUEENS
HOTEL • CASINO
LAS VEGAS

2-for-1 Lunch or Dinner Entrée in Magnolia's

Buy one lunch or dinner entrée in Magnolia's and get one entrée FREE! See reverse for more details.

A current American Casino Guide Discount Card must be presented when redeeming this coupon, or offer is void

Mike **Hammer**
-comedy magic show

2-for-1 Show Tickets

Buy one ticket to the Mike Hammer Comedy Magic Show and receive a second one FREE. See reverse for more details.

A current American Casino Guide Discount Card must be presented when redeeming this coupon, or offer is void

202 Fremont Street
Las Vegas, NV 89101
(702) 385-4011
(800) 634-6045
www.fourqueens.com

Strictly limited to one coupon per person per 12 month period. Coupon has no cash value. Must be 21 years or older. Points must be earned on day of redemption. Offer valid for Royal Players Club™ members only. Double points will be added to account within 48 hours. Management reserves the right to cancel or modify offer at any time without notice. Coupon is void if altered or duplicated. Offer expires December 27, 2015.

202 Fremont Street
Las Vegas, NV 89101
(702) 385-4011
(800) 634-6045
www.fourqueens.com

Strictly limited to one coupon per person per 12 month period. Must be 21 years or older. Must redeem coupon at the Royal Players Club to receive voucher for Magnolia's. Purchase one lunch or dinner entrée (equal or greater value) to receive the second one free. Offer valid only in Magnolia's. Coupon is void if altered or duplicated. Tax, alcoholic beverages and gratuity are not included. Not valid with any other offers or discounts. Management reserves the right to cancel or modify offer at any time. Coupon has no cash value. Offer expires December 27, 2015.

202 Fremont Street
Las Vegas, NV 89101
(877) 935-2844
mikehammershow.com

Show open to all ages. Must be 21 to redeem coupon. Must redeem coupon at the Four Queens Box Office to receive second ticket for free with purchase of one at full price. Coupon is void if altered or duplicated. Tax and box office fees are not included. Not valid with any other offers or discounts. Show times: 7pm Tuesday-Saturday. Subject to availability. Management reserves the right to cancel or modify offer at any time. Coupon has no cash value. Offer expires December 29, 2015.

Earn 250 Points, Get a Free Buffet
(Keep the points)

FREMONT
HOTEL & CASINO

Earn 250 base points playing slots, then present this original coupon and B Connected card to the B Connected Club to receive a voucher that will entitle bearer to one FREE breakfast, lunch or brunch buffet at the Paradise Buffet. See reverse side for details.

FREMONT
HOTEL & CASINO

One Free Room Night

Buy two nights and get the third night FREE! Valid Sunday through Thursday. Subject to availability. Excludes Holidays and blackout periods. For reservations, call (800) 634-6182 and reference offer: **ZACG15**

CALIFORNIA
HOTEL · CASINO · LAS VEGAS

FREMONT
HOTEL & CASINO

MAIN STREET
STATION
CASINO BREWERY HOTEL

New Members Play $25 Get $10

Present this coupon when signing up for a new B Connected card to be eligible for Play $25 and Get $10 slot play. See reverse for full details.

200 Fremont St
Las Vegas, NV 89101
(800) 634-6460
www.fremontcasino.com

Must be 21 or older and have an active B Connected card. Not valid on holidays. Earn 250 base points playing slots on the same day original coupon is presented to the B Connected Club for redemption. Limit one coupon per person. Excludes dinner and specialty night buffets. Coupon has no cash value, cannot be combined with any other offer, or used more than once. Reproduction, sale, barter, or transfer are prohibited and render this coupon void. Management reserves all rights to change or discontinue this offer without notice. Expires 12/30/2015. Offer Code: EYCA0ZZK6

Offer void if coupon is copied or sold

200 Fremont St
Las Vegas, NV 89101
(800) 634-6460
www.fremontcasino.com

This voucher entitles the bearer to one free room night at the Fremont Hotel and Casino, with the purchase of two room nights at the prevailing rate. Advance reservations required. Voucher must be presented upon check-in. Offer is not valid in conjunction with any other offer. Management reserves all rights to cancel this promotion without notification. Credit card required at the time of reservation and at check in. Guest is responsible for all incidental charges. Must be 21 or older. One free room per person. Offer expires 12/28/15. This voucher has no cash value, cannot be combined with any other offer or used more than once.

Offer void if coupon is copied or sold

California Hotel Casino	**Fremont Hotel & Casino**	**Main Street Station**
12 East Ogden Avenue	**200 Fremont St**	**200 North Main Street**
Las Vegas, NV 89101	**Las Vegas, NV 89101**	**Las Vegas, NV 89101**
(800) 634-6505	**(800) 634-6460**	**(800) 713-8933**
www.thecal.com	**www.fremontcasino.com**	**www.mainstreetcasino.com**

Present this coupon when signing up for a new B Connected card at your choice of casinos - the California, Fremont, or Main Street Station to be eligible for the Play & Get slot play. One Play & Get offer per new B Connected account. Slot play refers to non-cashable downloadable machine credits and will be uploaded to your B Connected account, pin number is required. Slot play is non-transferable and cannot be used with any other offer. You must be 21 or over to participate. Slot play will expire 24 hrs after coupon redemption. Management reserves the right to modify or cancel this promotion without prior notice. See the B Connected Club for additional details. Expires 12/30/2015. Offer code: TYFA0Z0K6

Offer void if coupon is copied or sold

GOLD COAST ®
HOTEL & CASINO · LAS VEGAS

Earn 200 Points, Get Free Buffet (Keep the points)

Earn 200 points playing slots then present this original coupon and
B Connected Card to the B Connected Club, and receive a voucher that
will entitle bearer to one FREE breakfast, lunch or regular dinner buffet.
See reverse side for details.

A current American Casino Guide Discount Card must be
presented when redeeming this coupon, or offer is void

GOLD COAST ® **$5 in Slot Dollars**
HOTEL & CASINO · LAS VEGAS **(With new enrollment)**

Present this original coupon and a valid government issued photo ID to the B
Connected Club when enrolling as a new member of the B Connected Club
and receive $5 worth of slot play. Downloadable slot play will be added to
new account. Offer limited to new members. Not valid with any other offer
or promotion. See reverse side for details.

A current American Casino Guide Discount Card must be
presented when redeeming this coupon, or offer is void

GOLD COAST ® **$10 Match Play**
HOTEL & CASINO · LAS VEGAS

Present this original coupon and B Connected Card to the
B Connected Club for a match play voucher. Voucher and equal
wager of real chips or cash should be presented to the dealer.
See reverse side for details.

A current American Casino Guide Discount Card must be
presented when redeeming this coupon, or offer is void

americancasinoguide.com

Gold Coast Hotel & Casino
4000 W. Flamingo Road
Las Vegas, NV 89103
(702) 367-7111 • (800) 331-5334
www.goldcoastcasino.com

Must be 21 or older and have an active B Connected Card. Not valid on Holidays. Earn 200 points playing slots on same day original coupon is presented to B Connected Club to obtain voucher. Limit one coupon per person. Excludes specialty night dinners. This coupon has no cash value, cannot be combined with any other offer or used more than once. Reproduction, sale, barter or transfer are prohibited and render this coupon void. Management reserves the right to change or discontinue this offer without notice. Expires 12/30/15.

Offer void if coupon is copied or sold

americancasinoguide.com

Gold Coast Hotel & Casino
4000 W. Flamingo Road
Las Vegas, NV 89103
(702) 367-7111 • (800) 331-5334
www.goldcoastcasino.com

Must be 21 or older and present a valid government issued photo ID. Limit one coupon per person. Valid for new members in B Connected club. This coupon has no cash value, cannot be combined with any other offer or used more than once. Reproduction, sale, barter or transfer are prohibited and render this coupon void. Management reserves the right to change or discontinue this offer without notice. Expires 12/30/15.

Offer void if coupon is copied or sold

americancasinoguide.com

GOLD COAST®
HOTEL & CASINO · LAS VEGAS

Gold Coast Hotel & Casino
4000 W. Flamingo Road
Las Vegas, NV 89103
(702) 367-7111 • (800) 331-5334
www.goldcoastcasino.com

Must be 21 or older and have an active B Connected Card. Limit one coupon per person and limit one coupon per wager. Coupon good for play on any Gold Coast casino table game but excludes live poker. Good for one decision on even-money bets only. Win or lose, coupon is claimed by the house. If you tie then the coupon may be re-bet. This coupon has no cash value, cannot be combined with any other offer or used more than once. Reproduction, sale, barter or transfer are prohibited and render this coupon void. Management reserves the right to change or discontinue this offer without notice. Expires 12/30/15.

Offer void if coupon is copied or sold

$25 FREE PLAY for earning 200 points, or $5 FREE PLAY for 50 points

Earn 200 points while playing with your Club 1906 card and receive $25 FREE slot play, or earn 50 points and receive $5 FREE slot play. Offer valid for new members only. See reverse side for full details.

GOLDEN GATE
HOTEL & CASINO

$25 Match Play for New Members

Bet $25 on any even-money bet and we'll pay you $50 if you win. Present this coupon at Club 1906 to receive your free $25 match play. Offer valid for new members only. See reverse side for full details.

GOLDEN GATE
HOTEL & CASINO

Free Calendar

Select from our annual "History of the Golden Gate" or our highly collectible "Girls of Golden Gate" 2015 calendars. See reverse side for full details.

GOLDEN GATE
HOTEL & CASINO

americancasinoguide.com

One Fremont Street
Las Vegas, NV 89101
(702) 385-1906
Reservations (800) 426-1906

Offer valid for new members only. Voucher must be surrendered to Club 1906 at time of sign-up and required points must be earned the same day. Limit one offer per account.

Valid government issued ID required to join Club 1906. Must be 21 or older. Membership is free. Management reserves all rights. No cash value. Offer expires December 29, 2015.

Offer void if coupon is copied or sold

---

americancasinoguide.com

One Fremont Street
Las Vegas, NV 89101
(702) 385-1906
Reservations (800) 426-1906

Offer valid for new members only. Voucher must be surrendered to Club 1906 at time of sign-up to receive free match play offer. Good for one bet only, win or lose, (pushes play again). Limit one offer per account.

Valid government issued ID required to join Club 1906. Must be 21 or older. Membership is free. Management reserves all rights. No cash value. Offer expires December 29, 2015.

Offer void if coupon is copied or sold

---

americancasinoguide.com

One Fremont Street
Las Vegas, NV 89101
(702) 385-1906
Reservations (800) 426-1906

Voucher must be surrendered to Club 1906 at time of redemption. Must be a member, or become a Club 1906 member to receive offer. Limit one per account per calendar year.

Valid government issued ID required to join Club 1906. Must be 21 or older. Membership is free. Management reserves all rights. No cash value. Offer valid January 1, 2015– December 29, 2015 while supplies last.

Offer void if coupon is copied or sold

Receive $60 in Poker Chips for $50

GOLDEN NUGGET
LAS VEGAS

Receive $60 in chips for a $50 buy-in in our non-smoking Poker Room. See reverse for more details.

$10 Free Slot Play For New Members

GOLDEN NUGGET
LAS VEGAS

Become a qualified member of the 24 Karat Club by earning 500 points and receive $10 in Free Slot Play. See reverse for more details.

GOLDEN NUGGET
LAS VEGAS

2-For-1 Drink at RUSH Lounge

Present this coupon at the RUSH Lounge to purchase one domestic beer or well drink at regular price and get a second domestic beer, or well drink, FREE! See reverse for details.

LAS VEGAS
129 E. Fremont Street
Las Vegas, NV 89101
(800) 777-4658
www.goldennugget.com

The ***Poker Room***

Redeemable only at the Poker Room Cashier's Cage. Not valid with any other offer. Management reserves the rights to alter or cancel this promotion at any time. Must be 21 years of age or older. Limit one coupon per person per calendar month. No cash value. Expires 12/30/15.

GOLDEN NUGGET

LAS VEGAS
129 E. Fremont Street
Las Vegas, NV 89101
(800) 777-4658
www.goldennugget.com

Offer not valid in conjunction with any other 24 Karat Club offer. Applies to new, first time members only. 500 points must be earned within first 72 hours of enrollment. Management reserves the right to alter or cancel this promotion at any time. Must be 21 years of age or older.

Free Slot Play credits have no cash value, can be used only for play and cannot be cashed out. Certificate must be redeemed prior to 12/30/15. Identification is required. LV15

LAS VEGAS
129 E. Fremont Street
Las Vegas, NV 89101
(800) 777-4658
www.goldennugget.com

Redeemable only at RUSH Lounge. Offer valid for one free domestic beer or well drink only at RUSH Lounge with the purchase of a second drink of equal or greater value. Not valid on holidays or with any other offer. Must be 21 years of age. Management reserves the right to alter or cancel this promotion at any time. Expires 12/30/15. Promo Code: ACG15.

AMERICAN CASINO GUIDE

GOLDEN NUGGET
LAS VEGAS

2-For-1
Buffet
(Monday-Friday)

Receive one FREE breakfast or lunch buffet with the purchase
of a second breakfast or lunch buffet at regular price.
See reverse for more details.

A current American Casino Guide Discount Card must be
presented when redeeming this coupon, or offer is void

AMERICAN CASINO GUIDE

GOLDEN NUGGET
LAS VEGAS

2-For-1
Show Tickets

Receive one complimentary ticket to Gordie Brown Live!
with the purchase of one ticket priced at $40 or more.
See reverse for more details.

A current American Casino Guide Discount Card must be
presented when redeeming this coupon, or offer is void

AMERICAN CASINO GUIDE

NINETEEN **FORTY SIX**
APPAREL & ACCESSORIES

Style **& TREND**

10% Off Purchase of $100 or More

Make a purchase of $100 or more at Style & Trend or 1946 and
get 10% off of your purchase! See reverse for full details.

A current American Casino Guide Discount Card must be
presented when redeeming this coupon, or offer is void

GOLDEN NUGGET
LAS VEGAS
129 E. Fremont Street
Las Vegas, NV 89101
(800) 777-4658
www.goldennugget.com

Coupon must be redeemed at the Golden Nugget Buffet. Offer valid for one free breakfast or lunch buffet Monday through Friday only with the purchase of a second buffet of equal or greater value. Not valid with any other offer. Based on availability. No cash value. Management reserves the rights to alter or cancel this promotion at any time. Expires 12/30/15. Promo Code: ACG15

GORDIE BROWN
COMEDY · MUSIC · IMPRESSIONS *Live*

Coupon must be redeemed at the Golden Nugget Box Office. Offer valid for one free ticket to Gordie Brown Live! with the purchase of a second ticket of equal or greater value. Valid on tickets priced $40 or higher only. Not valid with buffet package. Not valid with any other offer. Based on availability. No cash value. Management reserves the rights to alter or cancel this promotion at any time. Expires 12/30/15. Promo Code: ACG15

GOLDEN NUGGET
LAS VEGAS
129 E. Fremont Street
Las Vegas, NV 89101
(800) 777-4658
www.goldennugget.com

GOLDEN NUGGET
LAS VEGAS
129 E. Fremont Street
Las Vegas, NV 89101
(800) 777-4658
www.goldennugget.com

Redeemable only at Style & Trend or 1946. Not valid with any other offer. Management reserves the rights to alter or cancel this promotion at any time. Must be 21 years of age or older. Limit one coupon per person per calendar month. No cash value. Expires 12/30/15.

GVR

GREEN VALLEY RANCH

2-For-1 Buffet
(Sunday-Thursday)

Buy one Feast Buffet and get the second Feast Buffet free.
Offer valid Sunday-Thursday. See reverse for more details.

GVR

GREEN VALLEY RANCH

$20 For $10 at Grand Cafe

Present this coupon to your server before ordering to receive
$20 in food for only $10. See reverse for more details.

Häagen·Dazs®

Buy One Get One Free

Present this coupon at any Haagen Dazs shop listed on the back,
purchase your choice of any menu item and receive your choice
of a second menu item of equal or lesser value free!

GREEN VALLEY RANCH

2300 Paseo Verde Pkwy
Las Vegas, NV 89052
(702) 617-7777
www.greenvalleyranch.sclv.com

This voucher entitles bearer to one free breakfast, lunch or dinner in the Feast Buffet when accompanied by a full price, cash paying guest. Tax and gratuity not included. One voucher per person/subscriber. Voucher must be presented to cashier. Vouchers are not transferable and are not redeemable for cash. Must be 21 or older. Not a line pass. Not valid on holidays, Not valid with any other offer. Offer may be changed or discontinued at any time at the discretion of management. Original vouchers only. Offer is void if sold. Offer expires 12/23/15. Settle to: #88-942

GREEN VALLEY RANCH

2300 Paseo Verde Pkwy
Las Vegas, NV 89052
(702) 617-7777
www.greenvalleyranch.sclv.com

Present this Voucher to the Cashier at the Grand Cafe to receive $10.00 off a minimum check total of $20 or more (excluding alcohol). Gratuity not included. Offer valid for dine in only and valid 7 days per week. Limit one offer per check. Voucher is not transferable and not redeemable for cash. Must be 21 or older. Not a line pass. Not valid on holidays. Not valid with any other offer or menu specials. Offer may change or be discontinued at any time at the discretion of management. Original vouchers only. Offer is void if sold. Offer Valid at Green Valley Ranch resort only. Offer expires 12/23/15. Settle to: #41-310

MGM Grand Hotel - Food Court
New York New York Hotel
The Venetian Hotel
Fashion Show Mall

Must present coupon to cashier prior to ordering. Offer has no cash value. Not valid with any other offer. One coupon per person. Subject to change or cancellation without prior notice. Offer valid through December 31, 2015.

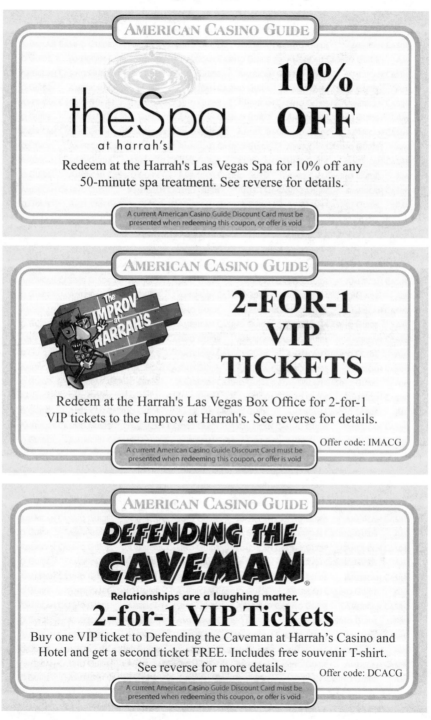

theSpa
at harrah's

10% OFF

Redeem at the Harrah's Las Vegas Spa for 10% off any
50-minute spa treatment. See reverse for details.

The IMPROV at HARRAH'S

2-FOR-1 VIP TICKETS

Redeem at the Harrah's Las Vegas Box Office for 2-for-1
VIP tickets to the Improv at Harrah's. See reverse for details.

Offer code: IMACG

DEFENDING THE CAVEMAN®

Relationships are a laughing matter.

2-for-1 VIP Tickets

Buy one VIP ticket to Defending the Caveman at Harrah's Casino and
Hotel and get a second ticket FREE. Includes free souvenir T-shirt.
See reverse for more details.

Offer code: DCACG

3475 Las Vegas Blvd. S.
Las Vegas, NV 89109
(702) 369-5000
harrahs.com

Valid at The Spa at Harrah's Las Vegas only. Limit 1 treatment per coupon. No cash value. Not valid on previously purchased services. Cannot be combined with any other offer. Subject to availability. Blackout dates may apply, including December 25 through 31. Management reserves all rights. Offer subject to change or cancellation without notification. Offer expires 12/30/15.

3475 Las Vegas Blvd. S.
Las Vegas, NV 89109
(702) 369-5000
harrahs.com

Valid at Harrah's Las Vegas only. Present coupon at time of purchase to redeem. Limit 4 per coupon. Valid on VIP tickets only. No cash value. Not valid on previously purchased tickets. Cannot be combined with any other offer. Subject to availability. Blackout dates may apply. Management reserves all rights. Offer subject to change or cancellation without notification. Offer expires 12/30/15.

Harrah's

DEFENDING THE CAVEMAN

Relationships are a laughing matter.

3475 Las Vegas Blvd S.
Las Vegas, NV 89109
(800) 214-9110
www.harrahslasvegas.com

Coupon must be redeemed at the Harrah's Las Vegas Box Office. Tax and box office fee apply. Limit one coupon per party. Not valid with any other offer. Based on availability. No cash value. Management reserves the right to alter or cancel this promotion at any time. Offer expires 12/30/15.

THE Mac King
COMEDY MAGIC SHOW

Two FREE Tickets With Drink Purchase

Receive two free tickets to The Mac King Comedy Magic Show with purchase of one drink per person. See reverse for details.

HOOTERS
Casino Hotel ◆ Las Vegas

Play $10 Get $10 in Free Play

Play $10 on slots or video poker and get $10 in Free Play. $10 in Free Play will be credited to your Rewards Club+ account once you have played $10 on any Hooters Casino slot or video poker machine. See reverse for full details.

Name_____ Club #_____

HOOTERS
Casino Hotel ◆ Las Vegas

$10 Match Play for Any Even-Money Table Game Bet

Make a $10 even-money bet at blackjack, craps or roulette with this coupon and your Rewards Club+ and receive a FREE $10 Match Bet! See reverse for full details.

Harrah's

3475 Las Vegas Blvd. S.
Las Vegas, NV 89109
(702) 369-5222
mackingshow.com

Show times Tuesday through Saturday at 1 p.m. and 3 p.m. Seating begins 45 minutes before show time. Seating is limited on a space available basis. Present this ticket at the Harrah's Las Vegas Box Office to redeem your free ticket for two. One drink minimum ($9.95 per person/plus tax & gratuity). Offer expires 12/31/15.

Additional Offer: Upgrade to VIP Line Pass & VIP Seating for only $5.00 per person and also receive 2-for-1 buffet. Offer expires 12/31/15.

115 East Tropicana Avenue
Las Vegas, Nevada 89109
(702) 739-9000
(800) 726-7366
www.hooterscasinohotel.com

Coupon must be presented to Rewards Club+ prior to play beginning. $10 in play must be recorded on Rewards Club+ card. Membership is free. Once the $10 in play threshold on a slot or video poker machines has been met, $10 in Free Play will be downloaded on to your Rewards Club+ card. Free Play must be played through once to cash out. Free Play cannot be used on any Wide Area Progressive machine. Limit one voucher per customer. Offer can only be used once per calendar year. No cash value. Not valid in conjunction with any other offer. Must be 21 years of age or older to redeem. Management reserves the right to alter, change or cancel without notice. A current American Casino Guide Discount Card must be presented when redeeming this coupon or offer is void. Offer expires December 30, 2015.

115 East Tropicana Avenue
Las Vegas, Nevada 89109
(702) 739-9000
(800) 726-7366
www.hooterscasinohotel.com

Must be 21 years of age or older and a Rewards Club+ member. Make a $10 minimum even-money bet at any blackjack, craps or roulette game, along with this original coupon (no photocopies), and receive a $10 Match Bet. Good for one decision on even money bets only. Win or lose, coupon is claimed by the house. If you tie, then coupon may be re-bet. No cash value. Limit: one coupon per customer, per year. Not valid with any other offer. Management reserves the right to alter, change or cancel without notice. Offer expires 12/31/15.

AMERICAN CASINO GUIDE

HOOTERS
Casino Hotel ◆ Las Vegas

Buy 10 Wings
Get 10 FREE!

Present this coupon to your server in Hooters Restaurant at Hooters Casino Hotel to receive 10 FREE wings when you buy 10 wings at regular price. See Reverse for full details.

Offer Code: 30555

A current American Casino Guide Discount Card must be presented when redeeming this coupon, or offer is void

---

AMERICAN CASINO GUIDE

JERRY'S NUGGET CASINO

$5 Table Games Match Play

Redeem at The MoreClub and receive a $5 table games match play. See reverse for details.

A current American Casino Guide Discount Card must be presented when redeeming this coupon, or offer is void

---

AMERICAN CASINO GUIDE

JERRY'S NUGGET CASINO

Free Blue Pack with Minimum Bingo Buy-In

Redeem at The MoreClub and receive a free blue pack when you play bingo. See reverse for details.

A current American Casino Guide Discount Card must be presented when redeeming this coupon, or offer is void

115 East Tropicana Avenue
Las Vegas, Nevada 89109
(702) 739-9000
(800) 726-7366
www.hooterscasinohotel.com

Present this coupon to your server in Hooters Restaurant at Hooters Casino Hotel, Las Vegas. Gratuity not included. Non-transferable. Must be a Rewards Club+ member. One offer per Rewards Club+ member. One offer per table. Offer good at Hooters Restaurant at Hooters Casino in Las Vegas only. Offer valid 24/7. Management reserves the right to alter, change or cancel without notice. Offer expires December 15, 2015.

1821 Las Vegas Boulevard North
N. Las Vegas, NV 89030
(702) 399-3000 • www.jerrysnugget.com

Limit one coupon per customer per month. Must be a MoreClub member. MoreClub membership is free. Present original coupon to The MoreClub and receive a $5 table games match play issued from The MoreClub Kiosk. No photocopies will be honored. Table games match play kiosk ticket good for 24 hours after issuance. A $5 minimum bet is required. Voucher surrendered after first hand. Good for one hand, one wager. Player rating required at time of play. Cannot be redeemed for cash. Not valid with any other offer. Must be 21 years of age or older to redeem. Management reserves all rights. Offer expires December 31, 2015.

1821 Las Vegas Boulevard North
N. Las Vegas, NV 89030
(702) 399-3000 • www.jerrysnugget.com

Limit one coupon per customer per month. Must be a MoreClub member. MoreClub membership is free. Present original coupon to The MoreClub and receive a free bingo blue pack in electronic or paper issued from The MoreClub Kiosk. No photocopies will be honored. Free blue pack kiosk ticket good for 24 hours after issuance. Electronic and validation fee not included for electronic blue pack. Minimum $4 bingo buy-in required for paper, $8 bingo buy-in for electronic. All bingo rules apply. Cannot be redeemed for cash. Not valid with any other offer. Must be 21 years of age or older to redeem. Management reserves all rights. Offer expires December 31, 2015.

AMERICAN CASINO GUIDE

FREE
Burger and
Milkshake

Present this coupon at any Johnny Rocket's listed on the back,
purchase any burger and milkshake and receive a second burger
and milkshake FREE! See reverse for details.

A current American Casino Guide Discount Card must be
presented when redeeming this coupon, or offer is void

AMERICAN CASINO GUIDE

Buy One Get One Free

Present this coupon at any L.A. Subs, purchase your choice of
any sub sandwich or salad and get a second sub sandwich
or salad of equal or lesser value free! See reverse for details.

A current American Casino Guide Discount Card must be
presented when redeeming this coupon, or offer is void

AMERICAN CASINO GUIDE

$5 Matchplay
on any Even
Money Bet

HOUSE OF JACKPOTS

Present this coupon at any blackjack, craps or roulette table, along with your
Royal Rewards Card, prior to the start of the play and we'll match your bet of
$5 if you win. See reverse for details.

A current American Casino Guide Discount Card must be
presented when redeeming this coupon, or offer is void

americancasinoguide.com

Fashion Show Mall • Bally's Hotel & Casino
Venetian Hotel Grand Canal Shops
Meadows Mall Food Court • Excalibur Hotel Casino
Flamingo Hotel Food Court
Mandalay Bay Food Court

Must present coupon to cashier prior to ordering. Offer has no cash value. Not valid with any other offer. One coupon per person. Subject to change or cancellation without prior notice. Offer valid through December 31, 2015.

americancasinoguide.com

Luxor Food Court
Flamingo Hotel Food Court

Must present coupon to cashier prior to ordering. Offer has no cash value. Not valid with any other offer. One coupon per person. Subject to change or cancellation without prior notice. Offer valid through December 31, 2015.

americancasinoguide.com

HOUSE OF JACKPOTS

18 E. Fremont Street
Las Vegas, NV 89101
(702) 385-1664
(800) 634-6532
www.vegasclubcasino.net

Limit: one coupon per person, per calendar month. Cannot be redeemed for cash. Must be a Royal Rewards member and 21 years of age or older. Cannot be combined with any other offers or promotion. Good for one decision on even-money bet only. Win or lose, coupon is claimed by the house. If you tie, then coupon may be re-bet.

Must present original coupon (no photocopies). Management reserves all rights. Offer may be changed or discontinued at anytime at the discretion of management. Offer expires 12/29/15.

430   **American Casino Guide - 2015**

HOUSE OF JACKPOTS

18 E. Fremont Street
Las Vegas, NV 89101
(702) 385-1664
(800) 634-6532
www.vegasclubcasino.net

Subject to availability. Not valid with any other offers. Excludes specialty drinks. Free drink of equal or lesser value. Gratuity not included.

Limit one per person. Coupon has no cash value. May not be combined with any other offer. Must be a Royal Rewards member and 21 years of age or older. Settle to Comp #C9321. Management reserves all rights. Expires 12/29/15.

HOUSE OF JACKPOTS

18 E. Fremont Street
Las Vegas, NV 89101
(702) 385-1664
(800) 634-6532
www.vegasclubcasino.net

Present this voucher to the Royal Rewards Center and receive $5 in FREE slot play. Limit one coupon per account per calendar year. Must present original coupon (no photocopies).

Must be a Royal Rewards member and 21 years of age or older. Not valid in conjunction with any other offer. Management reserves the right to cancel or change this offer at any time. Offer expires 12/29/15.

THE
LINQ
HOTEL &
CASINO

3535 Las Vegas Blvd. S
Las Vegas, NV 89109
(800) 351-7400
TheLinqlv.com

Limit 1 coupon per person. No cash value. Not valid on previously purchased services. Cannot be combined with any other offer. Subject to availability. Blackout dates may apply. Management reserves all rights. Offer subject to change or cancellation without notification. Offer expires 12/30/15.

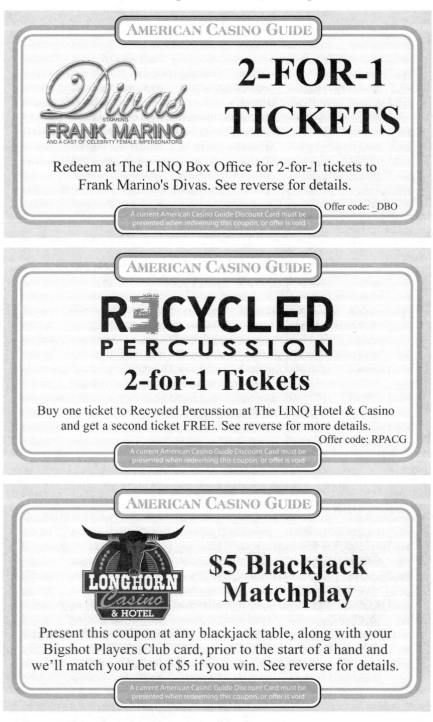

AMERICAN CASINO GUIDE

2-FOR-1 TICKETS

Divas
STARRING
FRANK MARINO
AND A CAST OF CELEBRITY FEMALE IMPERSONATORS

Redeem at The LINQ Box Office for 2-for-1 tickets to
Frank Marino's Divas. See reverse for details.

Offer code: _DBO

A current American Casino Guide Discount Card must be
presented when redeeming this coupon, or offer is void

AMERICAN CASINO GUIDE

R3CYCLED PERCUSSION
2-for-1 Tickets

Buy one ticket to Recycled Percussion at The LINQ Hotel & Casino
and get a second ticket FREE. See reverse for more details.

Offer code: RPACG

A current American Casino Guide Discount Card must be
presented when redeeming this coupon, or offer is void

AMERICAN CASINO GUIDE

LONGHORN *Casino* **& HOTEL**

$5 Blackjack Matchplay

Present this coupon at any blackjack table, along with your
Bigshot Players Club card, prior to the start of a hand and
we'll match your bet of $5 if you win. See reverse for details.

A current American Casino Guide Discount Card must be
presented when redeeming this coupon, or offer is void

THE LINQ HOTEL & CASINO

3535 Las Vegas Blvd. S
Las Vegas, NV 89109
(800) 351-7400
TheLinqlv.com

Present coupon at time of purchase to redeem. Limit 4 per coupon. No cash value. Not valid on previously purchased tickets. Cannot be combined with any other offer. Subject to availability. Blackout dates may apply. Management reserves all rights. Offer subject to change or cancellation without notification. Offer expires 12/30/15.

THE LINQ HOTEL & CASINO

3535 Las Vegas Blvd. S
Las Vegas, NV 89109
(800) 351-7400
TheLinqlv.com

Present coupon at time of purchase to redeem. Limit 4 per coupon. No cash value. Not valid on previously purchased tickets. Cannot be combined with any other offer. Subject to availability. Blackout dates may apply. Management reserves all rights. Offer subject to change or cancellation without notification. Offer expires 12/30/15.

LONGHORN Casino & HOTEL

5288 Boulder Highway
Las Vegas, Nevada 89122
(702) 435-9170
(800) 825-0880

Limit: one coupon per person, per month. Cannot be redeemed for cash. Must be 21 or older. Cannot be combined with any other offer or promotion. Non-transferable. Offer void if sold.

Must present original coupon (no photocopies). Not responsible for lost or stolen coupon. Management reserves all rights. Offer may be changed or discontinued at anytime at the discretion of management. Offer expires December 30, 2015.

AMERICAN CASINO GUIDE

2-for-1
Lunch or
Dinner Entrée

Buy one lunch or dinner entrée in our restaurant and get one entrée of equal or lesser value FREE! Present to server before ordering. See reverse for more details.

A current American Casino Guide Discount Card must be presented when redeeming this coupon, or offer is void

AMERICAN CASINO GUIDE

2,000 Slot Club Points
For New Members

Present this coupon at the Bigshot Players Club booth to receive 2,000 FREE slot club points when you join as a new member. See reverse for more details.

A current American Casino Guide Discount Card must be presented when redeeming this coupon, or offer is void

AMERICAN CASINO GUIDE

Free Deck of
Cards or Dice

Present this coupon at guest services and receive either a free deck of cards or a pair of dice. See reverse for more details.

A current American Casino Guide Discount Card must be presented when redeeming this coupon, or offer is void

5288 Boulder Highway
Las Vegas, Nevada 89122
(702) 435-9170
(800) 825-0880

Limit one coupon per person. Must be 21 years or older. Purchase one lunch or dinner entrée to receive the second one of equal or lesser value free. Not valid on take out orders. Coupon is void if altered or duplicated. Must present original coupon (no photocopies).

Tax, beverages and gratuity are not included. Not valid with any other offers or discounts. Management reserves the right to cancel or modify offer at any time. Coupon has no cash value. Offer expires December 30, 2015.

Offer void if coupon is copied or sold

5288 Boulder Highway
Las Vegas, Nevada 89122
(702) 435-9170
(800) 825-0880

Valid for new accounts only. Must be 21 or older. Cannot be combined with any other offer or promotion. Non-transferable. Offer void if sold. Please allow up to 72 hours for points to reflect on account balance.

Must present original coupon (no photocopies). Not responsible for lost or stolen coupon. Management reserves all rights. Offer may be changed or discontinued at anytime at the discretion of management. Offer expires December 30, 2015.

Offer void if coupon is copied or sold

(702) 399-3297 • (877) 333-9291
3227 Civic Center Drive
N. Las Vegas, NV 89030

Restrictions apply. See Players' club for complete rules. Limit one coupon per customer. **Must be a new member.** This offer is non-transferable, non-refundable and has no cash value. MUST mention ACG. Must present and surrender this coupon upon use. No exceptions. Not available in conjunction with any other offer, Management reserves all rights. Must be 21 or older. Offer subject to change or cancellation at any time without notice. Offer expires December 30, 2015.

Offer void if coupon is copied or sold

Buy One Entrée
Get One Free
(or 50% one entrée when dining alone)

Purchase one entrée at Lucy's Bar & Grill and get a second entrée for FREE, or get 50% off one entrée when dining alone. See reverse for details.

A current American Casino Guide Discount Card must be presented when redeeming this coupon, or offer is void

$10 Table Games
Match Bet

Place a $10 even-money bet with this voucher at Lucky Club, along with your players' card, and get an extra $10 if you win! See reverse for more details.

A current American Casino Guide Discount Card must be presented when redeeming this coupon, or offer is void

FREE Appetizer
With Purchase of
Two Entrees

Present this coupon to your server when ordering to get a FREE appetizer with the purchase of 2 entrees at Tacos & Tequila located inside the Luxor Las Vegas. See reverse for more details.

A current American Casino Guide Discount Card must be presented when redeeming this coupon, or offer is void

americancasinoguide.com

(702) 399-3297 • (877) 333-9291
3227 Civic Center Drive
N. Las Vegas, NV 89030

Present this original coupon to your server in Lucy's Bar & Grill, along with your My Points Las Vegas Club card, to receive one FREE entree with the purchase of another entree at the regular price, or 50% off a single entree when dining alone. The FREE entree must be of equal or lesser value. Not valid for to-go orders. Limit: one coupon per customer, per month. No cash value. Must be 21 years of age or older. Tax and gratuity not included. Management reserves all rights. Offer expires 12/30/15.

Offer void if coupon is copied or sold

americancasinoguide.com

(702) 399-3297 • (877) 333-9291
3227 Civic Center Drive
N. Las Vegas, NV 89030

Present this coupon to Lucky Club Players' Club for redemption. Valid for new and existing members. Limit one per calendar year. Offer is non-transferrable and has no cash value. Offer cannot be combined with any other offer. Management reserves all rights. Must be 21 years or older with a valid form of ID. Offer expires December 30, 2015.

Offer void if coupon is copied or sold

americancasinoguide.com

3500 Las Vegas Blvd S.
Las Vegas, NV 89109
(702) 262-4555
Luxor.com

Present this coupon to your server when ordering to get a FREE appetizer with the purchase of 2 entrees. Appetizer Sampler not available with this offer. Limit: one coupon per customer, per calendar month. No cash value. Must be 21 years of age or older. Tax and gratuity not included. Resale prohibited. Management reserves all rights. Offer expires 12/30/15.

Offer void if coupon is copied or sold

AMERICAN CASINO GUIDE

Madame Tussauds
LAS VEGAS

2-For-1 General Admission

Receive one FREE ticket with the purchase of a full-price adult general admission ticket at Madame Tussauds Interactive Wax Attraction located in front of the Venetian Resort on Las Vegas Boulevard. See reverse for details.

5106

A current American Casino Guide Discount Card must be presented when redeeming this coupon, or offer is void

---

AMERICAN CASINO GUIDE

MAIN STREET STATION
CASINO BREWERY HOTEL

Earn 250 points, Get a Free Buffet
(Keep the points)

Earn 250 base points playing slots, then present this original coupon and B Connected card to the B Connected Club to receive a voucher that will entitle bearer to one FREE breakfast, lunch or brunch buffet at the Garden Court Buffet. See reverse side for details.

A current American Casino Guide Discount Card must be presented when redeeming this coupon, or offer is void

---

AMERICAN CASINO GUIDE

MAIN STREET STATION
CASINO BREWERY HOTEL

One Free Room Night

Buy two nights and get the third night FREE! Valid Sunday through Thursday. Subject to availability. Excludes Holidays and blackout periods. For reservations, call (800) 465-0711 and reference offer: **ZACG15**

A current American Casino Guide Discount Card must be presented when redeeming this coupon, or offer is void

LAS VEGAS

Who would you like to meet at the world famous Madame Tussauds Las Vegas? Featuring over 100 lifelike wax figures of your favorite celebrities, Madame Tussauds removes the velvet ropes and allows you to get up close to your favorite stars!

Madame Tussauds Las Vegas is open daily at 10 a.m. For more information and pricing, please call (866) 841-3739 or visit madametussauds.com. Located in front of the Venetian Resort on Las Vegas Blvd (The Strip). Not valid with any other discount promotion. Expires December 31, 2015.

200 North Main Street
Las Vegas, NV 89101
(800) 713-8933
www.mainstreetcasino.com

Must be 21 or older and have an active B Connected card. Not valid on holidays. Earn 250 base points playing slots on the same day original coupon is presented to the B Connected Club for redemption. Limit one coupon per person. Excludes dinner and specialty night buffets. Coupon has no cash value, cannot be combined with any other offer, or used more than once. Reproduction, sale, barter, or transfer are prohibited and render this coupon void. Management reserves all rights to change or discontinue this offer without notice. Expires 12/30/2015. Offer code: GYCA0ZZK6

MAIN STREET
STATION
CASINO · BREWERY · HOTEL

200 North Main Street
Las Vegas, NV 89101
(800) 713-8933
www.mainstreetcasino.com

This voucher entitles the bearer to one free room night at the Main Street Station Casino Brewery Hotel, with the purchase of two room nights at the prevailing rate. Advance reservations required. Voucher must be presented upon check-in. Offer is not valid in conjunction with any other offer. Management reserves all rights to cancel this promotion without notification. Credit card required at the time of reservation and at check in. Guest is responsible for all incidental charges. Must be 21 or older. One free room per person. Offer expires December 28, 2015. This voucher has no cash value, cannot be combined with any other offer or used more than once.

New Members Play $25 Get $10

Present this coupon when signing up for a new B Connected
card to be eligible for Play $25 and Get $10 slot play.
See reverse for full details.

A current American Casino Guide Discount Card must be
presented when redeeming this coupon, or offer is void

Buy One Drink
Get One FREE

Buy one drink at The Crossroads at House of Blues Restaurant & Bar
and get a second drink FREE. See reverse for full details.

A current American Casino Guide Discount Card must be
presented when redeeming this coupon, or offer is void

Free Hat at HOB Company Store

Receive a FREE baseball cap at the House of Blues Company Store with
the purchase of a t-shirt of $25 or more. See reverse for full details.

A current American Casino Guide Discount Card must be
presented when redeeming this coupon, or offer is void

California Hotel Casino	**Fremont Hotel & Casino**	**Main Street Station**
12 East Ogden Avenue	200 Fremont St	200 North Main Street
Las Vegas, NV 89101	Las Vegas, NV 89101	Las Vegas, NV 89101
(800) 634-6505	(800) 634-6460	(800) 713-8933
www.thecal.com	www.fremontcasino.com	www.mainstreetcasino.com

Present this coupon when signing up for a new B Connected card at your choice of casinos - the California, Fremont, or Main Street Station to be eligible for the Play & Get slot play. One Play & Get offer per new B Connected account. Slot play refers to non-cashable downloadable machine credits and will be uploaded to your B Connected account, pin number is required. Slot play is non-transferable and cannot be used with any other offer. You must be 21 or over to participate. Slot play will expire 24 hrs after coupon redemption. Management reserves the right to modify or cancel this promotion without prior notice. See the B Connected Club for additional details. Expires 12/30/2015. Offer code:TYFA0Z0K6

Located at
Mandalay Bay Hotel & Casino
3950 Las Vegas Blvd South
Las Vegas, NV 89119
702-632-7600
www.houseofblues.com/lasvegas

Good for one domestic beer, well drink or house wine, valid at the bar only. Free drink must be of equal or lesser value. Must present this coupon when ordering drink. Limit one coupon per customer. Not valid with any other offers or on holidays. Offer is non-transferable and has no cash value. Must be 21+ with valid ID. Management reserves all rights. Expires 12/30/15.

Located at
Mandalay Bay Hotel & Casino
3950 Las Vegas Blvd South
Las Vegas, NV 89119
702-632-7600
www.houseofblues.com/lasvegas

T-shirt purchase of $25 or more required. Free baseball cap is a $20 value. Must present this coupon when purchasing retail item. Limit one coupon per customer. Not valid with any other offers. Not valid on previous purchases. Offer is non-transferable and has no cash value. Management reserves all rights. Expires 12/30/15

AMERICAN CASINO GUIDE

Family & Friends
50% Off Adult Ticket
to Gospel Brunch

Present this coupon when booking your Gospel Brunch ticket
to receive the 50% discount. See reverse for details.

A current American Casino Guide Discount Card must be
presented when redeeming this coupon, or offer is void

AMERICAN CASINO GUIDE

Buy One
Get One
Free

Present this coupon at any Nathan's listed on the back,
purchase your choice of any menu item and receive your
choice of a second menu item of equal or lesser value free!

A current American Casino Guide Discount Card must be
presented when redeeming this coupon, or offer is void

AMERICAN CASINO GUIDE

2-for-1 Admission

**Have a scream!
Ride The Roller Coaster
at New York-New York.**

The
**ROLLER
COASTER**
at New York - New York

**Purchase one Roller Coaster Pass
at regular price and receive one
free ride ticket.**

A current American Casino Guide Discount Card must be
presented when redeeming this coupon, or offer is void

Located at
Mandalay Bay Hotel & Casino
3950 Las Vegas Blvd South
Las Vegas, NV 89119
702-632-7600
www.houseofblues.com/lasvegas

Subject to availability. Must present coupon when booking adult Gospel Brunch ticket to receive discounted offer. Limit one coupon per customer. Not valid with any other offers or on holidays. Offer is non-transferable and has no cash value. Management reserves all rights. Expires 12/30/15.

MGM Grand Hotel • Palms Hotel and Casino
New York New York Hotel and Casino
Venetian Hotel Grand Canal Shoppes • Bally's Hotel
Luxor Hotel • Fashion Show Mall Food Court
Mandalay Bay Hotel And Casino

Must present coupon to cashier prior to ordering. Offer has no cash value. Not valid with any other offer. One coupon per person. Subject to change or cancellation without prior notice. Offer valid through December 31, 2015.

3790 Las Vegas Boulevard South
Las Vegas, NV 89109
(866) 815-4365

Height Restrictions apply. Hours of operation subject to weather conditions and other circumstances which may suspend service. Coupon is void if altered or duplicated. Must present original coupon (no photocopies). Not valid for re-rides. Expires 12/30/15.

NEW YORK PRETZEL

Buy One Get One Free

Present this coupon at any New York Pretzel listed on the back, purchase your choice of any menu item and receive your choice of a second menu item of equal or lesser value free!

Original CHICKEN TENDER

Free Hand Battered Chicken Tenders & Fresh Cut Fries

Present this coupon at Original Chicken Tender, buy any meal and receive a second meal of equal or lesser value free! See reverse for details.

Original CHICKEN TENDER

Buy One Breakfast Item Get One Free

Present this coupon at Original Chicken Tender, purchase any breakfast menu item and receive a second breakfast menu item of equal or lesser value FREE! See reverse for details.

Venetian Hotel Grand Canal Shoppes
MGM Grand Hotel - Star Lane Mall
New York New York Hotel - MGM Entrance

Must present coupon to cashier prior to ordering. Offer has no cash value. Not valid with any other offer. One coupon per person. Subject to change or cancellation without prior notice. Offer valid through December 31, 2015.

Luxor Food Court • MGM Grand Food Court
Monte Carlo Hotel Food Court

Must present coupon to cashier prior to ordering. Offer has no cash value. Not valid with any other offer. One coupon per person. Subject to change or cancellation without prior notice. Offer valid through December 31, 2015.

Luxor Food Court • MGM Grand Food Court
Monte Carlo Hotel Food Court

Must present coupon to cashier prior to ordering. Offer has no cash value. Not valid with any other offer. One coupon per person. Subject to change or cancellation without prior notice. Offer valid through December 31, 2015.

The ORLEANS
HOTEL & CASINO · LAS VEGAS

$10 Table Games Match Play

This coupon entitles the bearer to $10 in match play on any casino table game at The Orleans (except live poker). Present to your casino dealer. Good for one decision on even-money bets only. An equal wager of real chips or cash must accompany this coupon. See reverse side for details.

A current American Casino Guide Discount Card must be presented when redeeming this coupon, or offer is void

The ORLEANS
HOTEL & CASINO · LAS VEGAS

Two Showroom Tickets For
The Price of One

This coupon entitles the bearer to one free ticket of equal value for purchase of one ticket to any show in The Orleans Showroom. Present coupon at The Orleans Showroom box office. See reverse side for details.

A current American Casino Guide Discount Card must be presented when redeeming this coupon, or offer is void

The ORLEANS
HOTEL & CASINO · LAS VEGAS

Play $10 get $10 Free Slot Dollars

Play $10 on slots or video poker and get $10 free play. Upon playing $10 through any Orleans slot or video poker machine, you will be credited with $10 in free play. See reverse for details.

A current American Casino Guide Discount Card must be presented when redeeming this coupon, or offer is void

446 American Casino Guide - 2015

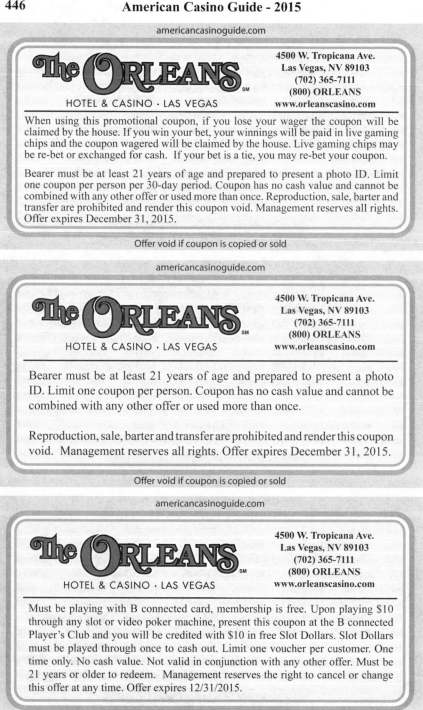

The ORLEANS℠
HOTEL & CASINO · LAS VEGAS

4500 W. Tropicana Ave.
Las Vegas, NV 89103
(702) 365-7111
(800) ORLEANS
www.orleanscasino.com

When using this promotional coupon, if you lose your wager the coupon will be claimed by the house. If you win your bet, your winnings will be paid in live gaming chips and the coupon wagered will be claimed by the house. Live gaming chips may be re-bet or exchanged for cash. If your bet is a tie, you may re-bet your coupon.

Bearer must be at least 21 years of age and prepared to present a photo ID. Limit one coupon per person per 30-day period. Coupon has no cash value and cannot be combined with any other offer or used more than once. Reproduction, sale, barter and transfer are prohibited and render this coupon void. Management reserves all rights. Offer expires December 31, 2015.

The ORLEANS℠
HOTEL & CASINO · LAS VEGAS

4500 W. Tropicana Ave.
Las Vegas, NV 89103
(702) 365-7111
(800) ORLEANS
www.orleanscasino.com

Bearer must be at least 21 years of age and prepared to present a photo ID. Limit one coupon per person. Coupon has no cash value and cannot be combined with any other offer or used more than once.

Reproduction, sale, barter and transfer are prohibited and render this coupon void. Management reserves all rights. Offer expires December 31, 2015.

The ORLEANS℠
HOTEL & CASINO · LAS VEGAS

4500 W. Tropicana Ave.
Las Vegas, NV 89103
(702) 365-7111
(800) ORLEANS
www.orleanscasino.com

Must be playing with B connected card, membership is free. Upon playing $10 through any slot or video poker machine, present this coupon at the B connected Player's Club and you will be credited with $10 in free Slot Dollars. Slot Dollars must be played through once to cash out. Limit one voucher per customer. One time only. No cash value. Not valid in conjunction with any other offer. Must be 21 years or older to redeem. Management reserves the right to cancel or change this offer at any time. Offer expires 12/31/2015.

2-For-1 Buffet
(Sunday-Thursday)

Buy one Feast Buffet and get the second Feast Buffet free.
Offer valid Sunday-Thursday. See reverse for more details.

PALACE STATION
HOTEL · CASINO

2-FOR-1 Fajitas in Cabo

Buy one Fajita and get the second Fajita Free. Offer valid 7 days
a week. See reverse for more details.

PALMS®
CASINO RESORT

$10 in FREE Slot Play!

Get $10 in free slot play when you've earned 400 base points on
slots or 3,000 base points on video poker in one 24-hour period
from 12:01am – 11:59pm. See reverse for complete details.

americancasinoguide.com

2411 W Sahara Ave
Las Vegas, NV 89102
(702) 367-2411
www.palacestation.sclv.com

This voucher entitles bearer to one free breakfast, lunch or dinner in the Feast Buffet when accompanied by a cash paying guest. Tax and gratuity not included. One voucher per person/subscriber. Voucher must be presented to cashier. Vouchers are not transferable and are not redeemable for cash. Must be 21 or older. Not a line pass. Not valid on holidays, Not valid with any other offer. Offer may be changed or discontinued at any time at the discretion of management. Original vouchers only. Offer is void if sold. Offer expires December 23, 2015. Settle to: #88-942

Offer void if coupon is copied or sold

americancasinoguide.com

2411 W Sahara Ave
Las Vegas, NV 89102
(702) 367-2411
www.palacestation.sclv.com

Tax and gratuity not included. One voucher per person/subscriber. Voucher must be presented to cashier. Vouchers are not transferable and are not redeemable for cash. Must be 21 or older. Not a line pass. Not valid on holidays. Not valid with any other offer. Offer may be changed or discontinued at any time at the discretion of management. Original vouchers only. Offer is void if sold. Offer expires December 23, 2015. Settle To: #20-400

Offer void if coupon is copied or sold

americancasinoguide.com

(702) 942-7777 • 1-866-942-7777
On Flamingo West of the Strip
Easy Access Convenient Parking
ww.palms.com

Present this coupon along with your Club Palms Card to the Club Palms Booth. Offer must be redeemed on day points earned. Not valid on manual adjustments or bonus points. Limit one coupon per customer. One time only. No cash value. Not valid in conjunction with any other offer. Must be 21 years of age or older to redeem. Management reserves the right to cancel or change this offer at any time. **Not valid on non-promotional machines.** Expires 12/31/15.

Offer void if coupon is copied or sold

PALMS. CASINO RESORT

$50 in FREE Slot Play!

Get $50 in free slot play when you've earned 2,000 base points on slots or 15,000 base points on video poker in one 24-hour period from 12:01am – 11:59pm. See reverse for complete details.

PALMS. CASINO RESORT

$10 Match Play for Any Even-Money Table Game Bet

Make a $10 even-money bet at blackjack, craps or roulette with this coupon and your Club Palms Card and receive a FREE $10 Match Bet!

Paris LAS VEGAS

20% Off One Item

Redeem at select Paris Las Vegas stores for 20% off one item. See reverse for details.

Offer code: GUIDE CPN

PALMS.
CASINO RESORT

(702) 942-7777 • 1-866-942-7777
On Flamingo West of the Strip
Easy Access Convenient Parking
ww.palms.com

Present this coupon along with your Club Palms Card to the Club Palms Booth Offer must be redeemed on day points earned. Not valid on manual adjustments or bonus points. Limit one coupon per customer. One time only. No cash value. Not valid in conjunction with any other offer. Must be 21 years of age or older to redeem. Management reserves the right to cancel or change this offer at any time. **Not valid on non-promotional machines.** Expires 12/31/15.

PALMS.
CASINO RESORT

(702) 942-7777 • 1-866-942-7777
On Flamingo West of the Strip
Easy Access Convenient Parking
ww.palms.com

Must be 21 years of age or older and a Club Palms member. Make a $10 minimum even-money bet at any blackjack, craps or roulette game, along with this original coupon (no photocopies), and receive a $10 Match Bet. Good for one decision on even money bets only. Win or lose, coupon is claimed by the house. If you tie, then coupon may be re-bet. No cash value. Limit: one coupon per customer, per year. Not valid with any other offer. Management reserves all rights. Offer expires 12/31/15.

3655 Las Vegas Blvd. S
Las Vegas, NV 89109
(702) 946-7000
ParisLasVegas.com

Valid at Paris Le Journal Shop, Eiffel Tour Shop, Petits Cheris and Glitz to Go Kiosk. Not valid on previous purchases. Limit 1 coupon per guest. No cash value. Cannot be combined with any other offer. Subject to availability. Blackout dates may apply. Management reserves all rights. Offer subject to change or cancellation without notification. Offer expires 12/30/15.

E**I**FFEL*TOWER*
E X P E R I E N C E
2-FOR-1 TICKETS

Redeem at the Paris Box Office for 2-for-1 admission to
the Eiffel Tower Ride. See reverse for details.

Offer code: AMCAS2012

A current American Casino Guide Discount Card must be
presented when redeeming this coupon, or offer is void

Anthony Cools   Free Upgrade to VIP Seating

Get a FREE upgrade to VIP seating with the purchase of a regular price
ticket to the Anthony Cools Hypnotism show. Valid for up to two tickets.
Coupon must be presented at the box office. See back for full details.

A current American Casino Guide Discount Card must be
presented when redeeming this coupon, or offer is void

ph planet hollywood
RESORT & CASINO • LAS VEGAS
2-FOR-1 DRINKS

Redeem at the Extra Bar or Playing Field Lounge at
Planet Hollywood Resort & Casino to get two drinks
for the price of one. See reverse for details.

PFL Offer code: ACG1B   EB Offer code: ACG2B

A current American Casino Guide Discount Card must be
presented when redeeming this coupon, or offer is void

3655 Las Vegas Blvd. S
Las Vegas, NV 89109
702-946-7000
ParisLasVegas.com

Present coupon at time of purchase to redeem. Limit 4 per coupon. No cash value. Not valid on previously purchased tickets or Express Pass Tickets. Cannot be combined with any other offer. Subject to availability. Service fees apply. Blackout dates may apply. Management reserves all rights. Offer subject to change or cancellation without notification. Offer expires 12/30/15

Paris Las Vegas Casino & Hotel
3655 Las Vegas Boulevard S.
Las Vegas, NV 89109
(702) 946-7000 or visit
www.parislasvegas.com

Subject to availability. Show times subject to change. Offers cannot be combined. Coupon must be presented at time of purchase and is only available through the box office. Management reserves all rights. Not for resale. Valid through 12/30/15. Offer Code: AMCAS2014

ph planet hollywood®
RESORT & CASINO • LAS VEGAS

3667 Las Vegas Blvd S
Las Vegas, NV 89109
(702) 785-5555
planethollywoodresort.com

Must be 21 with valid ID. Present coupon at time of purchase to redeem. Second drink must be of equal or lesser value. No cash value. Cannot be combined with any other offer. Subject to availability. Blackout dates may apply. Management reserves all rights. Offer subject to change or cancellation without notification. Offer expires 12/30/15

AMERICAN CASINO GUIDE

VTHEATER   SAXE THEATER

2-for-1 Show Tickets
Your choice of shows!

Zombie Burlesque • V The Ultimate Variety Show • Vegas! The Show
The Mentalist • B - A Tribute to The Beatles • And More!

Present this coupon at the box office when you purchase a full-price adult
show ticket and receive a second show ticket FREE! Or, purchase a single
full-price adult show ticket and get 50% off. See back for full details.

ACGF4ADG-001

A current American Casino Guide Discount Card must be
presented when redeeming this coupon, or offer is void

AMERICAN CASINO GUIDE

Plaza

Buy 1
Small Rainbow
Get 1 Free

Present this coupon to any Bingo Agent along with your Royal
Rewards Card and receive a free Small Rainbow with the
purchase of another. See reverse for details.

A current American Casino Guide Discount Card must be
presented when redeeming this coupon, or offer is void

AMERICAN CASINO GUIDE

Plaza

$5 FREE
Slot Play

Present this coupon to the Royal Rewards Center to
receive $5 in FREE Slot Play. See reverse for details.

A current American Casino Guide Discount Card must be
presented when redeeming this coupon, or offer is void

V THEATER   SAXE THEATER

In the Miracle Mile Shops at Planet Hollywood - 3663 Las Vegas Blvd.
For show information call (866) 932-1818

Present this voucher at the V Theater or Saxe Theater box office and receive one FREE show ticket when you purchase one adult ticket at the regular price, or receive 50% off one ticket. Voucher has no cash value and cannot be combined with any other offer or applied to prior purchase. Tax and fees apply. Good for up to four people. Seats subject to availability. Restrictions apply. Offer redeemable at the V Theater or Saxe Theater box offices only. Management reserves all rights. Offer expires December 30, 2015.

1 Main Street
Las Vegas, NV 89101
(702) 386-2110
(800) 634-6575
www.PlazaHotelCasino.com

Present this coupon to Bingo Attendant prior to game 1 of the Bingo session. Limit one coupon per session. Must present original coupon (no photocopies). Must be a Royal Rewards member and 21 years of age or older. Coupon has no cash value. Not valid in conjunction with any other offer. Management reserves the right to amend or cancel this promotion with 24 hours prior notice. Offer expires 12/29/15.

1 Main Street
Las Vegas, NV 89101
(702) 386-2110
(800) 634-6575
www.PlazaHotelCasino.com

Present this voucher to the Royal Rewards Center and receive $5 in FREE slot play. Limit one coupon per account per calendar year. Must present original coupon (no photocopies).

Must be a Royal Rewards member and 21 years of age or older. Not valid in conjunction with any other offer. Management reserves the right to cancel or change this offer at any time. Offer expires 12/29/15.

AMERICAN CASINO GUIDE

2-For-1 Drink

Redeem this coupon at any casino bar.
See reverse for details.

A current American Casino Guide Discount Card must be
presented when redeeming this coupon, or offer is void

AMERICAN CASINO GUIDE

RAMPART / CASINO
AT THE RESORT AT SUMMERLIN

$5 Match Play for Any Even-Money Table Game Bet

Make a $5 even-money bet on blackjack, craps or roulette
with this coupon and your Resort Rewards card and receive
a $5 Match Bet! See reverse for details.

A current American Casino Guide Discount Card must be
presented when redeeming this coupon, or offer is void

AMERICAN CASINO GUIDE

Rampart Buffet

2-For-1 Buffet
(or 50% off when dining alone)

Buy one buffet and get a second one FREE (or 50% off when dining
alone). When using as 2-for-1 coupon both buffets must be redeemed
on same visit. See reverse for more details.

A current American Casino Guide Discount Card must be
presented when redeeming this coupon, or offer is void

americancasinoguide.com

1 Main Street
Las Vegas, NV 89101
(702) 386-2110
(800) 634-6575
www.PlazaHotelCasino.com

Valid on well drinks, domestic beers, house wines, soda or water. Free drink of equal or lesser value. Gratuity not included. Limit one per person. Coupon has no cash value.

May not be combined with any other offer. Must be a Royal Rewards member and 21 years of age or older. Must be 21 years of age or older. Settle to Comp #82200. Management reserves all rights. Expires 12/29/15.

americancasinoguide.com

221 N. Rampart Boulevard
Las Vegas, NV 89128
(702) 507-5900
(877) 869-8777
www.RampartCasino.com

Must be 21 or older and a Resort Rewards member. Make a $5 even-money bet at any blackjack, craps or roulette game, with this original coupon (no photocopies), and your Resort Rewards card to receive a $5 Match Bet. Good for one decision on even money bets only. Win or lose, coupon is claimed by the house. If you tie, then coupon may be re-bet. No cash value. Limit: one coupon per customer, per year. Not valid with any other offer. Management reserves all rights. Valid through 12/30/15.

americancasinoguide.com

221 N. Rampart Boulevard
Las Vegas, NV 89128
(702) 507-5900
(877) 869-8777
www.RampartCasino.com

Present this coupon to the cashier at time of purchase. Must be 21 or older to reeem. Tax and gratuity not included. Coupon not redeeemable for cash. Must have Resort Rewards card. Original coupon (no photocopies) must be presented to the cashier. One coupon per customer. Not valid with any other coupon or offer. Management reserves all rights. Valid through 12/30/15.

AMERICAN CASINO GUIDE

SPA AQUAE

AT THE JW MARRIOTT, LAS VEGAS

30% Off
Spa

Redeem at the Spa Aquae at the Rampart Casino for 30% off any spa treatment. See reverse for details.

AMERICAN CASINO GUIDE

red rock
SM

CASINO · RESORT · SPA

2-For-1 Buffet
(Sunday-Thursday)

Buy one Feast Buffet and get the second Feast Buffet free. Offer valid Sunday-Thursday. See reverse for more details.

AMERICAN CASINO GUIDE

red rock
SM

CASINO · RESORT · SPA

$20 For $10
at Grand Cafe

Present this coupon to your server before ordering to receive $20 in food for only $10. See reverse for more details.

221 N. Rampart Boulevard
Las Vegas, NV 89128
(702) 507-5900
(877) 869-8777
www.RampartCasino.com

Limit one treatment per coupon. No cash value. Not valid on previously purchased services or on waxing. Cannot be combined with any other offer, package or discount. Subject to availability. Blackout dates may apply. Management reserves all rights. Offer subject to change or cancellation without notification. Valid through 12/30/15.

11011 W Charleston Blvd
Las Vegas, NV 89135
(702) 797-7777
www.redrock.sclv.com

This voucher entitles bearer to one free breakfast, lunch or dinner in the Feast Buffet when accompanied by a full price, cash paying guest. Tax and gratuity not included. One voucher per person/subscriber. Voucher must be presented to cashier. Vouchers are not transferable and are not redeemable for cash. Must be 21 or older. Not a line pass. Not valid on holidays, Not valid with any other offer. Offer may be changed or discontinued at any time at the discretion of management. Original vouchers only. Offer is void if sold. Offer expires 12/23/15. Settle to: #88-942

11011 W Charleston Blvd
Las Vegas, NV 89135
(702) 797-7777
www.redrock.sclv.com

Present this voucher to the cashier at the Grand Cafe to receive $10 off a minimum check total of $20 or more (excluding alcohol). Gratuity not included. Offer valid for dine in only and valid 7 days per week. Limit one offer per check. Voucher is not transferable and not redeemable for cash. Must be 21 or older. Not a line pass. Not valid on holidays. Not valid with any other offer or menu specials. Offer may change or be discontinued at any time at the discretion of management. Original vouchers only. Offer is void if sold. Offer valid at Red Rock Resort location only. Offer expires 12/23/15. Settle to: #41-310

CARNIVAL WORLD BUFFET

$5 Off

Redeem at the Carnival World Buffet® at Rio Las Vegas for $5 off buffet admission. See reverse for details.

Offer code: CB5TZ

A current American Casino Guide Discount Card must be presented when redeeming this coupon, or offer is void

VILLAGE SEAFOOD BUFFET

$10 Off

Redeem at the Village Seafood Buffet® at Rio Las Vegas for $10 off buffet admission. See reverse for details.

Offer code: 10VSB

A current American Casino Guide Discount Card must be presented when redeeming this coupon, or offer is void

VOODOO STEAK

$10 Off Entrée

Redeem at Voodoo Steak at Rio Las Vegas for $10 off your entrée. See reverse for details.

Offer code: ACGR1

A current American Casino Guide Discount Card must be presented when redeeming this coupon, or offer is void

americancasinoguide.com

3700 W. Flamingo Rd.
Las Vegas, NV 89103
(702) 777-7777
RioLasVegas.com

Present coupon at time of purchase to redeem. Limit 4 per coupon. Excludes Buffet of Buffets passes. No cash value. Not valid on previously purchased tickets. Cannot be combined with any other offer. Subject to availability. Blackout dates may apply. Management reserves all rights. Offer subject to change or cancellation without notification. Offer expires 12/30/15

americancasinoguide.com

3700 W. Flamingo Rd.
Las Vegas, NV 89103
(702) 777-7777
RioLasVegas.com

Present coupon at time of purchase to redeem. Limit 4 per coupon. Excludes Buffet of Buffets passes. No cash value. Not valid on previously purchased tickets. Cannot be combined with any other offer. Subject to availability. Blackout dates may apply. Management reserves all rights. Offer subject to change or cancellation without notification. Offer Expires 12/30/15

americancasinoguide.com

3700 W. Flamingo Rd.
Las Vegas, NV 89103
(702) 777-7777
RioLasVegas.com

Minimum purchase of 2 entrees. Tax & gratuity not included. No cash value. Not valid on previously purchased services. Cannot be combined with any other offer. Subject to availability. Blackout dates may apply. Management reserves all rights. Offer subject to change or cancellation without notification. Offer expires 12/30/15

2901 Las Vegas Blvd. S.
Las Vegas, NV 89109
(800) 634-3420
rivierahotel.com

Valid at the Comedy Club at the Riviera Las Vegas only. Present coupon at time of purchase to redeem. Limit 1 coupon per party. No cash value. Cannot be combined with any other offer. Subject to availability. Blackout dates may apply. Management reserves all rights. Offer subject to change or cancellation without notification. Offer expires 12/30/15.

2901 Las Vegas Blvd. S.
Las Vegas, NV 89109
(800) 634-3420
rivierahotel.com

Must be 21 years of age or older and a Riviera Rewards member. Make a $10 minimum even-money bet at any blackjack, craps or roulette game, along with this original coupon (no photocopies), and receive a $10 Match Bet. Good for one decision on even money bets only. Win or lose, coupon is claimed by the house. If you tie, then coupon may be re-bet. No cash value. Limit: one coupon per customer, per 12-month period. Not valid with any other offer. Management reserves all rights. Offer expires 12/30/15.

2901 Las Vegas Blvd. S.
Las Vegas, NV 89109
(800) 634-3420
rivierahotel.com

Show open to all ages. Must redeem coupon at the Riviera Box Office to receive second ticket for free with purchase of one at full price. Coupon is void if altered or duplicated. Tax and box office fees are not included. Not valid with any other offers or discounts. Not valid towards previously purchased tickets. Valid for up to 4 tickets. Subject to availability. Management reserves the right to cancel or modify offer at any time. Coupon has no cash value. Offer expires December 29, 2015.

2-for-1 VIP Show Tickets

Receive one complimentary ticket to Men The Experience with the purchase of one VIP ticket at full price. See reverse for more details.

Offer Code: ACGR/C

A current American Casino Guide Discount Card must be presented when redeeming this coupon, or offer is void

2-for-1 VIP Show Tickets

Receive one complimentary ticket to Forever Motor City with the purchase of one VIP ticket at full price. See reverse for more details.

Offer Code: ACGR/C

A current American Casino Guide Discount Card must be presented when redeeming this coupon, or offer is void

SAM'S TOWN®

Earn 200 Points, Get Free Buffet
(Keep the points)

Earn 200 points playing slots then present this original coupon and B Connected Card to the B Connected Club, and receive a voucher that will entitle bearer to one FREE breakfast, lunch or regular dinner buffet. See reverse side for details.

A current American Casino Guide Discount Card must be presented when redeeming this coupon, or offer is void

americancasinoguide.com

2901 Las Vegas Blvd. S.
Las Vegas, NV 89109
(800) 634-3420
rivierahotel.com

Must be 18 or older to redeem coupon. Must redeem coupon at the Riviera Box Office to receive second ticket for free with purchase of one at full price. Coupon is void if altered or duplicated. Tax and box office fees are not included. Not valid with any other offers or discounts. Not valid towards previously purchased tickets. Valid for up to 4 tickets. Subject to availability. Management reserves the right to cancel or modify offer at any time. Coupon has no cash value. Offer expires December 29, 2015.

Offer void if coupon is copied or sold

americancasinoguide.com

2901 Las Vegas Blvd. S.
Las Vegas, NV 89109
(800) 634-3420
rivierahotel.com

Show open to all ages. Must redeem coupon at the Riviera Box Office to receive second ticket for free with purchase of one at full price. Coupon is void if altered or duplicated. Tax and box office fees are not included. Not valid with any other offers or discounts. Not valid towards previously purchased tickets. Valid for up to 4 tickets. Subject to availability. Management reserves the right to cancel or modify offer at any time. Coupon has no cash value. Offer expires December 29, 2015.

Offer void if coupon is copied or sold

americancasinoguide.com

Sam's Town Hotel & Gambling Hall
5111 Boulder Highway
Las Vegas, NV 89122
(702) 456-7777 • (800) 897-8696
www.samstownlv.com

Must be 21 or older and have an active B Connected Card. Not valid on Holidays.Earn 200 points playing slots on same day original coupon is presented to B Connected Club to obtain voucher. Limit one coupon per person. Excludes specialty night dinners. This coupon has no cash value, cannot be combined with any other offer or used more than once. Reproduction, sale, barter or transfer are prohibited and render this coupon void. Management reserves the right to change or discontinue this offer without notice. Expires 12/30/15.

Offer void if coupon is copied or sold

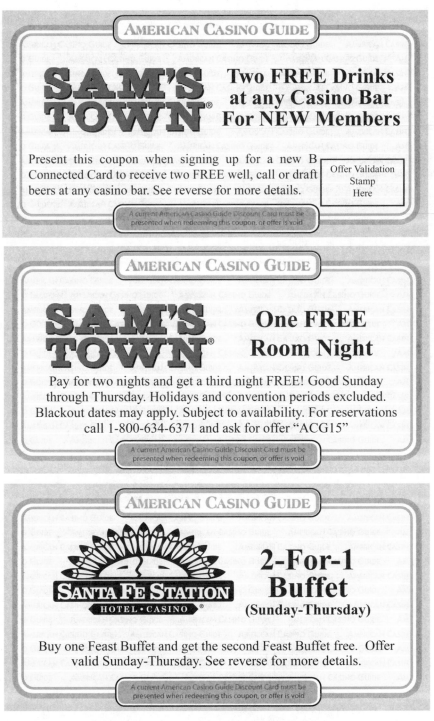

SAM'S TOWN®

Two FREE Drinks at any Casino Bar For NEW Members

Present this coupon when signing up for a new B Connected Card to receive two FREE well, call or draft beers at any casino bar. See reverse for more details.

Offer Validation Stamp Here

SAM'S TOWN®

One FREE Room Night

Pay for two nights and get a third night FREE! Good Sunday through Thursday. Holidays and convention periods excluded. Blackout dates may apply. Subject to availability. For reservations call 1-800-634-6371 and ask for offer "ACG15"

SANTA FE STATION
HOTEL · CASINO ®

2-For-1 Buffet
(Sunday-Thursday)

Buy one Feast Buffet and get the second Feast Buffet free. Offer valid Sunday-Thursday. See reverse for more details.

americancasinoguide.com

Sam's Town Hotel & Gambling Hall
5111 Boulder Highway
Las Vegas, NV 89122
(702) 456-7777 • (800) 897-8696
www.samstownlv.com

Present this coupon when signing up for a new B Connected card to receive two free well, call or draft beers at any casino bar. Must be 21 years of age or older. Coupon cannot be used in conjunction with any other offer. Management reserves right to change or cancel offer at any time. Must present B Connected Card with coupon for redemption. Coupon has no cash value. Expires 12/30/15. One per customer.

AM85994

Offer void if coupon is copied or sold

americancasinoguide.com

Sam's Town Hotel & Gambling Hall
5111 Boulder Highway
Las Vegas, NV 89122
(702) 456-7777 • (800) 897-8696
www.samstownlv.com

This voucher entitles the bearer to one free room night at Sam's Town Hotel & Casino, with the purchase of two nights at the prevailing rate. Must have advance reservations. Must present voucher upon check-in. Not valid in conjunction with any other offer. Management reserves the right to cancel this promotion at any time. Credit card or cash deposit required. Guest is responsible for all incidental charges. Must be 21 or older. Limit one free room per person. Offer expires 12/28/15.

Offer void if coupon is copied or sold

americancasinoguide.com

4949 N Rancho Dr
Las Vegas, NV 89108
(702) 658-4900
www. santafestation.sclv.com

This voucher entitles bearer to one free breakfast, lunch or dinner in the Feast Buffet when accompanied by a cash paying guest. Tax and gratuity not included. One voucher per person/subscriber. Voucher must be presented to cashier. Vouchers are not transferable and are not redeemable for cash. Must be 21 or older. Not a line pass. Not valid on holidays or specialty nights. Not valid with any other offer. Offer may be changed or discontinued at any time at the discretion of management. Original vouchers only. Offer is void if sold. Offer expires December 23, 2015. Settle to: #88-942

Offer void if coupon is copied or sold

AMERICAN CASINO GUIDE

SANTA FE STATION
HOTEL · CASINO

Free Margarita

Present this coupon to any casino bar for one Free Margarita.
See reverse for more details.

A current American Casino Guide Discount Card must be
presented when redeeming this coupon, or offer is void

AMERICAN CASINO GUIDE

SILVER NUGGET
CASINO

Buy One Entrée
Get One Free
(or 50% one entrée when dining alone)

Purchase one entrée at the Hometown Kitchen and get a
second entrée for FREE, or get 50% off one entrée
when dining alone. See reverse for details.

A current American Casino Guide Discount Card must be
presented when redeeming this coupon, or offer is void

AMERICAN CASINO GUIDE

SILVER NUGGET
CASINO

Free Deck of
Cards or Dice

Present this coupon at guest services and receive either a free deck
of cards or a pair of dice. See reverse for more details.

A current American Casino Guide Discount Card must be
presented when redeeming this coupon, or offer is void

4949 N Rancho Dr
Las Vegas, NV 89108
(702) 658-4900
www.santafestation.sclv.com

Present this coupon at time of payment. Tax and gratuity not included, valid with cash transactions only. No cash value. Not valid on holidays or with any other offer. Valid one time only. Must be 21 years of age or older. Limit one coupon per person. Valid at any casino bar inside Santa Fe Station. Management reserves all rights. Offer expires December 23, 2015. Settle to: #41-213

2140 Las Vegas Blvd. N.
N. Las Vegas, Nevada 89030
(702) 399-1111

Present this original coupon to your server in the Hometown Kitchen, along with your My Points Las Vegas Club card, to receive one FREE entree with the purchase of another entree at the regular price, or 50% off a single entree when dining alone. The FREE entree must be of equal or lesser value. Not valid for to-go orders. Limit: one coupon per customer, per month. No cash value. Must be 21 years of age or older. Tax and gratuity not included. Management reserves all rights. Offer expires 12/30/15.

2140 Las Vegas Blvd. N.
N. Las Vegas, Nevada 89030
(702) 399-1111

Restrictions apply. See Players' club for complete rules. Limit one coupon per customer. **Must be a new member.** This offer is non-transferable, non refundable and has no cash value. MUST mention ACG. Must present and surrender this coupon upon use. No exceptions. Not available in conjunction with any other offer, Management reserves all rights. Must be 21 or older. Offer subject to change or cancellation at any time without notice. Offer expires December 30, 2015.

SILVER NUGGET
CASINO

$5 in FREE Slot Play!

Get $5 in free slot play when you've earned 500 base points in one 24-hour period from 12:01am–11:59pm. See reverse for complete details.

SILVER SEVENS
HOTEL & CASINO

Buy One Night Get One Free!

Call 1-800-640-9777 to make your reservation. Offer Code: SSBOOK15

SILVER SEVENS
HOTEL & CASINO

Buy One Buffet Get One Free
(or 50% off one entrée when dining alone)

Purchase one buffet at the S7 Buffet and get the second one free, or get 50% off one buffet when dining alone. See reverse for details.

470   **American Casino Guide - 2015**

CASINO

2140 Las Vegas Blvd. N.
N. Las Vegas, Nevada 89030
(702) 399-1111

Restrictions apply. See Players' club for complete rules. Offer must be redeemed on day points earned. Not valid on manual adjustments or bonus points. Limit one coupon per customer. No cash value. Not valid in conjunction with any other offer. Must be 21 years of age or older to redeem. Management reserves the right to cancel or change this offer at any time. Expires 12/31/15.

Offer void if coupon is copied or sold

HOTEL & CASINO

Classic ✸ Las Vegas ✸ Fun

4100 Paradise Rd
Las Vegas, NV 89169
(702) 733-7000
www.silversevenscasino.com

Offer valid for any day of the week and cannot be booked online. Blackout dates may apply. Offer valid only after a purchase of one night at regularly published rates. Guest will receive free night on the lower of the two nightly rates. Offer cannot be combined with any other offer or promotional discount. No cash value. Resort fee applies on non-complimentary room nights. Credit card required when making reservation. Must present coupon at check-in. Must be 21 years of age or older to redeem this offer. Management reserves all rights to modify, change or cancel this offer at any time without prior notice. Offer Expires 12/28/15.

Offer void if coupon is copied or sold

HOTEL & CASINO

Classic ✸ Las Vegas ✸ Fun

4100 Paradise Rd
Las Vegas, NV 89169
(702) 733-7000
www.silversevenscasino.com

Present coupon to Buffet cashier. Must be an A-Play Club Card member to redeem offer. No cash value. Complimentary value good for up to $12.99. Receive one FREE buffet with the purchase of one buffet at regular price or receive 50% off one buffet. Limit one coupon per day, per party. Tax or gratuity not included. Must be 21 years of age or older to redeem this offer. Management reserves all rights to modify, change or cancel this offer at any time without prior notice. Settle to: 464. Offer Expires 12/28/15.

Offer void if coupon is copied or sold

SILVER SEVENS
HOTEL & CASINO

Buy One Entrée Get One Free
(or 50% off one entrée when dining alone)

Purchase one entrée at the Sterling Spoon Café and get a second entrée for FREE, or get 50% off one entrée when dining alone. See reverse for details.

SILVERTON
Casino • Hotel • Las Vegas

2-For-1 Seasons Buffet
(or 50% off when dining alone)

Must be a Silverton Rewards Club member. Must purchase one Seasons buffet at regular price, to receive a second buffet, of equal or lesser value, for free. Good for one time use only. See reverse for more details.

SILVERTON
Casino • Hotel • Las Vegas

New Members get $5 Free Play and a Free Gift

Plus get a Free Buffet when you Earn 50 points on First day

Must be a new Silverton Rewards Club member. Present this original coupon to the player's club when signing up. 50 points must be earned on day of sign up. You keep the points. See reverse for more details.

HOTEL & CASINO

Classic ✳ Las Vegas ✳ Fun

4100 Paradise Rd
Las Vegas, NV 89169
(702) 733-7000
www.silversevenscasino.com

Present coupon to Café cashier. Must be an A-Play Club Card member to redeem offer. No cash value. Receive one FREE entrée of equal or lesser value with the purchase of one entrée at regular price or receive 50% off one entrée. Limit one coupon per day, per party. Tax or gratuity not included. Must be 21 years of age or older to redeem this offer. Management reserves all rights to modify, change or cancel this offer at any time without prior notice. Settle to: 465. Offer Expires 12/28/15.

SILVERTON

Casino • Hotel • Las Vegas

Silverton Casino Hotel
3333 Blue Diamond Road
Las Vegas, NV 89139
www.silvertoncasino.com
702-263-7777 • 866-946-4373

Present this original coupon to the cashier at Seasons Buffet. Must be a Player's Club member, or sign up as a new club member to receive the offer. Player's Club membership is free. Limit one per customer. Offer is non-transferable, may not be used in conjunction with any other offer or promotion and has no cash value. Management reserves all rights. Must be 21 years of age or older, with a valid form of ID. Offer does not include gratuity. Offer void if sold. Settle to #D148 Expires 12/30/15.

SILVERTON

Casino • Hotel • Las Vegas

Silverton Casino Hotel
3333 Blue Diamond Road
Las Vegas, NV 89139
www.silvertoncasino.com
702-263-7777 • 866-946-4373

Must be a new Silverton Rewards Club Member. Redeem at Silverton Rewards Club. Silverton is not responsible for free slot play downloaded and inadvertently abandoned. Must be 21 years of age or older. Management reserves all rights. Silverton encourages responsible gaming. For help and information on problem gambling, please call the 24-hour Problem Gamblers Help Line at (800) 522-4700. Expires 12/30/15.

9777 S Las Vegas Blvd
Las Vegas, NV 89183
(702) 796-7111• (866) 791-7626
www.southpointcasino.com

Must be 21 or older and have an activeThe Club Card. Not valid on Holidays. Earn 300 points playing slots on same day original coupon is presented to The Club to obtain voucher. Limit one coupon per person. Excludes specialty night dinners. This coupon has no cash value, cannot be combined with any other offer or used more than once. Reproduction, sale, barter or transfer are prohibited and render this coupon void. Management reserves the right to change or discontinue this offer without notice. Expires 12/30/15.

9777 S Las Vegas Blvd
Las Vegas, NV 89183
(702) 796-7111• (866) 791-7626
www.southpointcasino.com

Must be 21 or older and present a valid government issued photo ID. Limit one coupon per person. Valid for new members in The Club. This coupon has no cash value, cannot be combined with any other offer or used more than once. Reproduction, sale, barter or transfer are prohibited and render this coupon void. Management reserves the right to change or discontinue this offer without notice. Expires 12/30/15.

STRATOSPHERE
HOTEL | **CASINO** | TOWER

For a glimpse of Frankie Moreno live and to view special offers, go to StratosphereHotel.com

OFFER CODE: ACG_FRANKIE
(Coupon must be presented at the Stratosphere Ticket Center.)

Management reserves all rights. Valid through December 30, 2015. Blackout dates apply. Contains Adult content. Ages 13-18 require accompanying parent or adult guardian. Subject to availability. Show times subject to change. Offers cannot be combined. Not for resale.Offer void if coupon is copied or sold.

PIN UP
STRATOSPHERE

**Two-For-One
Show Tickets**

Get one FREE PIN UP at Stratosphere ticket
with the purchase of one PIN UP ticket at full price.
(See back for full details.)

2000 Las Vegas Blvd. S. • Las Vegas, NV 89104 • 800.99.TOWER • 702.380.7777

A current American Casino Guide Discount Card must be
presented when redeeming this coupon, or offer is void

STRATOSPHERE
HOTEL | **CASINO** | TOWER

**Two-For-One
Tower Admission
Tickets**

Get one FREE Tower Admission ticket with the purchase
of one Tower Admission ticket at full price.
(See back for full details.)

2000 Las Vegas Blvd. S. • Las Vegas, NV 89104 • 800.99.TOWER • 702.380.7777

A current American Casino Guide Discount Card must be
presented when redeeming this coupon, or offer is void

SUNCOAST
HOTEL & CASINO · LAS VEGAS

**2-For-1
Breakfast or
Lunch Buffet**
(or 50% off when dining alone)

Buy one breakfast or lunch buffet and get a second one FREE (or 50% off
when dining alone). Offer valid Monday–Saturday. Coupon has no cash
value, must be 21 years of age or older. Must be a B Connected member
to redeem. See reverse for full details.

A current American Casino Guide Discount Card must be
presented when redeeming this coupon, or offer is void

STRATOSPHERE

HOTEL | **CASINO** | TOWER

For a glimpse of PIN UP™ live and to view special offers, go to StratosphereHotel.com

OFFER CODE: ACG_PINUP

(Coupon must be presented at the Stratosphere Ticket Center.)

Management reserves all rights. Valid through December 30, 2015. Blackout dates may apply. Must be at least 21 years of age to attend the show. Subject to availability. Show times subject to change. Offers cannot be combined. Not for resale. Offer void if coupon is copied or sold.

Offer void if coupon is copied or sold

STRATOSPHERE

HOTEL | **CASINO** | TOWER

OFFER CODE: ACG_TWR

To view special offers, go to StratosphereHotel.com
(Coupon must be presented at the Stratosphere Ticket Center.)

Management reserves all rights. Valid through December 30, 2015. Must be at least 18 years of age unless accompanied by an adult. Subject to availability. Offers cannot be combined. Not for resale. Offer void if coupon is copied or sold.

Offer void if coupon is copied or sold

SUNCOAST

HOTEL & CASINO · LAS VEGAS

(702) 636-7111 · (877) 677-7111
9090 Alta Dr
www.suncoastcasino.com

Present this coupon to St. Tropez Buffet cashier. Tax and Gratuity is not included Original coupon (no photocopies) must be presented at the time of purchase. This offer is not valid with any other offer or promotion and is not valid on holidays. This offer is void if sold. Management reserves the right to change or cancel this offer at anytime. Offer expires 12/20/15.

Offer Code: SBFAO14K6

B Connected Membership # _____

Offer void if coupon is copied or sold

5X Points!

Present this coupon to the B Connected Club and receive 5X points for one day's play from 12:01am-11:59pm. See reverse for more details.

A current American Casino Guide Discount Card must be presented when redeeming this coupon, or offer is void

SUNSET STATION
HOTEL · CASINO

2-For-1 Buffet
(Sunday-Thursday)

Buy one Feast Buffet and get the second Feast Buffet free. Offer valid Sunday-Thursday. See reverse for more details.

A current American Casino Guide Discount Card must be presented when redeeming this coupon, or offer is void

SUNSET STATION
HOTEL · CASINO

$50 For $25 at Sonoma Cellar Steakhouse

Present this coupon to your server before ordering to receive $50 in food for $25. See reverse for more details.

A current American Casino Guide Discount Card must be presented when redeeming this coupon, or offer is void

HOTEL & CASINO · LAS VEGAS

(702) 636-7111 • (877) 677-7111
9090 Alta Dr
www.suncoastcasino.com

Present this coupon to the B Connected Club with your B Connected Membership card. This offer cannot be used with any other offer or point multiplier offer. Must be 21 years of age. Maximum 100,000 points. Management reserves the right to change or cancel this offer at any time. Limit one coupon per person. Offer Expires 12/20/15

Group Codes: 5XAMER15E 5XAMER15R 5XAMERI5S

Offer void if coupon is copied or sold

1301 W Sunset Rd
Henderson, NV 89014
(702) 547-7715
www.sunsetstation.sclv.com

This voucher entitles bearer to one free breakfast, lunch or dinner in the Feast Buffet when accompanied by a cash paying guest. Tax and gratuity not included. One voucher per person/subscriber. Voucher must be presented to cashier. Vouchers are not transferable and are not redeemable for cash. Must be 21 or older. Not a line pass. Not valid on holidays, Not valid with any other offer. Offer may be changed or discontinued at any time at the discretion of management. Original vouchers only. Offer is void if sold. Offer expires December 23, 2015. Settle to: #88-942

Offer void if coupon is copied or sold

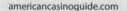

1301 W Sunset Rd
Henderson, NV 89014
(702) 547-7715
www.sunsetstation.sclv.com

This voucher may be taken to Sonoma Cellar Steakhouse for $25 for $50 in dining. Does not include tax or gratuity, must use full dollar amount in dining. No cash value. Offer is not to be combined with any other offer or discount. Offer good for dine in only. One coupon per table of 4 and max 4 guests per table. Offer is for cash paying guests only. Valid at Sunset Station Only. Management reserves all rights. Coupon must accompany book to be valid. Offer expires December 23, 2015. Settle To: #41-318

Offer void if coupon is copied or sold

2-For-1 Buffet
(Sunday-Thursday)

TEXAS STATION
Gambling Hall & Hotel

Buy one Feast Buffet and get the second Feast Buffet Free. Offer valid Sunday-Thursday. See reverse for more details.

A current American Casino Guide Discount Card must be presented when redeeming this coupon, or offer is void

$10 For $5 at Grand Cafe

TEXAS STATION
Gambling Hall & Hotel

Present this coupon to your server before ordering to receive $10 in food for only $5. See reverse for more details.

A current American Casino Guide Discount Card must be presented when redeeming this coupon, or offer is void

TUSCANY *SUITES & CASINO*

$10 Table Games Match Play

This coupon entitles the bearer to $10 in match play on any even-money bet. Present to your casino dealer. Good for one decision on even-money bets only. An equal wager of real chips or cash must accompany this coupon. See reverse side for details.

A current American Casino Guide Discount Card must be presented when redeeming this coupon, or offer is void

Gambling Hall & Hotel

2101 Texas Star Ln
North Las Vegas, NV 89032
(702) 631-1000
www.texasstation.sclv.com

This voucher entitles bearer to one free breakfast, lunch or dinner in the Feast Buffet when accompanied by a cash paying guest. Tax and gratuity not included. One voucher per person/subscriber. Voucher must be presented to cashier. Vouchers are not transferable and are not redeemable for cash. Must be 21 or older. Not a line pass. Not valid on holidays, Not valid with any other offer. Offer may be changed or discontinued at any time at the discretion of management. Original vouchers only. Offer is void if sold. Offer expires December 23, 2015. Settle to: #88-942

Gambling Hall & Hotel

2101 Texas Star Ln
North Las Vegas, NV 89032
(702) 631-1000
www.texasstation.sclv.com

Present this voucher to the server/cashier. Valid only at Texas Station Grand Cafe. Dine in only. Offer is non-transferable. Cannot be combined with any other offer. Limit one offer per party. Tax and gratuity not included. No cash value/change will be given. Not valid on holidays. Valid one time only. Management reserves all rights. Offer expires December 23, 2015. Settle To: #41-310

255 E Flamingo Road
Las Vegas, NV 89169
(702) 893-8933 • (877) 887-2261
www.tuscanylv.com

When using this promotional coupon, if you lose your wager the coupon will be claimed by the house. If you win your bet, your winnings will be paid in live gaming chips and the coupon wagered will be claimed by the house. Live gaming chips may be re-bet or exchanged for cash. If your bet is a tie, you may re-bet your coupon.

Bearer must be at least 21 years of age and prepared to present a photo ID. Limit one coupon per person per 30-day period. Coupon has no cash value and cannot be combined with any other offer or used more than once. Reproduction, sale, barter and transfer are prohibited and render this coupon void. Management reserves all rights. Offer expires 12/30/15.

Cantina Marilyn's Café

Mexican Restaurant

2-For-1 Entree

(or 50% off one item when dining alone)

Present this coupon, along with your Tuscany Player's Club Card, to your server at The Cantina or Marilyn's cafe to receive one FREE menu item when you purchase one item at the regular price, or receive 50% off one item when dining alone. See reverse for more details.

A current American Casino Guide Discount Card must be presented when redeeming this coupon, or offer is void

TUSCANY
SUITES & CASINO

$10 Free Slot Play

This coupon entitles the bearer to $10 in free slot play and is valid for new or current members. Present this coupon to the Tuscany Player's Club to redeem. See reverse side for details.

A current American Casino Guide Discount Card must be presented when redeeming this coupon, or offer is void

VEGAS BALLOON RIDES

$100 off any Balloon Flight

Present this coupon at time of purchase to receive $100 off the regular price of any Balloon flight. See reverse for details.

A current American Casino Guide Discount Card must be presented when redeeming this coupon, or offer is void

255 E Flamingo Road
Las Vegas, NV 89169
(702) 893-8933 • (877) 887-2261
www.tuscanylv.com

Present this original coupon to your server, along with your Tuscany Player's Club Card, to receive one FREE menu item from the regular menu with the purchase of another menu item at the regular price (or 50% off one item if dining alone). The FREE item must be of equal or lesser value. Dine-in only. Limit: one coupon per customer, per calendar month. No cash value. Must be 21 years of age or older. Tax and gratuity not included. Resale prohibited. Management reserves all rights. Offer expires 12/30/15.

255 E Flamingo Road
Las Vegas, NV 89169
(702) 893-8933 • (877) 887-2261
www.tuscanylv.com

Bearer must be at least 21 years of age and prepared to present a photo ID. Limit one coupon per person per 30-day period. Coupon has no cash value and cannot be combined with any other offer or used more than once. Present this coupon to the Tuscany Players Club to redeem. Reproduction, sale, barter and transfer are prohibited and render this coupon void. Management reserves all rights. Offer expires 12/30/15.

VEGAS BALLOON RIDES

4390 Polaris Ave
Las Vegas, Nevada 89103
(702) 553-3039
vegasballoonrides.com

Present this coupon at time of purchase to receive $100 off the regular price of any balloon flight. No cash value. Offer valid for all party members.

This adventure includes roundtrip transportation, a 1-hour balloon flight, a champagne toast, spectacular views, and memories that will last a lifetime. Flights subject to weather conditions. Management reserves all rights and may change or cancel this promotion at any time without notice. Offer is valid through December 23, 2015.

AMERICAN CASINO GUIDE

Bella Panini
Buy One Get One Free

Present this coupon at Bella Panini in the Venetian Hotel Grand Canal Shoppes, purchase your choice of any menu item and receive your choice of a second menu item of equal or lesser value free!

A current American Casino Guide Discount Card must be presented when redeeming this coupon, or offer is void

---

AMERICAN CASINO GUIDE

GRAND CANAL SHOPPES
THE VENETIAN | THE PALAZZO

FASHION SHOW
LAS VEGAS

Free Savings Book

Enjoy thousands in savings throughout the Strip's premier shopping destinations! Present this coupon at the Fashion Show Concierge Desk or the Apothecary at Grand Canal Shoppes. While supplies last. Expires 12/31/15.

A current American Casino Guide Discount Card must be presented when redeeming this coupon, or offer is void

---

AMERICAN CASINO GUIDE

BURGER *San Gennaro*

Buy One Get One Free

Present this coupon at the San Gennaro Burger in the Venetian Hotel Grand Canal Shops, purchase your choice of any menu item and receive your choice of a second menu item of equal or lesser value free!

A current American Casino Guide Discount Card must be presented when redeeming this coupon, or offer is void

Bella Panini

Venetian Hotel Grand Canal Shoppes

Must present coupon to cashier prior to ordering. Offer has no cash value. Not valid with any other offer. One coupon per person. Subject to change or cancellation without prior notice. Offer valid through December 31, 2015.

GRAND CANAL SHOPPES

THE VENETIAN® | THE PALAZZO®

Adjacent to The Palazzo across
from Fashion Show and TI
24-Hour Shopping Line
(702) 414-4500
www.thegrandcanalshoppes.com

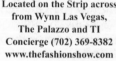

Located on the Strip across
from Wynn Las Vegas,
The Palazzo and TI
Concierge (702) 369-8382
www.thefashionshow.com

Venetian Hotel Casino Floor

Must present coupon to cashier prior to ordering. Offer has no cash value. Not valid with any other offer. One coupon per person. Subject to change or cancellation without prior notice. Offer valid through December 31, 2015.

americancasinoguide.com

1901 N Rancho Dr
Las Vegas, NV 89106
(702) 648-3801
www.wildfire.sclv.com

This voucher entitles bearer to $20 worth of Wild Grill Dining for only $10. **Offer is valid at any Wild Grill including Wildfire Boulder, Wildfire Lanes, Wildfire Rancho, or Wildfire Sunset.** Tax and gratuity not included. One voucher per person/subscriber. Voucher must be presented to cashier. Vouchers are not transferable and are not redeemable for cash. Must be 21 or older. Not a line pass. Not valid on holidays. Not valid with any other offer. Offer may be changed or discontinued at any time at the discretion of management. Original vouchers only. Offer is void if sold. Offer expires 12/23/15. Settle to: #88-113

Offer void if coupon is copied or sold

americancasinoguide.com

2470 Chandler Ave Suite 11
Las Vegas, NV 89120
(702) 792-5050
wildwesthorsebackadventures.com

Present this coupon at time of purchase to receive $40 off the regular price of the sunset dinner ride. No cash value. Offer valid for all party members.

This adventure includes roundtrip transportation, a 1.5 hour trail ride in beautiful Glendale, a mouthwatering steak BBQ dinner, spectacular views, and memories that will last a lifetime. Management reserves all rights and may change or cancel this promotion at any time without notice. Offer is valid through December 23, 2015.

Offer void if coupon is copied or sold

americancasinoguide.com

2100 S Casino Dr
Laughlin, NV 89029
(702) 298-4000
(800) 477-4837
www.coloradobelle.com

Must be at least 21 with valid photo ID. Subject to availability. Credit Card required to reserve room. Rate based on standard room. Valid Sunday – Wednesday. Excludes holidays and special events. Subject to change/cancellation. Limit one coupon per stay. Non-negotiable. No cash value. May not be redeemed by Edgewater or Colorado Belle employees. Management reserves all rights. Valid through 12/29/2015.

Offer void if coupon is copied or sold

COLORADO BELLE
CASINO · RESORT · LAUGHLIN

FREE Pints Draft Beer

Buy one regularly priced entree and receive a free Pints draft Beer! Redeem this coupon at Colorado Belle's Pints Brewery. Must be at least 21. See reverese for details.

Comp# 63150

COLORADO BELLE
CASINO · RESORT · LAUGHLIN

$10 FREE Slot Play!

Earn 1,000 base points on your player's card and receive $10 Free Slot Play. Redeem this coupon at Colorado Belle Casino Services. See reverse for details.

EDGEWATER
CASINO · RESORT · LAUGHLIN

One FREE Night!

Buy one night at $49 and get your second night FREE!
Advance reservations required.Call (877) 401-8896
Mon-Fri 9am – 4:30pm. Mention Code ACGEW.

COLORADO BELLE
CASINO · RESORT · LAUGHLIN

2100 S Casino Dr
Laughlin, NV 89029
(702) 298-4000
(800) 477-4837
www.coloradobelle.com

Gratuity not included. Must be at least 21. Subject to change/cancellation. No cash value, non-refundable, non-negotiable. Only original coupons accepted. May not be redeemed by Edgewater/Colorado Belle employees. May not be combined with any other offer/discount. Valid through 12/29/2015. Comp # 63150

COLORADO BELLE
CASINO · RESORT · LAUGHLIN

2100 S Casino Dr
Laughlin, NV 89029
(702) 298-4000
(800) 477-4837
www.coloradobelle.com

Earn 1,000 base points on your player's card to receive $10 Free Slot Play. Must be at least 21. Management reserves all rights. Offer expires 12/29/15.

Name: _____

Address: _____

City: _____ State: _____ Zip: _____

Clerk: _____ Valid: _____

EDGEWATER
CASINO · RESORT · LAUGHLIN

2020 S Casino Dr
Laughlin, NV 89029
(702) 298-2453
(800) 667-4837
www.edgewater-casino.com

Must be at least 21 with valid photo ID. Subject to availability. Credit Card required to reserve room. Rate based on standard room. Valid Sunday – Wednesday. Excludes holidays and special events. Subject to change/cancellation. Limit one coupon per stay. Non-negotiable. No cash value. May not be redeemed by Edgewater or Colorado Belle employees. Management reserves all rights. Valid through 12/29/2015.

AMERICAN CASINO GUIDE

EDGEWATER
CASINO • RESORT • LAUGHLIN

FREE
Buffet!

Buy one buffet and receive the second buffet FREE!
Redeem this coupon at Edgewater's Grand Buffet.
Must be at least 21. Comp # 63025

A current American Casino Guide Discount Card must be
presented when redeeming this coupon, or offer is void

AMERICAN CASINO GUIDE

EDGEWATER
CASINO • RESORT • LAUGHLIN

$10 FREE
Slot Play!

Earn 1,000 base points on your player's card and receive $10 free
Slot Play. Redeem this coupon at Edgewater Casino Services.
See reverse for details.

A current American Casino Guide Discount Card must be
presented when redeeming this coupon, or offer is void

AMERICAN CASINO GUIDE

Harrah's
LAUGHLIN

FRESH MARKET SQUARE
• BUFFET •

Buy One Buffet - Get One FREE!

Present this coupon at the Fresh Market Square Buffet at Harrah's Laughlin
at time of purchase. Buy one buffet (brunch or dinner) and receive one buffet
free! Valid at Harrah's Laughlin only. Offer code: 176

A current American Casino Guide Discount Card must be
presented when redeeming this coupon, or offer is void

2020 S Casino Dr
Laughlin, NV 89029
(702) 298-2453
(800) 667-4837
www.edgewater-casino.com

Gratuity not included. Must be at least 21. Subject to change/cancellation. No cash value, non-refundable, non-negotiable. Only original coupons accepted. May not be redeemed by Edgewater/Colorado Belle employees. May not be combined with any other offer/discount. Valid through 12/29/2015. Comp # 63025

2020 S Casino Dr
Laughlin, NV 89029
(702) 298-2453
(800) 667-4837
www.edgewater-casino.com

Earn 1,000 base points on your player's card to receive $10 Free Slot Play. Must be at least 21. Management reserves all rights. Offer expires 12/29/15.

Name: _____

Address: _____

City: _____ State: _____ Zip: _____

Clerk: _____ Valid: _____

2900 South Casino Drive
Laughlin, Nevada 89029
(702) 298-4600 • (800) HARRAHS
www.harrahs.com

Management reserves the right to modify this offer at any time without prior notice. Original coupon must be presented (no photocopies). Not valid on weekends (Friday/Saturday) or holidays. Cannot be used in conjunction with any other offer. Must be 21 or older to redeem. Coupon has no cash value. Limit one coupon per person per visit. Subject to availability. Gratuity not included. Offer valid through 12/15/15. Must be 21 years or older to gamble. Know When To Stop Before You Start.® Gambling Problem? Call 1-800-522-4700. ©2014, Caesars License Company, LLC.

AMERICAN CASINO GUIDE

Harrah's
LAUGHLIN
Beach Café

Buy One Entree - Get One FREE!

Present this coupon at the Beach Cafe at Harrah's Laughlin at time of seating.
Buy one entree at the Beach Cafe and receive one entree of equal
or lesser value FREE! Valid at Harrah's Laughlin only. Offer code: 176

A current American Casino Guide Discount Card must be
presented when redeeming this coupon, or offer is void

AMERICAN CASINO GUIDE

GOLD TOWN
CASINO • PAHRUMP, NV

LAKESIDE CASINO & RV PARK
PAHRUMP, NV

PAHRUMP NUGGET
HOTEL • CASINO
PAHRUMP, NV

2-for-1 Entrée

Present this coupon to the players club for a 2-for-1 entrée at the Pahrump
Nugget Café, Gold Town Café or Lakeside Café. Not valid with any
other offers. See reverse for more details.

A current American Casino Guide Discount Card must be
presented when redeeming this coupon, or offer is void

AMERICAN CASINO GUIDE

GOLD TOWN
CASINO • PAHRUMP, NV

LAKESIDE CASINO & RV PARK
PAHRUMP, NV

PAHRUMP NUGGET
HOTEL • CASINO
PAHRUMP, NV

$10 in FREE Slot Play

New members only, present this coupon at the players club booth at the
Pahrump Nugget, Gold Town or Lakeside casino and receive $10 in FREE
slot play! See reverse for more details.

A current American Casino Guide Discount Card must be
presented when redeeming this coupon, or offer is void

2900 South Casino Drive
Laughlin, Nevada 89029
(702) 298-4600 • (800) HARRAHS
www.harrahs.com

Management reserves the right to modify this offer at any time without prior notice. Original coupon must be presented (no photocopies). Not valid on weekends (Friday/Saturday) or holidays. Cannot be used in conjunction with any other offer. Must be 21 or older to redeem. Limit one coupon per person per visit. Subject to availability. Gratuity not included. Offer valid through 12/15/15. Must be 21 years or older to gamble. Know When To Stop Before You Start.® Gambling Problem? Call 1-800-522-4700. ©2014, Caesars License Company, LLC.

CASINO GROUP
PAHRUMP, NV

681 S. Highway 160
Pahrump, NV 89048
(775) 751-6500
(866) 751-6500
www.pahrumpnugget.com

Present this coupon to the players club. Excludes Nye County residents. Must be at least 21 years of age. Must show a valid photo I.D. and a players club card.

Limit one coupon per person. Not valid with any other offer. Coupon has no cash value. Management reserves the right to cancel or modify this offer at any time. Max value $10. Resale prohibited. Expires 12/31/15.

CASINO GROUP
PAHRUMP, NV

681 S. Highway 160
Pahrump, NV 89048
(775) 751-6500
(866) 751-6500
www.pahrumpnugget.com

This coupon is valid for new player club members only. Not valid with any other offer or discount. Limit one coupon per person. Excludes Nye County residents. Must be at least 21 years of age. Must show a valid photo I.D. Coupon has no cash value. Management reserves the right to cancel or modify this offer at any time. Offer expires 12/31/15.

AMERICAN CASINO GUIDE

LAKESIDE CASINO & RV PARK
PAHRUMP, NV

PAHRUMP NUGGET
HOTEL • CASINO
PAHRUMP, NV

One FREE Hotel or RV Night Stay!

Pay for one room night at the full rate and receive the second room night FREE at either the Pahrump Nugget or RV Space at Lakeside.
See reverse side for more details.

A current American Casino Guide Discount Card must be presented when redeeming this coupon, or offer is void

---

AMERICAN CASINO GUIDE

2-4-1 Breakfast or Lunch Buffet
in Toucan Charlie's Buffet & Grille

Atlantis
CASINO RESORT SPA • RENO ™

Present this coupon with your Club Paradise card to the cashier at Toucan Charlie's Buffet & Grille and receive one *free* breakfast or lunch buffet with the purchase of a second buffet at the regular price. *See back for details.*

A current American Casino Guide Discount Card must be presented when redeeming this coupon, or offer is void

---

AMERICAN CASINO GUIDE

$5 wins $10 Match Play

Atlantis
CASINO RESORT SPA • RENO ™

Present this coupon with a $5 wager and receive $10 when you win an even money bet at any blackjack, roulette, craps, Pai Gow Poker game or Mini-Baccarat. *See back for details.*

A current American Casino Guide Discount Card must be presented when redeeming this coupon, or offer is void

americancasinoguide.com

CASINO GROUP
PAHRUMP, NV

681 S. Highway 160
Pahrump, NV 89048
(775) 751-6500
(866) 751-6500
www.pahrumpnugget.com

Valid Sunday through Thursday for consecutive night stays in the same room or space. Excludes Nye county residents. Holidays and special events excluded. Subject to availability. Must have advance reservations by calling 866-751-6500 or 888-558-5253 and must advise the Pahrump Nugget Hotel agent or Lakeside RV agent that you are calling for the American Casino Guide offer. Must present and surrender this coupon upon check-in. No exceptions. Management reserves the right to modify or cancel this promotion at any time. Not valid with any other offer. Customer required to place credit card on file at check-in. Customer responsible for all other additional charges. Must be 21 or older. Limit one free room or RV Space per coupon. Expires 12/31/15.

Offer void if coupon is copied or sold

americancasinoguide.com

CASINO RESORT SPA • RENO

3800 S. Virginia Street | Reno NV 89502
800.723.6500 | atlantiscasino.com

Expires December 30, 2015. Valid Monday–Saturday. Excludes holidays or special events. No cash value. Gratuity not included. Must be 21. Not valid in combination with any other offer. Non-transferable. Management reserves all rights. Must be a Club Paradise member. *Not a Club Paradise member? Join today! It's fun, it's easy, it's free.*

Club Paradise #_____

1 5 A C G T C

Offer void if coupon is copied or sold

americancasinoguide.com

CASINO RESORT SPA • RENO

3800 S. Virginia Street | Reno NV 89502
800.723.6500 | atlantiscasino.com

Expires December 30, 2015. Limit one coupon per guest. No cash value. Must be 21. Not valid in combination with any other offer. Non-transferable. Management reserves all rights. Must be a Club Paradise member. *Not a Club Paradise member? Join today! It's fun, it's easy, it's free.*

Club Paradise #_____

1 5 A C G M P

Offer void if coupon is copied or sold

Harrah's
RENO

Buy One
Carvings® Buffet
Get One FREE!

Receive one Carvings Buffet FREE with the purchase of a full price Carvings Buffet. Present this coupon and Total Rewards® card to the Carvings Buffet cashier at Harrah's Reno prior to seating. Valid at Harrah's Reno only. See reverse for details. Coupon code: CG2F1

A current American Casino Guide Discount Card must be presented when redeeming this coupon, or offer is void

FIESTA BUFFET
BUY ONE BUFFET AND RECEIVE A
SECOND BUFFET FOR FREE!
Present this coupon and your Trop Advantage® Club Card at the buffet to receive your offer.

TROPICANA
ATLANTIC CITY

1-800-THE TROP • www.tropicana.net • Brighton and Boardwalk, Atlantic City, NJ 08401

A current American Casino Guide Discount Card must be presented when redeeming this coupon, or offer is void

Don't miss the 2016 edition of the American Casino Guide

**Completely Updated
More Casinos! • More Coupons!**

On Sale - November 1, 2015

**Ask for ISBN #978-1-883768-25-6
at your favorite bookstore or call (800) 741-1596
or order online at: americancasinoguide.com**

A current American Casino Guide Discount Card must be presented when redeeming this coupon, or offer is void

219 North Center Street
Reno, Nevada 89501
(775) 786-3232 • (800) HARRAHS
www.harrahs.com

Cannot be combined with any other offer. Gratuity not included. Management reserves the right to change or discontinue offer without notice. Restrictions apply. Must be 21 or older to gamble. Know When To Stop Before You Start. ® Gambling Problem? Call 1-800-522-4700. ©2014, Caesars License Company, LLC. Offer valid through December 30, 2015.

Buy one buffet and receive a second buffet for free. Use Code CP215. Cannot be combined with any other offer. Not valid on holiday weekends. Must have Trop Advantage® Card to redeem. Offer valid for two people per group only. Certain restrictions apply. No cash value. Original coupon only, no photocopies will be accepted. Tropicana has the right to reserve or cancel this promotion at any time. Must be 21 to participate. Gambling Problem? Call 1-800-GAMBLER.
Valid through December 31, 2015
American Casino Guide 2015

1-800-THE TROP • www.tropicana.net • Brighton and Boardwalk, Atlantic City, NJ 08401

Don't miss the 2016 edition of the American Casino Guide

Completely Updated
More Casinos! • More Coupons!

On Sale - November 1, 2015

Ask for ISBN #978-1-883768-25-6
at your favorite bookstore or call (800) 741-1596
or order online at: americancasinoguide.com